Colonial Adventures: Commercial Law and Practice in the Making

Legal History Library

VOLUME 45

The titles published in this series are listed at *brill.com/lhl*

Colonial Adventures: Commercial Law and Practice in the Making

Edited by

Serge Dauchy, Heikki Pihlajamäki,
Albrecht Cordes and Dave De ruysscher

BRILL
NIJHOFF

LEIDEN | BOSTON

Cover illustration: Joseph Vernet, Intérieur du port de Marseille, 1754. Collection of the Musée national de la Marine, actually in the reserves of the Louvre inventory n° MnM 5 OA 3 D (Musée de la Marine) – INV 8294 (Louvre).

Names: Dauchy, Serge, editor. | Pihlajamäki, Heikki, 1961- editor. | Cordes, Albrecht, editor. | ruysscher, Dave De, editor.
Title: Colonial adventures : commercial law and practice in the making / edited by Serge Dauchy, Heikki Pihlajamäki, Albrecht Cordes, and Dave De ruysscher.
Description: Leiden, The Netherlands : Koninklijke Brill NV, [2021] | Series: Legal history library, 1874–1793 ; volume 45 | Includes bibliographical references and index.
Identifiers: LCCN 2020037967 | ISBN 9789004442931 (hardback) | ISBN 9789004443075 (ebook)
Subjects: LCSH: Commercial law--History. | Corporation law--History. | Customary law--History.
Classification: LCC K1006 .C65 2021 | DDC 346.0709--dc23
LC record available at https://lccn.loc.gov/2020037967

Typeface for the Latin, Greek, and Cyrillic scripts: "Brill". See and download: brill.com/brill-typeface.

ISSN 1874-1793
ISBN 978-90-04-44293-1 (hardback)
ISBN 978-90-04-44307-5 (e-book)

This book is printed on acid-free paper and produced in a sustainable manner.

Contents

Acknowledgements

This book is based on the papers that were presented at the international workshop 'The Influence of Colonies on Commercial Law and Practice', which was held in Fiskars, Finland, in 2016. The workshop had been organized within the framework of the project 'The Making of Commercial Law: Common Practices and National Legal Rules from the Early Modern to the Modern Period' under the supervision of Heikki Pihlajamäki (University of Helsinki).

This is the fourth and final book of the series including *The Company in Law and Practice: Did Size Matter? Middle Ages – Nineteenth Century* (2017), *Understanding the Sources of Early Modern and Modern Commercial Law: Courts, Statutes, Contracts, and Legal Scholarship* (2018) and *Migrating Words, Migrating Merchants, Migrating Law* (2019).

The project and the conferences, as well as this book and the previous ones have been funded by the Academy of Finland and the Finnish Cultural Foundation, and they have also benefited from logistical support from the University of Helsinki.

In addition to the contributors of this volume, we would like to thank Katja Tikka and Jussi Sallila for helping to organize the workshop, Sofia Söderholm for the technical editing of the volume and Sara Roberts for the language editing.

Serge Dauchy, Albrecht Cordes, Dave De ruysscher and Heikki Pihlajamäki
Lille, 30 March 2020

Notes on Contributors

Alexander Claver
PhD at the Vrije Universiteit Amsterdam, is an independent scholar with a special interest in the entrepreneurial and economic history of colonial Indonesia.

Alain Clément (†)
was Associate Professor in Economy and Researcher in the History of Economic Thought at the University of Tours.

Oscar Cruz Barney
is Professor of Law and Legal History at the Universidad National Autónoma de Mexico and National Researcher Level III at the Institute of Legal Research of UNAM. He is Academician of the Mexican Academy of Jurisprudence and Legislation.

Bas De Roo
PhD in History at Ghent University, is researcher at Geheugen Collectief.

Paul du Plessis
is Professor of Roman Law at the Law School of the University of Edinburgh.

Bernard Durand
is Emeritus Professor in Legal History and Honorary Dean of the Law Faculty of the University of Montpellier.

David Gilles
is Professor at the Faculty of Law of the University of Sherbrooke and Director of the *Revue de droit de l'Université de Sherbrooke*.

Phillip Lipton
is an affiliate in the Department of Business Law and Taxation, Monash University (Melbourne).

Petra Mahy
is Senior Lecturer at the Department of Business Law and Taxation, Monash University (Melbourne).

David Mirhady
is Professor in the Department of Humanities at Simon Fraser University (Vancouver), with special interests in Greek Law and Rhetoric.

M.C. Mirow
is Professor of Law at Florida International University (Miami).

Luigi Nuzzo
is Professor in Medieval and Modern Legal History at the University of Salento (Lecce).

Umakanth Varottil
is Associate Professor at the Faculty of Law of the National University of Singapore.

Jakob Zollmann
is researcher at the Center for Global Constitutionalism at the WZB Berlin Social Science Center.

INTRODUCTION

Colonial Adventures: Commercial Law and Practice in the Making

Serge Dauchy, Albrecht Cordes, Dave De ruysscher and Heikki Pihlajamäki

Adam Smith's *The Wealth of Nations* (1776) is generally considered to be a denunciation of the ravages caused by colonial expansion, and in particular by the mercantile system and its main instrument, the charter companies. From the destruction of the pepper of the Moluccas and the depopulation of these islands by the Dutch East India Company to that of the opium or rice crops of Bengal by the English Company, the accumulation of examples in Chapter VII of Book IV is impressive. According to Smith, the interests which triggered the first settlements of European colonies in America and in the West Indies were not altogether as obvious as those which had instigated the establishment of the ancient Greece and Roman colonies. The latters' motives derived from clear and evident utilitarian considerations, i.e. the lack of agricultural land, while it was 'the great profits of the Venetians' and 'the sacrilegious thirst for gold of the Portuguese' which drove the former. The ancient colonies were in other words the result of objective necessities, whereas the modern colonial expansion was merely the product of an illusion.[1] Thus, according to Smith, the colonial project in Early Modern Times was as such nothing more than the most spectacular expression of the mercantile system, a project characterized by the confusion between particular and general interests.

The present volume is not an attempt to settle the controversy over the political and economic reasons and consequences of colonization, whether specifically the European colonization from the 16th until the 20th century or other forms of colonization. Its purpose is to examine the influence of colonial expansion and maritime trade on the development of commercial law and practices. One should never lose sight of the fact that colonization is intrinsically linked to trade. In ancient times, trading hubs around the Mediterranean provided a bridge to inland trade opportunities. Those trade centres were often the forerunners of permanent colonial settlements providing large

1 D. Diatkine, 'Adam Smith et le projet colonial ou l'avenu d'une illusion', *Cahiers d'Economie politique* 27–28 (1996), 21–38.

 | DOI:10.1163/9789004443075_002

opportunities for the export of luxury goods and the extraction of agricultural products. Similarly, Columbus's voyages were from the beginning regarded as trade enterprises, originally the exploration of new maritime roads to Asia, whereas the French and English colonization initiatives were also often planned within the broader framework of mercantilist policies.

It has been sufficiently demonstrated that law interacts with its political, economic and social context. Commercial law and practice in particular had to adapt to the requirements of overseas trade and settlement. On the other side, as colonial empires expanded, legal provisions were transplanted to the colonies and subsequently adapted to local particularities, depending on the different forms of colonial government. The influence of the 'colonial epic' on economic activities and its legal framework should however not be considered as an exclusively one-way process. It has for example been emphasized that British colonial trade was regulated by a complex body of statutes which was constantly being supplemented or amended in order to ensure the prosperity of homeland manufacturers and entrepreneurs amid the shifting commercial and political conditions.[2]

The studies gathered in this volume cover a long period, from Ancient Greece to the colonial empires of the 19th and early 20th centuries, and illustrate very different experiences, from the American continent to Australia, and from Asia to Africa. They all address the questions how and to what extent the making of commercial law was indebted to colonial developments. Did the colonial power and local authorities consciously reshape the law in order to further commercial – not to say imperialist – objectives, and did the expansion of the colonizers' legal systems shadow military conquest and economic penetration?[3] Or was the law simply brought in line with the new colonial imperatives and commercial practices?

The first two contributions in this volume remind us that the first colonial experiences and the first waves of settlement in the Western World date back to Greek and Roman ancient times. David Mirhardy highlights the legal and financial issues that already arose in Athens during the 4th century B.C. as a result of maritime trade with its colonies, on which the city strongly depended for the import of grain. Several of Demosthenes's speeches illustrate the complexity of these issues, specifically relating to the commercial relations with Sicily, Crimea and Egypt. Demosthenes's speech *Against Apaturius*, for

2 W.S. Holdsworth, *A History of English Law*, vol. 15, ed. by A.L. Goodhart and H.G. Hanbury (London, Methuen, 1965).

3 J.R. Schmidhauser, 'Legal Imperialism : Its Enduring Impact on Colonial and Post-Colonial Judicial Systems', *International Political Science Review* 13, 3 (1992), 321–334.

example, demonstrates the difficulties of financing maritime trade. The many lawsuits where loans or profit sharing were central issues, often involving Athenians and non-Athenians, led the courts to adapt the legal system and to adjust the traditional *paragraph* procedure, especially with regard to the risks of maritime voyages. Slaves could act as merchants and skippers, some – as Lampis in Demosthenes's *Against Phormio* – even had the ability to lend large sums of money. Because the democratic courts precluded slaves from testifying, the authorities also had to manage new patterns of conflict resolution, in particular through private arbitration.

Paul Du Plessis analyzes commercial practice in the remote Roman province of Britain at the turn of the first and second centuries A.D. The Vindolanda tablets used by the Romans to communicate across distances highlight a 'ground up approach', focusing on law in action. The central issue they raise is the application of Roman Law at the provincial level. In other words, did the formalized rules of Roman law as a territorially based system radiate from the centre to the peripheral colonies and did they suppress local customary law? The tablets show that is was important to fulfil contractual obligations promptly and that mutual trust and informal agreements between business partners were therefore paramount. The author supports the idea that, when studying commercial law and practice, we should not ask what the law (i.e. the existing doctrinal sources) was in a particular situation, but rather how merchants turned to legal principles and legalistic language for assistance and security. The Vindolanda tablets suggest that merchants, and more generally Roman trade, operated within networks of associations which mainly relied on some form of mercantile customs.

The next three contributions illustrate the influence of European colonial expansion during the Early Modern Period on the development of commercial law and practice. As Oscar Cruz Barney reminds us, monopoly and the principle of a single port of departure and arrival characterized the Habsburgs' trade policy in the Indies. In that light, the foundation of the *Casa de contratacion de Indias* in Seville in 1503 marks the Spanish authorities' will to ascertain state control over trade with the American colonies. The *Casa* was a governing agency with political, fiscal and judicial attributions. The progress of colonization during the 16th century drove the Spanish Crown to issue an important body of regulations in order to manage the navigational system (through convoys) and trade regime with the Indies. Many of these regulations were also intended to curb illegal trade and contraband. In 1543, the Crown moreover established an autonomous commercial jurisdiction composed by lay judges with expertise in international trade and its customs. The *Consulado de Cargadores a Indias* of Seville was competent to settle all disputes relating to the trade of goods for or from the Indies. Consulates were also set up in Mexico and Lima. Colonization gave thus birth to specialized institutions and a legal system specific to the Indies.

This was still true in the late 18th and early 19th century, as recently discovered records relating to East Florida show. A commercial dispute between residents of Saint Augustine and Panton Leslie & Co., a British firm run by Scots trading with native Americans, confirms that commercial law, even on the edges of the Spanish colonial empire, was based on specific licenses and regulations issued by the Crown. In 1802, some citizens of Saint Augustine petitioned the governor of the province. They argued that Panton Leslie had abused the privileges granted by the Spanish Crown by operating beyond its license and by denying Spaniards to benefit from Indian trade. The case, first handled by the governor's legal officer, was eventually sent to the Captain General in Havana for final determination. The records reflect the problems with regard to the applicability of the authorities of commercial law and their adaptation in this particular forum. Despite their remoteness from judicial and political centres and the lack of lawyers, local actors were apparently familiar with business terminology and legal arguments. Moreover, Matthew Mirow rightly emphasizes that the nature of trade management and commercial dispute resolution within empires was not simply one of economic benefit. They were closely linked to Spain's concern to maintain peaceful relationship with the Indian Nations and thus referred to the question of European inter-imperial sovereignty and trade competition.

Like Florida, New-France also experienced a change in sovereignty, as both territories were ceded to Great Britain following the Treaty of Paris of 1763. Canadian commercial law is therefor largely indebted to English law. However, as David Gilles reminds us, the French legal foundations should not be overlooked. In Quebec, the first provisions relating to commercial law were originally transplants from France. As can be observed in other Ancient Regime colonies, these transplants actually experienced two waves. In a first stage, settlers moving to the colony took their law with them. In the second, the colonizing power imposed its codes (Navy ordinance of 1681), applicable either to the settlers only or to the indigenous populations as well. In New France, commercial regulations were subsequently influenced by English common law. This legal 'remodelling' focused both on finding practical solutions to local problems as on asserting imperial sovereignty by imposing state-centred law. Based on case studies, this paper traces the shifts in the peculiar Quebec system characterized by plural legal orders. The transplant of a foreign (English) legal system to an unreceptive (French) society resulted with the passing of the Quebec

Act in 1774 in what the author describes as a Civil and Common law 'mashup' but ultimately a same commercial practice.

Alain Clément reminds us that overseas trade and colonial adventure were from the very beginning underpinned by economic theory with its share of debates and controversies. He offers a complete overview of the different – mainly English – attitudes towards the interconnection between colonization and enrichment and of the mercantilist disputes about balance of trade and monetary drains. Among the many mercantilist views of the Early Modern Times, Clément identifies three main orientations. First, some held that colonial settlements were based on demographic and economic arguments. They believed that settlements were a way to get rid of the poor and unemployed and, at the same time, an opportunity to open new markets for the benefit of homeland trade and manufacturing. Others defended a colonial policy limited to trade posts that would implement a one-way trade in raw materials and avoid dependency on other European nations. Finally, there was also a more sceptical approach considering colonization as a source of impoverishment that prefigured the liberal critics of the 18th century. They were particularly critical of protectionism and advocated free trade in favour of national interest.

The 19th century, the era of the Industrial Revolution and the emergence of nation-states, saw the number of colonial empires multiply and spread to all the continents. Whereas the American continent had largely gained independence, the European powers shared the rest of the world and established their political and economic power on every continent. The 19th century was above all the century of codification. Within a short span of time, a reception of the Napoleonic codes, for example, occurred in counties which had a historical, cultural and legal background entirely independent from France. At the same time, legal and institutional transplants took place in the expanding French and British settlers colonies.

Phillip Lipton's paper deals with such a transplant and adaptation of English commercial law and practice in the Australian colony of Victoria during the 19th century. He examines the common assumption that colonial developments were largely a bland imitation of the central country's law and practice with few, if any, distinguishing features apart from minor local innovations introduced at a very late stage. The underlying issue of the Victoria experience is whether that successful transplant of English company law in 1864 facilitated the colony's economic development or whether it only served the colonizers' interests. Lipton concludes that the transplant of efficient law and institutions effectively contributed to the significantly swift expansion and wealth of the settler societies in 19th century Victoria. However, the Australian ability to adapt the transplanted corporate law to the local realities – in particular the requirements of the mining industry – played an important role in the colony's economic and commercial development. The transition to large scale underground mining, for example, led to pass the 1858 and 1860 legislation which simplified the procedure for creating companies and introduced limited liability.

Petra Mahy undertook a comparative study of legal transplants and the development of company law in the former colonies of Southeast Asia. Transplants of company law fitted in a general extension of the colonizers' legal systems to their overseas territories. The colonial legal system was often based on a policy of racial segregation or on a paternalistic attempt to encourage indigenous people to adhere to the standards of Western civilization. In Southeast Asia, the colonial context — and the specific policy of each colonial power – appears to have been decisive for the outcome of transplanted company law and its subsequent development. The demands for legal provisions (or for the update of law originally only applicable in the colonial power's homeland) and the responsiveness of the lawmakers, both in the colonial mainland and in the colonies, appears to be the key determinant factors for the evolution of commercial law and commercial practice, although often only to the advantage of a small group of colonial entrepreneurs.

Alexander Claver's paper on colonial law in the Dutch East Indies provides a specific example of a policy of legal segregation and its unexpected consequences on commercial practice. In the 19th century Dutch East Indies, control over the legal system was viewed as an important feature of successful colonial policy implementation. Accordingly, courts were turned into tools of colonial administration. In that respect, the Dutch authorities also introduced a legal system based on racial segregation. To ensure their political, economic and commercial dominant position, they granted the different communities differential access (entailing also denial) to law and justice. However, such legal segregation finally backfired and turned against the colonizers. The Chinese minority turned the restrictive commercial legislation into profitable opportunities, to the discontent of the European traders. In particular, they perverted the bankruptcy provisions by claiming successfully before the courts that they were unskilled in bookkeeping, and furthermore authorized to keep their records and accounting in Chinese. Moreover, the Chinese community did not hesitate to resort to trade boycotts to defend their interests. Calver's study stresses the interweaving of commercial and legal strategies and the paramount importance of legal security in business relations.

Umakanth Varottil focuses on the managing agency system, a distinct type of corporate governance that emerged in India before spreading to other British colonies in Asia. The system did not receive any official recognition under Indian law and the colonial government refused to legislate on the matter until 1936. The reason was that originally, it had been conceived to fill a gap in the entrepreneurial needs of British business in India and therefore arose from specific colonial influences on corporate law. Varottil's study relates the evolution of the managing agency system from the early 19th century until Indian independence. It outlines the relationship between the company's (Indian) shareholders and its (British) managing agent, and the problems that arose from its operation in practice. The author also questions the reasons behind a century of legal inaction, which in the 20th century first led to a restrictive legislative response, and finally to the abolition of the system. Varottil argues that corporate law in India until 1936 was essentially a transplant of English company law. Because the managing agency system was a concept which was alien to English law and specific to the Indian colonial environment, it was left untouched.

The German Empire provides an interesting counter-example because it remained for a long time outside the European scramble for colonies. Towards the end of the 19th century, Bismarck still expressed his hostility against colonial expansion, expressing only half-heartedly the possibility of German protectorates financed and administered by trade companies. It was not until 1906, and under pressure from trade lobbies, that a Colonial Office reporting directly to the Imperial Foreign Office was set up in the (vain) hope of making a profit from the colonies. In that atypical context, Jacob Zollmann examines the reality of the German governmental foreign trade policy and the place of the law, mainly in the form of local administrative decrees. This brings us back to the central issues of this volume: what were the main objectives of commercial regulations and was actually colonial about them?

The interaction between the colonial state and private enterprises is also at the heart of the Bas de Roo's study. He focuses more particularly on customs law in the Congo Free State and pre-war Belgian Congo. Merchants and entrepreneurs indeed needed State authorities to secure public order, labour mobilization and price policies but at the same time they expressed their discontent with economic regulations and tax burden. Bas de Roo argues that commercial law making in the pre-war period can therefor only be understood by taking into account the continuous interaction between the private and the public sector. The Free state had to face a striking lack of income, forcing Leopold II to constantly negotiate tariffs (with trading firms he mistrusted) in order to avert the threat of colonial bankruptcy. In the 1890s, more and more voices were raised in Brussels to point the lack of efforts on the part of private enterprises to contribute to the colonial effort. When Belgium took over the administration of Congo in 1908, the colonial fiscal system was therefore completely reformed and customs duties significantly raised in return for the abolition of the monopolistic domanial system. Increase trade in order to increase tax revenues seems to have been the new credo of the Belgian administration in the years before the outbreak of the war.

Finally, Luigi Nuzzo reminds us that, beyond the legal and institutional realities, we should not forget the paramount importance of the colonial discourse and the political environment. That is the topic of his contribution dealing with foreign concessions in Tianjin (Tientsin) during the late 19th and early 20th centuries. Commercial activities in China depended mostly on international treaties which secured settlements, the opening of harbours or the right to trade without local intermediaries. Ten foreign concessions (seven of them controlled by Western European powers) coexisted and each of them tried to obtain a clause of most favoured nation. The author studies the Western discourse on international law and its projection outside its traditional borders, or what he calls a 'spatialized legal discourse'. Rather than transplanting law, which was simply unthinkable in China, Western legal concepts were interpreted in a non-European context. Moreover, the Western nations developed the principle of extraterritoriality in order to shield their nationals from foreign legislation and placed them under the jurisdiction of their consuls. The development of entrepreneurial and commercial activities in the Tianjin concession, i.e. outside the usual framework of colonial possessions, provides an interesting point of comparison, because it was totally dependent on international treaties and public law regulations.

The various contributions in this volume show that the influence of colonies on the development of commercial law and practice invariably leads back to the question of legal transplants. The initial introduction of commercial regulations in the colonies – which in a first stage consisted merely of warehouses and trading counters – was mostly incidental to a progressive extension of the colonizers' legal system applicable only to the overseas settlers themselves. The transplant of law and the replication of institutions therefore mostly occurred in a more exacting way, expressing legal imperialism and trade control by the colonial power, often underpinned by a policy of racial segregation. In such cases, the transplanted company law underwent either long periods of legal stagnation or adaptations for the sole benefit of European merchants. However, legal provisions could also be transplanted in a more innovative and flexible way in order to suit the local economic and commercial environment. In essence, both legal transplants and local specific regulations depended on the willingness of the various actors to adopt legal forms suited to the local and/or national commercial and economic environment. Rather than speaking of the influence of the 'colonial phenomenon' on the development of commercial law and practices, it seems therefore more appropriate to address the question, whether or not commercial law, institutions and practices adapted – or were adapted – to the colonial contexts. Did they adapt to the expectations of the colonial powers, as in ancient Greece and in the mercantilist experiments of Europe in modern times, which were mostly concerned with developing trade (i.e. finding raw materials and outlets for manufactured goods), or with asserting their political position on the international scene? Were they remodelled in response to the particular demands of companies, specific business sectors or settlers' communities? Could they also be circumvented, or even diverted, from their initial objectives, in particular when racial criteria determined commercial activities? It is to these questions that the present volume attempts to provide some answers or avenues for further research. It is clear, however, that much research still needs to be done on the subject.

The Rhetoric of Commercial Law in 4th-Century BCE Athens

David Mirhady

There are several law court speeches from 4th-century BCE Athens that deal with disputes over bottomry loans: the Athenians needed grain from Sicily, Crimea, and Egypt, and they exported olive oil, pottery, and other value added goods in return.[1] They had to innovate their legal processes in various ways both to manage the risks of sea voyages and to expedite disputes for traders for whom time was money. Bottomry allowed for risk to be spread over several lenders. Edward Cohen has recently noted the *supra*-nationality of access, the rapidity and rigor of legal process, and the enforcement of judges as some of the unique characteristics of these cases.[2] There are several legal issues that arose in Athens as a result of overseas trade with what may be considered Greek 'colonies': first, the special characteristics that led to the apparently common use of the *paragraphe* procedure, by which the defendant turned the tables and counter-prosecuted the prosecutor for illegal prosecution; second, the related use of written contracts (*syngraphai*), the existence of which was necessary for litigation over maritime disputes; third, resort to argumentation based on ethnicities, where Athenians were often matched up against non-Athenians of various stripes; and lastly, the ambiguous status of the slaves who were, at least in some cases, delegated to carry out overseas trade. These cases challenged Athens' normal exclusions of slaves from participation in its democratic law courts.

Athens depended greatly on the importation of grain, particularly wheat. Although its climate was excellent for growing olives and grapes, and it could largely supply its own needs for barley, wheat had to be imported from Sicily, Crimea, and Egypt.[3] Athens therefore had a great interest in promoting the grain trade, both by Athenians and by non-Athenians. Although it had few

1 The best discussion of these speeches, and ancient Greek maritime trade in general, is by Signe Isager and Mogens Herman Hansen, *Aspects of Athenian Society in the Fourth Century BC: A Historical Introduction to and Commentary on the Paragraphe Speeches and the Speech Against Dionysodorus in the Corpus Demosthenicum* (Odense: Odense Universitetsforlag, 1975).

2 Edward E. Cohen, 'Commercial Law', in Michael Gagarin and David Cohen (eds.), *The Cambridge Companion to Ancient Greek Law* (Cambridge: Cambridge University Press, 2005), 290–302, 300.

3 Isager and Hansen, *Aspects*, 19–33.

 | DOI:10.1163/9789004443075_003

overseas colonies as such,[4] Athens' large population and naval forces made it the dominant player in the eastern Mediterranean grain trade through the fifth and fourth centuries.

The *paragraphe* procedure actually appears to have come about just after the end of the Peloponnesian War (431–404 BC) as a result of the seizure of power in Athens by the so-called Thirty Tyrants and the civil war that toppled them. The Athenians then collectively swore, 'not to remember past wrongs' and instituted the *paragraphe* procedure in order to forestall litigation that was based on such past wrongs. As the years passed, however, new uses for the procedure were found. Since Athens' democratic judges had to make decisions about both questions of law and questions of fact, it became useful to have a procedure whereby such questions could be separated. The *paragraphe*, which ostensibly isolated the question of the admissibility of the suit, served also to decide the question of law while simultaneously risking only a small fraction of the contested amounts.[5] Moreover, because many of the questions of fact may have turned on events and so witnesses who were far from Athens' law courts, the *paragraphe* also allowed for a much more superficial debate on those points.

Demosthenes' speech *Against Zenothemis* is that of a defendant, Demon, an Athenian who financed a merchant, Protus, a non-Athenian (*xenos*) who may have been resident in Athens as a 'metic',[6] to sail to Syracuse aboard a ship owned by Hegestratus of Massilia (Marseille), to buy grain there, and to sail it back to Athens, where Protus hoped to sell the grain and repay the loan to Demon at a profit. Zenothemis is another Massiliote, Hegestratus' business partner, who sailed with him and claimed likewise to own a portion of the cargo. Demon explains that there was no contract (*symbolaion*) or written agreement (*syngraphe*) between himself and Zenothemis, facts that Zenothemis does not contest even though they are required for a prosecution under the maritime laws. Zenothemis claims in his charge, however, that he made a loan to Hegestratus, a skipper (*naukleros*), with whom he did have a written agreement, and that after Hegestratus was lost at sea, the speaker and his friends illegally appropriated the shipment in Athens. Demon's goal in his speech is, he says,

4 In the ancient Greek context a colony (*apoikia*) was an independent state. Many Greek cities set up such colonies in Italy, Sicily, France, and Libya, through the 7th and 6th centuries. The Athenians preferred cleruchies, generally on conquered territory, both Greek and non-Greek, where settlers got each got a lot (*kleros*) of land but kept their Athenian citizenship.

5 The loser of the *paragraphe* procedure had to pay *epobelia*, that is, an obol on every drachma under dispute. There were six obols in a drachma.

6 Demosthenes, 32 *Against Zenothemis*, 29, says that a suit against Protus might have been brought before the Polemarch, who dealt with cases involving foreigners and metics.

simultaneously to demonstrate that the suit is inadmissible and to show both Zenothemis' plotting (*epiboule*) and his baseness (*poneria*).[7]

Although a citizen of Massilia (Marseille), Zenothemis is described as an underling (*hyperetes*) of Hegestratus. The two of them took out loans in Syracuse for a purported shipment of grain, each one attesting for the other that the grain was his. Demon claims that they had credibility to do this because one of them was the skipper and the other a passenger. However, he claims that the money was sent directly to Massilia, their home, and that no grain was bought with that money, let alone placed on the ship. Since the written agreements stated that the loans were to be repaid only if the ship safely reached port, in order to cheat the lenders, Hegestratus and Zenothemis planned to sink the ship. A couple days out from Syracuse, Hegestratus attempted to cut through the hull of the boat and was caught doing so. He flung himself into the sea in an attempt to escape, but, because it was night, he missed the trailing dingy and drowned.

Zenothemis attempted to persuade the second officer and the sailors to abandon ship, but they managed instead to bring it to Cephallenia on the west coast of Greece. There, again, together with others from Massilia, Zenothemis tried to persuade the authorities to have the boat sail there instead of to Athens, claiming that the money and the lenders were from there, but the Cephallenian magistrates decided that the ship should proceed to Athens, from which it had embarked. Because of a decline in grain prices, however, in Athens Protus abandoned the grain to his lender, who seized it to cover his loan, and Zenothemis has brought suit against him as a result. The case turns on the question of admissibility, which relies on the existence of a maritime contract, and our speaker does acknowledge that Zenothemis has one, but claims that it was composed belatedly and fraudulently between Hegestratus and Zenothemis, who, as business partners, would not have needed one. The case clearly involves many facts for which witnesses are now at quite a distance. The only witnesses that are introduced are fellow creditors, like the speaker, who seem not to have sailed to Syracuse.

As interesting as the legal question over the existence of the contract is, the rhetorical strategy of Demon, which puts great emphasis on *ad hominem* attacks against Zenothemis, is that he is depraved and so on. Part of that attack is directed toward his ethnicity, that he, Hegestratus, and others are part of a Massiliote gang that has corrupted Athens' maritime trade. Demon posits the existence of a gang of Athenian criminals in Piraeus, with whom Zenothemis

---

7 Dem. 32.2. He repeats baseness and adds audacity (*tolme*) in the next section. He adds shamelessness later (32.9).

and his group conspired. Demon's own borrower Protus appears to be linked to these men, which accounts for his having abandoned the case. On the other side, Demon mentions his own familial relationship to Demosthenes, one of Athens' leading politicians. Although the argumentation of the speech appears to privilege the legal issues, its resort to ethnic attacks and its political background raise questions about the evenhandedness of Athens' courts with regard to foreign traders.

The complexity of financing maritime trade and maritime contracts is illustrated by another Demosthenic speech, *Against Apaturius*.[8] In this case Apaturius, a merchant from Byzantium, needed relief from a debt of 4,000 drachmas that had been lent to him on the security of his ship. He got a promise of 1,000 from a fellow Byzantine, an exile named Parmeno, and with the help of the speaker he got the remaining 3,000 from an Athenian banker, Heraclides, with the speaker guaranteeing that amount. The case illustrates nicely that not all those who financed maritime trade were bankers, whose principal function was actually currency exchange.

In this case, however, Heraclides' bank failed. The speaker thus took over as lender of the 3,000 drachmas and supported Parmeno's claim to the other 1,000. When Apaturius tried to leave Athens, the speaker and Parmeno seized the ship and its crew of slaves. He then found new lenders to cover Heraclides' 3,000, and supported Parmeno for his 1,000. The ship was sold for the full 4,000 drachmas, the money returned, and releases were granted all around. Normally the granting of releases would indicate that there was no longer a contract or obligation (the word *symbolaion* covers both ideas). Nevertheless, litigation arose over the seizure and the violence associated with it, and attempts at arbitration were frustrated. Here no aspersions are made against the Byzantines; there is one on each side to the dispute. But it is interesting to reflect that Byzantium served as a go-between between Athens and the Black Sea much as Syracuse and Cephallenia served in this way for Sicilian grain.

The involvement of even more ethnicities is illustrated in the speech *Against Lacritus*.[9] Here the speaker, an Athenian named Androcles, and a Euboean named Nausicrates have jointly loaned 3,000 drachmas to Artemo and Apollodorus of Phaselis, a Bithynian city on the southern coast of Turkey. They proposed to sail from Athens to Mende, on the west coast of the northern Aegean peninsula of Chalcidice, where they were to buy wine for shipment to Crimea. There they would buy other goods, presumably wheat, and return to sell it in Athens. But that is not what happened. Androcles charges that they used the

8 Demosthenes, 33 *Against Apaturius*.

9 Demosthenes, 35 *Against Lacritus*.

money for themselves, failed to buy sufficient wine in Mende, passed some of the money along to a compatriot in Crimea, and then the ship returned to Athens, where it did not enter the Piraeus harbor, where its cargo could be registered and taxed appropriately, but used an alternate harbor known as the Thieves Harbor. Artemo died along the way, so Androcles is suing Lacritus, Artemo's brother, who has, he says, inherited Artemo's debts.

The question of whether or not Athenian law allowed the inheritance of such contractual debts is an active one between the parties.[10] But the speaker also seems determined to base his case on his opponents' failure to fulfill the terms of the contract, as well as his ethnicity as a Phaselite and his activity as a student of sophistry. He notes that Phaselites have more litigation in Athens' courts than any other foreigners. It seems striking that Phaselis, like Massilia in the west, is outside the path between Athens and Crimea, as Massilia is far off the path between Syracuse and Athens. If Androcles is right about the amount of their litigation, that may well have also been a function of the amount of the Phaselites' maritime trading activity involving Athens. Phaselis is on the trade route to Egypt.

After speeches touching on trade with Sicily and Crimea, I would also like to turn to the Demosthenic speech *Against Dionysodorus*, which in fact concerns trade with Egypt.[11] The speech is very late, after the death of Alexander the Great and Athens' failed revolt against the Macedonians in 323/2. Athens' navy is now powerless, so while its large market still demands respect, its laws that required lenders to bring grain nowhere other than to Athens must no longer have been utmost in the minds of skippers who thought that they might get a better price elsewhere. In addition, Alexander's Egyptian administrator Cleomenes of Naucratis has for several years kept a firm and profitable hand on the Egyptian grain trade.

One year before, the speaker and a colleague loaned 3,000 drachmas to Dionysodorus and Parmeniscus on the basis of a maritime contract that stipulated that Parmeniscus sail to Egypt, buy grain, and bring it back to Athens. Parmeniscus did sail to Egypt and bought grain, but before he returned he was informed that a large flotilla of grain ships had arrived in Athens from Sicily, which depressed Athens' prices. So Parmeniscus stopped at Rhodes on the return voyage, offloaded his cargo there, and made an additional run to Egypt, which was facilitated by a longer sailing season in the southern waters between Rhodes and Egypt. On this basis, however, he and Dionysodorus want to prorate the interest for the shorter return trip to Rhodes.

10 Isager and Hansen, *Aspects*, 72–75.
11 Demosthenes, *Against Dionysodorus*, 56.

The speaker cries foul inasmuch as Athens' laws still proscribe lending for the conveyance of grain other than to Athens and, in any case, the conveyance to Rhodes was not what was called for in the maritime contract. Despite the fact that time goes on and he is not yet receiving back even a lesser amount, which he might lend out again, he remains insistent on repayment of the full amount. If he wished to insist on the letter of Athens' law that demanded conveyance to Athens, it would seem as if he might have brought suit against Dionysodrus for contravention of that statute, which would presumably have entailed a severe punishment. But the possibility of such a suit is not mentioned, which suggests that it may have become a dead letter.

In this speech there are no slurs against the ethnicity of the opponents. The speaker does describe them as underlings and associates of Cleomenes and alludes to his successes at price fixing. But in a later passage he says that some Athenian citizens, who happened to overhear the parties disputing the amount of the repayment, advised them to take the amount prorated to Rhodes and settle their dispute about that, but to keep open the dispute about the remaining money. He refers to the Athenians as 'your citizens', which suggests that none of the parties to the dispute were themselves Athenian. Since Dionysodorus seems to be resident at Athens, he was probably a metic, a resident alien, and the speaker and his colleague Parmeniscus were likely also metics. None is referred to with either an ethnic reference or a reference to an Athenian deme membership, all perhaps a result of a new, cosmopolitan worldview that is taking hold as a result of Alexander's conquests.

Finally I arrive at the last of the issues that I outlined at the outset, particularly as it pertains to a slave named Lampis, who is discussed at length in Demosthenes' *Against Phormio*,[12] which concerns trade from Athens to Crimea (Bosporus) and back. Although Lampis is described as a skipper, a *naukleros*, he is also described as a 'servant', an *oiketes*, of a man named Dion of Bosporus and as a 'child' (*pais*), a term that seems to be used only of actual children and of slaves.[13] But he clearly lived and worked independently of his owner and was able to carry on business, making and accepting loans and negotiating deals, as well as running his ship. However, although he is described as a witness (*martys*) before a private arbitrator, he does not testify before a popular court (*dikasterion*). The speaker's opponents appear to have requested private arbitration specifically in order to avoid the more stringent evidentiary rules of

12 Demosthenes, 34 *Against Phormio*.

13 Dem. 34.5, 10. It seems to be used of a slave crew of a ship, both in Dem. 34.10 and 33.8. See H.G. Liddell and R. Scott, *A Greek-English Lexicon*, revised and augmented throughout by Sir Henry Stuart Jones (Oxford: Oxford University Press, 1996) *s.v.* III.

the popular court, which precluded slaves from testifying.[14] Before the private arbitrator, moreover, Lampis changed his story and testified 'whatever he wanted' with the claim that he had been out of his mind when he had agreed to support the speaker's position. An Athenian expected such fickleness from a slave, but no one in the dispute raises the possibility of a challenge to torture Lampis as a means of ending the dispute. Even though Lampis' owner was quite remote from him, given how common torture-challenges occur in Athenian forensic oratory, the possibility of it might be expected unless Lampis enjoyed some special slave status that prevented it. His responsibilities as a skipper may have entailed such a status. To be sure, it appears that the speaker's opponent Phormio is relying upon Lampis' testimony before the arbitrator as if it had been introduced by a legal witness before the popular court. But the speaker says repeatedly that there is no witness concerning whether Lampis had received repayment of the loan because, in fact, it never happened.

Lampis plays a curious role. As a businessman and skipper, he had the resources to lend the merchant Phormio 1,000 drachmas, which was in addition to loans Phormio received from Phormio's opponents in the litigation and from a Phoenician named Theodorus (34.6). After Lampis' ship sank on the return voyage and even after the litigation had begun, he is said to have skippered another, large shipment from Bosporus to Acanthus. Since it originated in Bosporus, that expedition was probably under the more direct control of his owner Dion. However, Lampis, his wife, and children seem nevertheless to have been principally resident in Athens.

Most translators render *naukleros* as 'ship owner', but clearly many ship owners do not sail with their ships as *naukleroi* do. Lampis' crew belonged to Dion, and presumably his ship did as well.[15] Unlike a 'shipper', who conveys goods with someone else, the *naukleros* is the ship's master, though sometimes that person is also the owner. Being *naukleros* is clearly a more responsible position than 'captain', *gubernetes*, who directs the actual sailing of the ship, and it is also distinct from the merchants (*emporoi*) who have their goods shipped and who, like Phormio, often accompany their goods. As a skipper, however, Lampis is described as irresponsible. When he was to depart from Crimaea his ship was already overloaded. Nevertheless he took on an additional cargo of one thousand animal hides, which is what caused the ship to wreck. Although he and his crew escaped in the dingy, thirty others died and the cargo was lost.

14 Deborah Kamen, *Status in Classical Athens* (Princeton: Princeton University Press, 2013), 19–23, outlines the issues in a discussion of 'privileged slaves'.

15 See Isager and Hansen, *Aspects*, 65.

When Chrysippus, the speaker, approached Lampis as soon as he had returned to Athens after the shipwreck, Lampis said that Phormio neither put goods on board the ship for the return voyage, according to the contract, nor gave him the repayment in Bosporus. If he had loaded the cargo, then according to the rules of bottomry loans the debt would have been nullified by the sinking. Even the conveyance of the repayment and its sinking might have nullified the debt. But since the repayment appears to have been withheld in Bosporus, where Phormio stayed instead of returning on the doomed ship, Chrysippus and his partner approached Phormio for repayment when he returned to Athens. When he refused, they launched litigation to recover their money.

Initially Lampis was helpful. When Chrysippus approached him again and explained that Phormio was refusing to pay, Lampis led the speaker to where Phormio was so that a summons could be served on him before witnesses. Lampis did not alert Chrysippus at that time that he had received the money and then lost it on the doomed ship, nor did Phormio protest that he had. Lampis was at the time unconcerned, and Phormio was taking refuge in the fact that Lampis' ship had sunk. The men Chrysippus had taken along to witness the summons corroborate that Lampis and Phormio were silent about the repayment when Chrysippus confronted them. Chrysippus also introduces his initial statement from his summons, the *enklema*, which gives no suggestion that Phormio would take refuge in Lampis as a defense witness – Chrysippus actually claims that this document is his strongest proof – nor did Phormio's *paragraphe* say that he had returned the money even though the *enklema* explicitly stated that Phormio had neither shipped goods nor returned the money.

Just before the case came to the democratic court, the two parties agreed to refer it to a private arbitrator. Chrysippus says that the private arbitration gave Lampis the opportunity to change his story. He claims that Lampis now split the money with Phormio and testified the opposite of what he had said before. It should be understood that private arbitrations have whatever rules of evidence the arbitrator chooses. Unlike in the democratic courts or before public arbitrators, where only free adult males could testify, both women and slaves, and presumably even children, could appear before a private arbitrator. To Chrysippus, who had anticipated that Lampis would corroborate his story, that would have appeared an advantage to him. But he was deceived.

This arbitration was done 'according to terms' (*kata synthekas*), which might have regulated evidentiary matters somewhat, but Chrysippus says that Lampis thought himself safe to testify whatever he wanted. There could be no suit for false testimony as there might have been if false testimony were given in a democratic court:

> For it is not the same thing, men of Athens, to give false testimony while face to face with you and to do so before an arbitrator. With you heavy indignation and severe penalty await those who bear false witness; but before an arbitrator they give what testimony they please without risk and without shame (ἀκινδύνως καὶ ἀναισχύντως μαρτυροῦσιν ὅ τι ἂν βούλωνται).[16]

The arbitrator heard the parties several times but eventually referred the case to the democratic court.[17]

Lampis is never described as a *doulos*, the most explicit word for slave, but he is described as an *oiketes* and a *pais*, both times as belonging to Dion. I have mentioned his irresponsible behavior as skipper. Before the arbitrator he said that he was not himself when he told Chrysippus, before witnesses, that he had not received money from Phormio. In his account, Chrysippus does not draw explicit attention at this point to Lampis' status as slave. He says instead that Lampis played the rogue (πονηρὸς ὤν). As soon as he got money from Phormio he claimed to be himself again and to remember everything. He behaves contemptuously of Chrysippus and even more dangerously than Phormio had towards the Athenians since he was involved in transporting grain to Acanthus even though he, his wife, and children lived in Athens and grain was being rationed there.

Chrysippus describes Lampis as a witness, partner, and, finally, an accomplice of Phormio. At the time Lampis claims he accepted the money from Phormio, he did not summon either Chrysippus' slave (τὸν παῖδα παραλαβόντα τὸν ἐμόν) or his partner to witness the fact, although that was the common practice when making and returning loans. He also characterizes Lampis' initial statement to himself that he had not received the money as 'testimony', *marturia*, although that was not in any kind of judicial situation. He has witnesses in court to provide testimony that Lampis had denied receiving the money. Phormio likewise provides witnesses about Lampis' so called 'testimony' for him. Chrysippus cannot sue them for false testimony since they are telling the truth: Lampis had recanted and claimed that he got the money, which then sank with the ship. But Lampis' testimony before the private arbitrator was not produced before the court because it was not common practice for

16 Demosthenes, 34.19.

17 Chrysippus says that the arbitrator's friendship with Phormio precluded his deciding against him, and his fear of perjury precluded deciding the case, on oath, in Phormio's favour.

private arbitrators to pass on their testimony to the popular court as public arbitrators did.

My view is that, as a slave, Lampis could not appear as a witness in an Athenian court. In his recent translation, MacDowell says that Lampis does not appear because he is again on a shipping voyage when the trial takes place.[18] That he was away may be right. However, although Chrysippus does not put explicit emphasis on Lampis' status as a slave, his description of his behaviour is certainly consistent with what Athenians expected from slaves. He is an irresponsible skipper who overloads his boat, and he says one thing one moment and another thing the next depending on his assessment of his immediate bodily welfare.[19] In Athens, normally, challenges were made to have slaves tortured in the belief that torture, when bilaterally administered, would get to the truth. Normally the owner surrendered the slave to his opponent in the litigation. The opponent did the torturing and the owner stood by to see that things did not get out of hand.

But Lampis' owner is hundreds of kilometers away in Crimea. He was not a party to the suit. It is hard to imagine what inducement could have led him to give permission for torture to take place. Beyond that, Lampis seems to have been a slave with a special status. For better or worse he is put in charge of trading ships, which seems to preclude his being tortured. We likewise know of Phormio and Pasio, who both ran banks as slaves for their owners before they were freed, and the operator of the perfume business and his son, who are the object of the dispute in Hyperides' speech *Against Athenogenes*. No one ever suggests torturing any of them even though they would appear to have known a lot that would have been relevant to various legal disputes. Hyperides points out that the owners are liable for all the slaves' legal obligations.[20] Although the bankers' owners were in town and might have given permission for torture to take place, banks operated in an atmosphere where trust was at a premium, so clearly the normal Athenian distrust of slaves that led them to torture slaves was put aside. In the case of the perfume business, Hyperides' client was in fact interested in being the lover of the son of the slave who operated the perfume business, so it is no wonder that he was not interested in torture in that case.

Most of the parties to the dispute in Demosthenes 34 appear to have been metics. Even the private arbitrator, Theodotus, was a privileged alien who did

18 Douglas MacDowell, *Demosthenes, Speeches 27–38* (Austin: University of Texas Press, 2004), 113.

19 See David Mirhady, 'The Athenian Rationale for Torture', in Jonathan Edmondson and Virgina Hunter (eds.), *Law and Social Status in Classical Athens* (Oxford: Oxford University Press, 2000), 53–74.

20 Hyperides, *Against Athenogenes*, 22. See also Andocides 1.87 and Demosthenes, 23.87.

not have to pay the metic tax. In conducting international trade the Athenians had to make compromises with their own legal system, since they dealt not only with other Greek poleis but with peoples on the borders of the Greek world for whom status distinctions between slave and free, while likely still present in their general outlines, could have had very different implications, as we find even in the Greek city of Gortyn. Ambitious businessmen, both Athenian and non-Athenian, will have wanted to expand their profits not just through business partners with equal status but through agents, such as Lampis, with whom they did not have to share all the profits since they were in a very real sense subservient to them.

In facilitating Athens' overseas grain trade the Athenian legal system had to make adjustments. They applied the *paragraphe* procedure from other contexts in order to deal expeditiously with disputes over maritime contracts. They gave increased status to the existence of written documents that attested to the existence of such maritime contracts. They found themselves under the influence of rhetorical techniques that called into question the credibility of various sorts of non-Athenians, calling into question their evenhandedness. And they found themselves confronted with slaves who took on roles for their foreign owners and who challenged Athenian rules of evidence.

Trading along Hadrian's Wall

Paul du Plessis

1 Introduction

Sometime towards the end of the first century/start of the second century AD, two business partners in the Roman province of Britain corresponded by letter regarding their joint business activities (Tab. Vindol. II 343). One partner resided at (or near) Catterick in North Yorkshire, the location of a prominent leather tannery, the other in the small town that had sprung up outside the large Roman military fort at Vindolanda. Through historical accident, their correspondence was preserved among the Vindolanda tablets, small rectangles of birch and fir wood roughly the size of a small postcard, used by the Romans to communicate across distances.[1]

2 The Text in Question

The letter in question reads as follows:

> (i) Octavius to his brother Candidus, greetings. The hundred pounds of sinew from Marinus – I will settle up. From the time when you wrote about this matter, he has not even mentioned it to me. I have several times written to you that I have bought about five thousand *modii* of ears of grain, on account of which I need cash. Unless you send me some cash, (ii) at least five hundred *denarii*, the result will be that I shall lose what I have laid out as a deposit, about three hundred *denarii*, and I shall be embarrassed. So, I ask you, send me some cash as soon as possible. The hides which you write are at Cataractonium – write that they be given to me and the wagon about which you write. And write to me what is with that wagon. I would have already been to collect them except that I did not care to injure the animals while the roads are bad. See with Tertius about the 8½ *denarii* which he received from Fatalis. He has not credited them to my account. (iii) Know that I have completed the 170 hides and I have 119 (?) *modii* of threshed *bracis*. Make sure that you send me cash so

1 Alan K. Bowman, *Life and Letters on the Roman Frontier: Vindolanda and Its People*, rev., expanded and updated ed. (London: British Museum, 2003), 6–12.

 | DOI:10.1163/9789004443075_004

> that I may have ears of grain on the threshing-floor. Moreover, I have already finished threshing all that I had. A messmate of our friend Frontius has been here. He was wanting me to allocate (?) him hides and that being so, was ready to give cash. I told him I would give him the hides by the Kalends of March. (iv) He decided that he would come on The Ides of January. He did not turn up nor did he take any trouble to obtain them since he had hides. If he had given the cash, I would have given him them. I hear that Frontinius Iulius has for sale at a high price the leather-making (things) which he bought here for five *denarii* apiece. Greet Spectatus and ... and Firmus. I have received letters from Gleuco. Farewell. (Back) (Deliver) at Vindolanda. [Bowman translation].[2]

The letter consists of four leaves of wood (marked i–iv) that were strung together and folded, like a concertina, to preserve the privacy of the correspondence. It was bound together on the outside with a leather thong, but it does not appear to have been sealed like other Roman commercial documents (such as contracts) where the sealing preserved the *fides* of the parties to the document.

3 Analysis

The significance of this tablet resides in the fact that it provides us with quite a bit of information about 'commercial practice' rather than formalised rules of Roman law as laid down in the main sources of Roman law, i.e. the Justinianic compilation. Furthermore, as a document from the Roman West, and more specifically from a Roman 'frontier province' (a term commonly employed when describing Roman Britain), it provides a welcome counterbalance to the rich body of documentation found in the East (Egypt being our prime example and the source of countless papyri).[3] For all these reasons, as well as for some that will be discussed below, this document deserves closer scrutiny.

Before this can be done, however, a few general remarks are required about Roman 'commercial law'. The first and most obvious point to make is that 'Roman commercial law' is a modern category. There is no evidence in the legal

2 Bowman, *Life and Letters on the Roman Frontier*, 144–146.

3 On legal practice, see now the excellent collection of translated materials in James G. Keenan, Joseph Gilbert Manning and Uri Yiftach-Firanko (eds.), *Law and Legal Practice in Egypt from Alexander to the Arab Conquest: A Selection of Papyrological Sources in Translation, with Introductions and Commentary* (Cambridge: Cambridge University Press 2014) generally.

sources that the Roman jurists or the Roman Imperial bureaucracy ever conceived of or ring-fenced part of their private law as 'applied private law', i.e. 'commercial law'. This is also in keeping with modern debates about the extent to which the Romans understood 'economic theory'. In second place, as with so many areas of the study of the Roman world, scholars from different disciplines have approached the matter from their own disciplinary perspectives while paying little attention to the work undertaken in related fields. This is particularly evident in the study of Roman commercial law. In the last thirty years, two significant strands of scholarship have developed in this discourse. The first, located largely in the fields of ancient history (but increasingly also economic history), is based on the pioneering work of Moses Finley from the early 1970s on the ancient economy.[4] Thus, since the 1970s, scholars have investigated fundamental questions such as whether the Romans had a concept of 'economics', what the main features of this 'economy' were (and whether it was 'primitive' or 'sophisticated') and how this relates to issues of trade (especially the provision of grain) and monetary policy (minting of coins, tax collecting, etc.).[5] The academic debate in this area continues to be lively, but the current state of it is a far cry from Finley's original work. During the last twenty years, owing primarily to the work of Walter Scheidel, Dennis Kehoe and Bruce Frier, the study of the Roman economy has come under the influence of New Institutional Economics.[6] This movement, originating the USA in the 1970s, has moved away from the macro-level studies of the Roman economy characteristic of Finley's work (i.e. classical economics) and have begun to focus on 'institutions' in an attempt to explain Roman economic behaviour. The latter two scholars, especially, have chosen law as an 'institution' to be studied in order to uncover more information about Roman economics. The second strand of scholarship, largely confined to Italian Roman-law circles, have portioned off a section of Roman private law under the heading Roman 'commercial law' and have discussed the rules of law and their economic implications

4 M.I. Finley, *The Ancient Economy* (Berkeley: University of California Press, 1973).

5 Comprehensively summarised in Walter Scheidel, Ian Morris and Richard P. Saller (eds.), *The Cambridge Economic History of the Greco-Roman World* (Cambridge: Cambridge University Press, 2007); Walter Scheidel, *The Cambridge Companion to the Roman Economy* (Cambridge: Cambridge University Press, 2012) generally.

6 A good example of this method may be found in the recently published – Legal Documents in Ancient Societies (Conference), Dennis P. Kehoe, David M. Ratzan and Uri Yiftach, D.C. Center for Hellenic Studies (Washington, New York University), and Institute for the Study of the Ancient World, (eds.) *Law and Transaction Costs in the Ancient Economy* (2015).

(e.g. partnerships, *peculium*, carriage) in great detail.[7] These works, while admirable, continue to focus on formal rules of law and thus far, has not engaged to any great extent with the works of Scheidel, Kehoe or Frier.[8] As this brief survey has shown, therefore, much work still needs to be done concerning the integration of macro-level narratives about the Roman economy with micro-level narratives concerning the rules of Roman law, especially in light of more recent approaches employing New Institutional Economics.

Having set the scene, I now wish to proceed to the letter in hand. As an example of 'commercial practice' a document of this kind forms an important part of what one might call 'law in action' (to use Roscoe Pound's phrase) and thus provides a counterbalance to the doctrinal rules of Roman law.[9] But 'law in action' in the Roman context is complicated by a number of factors. Of these, the main issue relates to the application of Roman law in the provinces. The issue is this: for the majority of the duration of the Roman Empire; Roman law was not a territorially based legal order. Rather, it was connected to Roman citizenship in the sense that only Roman citizens (or foreigners who had been granted the *ius commercii*) could access Roman law.[10] According to the traditional narrative, based on the works of Ludwig Mitteis (1859–1921), the main effect of the *Constitutio Antoniniana* of 212 AD was to suppress any local customary law that may have existed prior to this date and to render Roman law '*Reichsrecht*' with territorial application.[11] Since then, the Mitteis thesis has come under sustained pressure, especially concerning Roman Egypt as records of court cases and petitions have painted a rather different picture.[12] In light of the overwhelming evidence gathered in the last century, most scholars now reject the Mitteis thesis and argue that both before and after 212 AD, the application of Roman law on a provincial level was much more selective (both in

7 Pietro Cerami, Andrea Di Porto and Aldo Petrucci, *Diritto commerciale romano: profilo storico* (Torino: G. Giappichelli, 2004) is a good example of this approach.

8 This may be seen in earlier works on the topic, such as, Generoso Melillo, *Economia e giurisprudenza a Roma: contributo al lessico economico dei giuristi romani* (Napoli: Liguori, 1978); Francesco De Martino, *Diritto, economia e società nel mondo romano* (Napoli: Jovene, 1995).

9 Roscoe Pound, 'Law in Books and Law in Action', *American Law Review* 44 (1910), 12.

10 For the use of 'fictions' to involve non-citizens in Roman law, see now Clifford Ando, 'Fact, Fiction, and Social Reality in Roman Law', *Law and Philosophy Library* 110 (2015), 295–324.

11 Ludwig Mitteis, *Reichsrecht und Volksrecht in den östlichen Provinzen des Römischen Kaiserreichs mit Beiträgen zur Kenntniss des griechischen Rechts und der spätrömischen Rechtsentwicklung* (Leipzig: Teubner, 1891).

12 Keenan, Manning and Yiftach-Firanko, *Law and Legal Practice in Egypt from Alexander to the Arab Conquest*, generally.

terms of topics and audience) than previously imagined. Furthermore, it is clear that the effect of the Imperial decree in 212 AD was not to render Roman law a territorially based legal order applicable to all free citizens within the Empire (although what it was intended to do remains debated).

In light of this rejection of Mitteis's thesis, it has become much more difficult to provide a picture of the application of Roman law in a provincial context. If the Roman state did not in all instances impose Roman law from above as a modern state would, then it becomes necessary to identify when and to what extent individuals would access Roman law. Phrased differently, one has to investigate the 'legal consciousness' (to use a modern socio-legal term) of individual actors to a dispute.[13] Caroline Humfress[14] and Georgy Kantor[15] have done much to further this approach in recent years. They have focused on 'from the ground up' issues such as local knowledge of the law, dispute resolution options available to the parties and individual choices when accessing Roman law. Investigations of this kind have, however, as a rule focused on the Eastern part of the Roman Empire owing to the preservation of ample material from legal practice.

This is not an unimportant point. Traditionally, investigations into the existence of local custom under Roman rule have tended to focus on the East, not only because of the substantial preservation of material but also because of cultural associations with the supposed sophistication of the Greek-speaking East. Although the available evidence does not permit modern scholars to conclude whether the Roman state ever had anything approaching an official policy about the engagement with different peoples in the Roman Empire (and by implication also the retention of indigenous systems of knowledge and of customary law), there does seem to have been a different approach to people in the Greek-speaking East than in the Latin West. As Caroline Humfress puts it:

> In contrast to the Hellenized provinces of the East, the Western provinces – and especially those within the Libyan, Iberian, Celtic and Germanic linguistic zones – seem to present a relatively "barren" pre-Roman

13 David Nelken, 'Defining and Using the Concept of Legal Culture', in Esin Örücü and David Nelken (eds.), *Comparative Law: A Handbook* (Oxford: Hart Publishing, 2007), 109–132; David Nelken, *Using Legal Culture* (London: Wildy, Simmonds & Hill, 2012) generally.

14 Caroline Humfress, 'Law's Empire: Roman Universalism and Legal Practice', in Claudia Rapp and H.A. Drake (eds.), *The City in the Classical and Post-Classical World* (Cambridge: Cambridge University Press, 2014), 81–108, generally.

15 Georgy Kantor, 'Ideas of Law in Hellenistic and Roman Legal Practice', in Paul Dresch and Hannah Skoda (eds.), *Legalism: Anthropology and History* (Oxford: Oxford University Press, 2012) generally.

> legal landscape. Notwithstanding the highly technical nineteenth-century vocabulary and early twentieth-century debates over the concept of *Volksrecht* and the continuing scholarly discussions of the persistence of 'Germanic legal customs' or 'Germanic customary law', the prevailing sense is that the legal Romanization in the West was a simpler process than in the East:...[16]

It is not my intention to enter into the complex and multi-faceted debate concerning 'Romanization'. For the moment, I wish to focus on the implications of Humfress's statement for the legal landscape of Roman Britain. There is virtually no evidence that the Roman government in Roman Britain attempted to engage in any systematic way with the indigenous systems of knowledge of the local population. Although information is sparse, comments such as those by Julius Caesar in *De Bello Gallico* V.14: 'The people of Kent are the most civilised of all the Britons. They have a way of life that is almost identical to that of the Gauls' are telling, especially in the choice of words. To this one may compare the intelligence report (Tab. Vindol. II 164) regarding the natives in the north: '...The cavalry do not use swords nor do the wretched [little] Britons (*Brittunculi*) mount in order to throw javelins'. [Bowman translation]. Early works of an anthropological nature such as those of Julius Caesar and of Tacitus, though clearly biased in favour of the Romans, do seem to suggest that the Romans had a complicated relationship with the local inhabitants of Britain and that there was clearly an element of judgement regarding their lack of 'civilisation' when it came to matters of society and of the retention of local systems of knowledge.

This then brings us to the letter under discussion. How should we interpret this work within the larger context of the provincial application of Roman law? First and foremost, the legal landscape of Roman law in the Roman province of Britain needs to be set out.[17] Despite the abundance of source material (mostly material culture), knowledge of Roman law in Roman Britain is somewhat sparse.[18] Legally speaking, as an Imperial province,[19] it was governed by an

16 Caroline Humfress, *Law and custom under Rome* (Centre for Hellenic Studies, 2011) http://eprints.bbk.ac.uk/4918/1/4918.pdf., 44.

17 For a good survey, see B.C. Burnham, A.S. Esmonde Cleary, L.J.F. Keppie, M.W. C. Hassall and R.S.O. Tomlin, 'Roman Britain in 1992' *Britannia* 24 (1993), 267–322, generally.

18 The main works are Eric Birley, *Roman Britain, and the Roman Army: Collected Papers* (Kendal: T. Wilson, 1953); Eric Birley, *Law in Roman Britain* (Berlin: Walter de Gruyter, 1980); Łukasz Jan Korporowicz, 'Roman Law in Roman Britain: An Introductory Survey', *The Journal of Legal History* 33:2 (2012), 133–150.

19 And on this matter, the excellent work by D.J. Mattingly, *An Imperial Possession: Britain in the Roman Empire, 54 BC–AD 409* (London: Allen Lane, 2006).

Imperial Legate (*Propraetor*) who had the right to hear appeals from local courts (as any governor of a province did in the Roman Empire).[20] The court of the governor seems not have been a static entity and there is evidence that it moved around (much like similar gubernatorial courts in other provinces of the Roman Empire). We also have evidence of the existence of a legal deputy to the governor, the *legatus iuridicus*, who seems to have dealt with matters of law and jurisdiction on behalf of the governor when the latter was occupied with military matters. Such an office is known from at least the mid-first century AD and although the names of quite a few individuals are known from the epigraphic record (including one of the famous Roman jurists), it is unclear whether this was a permanent office. Apart from the governor, who had a fairly small retinue of permanent staff, the province was managed on a fiscal level by a *procurator* in charge of tax collection and directly answerable to Rome, who seems to have had his headquarters in London. On a municipal level, the existence of only four cities with the status of a Roman *colonia* (i.e. populated by veterans) and a small number of *municipia* are known. If the municipal charters of Roman cities elsewhere in the Roman Empire (e.g. the Flavian Municipal Laws and the *Lex Irnitana*) are taken as a comparator, we assume that Roman law must have applied also in these cities, but we have no record either of these charters or of the application of the law on this level.

Thus far the legal landscape of Roman Britain. So how do we go about locating this letter within this landscape? Although Birley and recently Korporowicz have set out general surveys of Roman law in Roman Britain, these have focused on general matters and have not approached the issue 'from the ground up' as suggested by Humfress. To that end, this contribution will attempt to do so by focusing not on general surveys, but on this document in particular.

Let us take the parties first. We do not know the status of these individuals. They do not address one another with the usual *tria nomina* used by Roman citizens, and we cannot, therefore, assume that they were.[21] Most likely, according to the general interpretation, they were civilian traders operating in Roman Britain who had followed the army there to peddle their wares. The names are too generic to speculate about their origins. In all likelihood, they were *libertini*. Whether they had Roman citizenship is impossible to tell. If they had been properly manumitted, they would of course have had Roman citizenship, but we simply do not have the information. To this may be added

20 Anthony Richard Birley, *The Roman Government of Britain* (Oxford: Oxford University Press, 2005) generally.

21 Andreas Kakoschke, *Die Personennamen Im Römischen Britannien* (Hildesheim: Olms-Weidmann, 2011).

the fact that most of the nakedly commercial transactions under Roman law were not confined to the *ius civile*:

> D. 18, 1, 1, 2 Paul. 33 ad ed.
> Est autem emptio iuris gentium, et ideo consensu peragitur et inter absentes contrahi potest et per nuntium et per litteras.

The fact that one party addressed the other as 'brother' cannot be used to infer that they were necessarily related. This salutation is frequently used in these tablets even where the parties are clearly not related and even of different statuses.

The most pressing matter, discussed at the start of this letter, concerns the sale of a large quantity of wheat. From the context, it seems that the parties had agreed to purchase a large amount of wheat. One party had laid down a deposit and is now seeking to close the deal by paying the remainder. He is, therefore, writing to his business partner (not for the first time it seems) to provide him with the remainder. Two aspects of this transaction are noteworthy. The first is the issue of the deposit (perhaps not the best translation of *arra* in this context). According to Octavius, he will forfeit the *arra* if the money is not paid. Although there is some debate in Roman-law circles about the exact function of the *arra* (whether merely as a token of good faith or something more), the forfeit seems compatible with Roman law as handed down in the doctrinal sources (e.g. D. 18, 1, 35 Gai. 10 ad ed. provinc.; I. 3, 23pr). Max Kaser, in his shortened *Studienbuch* on Roman private law, describes it as follows:

> [*A*]*rra* as it was known to the Greek systems, following the Semitic example, was unnecessary, at least in the developed Roman law. ...In preclassical and classical law the giving of a ring or a sum of money by the buyer to the vendor occurred in order to give force to the conclusion of the contract. After the performance of the contract the ring was reclaimed in the *actio empti*, and the sum of money was set-off against the purchase price (Ulp. D.19.1.11.6). Under Justinian *arra*, in keeping with the Greek pattern, was to secure the future conclusion of a contract of sale when the parties had decided to employ the written type (*ante* I, 4). A party who withdrew from the (pre-contractual) agreement of future conclusion of the sale after the *arra* had been given, suffered legal disadvantages: the giver forfeited the *arra* to the other party, the recipient had to repay double the amount of the *arra*. [Kaser (translation Dannenbring) 41.2.1]

In light of the statement above, it would seem that the way in which the parties employed the term in this letter is closer to the Justinianic (and thus by implication Greek) practice, than the practice in classical Roman law. But this would perhaps be a step too far. There could be a variety of different reasons why the parties deviated from what is understood to be classical Roman law, ranging from scribal convention to incomplete or inaccurate knowledge of the law. This shows exactly why a 'gap-analysis' of legal practice with doctrinal legal scholarship is such a slippery slope.

The other aspect of this first transaction that deserves comment is the observation that the failure of the transaction will cause 'embarrassment'.[22] This statement is unique as it demonstrates one of the most important features of Roman commerce. For traders in a frontier province, reputation was key.[23] Modern contract-law theorists would call this 'relational contract theory'.[24] The Romans probably read elements of this into the term *bona fides*.[25] Where the parties and their business was dependent upon the continuing trust of other traders, it was important to fulfil all contractual obligations promptly and not to renege on contracts. This would create a bad atmosphere and might harm future business. It may also explain the rather anxious tone of the letter. To my knowledge, it is one of the few documents from the Latin West where the notion of 'financial embarrassment' is spelled out in so many words.

The second transaction that requires closer scrutiny concerns the carriage of a lot of hides. The hides are, at the time the letter was written, still at Catterick and needed to make their way to Vindolanda, no doubt for sale to the army. The issues raised here concern the release of the hides and their transport. When placing this into the larger context of the significance of land transport in the Roman Empire, these statements acquire new meaning. It is conventionally stated that land transport was of lesser significance that transport by water, owing to the state of the roads as well as the nature of Roman

22 There are seven instances where permutations of the verb *erubesco* (to redden or blush) appear in Roman legal sources, but none of these refer to 'financial embarrassment'. But see now information about the Bloomberg tablets recently unearthed in London: https://www.theguardian.com/uk-news/2016/jun/01/tablets-unearthed-city-glimpse-roman-london-bloomberg last accessed 16 June 2016.

23 On all this, see Barbara Abatino, Giuseppe Dari-Mattiacci and Enrico C. Perotti, 'Depersonalization of Business in Ancient Rome', *Oxford Journal of Legal Studies* 31:2 (2011), 365–389, generally.

24 The standard work remains Ian R. MacNeil and David Campbell, *The Relational Theory of Contract: Selected Works of Ian MacNeil* (London: Sweet & Maxwell, 2001).

25 Riccardo Cardilli, *Bona fides tra storia e sistema* (Torino: G. Giappichelli, 2004) generally.

cart-technology.[26] Here we find this in action. The observation 'I would have gone to collect the hides, but I did not want to injure the pack animals when the roads were bad' is telling. Land transport was cumbersome and potentially dangerous to the animals. There is a suggestion here that the party at Vindolanda may have access to a wagon and could, therefore, send the wagon to pick the hides up. One cannot push this too far, given the brevity of the statement, but it raises the tantalising question whether the party at Vindolanda might have somehow had access to the state transport system and could, therefore, move goods with greater ease than a private individual.[27]

The last aspect of this transaction (it may or may not be connected to the movement of the hides since the letter is written in a rather 'stream of consciousness' fashion) concerns an account held by Octavius with one Tertius. Again, the comment is so brief that one cannot push it too far, but it would be tempting to suggest that Tertius was a moneylender operating out of Vindolanda and that Octavius was enquiring through his business partner about a credit to his account from one Fatalis that has seemingly not yet shown in his account.[28] As Bowman observers: 'The movement of small sums of money between individuals is well attested'.[29] How Octavius would have known that the credit from Fatalis did not yet show is a mystery, but we can safely assume, given the number of Vindolanda tablets that have been recovered, that information was shared between locations on a regular basis.

The final transaction that I wish to focus on concerns the sale of hides to an acquaintance of a friend of theirs. This, again, shows the 'relational contract' in all its glory. An acquaintance of a friend of theirs had arrived to purchase some hides. The hides were not ready, but an informal agreement had been reached that he would return but never did. One gets the distinct impression here that Octavius is expressing his displeasure at being taken for a ride by someone who had been referred to them by a friend. To me, this again shows the complexity of 'networks of association' and how these operated in Roman commerce.[30]

26 The economics of land transport are discussed in Susan D. Martin, 'Servum Meum Mulionem Conduxisti: Mules, Muleteers and Transportation in Classical Roman Law', *Transactions of the American Philological Association (1974–)* 120 (1990), 301–314, generally.

27 Compare the observation in Tab. Vindol. II 255, a letter between Clodius Super and Flavius Cerialis where the statement occurs 'I am a commissariat officer now and have access to transport'.

28 Jean Andreau, *Banking and Business in the Roman World* (Cambridge: Cambridge University Press, 1999) generally.

29 Bowman, *Life and Letters on the Roman Frontier*, 74.

30 See, for example, Neville Morley, *Trade in Classical Antiquity* (Cambridge: Cambridge University Press, 2007); Helen Parkins and Christopher John Smith, *Trade, Traders and the Ancient City* (London: Routledge, 1998).

4 Conclusions

Although the law features quite significantly in this letter, it is not at the forefront of the discussion between the business partners. They are concerned primarily with the continuing profitability of their undertaking within a larger context where trust among merchants, good faith if you will, was paramount. Thus, this letter provides us with commercial substratum that underpinned much of Roman commercial law. But this is far from the entire affair.

Traditionally, and especially about examples of legal practice from Graeco-Roman Egypt, scholars have tended to ask 'what law is this?' They have then proceeded to compare the case of legal practice to existing doctrinal sources with the aim either to show (a) that the individuals in question followed the law (whatever this may be) or (b) that they deviated from the law (or were perhaps even ignorant of it). It does not take much to appreciate that such a methodology is based on a view of law as a territorially based system radiating out from the centre. As recent research has begun to question whether Roman law ever operated in this fashion, this question about the nature of the law should be abandoned and replaced a more useful one, namely 'what did the parties to this letter think that they were doing?'[31] Phrased in this manner, it opens up a new vista of enquiry.

Unless new evidence comes to light, it will not be possible to establish the status of the two parties to the letter. If we assume that they were not slaves (and there is no reason to assume that they were), then Roman law was certainly potentially available to them. What is far more interesting (and revealing) is what the parties thought that they were doing. In his 1976 work, *The Behavior of Law*, Donald Black set out his theory of 'pure sociology'.[32] This theory is an attempt to explain why certain situations attract more law than others. Thus, according to Black, the amount of law a situation (used here in the sense of a conflict) will attract depends on sociological factors such as the 'social status' and 'social distance' of the parties. In essence, the better the parties know one another, the less law they will resort to. This, to my mind, beautifully explains the issues raised in the letter. Instead of asking what the law is in this situation, we should rather ask what the parties thought the law was and how and when they turned to it for assistance. Objectively, here at the very edge of the Roman Empire (if the wall really represented an 'edge', of which I am sceptical), these two partners were using legalistic language as if they had a court right on their doorstep to which they could turn if matters went badly

31 See generally Humfress, *Law and custom under Rome*.

32 Donald J. Black, *The Behavior of Law* (New York: Academic Press, 1976) generally.

wrong. But, as I have set out above, this clearly was not the case in a province as remote and underdeveloped as Roman Britain. The nearest *colonia* (where Roman law applied in theory) was very far away and who knows how long it might take for the travelling court of the governor to show up. It seems much more likely that what the business partners were relying on in this case was 'mercantile custom'[33] for want of a better phrase (knowing full well how complex the debate about the origins of the *lex mercatoria* in Antiquity is), supported by 'relational contract theory' and 'networks of association'. In recent years, much has been made about traders in the Roman Empire. In my view, the role of traders and other lower level legal functionaries such as scribes and notaries in the spread of Roman law needs to be studied in much greater detail.[34]

33 Armin von Bogdandy and Sergio Dellavalle, 'The Lex Mercatoria of Systems Theory: Localisation, Reconstruction and Criticism from a Public Law Perspective', *Transnational Legal Theory* 4:1 (2015), 59–82, generally.

34 Gérard Minaud, *Les gens de commerce et le droit à Rome* (Aix-en-Provence: Presses universitaires d'Aix-Marseille, 2011) generally.

Trade and Law in New Spain in the Sixteenth and Seventeenth Centuries

Oscar Cruz Barney

1 Introduction

With the discovery of America, a sudden and unexpected growth on the Castilian horizons occurs, with a long series of discoveries initiated by Cristobal Colón. After the arrival of the conquerors came the merchants, who were willing to risk their money on different enterprises of conquest and discovery.[1] The Columbus voyage was planned from the beginning as a trade enterprise, a search of a new maritime route to Asia. The *Capitulaciones de Santa Fe* of April 17, 1492 stated that any merchandise that was found, gained, traded or acquired on the new lands were to belong exclusively to the monarchs. A tenth of the benefits belonged to Cristobal Colon. A monopoly on trade was established for the Catholic Kings.[2] As Ruiz Rivera and García Bernal stated, 'the abandonment of the Indies trade monopoly rights by the Catholic Kings and the substitution of Colon marked the beginning of the discovery and salvage journeys', also called minor journeys or 'Andalusians'. From that moment on, the trade merchants started to include the Atlantic journeys in their business possibilities.[3] A new trade was born: the transatlantic trade.[4]

When the great news regarding the economic possibilities offered by the newly discovered lands was received in Europe, a 'new phase for the European powers of that time is started, generally under the sign of dispute and common rivalry',[5] but it also allowed strong trade and financial networks to be established that made possible the trade with and within the Indies.

1 Julián B. Ruiz Rivera and Manuela Cristina García Bernal, *Cargadores a Indias* (Madrid: Editorial Mapfre, 1992), 15.

2 Ruiz Rivera and García Bernal, *Cargadores a Indias*, 17.

3 Ruiz Rivera and García Bernal, *Cargadores a Indias*, 27–28.

4 Luisa Brunori, *Societas quid sit. La société commerciale dans l'élaboration de la Seconde Scolastique*, Preface de Jean Hilaire, (Paris: Mare & Martin, Collection des Presses Universitaires de Sceaux, Université Paris Sud, 2015), 19.

5 Manuel Bustos Rodríguez, 'El apoderado en el comercio de América a través de Cádiz (siglos XVII y XVIII)', in *Andalucía y América: Actas del II Congreso de Historia de Andalucía* (Cordoba, 1994), 155.

 | DOI:10.1163/9789004443075_005

Many of the Atlantic trade regulations date from the seventeenth century, with the creation of a privately owned and operated regime. In the same way that the conquest of Hispanic America was made by individuals, trade was also in their hands, with the adoption by the Castilian Crown of a liberal policy regarding trade and commerce between conquerors and locals, even though limitations to trade would still be in force.[6] The economic ideas of mercantilism were in the mind of the Castilian Crown when the discovery and conquest of America were carried out: the capitalist and monetary economic growth, and the rising of the nation states[7] determined the issuing of regulations for international trade, which allowed for a favourable balance of payments, even though a royal trade monopoly was established in the first place and expanded later. Mercantilism caused the New Spain Economy to depend on Spain's Economy during the enforcement of the Fleets and Galleons System, until the implementation of free trade in 1778.[8]

2 The Habsburg Period

The two main principles that characterized the Habsburgs' trade policy were, according to Beatriz Bernal, those of monopoly, and of single port of departure and arrival. In fact, trade monopoly was the basic principle of all the Hispanic trade systems in the Indies.[9] Still, we have to consider the opinion of Moreyra Paz Soldan who thinks that 'Spain's trade monopoly in America was more apparent than real during the seventeenth century'.[10]

From the first regulations issued by Colon's regime, the main and distinctive features of the trading system were clear: it was a system that controlled and

6 José Antonio Caballero Juárez, *El régimen jurídico de las armadas de la Carrera de Indias, siglos XVI y XVII* (México: Universidad nacional autónoma de México, 1997), 19.

7 Marcelo Bitar Letayf, *Los economistas españoles del siglo XVIII y sus ideas sobre el comercio con las Indias*, 2nd ed. (México: Instituto Mexicano de Comercio Exterior, 1975), 27. See also Hira de Gortari Palacios, 'El comercio novohispano a través de Veracruz', *Historia Mexicana* (México, 1968), 429.

8 Sergio Florescano, 'Política mercantilista española y sus implicaciones económicas en la Nueva España', *Historia Mexicana* (México, 1968), 456–457.

9 Antonio García-Baquero González, *La Carrera de Indias: suma de la contratación y océano de negocios* (Sevilla: Algaida, 1992), 19.

10 Manuel Moreyra Paz Soldán, 'El ilusorio monopolio comercial de flotas y galeones y la decadencia de España', in *Estudios históricos* (Lima, 1994), 111.

registered every sailor, official or passenger to the Indies, and also all the merchandise embarked by them. On April 10, 1495, subjects of Castile were allowed to ask for permission to emigrate to the Indies and to ply their trade.[11] Departures and arrivals of the ships were controlled at first by the implementation of Cadiz as the only port authorized for departures and arrivals from the Indies. It was in Cadiz where customs controls were established.[12] A tenth of the tonnage of every ship was reserved for the use of the Crown, free of freight, and also a tenth and later a fifth of the income resulting from business traffic. In 1497, the payment of *almojarifazgo*, *almirantazgo*[13] and any other tax burden on the goods exported to the Indies were dispensed by the Crown, as was the payment of *alcabala* on its first sale in Spain. In fact, the Crown imposed no custom taxes on the ports of the Peninsula until 1543.[14]

2.1 *The* Casa de Contratación de Sevilla

The state agency that controlled and managed trade between Spain and the Indies was the *Casa de Contratación de Sevilla* (House of Trade of Seville), founded in 1503, as 'an answer given by the Catholic Kings to the problems related to the incipient trade with the Indies',[15] and Seville was chosen for the headquarters of the *Casa* which was based at the Royal Palace or *Alcazar*, over an old Muslim palace.[16] The *Casa* was created to manage the trade and the monopoly over all goods coming from the Indies. It issued the permits to travel to the Indies, performed the inspections of merchandise and ships, regulated the departing of the ships, acted as a civil and commercial tribunal, promoted geographical and nautical studies and was in charge of the preparation and examination of the pilots who wanted to undertake the *Carrera de Indias*.[17] Regarding taxes, the *Casa* was in charge of collecting the *quinto real* that was a tax of 20% imposed by Spain on every import of silver and gold from America.

11 Clarence H. Haring, *Comercio y navegación entre España y las Indias, en la época de los Habsburgos*, (trans.) Emma Salinas (México: Fondo De Cultura Economica, 1984), 5.

12 Caballero Juárez, *El régimen jurídico*, 19.

13 Miguel Lerdo de Tejada, *Comercio exterior de México desde la conquista hasta hoy* (México: Impreso por R. Rafael, 1853), 15.

14 Haring, *Comercio y navegación*, 7.

15 Caballero Juárez, *El régimen jurídico*, 20.

16 Pablo Emilio Pérez-Mallaina Bueno, 'Sevilla y la Carrera de Indias en el siglo XVI', in *Exposición Universal Sevilla 1992, Pabellón Temático Navegación* (Seville, 1992), 128.

17 María del Carmen Borrego Pla, 'Maestres y pilotos de la Bahía Gaditana en la Carrera de Indias hasta 1700', in *Andalucía y* América, 131.

It also collected the profits of all the Crown properties, and managed the 'Average Tax' or *Avería*, which was a mechanism of financing the defence of the ships that participated in the Atlantic navigation to the Indies, or *Carrera de Indias*.[18]

Why did the Crown choose Seville? Mainly because of the security that a river port offered to the management and control of trade and the wealth coming from the Indies, including the collection of trade taxes, migration to and from the new lands, as well as managing the trade of weapons and books. The task was easier in a river port such as Seville, and it was also much more safer against attacks from other powers, since it was at a long distance from open seas. Also, in Seville, important investors were ready to play their role in the trade with the Indies.[19] The headquarters of the *Casa* remained in Seville until 1717, when it was forced to move to Cadiz.[20]

The life of the *Casa de Contratación* can be divided in two large phases: first the Seville stage, and second, the Cadiz stage. The Seville stage begins with the creation of the *Casa* to establish an organized and managed trade between Spain and the Indies, controlled by the *Casa*. It was the first trade agency especially created to take care of the discoveries. At first, in 1493, the Catholic Kings appointed Juan Rodríguez de Fonseca to cooperate with Cristobal Colón on his second journey to America. Colon was instructed to avoid the transportation of goods for sale, since trade was for the Crown only and was to be made by its officials. Fonseca kept control of all the trade with the Indies, from his appointment until the creation of the *Casa de Contratación* in 1503.[21] The first ordinances of the *Casa* were issued in Alcalá de Henares on January 20th, 1503, with only 20 articles.[22] By February 14th, three employees were appointed to be in charge of the new agency: a treasurer, Doctor Sancho de Matienzo, Canon of Seville Cathedral; an accountant, Secretary Jimeno de Briviezca; and a factor, Francisco Pinelo, who was Genoese.[23] The *Casa de Contratación* was the governing agency of trade with the Indies, with politic, judicial, fiscal and scientific

18 Eduardo Martiré, 'El marco jurídico del tráfico con las Indias españolas', in Carlos Petit (ed.), *Del Ius Mercatorum al Derecho Mercantil* (Madrid: Marcial Pons, 1997), 229–230. The Avería was also a 'kind of obligatory insurance tax levied on vessels to cover damage to merchandise'. See Francois Chevalier, *Law and society in colonial Mexico* (USA, 1970), 321.

19 García-Baquero González, *La Carrera de Indias*, 31.

20 Angel Montenegro Duque, *Historia de España*, vol. 10 (Madrid, 1991), 270.

21 Haring, *Comercio y navegación*, 3, 27–28.

22 Joseph de Veytia Linaje, *Norte de la Contratación de las Indias Occidentales* (Sevilla, 1672), Lib.I, Cap.I, Núm. 1.

23 Haring, *Comercio y navegación*, 28.

attributions.[24] The *Casa* was responsible for everything to do with trade between Spain and the Indies: customs, commerce, and administrative issues. Goods and equipment necessary for the travel to Indies had to be stored, bargained for, and sold on its premises. Also all goods that arrived from the Indies had to go through the *Casa*. The officers of the agency had to be knowledgeable of the Indies' needs in order to be able to answer to them. The *Casa* was responsible for keeping a record and for managing every operation made on behalf of the Royal Treasury, and was also responsible for rigging out the ships that were going to be used for the travel to the Indies. The appointment of the captains and scriveners for every expedition was also within the powers of the *Casa*. Captains received the navigational and trade instructions from the aforementioned *Casa* officials.

Since 1509 the Crown had issued regulations to bring more security to the ships, with an attempt to avoid every possible risk, stating the minimum number of crew members, equipment and weaponry for defence against pirates.[25] The 1503 ordinances were in place for seven years, until some competency troubles with the Seville City Council and local judicial authorities forced the issuing of new ones on 15 June 1510. With only 35 articles, this new ordinance started important changes to the judicial powers of the *Casa*. Every judicial and treasury matter was to be taken care of in a collegial manner by the agency. Registry, letter and account books had to be opened. One of the books was for keeping a record of every document and communication sent to and received by the Indies authorities; a second book was to write down the inputs and outputs of royal property; and a third book was to keep a record of the goods stored for the preparation of the fleets, together with a handbook for acquisition of materials.[26]

The ordinances of 1510 also established regulations for the preparation for travels and expeditions. In order to travel to the Indies, every private ship had to be examined by the *Casa* officials who would issue a certificate of its capacity and tonnage, keeping a record of the goods embarked. No one could travel to the Indies without a permit. The *Casa* was responsible of the administration of the Probate Court (*Juzgado de Bienes de Difuntos*[27]), which had a mirror institution in Mexico and Peru. An ordinance also prohibited the *Casa* to act before courts without the proper counsel of a lawyer. On May 1511 the ordinance

24 José María Ots Capdequí, *El Estado español en las Indias* (Mexico: Fondo de Cultura Economica 1986), 63.

25 Caballero Juárez, *El régimen jurídico*, 22.

26 García-Baquero González, *La Carrera de Indias*, 61.

27 A court in charge for the administration of estates.

was modified by the inclusion of 17 new articles.[28] In addition, in September the Crown granted the *Casa*, by a Royal Decree, full jurisdiction over civil and criminal matters regarding trade and navigations with the Indies, and in every case related to contracts, trade companies, insurances and freights according to the regulations of the *Consulado de Burgos*.[29] From that point, the *Casa* officials were to be named *Jueces de la Contratación*. The *Casa de Contratación* not only organized and managed the trade, but also developed scientific and scholarly tasks, such as the creation in 1508 of the *Piloto Mayor*,[30] which was to examine the pilots that would work on the *Carrera de Indias*, and also to draw the maps and navigation charts from the information provided by the explorers and navigators.[31] From 1519, the maps were in the charge of the mapmaker of the *Casa*, and the technical issues remained as part the tasks of the *Piloto Mayor*. Three years later, in 1522, a Chair on Navigation and Cosmography Arts was created,[32] giving life to the first and most important navigation school in modern Europe, with Americo Vespucci as the first *Piloto Mayor*.[33] Other *Pilotos Mayores* included Juan Díaz de Solís; Sebastián Caboto; Rodrigo Zamorano;[34] Francisco de Ruesta; Juan Cruzado de la Cruz; and Francisco Antonio de Orbe.[35]

Due to the necessity of better controlling trade and because of the creation of the *Council of the Indies* in 1524, new ordinances for the *Casa* were issued in 1531. The new ordinances had 62 articles, including the regulations of the 1510 ordinances. The new ordinances included specific regulations on the *Casa* staff obligations, working hours and residence. Also, the 1531 ordinances contains provisions on fleet organization, instructions to captains and crewmembers, searches, punishments and frauds.[36] In 1534, 1536 and 1543, regulations on

28 García-Baquero González, *La Carrera de Indias*, 37.

29 García-Baquero González, *La Carrera de Indias*, 62.

30 Ots Capdequí, *El Estado español en las Indias*, 63.

31 García-Baquero González, *La Carrera de Indias*, 62.

32 José Luis Comellas, *Sevilla, Cádiz y América: El trasiego y el tráfico* (Malaga: Editorial Argual, 1992), 61.

33 Haring, *Comercio y navegación*, 44.

34 Zamorano was the author of the well known works *Compendio de la Arte de Navegar* (Imp. Alonso de la Barrera, Seville, 1581) and *Cronologia y Repertorio de la Razon de los Tiempos. El mas copioso que hasta oi se ha visto* (Imp. Andrea Pescioni y Juan de Leon, Seville, 1585). The *Compendio* was printed in 1582, 1586, 1591 and 1698. There is a facsimile edition of the 1582 edition by Librerías París-Valencia, Valencia, 1995. The *Cronologia* was printed in 1594 and 1621. See Antonio Palau y Dulcet, *Manual del librero hispano-americano*, VII (Madrid, reprint from the first edition, 1990), 247.

35 Comellas, *Sevilla, Cádiz y América*, 61.

36 See Oscar Cruz Barney, *El régimen jurídico de los Consulados de Comercio Indianos: 1784–1795* (México: Universidad Nacional Autónoma de México, 2001), Cap. I.

weaponry, crews and supplies for the fleets were issued. In 1539 the *Casa* was granted exclusive jurisdiction over civil and criminal matters related to the regulations regarding transatlantic trade, and also over common law crimes perpetrated on board the ships. In 1552 new ordinances were issued, this time considerably larger than the older ones: 200 articles that according to García-Baquero are the most complete collection of regulations on the *Casa de Contratación* for the sixteenth century.[37] The ordinances paid special attention to the tasks of the *Casa* staff and the navigational and trade regime. The ordinances were reprinted in 1585, and were used to write the ninth book of the *Compilation of Laws of the Kingdoms of the Indies* of 1680. Now, the *Casa de Contratación of Seville* would became the centre of the *Carrera de Indias*, 'without their permission and consent, nothing could be sent or bring from the Indies; it regulates and supervise the ships conditions and crews; controls migration; works on the protection and defence of the maritime routes used by their pilots and mapmakers and in sum, it watches for the enforcement of every laws and ordinances regarding transatlantic trade'.[38] Finally, the *Casa de Contratación* was the Monarch's advisory body on treasury matters.

As the *Casa de Contratación* consolidated its position, the number of employees grew significantly: from its original three officials, it increased to three judges, one lawyer, one fiscal, one scribe, two ship inspectors, one *Piloto Mayor*, several mapmakers, one auxiliary treasurer, four officials, three accountant scribes, one jailer, and one doorman. In 1579 a President of the *Casa* was appointed, and in 1538 the *Casa* also became an *Audiencia* or Supreme Tribunal, with two courts, one of justice and one of government. This structure remained until the Bourbon reforms of the eighteenth century.

The *Casa* was affected by the sale of public offices by the Crown. Almost all the offices were subject to be sold, except those that included justice: officers such as the *Corregidor*, *Oidores* of the *Audiencias* and *Chancillerías*, the *Consejeros* of the Royal Council,[39] the three *oidores* or judges of the *Audiencia*, and the fiscal. The Crown made the sale as a donation to an individual, recognizing his special services rendered to the Monarchy. At the *Casa de Contratación* they used two mechanisms for these sales.

37 García-Baquero González, *La Carrera de Indias*, 64.

38 García-Baquero González, *La Carrera de Indias*.

39 See Francisco Tomás y Valiente, *Gobierno e instituciones en la España del antiguo régimen* (Madrid: Alianza Editorial, 1982), 163.

2.1.1 Perpetuity Sales or by *juros de heredad*

In this case the sale granted the acquirer of the position or office the possibility of transmitting it by hereditary means, to perform it personally or through a lieutenant and to designate, in addition, all the subordinate personnel that required, which deprived the *Casa de Contratación* of the control over such employees.

2.1.2 Expectancy Sales or Future Successions

This kind of sale was made with respect to those job titles that were occupied at the time of the sale. The buyer have the right to succeed the officer when he retired or was removed from office. The Crown also created supernumerary officers.

The Crown also decided to create hereditary offices, with the right to designate the employees. Those job titles were given to those individuals who had special merits or had rendered special services to the Monarchy.

These changes had different consequences. First, there was an impact on the number of employees, increasing from 24 in 1552 to 110 in 1687, with the consequent increase in salaries and expenses. Secondly, there was a decrease in the seriousness and the rigour of the officials, which was accompanied by a dangerous non-compliance of the ordinances.[40]

In 1526, Emperor Charles V liberalized the regime by opening the possibility of trading with the Indies to non-Castilian subjects. Perhaps because of the pressure put on him by foreign bankers, liberalization was repealed by his son Philip II in 1573 who only maintained the privilege for Cadiz. Charles V created the *Casa de Contratación* of La Coruña to manage the trade with the Molucas, giving privileges in 1529 to Bayona, Bilbao, Laredo, Avilés, San Sebastián, Cádiz, Málaga, and Cartagena. For the first time, in 1537 the Royal Armada escorted a fleet of trading vessels to the Caribbean.[41]

2.2 *The Convoy System: Fleets and Galleons*

In 1564, Philip II organized the convoy system that allowed better control from the authorities and also a much more effective defence against pirates and privateers.[42] '...[A]s the wealth extracted from Spain's colonies grew, piracy

40 García-Baquero González, *La Carrera de Indias*, 66–68.

41 Jeremy Baskes, *Staying afloat: Risk and uncertainty in Spanish Atlantic World Trade, 1760–1820* (Stanford, California: Stanford University Press, 2013), 62. See also Nicolas del Castillo Mathieu, 'Las 18 flotas de galeones a Tierra Firme (1650–1700)', *Anuario de estudios americanos, suplemento* 47:2 (1990), 83–129.

42 Beatriz Bernal, 'La política comercial marítima de España en Indias', in *Estudios en homenaje a Jorge Barrera Graf* I (México: Univ. Nacional Autónoma, 1989) 216. See also María

became an increasingly alarming problem, leading the Crown to issue a series of edicts designed to protect the valuable cargoes'.[43] It was a step forward from the navigation system which had been used by the *Casa de Contratación* since 1526.[44]

Since 1543, fleets had departed twice a year from Seville, the first departure during spring, in April, heading up to the Gulf of Mexico, Honduras and Las Antillas; and the second in August, to Tierra Firme (Gulf of Panama), with stopovers in Cartagena, Santa Marta and other ports in the north of South America. When the fleets returned to Spain the following March, they assembled at La Habana and made the journey back together. It was not always possible to send the fleets on a regular basis.

The fleet from Tierra Firme carried Peruvian silver, and was escorted by the galleons from which that fleet received its name ('galleons'). The fleet from New Spain was simply known as 'fleet', and was escorted by warships with lesser firepower. 15 to 90 vessels, depending on the economic and security conditions, made up each group of fleets or galleons.[45]

Together with Seville, two more ports participated in the transatlantic trade: Cadiz since 1531, and the Canary Islands since 1508, both obligatory stopovers under the supervision of an agent from the *Casa de Contratación of Seville*. In America, the ports authorized to trade with Spain were Veracruz in New Spain (which was the trade axis between Seville and Mexico City during the seventeenth century),[46] Cartagena in Nueva Granada, and Nombre de Dios or Puerto Bello at the Panama Isthmus. Acapulco in New Spain had a permanent permit to trade with the Far East through Manila, receiving the *Nao de China* (New Spain vessels returning from Manila). At one point, Cadiz grew from being a complementary port to being the home port of the *Carrera de Indias*.[47]

---

del Cármen Velázquez, *El estado de guerra en Nueva España, 1760–1808*, 2nd ed. (México: El Colegio de México, Centro de Estudios Históricos, 1997), 17.

43 Baskes, *Staying afloat*, 62.

44 First used in 1522. See Esteban Mira Caballos, 'La navegación entre España y América en la primera mitad del siglo XVI: algunas precisiones', *Revista de historia naval* 16:62 (1998), 68–69.

45 About the fleets see Mervyn Francis Lang, *Las flotas de la Nueva España (1630–1710): Despacho, azogue, comercio* (Sevilla-Bogotá, 1998).

46 Pablo Montero et al., *Ulúa, puente intercontinental en el siglo XVII* (México: Instituto Nacional de Antropología e Historia, 1997), 56–57. Also Pierre Chaunu, 'Veracruz en la segunda mitad del siglo XVI y primera del XVII', *Historia Mexicana* 36 abril-junio (1960), 528–531.

47 García-Baquero González, *La Carrera de Indias*, 33. Also, Montenegro Duque, *Historia de España*, 265.

Either way, not all the trade between Spain and the Indies was made through the convoy system, and occasionally the use of vessels from outside the system was allowed. These were known as *navíos de registro*.[48] Some ports of the Indies were authorized to trade directly with Spain using these *navios de registro* and were subjected to a special tax regime. This was the case for Caracas, Buenos Aires (with the authorization of having two *navíos de registro*), Maracaibo, Puerto Rico, Santo Domingo, La Habana, Matanzas, Trujillo and Campeche.[49]

The Spanish merchants had to deal with heavy taxes that, combined with the attractive American markets, provoked the creation of a parallel contraband market involving Spanish and foreigners, with consequent losses to the formal trade, and these posed a serious challenge to the security and defence of the possessions of the Spanish Crown,[50] where the fleet system was unable to oppose the illegal trade effectively.[51] The penalty for the crime of smuggling, confiscation, was called *comiso* (seizure), and it consisted of the loss or confiscation of the goods being smuggled.[52] Confiscated goods passed to the domain of the Royal Treasury.

The Spanish economy was unable to supply the markets of its American possessions due to poor or inadequate management of the political-administrative apparatus that did not allow adequate supply in times, qualities and quantities required.[53] The economies of Spain's European rivals were increasing in power. As a result, an illicit trade emerged between the inhabitants of the Spanish possessions in America and the colonies of England, Holland and France, to such an extent that the Indies became the main consumer market of goods from these three countries.[54]

Another cause of this illegal trade was the closeness of the European colonies in respect to the Spanish possessions and kingdoms, since communications between them offered no major difficulties for its inhabitants. Tax burdens established by the Spanish Crown constituted an incentive for smugglers, who established large commercial networks to supply the vast market of the

48 Bernal, 'La política comercial marítima', 217.

49 Martiré, 'El marco jurídico del tráfico', 231–232.

50 Oscar Cruz Barney, *El régimen jurídico del corso marítimo: el mundo indiano y el México del siglo XIX* (México: Universidad nacional autónoma de México, 1997), 228–242.

51 Montenegro Duque, *Historia de España*, 267.

52 Antonio Xavier Pérez y López, *Teatro de la legislación universal de España e Indias* IX (Madrid, 1744), 113.

53 See Ramón Aizpurua, *Curazao y la Costa de Caracas: Introducción al estudio del contrabando en la provincia de Venezuela en tiempos de la Compañía Guipuzcoana 1730–1780* (Caracas: Academia Nacional de la Historia, 1993).

54 Héctor R. Feliciano Ramos, *El contrabando inglés en el Caribe y Golfo de México (1748–1778)* (Sevilla: Diputación de Sevilla, 1990), 9.

Indies.[55] Moreover, population growth and the increase in manufacturing production resulted in an increase in consumption and the search for new markets to sell these products. The collapse of the fleet system and the rise of smuggling had to combine with the reforms of the Bourbon house. Thus, the legal regime in force had to be updated to try to deal with the nautical progress and the development of smuggling.[56]

Throughout the eighteenth century the Spanish Crown implemented a series of measures, including traditional and innovative ones, to try to curb the illicit trade. Such measures included coastal surveillance militias, Royal Coastguards (corsairs, or from the Royal Navy), the creation of privileged trading companies that provided enough supply to the Indies market and also provided surveillance services and the repression of smuggling, and surveillance of shipping routes. In addition, legislation was issued to fight smuggling, increase diplomatic actions and of course to strengthen Spanish Privateering. The Crown even ordered the Governors of the ports to eradicate the belief among the population that it was not a sin to commit fraud against the Royal Treasury.[57]

All of these efforts '...were insufficient to eliminate, or at least substantially alleviate the current crisis'.[58] Feliciano Ramos notes that in relation to the English contraband in the first half of the eighteenth century, it can be classified into three types, according to the subjects who performed the activity: that performed by the South Sea Company, that conducted by private British subjects, and finally that performed by subjects of the Spanish Crown from Spain or America.[59] Julio C. Guillamondegui argues that the main defect in vitiating

55 Feliciano Ramos, *El contrabando inglés*, 11.

56 See Alamiro de Avila Martel y Bernardino Bravo Lira, 'Nuevo régimen del comercio marítimo del siglo XVIII y su aplicación en el Pacífico Sur', *Revista chilena de historia del derecho* 5 (1969), 136.

57 *Real Orden de 15 de Septiembre de 1776 a los Governadores de los Puertos para que se dediquen como deben á desarraigar en sus respectivos distritos el perjudicial error de no ser pecaminosos los fraudes contra el Real Erario*, AGN, Bandos, vol. 10. Exp. 3, Fs. 5. The guards or government ministers that not fulfil their job as they should and permitted the transfer of forbidden goods from one place to another sinned mortally, and were forced to refund the damage directly to the King. See Universidad del Convento de Santiago de la Ciudad de Pamplona, *Promptuario de la theologia moral, que ha compuesto el convento de Santiago, Univerſidad de Pamplona, del Sagrado Orden de Predicadores, ſiguiendo por la mayor parte las Doctrinas del M.R.P. Maestro Fr. Francifco Larraga, Prior que ſue de dicho Convento, en el que ſe reforman, y corrigen muchas de ſus opiniones: y se ilustra con la explicacion de varias Conſtituciones de N.SS.P. Benedicto XIV* (Puebla, 1766), trat. XLIV, n. III, 1766, 388.

58 Feliciano Ramos, *El contrabando inglés*, 23.

59 On the coastguards in new Spain, see Oscar Cruz Barney, 'El régimen jurídico de los guardacostas novohispanos en la segunda mitad del siglo XVIII', *Revista de historia naval*

the Indies' mercantile system was not the lack of protection against illicit trade abroad, but the same internal structure of the Spanish commercial organization with regard to the territories of the Indies.[60] During the last decade of the seventeenth century the number of fleets bound for the Indies was reduced and they lost their periodicity. Due to the circumstances of the time, only seven fleets departed from Seville between 1690 and 1699, with the war of succession interrupting communications a year later.[61]

3 The *Consulados*

The *Consulados* were associations for trade promotion and the defence of its members, who were resident merchants who filled the requirements of age, property and occupation.[62] Consulates were created due to the need for specialized justice in commercial matters.[63] In this sense, they acted as special trade courts to resolve commercial disputes between its members with the express prohibition that ordinary courts intervened in such matters.[64] In 1494 the Catholic Kings in Burgos gave a pragmatic to spread both jurisdictions: civil and commercial, allowing the Consulates to act as Trade Courts.[65] Vas Mingo

16:60 (1998). Also: Oscar Cruz Barney, 'El régimen jurídico de los guardacostas novohispanos en la segunda mitad del siglo XVIII: la obra del virrey Juan Vicente de Güemes Pacheco de Padilla y Horcasitas, segundo conde de Revillagigedo', *Anuario mexicano de historia del derecho. Memorias del VII Congreso de Historia del Derecho Mexicano* X (1998); and Oscar Cruz Barney, 'La instrucción para gobierno de los bajeles guardacostas de Indias de 10. de octubre de 1803 en la Nueva España', *Anuario mexicano de historia del derecho* 11–12 (1999–2000).

60 Julio C. Guillamondegui, 'La repercusión inmediata del Reglamento de Comercio Libre de 1778. Una solicitud de creación del Consulado de Buenos Aires', in *III Congreso del Instituto Internacional de Historia del Derecho Indiano, Actas y Estudios* (Madrid: Instituto Nacional de Estudios Jurídicos, 1973), 985.

61 Caballero Juárez, *El régimen jurídico*, 76.

62 Robert Smith, 'Los consulados de comerciantes en Nueva España', in *Los consulados de comerciantes en Nueva España* (México: Instituto Mexicano de Comercio Exterior, 1976), 15.

63 Héctor Noejovich Ch., 'La institución consular y el derecho comercial: conceptos, evolución y pervivencias', in Bernd Hausberger and Antonio Ibarra (eds.), *Comercio y poder en América colonial: Los consulados de comerciantes, siglos XVII–XIX* (Madrid: Iberoamericana, 2003), 25.

64 For a history of the Mexican Trade Jurisdiction see Cruz Barney, Oscar, *Historia de la Jurisdicción Mercantil en México,* México, IIJ-UNAM, Universidad Panamericana, Porrúa, 2006.

65 *Nueva Recopilación*, Ley XII, Tít. XIII, Lib. III. We use the 1772 print *Leyes de Recopilación*, I–II (Madrid, 1772); *Tomo tercero de Autos Acordados, que contiene nueve libros, por el orden de títulos de las Leyes de Recopilación* (Madrid, 1772).

and Luque Talaván argue that 'the autonomy of the commercial jurisdiction from ordinary jurisdiction was a major step in stabilizing the Castilian trade from the legal point of view, as well as laying the necessary foundations to address the monumental Indies trade…'.[66]

The judges or consuls and the Prior were elected annually, and were taken from two or three of its members. For its importance in solving commercial disputes, given the need for expeditious resolutions, arbitration was a direct antecedent of the consular jurisdiction.[67] No jurists or professional judges intervened, but instead, merchants who were knowledgeable of the trade, its problems and its customs. Disputes were settled on the basis of *usus mercatorum* or usage of trade and the written rules of each Consulate.[68] It must be emphasized that from 1494 at the Consulate of Burgos, the decisions dictated by the Prior and Consuls had the characteristics of arbitration coupled with an undeniable enforceability.[69] Two ways to solve the disputes were available: the special jurisdiction of the Consulate and traditional arbitration. Juan de Hevia Bolaños maintained in this sense the distinction between pure arbitration proceedings and the proceedings before the Trade Consulates.[70]

The first Consulate in Castille was the one of Burgos, created by a *pragmática* of the Catholic Kings given in Medina de Campo on 21 July 1494 at the request of local merchants.[71] After their first ordinances on charters, and with the authorization of the Emperor in 1520, the Consulate of Burgos saw its first ordinances confirmed in Valladolid on 18 September 1538.[72] The Consulate received its second ordinances in 1572, improving on the previous ones, particularly with regard to maritime insurance, and inserting three formats for issuing them.[73]

---

66 Marta Milagros del Vas Mingo and Miguel Luque Talaván, 'La avería de disminución…', 28, 119 and 120.

67 Marta Milagros del Vas Mingo, 'Los Consulados en el tráfico indiano', in José Andrés-Gallego (coord.), *Colección Proyectos Históricos Tavera, I: Nuevas Aportaciones a la Historia Jurídica de Iberoamerica* (CD) (Madrid: Fundación Histórica Tavera, 2000), 11.

68 Francisco Tomás y Valiente, *Manual de historia del derecho español* (Madrid: Tecnos, 1987), 352–353; Santos M. Coronas González, *Manual de historia del derecho español* (Valencia: Tirant lo blanch, 1996), 353–354.

69 José María de la Cuesta Sáenz, 'Consulados y arbitrajes', *Actas del V Centenario del Consulado de Burgos, II: Conferencias 'Burgos y el Consulado'* (Burgos, 1994), 318.

70 Juan de Hevia Bolaños, *Curia Philipica* (Madrid, 1783), Lib. II, Caps. XIV and XV. In the same position, Cuesta Sáenz, 'Consulados y arbitrajes', 320.

71 Included in the *Nueva Recopilación* como ley 1ª, título 13, libro 3°. See *Ordenanzas del Consulado y Casa de Contratación de Burgos, aprobadas por el rey, Felipe II en 1572, Ordenanzas del Consulado de Burgos* (Valladolid: Lex Nova, 1988).

72 Manuel Basas Fernández, *El Consulado de Burgos en el siglo XVI* (Madrid, 1963), 41.

73 *Novísima Recopilación* Ley III, Tít. II, Lib. IX.

According to Gil Blanco, the importance of the Indies trade and the rising costs of maintenance and commercial litigation resulting from trade liberalization were the main reasons for authorizing the creation of the *Consulado de Cargadores a Indias* of Seville.[74] It was created by Royal Provision on August 23th, 1543,[75] and its ordinances were approved by Royal Provision on July 14th, 1556, bearing in mind the organization and functioning of the Consulate of Burgos.[76] The ordinances stated that the Consulate would have a Prior and two consuls, elected from among the traders, who would decide on any dispute relating to the trade of goods for or from the Indies, including freight, insurance, partnerships, contracts and commissions.[77] The activities of the Consulate of Seville were divided into three by García Fuentes: legal, commercial, and financial.[78] The Consulate heard lawsuits arising from the exercise of trade, financing through loans and grants to Indies trade, and by delegation of the *Casa de Contratación,* functions related to traffic control with the Indies, controlling marine insurance, tonnage and fleet dispatch,. oreover, the Consulate collected the taxes for infants, markets, average (*avería*) and tonnage.[79] Along with the Consulate, another institution was the University of the Masters and Pilots of the Naos of Navigation of the Indies (*Universidad de los Maestres e Pilotos de las Naos de la Navegación de las Indias*), which brought together the owners of the vessels and their captains who participate in the *Carrera de Indias*, with devotional purposes, chapel, religious festivals and caring tasks.[80] The *Casa de Contratación de Sevilla* played a key role, closely related to the Seville Consulate whose headquarters would be precisely the *Casa* itself. The Consulate remained in a close relationship with the *Casa de Contratación,* which handled the appeals regarding consular rulings, implementation and

---

74 Emiliano Gil Blanco, 'La realidad del tráfico veracruzano y su contraste con las políticas de los consulados de Sevilla y México', *Novahispania* 2 (1996), 163.

75 See also Ruiz Rivera and García Bernal, *Cargadores a Indias*, 52–67.

76 José Luis Comellas argues that the definitive ordinances ate from 1522. See Comellas, *Sevilla, Cádiz y América*, 63.

77 Robert Sidney Smith, *Historia de los Consulados de Mar (1250–1700)*, (trans.) E. Riambau (Barcelona: Península, 1978), 121. On trade and risks and insurances see Oscar Cruz Barney, *El riesgo en el comercio hispano-indiano: préstamos y seguros marítimos durante los siglos XVI a XIX* (México: Universidad Nacional Autónoma de México, 1998). Also Marta Milagros del Vas Mingo and Miguel Luque Talaván, 'La avería de disminución…'. The Consulate soon entered into a jurisdictional conflict with the *Casa* de Contratación, which in the end was solved by the Council of the Indies. See Eduardo Trueba and José Llavador, *Jurisdicción marítima y la práctica jurídica en Sevilla (siglo XVI)* (Valencia, 1993), 53.

78 Lutgardo García Fuentes, *El comercio español con América 1650–1799* (Sevilla, 1980), 23–25.

79 García Fuentes, *El comercio español con América*, 27.

80 Comellas, *Sevilla, Cádiz y América*, 64.

the accountability of the body in the collection of taxes. In the second half of the seventeenth century, the *Casa* lost the initiative in matters relating to commercial traffic with the Indies: 'the *Casa* was relegated to a second place, it will be towed by the Consulate of Commerce of Seville, true governing organ of the trade with Indies'.[81]

In late sixteenth-century Mexico, a group of traders made plans to organize its own separate guild from the Consulate of Seville[82] Thus, in June 15th, 1592, Philip II issued a charter creating the first trade guild of America, which was received by Mexico City council on March 13th, 1593, and proceeded to organize the guild and the court immediately.[83] With no major objections to the project of the Consulate, on May 17th, the Superior Tribunal authorized the creation of the guild and provided for the integration of an appellate court under the administration of a treasury official as an appellate judge. Two scribes of the *camera* and three affiliated *rapporteurs* to the Superior Tribunal objected to the creation of the Consulate, as this could undermine the royal authority. However, his opposition did not prevent its creation and November 8, 1594 the *Audiencia* was instructed to protect the new institution, pronouncing their definitive resolution on June 20th, 1595.[84] Its ordinances were ratified by the Crown in 1604 and published in 1636, stating that in every case that was

81 García Fuentes, *El comercio español*, 29.

82 See *Ordenanzas del Consulado de la Universidad de los Mercaderes de esta Nueva España, confirmadas por el Rey Nuestro Señor. Impressas siendo Prior, y Consules en él, Clemente de Valdes, Domingo de Varahinca, y Pedro Lopez de Cobarrubias, año de 1636. y reimpresas siendo Prior, y Consules los señores Theniente Coronel D. Juan Jofeph Perezcano, D. Gabriel Gutierrez de Teran, y D. Jofeph de Zevallos, en el 1772* (México, 1772), 5.

83 On the Mexican Consulate see Rubén Ruíz Guerra, 'El Consulado de Comerciantes de la Ciudad de México', in José Luis Soberanes Fernández (coord.), *Memoria del III Congreso de Historia del Derecho Mexicano* (México: Univ. Nacional Autónoma de México, 1984); and Ana Ma. Barrero García, 'Notas para una nueva edición de las Ordenanzas del Consulado de la Universidad de Mercaderes de Nueva España', in Beatriz Bernal, (coord.), *Memoria del IV Congreso de Historia del Derecho Mexicano* I (México, 1988). See also Guillermina del Valle Pavón, 'Apertura comercial del imperio y reconstitución de facciones en el Consulado de México: el conflicto electoral de 1787', in Guillermina del Valle Pavón (coord.), *Mercaderes, comercio y consulados de Nueva España en el siglo XVIII* (México: Instituto de Investigaciones, 2003). For the Consulado of Phillipines see Carmen Yuste, 'La fundación de la Junta de Profesores Comerciantes o Consulado de Filipinas. Circunscripción, atribuciones y competencias', *Revista Mexicana de Historia del Derecho* XXVIII (2013), 111–130.

84 See Robert Sidney Smith, José Ramírez Flores and Leonardo Pasquel, *Los consulados de comerciantes en Nueva España* (México: Instituto Mexicano de Comercio Exterior, 1976), 18.

not contemplated by them, the Consulate was to use the Ordinnances of the Consulates of Burgos and Seville.[85]

The *Consulado de Nueva España* was under the regulations contained in the ordinances of Burgos and Seville[86] during their first two years of life until the development of their own ordinances in 1603, which were confirmed by the King in 1604, and printed for the first time in 1636, the second in 1772, and the third and final in 1816.[87] The Ordinances of the Consulate of New Spain were led to the election of a Prior, consuls, and the organization of the Consulate and the procedures to be followed before it, applying on a supplementary basis the provisions of the Ordinances of the Consulate of Seville and Burgos, and so it will be regulated by the *Recopilación de leyes de los Reynos de las Indias de 1680*.[88] In this sense, as Robert Smith stated, 'the only express purpose of the Royal Decrees that created the Consulates of Mexico and Lima was to provide a commercial court, but the Consulate court structure presupposed the organization of a university of merchants or guild'.[89]

The next Consulate in the Indies was the one in Lima, whose first mention dates back to 1592 when the Council of the City of Kings requested before the Court in Spain the privilege of having their Consulate.[90] This was established by a decree of December 29th, 1593, although it did not begin its corporate life until February 21th, 1613, under the viceroyalty of the Marquis of Montesclaros, serving as Prior, and Consuls Miguel Ochoa, D. Pedro Gonzalez Refolio and D. Juan de la Fuente respectively.[91] The first ordinances of the Consulate of Lima were confirmed on March 30th, 1627, following the ones of Seville and Mexico, and are included in book IX of the *Recopilación de Indias* of 1680.[92] These ordinances were printed in 1630, 1635, 1680, 1723 (in the press of Francisco Sobrino,

---

85 Francisco R. Calderón, *Historia económica de la Nueva España en tiempo de los Austrias* (México: Fondo de Cultura Económica, 1995), 460. See also Manuel Cervantes Rendón, *El derecho mercantil terrestre de la Nueva España* (México: A. Mijares y hno., 1930), 14–15.

86 *Ordenanzas del Consulado de la Nueva España, Auto de el Acuerdo de la Real Audiencia de México, a veinte de junio de mil quinientos noventa y cinco*, 10.

87 Juan N. Rodríguez de San Miguel, *Pandectas hispano-megicanas* 3 (Méjico, 1852), 353. See also *Reales cédulas y provisiones a que deben sujetarse los cónsules, licencia de S.M. para hacer las Ordenanzas del Consulado de la Nueva España, limitaciones de la póliza pasada y seguro de las naos de las Indias*, vol. 2 (AGN, Reales Cédulas Duplicadas), Exp. 513, Fojas. 300 vta.-311. 15 de junio de 1592.

88 *Recopilación de Indias*, Lib.IX, Tít.XXXXVI, Ley. 75.

89 Smith, Ramírez Flores and Pasquel, *Los consulados*, 21.

90 María Encarnación Rodríguez Vicente, *El Tribunal del Consulado de Lima en la primera mitad del siglo XVII* (Madrid: Cultura Hispánica, 1960), 17.

91 Rodríguez Vicente, *El Tribunal del Consulado*, 31.

92 They can be consulted as an appendix of the work of María Encarnación Rodríguez Vicente already quoted.

being Prior Beytia and Aguirre), 1768 and 1820. Manuel Moreyra states that the content of the decree of creation of the Consulate of Lima in 1593 is brief, and mainly referred to the desirability of founding it on the model of Burgos and Seville.[93]

In the eighteenth century, Lima was the main centre of European product distribution in South America. The Consulate of Lima was one of the 'engines of economic life in Lima and throughout the Viceroyalty, not only from an information item or consultant but from the executive side'.[94] According to Turiso Sebastián in the eighteenth century, all, from the Viceroy to the judges and magistrates, to the last of the governed with a small capital, were part of the commercial dynamics.[95]

Consulates were composed of the Prior, the consuls, deputies, voters, scribe, bailiff, keeper and receiver. Those responsible for the administration of justice were the Prior and two consuls, as supreme authorities with legal and administrative functions.[96] In the exercise of its judicial functions they were considered to be royal judges. Consuls exercised their functions temporarily under their respective ordinances. The appellate judge was one of the judges (*oidores*) of the Superior Tribunal appointed by the Viceroy in each viceroyalty.[97]

The Prior and consuls of the Consulate of Lima and Mexico could resolve disputes and disputes between merchants on purchases, sales, exchanges, trades, bankruptcy, insurance, accounts, companies, factories, pack trains and ships charters, freight, 'and everything else they can and must solve as the Confulados of Burgos, and Seville…'[98]

The Consulate was expected to bring the lawsuit as soon as possible, and could be solved either unanimously or by majority. All three must sign the verdict, registering their votes in the book kept by the Secretary of the respective Consulate for this purpose. The prior and consuls were to resolve lawsuits in good faith and with the greatest speed possible.[99]

93 Manuel Moreyra Paz Soldán, 'El Tribunal del Consulado de Lima', *Estudios históricos* (Lima, 1994), 309.

94 Jesús Turiso Sebastián, *Comerciantes españoles en la Lima Borbónica: Anatomía de una elite de poder (1701–1761)* (Valladolid: Universidad de Valladolid, 2002), 92–93.

95 Sebastián, *Comerciantes españoles en la Lima Borbónica*, 93.

96 The Mexican Consulate jurisdiction covered México City, New Spain, Nueva Galicia, Nueva Vizcaya, Guatemala, Yucatán and Soconusco. See Christiana Renate Borchart de Moreno, *Los mercaderes y el capitalismo en México (1759–1778)*, (trans.) Alejandro Zenker (México: Fondo de cultura economica, 1984), 22.

97 Enrique Gacto Fernández, *Historia de la jurisdicción mercantil en España* (Sevilla: Universidad de Sevilla, 1971), 50; *Ordenanzas del Consulado de la Nueva España*, fol. 58.

98 *Recopilación de Indias*, Lib. IX, Tít. XXXXVI, Ley 28.

99 *Recopilación de Indias*, Lib. IX, Tít. XXXXVI, Ley 30.

It was possible to challenge the Prior and consuls. At the Consulate of Lima it was not possible to challenge both the Prior and the three consuls, but only two of them, and with causes for it. In Mexico, When the Prior and consuls were challenged, it was to be with just causes and according to law.[100]

With regard to conflicts of jurisdiction between the ordinary courts and consulates, in the case of the Consulate of Mexico, the Viceroy was, according to a Royal Decree of 18 June 1597, responsible for the resolution of the conflict. In Lima, according to Juan de Solorzano y Pereira, the Superior Tribunal (*Audiencia*), through the Chamber of Relations, solved such disputes. According to Hevia Bolaños, it was the Viceroy.[101]

4 Conclusion

The regulation of trade and navigation between Spain and the Indies during the sixteenth and seventeenth centuries show a clear intention to confirm the exclusive presence of the Hispanic Government over America. This was a huge effort of organization and regulatory measures that in some cases proved to have little effect (i.e. smuggling), but in others worked very well (i.e. migration policies). The Law of the Indies developed to become highly specialized due to the necessity for control and security, and gave birth to a legal system which was exclusive for the Indies. The Consulates form a highly important aspect to the study of Spanish-Indies trade relations. These were institutions with a long tradition dating back to the Consulate of the Sea, through the Consulates of Burgos, Sevilla, Mexico and Lima.

100 *Recopilación de Indias,* Lib. IX, Tít. XXXXVI, Leyes 31 and 32. For the Consulate of Lima in the eighteenth century see Cármen Parrón Salas, *De las reformas borbónicas a la república: el Consulado y el comercio marítimo de Lima, 1778–1821* (Murcia: Academia General del Aire, 1995) and the book already quoted of Jesús Turiso Sebastián.

101 Juan de Solorzano y Pereyra, *Política indiana* (Madrid, 1930), Lib. VI, Cap. XIV, Núm. 26; de Hevia Bolaños, *Curia Philipica,* Lib.II, Cap. XV, Núm. 29, 443–444.

Scots Traders and Spanish Law in East Florida

M.C. Mirow

1 Introduction

In 1802, a few leading residents of Saint Augustine, the capital of Spanish East Florida, brought suit against Panton, Leslie, and Company, a British firm run by Scots who had successfully traded with Native Americans for several decades in the region. The residents, led by Francisco Sánchez, claimed that Panton Leslie was blocking their access to trade with Indians through its facilities near Picolata, approximately 22 kilometers west of the city on the Saint Johns River.[1] They requested that the firm move its trading operations into Saint Augustine or, in the alternative, that Panton Leslie be expelled from the province. They based their claim on allegations of Panton Leslie's hindering trade through monopoly, of its illegal evasion of duties, and of its abuse of privileges granted by the Spanish crown. The petition alleged damages both to the royal fisc and to the public at large through the firm's excessive and monopolistic trading practices.

The central issue of the dispute related to the scope and interpretation of numerous royal orders and decrees issued by the Spanish crown. Other important yet ancillary issues included the representative capacity of Sánchez and his co-plaintiffs; the payment of duties by Panton Leslie in specific instances; the management of economic, political, and military aspects of native populations; the causes of instability and disruption in the region; the actions of Panton Leslie's principals, agents, and employees; and the appropriateness of the forum considering the general lack of legally trained individuals in the city.

This study tells the story of a commercial lawsuit found in the primary records of the dispute extant in the East Florida Papers held by the Library of Congress. The record of the case consists of approximately 1000 folios and reveals that the Spanish colonial legal system in a small city was capable not only of producing voluminous texts related to legal issues but also of engaging in a high level of legal argumentation and sophistication. In the end, however, the governor decided to transfer the case to the Captain General in Havana for final determination. This action ensured that legal historians would have an

1 Although some documents studied here use 'Picalata', 'Picolata', the accepted term, is used throughout this contribution.

 | DOI:10.1163/9789004443075_006

almost complete record of the pleadings, rulings, sources, and evidence submitted to the governor to resolve the dispute.

Commercial law in Spanish East Florida was based on specific agreements and licenses issued by the crown and general regulations concerning shipping and duties. In the context of overlapping imperial interests and native populations, commerce and commercial law encompassed more than the relationship between merchants and national economic policy. Careful management of trade ensured tranquility in Spain's relationship to a varied community of Indian nations and impeded economic, political, and military encroachment by the United States into the northern regions of the Spanish empire. Although focused on a single, large dispute, this study demonstrates that commercial law touched on questions of European inter-imperial sovereignty, Spanish and British intra-imperial trade competition, American political geography, relationships with native populations and their exercise of power, and the application of colonial legality in the context of overlapping regimes in which commercial actors could have multiple and conflicting alliances and identities.

2 A Brief History of Panton, Leslie, and Company with Special Reference to East Florida

The trading firm of Panton, Leslie and Company was a complex and lucrative commercial enterprise in the southeastern region of North America.[2] In the late eighteenth and early nineteenth centuries, the firm had over fifteen trading outposts and company stores that covered a region now encompassing the states of Florida, Alabama, Mississippi, Louisiana, and Tennessee. In the eastern areas of its influence, it traded with Seminoles and Lower Creeks; in the west, with Choctaw and Chickasaw. Panton Leslie representatives in the Bahamas, London, Glasgow, and Madrid represented its commercial and legal interests. Although Panton Leslie diversified its activities with land deals and various forms of international trade, including enslaved humans, its core business

2 The firm used two principle names during its existence, 'Panton, Leslie, and Company' from approximately 1783 until 1804, with the composition of the partnership changing in 1792 when John Forbes, John Forrester, and Robert Leslie joined the firm, and then 'John Forbes and Company' from 1804 to 1847. William S. Coker and Thomas D. Watson, *Indian Traders of the Southeastern Spanish Borderlands: Panton, Leslie & Company and John Forbes & Company, 1783–1847* (Pensacola: University of West Florida Press, 1986), 363. Forbes and Company continued to use the name Panton, Leslie, and Company in East Florida even after it used Forbes and Company elsewhere in its economic sphere. Because this study focuses on East Florida, it uses 'Panton Leslie' to refer to the firm during its entire life span.

was trading English guns, gunpowder, and shot for deerskins. European powers and competitors always alleged that along with licit trade, success in the world of international trade was linked to smuggling and the evasion of duties.[3] It appears that establish practice often merged licit and illicit trade.[4] Because Panton Leslie extended credit in many of its transactions, Native American tribes and European powers quickly became indebted to the firm which carved out a unique place for itself in the politically tumultuous colonial world of the southeast of North America. Panton Leslie closely followed political and diplomatic tensions and accords as the firm was often the recipient of particular favors and privileges extended by one government or another.[5]

In the mid-1770s, British loyalists shifted their activities south to the British provinces of East and West Florida. A loyalist and trader, William Panton fled from Georgia in 1776 to Saint Augustine, the capital of British East Florida, and in late 1782 or early 1783, formed Panton, Leslie, and Company with four other refugees.[6] Scots loyalists leaving former northern British colonies for the relative safety and stability of East Florida was common.[7] Panton had been an apprentice with the Scots trading firm of John Gordon and Company in Charleston, South Carolina, from 1765 to 1772.[8]

William Panton was born near Fraserburgh, Scotland, in the early 1740s, and little is known about his life before his arrival in Charleston, South Carolina, in 1765. Panton first appears as a merchant in 1774 when he with another offers to sell a newly arrived cargo of 65 enslaved humans, and he established other short-lived partnerships in the late 1770s and early 1780s.[9]

William Panton's first set of partners were John Leslie, Thomas Forbes, Charles McLatchy, and William Alexander. Most of the partners had come from the string of coastal villages along Moray Firth, north of the Grampian Mountains and Aberdeen, to work in Indian trade in the southern trading cities of Charleston, Savannah, and Saint Augustine before the American Revolution. John Leslie was baptized in Rothes, Scotland, in 1749, and his brother Robert who later became a junior partner in Panton Leslie was baptized there in 1758. They were brothers of the well-known Scots minister and local author

3 Coker and Watson, *Indian Traders*, ix, 12, 34–36, 61–62, 127, 365.

4 T.M. Devine, *Scotland's Empire: The Origins of the Global Diaspora* (London: Allen Lane 2003), 33, 66, 75–76, 93.

5 Coker and Watson, *Indian Traders*, xiii.

6 Coker and Watson, *Indian Traders*, ix, x.

7 David Dobson, *Scottish Emigration to Colonial America, 1607–1785* (Athens: University of Georgia Press, 2004), 167–171.

8 Coker and Watson, *Indian Traders*, 15.

9 Coker and Watson, *Indian Traders*, 18, 24–26.

William Leslie. Thomas and John Forbes were from Gamrie, County of Banff; John arrived in Saint Augustine, East Florida, in 1784, and his older brother Thomas had worked in Indian trade for over fifteen years by the time of his death in 1808.[10] Less is known about Charles McLatchy and William Alexander; it is clear, however, that both were from Scotland.[11]

It seems highly unlikely that the partners of Panton Leslie expected that Spain would take possession of East Florida almost immediately after the partnership was established in late 1782 or early 1783. The British withdrawal from South Carolina and Georgia in 1782 disrupted Indian trade in the region, and thousands of Creeks crossed into British East Florida. To stabilize trade and to create a buffer with the United States, British authorities granted Panton Leslie a license in January 1783 to continue its trade with Indians.[12]

Two months later, in April 1783, Britain ceded East Florida to Spain, and Saint Augustine began the process of peacefully transferring power from British to Spanish authority over the next two years. Three of the original Panton Leslie partners remained in East Florida, Panton, Leslie, and McLatchy; Forbes and Alexander went to the Bahamas where they maintained their ties to the firm. Meeting Spanish representatives in London, Thomas Forbes argued for Panton Leslie's continuation in East Florida to trade with the Indians. Only Panton Leslie had the established trade network, resources, and personal connections to provide an effective buffer against the United States and its expansion into Spanish territory and trade. Only England could provide the trade goods that were most appreciated by the Seminoles and Lower Creeks. Indeed the Seminoles, an important offshoot of the Lower Creeks, were led by Alexander McGillivray, himself a wealthy half-Scot with strong British loyalist ties and a share in Panton Leslie profits. Spain granted Panton Leslie a license to trade in East Florida as long as it conducted its trade under the *Reglamento de Comercio Libre* of 1778 that required that goods be cleared through particular Spanish ports.[13]

Panton Leslie's relationship with Spain was unique. Spain usually used its own trading system, and granting a monopoly of trade to a foreign company loyal to another crown was highly unusual. Spain had no merchants ready to step into the shoes of Panton Leslie, and the firm had access to highly-regarded English goods, an established trade network, ships, knowledge of the customary

10 Coker and Watson, *Indian Traders*, 15, 19, 20–23.

11 Coker and Watson, *Indian Traders*, 21. It is not known if this William Alexander was related to the Edinburgh trading firm of William Alexander and Sons active in the 1750s and 1760s. Devine, *Scotland's Empire*, 80.

12 Coker and Watson, *Indian Traders*, 43, 50.

13 Coker and Watson, *Indian Traders*, 43–45, 51–55.

practices, and personal contacts with McGillivray, the leader of the Seminoles. Panton Leslie was in a position to press for more favorable trade conditions such as the reduction or elimination of duties, the easing of restrictions concerning access to non-Spanish ports, and the ability to trade in goods that were not originally encompassed in a trade that was exclusively directed towards native populations.[14]

The Spanish strategy of using Panton Leslie as a trading buffer with the United States was effective during the late 1780s despite U.S. efforts to make inroads into Indian trade in the west and other merchants' attempts to topple Panton Leslie's monopoly. The Creeks at times led or joined violent expeditions to keep U.S. forays in check. Nonetheless, by the late 1780s, an English trader from Nassau, William Augustus Bowles, began to nudge Panton Leslie from its secure position, and the relationship between McGillivray and Spain grew distant. McGillivray and the Creek were courted by the United States, and Bowles physically and diplomatically attacked Panton Leslie's interests. Near the beginning of 1789, William Panton doubted that continued trade would be stable and profitable in the region, and he began to collect and to liquidate the extensive outstanding debts he held, especially those extended to Indian nations. McGillivray died in 1793 creating a power vacuum in Creek leadership. In the same year, French privateering through U.S. ports impeded Atlantic trade for Panton Leslie and its ability to obtain goods diminished while its insurance costs increased three- to six-fold. The Treaty of San Lorenzo in 1795 placed most of Panton Leslie's business in territory now held by the United States.[15]

Conditions for peaceful and profitable trade decreased as Spain and Great Britain entered into the Anglo-Spanish War in 1797 and Britain blockaded Spanish colonies in the Americas. This might have been an unworkable situation for a British firm operating out of Spanish colonies. For reasons of state centering on maintaining supportive and peaceful relations with Indians, Spain permitted Panton Leslie to continue its activities throughout the war. Spain subjected Panton Leslie to closer scrutiny as the firm asserted variances from the strict letter of Spanish trade law based on its established customary and earlier permitted practices. William Panton and the employees of Panton Leslie swore an oath not to impede Spain's prosecution of the war or to give aid to Spain's enemies.[16]

These arrangements, however, only satisfied one side of the parties at war. Panton Leslie needed legal opinions concerning its activities relative to British

14 Coker and Watson, *Indian Traders*, 66–72, 109, 128–129, 134, 367–368.

15 Coker and Watson, *Indian Traders*, 93–125, 135–156, 177, 182–194, 369.

16 Coker and Watson, *Indian Traders*, 203–209.

interests to protect it trade from seizure by British forces as prize. Admiralty law experts Sir William Scott and Sir John Nicholls concluded that Panton Leslie ships were subject to seizure and one expert even asserted that Britain could consider Panton and his partners Spanish subjects. Although Panton Leslie successfully turned to James Gardiner and Company in Charleston, South Carolina, as a neutral intermediary through the guise of 'broken voyages', William Panton became increasingly discouraged and contemplated leaving Florida. Panton Leslie's formerly excellent relations with it London correspondent, Strachan and MacKenzie, fell apart as the London firm sought to collect on debts owed by Panton Leslie. Panton Leslie had wisely obtained an order-in-council protecting its assets for two years as it supposedly withdrew its property from the Floridas. In the late 1790s, Panton Leslie faced almost insurmountable obstacles because its major goods for trade included guns and gunpowder, equally suited to taking pelts and waging war. The firm later leveraged claims against Spain for economic damage from the war, estimated at over £41,000, into significant trade concessions.[17]

By the first years of the nineteenth century as Bowles reinvigorated his challenges to Panton Leslie's control of Indian trade, Panton Leslie turned towards collecting its debts. Most Indians indebted to Panton Leslie now resided within the United States, and the United States property and law would necessarily be part of Panton Leslie's resolution of its claims. Panton Leslie pursued land to satisfy debts, most likely because land was the only asset held by those in debt to the firm.[18]

In February 1801, William Panton died and John Forbes took over leadership of Panton Leslie in April of the same year.[19] It is in this context that the litigation explored here between some Spanish residents of Saint Augustine and Panton Leslie is examined.

3 Saint Augustine v. Panton Leslie, 1802

In 1793, John Forrester, Panton Leslie's agent in Saint Augustine, opened a trading post on the Saint Johns River, opposite an area known as Picolata on the east bank of the river. This was an effort to protect Panton Leslie's property at the Saint Marys store because it was subject to raids from Georgians across the Saint Marys River and Indians allied with Bowles. For years, Panton Leslie had

17 Coker and Watson, *Indian Traders*, 212–225.
18 Coker and Watson, *Indian Traders*, 226–233.
19 Coker and Watson, *Indian Traders*, 234–235.

been aware of its exposure in the area. As part of Bowles's resurgence in attacking Panton Leslie, a group of Indians under Bowles's leadership attacked Francisco Fatio's plantation near Picolata on 31 August 1801 and stole thirty-eight slaves. Nonetheless, with a change of leadership in the Bahamas, Bowles fell out of favor, and John Forrester helped negotiate a treaty between Seminoles and Spain through which Seminoles agreed to return the stolen slaves and to withdraw any support from Bowles.[20] At the time Forrester was described as a being:

> thirty-seven years old, son of Scottish parents, born in Georgia, a sworn vassal of His Majesty [of Spain], has served in this city [of Saint Augustine] in various trading firms since 1776 until 1781 when he went to Panton Leslie and Company of which he has been a member since 1790. He married in 1791 with Isabel Green daughter of this province with whom he has two sons, one of nine and the other of seven years. He served in the firm in Penzacola six months and three in the trading post of Apalacha. He is a Protestant and of irreproachable conduct.[21]

Forrester and the Picolata trading post were not without their detractors beyond Bowles. In the middle of June 1802, a number of leading citizens (*vecinos*) of the city of Saint Augustine petitioned the governor of the province for redress against Panton Leslie. The petition sought to stop Panton Leslie from operating its trading post at Picolata and, in the alternative, to expel the trading firm from East Florida. The immediate issue was the imminent re-establishment of the Picolata trading post in the same month after it had been closed following the murder of William Brady near the post. The main arguments of the petition were that Panton Leslie had abused the privileges granted to it by the Spanish crown by operating beyond the scope of its license, by fraudulently avoiding duties on goods, by operating as an exclusive monopoly in Indian trade, and by denying Spaniards the right to benefit from Indian trade. Thus, claiming representative collective capacity, Sánchez and his co-plaintiffs claimed damage to the citizens of the city and to the fisc of the crown.[22] The governor ordered that the petition be sent to his legal officer or *asesor*, Licenciado José de Ortega, for his careful consideration.[23]

20 Coker and Watson, *Indian Traders*, 32, 165, 238–239.

21 Washington, D.C., Library of Congress, East Florida Papers, Oficio no. 608, 9 November 1802, Reel 157, Part II, fols. 156–156v (hereafter 'E.F.P.').

22 The petition is in poor condition and these arguments have been reconstructed from subsequent pleadings in the case. Petition, 14 June 1802, E.F.P., Reel 157, Part I, fols. 1–3v, 6.

23 Decree, 22 June 1802, E.F.P., Reel 157, Part I, fol. 4v.

One of the few legally trained individuals in the entire province, Ortega issued a *dictamen* that was incorporated into the governor's decree. The dictamen states that Ortega had surveyed the documents related to Panton Leslie and that it was permitted to trade with Indians by royal order under specific rules.[24] He was also ordered to examine the *Autos*, papers, instructions, and receipts related to the firm in the offices of the crown, the tax assessor and the treasury to determine Panton Leslie's payment of duties in possible prejudice to the royal treasury. Ortega responded that he would need the assistance of these offices to assemble the necessary documents, and the governor, Enrique White, issued a decree accordingly.[25]

Perhaps aware that his petition had some traction with the governor, Sánchez was ready with another more extensive petition delivered to the governor the following day.[26] He and his co-plaintiffs repeated that the resumption of trade at Picolata would be prejudicial to the king and to the public. They requested that Panton Leslie halt its restocking of the trading post and that the governor order the firm not to conduct Indian trade outside the city. They suggested that the petition be supplemented with the texts of the royal orders related to Panton Leslie and that if the governor was not able to grant the relief they requested that the cause be forwarded to the king to remedy

24 Dictamen, 10 July 1802, E.F.P., Reel 157, Part I, fols. 4v–5v. Complete texts of many of the royal orders and other governing documents are found in the file. E.F.P., Reel 157, Part II, fols. 85–94 (R.O., 9 June 1793); E.F.P., Reel 157, Part II, fols. 94–96 (Edict interpreting R.O. 9 June 1793); E.F.P., Reel 157, Part II, fols. 96v–97v (Edict, 2 September 1802); E.F.P., Reel 157, Part II, fols. 107v–109v (Governor White's talk with Seminoles, 18 June 1800); E.F.P., Reel 157, Part II, fols.109v–115v (correspondence between Seminoles and White); E.F.P., Reel 157, Part II, fols. 115v–129 (correspondence related to Mickosukees); E.F.P., Reel 157, Part II, fols. 157v–162v (Treaty of Peace of Apalache, 20 August 1802); E.F.P., Reel 157, Part II, fols. 162v–175v (Treaty of Peace of Pensacola and related points about treaty, 1 June 1784); E.F.P., Reel 157, Part II, fols. 218v-219 (Edict, 10 November 1801, regarding sale of gunpowder to Indians); E.F.P., Reel 157, Part II, fols. 221–222 (Edict, 7 March 1803, regarding trade with Indians outside city); E.F.P., Reel 157, Part III, ff. 10v-12v (R.O. 20 June 1784); E.F.P., Reel 157, Part III, fols. 11v–12v (R.O. 18 May 1786); E.F.P., Reel 157, Part III, fols. 13–14 (R.O. 11 May 1786); E.F.P., Reel 157, Part III, fols. 14–15v (R.O. 9 August 1788); E.F.P., Reel 157, Part III, fols. 15v–18 (R.O. 26 June 1788).

25 Decree, 16 July 1802, E.F.P., Reel 157, Part I, fol. 5v.

26 Petition, 17 July 1802, E.F.P., Reel 157, Part I, fols. 5v–12. The signatories of this petition can easily be made out: Francisco Xavier Sánchez, Francisco Pellicer, Pedro Cocifacio, José Pezo de Borgo, Pedro Fornells, Juan Cavedo, Vicente Mexía, Francisco Felipe Fatio, Alexander Crighton, Jorge Fleming, Mateo Guardarrama, Francisco Miranda, Bernardino Sánchez, José Sánchez, Nicolas Sánchez, Francisco Richard, Juan Gianapoly, and Antonio Mabrunmary.

the continuous injuries they suffer from the 'privileged and exclusive Indian trade' granted to Panton Leslie.[27]

3.1 *Arguments in the Petitions of the Leading Men (Vecinos), Sánchez and His Co-plaintiffs*

As Sánchez and his co-plaintiffs filed their complaint, they asserted that Panton Leslie was preparing to deliver horse-loads of gunpowder and munitions to Picolata for trade with the Indians which would lead to greater disruption and violence in the province. A general theme used by the petitioners was that peaceful relations between Spain and the Indians would never be possible while Panton Leslie served as an intermediary between them. Peaceful conditions would lead to greater direct trade with the Indians, which would, in turn, increase the royal treasury. Nonetheless, the trading post at Picolata isolated Indians and impeded their access to the city to trade, and the petition asserted that Panton Leslie effectively controlled not only this physically important river crossing at Picolata but also the flow of information to Indians to ensure that they feared trading directly with Spaniards. Direct trade was necessary to establish a more lasting peace with the Indians which Panton Leslie had not been able to attain.[28]

By establishing a monopoly in trade, the petition argued, Panton Leslie inflated prices while avoiding payments of duties and defrauding the king. Even the presence of Bowles as competition to Panton Leslie indicated that monopolistic control of trade was not necessary. Elsewhere, Sánchez alleged that Panton Leslie paid 10,000 pesos annually for exclusive trade with the Indians.[29]

Panton Leslie had additionally expanded into forms of trade that were not covered by its original permission to trade with Indians. As Panton Leslie traded in cattle, it sold meat and traded in leather goods, markets earlier served by Spanish merchants in the city.[30] The petition concluded by requesting that the transportation across the river at Picolata by floats (*flata*) and by trails be turned over to a Spaniard so that 'the Indians can bring their horses and cargo to this city and the others that travel to sell in it so that the noxious influences of the said firm with the Indians is avoided'.[31] The governor again referred the petition to his asesor, Ortega.[32]

27 Petition, 17 July 1802, E.F.P., Reel 157, Part 1, fols. 6–7.
28 Petition, 17 July 1802, E.F.P., Reel 157, Part 1, fols. 7v–9, 11–11v.
29 Petition, undated (July 1802), E.F.P., Reel 157, Part 1, fols. 10, 13v.
30 Petition, 17 July 1802, E.F.P., Reel 157, Part 1, fols. 9–9v.
31 Petition, 17 July 1802, E.F.P., Reel 157, Part 1, fol. 11.
32 Decreto, 17 July 1802, E.F.P., Reel 157, Part 1, fols. 12–12v.

The petitioners did not let up. In an undated petition from the second half of July, 1802, Sánchez continued his attack on Panton Leslie.[33] He now turned his attention to John Forrester, the chief representative of Panton Leslie in Saint Augustine, who travelled with Chief Payne and an interpreter, Dermant, to Indian settlements to enter into a peace treaty. The petitioners doubted the peaceful aims of this action because Indian hostilities in the region continued, especially from the Micosuky under the chief that Forrester was supposed to have subdued.[34] Without specific allegations, the petition also characterized Dermant as someone who was already supposed to have been expelled from the province because of his 'perverse character and very bad conduct'.[35] The petitioners asserted that Dermant, as a representative of Panton Leslie, had lied to the Indians to encourage them to trade at Picolata by telling them it was not safe to trade in the city where the Spaniard did not like them and would kill them. Forrester too upheld the necessity of the Picolata trading post, and thus the Panton Leslie team had more than establishing peace on their minds when they travelled to the Indian towns. This petition again concluded that action was necessary to avoid irreparable damage to the province, its inhabitants, and the interests of the king. The remedy was the suspension, even temporary, of the trading post at Picolata and of Panton Leslie's operations in the province.[36] The decree of the governor indicated he would grant the relief, provided that the petitioners were able to establish the facts complained of in the petition. For this reason, Ortega was instructed to inform the secretary of the government (*Escribano del Gobierno*) to assemble the required documents quickly to avoid further damage.[37]

In response to the various petitions and directions from the governor, Ortega prepared a lengthy dictamen that deeply examined the legal substance and nature of the dispute.[38] He reviewed the available documents, royal orders, and over 50 files from the customs department from 1785 until 17 April 1802 with special attention given to the payments for duties and the goods imported and exported by Panton Leslie. He divided his dictamen into three parts: (1) the establishment of Panton Leslie and its relationship with Spain; (2) its failure to observe the rules established for its trade with the Indians and the damage

33 Petition, undated (July 1802), E.F.P., Reel 157, Part I, fols. 12v–17.

34 Petition, undated (July 1802), E.F.P., Reel 157, Part I, f. 13–13v. The file of the case contains correspondence with and reports to the Captain General concerning the state of the province during the period. E.F.P., Reel 157, Part II, ff. 136v–157.

35 Petition, undated (July 1802), E.F.P., Reel 157, Part I, fol. 13v.

36 Petition, undated (July 1802), E.F.P., Reel 157, Part I, fols. 14–16.

37 Decree, 31 July 1802, E.F.P., Reel 157, Part I, fols. 17–17v.

38 Dictamen, 23 August 1802, E.F.P., Reel 157, Part I, fols. 18–49.

perpetrated on the king and public; and (3) an examination of the injures arising specifically from its operation of a trading post in a sparsely populated area and from its inability to advance royal policies. The dictamen stated that this analysis would lead to a determination of whether or not Panton Leslie should remain in the province.[39]

The dictamen provided a detailed description of the royal orders creating the unusual relationship between these Scots traders and the Spanish crown. Ortega surveyed the royal orders recognizing Panton Leslie on the recommendation of the English with the requirement that the firm trade in Spanish goods according to the requirements of the *Reglamento de Comercio Libre* of 1778.[40] Other royal orders continued Panton Leslie's activities to maintain tranquility in the province, permitted the firm to use British goods because these were more appreciated by Indians, required oaths of fidelity and obedience to the king (with appropriate modifications for nation and religion), addressed Indian declarations of war against the United States to reclaim land, and incorporated the agreements of the congress held in Louisiana with Indian nations.[41] Ortega had access to the specific texts and clearly set out the language of these orders as they related to Panton Leslie's privileges. It is not necessary here to chronicle the specificity of description provided by Ortega who knew that the question of Panton Leslie's continuation in East Florida might very will hinge on the interpretation of language within these orders. Ortega importantly included a discussion of the royal order that exempted Panton Leslie from the required six percent duty on imports and exports when they were part of Indian trade with an associated list of provisions to avoid abuse and to establish prices.[42] According to Ortega, the intent of the royal orders from the late 1780s was to give Panton Leslie control of Indian trade at Pensacola, in West Florida, and to give another trader, Mather, control of Indian trade at Mobile, with no one allowed to trade along the Mississippi River. Rum and salt were to be obtained in Havana at Spanish prices.[43]

With these and other royal orders in mind, Orgeta came to the conclusion that Panton Leslie had violated many of their provisions. He focused on the firm's use of English goods, its shipments from New Providence, Bahamas, its lack of truthfulness in registers and documents, its lack of records in some instances, its valuation of cargo, and its excessive use of its exemption from

39 Dictamen, 23 August 1802, E.F.P., Reel 157, Part I, fols. 18–19v.

40 Dictamen, 23 August 1802, E.F.P., Reel 157, Part I, fols. 19v–20 (R.O. 20 July 1784).

41 Dictamen, 23 August 1802, E.F.P., Reel 157, Part I, fols. 20–21v (RR.OO. 8 May 1786, 11 May 1786). For an oath by Forrester, a protestant, see E.F.P., Reel 157, Part II, fols. 103v–104.

42 Dictamen, 23 August 1802, E.F.P., Reel 157, Part I, fol. 23v (citing R.O. 23 March 1789).

43 Dictamen, 23 August 1802, E.F.P., Reel 157, Part I, fols. 24–24v.

taxation. From records of shipments, he surmised that the volume of goods and their duty-free status had not complied with the royal orders, especially in the characterization of goods for Indian trade which turned out to be clearly for Spanish consumption. Ortega noted that in just one year from 1800 to 1801, just one ship undertook eleven voyages from Charleston with goods that, for the most part, resulted in no duties being paid. Such quantity of goods could not have been exclusively for Indian trade. Panton Leslie similarly had not followed the provisions requiring that rum and salt come from Havana.[44]

Turning from Panton Leslie's general conduct in trade, Ortega next addressed the firm's trading post in Picolata. Ortega concluded that the post was not consistent with the creation and maintenance of the firm in the province. Ortega first argued by analogy from the prohibition of trade on the Mississippi River. The royal order prohibiting British traders from the Mississippi River was based on several policy considerations. In the event of hostilities between Spain and Britain, Spain did not want British traders to have established influence over the tribes along the Mississippi River. It also did not want Britain to gain strategic knowledge of the region from extensive trade. Additional considerations were the easy avoidance of inspections and ability to circumvent duty payments at an unsupervised and isolated trading post. For the same reasons, Britain should be denied trading posts in any deserted areas and this included the trading post at Picolata. Indeed, even Spaniards were prohibited from establishing trading posts in deserted areas for the same reasons. Under several royal orders, trading posts in unpopulated areas, in hidden places, and in forests were prohibited in Indian trade. The possibility of abuse was just too high. If Spaniards were prohibited from establishing isolated trading posts, then foreign, British traders should, even more so, be prohibited.[45] Ortega adopted the concerns expressed by Sánchez that by its exclusive trade with the Indians, Panton Leslie had effectively cut off Indians from coming into Saint Augustine. This isolation not only had impeded better social relations with the Indians but also had hindered the crown policy of introducing Christianity to the Indian nations. Ortega noted that the trading posts in unpopulated areas tied Indians to British firms and placed Spain at a linguistic disadvantage. Indians gained familiarity with English rather than Spanish, again impeding direct communication with Spaniards in Spanish.[46]

44 Dictamen, 23 August 1802, E.F.P., Reel 157, Part 1, fols. 25–35v.

45 Dictamen, 23 August 1802, E.F.P., Reel 157, Part 1, fols. 36–37, 39–40 (citing an agreement with Indians in Pensacola in 1784, and royal orders from May 1786 and March 1789).

46 Dictamen, 23 August 1802, E.F.P., Reel 157, Part 1, fols. 37–38, 41–41v.

Ortega then turned to the actions of Forrester. He described the relatively stability of the period when John Leslie represented Panton Leslie with the leading Seminole Alexander McGillivray. This good state of affairs eroded with the death of McGillivray in 1793 and Leslie's departure to London in 1798. Since then Forrester's tenure as the representative for Panton Leslie had been punctuated by his sudden flight to the United States during an increase in Indian and other hostilities, his return to Saint Augustine only when the petition had been filed, and his unwillingness to join the local militia to aid in the common defense of the province.[47]

Ortega also questioned the policy of maintaining tranquility in the region as a justification for Panton Leslie's exclusive trade with Indians. Recent hostilities and instability arising from William Bowles's disruption demonstrated that Panton Leslie was not able to assure peace. Ortega properly attributed Bowles as the primary agitator of hostilities in the region as he used violent methods to destabilize Panton Leslie's monopoly. Nonetheless, the newest treaty with the Indians indicated that most Indian nations would work collectively to remove Bowles from his power and from the region. Furthermore, the stability resulting from trade between Panton Leslie and the Seminoles under McGillivray had been essential to Spanish aims of keeping the U.S. influence in check in the 1780s and early 1790s. Now, however, most territorial questions between the United States and Spain were resolved by the Treaty of 1795, and this reason for granting special privileges to Panton Leslie disappeared.[48]

Ortega's interpretation of the facts was not favorable to Panton Leslie. In the final portion of the dictamen, Ortega concludes that through greed and abuse, Panton Leslie had damaged the royal revenue and the public. Panton Leslie's trading post in Picolata was inconsistent with the royal orders; the firm had supplied the crown at elevated prices and had profited as an intermediary of the Indian gifts necessary to grease the wheels of trade. It had evaded duties and continued to use English goods after it was no longer necessary to do so. It had brought in significant quantities of goods from the United States with whom Spain was now in a position to trade directly without intermediaries.[49]

Panton Leslie's more recent actions of gobbling up land in the region as payment of debt or through other means of acquisition were also detrimental to Spanish inhabitants. Panton Leslie was evading duties on these activities. Panton Leslie was cattle ranching, running a slaughterhouse and blacksmithing

47 Dictamen, 23 August 1802, E.F.P., Reel 157, Part 1, fols. 38v–39.
48 Dictamen, 23 August 1802, E.F.P., Reel 157, Part 1, fols. 41, 43–43v, 44.
49 Dictamen, 23 August 1802, E.F.P., Reel 157, Part 1, fols. 45–46.

shop, and was trading in meat, hides, and leather goods. These were all beyond the scope of its charge to trade with Indians.[50]

Thus, Ortega concluded that the trading post should be permanently suspended and Panton Leslie should be expelled from the province.[51] Ortega cautioned that the governor could not act directly on the dictamen. Explaining the odd nature of the case and the fact that Panton Leslie still had not be heard on the case, Ortega included in his advice to the governor:

> But as [Panton Leslie] has not been heard in justice, [this decision] is not able, in my view, to be imposed due to the lack of jurisdiction of the court, and of the *Contaduria* who exercises the functions for the fiscal of the royal treasury (more than that of the asesor in which role I have served in this case) until the determination of His Majesty who ought to decide the mode and form of such proceeding. I am of the opinion that in the Junta of War, if you decide this file and the documents that must be added are viewed, it is to be decided what is best, to order the closure of the trading post in an unpopulated area.[52]

To make an informed decision, the governor ordered that all the documents cited in the dictamen be provided to him in authorized copies by the secretary of the government. As the governor was deciding on the points of the dictamen and to preserve royal interests, Panton Leslie was ordered not to engage in any of the tricks described in the dictamen.[53] There was, however, already a substantial amount of supporting documentation available in the case. The Contaduria, the office charged with keeping accounts of shipping duties and other royal revenues, had supplied an itemized list of payments of duties by Panton Leslie to the secretary of the government. It included payments made from 1794 to 1801, a list of items recognized for Indian trade, a list of items related to supplying the firm itself, the text of the trade treaty between Spain and Indians in Pensacola from 1 June 1784, and the text of the Saint Augustine agreement between Spain and Panton Leslie from 31 July 1784.[54] The governor was also supplied with numerous records of vessels arriving in East Florida from 1784 to 1802 under Panton Leslie with lists of goods and duties paid.[55]

50 Dictamen, 23 August 1802, E.F.P., Reel 157, Part 1, fols. 46–47.
51 Dictamen, 23 August 1802, E.F.P., Reel 157, Part 1, fols. 47–47v.
52 Dictamen, 23 August 1802, E.F.P., Reel 157, Part 1, fols. 47v–48.
53 Decreto, 26 August 1802, E.F.P., Reel 157, fols. 49–49v.
54 Relación, 17 July 1802, E.F.P., Reel 157, fols. 49v–64.
55 List of Descargas prepared by José de Zubizarreta, 20 September 1802, E.F.P., Reel 157, fols. 64–188.

The memorial between the governor of East Florida and Panton Leslie was particularly important for its presentation of the obligations of the parties and the underlying policies of the agreement. For example, Panton Leslie emphasized its long practice of trade with Indian nations and its considerable influence among these populations. The firm was familiar with the use, customs, and languages of trade with Indians, and it had their trust. It promised its loyal action to accustom the Indians to the Spanish crown and its expertise in providing the gifts commonly distributed to Indians. Panton Leslie noted that Indians did not like Spanish goods and that the quality of pelts exported through Spain was poorer due to their movement though several ports and warmer climates. For these reasons, English goods were necessary and payment with pelts directly in Britain was preferable. Nonetheless, Panton Leslie stated that British goods would be used only for Indian trade and that all trade would be conducted according to Spanish law.[56] Members of Panton Leslie in East Florida would swear an oath of obedience and faithfulness to the Spanish crown in accordance with their religious profession and would be extended tolerance for their religious beliefs 'until, perhaps, a combination of the errors of the protestant doctrine may be the cause of our conversion to the Catholic faith'.[57] If war broke out between Britain and Spain, the members of Panton Leslie would not take any personal action against Spain.[58]

A month after the governor's decree requesting documents and admonishing Panton Leslie to conduct its trade according to the royal orders, Sánchez sent another petition to the governor. The petition asserted that the violations continued although operations at Picolata had ceased because of hostilities in the area and specifically because of fear after the murder of William Brady. Now the petitioners complained that on wrapping up its trade at Picolata, Panton Leslie did not bring its goods to the city but instead had transferred them to John Forrester's house which was still far from the city and which served as a continuing location for hidden trade with the Indians. The petitioners also alleged that Panton Leslie continued its illicit trade to and from the United States. They repeated their concerns that this isolated trade hindered better relationships with the Indians and that the head and guard of the Picolata trading post, Dermant, continued to tell Indians that no Spaniard had the right to trade with Indians and that only Panton Leslie could do so. For this reason, the petition requested that Dermant be removed from Picolata.[59] Another

56 Memorial, 31 July 1784, E.F.P., Reel 157, fols. 58v, 59v–60v, 61v.

57 Memorial, 31 July 1784, E.F.P., Reel 157, fols. 62–63, quote at fol. 63.

58 Memorial, 31 July 1784, E.F.P., Reel 157, fol. 62v.

59 Petition, 23 September 1802, E.F.P., Reel 157, fols. 188–195.

petition complained that Dermant was impeding Indian passage to the city through Picolata in other ways.[60]

Several additional petitions from Sánchez and his co-plaintiffs followed over the next few weeks and months. Many of the points of these new petitions repeated the allegations and demands of the petitions already submitted. They added that Panton Leslie was now storing goods at the house of John Forrester's neighbour, that the firm should return all its goods to the city, and that the privilege of Indian trade was personal to Panton and did not extend to the firm.[61] One petition sought to establish a theory of privileges to apply to Panton Leslie. Somewhat unusual for the tone and level of argument in these petitions, the passage stated:

> And being that it is given that a privilege is always disfavored for being against the *derecho comun* and that the intent of the Legislator in concessions of this nature, wanting to be favorable to some with the look of not being injurious (*gravoso*) to others, we find that this is the case that makes *epikeia* pour over all those suitable remedies, that modifying the most severe restrictions ought to create a plain discourse under which, until now, has run all the matters of this firm.[62]

The governor referred these petitions to asesor Ortega. By the beginning of November 1802, the petitioners noted that Panton Leslie had not responded to any of its petitions and urged the governor to secure a reply from the firm and to set a first hearing on the case.[63]

3.2 *Panton Leslie Responds*

By mid-October 1802, Felipe Roberto (Phillip Robert) Yonge had been called in to help with legal aspects of the case for Panton Leslie. He is described in the clerk's notification of the parties as '*dependiente de y uno de los Apoderados de la Casa de Panton Leslie y Compañia en esta Ciudad*'.[64] Yonge, an important legal figure throughout the British and Spanish periods, was an attorney for Panton Leslie in August 1802, and had previously served the firm as a clerk, attorney, and head of the Saint Augustine branch.[65] He petitioned for an extension

60 Petition, September 1802, E.F.P., Reel 157, fols. 195–198v (no day provided).

61 Petition, late September or early October 1802, E.F.P., Reel 157, fols. 199–200 (no day provided).

62 Petition, late September or early October 1802, E.F.P., Reel 157, fol. 200v.

63 Decree, 6 November 1802, E.F.P., Reel 157, fols. 202–203v.

64 Notification, 23 October 1802, E.F.P., Reel 157, fols. 202v–203.

65 Coker and Watson, *Indian Traders*, 274–275.

of 20 days to respond based on three reasons. First, he was the only member of Panton Leslie who would understand the legal aspects of the demands of Sánchez's petitions, but as he was also employed by the Royal Treasury (*Real Hacienda*), he should be excused from responding. Related to the first point, the dearth of lawyers (*profesores*) in the city meant that there was no one with whom he could consult. His third reason for not responding was that he had only a short time to study the rulings of the court, and because he was working in English with translations to and from Spanish, he needed more time to ensure the accuracy of the texts.[66] He was granted 15 days.[67] In a subsequent petition he requested nine more days because Forrester was ill.[68] Obtaining proof of Forrester's poor health from a doctor, the governor granted the extension.[69]

Nearly half a year had passed since Sánchez's first petition. A substantial body of documentation and numerous petitions with sound arguments had come before the governor. Asesor Ortega had supported the propositions in the petitions and added his own arguments against Panton Leslie. It seemed unlikely that Panton Leslie would continue its trade in Picolata or, for that matter, anywhere within East Florida.

In December 1802, Yonge responded for Panton Leslie.[70] He first described the establishment of Panton Leslie's rights to trade in East Florida under Spain. The firm had acquired the rights to continue its commerce with Indians with the same conditions it had conducted this trade under Britain. This was the result of its long experience and the recommendation the firm received from British authorities to the Captain General of Havana who sanctioned this arrangement. Instead of denying Panton Leslie's influence over the Indians, Yonge described a firm that exerted its influence always in the prudent service of the Spanish crown, and Forrester and Dermant had acted accordingly. Panton Leslie had to use English goods because Spain did not produce the articles required by Indians. This led to a series of royal orders and agreement that recognized Panton Leslie's unique contribution not only to commerce with the Indians but also to Spain's political and diplomatic goals in the region. Panton Leslie was a trusted representative of Spain in negotiations with Indians and severed the country in this capacity. Yonge disputed Ortega's reasoning and conclusions with his own interpretation of the royal orders, decrees, and letters. Without

66 Petition, November 1802, E.F.P., Reel 157, fols. 204–205 (no day provided).

67 Decree, 9 November 1802, E.F.P., Reel 157, fol. 205.

68 Petition, November 1802, E.F.P., Reel 157, fols. 205v–206 (no day provided).

69 Decree, 23 November 1802, E.F.P., Reel 157, fols. 206–206v.

70 Petition, 4 December 1802, E.F.P., Reel 157, Part 1, fols. 207–227v.

Panton Leslie's adaptive strategy of continuing trade, the Indians and their needs would have been abandoned leading to hostility and war.[71]

As an example of his skill as an advocate for Paton Leslie, Yonge dismantled the analogy Ortega tried to construct between the prohibition of trade on the Mississippi River and a prohibition of a trading post in Picolata. Yonge argued that the policies behind the Mississippi River prohibitions were unknown and that Panton had express permission to trade on the Mississippi from Spain. Yonge argued that Spain recognized the need for such trading posts to maintain stability and to avoid the ill social effects of intoxicated Indians roaming the city after successfully trading pelts. Instability, murders, and robberies in the region were not the product of the trading post in Picolata; they were the product of Bowles and the groups of Indians associated with him.[72]

Any monopolistic practices were necessitated by the trade with which Panton Leslie was entrusted; it was the only way for Panton Leslie to provide the needed leather goods that were shipped from East Florida to Havana to Spain. Yonge similarly did not dispute the facts of Panton Leslie's movement of goods after the closure of Picolata, of its use of small boats for trade, or of Dermant's continuation at Picolata. Nonetheless, he asserted that these and other actions questioned by Ortega were always done with the governor's permission or under the color of royal order.[73]

To demonstrate Panton Leslie's service to the crown, Yonge returned to the theme of good Indian trade securing peace. He mentioned that Panton Leslie had to deal with France, England, United States, and Indians and had suffered financial losses that would have easily ruined other merchants. Panton Leslie had loyally stayed the course though the recent war that increased the price of goods purchased by the firm and increased the cost of shipping and insurance. It continued this trade to keep peace and with the understanding that it would be permitted to continue trade to recoup its losses. Panton Leslie, argued Yonge, had provided good service to Spain and deserved to continue.[74]

---

71 Petition, 4 December 1802, E.F.P., Reel 157, Part I, fols. 207–211v, 212, 218–218v.

72 Petition, 4 December 1802, E.F.P., Reel 157, Part I, fols. 213–216, 220v.

73 Petition, 4 December 1802, E.F.P., Reel 157, Part I, fols. 216v–217, 221–222. Petitions, decrees for passports, certificates, and polizas indicating that Panton Leslie acted with oversight and permission are found at E.F.P., Reel 157, Part II, fols. 175v–221. Panton Leslie even sought permission on 18 March 1803 to take delivery of cattle at Picolata to satisfy Indian debts after an edict on 7 March 1803 prohibited Indian trade in unpopulated areas. Panton Leslie argued that the reasonable expectations at the time of creation of the debt was that it could be satisfied at the trading post. The governor granted permission for the delivery. Petition and Decree, 18 March 1803, E.F.P., Reel 157, Part II, fols. 222–223v.

74 Petition, 4 December 1802, E.F.P., Reel 157, Part I, fols. 222–223v.

From the argument based on policy, Yonge next attacks the ability of Sánchez and his co-plaintiffs to serve as representatives. Yonge's petition stated:

> I ought to point out to you that the representations have been signed by some few inhabitants of the province in the name of all, and I doubt that they have this authority, not one power appearing [in the pleadings], and because there are many respectable subjects of different opinion to theirs, I am obligated to request certifications or declarations that the court make available.[75]

Yonge addressed those who sought to restrict Forrester's movement. Yonge stated that there was duplicity in those who signed because they knew they were impeding his ability to manage his property leading to its being subject to robbery and destruction. They signed without personally knowing the content of the petition, and Yonge would show that others refused to sign for this reason. Thus, Yonge requested that the court call the signatories one-by-one to examine each one of his knowledge of the representations and that the judge punish those who did not know.[76] In this regard, Yonge revealed his knowledge of colonial Spanish law and its insistence on proper, written delegation of authority for one person to act for another. The force of this argument should not be discounted.

Yonge also sought to diffuse an underlying theme put forward by Sánchez that Panton Leslie should not trade in the province because it was a foreign firm. Yonge used the transitory nature of Spanish, English, and Spanish rule in the region to his advantage. Yonge asked rhetorically:

> What does it matter that Don Francisco Sánchez was born in the province when the Spanish were its rulers and that he calls himself Spanish, if under British rule he was English? This shows that he is neither Spanish nor English but a guardian of his own convenience.[77]

Thus, Sánchez's shifting citizenship undermined his assertions that he was acting for the best interests of the Spanish crown to whom his allegiance was embarrassingly fluid. And questions of national allegiance were not the only reason to distrust Sánchez and his co-plaintiffs. Yonge impugned their class and education; they were a group of tavern owners and tradesmen (*taberneros y*

75 Petition, 4 December 1802, E.F.P., Reel 157, Part 1, fol. 223v.
76 Petition, 4 December 1802, E.F.P., Reel 157, Part 1, fol. 224.
77 Petition, 4 December 1802, E.F.P., Reel 157, Part 1, fol. 224v.

artesanos) who widely overstated Panton Leslie's earning because they did not understand the operating expenses of the business that included losses through confiscation and natural conditions, the costs of acquiring goods at the point of origin, and associated fees paid to governments. This was just one example of their desire to give a false impression of all the acts of Panton Leslie.[78]

Yonge stated that he was ready to answer for Panton Leslie in any tribunal or to one and all inhabitants for its compliance with the rules governing its trade with Indians.[79] All he sought was a regular and just inquisition into Panton Leslie's operation. Yonge requested five forms of relief: (1) his opponents should supply a more reasonable complaint than the petitions filed with the governor; (2) they should give surety (*cargo de seguranza*) to pursue their claim; (3) they should provide sufficient notice to Panton Leslie; (4) the litigation should be removed to a location where there was a sufficient number of lawyers; and (5) Panton Leslie denied any damage to the city or its inhabitants.[80]

Shortly afterwards, Yonge filed another petition on behalf of Panton Leslie. Yonge repeated his objection to the representative capacity of the signatories and indicated that different individuals signed the statement against Panton Leslie for different, and deceptive, reasons. Yonge described at length the relationship between Felipe Fatio and Forrester as Forrester attempted to recover Fatio's slaves from the Micosuky. Forrester's actions led to a significant dispute between him and Fatio over the return of the slaves Forrester had seized and the costs associated with their recovery and maintenance. Yonge again steered the argument towards the content of the royal orders and justified Panton Leslie's actions in relation to the language of the orders. Furthermore, much of Panton Leslie's trade was at the request of the government, and if it was responsible for supplying goods to non-Indian consumers, it did so only because it was fulfilling requests coming directly from the government which then should be responsible for any expansion of Panton Leslie's activities.[81]

The governor ordered that English documents be translated into Spanish and that notice of Panton Leslie's petition be given to the other parties.[82] Numerous supporting documents were appended to the record in Spanish including statements related to Panton's permission to operate on the Mississippi River, permissions extended to Panton Leslie in New Orleans in 1789,

78 Petition, 4 December 1802, E.F.P., Reel 157, Part I, fols. 226–226v.
79 Petition, 4 December 1802, E.F.P., Reel 157, Part I, fol. 212v.
80 Petition, 4 December 1802, E.F.P., Reel 157, Part I, fols. 212v, 227–227v.
81 Petition, December 1802, E.F.P., Reel 157, Part III, fols. 1–10v (no day provided).
82 Decree, 15 January 1803, E.F.P., Reel 157, Part I, fols. 227v–228.

extracts from an agreement with Alexander McGillivray, copies of correspondence between Panton and Corondocet, correspondence from governor Juan Quesada chronicling John Leslie's services to the Spanish crown and commissioning Forrester, and correspondence with high-level representatives of Spain.[83]

3.3 *Sánchez Responds*

Sánchez and his co-plaintiffs reiterated their claim in another petition responding to Panton Leslie.[84] The substantive claims were the same as in prior petitions. Perhaps sensing the quality of Yonge's response, the petitioners sought to benefit from the unusual nature of their claim:

> It is not doubted and quite clear, Señor Governor, that what we ask for the leading citizens whom we represent, the observance and compliance of the sovereign dispositions in this matter of our complaint and damages, ought not to be understood as a suit between parties, that precisely it must be determined with pleadings (*traslados*), because this has stopped being civil and ordinary. [This] matter of yours is criminal and executive, as now we have indicated, [and] gives occasion to parties with sinister proofs and reports. They destroy the common good until it finally tires the population by advancing their demands.
>
> In civil and criminal suits between parties, although they have laws that work in their favor, there are also arguments, terms, and occasions that pull apart their pretensions. This requires that [this case] no longer follows the royal ordinances under which the said firm should conduct its trade and commerce as it is now provided, and as intended, considering principally the conservation of the province.[85]

This tactic by Sánchez indicates that he felt the legal arguments were in favor of Panton Leslie after reviewing Yonge's petition. The case was no longer an ordinary civil matter and required exceptional executive action to remedy Panton Leslie's breaches. Furthermore, this most recent petition recognized that there were some irregularities in the role of the asesor:

> Having noted in the decrees of various rulings the signature of the asesor is not found, [the case] proceeded without consultation [of the asesor]

83 E.F.P., Reel 157, Part 1, fols. 228v–242.
84 Petition, 5 February 1803, E.F.P., Reel 157, Part 1, fols. 251v–257v.
85 Petition, 5 February 1803, E.F.P., Reel 157, Part 1, fols. 253v–254v.

> and this being contrary to the laws and royal orders which precisely oblige judges so that all their rulings are with an asesor, and not conforming itself with the dictamen. From this it is observed what was prevented in this matter. We request consultation [of an asesor] from now on, otherwise we shall return to the hard precision of protesting against all that has been done as null and illegal and appeal to a superior court for the justice we seek.[86]

The governor's more moderate tone in his recent decrees issued without consultation with the asesor were at the heart of this complaint. If Yonge was going to insist on the strict application of law, then Sánchez could also invoke procedural requirements that would enable their supporter, the asesor, to opine on the next ruling to be issued by the governor. This petition was, as one might expect, ordered to be delivered to the asesor for his consultation.[87]

3.4 *Ortega's Dictamen*

Back in the loop as Asesor, Ortega issued his dictamen on Sánchez's petition. Ortega thought that the situation needed new sovereign orders to resolve the issues presented in the petitions. He analyzed provisions of the *Real Ordenanza de Intendentes de 1786* to find that generally exemptions and liberties were to apply to Indian trade and even to permit trade in hidden as well as public spaces. Thus, Panton Leslie was to obey the extant royal letters and orders until the crown produced a new royal resolution.[88] This was the general rule.

Nonetheless, when a privilege was exercised poorly, the holder of the privilege should lose it, Ortega argued. The loss of a privilege was supported by a rule of interpretation that when doubt arose about the exercise of a privilege the doubt should be decided in favor of the sovereign and against the holder of the privilege. The governor should examine Panton Leslie's actions in this light. Before a determination was made, the governor would have to require the production of more documents and would also need to decide where the cause should be heard while waiting for sovereign action on the matter. Furthermore, Ortega found that Sánchez and his co-plaintiffs had appropriate representative capacity or standing to bring the claim; any member of the public who was injured by an abuse was a legitimate interested party to reclaim the injury as long as the allegations were pleaded with particularity.[89]

86 Petition, 5 February 1803, E.F.P., Reel 157, Part 1, fols. 256v–257.
87 Decree, 5 February 1803, E.F.P., Reel 157, Part 1, fols. 257–257v.
88 Dictamen, 2 March 1803, E.F.P., Reel 157, Part 1, fols. 257v–259v.
89 Dictamen, 2 March 1803, E.F.P., Reel 157, Part 1, fols. 259v–261v.

Following the dictamen, the governor's decree ordered the closure of Panton Leslie's trading posts on the Saint Johns River and the construction of means of transportation across the river. The governor restricted Panton Leslie from moving or buying any goods and ordered appropriate fines and costs.[90]

3.5 *Panton Leslie Gathers Local Support and Sánchez Responds*

The matter was far from settled. Another document, labeled a 'presentation', demonstrated public support for Panton Leslie. The presentation gave voice to supporters of Panton Leslie who were property and plantation owners along the Saint Johns River. Perhaps Yonge had waited until the court determined the question of whether a few individuals could speak for the population as a whole before deciding to file his own petition with a list of signatures attached. This was a clever tactic. Signed on 7 January 1803 but filed with the court on 7 March 1803, the document noted that there was an earlier petition that purposes to speak for all the inhabitants requesting that the trading post be moved. This writing protested the petition because the signatories of the presentation were not consulted and because the remedies suggested by Sánchez would injure the prosperity of the province and lead to its destruction. Panton Leslie's trading posts were necessary to maintain the 'savages' in peace along the frontier; without them, the signatories were worried about Indian raids and hostilities. The presentation was signed by more than 75 individuals, eclipsing the apparent collective representation of the handful of leading men who had started the suit.[91]

Shortly after this statement of support for Panton Leslie, Sánchez and his co-plaintiffs submitted a 160 page petition restating and elaborating on their earlier claims.[92] Their concern was not just about ejecting Panton Leslie, it was about the benefits that foreigners had for over eighteen years. On assuming control of the province, Spain did not know the Indians or the character of its neighbours, and thus, at the time it made sense to give Panton Leslie permission to trade with Indians. Indians also preferred English goods and the leader of the Seminoles, Alexander McGillivray, was already closely connected to Panton Leslie. There were also disputes with the United States along the Mississippi River. These reasons, so persuasive eighteen years ago, no longer existed. Indeed, the leading men asked the court to consider why it was still necessary to rely on foreigners, particularly when Panton Leslie had been incapable

90 Decree, 7 March 1803, E.F.P., Reel 157, Part I, fols. 262–264.

91 Presentation, 7 January 1803, E.F.P., Reel 157, Part I, fols. 264–267v.

92 Petition, 12 March 1803, E.F.P., Reel 157, Part II, fols. 1–80.

of stopping the recent flood of Indians from the United States to Spanish territory. The petition repeated the allegations of abuse of royal benefits, fraud, trade beyond the limits imposed by royal orders, and Panton Leslie's control of gifts to the Indians. Instead of limiting its trade to Indians, Panton Leslie supplied everyone from individuals in the city to troops in the fort. Furthermore, although the members of Panton Leslie took the appropriate oaths to trade in Spain, they did not take up arms to protect it when necessary. Even when Spain was at war with Britain, the ships of Panton Leslie entered freely from the Bahamas laden with goods that were most likely made by Spanish prisoners. To watch a ship under enemy flag enter an East Florida port as required by the crown's agreement with Panton Leslie was too much to ask of any loyal Spaniard. Panton Leslie and particularly its trading posts in unpopulated areas had not produced the peace expected through its exclusive trade with Indians. The region was filled with unrest and hostilities. And Bowles had not helped the situation, but Panton Leslie was unable to control him. Panton Leslie had expanded its operations far beyond the scope of its royal permission into blacksmithing, leather goods, and meat. Panton Leslie did not need all the land that it obtained from the government. Forrester's travels and communications with Indians and Dermant's activities particularly in relation to the trading post at Picolata were suspect.[93]

Sánchez and his co-plaintiffs also addressed their representative capacity:

> It would be silly to sustain that we are empowered for all the inhabitants of the province to represent our complaints, but as the circumstance is material so that the causes be true and constant that have obliged us [to act], to find them, nothing is lost of our representations. We know well that not all are of our opinion, and that the firm of Panton Leslie has and has had respectable countrymen, friends, and protectors, but also it should be noted that the same protection has been the cause through which your Majesty has lost many thousands of pesos and that we have been defrauded of the use of so many rights that belong to us. Nonetheless, if this case had to be decided by a plurality of votes, we would have the relief of seeing it concluded in a few days being quickly presented to the court if it was up to a list of all those of our opinion for the removal of Panton and Company.[94]

93 Petition, 12 March 1803, E.F.P., Reel 157, Part II, fols. 1–1v, 5v–7, 9–18v, 21, 22–32v, 35–36–37, 47–49, 56v, 60.

94 Petition, 12 March 1803, E.F.P., Reel 157, Part II, fols. 33–34.

The leading men offered to supply a list of individuals supporting their position and asserted that it would be much longer than the list of Panton Leslie supporters.[95]

Insulted by being called poor tavern owners and tradesmen, Sánchez and his co-plaintiffs joined in the arguments related to class. Panton Leslie was nothing more than a few rich British merchants with offices in London. In East Florida, like Panton Leslie, Sánchez and his co-plaintiffs were dedicated to agriculture and trade. This implied that they were completely able to replace Panton Leslie in its activities, and they were tired of being excluded from such a lucrative trade.[96] The haughtiness of Panton Leslie precluded it not only from military assistance in the province but also from providing needed economic assistance. Despite its successes in trade, Panton Leslie did not step in to help the citizens of Saint Augustine with financial assistance. With tongue in cheek, the leading men argued that Forrester could not be blamed for this because a person of his high character should not be associated with tavern owners and tradesmen nor mix his money with theirs. Forrester had to maintain his distance from the ordinary people. When the Spaniards and settlers abandoned their wives, children, slaves, crops and land to join the militias and fight against a common enemy, Panton Leslie was too good to join in this concerted action and instead swept up cattle and goods and blocked any trade the Spaniards might undertake. This petition expanded the enquiry from merely Panton Leslie's financial compliance and requested that government officials provide certificates of how the firm assisted in the defense of the province.[97]

Repeating the allegations of earlier petitions, this petition then presented a detailed analysis of the royal orders and letters to conclude on each point that Panton Leslie had violated its obligations. The main problem according to this petition was Panton Leslie's importation of prohibited goods and non-payment of duties. Panton Leslie had also violated the broad policies that justified its introduction into Spanish trade. In eighteen years, Panton Leslie had not assisted in the return of one cow, horse, slave, or any other piece of property taken by Indians nor had it advanced peace in the region through its commercial influence.[98] Even if all the good acts Panton Leslie was supposed to have

95 Petition, 12 March 1803, E.F.P., Reel 157, Part II, fol. 34.

96 Petition, 12 March 1803, E.F.P., Reel 157, Part II, fols. 37v–38v, 42v. A supplement to the petition lists the property of Francisco Fatio, Francisco Sánchez, and Manuel Solano, each with assets of between 70,000 and 157,000 pesos. They indicated their willingness to take over Panton Leslie's trade. Petition, 12 March 1803, E.F.P., Reel 157, Part II, fols. 75v–77v.

97 Petition, 12 March 1803, E.F.P., Reel 157, Part II, fols. 43–44v.

98 Petition, 12 March 1803, E.F.P., Reel 157, Part II, f. 61v–70. A supplement to the petition carefully lists deaths, those wounded, and robberies by race during the period. Petition, 12 March 1803, E.F.P., Reel 157, Part II, fol. 78.

done were conceded, the firm still should not remain in East Florida. If it remained, Spain would forever give up its possible union with the Indians. It is only through trade and communication, particularly though mixed sexual union although criminal and shameful to Christians, argued the petition, that Spaniards and Indians would eventually create a society where both groups live well. The British have served as an example of this. Such racial mixing diminished the influence of others on Indians and reduced hostility.[99]

The petition asserted that Spain was now enslaved by a foreign firm with fatal consequences. The only solution was to expel Panton Leslie.[100]

3.6 *More on Documents, the Contador's Reply, and Resolution*

A number of petitions related to the production of documents, a summary of Panton Leslie's costs, and their translation followed the substantive pleadings.[101] Yonge again raised his concern that there was a lack of 'profesores' of law or lawyers in the city to advise him.[102] Asesor Ortega issued a dictamen requiring the production and translation of documents related to the dispute, and the governor issued his decree accordingly.[103] After several other petitions related to the production of documents, asesor Orgeta, perhaps aligning himself with Sánchez's theory that this was no ordinary civil dispute that could be resolved in the ordinary course of litigation, opined that the when he was sent to obtain the requested documents, he determined they were impossible to obtain. The governor had asked him to sort through nineteen years of records that were not indexed in a way that the materials related to Panton Leslie were readily available. Indeed, the contador of the royal treasury, Gonzalo Zamorano, stated that he could not supply the documents even if given a year to find them. Instead, the contador offered his impression of the documents related to Panton Leslie and concluded that it had defrauded the treasury.[104] The governor confirmed the dictamen in his decree.[105]

The contador now found it necessary to justify his inability to get the document as requested. He first objected that the ruling had its origin in a petition in a civil case instigated by various citizens, Sánchez and his co-plaintiffs. The

99 Petition, 12 March 1803, E.F.P., Reel 157, Part II, fols. 66–66v. On sexual relations and the expansion of the British empire see Devine, *Scotland's Empire*, 201–202.

100 Petition, 12 March 1803, E.F.P., Reel 157, Part II, fols. 66v, 67v, 70–72v.

101 E.P.F., Reel 157, Part I, fols. 267v–277v

102 Petition, 5 May 1803, E.F.P., Reel 157, Part I, fol. 277v.

103 Dictamen, 17 May 1803, Reel 157, Part I, fols. 278v–283v; Decree, 17 May 1803, Reel 157, Part I, fol. 283v.

104 Dictamen, 20 June 1803, E.F.P., Reel 157, Part I, fols. 285v–289v.

105 Decree, 21 June 1803, E.F.P., Reel 157, Part I, fols. 289v–290.

contador asserted that requests to examine the records of the Royal Treasury should come directly from the governor and not through the petition of a few individuals. While the contador stated he would obey the ruling, he stated he had many other more pressing duties and activities to undertake in his office and he had only one person who wrote in his office (*escribiente*) because the one and only official scribe (*escribano*) left in 1797. The request was not consistent with the organization of the documents in the office, but it was his impression, although difficult to determine, that the amounts due to the treasury from Panton Leslie were different from the amounts the firm had paid. It was not his responsibility to search the records in the manner requested, and in fact, a similar recent request for documents related to Louisiana had produced very few documents. The contador offered a long list of goods used by the firm.[106]

The contador then went on the offensive. To accuse the governor and the head of the Royal Treasury of the gravest crimes was a silly thing for Sánchez to do. The office of the contador had all the documentation required to establish Panton Leslie's rights, and the asesor has acted more like a party to the case than someone offering impartial consultation. Indeed, Ortega should not serve as asesor in this case because of his close relationship to Francisco Sánchez with whom he was an intimate friend; two of Sánchez's four nephews, apparently signatories to the petitions, were married to sisters of the asesor's wife. A relative of the asesor was a competitor of Panton Leslie, and it was odd that the asesor accused the office of the contador as colluding in such a large-scale fraud. Because there was no one serving as a legally trained prosecutor (*fiscal*) and because there was no other lawyer than the asesor, the contador exercised the function of the prosecutor of the royal treasury (*fiscal de Real Hacienda*) despite his lack of legal training. Furthermore, according to the contador, the Royal Treasury was not within the jurisdiction of the asesor. Only the court of the royal treasury in Havana (*Real Tribunal y Audiencia de Cuentas de la Havana*) could direct the provincial treasury offices to provide information. In such a scandalous matter, the contador warned, all the actions of the governor and asesor Ortega would eventually be reviewed by the Royal *Audiencia*.[107]

A further set of petitions led the governor again to order the production of the documents.[108] It appears that the documents were eventually compiled. On 2 July 1803, the secretary of the government, Zubizarreta, certified he had done what was required by the rulings of the governor and had also supplied

106 Petition, 30 June 1803, E.F.P., Reel 157, Part 1, fols. 291–297, 299.

107 Petition, 30 June 1803, E.F.P., Reel 157, Part 1, fols. 300–305v.

108 Decree, 5 July 1803, E.F.P., Reel 157, Part 1, fols. 290v–291.

whatever information he had on John Leslie until 1798 when Leslie returned to London.[109]

The contador's petition, however, had raised new legal issues, and the asesor was infuriated by its allegations. He responded by accusing the contador both of a *libelo infamatorio* and of not following the decrees in the case by interpreting the royal orders in favor of Panton Leslie's fraudulent actions. Furthermore, the advice of the asesor was not binding on the governor as judge who could independently disapprove of the asesor's reasoning or suspend execution for just cause.[110]

The contador's petition had offended the reputation of the asesor so greatly that he was provoked to invite the contador 'to the country with equal arms'.[111] Although the asesor pardoned the contador in the earthly realm, he did not pardon him in the 'eternal forum' (*el fuero aeterno*) because even great saints would permit him to defend himself when he was exposed to guilt and punishment in a human court.[112] Asesor Ortega first addressed his relationship to Francisco Sánchez and his four nephews. He stated that his wife had no sisters, and that it was strange indeed that the contador should have better knowledge of his wife's genealogy than he did. Furthermore, when his close friend witnessed a fraud to the public, should the asesor not act merely because of their friendship? According to the asesor, the contador was clearly lying under oath, a crime bringing the severest punishments and leading to the contador's loss of public position and honor. The allegations of the contador were so serious that the governor should separate this matter into another case, and the asesor offered to resign his functions in the principal case so that he could better defend himself and prosecute the contador.[113]

Governor Enrique White was now sitting on top of a highly passionate dispute between two of the most important royal and legal officials in the province. The contador was in charge of the daily management of finances, and the asesor was, indeed, second in command as *Teniente de Gobernador, Auditor de*

---

109 Concuerda and Certificación, 2 July 1803, E.F.P., Reel 157, Part II, fols. 223v–225v. Although it appears that the documentation found was incorporated into the various parts of the file forwarded to Captain General, there are some additional documents and lists immediately following this certificate. E.F.P., Reel 157, Part II, fols. 225v–235. The file also contains an annual itemized list of payments made by Panton Leslie for imports. E.F.P., Reel 157, Part III, fol. 22.

110 Instancia, 7 July 1803, E.F.P., Reel 157, Part I, fols. 306v–307v.

111 Instancia, 7 July 1803, E.F.P., Reel 157, Part I, fol. 308v.

112 Instancia, 7 July 1803, E.F.P., Reel 157, Part I, fols. 308v–309.

113 Instancia, 7 July 1803, E.F.P., Reel 157, Part I, fols. 310–313v.

Guerra, y Asesor General de esta Plaza y Provincia.[114] Governor White wisely chose to send the file to the Captain General.[115]

The insulted asesor, however, was not finished and did not agree with the governor's passing the dispute along to the Captain General. Orgeta served only because there was no other 'professor of law' or lawyer in the entire province, and his job was not merely to put the decision of the governor into proper form but to determine the truth as the main object of judicial investigation. The *libelo infamatorio* was sent to him not in the ordinary course of the principal case, but rather for him to defend the allegations made by the contador. The governor should hear the case as a first instance judge. The governor denied the relief sought by asesor Ortega who petitioned the governor again complaining that the main case against Panton Leslie had not proceeded and who requested a bond (*fianza*). Pending the decision of the Captain General, the governor denied the requirement of a bond.[116]

The question of producing and compiling the necessary documents still had not been entirely resolved. Attempting to comply with the decree requiring the production of documents, contador Zamorano produced 99 pages of documents on 2 August 1803.[117] The following day, Ortega requested even fuller documentation setting out the purchases and sales of the firm and the certificates reporting the deposits of cargo by the firm.[118] The secretary of the government, Zubizarrata certified that these additional documents could not be turned over.[119]

The case was now at a complete impasse; perhaps persuaded by the governor, asesor Ortega prepared a dictamen that all of the decrees and supporting documents be compiled and sent to the Captain General for his determination. The parties were permitted to inspect and complete the record with appropriate costs assessed.[120] The governor signed a decree in accordance with the dictamen.[121] The record was compiled into three parts on 4 October 1803 and certified by José de Zubizarreta for transmittal to the Capitan General.[122]

114 Petition, 20 July 1803, E.F.P., Reel 157, Part I, fol. 314v.

115 Decree, 12 July 1803, E.F.P., Reel 157, Part I, fol. 314.

116 Decree, 27 July 1803, E.F.P., Reel 157, Part I, fols. 314–319v, 321v.

117 Nota, 2 August 1803, E.F.P. Reel 157, Part I, fols. 322–322v.

118 Dictamen, 3 August 1803, E.F.P., Reel 157, Part I, fols. 322v–325.

119 Certificación, 9 August 1803, E.F.P., Reel 157, Part I, fols. 325v–326.

120 Dictamen, 12 September 1803, E.F.P., Reel 157, Part I, fols. 326–328.

121 Decree, 13 September 1803, E.F.P., Reel 157, Part I, fols. 328–328v.

122 Concuerdas, 4 October 1803, E.F.P., Reel 157, Part I, fols. 329–329v; E.F.P., Reel 157, Part II, fol. 235v.

The dispute had already been decided in favor of Panton Leslie. On 28 October 1802, the Captain General responded to the governor's query about closing the trading post at Picolata. The Captain General responded that closing Panton Leslie's trading posts in unpopulated areas 'in whatever way you look at it is very prejudicial to the State and to royal interests'.[123] Although the disposition of the case before the Captain General after the file was sent to him in October 1803 is not known, Panton Leslie continued to trade in East Florida for another fifteen years.[124] It has not been determined when the Picolata trading post was permanently closed. It seems unlikely that it engaged in any significant trade after this dispute.

4 Conclusion

This chronicle of commercial litigation threatening Panton Leslie's trading post at Picolata and the firm's very existence in East Florida demonstrates both the legal sophistication and institutional limits of local actors in a small northern outpost of the Spanish empire. The parties, the asesor and the governor as judge engaged with the legal sources and facts in ways that indicated a high regard for the authority of the sources, the applicability of these sources to the dispute, and the importance of established facts as maintained through a relatively sophisticated state apparatus of officials, offices, and institutions. The parties considered and argued about the proper interpretation of royal orders, governors' edicts, official correspondence, and other documents that shaped the dispute. They employed legal arguments and adapted these arguments to the forum and its expectations.

Sánchez, Forrester, Ortega, Yonge, and White had to address issues within their colonial context. East Florida contained a mix of interests: English, Scottish, British, U.S., Spanish peninsular and creole, Seminole, Lower Creek, Micosuky (and those of other Indian nations not described in this study). East Florida trade flowed from and through the Spanish and British Caribbean and from and through the United States. Each group brought different and competing ideas of commerce, law, and practices. There were different languages, expectations, and cultures. For example, the Bahamian Englishman Bowles bid for Panton Leslie's business may have represented broader regional tensions in Britain between English traders and Scots traders throughout the empire. The issues involved the nature and goals of commerce in empires and the mediating

123 Contesta, 28 October 1802, E.F.P., Reel 157, Part II, fol. 155v.

124 Coker and Watson, *Indian Traders*, 329, 370.

quality of commercial and social relations with Native Americans who were perceived in their different nations and at different moments, and also collectively and simultaneously, as needed commercial partners, murderous and hostile enemies, and important buffer populations that kept U.S. economic and territorial ambitions at bay. Interests and identities of different communities overlapped in many instances. Alexander McGillivray, son of a Scotsman, led the Seminoles to establish their political and economic bargains with the British and Spanish.

Concerning commercial legal culture, the issues debated in the pleadings centered on Panton Leslie's compliance with its unique trade status as delineated in a series of royal orders and agreements. These documents provided the core of the sources of commercial law that governed Panton Leslie's actions. The main areas of potential violation were payment of duties, smuggling and fraud in imports and exports, and trading beyond the scope of royal permissions. In arguing about Panton Leslie, parties employed the applicable language of these orders and other general royal provisions related to trade. In this context, Sánchez, Forrester, Ortega, and Yonge, despite their remoteness from imperial economic and commercial centers, did not play fast and loose with the legal sources or arguments. The *derecho vulgar* observed by Cutter in other contexts and in another regions of Northern New Spain does not appear to guide the governor, his asesor, or the representatives of Panton Leslie in this dispute.[125]

Some specific legal issues are worth discussing because they demonstrate the detailed legal thought employed by the parties. Throughout the documents, Sánchez and his co-plaintiffs claimed to represent themselves, other leading individuals, and the inhabitants of the city.[126] The first few petitions were signed by all of the interested petitioners, but later in the proceedings, they found this process cumbersome and offered a different form of signing their petitions and other document. In the undated petition from July 1802, the petitioners turn to a system of representatives of groups within the community. The petitioners ask that to avoid the inconvenience of gathering signatures each time that the governor allow three individuals to sign 'for the class of merchants' and three others 'for the class of farmers'.[127] To some extent the

125 Charles R. Cutter, *The Legal Culture of Northern New Spain* (Albuquerque: University of New Mexico Press, 1995).

126 Petition, 17 July 1802, E.F.P., Reel 157, Part 1, fol. 5v.

127 Petition, undated (July 1802), E.F.P., Reel 157, Part 1, fols. 16–16v.

tribunal had already accepted this practice by giving notice of petitions, dictamens, and decrees only to one representative, Francisco Xavier Sánchez.[128]

Yonge's first response to the petition describes the group of petitioners narrowly as 'some of the leading men of the city'.[129] After asesor Ortega determined that individuals had standing to bring the action because of the harm done to them, Yonge responded with a petition countering Sánchez's petition with a list of over 75 supporters of Panton Leslie who claimed that the closure of the Picolata post and of Panton Leslie would be detrimental to them.

Even if the petitioners passed the hurdle of their collective representative capacity, the language of their petition indicated the tentative quality of whether this issue was appropriate for a tribunal. One petition requested that the governor consider their claim 'not only as judge but also as father of so many who live in the province'.[130] At another point in the case, Sánchez sought to re-characterize the dispute as not being justiciable as an ordinary civil claim. The issues of public benefit and royal rights meant that greater procedural leeway should be extended to the leading men.

The role of the asesor was particular difficult in the context of this case. The lack of lawyers in Saint Augustine led the asesor to continue his function even after he was accused of bias and after these accusations led to a separate dispute with the contador that he wished to separate from the main case and defend individually. The asesor's interest in the litigation was a complicating factor in the parties' ability to obtain an impartial result at the local level.[131]

The dispute reveals that the nature of commercial enterprise within empires was not simply one of economic benefit. At various points in the dispute the documents on both sides argued that Panton Leslie was expected to manage native populations, ensure peace in the region, advance the interests of the Spanish crown, and work for the Spanish defense of East Florida, even when Britain was at war with Spain. Trading companies were woven into the political fabric of imperial administration. Surely these activities and benefits were the reasons of state that prompted the Captain General to support Panton Leslie and its trading posts in unpopulated areas. In this context, Sánchez argued that for Spain to coexists with native populations and eventually to have Indian

128 Early notifications by the escribano to the parties stated that notice was given to the individuals who signed the petition. Notification, 17 July 1802, E.F.P., Reel 157, Part I, fol. 12v; Notification, 23 July 1802, E.F.P., Reel 157, Part I, fols. 17v–18.

129 Petition, November 1802, E.F.P., Reel 157, Part 1, f. 264 (no day provided).

130 Petition, 17 July 1802, E.F.P., Reel 157, Part I, fol. 10v.

131 Yonge joined the contador's concerns about the impartiality of the asesor. Petition, December 1802, E.F.P., Reel 157, Part III, fol. 5 (no day provided).

populations join its polity, the foreign, English, trading house of Panton Leslie had to be removed as an intermediary between them.[132] This argument failed.

The arguments based on class and local ability also failed. The Captain Governor and most likely the governor had no qualms about the high status of Panton Leslie. Indeed, as a representative of the Spanish crown and an actor in international economic and political affairs, Panton Leslie's elite reputation was most likely a neutral or even positive attribute.

It appears that Panton Leslie had the better legal arguments based on the sources, particularly if Spain was bound by the regular determinations of its customs and revenue officials. The policy arguments for overturning a series of royal privileges were not compelling in the face of the text of the royal orders. The allegations of avoiding duties, abuse of privilege, and importing the wrong goods from the wrong place for the wrong purchasers were all most likely founded in fact, but the technicalities involved in establishing them in the context of a civil suit in a provincial capital proved to be insurmountable. This led to the ancillary disputes about the production and preparation of supporting documents.

This extensive legal battle also has some explanatory benefit on the shift of Panton Leslie away from trade to debt collection and property management in the early years of the nineteenth century. William Panton died in 1801 and Bowles's attacks against Panton Leslie had significantly disrupted its ability to trade profitably. The suit by Sánchez and his co-plaintiffs must be added to these causes of the firm's shift from Indian trade to debt collection and land management. The case surely absorbed time and resources. It also created an atmosphere of uncertainly under which the firm would have to operate. Every shipment and every transaction after the case would be subject to the greatest and most jealous scrutiny by at least a portion of Saint Augustine's population. Panton Leslie's success was a hollow victory.

132 Petition, 17 July 1802, E.F.P., Reel 157, Part 1, fol. 8.

How to 'Mash Up' Lex Mercatoria from Civil Law to Common Law: The Genesis of Lex Mercatoria in Lower-Canada History 1760–1866

David Gilles

1 Introduction

By all contemporary accounts, Canadian commercial law was deeply and persistently in debt to English law, but French influences should not be overlooked. In 1766, the Lords of the Board of Trade and Plantations summarized the problems existing in Quebec in the following manner:

> 'The Circumstances in the State of that Province, which appear to be the most important are: First, the unsettled State of Ecclesiastical Affairs, and the complaints and Representations of His Majesty's new subjects on that head. Secondly, The defective and partial Establishments of Judicature in respect to the constitution of the Courts of Justice, and their Rules and forms of proceeding; and Thirdly, The want of such a complete Constitution of Civil Government, as may be competent to the forming those Regulations essential to the Peace, Happiness and Welfare of the People, and the support of every necessary Establishment'.[1]

Strangely, as is shown in these lines, the British institution in charge of the economy of the colony essentially focussed on non-economic problems in the new province. There were many economic problems in the new Province of Quebec, but they were connected to larger legal issues. The essential thesis of this paper is that while Canadian commercial law began as a legal transplant from France, England's common law influence changed it during the period from 1760 to the enactment of the Lower Canada Civil Code (L.-C. C.C.) in 1866. The capitulation of Montreal on 8 September 1760 marked the end of French sovereignty in Canada and its incorporation in the English Empire.[2] The *Lex Mercatoria* had been progressively decoupled from its original civil

1 Report of the Lords of the Board of Trade and Plantations, Whitehall, 16 May 1766.

2 P.J. Marshall, 'The Incorporation of Quebec in the British Empire, 1763–1774', in V. Bever Platt and D.C. Skaggs (eds.), *Of Mother Country and Plantations: Proceedings of the Twenty-Seventh Conference in Early American History* (Bowling Green: Bowling Green University, 1970), 42–62.

 | DOI:10.1163/9789004443075_007

source with subsequent amendments and reforms, such as the Quebec Act. These reforms were focused either on finding solutions to local problems, reflecting imperial motivations, improving trade modernity or borrowing from other jurisdictional schemes. Thus, they reflected a convergent relationship between British judicial tradition and French private law norms.

Focusing on colonial legal politics and laws and the interrelation of local and indigenous cultural contests and institutional change, this paper uses 'case law studies' to trace a shift in plural legal orders – from the ancient law of the French empire[3] to the state-centred law of the colonial English Lower-Canada. One major trend in North American history in this period, including in the history of post-conquest New France, 'is towards transnational histories, whether framed as the new imperial history, as Atlantic history, or as the history of borderlands'.[4] In this paper we prefer a nationally-based history of law, justice and law system formation that 'must necessarily be framed in a wider, comparative context'.[5] The case of imperial transplantation of foreign legal systems to unreceptive colonies is a difficult one to resolve for legal historians, especially in Quebec.[6] Legal transplantation takes place when a people moves into a different territory where there is no comparable civilisation, and takes its law with it. This is what the French did first, and then what the English had to do in the 1760s. As Warren Swain said about English law, there were significant obstacles in the way of adapting rules of law in order to promote trade and commerce in the eighteenth century.[7]

Mercantilism was the generally accepted theory that directed English[8] and French colonial developments until the beginning of the nineteenth century. Colonies, it was believed, existed for the benefit of the mother country; that is,

3 See C. Hodson and B. Rushforth, 'Absolutely Atlantic: Colonialism and the Early Modern French State in Recent Historiography', *History Compass* 8:1 (2010), 101–117.

4 Donald Fyson, 'Between the Ancien Regime and Liberal Modernity: Law, Justice and State Formation in Colonial Quebec, 1760–1867', *History Compass* 12:5 (2014), 412–432, 413.

5 Fyson, *Between the Ancien Regime and Liberal Modernity*.

6 See L.A. Knafla and T.L. Chapman, 'Criminal Justice in Canada: A Comparative Study of the Maritimes and Lower Canada, 1760–1812', *Osgoode Hall Law Journal* 21:2 (1983), 245–274. Evelyn Kolish, 'The Impact of the Change in Legal Metropolis on the Development of Lower Canada's Legal System', *Canadian Journal of Law and Society* 3 (1988), 1–25; Evelyn Kolish, *Nationalismes et conflits de droits: le débat du droit privé au Québec, 1760–1840* (LaSalle: Hurtubise HMH, 1994); Jacques L'Heureux, 'L'organisation judiciaire au Québec de 1764 à 1774', *Revue générale de droit* 1:2 (1970), 266–331.

7 Warren Swain, 'Lawyers, merchants and the law of contract in the long eighteenth century', in Matthew Dyson and David Ibbetson, *Law and Legal Process: Substantive Law and Procedure in English Legal History* (Cambridge: Cambridge University Press, 2013), 186.

8 On British mercantilism in colonial territories, see Claire Priest, 'Law and Commerce 1580–1815', in Michael Grossberg and Christopher Tomlins (eds.), *The Cambridge History of Law in America*, vol. I (Cambridge: Cambridge University Press, 2008), 402–433.

they were to supply her with the raw products she needed, and at the same time was to provide an expanding market for her manufactured goods. By this system, colonies were encouraged to supply commodities which England could not produce, but were discouraged from competing with the motherland's enterprises. The mercantile system implies a monopoly of trade and shipping by the mother country. If the aim of colonial mercantilism was, for both France and England, the welfare of the mother country, their methods of implementing it were quite different. French mercantilism was, under the *ancien régime,* a form of 'Colbertism', characterised by strong state control. For England, on the other hand, the Board of Trade and local Governor relied largely on recommendations for the colonies. To aggravate matters, the Crown and Parliament 'placed their faith in private informers to enforce these laws in English markets. Mercantile influence was strongest when the common law and the French law were sketchiest. As the law became clear, the merits of certainty began to trump those of commercial flexibility. The use of private agents of enforcement did not enjoy even an iota of market efficiency because the state had, in effect, empowered individuals to enforce its regulations for personal gain by reaping profits from their neighbours' industry'.[9] Modern commercial laws, based on corporate activity and finance, took shape in England only at the end of the eighteenth century, and rose to prominence during the nineteenth century.[10]

After the conquest of Quebec, attempts were made to revitalize its economic position, which had been greatly injured during the Seven Years War. One of the objectives of the colonial authorities was to render the colony more self-sufficient, while at the same time furthering the economic development of the empire[11] We will examine the ways in which commercial questions were shaped by social engineering efforts,[12] legal initiatives and political expectations, and the consequences of these influences for the commercial law of Quebec as codified in 1866. This history is a history of legal transplantation, a history of 'adaptation-interpretation'. The latter concept denotes the reality that when European laws were transplanted to colonial territories, there was first a period of adaptation, a colonial blend from different legal roots and

9 C.E. Smith, 'Economic Liberty and the Official Law Books in Colonial Massachusetts', *Cato Journal* 27:3 (2007), 411–430, 423.

10 R.C. Hunt, *The Development of Business Corporations in England* (New York: Russell & Russell, 1969; orig. 1936); P.L. Cottrell, *Industrial Finance, 1830–1914* (New York: Methuen, 1979).

11 E. Mancke, 'Another British America: A Canadian Model for the Early Modern British Empire', *Journal of Imperial and Commonwealth History* 25:1 (1997), 1–36.

12 I. McKay, 'The Liberal Order Framework: A Prospectus for a Reconnaissance of Canadian History', *Canadian Historical Review* 81:4 (2000), 617–645.

then, once the colonial population identified with the law they had engineered, it became their own law, with a cultural crush of the ancient roots. Usually, legal transplantation is most suitable for a small jurisdiction, like Quebec, but cultural differences can lead to contestation and incomprehension. There could be tremendous benefits for a small colony, to receive transplanted laws from Europe, especially during a period of colonial conflicts when the European power is unable to establish a colonial assembly because the majority of the population on the territory is foreign. Still, to create a system of laws that would be well received locally was an ambitious aim for colonial authorities. Province population renounced easily to their own customs and preferred to deal with 'metropole' laws, French law on the one hand,[13] and English law on the other.

Our question is: did the commercial law of Quebec in 1866 represent the last gasp of the *ancien régime* in Quebec, steeped in institutions and practices inherited from early modern France, or did it herald the beginnings of a modern and liberal legal system, expressed in common law practices? Or, alternatively, was the modernity of the commercial law initiated in 1866 the result of a 'mashup' of competing legal traditions?

The rise of capitalist property and labour relations well before the 1840s was undoubtedly due in part to the influence of industrial capitalism developing elsewhere and notably in Britain. These are in fact some of the main issues in the broader development of law in colonial Quebec, from the British conquest of Quebec in 1759/1760, through to the codification of 1866, which added another important layer to the apparatus of its legal system. At the same time, there were few legal interventions regarding economic institutions until the 1840s. In fact, between the passage of the Bubble Act in 1720 and the sweeping reforms of the General Incorporation Act of 1844, the legal framework of business organization in England remained remarkably stagnant despite the profound economic and structural changes wrought by the Industrial Revolution. Even in England, during the eighteenth century, through the different organizational forms of business, the joint-stock corporation did not gain dominance.[14] There was a full range of possible forms of organization of enterprises available to business persons in the colonial empire, from the proprietorship to the joint-stock corporation and beyond.[15] As in England, it was the corporation, and not the trust or the partnership, which came to dominate business in

13 T. Mathew, 'Law-French', *Law Quarterly Review* 54 (1938), 358–369.

14 Harris Ron, *Industrializing English Law: Entrepreneurship and Business Organization, 1720–1844* (Cambridge: Cambridge University Press, 2000), 85.

15 Ron, *Industrializing English Law*, 16.

Canada by the second half of the nineteenth century. Nevertheless, the form of businesses was not a crucial topic of debate in Lower Canada during our period. There are four principal legal themes revealed by sources, all in connection with the interaction of civil and common law: real estate property, debt imprisonment and bankruptcy laws, the efficient regulation of trade, local and international, and the role of the jury[16] in private law.

Largely speaking, in the civil law, recent work has underscored the relative continuity in practices across the imperial divide and partially invalidated the postulates of administrative chaos, passive resistance from French Canadians against English institutions, and the illegitimacy of the latter.[17] Instead, there was a development of a hybrid judicial culture, at least partially pluralistic, by means of which both French and British Canadians adapted with greater or lesser success to new legal realities.

Social organization and legal transplantations are sometimes difficult to separate from economic and spatial organization. As a territorial entity, the boundaries of post-Conquest Quebec, under its various names (the Province of Quebec, Lower Canada and Canada East) varied considerably across the period, from the narrow quadrangle defined in 1763 that framed the main Canadian settlements and part of the surrounding First Nation lands, to a vast sprawl over most of the Great Lakes region (but only very briefly), and back to the southern part of the current-day Canadian province. We will focus on the Saint Lawrence lowlands, which were dominated by the white settler society progressively implanted since the seventeenth century and made up largely of settlers of French and, increasingly, British origin from 1760, though with a minority population of Natives settled in missions. Beyond this white settlement area, there were Native lands to the north and west, controlled by sovereign nations whose history and life were considerably less framed by European borders and European conceptions of commercial law, but still involved in the commercial fur trade.

This paper will focus on the formation of commercial law in the white-settler-dominated zone. The laws of Admiralty, marine insurance, commercial paper and sale of goods were not, supposedly, merely English or French laws, but part of an international body of rules. In 1760, the commerce of the colony

16 D. Fyson, 'Jurys, participation civique et représentation au Québec et au Bas-Canada: les grands jurys du district de Montréal (1764–1832)', *Revue d'histoire de l'Amérique française* 55:1 (2001), 85–120.

17 See André Morel, 'La réaction des Canadiens devant l'administration de la justice de 1764 à 1774: une forme de résistance passive', *Revue du Barreau* 20:2 (1960), 55–63; André Morel, 'La réception du droit criminel anglais au Québec (1760–1892)', *Revue juridique Thémis* 13:2–3 (1978), 449–541.

had been disrupted and had not yet established itself on a firm basis. To that extent, the English commercial law had a significant effect in radically altering the course of lower-Canadian commercial law. As for economic trends, during the period of French domination, the Saint Lawrence lowlands were under seigniorial land ownership,[18] with little commercial activity, mostly restricted to fur and colonial trade. There was no real industry – except the forges of St. Maurice – and poor conditions for investment. The Canadian population in 1760 was strung out narrowly along the coast and around the St Lawrence. Commerce was, in large measure, ocean and fur commerce. As waves of human beings moved into the vast Canadian interior, the lakes and rivers served as arteries of commerce as important as turnpikes and roads. To determine jurisdiction over rivers for example, in the English tradition, the Admiralty had power only over matters 'within the ebb and flow of the tide'. But, if the 'ebb and flow of the tide' was a good enough criterion in England, which is a continental country, for Canada and the U.S., that contain the Great Lakes and huge rivers, it was not an efficient criteria.

How did commercial law in Quebec adapt in that crucial locus of encounter between legal traditions and society? Our intent is not to advance an overarching interpretative framework for legal change in Canada; rather, it is to offer a brief and necessarily partial overview of the field, structured around three key periods. The first concerns the Conquest as a point of rupture, with the imposition of a British colonial state and international English commercial law on top of a largely French society. Conflicts and cultural fights marked this period. The second focuses on the hybrid nature of commercial law after the Quebec Act, and the 'path of law' to trade and commercial modernity, ultimately leading to a system of law reflective of two distinct sources. The third period surrounds the debate about the creation of the Lower Canada civil code in 1857, in which the authors of the Code used French and common law influences to draft a new commercial law framework.

Debates among jurists, merchants[19] and politicians centred on the sources of *Lex Mercatoria* marked each of these three periods. Commercial law did not become the object of juristic reflection until the political troubles following

18 B. Grenier, *Brève histoire du régime seigneurial* (Montreal: Boréal, 2012); J.-P. Garneau, 'Réflexions sur la régulation juridique du régime seigneurial canadien', in B. Grenier and A. Laberge (eds.), *Le Régime seigneurial au Québec 150 ans après* (Quebec: CIEQ, 2009), 61–77.

19 On merchants' thinking in Quebec at the time, see J. Igartua, 'The Merchants and Negociants of Montreal, 1750–1775: A Study in Socio-Economic History' (Ph. D Thesis, Michigan State University, 1974).

the Royal Proclamation in 1763.[20] After 1763, French-Canadians, English merchants and loyalists challenged jurists and political leaders to change the legal compromise in the colony, and after 1774, it was the slow transformation of the main economic institutions from its civil roots to a common law architecture, which led to a blending of legal sources in the codification process.

The chapter on commercial law in the 1866 Civil Code of Lower Canada represents not only a significant departure from its colonial origins, but also a big divergence between both French and English legal orders. The new commercial Law of Quebec is, at this period, a compendium of each part of these legal traditions.

2 The Conquest as a Moment of Legal and Commercial Choice

The implantation of the mercantile system was at the heart of the negotiations after the Conquest. During the Treaty of Paris negotiations, France wanted Guadeloupe and Martinique because they offered easy profits without investment. For the English, Canada was preferred to Guadeloupe because of the opportunities that it offered for English settlement and production. In so far as the colony's trade was concerned, it would enter the British mercantile system, as did that of the other colonies, even if the local population differed from the British world in language, religion, customs and laws. At the beginning of the post Conquest period, when land mattered because of the families it could sustain, the primary impact of choice of law on the economy lay in its potential to regulate the economy by restraining what could later be described as market forces, and promoting order and control of the local economy.

One of England's major problems consisted in giving its newly acquired territory a government suited to its unique character. How should a region, populated by a rival European people that had colonized it, be administered? The problem was further complicated by the presence of a small English minority, as well as the proximity of a large British group to the south. Choices were difficult, and Britain had to invent a new way of colonisation. The Colonial Office was badly organized, for the American colonies were under the management of the Secretary of State for the southern department, who also directed policy in different territories. The Board of Trade and Plantations was largely responsible for advising on colonial matters. Nobody was effectively in charge of colonial issues or the choice of administrative and legal frameworks. After the

20 Proclamation of Oct. 7th, 1763, Adam Shortt and Arthur G. Doughty, *Constitutional Documents 1759–1791* (Ottawa, 1921), 163–168.

military defeat of the French, British merchants began moving into the Province of Quebec, crowding out their former rivals. Colonialism became a framework for the politics of legal pluralism, though particular patterns and outcomes varied. Wherever a group imposed law on newly-acquired territories and subordinated peoples, strategic decisions were made about the extent and nature of the legal control exerted from the centre. The strategies of rule included aggressive attempts to impose legal systems melting pot.[21] This is why French Canadian historians once saw the conquest as bringing a clash of legal and institutional cultures that played out most notably in the ultimately successful battles of the French-Canadians to preserve their traditions. More common, though, were conscious efforts to retain elements of existing institutions and limit legal change as a way of sustaining social order. For Quebec, the Royal Proclamation of 1763 constituted an aggressive incursion, and the Quebec Act represented accommodation. Conquered and colonized groups often respond to the imposition of law in ways that, progressively, include accommodation, advocacy within the system, and outright rebellion. For Lower-Canada, the rebellion appeared – militarily speaking – in 1837–1838, but the aim of that rebellion was not commercial, but cultural, linguistic and political.

These legal contests were central to the construction of a colonial rule in Canada and key to the formation of larger patterns of global structuring. Precisely because imperial and colonial polities contained multiple legal orientations, the location of political authority was not uniform across different laws.[22] After a period of military rule where much of French civil law was maintained[23] though administered by military tribunals (1759–1764), French law was in theory almost entirely replaced by English civil and criminal law and justice[24] pursuant to the Royal Proclamation. In commercial law, like private law, it is easy to put the emphasis on the difficulty of reconciling legal

21 Lauren A. Benton, *Law and Colonial Cultures: Legal Regimes in World History, 1400–1900* (Cambridge: Cambridge University Press, 2002), 3.

22 See P. Lawson, *The Imperial Challenge: Quebec and Britain in the Age of the American Revolution* (Montreal: McGill-Queen's University Press, 1989).

23 D. Hay, 'Civilians Tried in Military Courts: Quebec, 1759–64', in F.M. Greenwood and Barry Wright (eds.), *Canadian State Trials. Volume 1: Law, Politics, and Security Measures, 1608–1837* (Toronto: Osgoode Society for Canadian Legal History and University of Toronto Press, 1997), 114–128; J. M. Fecteau and D. Hay, '"Government by Will and Pleasure Instead of Law": Military Justice and the Legal System in Quebec, 1775–83', in F.M. Greenwood and Barry Wright (eds.), *Canadian State Trials. Volume 1: Law, Politics, and Security Measures, 1608–1837* (Toronto: Osgoode Society for Canadian Legal History and University of Toronto Press, 1997), 129–171.

24 For justice institutions after the British Conquest, see Luc Huppé, *Histoire des institutions judiciaires du Canada* (Montreal: Wilson & Lafleur, 2007).

traditions and on the confusion engendered by the rapidly shifting legal landscape. As seen in the Royal Proclamation and in the instructions given to Governor Murray,[25] British policy in 1763 seems to have been oriented towards establishing English laws and language, as well as the Protestant religion. Opposition to the proposed policy soon appeared in the form of protests from the French-Canadians as well as from Murray and officials in England, resulting in a general mitigation of the letter of the law. As Donald Fyson says:

> 'Even in the first decades of British rule, analysts were divided over the effects of the change in empires: was it a beneficial event that had brought British liberties to a colony formerly crushed under the weight of French absolutism, or was it the ultimate disaster for the Canadians, cut off from their former "metropolis" and forced to live under alien rulers and alien institutions?'.[26]

The introduction of English commercial law into Quebec can be demarcated by two main events: (A) the Quebec Conquest and the debates around private law choice and (B) the imprisonment for debt debate.

2.1 *Debates about Commercial Practices and Private Law*

Because English common law is accurately summarized as 'judge-made law', based on the English heritage of the majority of new settlers, English common law is an obvious source and explanation for colonial Canadian law. But several innovations that the English legal profession and Parliament were, at best, slow to act upon were demands for the English characteristic of common law from 'Law-French' pleading in courts.[27] There was soon a divide between partisans of the re-introduction of French law on one side, and defenders of the strengths of the common law on the other. The legal conflicts between the colonized and the colonizers were further shaped by other tensions that divided the two sides, such as their commercial practices. Jurisdictional jockeying by competing colonial authorities was a universal feature of the colonial order in Quebec.[28] It called up and altered cultural distinctions, as competing colonial authorities tied their jurisdictional claims to representations of their

25 Instructions to Governor Murray, Dec. 7, 1763, Shortt and Doughty, *Constitutional* Documents, 181–205.

26 Donald Fyson, 'Between the *ancien régime* and liberal modernity: Law, justice and state formation in colonial Quebec, 1760–1867', *History Compass* 12:5 (2014), 412–432.

27 See Hilda Neatby, *The Administration of Justice under the Quebec Act* (Minneapolis: Minnesota University Press, 1933).

28 Benton, *Law and colonial* cultures, 3.

(special or superior) relationship to the French-speaking population, or sought to delegitimize other legal authorities by depicting them as being tainted by French culture.[29] Factions within the colonized population, too, entered into conflicts with one another because of different interests in the legal order and perceptions of it. For French Canadians, civil law was seen as one of the bastions of their identity. Since 1763, there had been frequent instances of tension between new and ancient subjects, and an overarching sense of colonial superiority and entitlement among many of the latter. Board of Trade recommendations for administering the new territories had been contained in three major documents: the Royal Proclamation of 7 October 1763; Murray's commission as governor (21 November 1763); and Murray's instructions (7 December 1763). The first move was, in line with the Royal Proclamation, to make the substitution from French law to English common law. However, 98% of the population was French, and did not understand the new settlers' language or laws. The aim of the Proclamation was to integrate new subjects to the ancient subjects' traditions, and to build one colonial people, directly linked to royal will and Parliamentary decision-making. For economic purposes, the Imperial authorities in London regarded the collection and disposition of the public revenue of Quebec as a prerogative of the Crown. The revenues of the colonial government were quite limited in the first years after the conquest, however, consisting chiefly of duties on spirits. This was a conflict point between merchants and authorities. In August 1766, Paulus Aemilius Irving, crown officer, had informed the Lords of the Treasury that it would be difficult to force the importers of wine, rum and other liquors[30] to pay the duties that had been collected during the French regime.[31] It proved impossible to collect duties, as they were at this time abhorrent to the Quebec merchants, who felt the influence of American resistance to taxation without representation. Merchants used civil juries to win their points on this question, but they would pay dearly for this victory, however, as the jury system was removed in 1774.

The Royal Proclamation of 7 October 1763 promised that an Assembly would be called as soon as circumstances would permit. Legislative and taxation powers were to be exercised by the Governor, the Council and the Assembly.

---

29 See Hilda Neatby, *Quebec: The Revolutionary Age, 1760–1791* (Toronto: McClelland & Stewart, 1966).

30 Several factors had been working against this trade, however, such as the high price and poor quality of English rum which favoured the sale of American spirits. As nothing had been traded in return, this had resulted in a drain of currency from the Province. Colonial Authorities favoured a direct exchange of products between Canada and the West Indies.

31 Irving to Lords of Trade and Plantations, Quebec, 21 July 1766, BAC, Q 3: 218–220.

The same provisions were repeated in Murray's commission and instructions. An attractive form of government had been promised for the newly-acquired colony to appeal to new settlers. On 19 April 1765, a group of London merchants trading in Canada petitioned the Lords of Trade and Plantations with this purpose in mind. They claimed that because of the promise that had been made in 1763, many important merchants had settled in Canada to carry on trade, but had been disappointed in their hopes by the arbitrariness of the government administering the colony. They wrote that:

> '[…] a military Government is entirely incompatible with the Spirit & Genius of Commerce; & that a civil Administration, with a regular House of Representatives, is the only Means to make this Infant Colony flourish, & become useful to the Mother Country'.[32]

The Canada Committee in 1768 expressed the idea that the trade of the Province could only be recovered by means of an Assembly. In 1770, Quebec merchants presented a petition requesting that an Assembly be called that would work for the best interests of both old and new subjects.[33] It was not only the British merchants who were asking for political reform and the establishment of an Assembly. There was a group of French Canadians, old colonists and merchants, who had adopted a commercial outlook that was much closer to the economic ideas of the English trading minority than to those of the old 'Seigneurs'. Lieutenant-Governor Carleton took on the cause of the English merchants, opposing himself to the Murray faction – the French party. This led him to crush the opposition by dismissing two of their leaders, Irving and Mabane, from the Governor's Council. A few months later, Carleton converted to the 'French Party', and throughout his stay in Quebec he strove to further their cause. This was expressed through his relentless opposition to the merchants' agitation for an Assembly, and by his repeated demands that Canadian lords be awarded positions of honour. This was one of the factors that irritated the English government and led it to oppose several of the Lieutenant-Governor's attempts at reform.

32 Petition of London Merchants trading to Canada to the Lords of Trade and Plantations, London, 18 April 1765, BAC, MG11, CO 42, Quebec and Lower Canada Papers, vol. 2, pt. 1: 112.

33 Petition of the British Freeholders, Merchants and Traders in the Province of Quebec to the King, Quebec, no date but probably 1770, BAC, Q 7, 359–562.

Essentially, English legal knowledge promotion was monopolized by some lawyers who presented their arguments in a foreign language,[34] and by English merchants, linked with London, Boston and New York, who were lobbying for a coherent British legal system in Quebec.[35] Colonial authorities, like governors Murray and Carleton, some London lawyers (William Hey, Thurlow) and the majority of the French population, were more pragmatic,[36] and pleaded for a mixed system, French laws for private law, and English laws for public law. The colonial authority failed to issue officially and free of charge the statutes that now governed the territory and to assimilate French Canadians to English tradition.[37] In fact, the governors sent to administer the 'newly-acquired' colony soon realized that to keep Quebec British, the system in existence before 1760 had to be re-established as far as circumstances permitted. Murray and Carleton thus began to re-instate the system of privileges and French law, by the creation, in 1764, of the Common Law Pleas court, where French Canadians could plead in French and apply old French law, even if the judges were English and without any knowledge of French language and law. This strange mitigation of rights and courts – a common law jurisdiction applying French law in

34 J.-Ph. Garneau, 'Gérer la différence dans le Québec britannique: l'exemple de la langue (1760–1840)', in L. Derocher et al. (eds.), *L'État canadien et la diversité culturelle et religieuse, 1800–1914* (Quebec: Presses de l'Université du Québec, 2009), 21–48.

35 On 17 February 1766, additional instructions were sent to Murray, whereby Canadian lawyers were to be permitted to plead in both courts on an equal footing with the English barristers, and juries were to be chosen as dictated by the nationality of the litigants. See D. Fyson, 'Judicial Auxiliaries Across Legal Regimes: From New France to Lower Canada', in C. Dolan (ed.), *Entre justice et justiciables: les auxiliaires de la justice du Moyen Âge au xxe siècle* (Sainte-Foy: Presses de l'Université Laval, 2005), 383–403; David Gilles, 'Le notariat canadien face à la Conquête anglaise de 1760: l'exemple des notaires Panet', in Vincent Bernaudeau, Jean-Pierre Nandrin, Bénédicte Rochet, Xavier Rousseaux and Axel Tixhon (dir.), *Les praticiens du droit du Moyen Âge à l'époque Contemporaine: Approches prosopographiques, Belgique, Canada, France, Italie* (Rennes: Presses Universitaires de Rennes, 2008), 189–207; J.-P. Garneau, 'Civil Law, Legal Practitioners, and Everyday Justice in the Decades following the Quebec Act of 1774', in C. Backhouse and W.W. Pue (eds.), *The Promise and Perils of Law: Lawyers in Canadian History* (Toronto: Irwin Law, 2009), 129–139.

36 M. Morin, 'Les revendications des nouveaux sujets, francophones et catholiques, de la Province de Québec, 1764–1774', in G.B. Baker and D. Fyson (eds.), *Essays in the History of Canadian Law, vol XI: Quebec and the Canadas* (Toronto: Osgoode Society for Canadian Legal History and University of Toronto Press, 2013).

37 Donald Fyson, 'The Canadiens and British Institutions of Local Governance in Quebec, from the Conquest to the Rebellions', in Nancy Christie (ed.), *Transatlantic Subjects: Ideas, Institutions and Identities in Post-Revolutionary British North America* (Montreal: McGill-Queen's University Press, 2008), 45–82; Charles-Philippe Courtois (ed.), *La Conquête, une anthologie* (Montréal: Typo, 2009), 446.

a British colony – could be easily explained. Authorities feared that the new subjects might join their former mother country in opposing Great Britain in the eventuality of war, which led them to attempt to gain the allegiance of the Canadians, by ensuring the support of French traditions, laws, and the privileges of church and nobility. On the other hand, authorities refused to call a colonial Assembly, where the French would be the majority. This choice was equally difficult to understand for both English and French Canadian subjects.

2.1.1 Private Law Choice

The '*Coutume de Paris*' had been the common law of New France. England's problem was that two settlers' cultures would now occupy the continent.[38] The gravity of this problem does not seem to have been realized at first, as the English minority living in the province were promised British law. It was hoped that this would serve to attract English colonists who would thus soon outnumber the old inhabitants.[39] By the Royal Proclamation of 7 October 1763, and by Murray's commission and instructions, it was proclaimed that English law was to be introduced into the colony. All court offices were to be filled by English Protestants, as Roman Catholics could not take the Test against transubstantiation, and thus were barred from all official functions. The Ordinance of 17 September 1764, establishing courts of judicature,[40] was to mark the theoretical end of French law and the beginning of English law in the Province of Quebec but, in fact, it was an illusion.[41] In 1767, Carleton noted that although English law was supposed to have been introduced in 1764, the Canadians still

38 See Donald Fyson, 'Minority Groups and the Law in Quebec, 1760–1867', in G.B. Baker and Donald Fyson (eds.), *Essays in the History of Canadian Law, vol. XI: Quebec and the Canadas* (Toronto: Osgoode Society for Canadian Legal History and University of Toronto Press, 2013), 278–329.

39 W. Smith, 'The Struggle over the Laws of Canada, 1763–1783', *The Canadian Historical Review* 1 (1920), 166.

40 This Act established a Court of King's Bench presided over by the Chief Justice; a Court of Common Pleas which was intended to be for the French-Canadians only, presided over by three English judges; and justices of the peace to determine minor cases; Smith, 'The Struggle over the Laws of Canada', 168.

41 See David Gilles, 'L'arbitrage notarié, instrument idoine de conciliation des traditions juridiques après la Conquête britannique? (1760–1784)', *McGill Law Journal* 57:1 (2011), 1–52; Donald Fyson, 'The Canadians and the Conquest of Quebec: Interpretations, Realities, Ambiguities', in S. Gervais et al. (eds.), *Quebec Questions: Quebec Studies for the Twenty-First Century* (Toronto: Oxford University Press, 2011), 18–33; Donald Fyson, 'The Conquered and the Conqueror: The Mutual Adaptation of the Canadians and the British in Quebec, 1759–1775', in P.A. Buckner and J.G. Reid (eds.), *Revisiting 1759: The Conquest of Canada in Historical Perspective* (Toronto: University of Toronto Press, 2012), 190–217.

conducted their affairs according to their former laws, leading to numerous reversals of lower court decisions by the courts.[42] With the establishment of the courts of judicature, Murray had declared that English law would prevail in the Province of Quebec, implying that land was to be granted according to the English system.[43] In reality, there was no change in land ownership; the English system of land tenure was not adopted at this time. For colonial authorities, the seigneurial system had kept the inhabitants in check and had provided law and order in the colony. For Carleton:

> 'The Canadian Tenures differ, it is true, from those in the other Parts of His Majesty's American Dominions, but if Confirmed, and I cannot see how it well can be avoided, without entirely over-setting the Properties of the People, will ever secure a proper Subordination from this Province to Great Britain; if it's detached Situation be constantly Rembered (sic), and that on the Canadian Stock we can only depend for an Increase of Population therein, the Policy of Continuing to them their Customs and Usages will be sufficiently Evinced'.[44]

Carleton concluded that the vacant lands in the interior part of the province ought to be granted *en fief et seigneurie*. Land in new territories would be reserved for the English colonists, and granted to them in free and common socage. On 2 July 1771 the English government sent additional instructions to the Governor[45] whereby lands were to be granted *en fief et seigneurie*, with the reservation that judicial powers were not to be exercised by the seigneurs.

---

42 'A few Disputes have already appeared, where the English Law gives to ones what by the Canadian Law would belong to another; A Case of this Sort, not easy to determine, lies at present in Chancery; if decided for the Canadian, on the Principle, that Promulgation is necessary to give Force to Laws, the uniformity of the Courts of Justice thereby will be still further destroyed, Chancery reversing the Judgments of the Supreme Court, as that Court reverses those of the Common Pleas. The People notwithstanding continue to regulate their Transactions by Their Ancient Laws, tho' unknown and unauthorised in the Supreme Court, where most of the Transaction would be declared Invalid', Carleton to Shelburne, Quebec, 24 December 1767, BAC, Q 5–1, 318.

43 See Michel Morin, 'La perception de l'ancien droit et du nouveau droit français au Bas-Canada, 1774–1866', in H.P. Glenn (ed.), *Droit québécois et droit français: communauté, autonomie, concordance* (Montreal: Yvon Blais, 1993), 1–41.

44 Carleton to Shelburne, Quebec, 12 April 1768, BAC, Q 5–2, 479.

45 Shortt and Doughty, *Constitutional Documents*, 422.

2.1.2 Merchant Aspirations

Merchants were the first immigrant group settled in the new Province, and they made up the first political minority group in Canadian politics.[46] Opposition to the colonial policy pursued by Murray appeared quickly,[47] first in the form of the representations of the Grand Jury in October 1764.[48] These claimed that:

> 'The Grand Jury must be considered at present as the only Body representative of the Colony, they, as British Subjects, have a right to be consulted, before any Ordinance that may affect the Body that they represent, be passed into a Law, And as it must happen that Taxes be levied for the necessary Expenses or Improvement of the Colony in Order to prevent all abuses & embezzlements or wrong application of the public money'.[49]

The merchants soon organized their opposition, naming Fowler Walker (19 April 1765), who was to play a major role in Murray's recall, as their agent in London. London merchants were also quite active at the same time.[50] By expressing sympathy and admiration for the Canadians, Murray brought upon himself the wrath of the English mercantile minority. He was soon involved in a quarrel with them.[51] Guy Carleton was commissioned on 7 April 1766 to replace Governor Murray and resolve this problem. For almost three years he had been merely Murray's deputy. His main task consisted of gaining the allegiance of the Canadians, restoring peace between colonial subjects[52] and

---

46 See D. Milobar, 'The Origins of British-Quebec Merchant Ideology: New France, the British Atlantic and the Constitutional Periphery, 1720–70', *Journal of Imperial and Commonwealth History* 24:3 (1996), 364–390.

47 Petition of the Quebec Traders to the King, Shortt and Doughty, *Constitutional* Documents, 232–235.

48 Presentments of the Grand Jury of Quebec, oct. 16, 1764, Shortt and Doughty, *Constitutional Documents*, 212–214.

49 Shortt and Doughty, *Constitutional Documents*, 213.

50 Petition of the Merchants to the King, Shortt and Doughty, *Constitutional Documents*, 235–236.

51 Alfred L. Burt, *The Old Province of Quebec* (Toronto: The Ryerson Press, 1933), 102.

52 '[…] from many concurrent Circumstances, the Minds of the King's British Subjects here have been so heated, the most trifling Matter occasions a fresh Stir; on my first Arrival, I had conceived some Hopes, that letting all things rest as they were for some time, would by Degrees bring all Parties into better Temper, and believe it would have had the intended Effect, only for this unlucky Affair of Walker's, in which too many Persons of note in the Province were interested, not to set the Humours afloat again; It must therefore be a Work of Time, and it will require great Attention and Management from the King's Servants on this side of the Water, to restore them to a State of perfect Tranquillity and Good

saving the colony from the absorbing force of its southern neighbours. He had been supplied with experienced and capable legal advisors in the persons of Chief Justice Hey and Attorney General Maseres. For commercial laws, Governors had to face the rivalry existing in the colony, expressed by merchants and traders of the city of Quebec, who demanded that free trade be restored.[53]

Even among English merchants, there were tensions around free trade questions. The Proclamation led to great unrest in the Province of Quebec, the fur traders agitating to obtain the right of free trade. Dunn and Gray vs. Allsopp is an important judgment about the interpretation of the Royal Proclamation. Murray, in 1762, had granted to Thomas Dunn and John Gray a monopoly of the King's posts, among which the most important were Tadoussac and Chicoutimi. On 9 March 1765, several Quebec merchants (Allsopp, Howard and Chinn), basing their arguments on the Royal Proclamation of 7 October 1765, that had declared trade free and open to everyone, applied to the Governor and Council for permission to trade in the King's Domain, part of the colonial territories under the crown's direct management. Murray's proclamation of 31 June 1765 declared trade free and open to all British subjects as mentioned in the Royal Proclamation. Dunn and Gray thought that they still had a right to the privilege granted three years earlier. They were supported in their claim by the Governor and Council, who declared that no one else was able to trade at these posts. It was the start of a commercial war between two groups of merchants. George Allsopp, along with Walker and Eleazar Levy, were the leaders of the malcontents. A clash developed in the fur trade as a result of their activities. Both Canadian and London merchants presented petitions for the opening of the King's domain. On 26 June 1767 an Order-in-Council was issued dismissing the petition of the merchants demanding free trade.[54] Colonial authorities believed that the best way of assuring the development of the colony's fur trade lay in permitting the merchants to trade freely with the Indians of the interior country, while at the same time placing

Humour with each other; I can depend entirely upon Mr. Hey, with his Assistance, and the Support of Government at Home, I trust I shall yet succeed, notwithstanding the various opposite and contending Interests into which they are split; I have and can have no other View, than to fulfil His Majesty's most gracious Intentions to all His Subjects in General, by promoting the Welfare and Happiness of those He has been pleased to commit to my Charge, and to extinguish all Party among them'; Carleton to Shelburne, Trois Rivières, 15 March 1767, BAC, Q 4, 109–110.

53 The Address of the Merchants and Traders of the City of Quebec to Lt. Gov. Carleton, Quebec, 27 September 1766, BAC, Q 3, 344–348.

54 Order-in-Council dismissing the petition of Anthony Merry and others respecting their trade at the posts of Tadoussac and Chicoutimi, Court of St. James, 26 June 1767, BAC, CO42, vol.6, 181–183.

them under proper surveillance.[55] On the other hand, English merchants requested that the commissaries be obliged to give security for their good behaviour, so that if any injustices were committed, damages could easily be recovered.[56] After 1768, the State secretary for the American colony, Lord Hillsborough, decided that Imperial control of the Indian territory was to be replaced by provincial authority, to help the fur trade.

The English traders operating from Canada incessantly presented petitions to Carleton and to the home government for the granting of free trade. John Livingston and a group of merchants represented to Carleton in September 1766 that the regulations enacted to confine trade to certain forts would destroy commerce. They petitioned that trade with the Indians be free and open to all English subjects:[57] 'It is absolutely necessary that the Trade with the Indians should be free to all, the restraining it to Posts that are Garrisoned will entirely destroy it'.[58]

There was also a conflict between these two groups about the nomination of Allsopp[59] as Secretary Clerk of the Quebec Council and Clerk of the Enrolment. Murray had suspended Allsopp, under pressure from some Quebec merchants. On 2 April 1768, Carleton and his Council removed the suspension and reinstated Allsopp to his offices. Twenty Quebec merchants then presented a petition to the Governor a few days later, emphasizing the danger of reinstating him to the office of Secretary of the Province and Clerk of the Council and Registrar. They expressed the belief that the Province's economic life would suffer if such a man were permitted to hold those offices.[60]

For administrative purposes, Carleton wished to make his will as supreme as possible as chief administrator of the Province. A strong hand was required to administer the colony. Carleton said, on this mercantile conflict:

> 'The Disputes between Dunn and Company on one side, and Howard and Company on the other spring from a different Source, as your Lordship

55 Carleton to the Lords of Trade and Plantation, Quebec, 18 October 1766, BAC, Q3, 395.

56 Carleton to Johnson, Quebec, 27 March 1767, BAC, Q 4, 126.

57 John Livingston and a group of merchants to Carleton, Montreal, 20 September 1766, PAC, Q 4, 200–207.

58 'Sir Wm. Johnson's Regulations for the Indian Trade, and the Observations of the Quebec Merchants thereon', Quebec, March, 1768, BAC, Q 5–1, 393.

59 Gérald Lacombe, *Guy Carleton's views on Canadian problems, 1766–1770* (Thesis, Master of Arts, History, Ottawa University, 1965), 46. See, on Carleton, A. Lefort, *Le point de vue de Lord Dorchester sur les problèmes canadiens entre 1786 et 1791* (Thesis, Master of Arts, History, Ottawa University, 1964).

60 Petition of merchants and traders of Quebec to Carleton, Quebec, 28 April 1768, 28 BAC, Q 5–2, 629–632.

> will perceive in my Letter to the Lords of Trade. Government here declared that trade open in the Gazette; afterwards the Secretary of the Province, by the Governors Orders, made a verbal Declaration that no Body must trade there but Dunn and Company; Merchants cleared out regularly at the Custom House for those Parts, and quietly enjoyed that Trade near a year, there they were threatened with Prosecution by the King's Receiver General, and to crown all, Lieutenant Colonel Irving and Council, looking on the Trade to be open, yet granted an Order directed to one Party, to destroy, under the name of dwelling Houses, the Sheds of all others, which is such a Mockery of the King's Subjects, as must tend to their Ruin, and so unjust, that had the Council unanimously opposed it, I should have thought it my Duty to suspend that Order. This Inconsistency your Lordship, I believe, will allow, Cause sufficient to occasion much Contention, about a lucrative Trade. The Suspension, those given to Howard, did not arrive in Time, their Sheds were destroyed, and part of their Goods are brought up, in what Craft they could find in the Saguenay River, it being impossible to live there without Shelter'.[61]

This commercial dispute extended to a complete re-composition of the Council. After the conflict, Carleton removed Mabane and Irving from it.[62] Carleton established an adapted mercantile program aimed at strengthening commerce in the colony.[63] His plan was good, but it proved impossible to apply because

61 Carleton to Shelburne, Quebec, 29 October 1766, BAC, Q 3, 259–261.

62 Carleton to Shelburne, Quebec, 29 November 1766, BAC, Q 4, 40–41.

63 'Since the Conquest of this Province, her Commerce, forced out of its' usual and established Channel, has not yet settled into such a regular and uniform Course, as to allow of fixing her Consumption of those Commodities, upon which Taxes, with the least Inconveniency can be laid, with any Kind of Precision; The in closed Accounts will show, what the Imports of the several Articles, proposed for Taxation, amount to for three years past, The most certain Revenue, that can be raised, is undoubtedly upon Spirits, of which the Inhabitants are in the Custom to consume a considerable Quantity; Prom the high Price of Grain in England, which has raised the Price of British Spirits, and the bad quality of those imported, the People here have taken such a Distaste thereat, that the Colonies upon the Continent have been enabled to drive here a very gainful Trade by vast Importations of Rum, of their own Manufacturing, and vending the Produce of the West India Islands, on which they get considerable Profits; the more detrimental to this Country, that they drain it of the Species, as in Return they take nothing else, except Bills of Exchange. To divert a Trade so ruinous and Impoverishing to throw more of this Branch of Commerce into the Hands of the Mother Country, and to excite the People here to engage in a direct Trade to the West India Islands, where with the Produce of the Country, instead of ready Cash, they may purchase such Articles, as are wanted for their own Consumption, is the main Drift of the Scheme in closed; at the same Time it must be considered, that the very

of the opposition of the English merchants. For commercial purposes, the authorities thought that the Canadians could be helpful with past commercial practices, to learn the practices of the fur trade and native relations.[64]

There was also rivalry over the fisheries between two groups of merchants and Seigneurs. On the one hand, Tachet and Cugnet, two Canadian Seigneurs, asked for their lands and fisheries titles to be restored. This was followed by a petition by the other group, some of the Canadian merchants engaged in the same industry, who argued that in 1765 and 1766 Palliser had put an end to their cod, salmon and seal fisheries.[65] Carleton supported the Canadian lords, but Hey decided that the claims, as they stood, had no legal validity. This injustice was removed only a few years later when the Quebec Act was passed.[66]

In fact, during the years that followed the Treaty of Paris, fur trade and fisheries remained the colony's major economic activities. Manufacturing, such as the production of linen, potash and the distilling of rum, was developing

---

Imposing of these Duties, and a plentiful Harvest in Britain, may again shift the course of this Trade, and leave but a scanty Revenue for the Exigencies of Government; I must further observe to their Lordships, that as there is a considerable Quantity of Spirits actually on Hand, it may at first damp the Importation so much, it will not be prudent, for some Time absolutely to rely thereon; That it would be highly necessary, the raising these, or any other Duties, on Importation, should commence from the Opening of the Navigation, which may be commonly esteemed about the first of May, as it has scarcely ever been known, that foreign Vessells have arrived at Quebec before that Time, in Order to put all Importers of these Commodities upon an equal Footing; That all Vessells coming up the River should be obliged to enter at this Port, and break Bulk nowhere before their arrival here; A List of the Officers deemed Requisite for the Collection of these Duties, and of the Salaries that may be allowed them, is herewith likewise enclosed'; Carleton to Grey Cooper (Secretary to the Lords Commissioners of the Treasury), Quebec, 10 December 1767, BAC, Q 5-1, 303–305.

64 '[…] Whether they are right or wrong in their Opinion of the Indian Trade, I submit to those whom the King has appointed to direct and superintend[ant] the same, but the unanimous Opinion of all here, Canadians and British, is, that unless the present Restraints are taken off, that Trade must greatly suffer, this Province, be nearly ruined, Great Britain be a considerable Loser, and Prance the sole Gainer, as they must turn the greatest Part of the Furs down the Mississippi, instead of the St. Lawrence, they compute that a very large quantity of Merchandise formerly passed throw this Province to Nations unknown to Pontiac, and too distant to come to any of our Posts, and that so much is lost of the Consumption of British Manufactures. They say that their own Interest will always be a sufficient Reason and Motive to treat these People well, and to use their utmost Endeavours to keep them in Peace, and the Canadians will engage to take some English in every Canoe, to acquire a Knowledge of these Countries, and the Language, to show they have no Jealousy at their becoming acquainted with this Trade'; Carleton to Johnson, Quebec, 27 March 1767, BAC, Q 4, 123.

65 Burt, *The Old Province of Quebec*, 141.

66 Lacombe, *Guy Carleton's views on Canadian problems*, 181.

slowly. England maintained a strong control over the development of her colony's industries. She was to produce products needed by the mother country, such as staples and raw materials, but she was not to manufacture goods that would compete with British merchandise. As we have seen, the legal questions were not about economic questions but around procedural and judicial issues.

2.2 *Debates over Debt Imprisonment and Bankruptcy Laws*

One may perceive from this the main conflicts that appeared on the surface during Murray's and Carleton's administrations; that is, opposition between the mercantile element and the civil authorities. There were also issues of jealousy between the military and the merchants. Furthermore, the English element opposed itself to the leniency shown towards the Canadians. Unrest increased from the growing demands of the Canadians for the rights that had been promised to them in 1760. The most important job of Quebec's courts, as with other colonial courts, was to maintain lines of credit to perpetuate economic trends by assisting creditors in the collection of their debts. Notes, bills and bonds were instruments of a commercial economy, and were founded in part on French law. If creditors 'had no remedy' and 'would suffer a total loss' when debtors failed to pay what they owed, 'every prudent man'[67] would become very averse to giving credit, which would prove inimical to trade.

It was essential not to leave any creditor remediless in the recovery of a just debt, which neither law nor equity could permit. They had to ensure that no debtor be excused from payment of all debts, although writs of execution might be issued in a fashion that would ensure that debts of a higher nature be satisfied and paid first. Such a debt collection system, resulting from a blend of legal traditions, would lead to a decline in trade. The entry of a judgment, however, did not guarantee any form of debt payment, and British subjects were quite virulent against French legal traditions, with the English procedure adopted for Quebec's courts as well.

One of these British innovations was the establishment of debt imprisonment and the attempt to introduce English bankruptcy laws. As the new rulers wished to treat Canada as a British colony, liberty[68] and criminal justice was to

67 William E Nelson, *The Common Law in Colonial America: The Chesapeake and New England, 1660–1750*, (Oxford, Oxford University Press, 2016), 19.

68 P. Girard, 'Liberty, Order, and Pluralism: The Canadian Experience', in J.P. Greene (ed.), *Exclusionary Empire: English Liberty Overseas, 1600–1900* (Cambridge: Cambridge University Press, 2009), 160–190.

be granted to its subjects.[69] English economic rules were sought by some English merchants, but were not supported by the French Canadians, because some of the English legal frameworks were not familiar to the French legal system, such as debt imprisonment and bankruptcy laws.

As G.B. Warden wrote, the 'most persuasive object' of seventeenth century English law reformers was the twin dilemma of 'indebtedness and property'.[70] In England and its American colonies, debtors were imprisoned until the creditors had been repaid, in an era devoid of credit agencies, instant credit checks, or fine print on bills of sales.[71]

2.2.1 Bankruptcy Laws

The disagreement over the introduction of bankruptcy laws into the colony was an example of the unsettled status of the law at the time: in this case, whether the establishment of English laws had included its bankruptcy laws or not. At the start of this conflict, there was a symbolic case.

In October 1767, Levi Solomon, a respectable Jewish merchant unable to pay his debt, consulted Maseres, the Attorney General, as to the best way of reaching a settlement with his creditors. Maseres, believing that the bankruptcy laws had been introduced in 1763–1764 along with all the other English laws, proposed the creation of a bankruptcy commission, a common law institution that did not exist under French law. This institution existed in England, but not in Scotland, Ireland or in the American colonies.[72] A group of Quebec merchants petitioned for a recall of the commission, stressing that its proceedings would endanger their credit and property, and be detrimental to the province's trade.[73] The commission was recalled and the Lieutenant-Governor refused to give a decision before receiving advice from the Board of Trade.

---

69 On 1 July 1766, an ordinance had been passed by Irving and Council in pursuance of an order-in-council of 17 February, granting the Canadians more extended rights; An Ordinance to alter and amend an Ordinance of His Excellency, the Governor and His Majesty's Council of this Province, passed the seventeenth Day of September 1764, Quebec, 1 July 1766. BAC, Q 3, 181–184.

70 G.B. Warden, 'Notes and Documents: Law Reform in England and New England, 1620–1660', *William and Mary Quarterly* 35 (1978), 668–690, 681.

71 C.E. Smith, 'Economic Liberty and the Official Law Books in Colonial Massachusetts', *Cato Journal* 27:3 (2007), 411–430, 419.

72 See M.J. Horwitz, *The Transformation of American Law, 1780–1860* (Cambridge: Harvard University Press, 1977).

73 Memorial of Quebec Merchants to Carleton, Quebec, 17 November 1767, BAC, Q 5–1, 248–250.

> 'Having lately received an Application for a Commission of Bankruptcy, agreeable to the British Acts of Parliament in that Oa.se made and Provided, and as there was no Precedent of such a Commission's being issued since the Establishment of Civil Government in this Province, I consulted His Majesty's Attorney General thereupon, who was clearly of Opinion, the Laws relative thereto, as well as all the Laws of England, which existed upon the 17th of September 1764, were introduced here by the Ordinance of that Date, and that these therefore might be carried into Execution'.[74]

Carleton fixed the transplantation law problem in this case, and reported the merchants' reaction.

> 'But many of the People in Trade having taken the Alarm thereat, and represented, as your Lordships will see by the inclosed Petition, that it might very much endanger the Credit of the Merchants at this Place with their Correspondents in England, for whose sake, and for the Preservation of whose Rights, it was chiefly intended to put them in Execution, and the Canadians like-wise, from their not understanding those Laws, having conceived apprehensions, they might subject them to many Difficulties [...]'.[75]

Carleton expressed that legal transplantation raised an issue between fidelity to the legal standards of the home country and necessary adaptation to the colonial context:

> 'As the Commercial Interests of this Province are intimately united with those of the Mother Country, the British Merchants concerned in the Trade thereof must be the best Judges of the Advantages or Disadvantages likely to result to them from the Execution of these Laws, and whether there is any Foundation for the Complaint made by some, of partial Assignments having been the Consequence of the Want of such a Regulation, as well as of an Ordinance of this Province of the 9th of March 1765, to which I take the Liberty to refer Your Lordships'.[76]

---

74 Carleton to the Lords of Trade and Plantations, Quebec, 21 November 1767, BAC, CO 42, vol. 6, 236–237.

75 Carleton to the Lords of Trade and Plantations, Quebec, 21 November 1767, BAC, CO 42, vol. 6, 236.

76 Carleton to the Lords of Trade and Plantations, Quebec, 21 November 1767, BAC, CO 42, vol. 6, 237.

Awaiting the Lords of Trade's decision, Carleton tried to resolve the situation.[77] The Foreign Secretary of State made his decision. For Hillsborough, the Act of Bankruptcy was not to be applied in the province.[78]

2.2.2 Debt Process Recovery Reform

The reform of the justice system was another point of contention between merchants and authorities on debt questions. On 1 February 1770 a reform ordinance was passed,[79] whereby the powers of justices of the peace were greatly curtailed. Their authority in matters of private property was mostly taken away. To further alleviate the burden weighing upon the population, no houses or lands were to be sold for debts in the case of actions not exceeding twelve pounds, and in other cases, to be sold only on default of personal property. The main reason for this ordinance was that it was required to relieve the oppression weighing upon the Canadians. In fact, most of the law officers were bankrupt traders who sought to enrich themselves by exploiting the people, consuming exorbitant fees for the collection of minor debts.[80] 'After this ordinance,

77 'And until I could be entirely Satisfied herein, I Judged, as these Laws had never yet been put in Force. A further Suspension of the same, for about six Months, could not be attended with any Manifest Inconveniency; That every Creditor, in whatever Part of the Globe Situated, should equally and proportionally share in the Effects of his insolvent Debtor, Honor and Justice evidently Direct, How to attain this End is the Point in Question, in which the Merchants at Home are strongly interested, as the Balance of Trade hitherto, I apprehend has been greatly against this Province, the Impediments, thrown in the Way of the Fur Trade above, and of the Fisheries below, having very much curtailed the ancient and usual Resources of her Commerce', Carleton to the Lords of Trade and Plantations, Quebec, 21 November 1767, BAC, CO 42, vol. 6, 237.

78 Hillsborough to Carleton, Whitehall, 6 March 1768, BAC, Q 5–1, 344–350.

79 Cases of less than twelve pounds were to be judged by the Court of Common Pleas. To render justice more efficiently, the court at Montreal was to be independent of that of Quebec. Both of these were to sit throughout the year, except on prescribed holidays, and twice a year to permit the judges to go on their circuits. Special commissioners were to judge cases not exceeding three pounds; An Ordinance for the more effectual Administration of Justice…, Quebec, 1 February 1770, BAC, RG 1, B 1, vol. 5, 127–145.

80 'Your Lordship has been already informed, that the Protestants, who have settled or rather Sojourned here since the Conquest, are composed only of Traders, disbanded Soldiers, and Officers, the latter, one or two excepted, below the Rank of Captain; of those in the Commission of the Peace, such as prospered in Business, could not give up their Time to sit as Judges, and when several from Accidents and ill Judged Undertakings, became Bankrupts, they naturally sought to repair their broken Fortunes at the Expence of the People; Hence a Variety of Schemes to increase the Business and their own Emoluments, Bailiffs, of their own Creation, mostly French Soldiers, either disbanded, or Deserters, dispersed through the Parishes with blanks Citations, catching at every little Feud or Dissension among the People, exciting them on to their Ruin, and in a Manner forcing them to litigate, what, if left to themselves, might have been easily accommodated, putting them

Governor Carleton claimed that it was being opposed by the old subjects mainly because it deprived many of them of their means of subsistence':[81]

> 'The ordinance produced a Stir among some of them, or that a Regulation depriving so many of a most unfair Means of Subsistence, although raised under the specious Pretext and colour of the Law should engage these to struggle, for a Repeal of what was likely in so great a Degree to affect their private Circumstances, as well as the Influence and Sway they had acquired, in Consequence of the Powers they were before invested with'.[82]

Carleton opposed the view of Grant, a merchant leader who made trouble in London about this justice reform.[83] However, the Governor believed that he had made the correct/best choice for economic purposes.[84]

> 'Within these four or five Years between three or four hundred Families have been turned out of their Houses, obliged to sell their Lands, and seek new Habitations, a real Loss to Trade, as they become a Burthen to Society, and are years before they can be enabled to purchase our

---

to extravagant Costs for the Recovery of very small Sums, their Lands, at a Time there is the greatest Scarcity of Money, and consequently but few Purchasers, exposed to hasty Sales for Payment of the most trifling Debts, and the Money arising from these Sales consumed in exorbitant Fees, while the Creditors reap little Benefit from the Destruction of their unfortunate Debtors; This, My Lord, is but a very faint Sketch of the Distresses of the Canadians, and the Cause of much Reproach to our National Justice, and the King's Government'; Carleton to Hillsborough, Quebec, 28 March 1770, BAC 7, 7.

81 Lacombe, *Guy Carleton's views on Canadian* problems, 147.

82 Carleton to Hillsborough, Quebec, 25 April 1770, BAC, Q 7, 89.

83 'However I could not help observing to Mr. Charles Grant, who had all along put himself at the Head of this Affair, I was well assured, and that, some Time before the Ordinance was near perfected, He made this Declaration, that as he had not been consulted, tho' one of the most considerable Traders in the Country, He was resolved to oppose it; to this he made no Reply, I had been long informed, that one Mr. Shapherd, formerly in Trade here, who owed a considerable Sum to some Merchants in London of the name of Grant, which he had no other Means of discharging, than by the very Beneficial Employment, as He made it, of Cleric of the Peace of this District, which he had enjoyed for some Years, was determined to cause a Bustle, and pushed on this same Mr. Charles Grant to take the Part he has acted therein', Carleton to Hillsborough, Quebec, 25 April 1770, BAC, Q 7, 89.

84 '[…] the Lands not being liable to be sold for Debts under twelve Pounds Currency, I am well convinced, can be attended with no particular Inconvenience, for the Produce of the smallest Farms allowed by the French Regulation, about sixty Acres, which in my humble Opinion was a very prudent and political one, and ought to be kept up, besides the Stock, will considerably more than pay that Sum, exactly equal to nine Pounds Sterling', Carleton to Hillsborough, Quebec, 25 April 1770, BAC, Q 7, 91.

> Manufactures, and what is still a greater Hardship upon them, the Lands have not been sold for a sixth or eight of their Value, so that many Instances can be brought of Debtors being ruined, the Produce consumed in Fees, and the Creditor's Demand remaining undischarged'.[85]

During the same era in England, English common law protected real property from attachment for debts,[86] but debtors were routinely imprisoned until they repaid their creditors. 'While the English statutory definition of bankruptcy remained a convoluted one for centuries, it was consistently dependant on whether a debtor was a merchant or a member of the landed gentry'.[87] John Cooke explained that many people who sought repayment of 'just debts' had been unable to 'pay officers fees to recover them', so that a 'poor man cannot sue for his wages' but 'a matter of 20 shillings […] will cost him forty in the getting of it'.[88] In Quebec, the arrest of the person for debts and the practice of trading justice generated opposition to the English government.[89] For Carleton,

> 'A Trading Justice was likewise a new Practice, no Ways likely to make the Canadians relish British Government, there was not a Protestant Butcher or Publican, that became a Bankrupt, who did not apply to be made a Justice, they cantoned themselves upon the Country, and many of them rid the People with despotic Sway, imposed Fines, which they turned to their own Profit, and in a Manner looked upon themselves as the Legislators of the Province. To ease the poor People of such intolerable oppression, to render them useful to Great Britain, and the Society they live in, and that the only Order of Canadians most likely to reap any Advantage

85 Carleton to Hillsborough, Quebec, 25 April 1770, BAC, Q 7, 91.

86 See I. Duffy, 'English Bankrupts', *American Journal of Legal History* 24 (1980), 283–305; B. Mann, *Republic of Debtors* (Cambridge, Massachusetts: Harvard University Press, 2002).

87 C.E. Smith, 'Economic liberty and the official law books in colonial Massachusetts', *Cato Journal* 27:3 (2007), 411–430, 418.

88 J. Cooke, *The Vindication of the Professors and Profession of the Law* (1646). In Thomason Tracts, E320 (17), Reel 52 quoted by Smith, 'Economic liberty', 429. After the execution of Charles I in 1649, Parliament passed a series of laws aiming to reform creditor-debtor relations.

89 'It is but a few Months since sixteen Debtors were released out of the Gaol of Montreal, at the Expense of Government, by my Orders, whose Debts and Gaol Pees, the latter of which were above one half of the whole, did not amount to quite forty Pounds Sterling; What Effect this must have upon a People, to whom an Arrest of the Body for Debt was almost entirely unknown, I humbly submit'; Carleton to Hillsborough, Quebec, 25 April 1770, BAC, Q 7, 92.

> from the Change of Dominion, might feel the full Benefit of this Change, were the only Motives which guided my Conduct upon this Occasion, I shall be happy, if it procures the End proposed'.[90]

Already by the seventeenth century exactly the same concerns were to be found in England, where the population and several jurists challenged the practice of imprisonment for debt, the abuses of debt officers, and the costs of debt collection.[91]

The Protestant colonists were on the frontline of the opposition to the ordinance. They argued that such legislation would hurt the general interest of the colony and ruin many merchants, and that it would help debtors to defraud their creditors and give too much power to the Common Pleas Judges.[92]

The government of Quebec, from 1764 to 1774, was a welter of chaos and discontent; confusion reigned in the province during these years.[93] In reality, until May 1767, the British administration was more interested in the problem of the old American colonies than in the new ones. Attempts had been made by England to establish a legal framework that would both attract colonists and conciliate the Canadian population. Quebec's unique character presented problems for which no set and proven solutions existed. The British merchants

90 Carleton to Hillsborough, Quebec, 25 April 1770, BAC, Q 7, 92.

91 Smith, 'Economic liberty', 420.

92 Memorial of the merchants of London trading to Quebec to the Board of Trade, London, 11 July 1770, PAC, CO 42, vol. 7, 60–61.

93 The province's difficulties were ascribed to two major causes by Charles York, attorney general, and William Hey, solicitor general: '1st. The Attempt to carry on the Administration of Justice without the aid of the natives, not merely in new forms, but totally in an unknown tongue, by which means the partys Understood Nothing of what was pleaded or determined having neither Canadian Advocates or Solicitors to Conduct their Causes, nor Canadian jurors to give Verdicts, even in Causes between Canadians only, Nor Judges Conversant in the French language to declare the Laws, and to pronounce Judgement; This must cause the Real Mischiefs of Ignorance, oppression and Corruption, or else what is almost equal in Government to the mischiefs themselves, the suspension and Imputation of them. The second and great source of disorders was the Alarm taken at the Construction put upon his Majesty's Proclamation of Oct. 17th 1763. As if it were his Royal Intentions by his Judges and Officers in that Country, at once to abolish all the usages and Customs of Canada, with the rough hand of a Conqueror rather than with the true Spirit of a Lawful Sovereign, and not so much to extend the protection and Benefit of his English laws to His new subjects, by securing their laws, liberties and properties with more certainty than in former times, as to impose new, unnecessary and arbitrary Rules, especially in the Titles to Land, and in the Modes of Descent Alienation and Settlement, which tend to confound and subvert rights, instead of supporting them', 'Report of Attorney and Solicitor General Regarding the Civil Government of Quebec', from Dartmouth Papers, M 383, Shortt and Doughty, *Constitutional Documents*, 170.

wondered whether or not an Assembly would be convened. In this period many French and English laws ran concurrently, creating a disorderly and tense situation. The Canadians in some instances would follow English law, while in others they would follow French laws and customs, depending on the advantages that might be gained from one or the other. The population was uncertain as to the laws that were to be followed and was being incessantly exploited by minor government officials; justice began to be expensive, slow and complicated. As may be seen from these examples, some English laws had been introduced while others had not. Once more it had been vividly demonstrated that the colony was in need of a settled and fixed system of laws. The colony's Governor strove to alleviate the burden weighing upon the conquered people and took steps to restore the situation that existed prior to 1760, reintroducing the seigneurial system and the French judicial system on one hand, and on the other, seeking to introduce some British commercial advances and practices.

3 The Accommodation: Civil and Common Law 'Mashup'

From 1763 to 1774, the major domestic question continued to be the lack of a comprehensive legal code. This was not necessarily disadvantageous to commercial parties who were beginning to adopt standard forms when contracting. Where mercantile practice conflicted with French and English laws' confusion, judges proceeded with caution. Rivalry between British and Canadian settlers intensified in this period. The latter group received assistance from official circles both in the colony (Murray, Carleton,[94] Cugnet,[95] York, Hey) and in the mother country (Thurlow, De Grey).[96] Beyond the effects of the Conquest, there was also the more general issue of the nature of the *ancien régime*

94 For Carleton, '[…] [a]ll this Arrangement (French Laws), in one Hour, we overturned, by the Ordinance of the Seventeenth of September One Thousand seven hundred and sixty four, and Laws, ill adapted to the Genius of the Canadians, to the Situation of the Province, and to the Interests of Great Britain, unknown, and unpublished were introduced in their Stead; A Sort of Severity, if I remember right, never before practiced by any Conqueror, even where the People, without Capitulation, submitted to His will and Discretion', Carleton to Shelburne, Quebec, 24 December 1767, BAC, Q 5–1, 316.

95 See Silvio Normand, 'François-Joseph Cugnet et la reconstitution du droit de la Nouvelle-France', *Cahiers aixois d'histoire des droits de l'outre-mer français* 1 (2002), 127–145.

96 See David Gilles, 'Les acteurs de la norme coloniale face au droit métropolitain: de l'adaptation à l'appropriation (Canada XVIIe–XVIIIe s.)', *Clio@Thémis* 4 (2011), www.cliothemis.com.

commercial system. 1774 and the promulgation of the Quebec Act[97] marked the choice of French law for private law, accompanied by the formalization of the superiority of the British parliament for all international commercial questions. After his nomination and following a short time spent on the side of the British merchants' party, Carleton had begun a campaign – a process that had been started by Murray – which was to reach its conclusion with the passing of the Quebec Act in 1774. Up to that date the substantive law (English) of the province remained unchanged, although the administrative rules witnessed several alterations mainly in the direction desired by the Canadians.

3.1 *The Choice of the Quebec Act*

During the debates before the Quebec Act, Governor Carleton wished to retain French civil law and English criminal law while his assistants (Hey and Maseres) favoured English law, permitting the survival of a few minor French laws.[98] If Maseres stayed in this view, Hey, at the end of 1760s, adopted the Governor's view. Carleton discarded the draft of a report written by Maseres because it was too critical of his own views. Instead of this version, Carleton wrote a report himself, based on Hey's and his own views.[99] He wrote that in the Court of Common Pleas, Canadian laws and customs were to serve as the basis of the decisions in all actions between Canadians, being determined according to 'equity' in the French meaning. Carleton claimed that the best way of winning the allegiance of the Canadians lay in the imposition of as few English laws as possible. At any rate, applying all English legal frameworks would be impracticable until the population had been educated in the English language and laws. To please the old subjects, juries were to be called in tort cases. English commercial law was taken for granted. The colonial authority's goal had been to relieve the burden weighing on the Canadians and in this way succeed in winning their allegiance. As they could not be fitted into the English mould, it was to be re-cast so as to accommodate them. Accordingly, article 8 of the Quebec Act restored French private law, subject to such amendments as the local legislature was authorized to issue. Despite this provision, the legislature would intervene relatively moderately thereafter, with the exception of commercial law. The Quebec Act authorized the drafting of wills according to

---

97 An Act for making more effectual provision for the government of the Province of Quebec in North America [Acte de Québec], 1774 (R.-U.), 14 Geo. III, c. 83.

98 W.P.M. Kennedy and G. Lanctot, *Reports on the Laws of Quebec: 1767–1770* (Ottawa: F.A. Acland, 1931), 51–83.

99 Carleton and Hey's Report upon the Laws and Courts of Judicature in the Province of Quebec, Quebec, 15 September 1769, BM King's Manuscripts-207, BAC, MG 21, vol. 21, 1–50.

English rules;[100] it also introduced unlimited freedom of testamentary gifts, repealing at the same time the rules on legitimacy and the French Reserve.[101] The Quebec Act confirmed an order of 1771 about land ownership: seigneuries would continue to be granted until the mass exodus of the Loyalists to Quebec, but it was under the free and common socage statute that applied in the townships.[102] After the Quebec Act, French Canadians sought English constitutional liberty,[103] and to make English legal culture their own in cases where they thought it to their advantage.

After the proclamation of the Quebec Act, mercantile law (including marine, life and fire insurance) would be administered in accordance with the law in England at the time unless Quebec law made other provisions.[104] Section 18 of the Quebec Act only extended to the new possessions the effect of English acts regulating 'Trade of Commerce' in the British North American colonies.

3.2 *The 'Long March' to Commercial Modernity (1774–1857): Inserting the Common Law in a Civil Law Framework*

As we have seen, following the Quebec Act, the civil law saw several English 'innovations' such as imprisonment for debt and testamentary freedom. Most studies of law and justice in post-Conquest Quebec 'questioned the fundamental legitimacy of a British justice system staffed by British judges following largely English procedures (though applying French civil law) and saw it as an instance of colonial domination'.[105] But it's also possible to see there the establishment of a mixed legal culture, which was an improvement of colonial modernity, against two 'old' European law traditions. In England, the law governing sales of goods developed significantly at the end of eighteenth century and

100 André Morel, 'Un exemple de contact entre deux systèmes juridiques: le droit successoral du Québec', *Annales de l'Université de Poitiers*, 2nd series 4–5 (1963–1964), 19–32.

101 F.M. Greenwood, 'Lower Canada (Quebec): Transformation of Civil Law, from Higher Morality to Autonomous Will, 1774–1866', *Manitoba Law Journal* 23:1–2 (1996), 132–182.

102 See J. Little, '"The fostering care of Government": Lord Dalhousie's 1821 Survey of the Eastern Townships', *Histoire sociale/Social History* 43:85 (2010) 193–212; J. Little, *State and Society in Transition: The Politics of Institutional Reform in the Eastern Townships, 1838–1852* (Montreal: McGill-Queen's University Press, 1997).

103 Michel Morin, 'La découverte du droit constitutionnel britannique dans une colonie francophone: la Gazette de Québec, 1764–1774', *RJT* 47:2 (2013), 318–355.

104 Under the chairmanship of Chief Justice Smith (1786–1793), the Court of Appeal refused to apply the ordinance on trade enacted in 1673 by the king of France on the ground that it had not been registered by the Sovereign Council; Marine Leland, 'François-Joseph Cugnet 1720–1789' *Revue de l'Université Laval* XXI:4 (1966), 378–396; Bernard Clermont, *Initiation au droit des affaires du Québec* (Québec: PU Laval, 1986), 33.

105 Fyson, 'Between the *Ancien Régime* and Liberal Modernity', 414.

in the first half of the nineteenth century. Many of the leading cases were English. Two strains of law – contract and the law merchant –, were more or less godparents, French and English, of the law of sales. Some commercial trends were common to both, such as the concept of market overt, or open market, that suffused the merchant law. In market overt, goods were as freely transferable as bills, notes, and paper money. A buyer of goods in market overt acquired full rights to the goods, and if he bought in good faith and for value, his claims were superior to those of any prior owner, even if the goods had been stolen.[106]

3.2.1 Mixed Traditions, One Practice

After the choice of a mixed tradition for private law, the authorities needed to increase access to the French laws, English laws, the common law and jurisprudence. Access to *ancien régime* French doctrine was difficult for jurists in Lower-Canada,[107] even if the access to English statutes and judgments was not much easier.[108] In the seventeenth and eighteenth centuries, the official collection of Acts of Parliament was kept in the Tower of London, and it was left to private printers to issue printed editions of English law. In France, the link between French colonial law and *ancien régime* law was interrupted by the French revolution, and it could be difficult for Lower Canada lawyers to apply the old French doctrine. A legal publication process began after the Conquest in the colony, but at the beginning the legal literature was relatively scant.[109]

106 Lawrence M. Friedman, *A History of American Law* (New York: A Touchstone Book, 2005), 193.

107 J.-Ph Garneau, 'Les contours du barreau de Montréal au début du XIXe siècle: Réflexions sur les liens entre profession et pouvoir social dans la société bas-canadienne', in T. Nootens and J.-R. Thuot (eds.), *Les figures du pouvoir à travers le temps: Formes, pratiques et intérêts des groupes élitaires au Québec, XVIIe–XXe siècles* (Quebec: Presses de l'Université Laval, 2012), 77–86.

108 Access to law was an old claim in England and France. 'In the 1640s and 1650s pamphlets published in London regularly demanded that Parliament compile and distribute an official publication of existing statutory law. [...] At the time In 1647, a pamphlet entitled The Lawyers Bane urged members of Parliament to summarize and publish the mass of statutory law enacted over the centuries because men should understand those laws and ordinances by which their rights, privileges, interests, and estates are secured'; C.E. Smith, 'Economic liberty and the official law books in colonial Massachusetts', *Cato Journal* 27:3 (2007), 411–430, 413–414.

109 Silvio Normand, 'Les débuts de la littérature juridique québécoise, 1767–1840', in G. Blaine Baker and Donald Fyson (eds.), *Essays in the History of Canadian Law, volume XI: Quebec and the Canadas* (Toronto: Osgoode Society for Canadian Legal History and University of Toronto Press, 2013), 96–130; Silvio Normand, 'Profil des périodiques juridiques québécois au XIXe siècle', *Les Cahiers de droit* 34:1 (1993), 153–182.

There were only two or three books about commercial matters written during this period. If we exclude works about real property and general civil law, we have only A. Gorrie, *Synopsis of the Laws of Letting and Hiring*, Montreal, 1848; E.L. Montizambert, *Lecture on the Mercantile Law of Lower Canada*, Montréal, 1848; and D. Girouard, *Essai sur les Lettres de change*, Montréal, 1860.

There were few case reports published from 1774 to 1866 on civil and commercial matters. Some commercial judgments can be found in the Revue de Législation,[110] Lower-Canada Reports,[111] Pyke's[112] and Stuart's[113] Reports, The Lower Canada jurist,[114] The Law Reporter,[115] and the Montreal Condensed Reports.[116]

International commercial order depended upon the ability of different political authorities to recognize each other, even if that recognition fell short of formal diplomacy or treaty making. Commercial law worked both to tie together disparate parts of colonial empires, and to lay the basis for exchanges of all sorts between politically and culturally separate imperial or colonial powers. This is why the British Parliament conserved its international commercial law jurisdiction in the Quebec Act in 1774.

An ordinance of 17 September 1764 stated that trials could be decided by jury if one party asked for it.[117] According to an ordinance of 1777, English laws of evidence would be used to establish proof of the facts in commercial matters.[118] Section 10 of the ordinance on jury trials in civil cases (1785) reiterated that for all evidence in commercial cases, it would be English law that applied.[119] This rule, as was finally expressed in Art. 1206 Lower Canada Civil Code, was introduced along with trial by jury in commercial actions.[120] As Caron said during the writing of the Code, only the English rules of evidence

110 *Revue de législation et de jurisprudence*, 3 vol., 1840–1848.

111 *Décisions des tribunaux du Bas Canada/Lower Canada Reports*, 19 vol., 1850–1867.

112 *Pyke's Report of Cases argued and determined in the Court of King's Bench, for the District of Quebec in the Province of Lower Canada in Hilary Term*, 1 vol., 1811.

113 G.O. Stuart, *Reports of Cases*, 1 vol., 1834 for the years 1810–1835.

114 *Lower Canada Jurist/Collection de décisions du Bas-Canada*, 35 vol., 1856–1891.

115 *The Law Reporter/Journal de Jurisprudence*, 2 vol., 1854, for year 1853–1854.

116 *Montreal Condensed Reports/Précis des Décisions des Tribunaux du District de Montréal*, 1, for 1853–1854, 1854.

117 *Ordonnance établissant des cours civiles*, 17 septembre 1764, *D.C. I*, cit., 181.

118 *Ordonnance pour réglementer la procédure dans les cours de judicature civile de la province de Québec*, 17 Geo. III, c. 2, art. 7 (1777).

119 *D.C. I*, cit., 768.

120 'In Proof of all Facts concerning Commercial Matters Recourse shall be had, in all the Courts of civil Jurisdiction in this Province, to the Rules of Evidence laid down by the Laws of England'; 17 Geo. III, 1777, c. 2, s.7 and 25 Geo. III 1785, c.2, s.10.

should be applied, but once facts were proven, it was the Quebec law that ruled. The English Statute of Frauds applied, but not the Statute of Limitations: 'Only the English testimony of laws are in force in this country, even in the trade business. [I]n these cases, it is the only evidence that must be made and conducted according to the English system, but on the application of the law to proven facts, it is according to our law that we must decide. The status of Fraud is for us a part of the Testimony of rules, but not the Limitations Status [my transl.]'.[121] While the Quebec Act did not provide for this, commercial cases and claims resulting from bodily injury could be the subject of proceedings before a jury according to an Ordinance issued in 1785.[122] This Ordinance also required

> [...] tous et chaque particulier, qui auront des procès dans aucune des Cours des Plaidoyers communs fondés sur dettes, promesses, engagements et conventions, concernant le commerce seulement, entre négociants et négociants et entre marchands et marchands réputés et connus comme tels, suivant la loi, et aussi, concernant les injures personnelles qui doivent être compensées en dommages, pourront à l'option et choix de l'une des parties, avoir et obtenir qu'elles seront plaidées devant un corps de jurés pour avoir un verdict, tant pour déterminer le fait qui doit être établi, dans telles actions de commerce, que pour constater les dommages dans celles d'injures personnelles.[123]

In terms of bills of exchange, English law specifically played a supplementary role. For real property, there had been a mixed system since 1774. The land already colonised stayed under French law and the seigneurial regime. New lands given to British colonist were deeded in free and common socage. English common law's primary purpose in this regard was to make real property as secure as possible from any type of intrusion or summary confiscation.

121 *'Il n'y a que les lois de témoignage anglaises qui soient en force dans le pays, même dans les affaires de commerce – dans ces cas, c'est la preuve seulement qui doit être faite et conduite d'après le système anglais, mais quant à l'application de la loi aux faits prouvés, c'est d'après notre loi qu'il doit être statue. Le statut des Fraudes fait pour nous partie des règles de Témoignage, mais non le Statut des limitation'*, J.E.C. Brierley, 'Quebec's Civil Law Codification, Viewed and Reviewed', *McGill Law Journal* 14 (1968), 521, 555, note 78.

122 *Ordonnance qui règle les formes de procéder dans les Cours civiles de Judicature, et qui établit les procès par jurés dans les affaires de commerce, et d'injures personnelles qui doivent être compensées en dommages, en la Province de Québec*, 25 Geo. III, c. 2 (1785), *D.C. I*, 765.

123 *Ordonnance instituant les procès par jury*, O.Q. 1785, 25 Geo. III, c. 2, art. 9, *D.C. I*, 768, art. IX.

A consensus on real property's systemic integration into a market economy and under a uniform statute did not exist at the beginning of the nineteenth century. It was only later, in 1854 and 1857, that land tenure in Quebec changed to a modern legal framework.[124] In this manner, English law was specifically introduced to Lower Canada in particular fields such as wills, rules of evidence in commercial matters, ownership of new land, and bills of exchange.

By the 1820s and 1830s the choice between French and English law started to become a secondary issue, behind economics,[125] politics and liberal questions. In 1822, the Canada Trade Act introduced certain liberal practices, and began to change land tenure rules.[126] In the 1820s options were proposed to deal with the long-standing problem of secret mortgages on real property (often related to the dower rights of married women) that hindered the free property transfers that were essential to an increasingly capitalist society.[127] Titling or registering property[128] could discourage owners from leaving unofficial property regimes because those very processes alerted government to new sources of revenue through taxation or confiscation. Under the Union Act (1840),[129] the Parliament of United Canada legislated for both the former Lower Canada and for former Upper Canada, which in 1867 became Quebec and Ontario. As Michel Morin has written, in some cases, however, British laws were copied in Quebec legislation. However, their harmonization with the civil law system of Lower Canada was quite dysfunctional.[130]

The author of a pamphlet published in 1846 urged the need for the commercial laws of Canada to approximate as much as possible the most important trading relation tradition : 'Our position should make us desire to assimilate as

---

124 *An Act for settling the Law concerning lands held in Free and Common Soccage, in Lower Canada*, 20 Vict., S.C. 1857, c. 45 ; *An Act for the abolition of feudal rights and duties in Lower Canada*, 18 Vict., S.C., 1854, c.3.

125 G.L. Hogg, and G. Shulman, 'Wage Disputes and the Courts in Montreal, 1816–1835', in Donald Fyson, Colin Coates and Kathryn Harvey (eds.), *Class, Gender and the Law in Eighteenth and Nineteenth-Century Quebec: Sources and Perspectives* (Montreal: Montreal History Group, 1993), 127–143.

126 *An Act to regulate the Trade of the Provinces of Lower and Upper Canada, and for the Purposes relating to the said Provinces*, 3 Geo. 4, 1822, c. 119.

127 Donald Fyson, 'Between the *ancien régime* and liberal modernity', 416.

128 See Silvio Normand, and A. Hudon, 'Le contrôle des hypothèques secrètes au XIXe siècle: ou la difficile conciliation de deux cultures juridiques et de deux communautés ethniques', *Recueil de droit immobilier* (1990), 171–201.

129 *An Act to re-unite the Provinces of Upper and Lower Canada, and for the government of Canada*, 1840 (R.-U.), c. 35; L.R.C. (1985), App. II, no 4.

130 Michel Morin, 'Des juristes sédentaires. L'influence du droit anglais et du droit français sur l'interprétation du Code civil du Bas-Canada', *Revue du Barreau* 60 (2000), 247–386, 268.

much as possible our commercial code to those of England, the United States and Upper Canada because of our relationship with them [my transl.]'.[131]

3.2.2 Commercial Structures and Companies

Up to the beginning of the eighteenth century, English companies were usually royal enterprises and participation in the management and capital of such corporations was limited to a privileged few. In 1771, the South Sea Company was founded. In this company, government bonds, which formed the bulk of the national debt, became redeemable in exchange for shares in the South Sea Company.[132] We know that, in England during the seventeenth century, there was a substantial corporate inflation. The British Parliament had reacted vigorously with the Bubble Act (1720).

The Bubble Act[133] declared illegal certain undertakings that raised transferable stock without the authority of a royal charter or Act of Parliament, and outlawed undertakings acting under obsolete charters. It exempted from these prohibitions companies formed before 1718 and all partnerships, and some authorities suggest that the Bubble Act was passed to eliminate competition in favour of the South Sea Company. The main effect of the Bubble Act was to restrain for more than a century the incorporation of commercial enterprises: after the Great Bubble, companies remained unpopular in the public eye and, as a general rule, the Crown refused to grant charters to promoters of such associations.[134] The law prohibited the formation of new corporations, except those created by an Act of Parliament, and it made it criminal to act as a corporation without that authority.[135] This repressive law would in no way hinder the development of *de facto* joint stock companies which, using a deed of settlement (a concept akin to a trust) as a replacement form of legal organization, managed to partially circumvent the law.[136] Further, legal opinion at the time

131 *'Notre position doit nous faire desirer d'assimiler autant que possible notre code de commerce à ceux d'Angleterre, des États-Unis et du Haut Canada, en raison de nos rapports avec eux'* [anonymous], 'De la codification des lois du Canada', *Revue de Législation* (1846) 337, 339.

132 Robert Demers, 'From the Bubble Act to the pre-incorporation trust: investor protection in Quebec law', *Les Cahiers de droit* 18:2–3 (1977), 335–382.

133 *Bubble Act* (1720) 6 Geo. I c. 18, s. 18.

134 A.B. Dubois, *The English Business Company after the Bubble Act 1720–1800*, 1st ed. (New York: The Commonwealth Fund, 1938), 1–41; W.S. Holdsworth, 'The early history of commercial societies', *Juridical Review* 28 (1916), 340–344, 305.

135 See A.B. Du Bois, *The English Business Company after the Bubble Act, 1720–1800* (New York: Octagon, 1971).

136 M. Fecteau, 'Les "petites républiques": Les compagnies et la mise en place du droit corporatif moderne au Québec au milieu du 19e siècle', *Histoire sociale* 25:49 (1992), 35, 39.

favoured the view that the statute was only of local application and did not encompass the whole of the Empire.

As Robert Demers notes, a jurisdiction of civil law could adapt only with great difficulty to this type of legislation. In the eighteenth century, there was a massive debate about the enforcement of the Bubble Act in the colony of Quebec. By the Quebec Act, commercial law, except for a few modifications as we have seen, was to remain substantially the same as under the French *regime.* As a consequence, one can conclude as a matter of principle that the Crown did not intend to extend the application of the Bubble Act to the colony. The jurisprudence of the Province confirmed this opinion in White & al. v. The Ship Daedalus.[137] Justice William Scott refused to apply the statute for two main reasons: It was 'a statute for restraining certain unwarrantable extravagancies, projects and schemes, or as they were called in the language of the times, bubbles, and for protecting owners of ships from exorbitant and fraudulent insurances' and the statute was enacted to 'correct multiple frauds brought about by the abuses of bubble companies – but such a situation never arose in Canada'.[138] For Justice Scott, '[...] it is perfectly clear that such an act could not apply to America. There were no existing circumstances at that time to render it necessary to erect such corporations in that part of the world [...] if then, its policy did not extend to America, so neither did its prohibitions'.[139]

Finally, the establishment of modern local corporate law in 1847[140] was an important step in building commerce in Lower Canada,[141] as it was in France,[142] England, and the United States.[143] In Quebec, until the 1840s,[144] incorporation as a means of economic development was virtually reserved for undertakings

137 Stuart's Report, 11 December 1818, High Court of Admiralty, Division of Quebec, 130 sq.

138 Demers, 'From the Bubble Act to the pre-incorporation trust', 344.

139 Stuart's Report, 132.

140 J.-M. Fecteau, 'Les petites républiques', 35.

141 J.-M. Fecteau, 'Du droit d'association au droit social: essai sur la crise du droit libéral et l'émergence d'une alternative pluraliste à la norme étatique, 1850–1930', *Revue canadienne de droit et de société* 12:2 (1997), 143–157; J.-M. Fecteau, 'État et associationnisme au XIXe siècle québécois: éléments pour une problématique des rapports État/société dans la transition au capitalisme', in A. Greer and I. Radforth (eds.), *Colonial Leviathan: State Formation in Nineteenth-Century Canada* (Toronto: University of Toronto Press, 1992), 134–162.

142 A. Lebebvre-Teillard, *La société anonyme au 19e siècle, du code de Commerce à la loi de 1867: histoire d'un instrument juridique du développement capitaliste* (Paris: P.U.F., 1985).

143 See E. M. Dodd, *American Business Corporations untii 1860* (Cambridge, Mass.:, Harvard University Press, 1954).

144 See Pierre-Jean Beauregard, 'Les modes de formation des corporations commerciales au Québec, d'hier à aujourd'hui', thesis (M.A, Law) (Université de Montréal, 1975).

considered to be of public interest,[145] such as channels, public markets, toll bridges, banks and insurance buildings. Corporate law is the hearth of modern capitalism, and it redefined the relationship between government and profit-making associations. Companies are customized modes of associating people and capital for economic activity and, at the end, for making profit.

As Fecteau has written, in the 1840s there was no link between the words 'company' and 'corporation'. A company was an association of merchants and industrialists gathered more or less contingently, most often through an association framed by a partnership. A corporation was primarily a political entity and a specific legal form[146] of decentralization of sovereign power in the feudal system. Blackstone defined it as a 'little republic':

> 'If land he granted for the purposes of religion or learning to twenty individuals not incorporated, there is no legal way of continuing the property to any other persons for the same purposes, but by endless conveyances from one to the other, as often as the hands are changed. But when they are consolidated and united into a corporation, they and their successors are then considered as one person in law: as one person, they have one will, which is collected from the sense of the majority of the individuals: this one will may establish rules and orders for the regulation of the whole, which are a sort of municipal laws of this Little republic'.[147]

When the Union Act was passed,[148] there was no provision for corporations in Canadian law.[149] Ironically, it was under the French civil law – the archaic and feudal law – that we find the legal framework closer to modern law: *la société*

145 AW. Currie, 'Corporation Law before 1840', *Canadian Chartered Accountant*, May 1940, 331–336; AW. Currie, 'The First Dominion Companies Act', *Canadian Journal of Economies and Political Science* 28 (1962), 387–404.

146 In English law, incorporations obtained by express authorization were distinguished either by royal charter or charter of Parliament, those existing under the common law (corporations sole) by prescription (presumed ancestral charter) or *de facto*; C.T. Carr, *The General Principle of the Law of Corporations* (Cambridge: Cambridge University Press, 1905), 114–124.

147 W. Blackstone, *Commentaries on the Laws of England*, vol. 1 (Childs ed., 1765; 1864), 467–468.

148 F.E. Labrie and E.E. Palmer, 'The Pre-Confederation History of Corporations in Canada', in S. Ziegel (dir.), *Études sur le droit canadien des compagnies* (Toronto: Butterworths, 1972), 33–60.

149 F.W. Wenegast, *The Law of Canadian Companies* (Toronto: Burroughs, 1931), 20–27.

en commandite.[150] This is a legal instrument that helped to limit the liability of investors. Canadian MP William Merritt unsuccessfully in 1845 offered a bill to extend the French partnership '*société en commandite*' to Canada generally, and again, in 1847 for a 'general partnership', still inspired by the French law.[151]

After the small commercial adaptations that occurred in the eighteenth century and the beginning of the nineteenth century, there was a substantial need to rebuild an efficient *lex mercatoria* in Canada. The 1841 union of the formerly separate colonies of Lower Canada and Upper Canada,[152] one of the key solutions of British reformers to the crisis of the Rebellions, was unable to improve commercial development. Most of the state apparatus of the two colonial halves, including the judicial, educational and municipal systems, remained essentially independent, and Quebec was the inheritor of old European institutions, such as the seigneurial regime. We have to wait until 1847 to see the real change in legal and political thinking translate into action with the abrogation of the seigneurial regime. The place of the French civil law was secured during these years, even though in a number of ways it had been affected, as in commercial law, by provincial and imperial English legislation.[153] At the end of the 1840s, Lower Canada was in an altogether exceptional position: the private law was essentially and traditionally French in origin, but the principal French commercial law (the *Ordonnance sur le commerce* originating in France, 1680), was declared invalid. On the other hand, its judicial organization was inspired along English lines, and in the 1840s portions of English substantive law were introduced in particular instances, such as commercial law. Quebec law was, as Lord Durham concluded, a 'patchwork of the results of the interference, at different times, of different legislative powers [...], the law itself is a mass of incoherent and conflicting laws, part French, part English, and with the line between each very confusedly drawn'.[154] He pleaded for the full establishment of English laws in Quebec.[155]

150 According to M. Fecteau, 'Les petites républiques', 41.

151 'Histoire du droit des compagnies' in James Smith and Yvon Renaud, *Manuel des notaires. Droit québécois des corporations commerciales,* vol. 1 (Montréal: Traité-formulaires, 1973), 3–29.

152 See R.C.B. Risk, '19th Century Foundations of the Business Corporations in Ontario', *University of Toronto Law Journal* 23 (1973), 270–306.

153 Brierley, 'Quebec's Civil Law Codification', 532.

154 G.M., Craig, *Lord Durham's Report* (Toronto: McClelland and Stewart, 1963), 69.

155 Craig, *Lord Durham's Report*, 146.

4 The 'Appropriation': The 'Lower Canada Commercial Law' in the Lower Canada Codification (1866)

The mid-nineteenth century saw a fundamental change in the nature of the commercial system in Lower Canada.[156] In Quebec there had been a 'blockage' of developments in the law and government[157] up to the 1830s,[158] 'caused by conflict between an elected Assembly, dominated by reform-minded Canadians, and an appointed colonial executive, dominated by British-descended Tories'.[159]

The preamble to the 1857 Act,[160] which started the codification work, served the purpose of explaining the evils that the enactment was intended to remedy and the objects it was to achieve. There were four principal factors: the diversity and inaccessibility of legal sources, the language of the laws, the absence of legislative or doctrinal synthesis, and the availability of foreign models.[161] If legislation by way of statute, whether provincial or imperial, had traditionally been available in French translation since 1791, the *Coutume de Paris* was only unofficially translated and published in English in the early 1840s, after the Cugnet summaries published in 1775.[162] After six years of work by its draftsmen, the civil Code of Lower Canada entered into force on 1 August 1866.[163] Its leading ideas were that codification was required to order and co-ordinate the existing law, and to render all of it accessible in both the English and French languages. The Commissioners, Day, Caron and Morin, were instructed to proceed in the following manner: '[... to] reduce into one Code, to be called the Civil Code of Lower Canada, those provisions of the Laws of Lower Canada which relate to Civil Matters and are of a general and permanent character, whether they relate to Commercial Cases or to those of any other nature [...] They may suggest such amendments as they think desirable, but shall state

156 I. McKay, 'Canada as a Long Liberal Revolution: On Writing the History of Actually Existing Canadian Liberalisms, 1840s-1940s', in J.F. Constant and M. Ducharme (eds.), *Liberalism and Hegemony: Debating the Canadian Liberal Revolution* (Toronto: University of Toronto Press, 2009), 347–452.

157 Greer and Radforth, *Colonial Leviathan.*

158 E. Mancke, 'Early Modern Imperial Governance and the Origins of Canadian Political Culture', *Canadian Journal of Political Science* 32:1 (1999), 3–20.

159 Donald Fyson, 'Between the *ancien régime* and liberal modernity', 415.

160 *Acte concernant la Codification des Lois du Bas Canada, qui se rapportent aux matières civiles et à la procédure*, 20 Vict., c. 43, (1857).

161 Brierley, 'Quebec's Civil Law Codification', 534.

162 Brierley, 'Quebec's Civil Law Codification', 539.

163 See B. Young, *The Politics of Codification: The Lower Canadian Civil Code of 1866* (Montréal: Osgoode Society for Canadian Legal History and Mc Gill-Queen's University Press, 1994).

such amendments separately and distinctly, with the reasons on which they are found'.[164]

The codification of civil law (1866)[165] and of civil procedure (1867) was made under the influence of a newly ascendant legal profession, and the role of the authors of the codification is important.[166] At the same time, only a few Lower Canadian decisions were used in drafting the Code. 'Only 95 decisions are cited in the Reports relating to the civil and commercial law of Lower Canada; Professor Morel estimates that 72 decisions are invoked with respect to only sixty-four articles in the Reports on the first three Books of the Code'.[167]

In the minds of some jurists and politicians such as McCord, the Code could offer a 'standard of assimilation'[168] to which the laws of the other future Canadian common law provinces might adhere. As John Brierley wrote, 'for some, at the time, the Quebec Code did constitute a means by which the first goal might be achieved, but this was no more than an aspiration; for others, subsequent in time, the Code has been seen as an expression, in the realm of private law, of a new kind of "national" political unity [...]'.[169]

In commercial matters, the authors were led by the need to modify the laws relating to commerce in the light of commercial ties with the USA.[170] They had to compile all provisions dealing with 'commercial matters', to form part of the new Code in either a distinct title or a book. Caron, Day and Morin had to

164 Section 6 and 7, *An Act to provide for the Codification of the Laws of Lower Canada relative to Civil matters and Procedure,* 20 Vict. S.C. 1857, c. 43.

165 See André Morel, 'La codification devant l'opinion publique de l'époque', in Jacques Boucher and André Morel (dir.), *Livre du Centenaire du Code civil* I (Montréal, P.U.M., 1970), 27; Martin Broodman, John E.C. Brierley and Roderick A. MacDonald, *Quebec Civil Law. An introduction to Quebec Private Law* (Toronto: Edmond Montgomery Publication, 1993), 5–74; Sylvio Normand, 'La codification de 1866: contexte et impact', in Patrick Glenn (dir.), *Droit québécois et droit français: communauté, autonomie, concordance* (Cowansville: Éditions Yvon Blais, 1993), 43–62; Sylvio Normand and Donald Fyson, 'Le droit romain comme source du Code civil du Bas-Canada', *La Revue du notariat* 103 (2001), 87–113.

166 Silvio Normand, 'La codification de 1866: contexte et impact', in H.P. Glenn (ed.), *Droit québécois et droit français: communauté, autonomie, concordance* (Montreal: Yvon Blais, 1993), 43–62.

167 A. Morel, 'Apparition de la succession testamentaire', *R. du B.* 26 (1966), 499 quoted by Brierley, 'Quebec's Civil Law Codification', 521, 555, note 87.

168 Brierley, 'Quebec's Civil Law Codification', 521, 533.

169 Brierley, 'Quebec's Civil Law Codification', 532.

170 See J.W. Hurst, *The Legitimacy of the Business Corporation in the Law of the U.S., 1780–1970* (Charlottesville: University Press of Virginia, 1970); R.K. Newmyer, 'Justice Joseph Story's Doctrine of "Public and Private Corporations", and the Rise of the American Business Corporation', *De Paul Law Review* 25 (1976), 825–841.

translate English evidentiary laws in commercial matters in the Lower Canada Code. For the commercial provisions they used more Lower-Canadian and English jurisprudence and laws than they did of French. Even if new French 'doctrine' was well known by Lower-Canadian jurists,[171] commercial matters seemed to them to be linked with Canada's English roots. Blackstone, Russell, and Wharton are quoted in some parts of the Civil Code, but they were a really minor influence on the bulk of the code (Blackstone is quoted around twenty times in the *Code civil du Bas Canada*). We find most of their influence in corporate and commercial matters. These matters are almost exclusively linked to British legal doctrine and jurisprudence. For sections 352–364, on corporations, most quote Blackstone, and no French writers. For loans and pensions, the commissioners established a fourth chapter, based on the law of nations and not on the Napoleonic Code, where there is no equivalent set of rules.[172]

In its structure, the CcBC differed from the French Code on economic issues. It contained titles devoted to emphyteusis, corporations, *substitutions fidéicommissaires* and registration of real property rights. There was one major difference between the overall arrangement of the Lower Canada Code and the French Code: the inclusion of a fourth book devoted to commercial law, instead of a distinct code of commercial law. As Brierley reports, it was decided in 1862 that matters relating particularly to commerce, in so far as they deviated from and 'were not already included within "*la loi commune civile*" and could not be covered by provisions common to both, would be placed at the end of the Code in a separate title or special book which, in form and content, would observe as much as possible the French Code'.[173] It is remarkable to note that almost no amendments were proposed for this fourth book (1); all of the 334 commercial provisions were considered old, not innovative law.

Nevertheless, there were some innovations: article 1889 of the Quebec Civil Code read as follows: 'Joint-stock companies are formed either under the authority of a royal charter, or of an act of the legislature, and are governed by its provisions; or they are formed without such authority, and, in the later case, are subject to the same general rules as partnerships under a collective name'. The Civil Code introduced a distinction between incorporated and

171 See Eric H. Reiter, 'Imported Books, Imported Ideas: Reading European Jurisprudence in Mid-Nineteenth-Century Quebec', *Law and History Review* 22 (2004), 445–492; and Michel Morin, 'Portalis c. Bentham? Les objectifs assignés à la codification du droit civil et du droit pénal en France, en Angleterre et au Canada', in *Commission du droit Canada, La législation en question* (Ottawa, 2000), 141–217.

172 *Sixième rapport des commissaires, Code civil du Bas-Canada*, cit., xi

173 Brierley, 'Quebec's Civil Law Codification', 521, 562.

unincorporated companies. As Demers notes,[174] in drafting article 1889, the Commissioners referred exclusively to English sources, where the distinction is a valid one; however, they indicated in their commentaries under this article that they doubted whether in fact any such companies had ever existed in Quebec. Most subsequent Quebec writers accepted this proposition and the consensus has been that in fact unincorporated joint-stock companies were not to be found in the Province.

Nonetheless, if commercial law reflected British legal influence, the 'provisions forms' in the Code, as F.P. Walton has remarked, were not exactly the English law. Caron, Day and Morin engaged in a comparative exercise between French and British laws.[175] For them, commercial law was neither English nor French, because although French and Dutch jurists developed most of these provisions in the seventeenth and eighteenth centuries, their rules were applied by judges (like Justice Mansfield) and merchants from all European countries.[176] As Maurice Tancelin indicates, '(...) the complexity of the sources of Quebec civil code does not accommodate the current simplification of placing the origin of civil law provisions in French law and those of commercial law provisions in English law'.[177] In each part, Canadian codified law is a 'mashup law', a new law.

In discharging its obligation of incorporating, without alteration, the laws of general and permanent character then in force, the Code Commission performed a work of legal mix where Lower Canadians could appropriate laws and at the same time forgot their legal roots. When they read provisions about commercial matters, they thought, as our students do now, that they were linked to civilian roots, because they were in the Civil Code. In fact, especially in these matters, the legal roots were mixed. There was a transplantation effected with the duet of 'adaptation and appropriation'. After the Lower-Canada Civil Code, some of the doctrinal authorities stigmatized the apparent lack of French norms in Quebec commercial law. Loranger wrote:

> Quoiqu'on ne puisse dire que le droit commercial anglais lui-même soit en force parmi nous, on ne peut cependant se cacher que, dans les cas omis par le droit français, dont l'Ordonnance de commerce n'a pas été

---

174 Demers, 'From the Bubble Act to the pre-incorporation trust', 347.

175 Also H. Patrick Glenn, 'Quebec: Mixed and Monism', in Esin Orucu, Elspeth Attwooll, and Sean Coyle (eds.), *Studies in Legal Systems: Mixed and Mixing* (The Hague: Kluwer Law International, 1996), 1–15.

176 Frédéric Parker Walton, *Le domaine et l'interprétation du Code civil du Bas-Canada* (introduction and trans.) Maurice Tancelin (Toronto: Butterworths, 1980), 8.

177 Walton, *Le domaine et l'interprétation du Code civil du Bas-Canada*, 8.

> enregistrée au Conseil Supérieur, et par notre législation statutaire, les usages commerciaux de l'Angleterre avec laquelle nous sommes si étroitement liés par le commerce, ne soient en vigueur devant nos tribunaux.[178]

In the 1990s, La Porta, Lopez-de-Silanes, Shleifer and Vishny, experts at the World Bank, started to analyse links and competition between civil law and common law traditions in the economic world.[179] Based on an unconventional combination of sociology of religion, legal history, political theory and econometrics, this group argued that Protestant common law countries were better governed and offered superior business environments than did civil law countries of French or German 'legal origin'. Is Quebec's history a good example of this thesis? Did common law traditions bring modernity and crush French civil tradition? It seems not.

Economic development for Quebec was a success under British supremacy, even if there were some set-backs in the war of economic expansion. The contest between opposing traders and settlers from the thirteen American colonies and British merchants operating from Canada in the fur trade was one of the last issues before lumber dispute which arose by the end of the 19th century. The United States would succeed in controlling northwest commerce under the Treaty of Ghent (1812). But the loss of control of the fur trade was largely offset in the Province by the development of the timber trade and the affirmation of Quebec City as a hub of international trade and as a naval base. The years 1760–1860 were marked by economic development accompanied by law. Indeed, laws rarely initiated colonial economic upheavals. Accounting for change in the commercial law of Quebec between 1760 and 1866 requires addressing a range of factors, both local and transnational, and necessarily bicultural. At the same time, we see, through the lens of legal choices and mixed traditions, many commercial turning points where legal frameworks were essential in defining the economy and trade of the Province: debt collection, corporate status, international trade, land ownership, commercial jurisdiction, bills of exchange, torts, etc. The constant cultural contact between two major world legal cultures, as a result of the imperial context of British immigration and of the continuing vitality of French-Canadian culture, generated a mixed system in private law, and colonial commercial law is a perfect example of a

178 T.J.J. Loranger, *Commentaire sur le Code civil du Bas-Canada* (Montréal: A.E. Brassard, 1873), IV.

179 See Michèle and Henrik Schmiegelow, *Institutional competition between common law and civil law: Theory and policy* (Berlin: Springer Berlin Heidelberg, 2014), intro.

'mashup legal culture'. Lower Canada's colonial history demonstrates the relevance of the assertion of Chief Justice Willes of the London Common Pleas: 'Courts of law have always in mercantile affairs endeavoured to adapt rules of law to the course and method of trade in order to promote trade and commerce instead of doing it hurt'.[180]

180 Stone v. Rawlinson (1745) Willes 559, 561, quoted by Swain, 'Lawyers, merchants and the law of contract in the long eighteenth century', 186.

English Mercantilist Thought and the Matter of Colonies from the 17th to the First Half of the 18th Century

Alain Clément

European colonization began in the early 16th century with the discovery of the Americas.[1] One of the primary reasons behind the voyages of discovery was the shortage of ready money during the 15th century, which hampered the expansion of European trade. The Americas and Africa came to be included in the world economic circuit primarily as sources of silver and gold, and of labour through the Atlantic slave trade.[2] A growing taste for foodstuffs such as sugar promoted the cultivation of new lands outside Europe.[3] And there was the quest to break the Venetian and Genoese monopoly in spices and silk from the East.[4] The colonial adventure was therefore, from the outset, an economic, commercial and financial undertaking although not without its political, religious and humanistic motives.[5] Expeditions from Portugal and Spain were followed by others from France, from 1524 onwards under François I, albeit very modestly,[6] from Holland in 1595 for largely financial motives, and finally from England in the early 17th century for both commercial[7] and religious motives, prompting both territorial and commercial forms of colonization. However, it is important not to overlook the point that all these motives for embarking on colonial ventures were underpinned also by the economic theory of the time with its own contingent of debates and controversies. I will study more precisely the British case.

1 Note from the editors: This is a first draft prepared by Alain Clément for the conference organized in Fiskars in 2016. His sudden death in 2017 prevented him to complete or adapt his final paper.
2 Bartolomé Benassar, 'L'explosion planétaire (1415–vers 1570)', in Pierre Léon (ed.), *Histoire économique et sociale du monde*, tome 1 (Paris, Armand Colin 1977), 416–426.
3 Jean Meyer, *Histoire du sucre* (Paris, Desjonquères 1989).
4 Jacques Brasseul, *Histoire des faits économiques* (Paris, Armand Colin 1997).
5 Marc Ferro, *Histoire des colonisations* (Paris, Le Seuil 1994) ; Andrew Fitzmaurice, *Humanism and America, an intellectual history of English colonisation, 1500–1625* (Cambridge University Press 2003).
6 Jean Meyer et alii, *Histoire de la France coloniale* (Paris, Armand Colin 1991).
7 Immanuel Wallerstein, *The modern world system*, t. 1–2 (New-York, Academic Press 1974–1980).

 | DOI:10.1163/9789004443075_008

This was the great age of mercantilism when the pecuniary concerns of the ruling classes and thinkers alike contrasted with Aristotelian disdain for profit. Private enrichment was desirable because it was also indirectly the enrichment of Prince and State. Mercantilist policy was about a *favorable* balance of trade.[8] In this intellectual context, the colonial venture was highly significant for mercantilists because it could bolster the power and wealth of the State. It was a source of political power (competition among nations was continued in colonial conquests), a source of monetary enrichment (all states coveted gold and silver from overseas), and a source of enrichment through the supply of commodities (pepper and other spices, cotton, silk, indigo, coffee, tobacco, sugar, etc.) needed for the home nation's manufacturing activities.

Although there was a general consensus in favour of colonization, deep divergences remained about how colonization and enrichment were interconnected. Essentially there were three attitudes towards colonization. Colonization for settlement (Section 1) involved the colonized land being developed economically so as to enrich the home nation through exclusive trade, with such colonies being held to be mere extensions of the nation: Robinson,[9] Pollexfen,[10] Child,[11] Barbon,[12] North,[13] Cary,[14] and Davenant,[15] Gee,[16] Defoe,[17] Berkeley.[18]

8 Andrea Finkelstein, *Harmony and the Balance: An Intellectual History of Seventeenth-Century English Economic Thought* (Ann Arbor, University of Michigan Press 2000).

9 Henry Robinson, *Certain Proposals* (London, 1652).

10 John Pollexfen, *England and East India inconsitent in their manufactures* (London, 1697).

11 Josiah Child, *A New Discourse of Trade* (London, J. Hodges 1668; new ed. 1690).

12 Nicholas Barbon, *A Discourse of Trade* (London 1690; Reprint by Jacob H. Hollander, Baltimore, John Hopkins University, 1905).

13 Dudley North, *Discourses upon Trades* (London 1691), in J.-R. McCulloch (ed.), *Early English Tracts on Commerce* (London, 1856; Reprint Cambridge University Press 1954), 505–540.

14 John Cary, *An essay on the state of England* (Bristol 1695); John Cary, *A Discourse concerning the East- India trade showing how it is unprofitable to the kingdom of England* (London, E. Baldwin 1695), in Lars Magnusson (ed.), *Mercantilism*, vol. 2 (London, Routledge 1995).

15 Charles Davenant, 'An essay on the East India trade' (London 1696), in *The Political and Commercial Works, Collected and Revised by Sir Charles Whitworth* (London, R. Horsfield 1771; Reprint Gregg Press, 1967), I, 85–123.

16 Joshua Gee, *The trade and navigation of Great-Britain considered* (London, Bettesworth & Hicht, 1729), in Lars Magnusson, *Mercantilism*, vol. 4, 18–137.

17 Daniel Defoe, *Giving alms, no charity, and Employing the Poor* (London 1704); Daniel Defoe, *A plan of the English commerce* (London, Rivington 1728; Reprint Oxford, Blackwell 1974).

18 George Berkeley, *An essay toward preventing the ruin of Great-Britain* (London, J. Roberts, 1721), Reprint in Alexander Campbell Fraser (ed.), *The works of George Berkeley*, vol. 4,

The second view (Section 2), which is broadly compatible with the first form of colonization, saw the colony as a trading-post, a way of becoming rich through one-sided trade on unfair terms with virtually no significant investment in the colony: Misselden,[19] Mun,[20] Davenant,[21] Child,[22] Pollexfen,[23] Martyn,[24] Carry,[25] Blanch,[26] Gee.[27]

On the third view (Section 3), the colonial adventure was a source of impoverishment rather than of enrichment: Petty[28] and Coke.[29] These analysis prefigure the pre-liberal critics of the middle of the eighteenth century. Indeed, from the 1740s and running through 1765, the questions of colonial trade and the colonies were addressed from increasingly 'liberal' points of view. A more critical approach to the economic ideas of that period came to light with the

Miscellaneous Works (1994); George Berkeley, *The Querist: Containing Several Queries, Proposed to the Consideration of the Public* (Dublin, Risk, Ewing & Smith, 1735).

19 Edward Misselden, *Free Trade or the Meanes to make trade florish wherein the causes of the decay of Trade in this Kingdom are discovered* (London 1622, Reprint New York, Augustus Mc Kelley 1971) ; Edward Misselden, *The Circle of Commerce or the Ballance of Trade* (London 1623, Reprint New York, Augustus Mc. Kelley 1971).

20 Thomas Mun, *A discourse of trade from England into the East* (London 1621, reprint New York, Augustus Mc Kelley, 1971) ; Thomas Mun, *England's treasure by forraign trade or the Ballance of our Forraign Trade is the Rule of our Treasure* (London 1664, reprint New York, Augustus Mc Kelley 1965).

21 Davenant, *Essay on the East India Trade.*

22 Josiah Child, *A treatise concerning the East-India trade* (London 1697), in Lars Magnusson (ed.), 1995.

23 John Pollexfen, *A discourse of trade, coyn, paper credit* (London 1696).

24 Henry Martyn, (Anonymous attributed to), *Considerations on the East-India Trade* (London 1701, Reprint McCulloch 1856), 541–630.

25 Cary, *A discourse concerning the East-India trade*; John Cary, *Some considerations relating to the carrying on the linnen manufactures in the Kingdom of Ireland* (London, 1st ed. 1699, 1704); John Cary, *A discourse on trade and other matters relative to it* (*London: Osborne* 1745, Reprint *British Economic Thought in the 17*th *and 18*th *centuries*, vol. 2, London, Routledge/Thoemmes Press, 1992).

26 John Blanch, *The interest of England considered: in an essay upon wooll, our woollen-manufactures, and the improvement of trade* (London, Walter Kettilby, 1694); John Blanch, *The naked truth in an essay upon trade* (London, 1696).

27 Gee, *The trade and navigation of Great-Britain considered*, 18–137.

28 William Petty, *Political Arithmetick* (London, R. Clavel and H. Mortlock 1690), *in* Charles Hull (ed.), *The Economic Writings*, (Cambridge University Press, Reprint New York, Augustus Mc Kelley 1963), vol. I, 232–313; *The political Anatomy of Ireland, in The Economic Writings*, vol. I, 121–230.

29 Roger Coke, *A Discourse of Trade* (London, H. Brome 1670, Reprint New York, Johnson Reprint Corporation 1970).

publication of work by Townsend,[30] Wallace[31] and, on the subject of the colonies, Decker,[32] pre-cursors to Smith and Tucker's liberal approach.[33]

1 Colonial Settlement in the Service of the Nation: Self-Sufficiency and Enrichment

The defense is justified by two arguments: a demographic argumentation (A) and an economic argumentation (B).

1.1 *Colonies and Demographic Loss: Risk of Impoverishment or Source of Enrichment?*

1.1.1 The Colonies: An Opportunity for the Poor and for the Nation!

The demographic argument was naturally raised first because colonial settlement entailed emigration. However, most mercantilists considered the population to be the primary source of wealth. Any loss of population might therefore be perceived as impoverishment. However, the argument could be readily countered: colonies were a way out for the poor who were a burden on the nation. The mercantilists claimed that significant numbers of poor, beggars and unemployed were evidence of demographic congestion which the colonies could absorb without impoverishing the home nation.

The widespread impression of overpopulation made the idea of migration to the colonies more acceptable. Not only would the burden of the poor be lifted, but the colonists would work elsewhere producing wealth from which the home nation would benefit. This was a view shared by Francis Bacon in his *Essays* published in 1625 and Malynes, another significant mercantilist of the time: 'for unlesse the three impostumes of the world, namely, wars, famine, and pestilence, do purge that great body; all kingdomes and countries become very populous, and men hardly can live in quiet, or without danger. Merchants

30 Charles Townshend, *National thoughts recommended to the serious attention of the public* (London, Dodsley, 1751).

31 Robert Wallace, *A dissertation on the numbers of Mankind in Ancient and modern times* (London, 1753, Reprint London, Routledge, 1998).

32 Matthew Decker, *An essay on the causes of the decline of the foreign trade* (Dublin, F. Faulkner, 1744), in Lars Magnusson, *Mercantilism*, vol. 4, 38–271.

33 This was the period when Josiah Tucker published *A brief essay on the advantages and disadvantages which respectively attend France and Great Britain with regard to trade* in 1750 and *Elements of commerce and theory of taxes* in 1752. However, his contributions to the issue of the colonies and the debate in which he participated pertained to a slightly later period, contemporary to Smith, Burke and Anderson (Clément 2014). For these reasons, his writings will not be covered in this article.

therefore seeking to discover new countries, are much to be commended and cherished'.[34]

The opinion was again voiced in the final decades of the 17th century when the lower cost argument still prevailed. As Child reported, Virginia and Barbados were populated by 'A sort of loose vagrant people, vicious and destitute of means to live at home, (being either unfit for labour, or such as could find none to employ themselves about) [...] and these, I say, were such, as had there been no English foreign plantation in the world, could probably never have lived at home to do service for their country'.[35] Child claimed that had the Puritans not settled in New England they would have been driven out of the country and taken refuge in Germany or Holland, which would have directly benefited from their labour. The colonies were therefore not only a lesser evil, but they maintained the home nation's influence over people who would otherwise have been lost to it: 'His Majesty had had no foreign plantations, to which they might have resorted, England however must have lost them'.[36] By populating lands under English domination they contributed indirectly to the enrichment of the nation. Lastly, Child evoked the case of a country which was sometimes unable to feed all its people, in which case 'If there be encouragement for a hundred persons in London, (that is, a way how a hundred may live better than in the country) the evacuating of a fourth or third part of that number, must soon be supplied out of the country'.[37]

Davenant justified one of the functions of colonial settlement in very similar terms. For him, new lands of colonial expansion were best used as an outlet for the home nation's undesirables, who were a burden and would not entail any loss of earnings if they emigrated, being 'such sort of people, as their crimes and debaucheries would quickly destroy at home, or whom their wants would confine in prisons or force to beg, and so render them useless, and consequently a burthern to the public'.[38] There were two advantages, then, in colonies; initially they drew off people 'whom their vice or necessities would destroy at home'[39] and they prevented those same emigrants, who could nevertheless contribute to wealth creation, from increasing the prosperity of foreign states and in particular of Holland, Denmark and Sweden. Migration to those states would have been a double blow to England. Thus, for Davenant and Child, the

34 Gerard de Malynes, *The Maintenance of Free Trade* (London 1622, Reprint New York, Augustus Mc Kelley 1971), 164.
35 Child, *A New Discourse of Trade*, 197.
36 Child, *A New Discourse of Trade*, 200.
37 Child, *A New Discourse of Trade*, 200.
38 Davenant, *Discourses on the public revenue and on the trade* II, 3.
39 Davenant, *Discourses on the public revenue and on the trade* II, 3.

colonies were 'A place of refuge for these, peradventure, mistaken and misled people, where their labour and industry is more useful to their mother kingdom'.[40]

Occupying land in the New World should therefore benefit both the poor themselves and the entire nation of England. In addition, occupying land would not be contradictory to the interests of the native peoples, since colonists of the time could rely on the Lockean principle of land ownership: land belonged to whoever worked it. Now, as Child emphasised, the English had just 'wild heathens'.[41] The virgin land could therefore be occupied much as European land must have been at the beginnings of human history. Under these circumstances, colonists were not perceived as conquerors, like the Spaniards. They became simple occupiers, who remained relatively dependent on the mother country.

1.1.2 Populating the Colonies: The Poor and the Slaves during the First Part of the 18th Century

In the first decades of the 18th century, the authors deal with the demographic question, from the angle of poverty but they add the matter of slavery because it has already been seen that the demographic boom in the American colonies and the sugar islands owed very little to British migration over the course of that century. Migratory flows from Africa were the primary contributors to that boom, and no economists raised their voices to denounce the slave trade-based economy. On the contrary, servile manpower was not only considered useful but, moreover, was recognized as being relatively inexpensive: 'The supplying our plantations with negroes is of that extraordinary advantage to us'.[42] Gee even added that 'our profit is either more or less according to the numbers there employed'. This was due not only to the free cost of labor but, above all, to low purchase prices, such that '[w]ork may be done by the labour of slaves, almost as cheap as it is in India'.[43] This point of view was not unique. It was shared by Defoe, who clearly showed how the African slave trade represented 'an infinite advantage, considering that these negroes do not cost in the country above 30 to 50 shillings per head'.[44] In this way, the interest of the settlement colonies comes fully to bear, given that a servile labor force can produce goods that would not have been possible without the slave trade, as growing

40 Davenant, *Discourses on the public revenue and on the trade* II, 5.
41 Quoted by Pagden, *The Oxford history of the British empire*, 41.
42 Gee, *The trade and navigation of Great-Britain considered*, 18–137.
43 Gee, *The trade and navigation of Great-Britain considered*, 83.
44 Defoe, *A plan of the English commerce*, 183.

cotton, coffee, sugar and tobacco all require significant manpower. But although Defoe admitted the economic necessity to resort to servile labor, he lamented it on moral grounds,[45] particularly in his *Reformation of Manners*, and, in that sense, was one of the forerunners of the anti-slavery struggle.[46] However, the economic arguments prevailed, because the vast majority of writers did not mention that moral dimension of slavery, preferring instead to stress the exclusively merchant dimension. In fact, one of the themes linked to the black slave trade was the reorganization of African trade and the place of the Royal African Company. The Board of Trade discussed this question from 1707 to 1710,[47] following the criticism expressed by the Royal African Company. The latter cited the cost of slaves due to increased competition with independent slave traders. For its part, the Board of Trade noted that it was no longer crucial to have a regulated company, thus going against the theories maintained by Defoe, who was, for a time an agent of that Royal African Company whose interests he defended.

This use of servile labor does not however exclude possible recourse to the country's poor. For Berkeley, it was the State's responsibility to ensure employment for all,[48] without, however, directly employing them, although he did not rule out the option of public work programs to help them.[49] In his text, *The Querist* (1735), in which he outlines his program to encourage high employment levels in the face of chronic unemployment and to improve the people's standard of living, Berkeley mentioned several main lines[50] but no colonial

45 'The work of the islands, which is the planting canes and making sugar, whether in the field or in the sugar- works, is of that nature, the labor is so severe, the climate so hot, the food so coarse, that no Europeans were ever yet found could go through it-at least not to the profit of the planter. They must have people used to extremities of the wealther, entirely subjected to the government and correction of the cruelest masters, that they may be whipped forward like horses, that can live on what it next to the offal of food, like beasts, and never knew better; that have the strength of the ox and know no more of liberty; and that suffer everything the horse suffers, but being flayed when they are dead, which would be done too, if they could get 6d. For the hide – These they get their wealth from – and these, I doubt, they have much to answer about, as to cruelties and barbarities; which it is not my present work to inquire into' (Defoe, cited in Moore 1970, 290).

46 John Moore, *Daniel Defoe, Citizen of the Modern World* (Chicago and London, University of Chicago Press, 1970), 289–290.

47 Ian Steele, *Politics of Colonial Policy: The Role of the Board of Trade in Colonial Administration, 1696 – 1720* (Oxford University Press, 1968), 124–127.

48 Frank Petrella, 'George Berkeley's theory of economic policy and classical economic liberalism', *Southern Economic Journal*, 23–3 (1966), 275–284 (277).

49 T.W. Hutchison, 'Berkeley's Querist and its place in the economic thought of the Eighteenth century', *British Journal for the Philosophy of Science*, 4–13 (1953), 52–77.

50 Hutchison, *Berkeley's Querist.*

solution. And yet, the colonies were still a solution for poverty reduction – a solution that was defended, in particular, by Gee and Defoe. Gee assessed the agricultural colonies as an economic and social solution to the poverty endemic to Great Britain: 'I have had in view the raising and producing great plenty of materials in our plantations for setting the poor to work, the several employments arising from hemp, flax, silk, etc. will afford such variety, that there will be enough, not only for the robust and strong, but for the weakly, and even for children; and doubtless a good example and perseverance in the rules of industry will change the very inclinations of those idle vagrant persons, who now run about the kingdom and spend their time and what money they can any way come at, upon their debauches'.[51] However, over the course of that same century, Defoe found that, in England, there were more jobs than available workers, so he had difficulty understanding how the English people could still be doing charity for the poor. He remained convinced that charity paid more for some than the wages they would earn by working! 'When I have wanted a man for labouring work, and offer 9 shilling per week to strouling fellows at my door, they have frequently told me to my face, they could get more a begging', Defoe[52] was wont to say. Listing the various possible causes of the people's poverty, Defoe believed that he had uncovered it in their hereditary laziness. He wrote that there was 'nothing more frequent, than for an Englishman to work till he has got his pocket full of money, and then go and be idle, or perhaps drunk'.[53] He also believed in the virtues of a stay in the colonies because, as Gee similarly observed: 'When they are transported into the colonies, we are assured come to severe repentance for their past lives, and become very industrious'.[54] The author thought that the fact of becoming a landowner would encourage them to work: 'The prospect of having land of their own would induce them to continue their industry [...] They would marry young, increase and multiply, and supply themselves with every thing they want from us, but their food' [ibid.]. Aside from the economic interest of no longer having to support the poor in the parishes – which was becoming a real burden to the community, Defoe emphasized the 'curative' and enriching dimension of a stay in the colonies for all those poor people: 'Here you dispose of your encreasing numbers of poor; they go there poor, and come back rich; there they plant, trade, thrive, and encrease; even your transported felons, sent to Virginia instead of Tyburn; thousands of them, if we are not misinformed, have, by turning their

51 Gee, *The trade and navigation of Great-Britain considered*, 49–50.

52 Defoe, *Giving alms, no charity, and Employing the Poor*, 12.

53 Defoe, *Giving alms, no charity, and Employing the Poor*, 27.

54 Gee, *The trade and navigation of Great-Britain considered*, 66.

hands to industry and improvement, and which is best of all, to honesty, become rich substantial planters and merchants, settled large families, an been famous in the country; nay, we have seen many of them made magistrates, officers of militia, captains of the good ships, and master of good estates'.[55] In particular, he highlighted the interest – not compelled or forced, rather quite often voluntary – exhibited by poor Scotsman in the colonial experience, which was not the case among departures from England, he noted.[56] The emigration of the poor as a solution to idleness did not, however, rule out the fear of losing manpower whose absence might, according to Gee,[57] prove harmful to the home country's economy, a view that authors like Paterson did not appear to share.

1.2 *Enrichment by Supplying Staple Goods towards Self-Sufficiency?: The Economic Arguments*

The motives behind colonial settlement were essentially utilitarian for the English mercantilists. It was a way of removing undesirables from the country. Colonies meant England could run a balance of trade surplus with the new markets opening up, and they stimulated output and employment in the home nation. However, the colonies themselves had to remain under the sway of the home nation exclusively.

1.2.1 The Colonies Break the Link of Economic Dependance toward European Countries

The English mercantilists considered the colonies an important source of raw materials. In particular, salt for the conservation of fish, potash and dyes for the textile industry, and shipbuilding materials (pitch, timber, flax, hemp, rope, etc.) were products of great strategic importance, and dependence for them on other European nations was neither politically nor economically desirable. They entertained great optimism that all these products could be obtained at less expense from their colonies: 'that will all possible conveniency wee enlarge our forraigne plantations, and get farther footing in Barbarie, East and West Indies… Not only that wee may be better provide our selves of Canvas for Sailes, Masts, Timber, with all other things necessary for shipping within our own dominions, but also in that a little spot of ground, as England is, with its

55 Defoe, *A plan of the English commerce*, 273–274.

56 Huw V. Bowen, *Elites, Enterprise and the Making of the British Overseas Empire, 1688–1775* (Basingstoke, Macmillan Press 1996), 161.

57 Edgar Johnson, *Predecessors of Adam Smith: The Growth of British Economic Thought* (New York, 1937, Reprint 1965), 246.

dominions if it does not enlarge them, in future generations, and feare me will be found inconsiderable in respect of Spain, Portugal, the United Provinces, or any other European Nation, which shall have arrived to, and be armed with five or ten times a greater strength, power, and riches, either from their Asian, African, or American Dominions'.[58] By restricting imports from Europe, especially the Netherlands and France, England hoped to make huge savings on these imported goods. It also hoped to grow rich by manufacturing goods with raw materials from the colonies and selling them on the European market.

1.2.2 Colonies Have an Economic Advantage in Terms of Production, of Employment and of Outlet

The colonies were also an outlet for English industry and a spur to national employment: 'Every person sent abroad with the negroes and ustensils, he is constrained to employ, or that are employed with him, it being customary in most of our islands in America, upon every plantation, to employ eight or ten blacks for one white servant; I Say in this case we may reckon, that for provisions, clothes, and household goods, seamen, and all others employed about materials for building, fitting, and victualling of ships, every Englishman in Barbadoes, or Jamaica creates employment for four men at home'.[59] Pollexfen supported this view: 'Our trade to our plantations or West-India Colonies takes off great quantities of our products and manufactures, as well as provisions and handicraft wares'.[60]

Ultimately these authors wished to see the colonies develop economically as outlets: without activity there would be no market and with no market, no trade for the benefit of the mother country. Spain was certainly not the model to imitate as its colonists simply worked the gold and silver mines, which 'causes them to neglect in great measure cultivating of the earth, and producing commodities from the growth of it, which might give employment to a greater navy, as well as sustenance to a far greater number of people by sea and land'.[61] These economists came to realise that the economic development of the new lands would enrich England more than simple plunder ever could.

58 Robinson (1652), quoted by Knorr, *British colonial theories, 1570–1850*, 54.

59 Child, *A New Discourse of Trade*, 205.

60 Pollexfen, *England and East India inconsistent in their manufactures*, 86.

61 Child, *A New Discourse of Trade*, 241.

1.2.3 Colonies and the Target of Balance of Trade Surplus

The objective was to run a balance of trade surplus. This implied severe restraints on imports of luxury goods.[62] It was thought that the royal coffers could best be filled by reducing domestic consumption and developing exports of finished products. However, the first inklings of the impact of demand on economic dynamics were apparent: 'It is from fashion in cloths, and living in cities, that the king of France's revenues is so great'.[63] England was increasingly perceived as a large market to be supplied by satisfying domestic demand driven by desire, emulation, prodigality and the love of luxury: 'The main spur to trade, or rather to industry and ingenuity, is the exorbitant appetites of men, which they will take pains to gratify, and so be disposed to work'.[64] Luxury was no longer shunned or condemned because it was a goad to all industry.[65] For some mercantilists importing foreign goods could be justified 'because they dazzled people with their novelty and promoted industry by way of the acquisitive instinct'.[66] This was the position of Barbon,[67] of Cary[68] and of Thomas for whom foreign luxury goods were not the root of evil but 'true spurs to virtue, valour and the elevation of the mind, as well as the just rewards of industry'.[69] However, most of the colonies could also provide some of these luxury goods without adversely affecting the balance of trade. Indeed, Davenant argued 'This excess become less dangerous, when we can purchase them with the product of distant countries under our dominion'.[70]

1.2.4 The Conditions to Maintain the Advantages Got from the Colonies

The colonies could make a huge economic contribution to the metropolis provided that they remained in a state of dependence, that their output did not come into competition with domestic output. Child and Davenant did not fear competition from these lands for the home nation because manufacturing activities are 'the last work of a people settled 3 or 400 years, growing numerous,

62 Cosimo Perrotta, 'Is the mercantilist theory of the favourable balance of trade really erroneous ?', *History of political Economy*, vol. 23–2 (1991), 2, 301–335.

63 Barbon, *A Discourse of Trade*, 34.

64 North, *Discourses upon Trades*, 528.

65 Letwin, *The origin of scientific economics, the English economic thought 1660–1776*; J.O. Appleby, *Economic thought and ideology in the seventeenth century England*, (Princeton University Press 1978).

66 Appleby, *Economic thought and ideology in the seventeenth century England*, 171.

67 Barbon, *A Discourse of Trade*, 35–36.

68 Cary, *An essay on the state of England.*

69 Dalby Thomas, *An historical account of the West-India colonies* (1690), quoted by Appleby, *Economic thought and ideology in the seventeenth century* England, 171.

70 Davenant, *Discourses on the public revenue and on the trade* II, 12.

and wanting territory'[71] and 'All our American plantations, except that of New-England, produce Commodities of different natures from those of this kingdom, as sugar, tobacco, cocoa, wool, ginger, different sorts of dying'.[72] Even if the risk of competition appeared remote, it remained important to prevent the colony from developing to the extent that it could achieve its independence.

This idea of colonial dependence was initially developed by Child in *A New Discourse of Trade.* Colonial policy was 'to keep their external provinces and colonies in a subjection unto and dependency upon their mother-kingdom'.[73] Davenant went even further, arguing 'Colonies should not only be kept economically as much dependent as possible upon their mother country'[74] but they should not even be taught the art of war for fear it might contribute indirectly to their emancipation from the mother country: 'if we should go to cultivate among them the art of navigation, and teach them to have a naval force, they may set up for themselves and make the greatest part of our West-India trade precarious'.[75]

Such imposed dependence required a lawful basis, which was given in the maintenance of the Navigation Acts. The *Staple Act* of 1663 reserved trade with the colonies to the metropolis alone by forcing the colonies not to buy or sell goods other than with England. This state of dependence entailed a degree of reciprocity in that colonial products were generally granted a monopoly on the national market. Heckscher explains how tobacco production was prohibited in England so as to protect the interest of the colonies.[76] Child sought to limit the taxation of trade with other countries but nevertheless supported the legislation as the only way to profit from trade with the country's own colonies: 'If they (colonies) were not kept to the rules of the act of navigation, the consequence would be, that in a few years the benefit of them would be wholly lost to the nation'.[77] The liberalism of these defenders of the colonies had its limits! This liberalism was also seriously affected when the leaders of the East India Company, in particular Mun, Child and Davenant, examined colonial trading concessions.

71 Davenant, *Discourses on the public revenue and on the trade* II, 22.
72 Child, *A New Discourse of Trade*, 230.
73 Child, *A New Discourse of Trade*, 125.
74 Davenant, *Discourses on the public revenue and on the trade* II, 8–10.
75 Davenant, *Discourses on the public revenue and on the trade* II, 9.
76 Heckscher, *Mercantilism* II, 41.
77 Child, *A New Discourse of Trade*, 124–125.

1.3 *The Persistence of the same Economic Discourse during the First Part of the 18th Century*

1.3.1 Continuously Expanding Natural Riches: The El Dorado of the Colonies

The settlement colonies in America and the sugar islands entered a growing production phase in the early 18th century. Writers from that period assessed colonial wealth as and when the concrete effects of the first facilities began to be felt. For example, Gee saw Carolina as an El Dorado where '[t]he soil is generally fertile: The rice it produces is said to be the best in the world; and no country affords better silk than has been brought from thence [...] The olive tree grows wild [...] The indigo plant grows wild [...] The country has plenty of iron mines'.[78] The same evaluation was made of Pennsylvania and New England. The land there was abundant, unlimited and, like a number of other regions, located on the same latitude as Europe. Gee emphasized the opportunity that could even be created by growing certain European plants – like flax and hemp – in the colonies, and under far better conditions: 'Our land is too dear for raising hemp and flax, and what is grown here neither dresses so kindly, nor whitens so well as that which grows in warmer climates [...] Nothing empoverishes land more than hemp and flax for the land ought to be changed after three or four crops[79]'. In his optimism, he challenged the supply of silk from India, likewise considering that space and wilderness might (with no special effort) produced that sought-after good: 'If care was taken to cultivate and improve the raising of silk in our plantations Carolina, Virginia, Maryland, and Pennsylvania, would produce the best of silk [...] These countries produce vast numbers of white and other mulberry-trees, which grow wild, and spring up almost every where in great abundance, which looks as if nature had called us thither to propagate that manufacture'.[80] This point of view was also shared by Lindsay, who believed that the American colonies could supply England with flax, hemp and silk 'at easier rates than they can be imported from foreign parts'.[81]

Finally, to Defoe, the colonies made it possible to achieve that autarchy for basic products that was so dear to mercantilists: 'They [the colonies] are able to furnish a sufficient quantity of hemp, flax, tar, turpentine, fir, timber, deal boards, masts, yards, pipes, and hogshead-staves, to supply the whole demand

78 Gee, *The trade and navigation of Great-Britain considered*, 39.

79 *Ibidem*, 83.

80 *Ibidem*, 90.

81 Patrick Lindsay, *The interests of Scotland considered, with regard to its police in employing of the poor, its agriculture, its trade, its manufactures and fisheries* (Edinburgh, Fleming & Company, 1733), 135.

of Great-Britain and Ireland, so as that we should suffer no scarcity, or want of those goods, tho'we should absolutely prohibit their importation from any other place'.[82]

Those raw materials would give industry in the home country products for processing because, as noted by Gee, factories in Northern England and in Ireland only operated for part of the year, for want of sufficient quantities of flax and hemp. For that author, the colonists should really be encouraged to produce all the raw materials required by the motherland, and so it fell 'to the government, to endeavour by all possible means to encourage them in the raising of silk, hemp, flax, iron, pot-ash,[83] etc… by giving them competent bounties in the beginning, and sending over judicious and skillful Persons at the public charge, to assist and instruct them in the most proper methods of management'.[84] This supply of raw materials – to be encouraged by the State – could then generate more work for the factories and so reduce the number of unemployed people in the kingdom: 'It is a common opinion, that we have above a million of people in the three nations destitute of work; but if those rough materials should come to be raised in our plantations, there need not be one idle person'.[85]

1.3.2 A Large Market across the Atlantic at the Service of the Homeland

The colonies' natural riches, and the fact of putting the poor and the slaves under the colonists' management, jointly contributed to enriching the colonies and, indirectly, to enriching the home country, under certain conditions. One of the main conditions (see below) was for the colonists to personally lead sober lives, following the example of the citizens back home (who should also conform to such a way of life). Next, both the nature and the share of the riches to be sent back to the homeland were discussed, along with the conditions to be fulfilled in order to channel them.

Defoe showed that demographic growth in the American colonies was not detrimental to the homeland, while being further aware that said growth was becoming less and less linked to emigration from England. To him, this demographic growth fostered demand for manufactured goods, which stimulated trade, navigation, the employment of large numbers of sailors, factory jobs and, in the end, British power and prosperity. When all was said and done, the

82 Defoe, *A plan of the English commerce*, 263.

83 We know, however, that flax and hemp were not successful crops outside of Europe, including in America, although the resulting textiles were amply used in linens and bedding, as well as in ropes and sails (Braudel 1979, I, 285).

84 Gee, *The trade and navigation of Great-Britain considered*, 79.

85 *Ibidem*, 86.

colonies' economic development was necessary to the motherland's prosperity, on condition, of course, that the new wealth was channeled toward England. This was Keith's observation in 1740: 'The colonies take off and consume one sixth part of the woolen manufactures exported from Britain, which is the chief staple of England [...] they take off and consume more than double that value in linen and callicoes, which is either the product of Britain and Ireland, or partly the profitable returns made for that product carried to foreign countries. The luxury of the colonies which increases daily, consumes great quantities of English manufactured silk, haberdashery, household furniture, and trinkets of all sorts'.[86] This colonial market was one way of guaranteeing outlets for British products that had come to seem less sure, given that other clients were foreign and European countries, in particular. In fact, it was a captive market with no competition from other countries.

Nevertheless, in encouraging the production of those raw materials, there might be grounds for concern that the colonies could, in the long term, become competitors by processing those products into finished goods. Gee, who, it should be mentioned, had commercial interests and holdings in iron mines in Maryland and Virginia, did not believe in that harmful competition, so long as colonial activities were regulated and very seriously controlled.[87] For example, in his opinion, no wool manufacturers should be allowed to set up shop without first registering with the governor of each province.[88] The colonies economic activities in general should be encouraged, while still ensuring that wealth is not diverted to the colonies alone, whence his position in favor of the Navigation Acts. This conception was supported by other mercantilist writers, most of them merchants who supported protective and coercive measures with regard to the Empire's colonies: Blanch,[89] Brewster[90] and Cary[91] representing

86 Keith (1740), cited in Klauss Knorr, *British Colonial Theories, 1570–1850*, 95.

87 As a reminder, tobacco, cotton, indigo, ginger, dyewood, rice, molasses, hemp, caulking products, furs and copper could only be shipped to ports in the home country. The colonies could not buy directly from other countries. The Act of 1699 prohibited the sale of woolens from one colony to another, as well as their exportation to European markets. The Act of 1732 stipulated that beaver skins be sent to and worked in the home country. The Act of 1750 stated that iron and cast iron could not be processed in America (cf. Kaspi 1986).

88 Gee, *The trade and navigation of Great-Britain considered*, 80.

89 John Blanch, *The naked truth in an essay upon trade* (London 1696).

90 Francis Brewster, *Essays on trade and navigation* (London, ThoCockerill 1695); Francis Brewster, *New essays on trade*, (London, H. Walwyn 1702).

91 Cary, *A discourse concerning the East-India trade*; John Cary, *Some considerations relating to the carrying on the linnen manufactures in the Kingdom of Ireland* (London 1704).

interests in Ireland, and Seton[92] speaking for Scottish interests. While most of those analysts saw the colonies' economic development as more a source of wealth than injury to the home country, they were becoming more and more unfavorable toward the existence of companies with monopolies in Atlantic trade. This was the case, for example, of Gervaise,[93] one of the fierce champions of greater freedom in international trade. These analysts were also, for reasons of economic interests, supporters of regulated, protected global trade, including if that was to the detriment of the colonies.

2 Colonies as Trading Concessions in Question

In the East, the trading post was the basic structure of trade and nothing like a first step towards traditional settlement. It was, for Braudel, a purely commercial form of colonization with limited occupation of land,[94] with few exceptions. This form of colonization found supporters among mercantilists in England as a means of breaking the Venetian and Genoese monopoly of oriental spices and silk. Among its other advantages were that it opened the road to monetary enrichment without the need for significant material and human investment.

Unlike settlement, trading-based colonization did not contribute to the enrichment of the nation on the basis of territorial output but on the basis of immaterial investments: capacity to control trading networks, to control the seaways, to negotiate with the authorities of the countries in which trading concessions could be set up, to establish the right trading posts in the right places, etc. The Dutch provided the prime example. A number of authors showed that Holland became the world's richest nation through the re-export trade alone by virtue of the *Verenigde Oost-Indische Compagnie.*[95] The English adventurer Walter Raleigh commented in 1596 that the nation 'which holds the sea, holds the trade of the world, which holds the trade of the world, holds the richness of the world, which holds the richness of the world, holds the world

92 William Seton, *Some thoughts on ways and means for making this nation a gainer in foreign commerce*, (Edinburgh, James Watson 1705).

93 Isaac Gervaise, *The system or theory of the trade of the world* (London, Woodfall & Sold 1720), Reprint in Lars Magnusson, *Mercantilism*, vol. 4 (1995), 1–17.

94 Fernand Braudel, *Civilisation matérielle, économie et capitalisme* (Paris, Armand Colin 1979), III, 426–429.

95 See on this point Michel Morineau, *Les grandes compagnies des Indes Orientales* (Paris, P.U.F. 1994).

itself'.[96] This grand design whereby self-sufficiency would no longer be the essence of national power became widespread by the mid 17th century. Wealth became more immaterial. What became increasingly significant, as Fourquet[97] underlined in more modern terms, was the control of world networks of economic information: 'it (Amsterdam or London) knows where and what to buy, to whom to sell, it knows the supply markets and the outlet markets'.

This new form of colonial expansion was conducted under the authority and the responsibility of large private companies to which a monopoly was granted. The example was set by England, which created the *East India Company* by a decision of Queen Elisabeth in 1600. The United Provinces followed suit in 1602 with the VOC. In France, after several attempts, Colbert founded the Eastern Company of France mainly out of public monies.

This alternative form of colonial expansion, however, was not without its detractors. From the outset of the 17th century, the question of the drain on monetary resources was raised. Then, in the second half of the 17th century and in the first half of the 18th century, this form of trade came under fire from protectionists on the one side and liberals on the other. Finally, These debates were valuable in that they contributed to the emergence of a new concept (balance of trade) and of a new theory of international trade which was closer to the liberal analysis of the 18th century than the traditional mercantilist outlook.

2.1 *In the 17th Century, the Main Issue Remained the 'Monetary Drain'*

In England, trade with Asia grew over the course of the century. Unlike in France, economic rather than political motives underlay these new trading activities. England was hard hit by the international economic crisis of 1590–1640. This provided an incentive to find outlets other than on the traditional markets. Another form of trade was developed in response to the crisis: re-export trade. Interest in this form of trade also arose because demand for luxury goods imported from overseas was asserting itself among the aristocracy. New trade with the Indies (indigo, pepper,[98] cloves, etc.), the Levant (silk, cotton, etc.)

96 Quoted by Roland Marx, *Histoire de la Grande-Bretagne* (Paris, Armand Colin 1980), 91.

97 As Cole remarked of Colbert's colonial policy, over nearly 20 years, more certain knowledge of the road to the Indies, the newly acquired ability of merchants to do business in this region, and knowledge of manners and habits 'were all assets which could not figure on the balance sheet, but which formed a significant contribution from the company of Colbert to its successors', cf. C.W. Cole, *Colbert and a century of French mercantilism* (New York, 1939) 523. See also Fourquet, *Richesse et puissance*, 175.

98 Pepper remained the most significant import from Asia both in volume and in value from 1600–1640. Around 1623 a million and a half pounds of pepper were imported annually

and America (particularly tobacco) rose by 60 per cent between 1600 and 1640, as evidence of the refinement of consumer habits[99] and of taste for new textiles from the East Indies[100] from the mid 17th century. This new form of trade which was not clearly distinct from colonial expansion was conducted by private companies. The largest trading companies were based on the Dutch model, the most famous one being the East India Company. All were in the hands of merchants, the rising class in the 17th century.

The East India Company played a very decisive part in colonial expansion and the formation of the British Empire. The charter from Elizabeth in 1600 granted the new company a privilege of shipping with the Orient. It was initially made up of 218 members each of whom could withdraw its investment at the end of each expedition (it only became a joint stock company in 1657). The company came in for serious criticism from the outset, the most important charge being its responsibility for the 1620 crisis. The most severe criticism related to the export of gold and silver by the East India Company for the East Indies and the competition it imposed on domestic manufactured goods. This questioning and criticism fueled the first major controversy about the interest of overseas trade and the limits of bullionism. The company, which was accused of exporting specie[101] and providing no outlets for domestic production (English woolen cloth was not widely used in the tropics), imported spices, medicines, pepper, saltpeter, nutmeg, cloves and indigo for dyestuffs, cotton thread, silk and calico and then later tea and coffee. It was not the imports themselves that were contested but that they were a monopoly which could practice excessive sale prices on the English market.

with a peak at three million in 1626; see Kirti N. Chaudhuri, *The English East India Company. The study of early joint-stock Company, 1600–1640* (London 1965), 146.

99 Michel Morineau, in Pierre Léon (ed.), *Histoire économique et sociale du monde*, vol. 2, Les hésitations de la croissance, 1580–1730, tome 3, Inerties et révolutions, 1730–1840 (Paris, Armand Colin 1979), p. 190.

100 Calico appeared as a regular import in the years after 1610: 5000 pieces were imported in 1613, 26000 pieces in 1619, 123000 pieces in 1621, and 221500 in 1625; see Chaudhuri, *The English East India Company*, 193.

101 It is true that the East India Company's main export over this period was precious metal: in 1624, in 23 years, the company had exported £753, 336 in bullion and £351, 236 in manufactured goods (wool, leather, etc.). This was because of lack of demand for European products in Asia and it was an established fact despite the considerable efforts the company made. More specifically, it was the high price of metal in Asia that made it possible to buy cheaply but made English products much more expensive for potential consumers, Chaudhuri, *The English East India Company*, 120–122.

2.1.1 The Malynes-Misselden Polemic on the Role of the East Indies Trade in the Economic Crisis of 1620

Trade conducted by the East India Company in the early 17th century was the subject of a fierce polemic between two leading proponents of English mercantilism, Malynes and Misselden. For Malynes, the monetary species sent to the East Indies accounted for the lack of species in the country. Misselden[102] did not dispute this point: the money employed in this trade was the counterpart for imports of products such as indigo, calicoes, spices, and so was the source of monetary outflow. However, this trade made it possible to supplant the Persian merchants, it fueled a re-export trade throughout the rest of the world, it promoted the employment of great numbers of seamen in the use of English ships and of craftsmen in their construction. It was an excellent means of progressing in the art of navigation and in the employment of the poor.[103] Economic profit in terms of production and employment, and monetary profit seemed to him to far outweigh the disadvantages that this trade might entail. And so it had to be encouraged.

2.1.2 Thomas Mun: The Defence of Mercantilism through the Defence of the East India Company and the Concept of Balance of Trade

Mun, as a director of the East India Company, naturally sided with Misselden against Malynes and persuasively and accurately set out the arguments whereby trade with the East was an activity that enriched the kingdom despite the outgoings of gold and silver. In his 1621 and 1664 pamphlets[104] not only did he take the defence of his much criticized company but he developed an interesting conception of trade and finance, starting from the balance of trade. He began by challenging the claim that the export of cash was harmful to the economy. Prohibiting this would preclude any opportunity to engage in trade and so enrich the nation: 'if our commodities be over ballanced in value by forraign wares, our mony must be carried out'.[105] Like other economists of the time he considered that foreign trade alone brought wealth, provided, of course, that there was a trade surplus. This surplus money, Mun argued, had to be re-used in the international monetary circuit if it was to be a source of

102 Edward Misselden, *The Circle of Commerce or the Ballance of Trade* (London 1623, Reprint New York, Augustus Mc. Kelley 1971).

103 Misselden, *The Circle of Commerce or the Ballance of Trade*, 34–36.

104 The pamphlet published in 1664, i.e. 23 years after his death, was written before 1628.

105 Mun, *England's treasure by forraign trade*, 34.

continuous enrichment[106] 'and so by a continual and orderly change of one into the other grow rich'[107] i.e. in trading activity.

Mun acknowledged initially that there was a trade deficit with the Indies in absolute terms, since it appeared difficult to sell European goods on Eastern markets while at the same time Europeans, and the English in particular, sought to consume ever more products from the East. There was therefore a net outflow of money. But Mun showed that the accounts should reflect not only incomings and outgoings of money in trade between the two (England and the East Indies) but among all the countries with which England traded. It was the full balance of foreign trade which measured the degree of success and the enrichment or impoverishment of a nation, and not the partial balance between two countries alone.

Then, he showed that imports from the East Indies were the source of a lucrative re-export trade for England. This trade, he argued, came to supplant overland trade which was regulated by the Turks, who acted as intermediaries between Europe and the East. The sea route brought considerable savings 'So that by the substance, and summes of these accompts, it doth plainely appeare, that the buying of the said quantitie of raw-silkes, indico, and spices, may be performed in the Indies, so near one third part of the ready moneyes, which were accustomed to be sent into Turkey to provide the same; so that there will bee saved every year the value of £953,543 of ready money'[108] These purchases were to underlie a new trade between England and Europe. Re-export of goods bought in the East Indies and destined mostly for the continent was what enriched the nation, and so the distinction had to be drawn between imported goods for domestic consumption and imported goods for re-export to the continent: 'There is the same power in these Indian wares, to procure other sommes of ready moneyes to be brought into this kingdom'.[109]

Mun also showed that trade with India was advantageous to England not just for the trade surplus[110] but also in terms of national employment,

---

106 Mun thought of this as the circuit of capital. See Steiner, in Béraud and Faccarello (eds), *Nouvelle histoire de la pensée économique*, vol. 1 (Paris, La Découverte 1992), 116–121.

107 Mun, *England's treasure by forraign trade*, 16.

108 Pepper was another significant example Mun gave: 'suppose pepper to be worth here two shillings the pound constantly, if then it be brought from the Dutch at Amsterdam, the Merchant may give there twenty pence the pound, and gain well by the bargain; but if he fetch this pepper from the East Indies, he must not give above three pence the pound at the most, which is a mighty advantage, not only in that part which serveth for our own use, but also for that quantity which we transport yearly unto divers other nations to be sold at a higher price'; Mun, *A discourse of trade from England into the East*, 10–12.

109 Mun, *A discourse of trade from England into the East*, p. 26.

110 Thomas, *Mercantilism and East India trade*, 12.

production (shipbuilding), and the processing of staple commodities, which were imported and used as raw materials by English manufacturers and then re-sold on the European market. This was what happened with the imported dyes, which created employment in the textile industry. It was also true of imported raw silk, which promoted employment in a new national productive activity, weaving: 'We get more by the Indian wares than the Indians themselves [...] I will remember a notable increase in our manufacture of winding and twisting only of forraign raw silk, which within 35 years to my knowledge did not employ more than 300 people in the City and suburbs of London, where at this present time it doth set on work above fourteen thousands souls'.[111] The outgoings of gold and silver were thus perceived not as a loss but as a form of investment, a prepayment for the development of manufactures and the English export trade. To conclude: 'It is not therefore the keeping of our mony in the kingdom, but the necessity and use of our wares in forraign countries, and our want of their commodities that causeth the vent and consumption on all sides, which makes a quick and ample trade'.[112]

2.2 *New Debates, New Challenges: The Calico Controversy at the End of the 17th Century*

Much criticism was levelled at the East India Company in the late 17th century. Some attacked the harmful competition of Eastern products for the wool trade; others denounced what were seen as exorbitant privileges granted to the East India Company. It is important to note that the changes in the economic context largely explain the new polemic that raged in the second half of the century about trade with the Indies.[113]

Debate about the role of the East India Company was largely open because this period saw a sharp upturn in the volume of trade.[114] Trade thrived particularly between 1660 and 1700 while the polemic between supporters and opponents of the state company grew in amplitude. Exports were mostly to provide

111 Mun, *England's treasure by forraign trade*, 10–11.

112 Mun, *England's treasure by forraign trade*, 17.

113 Despite the polemics of the earlier period, Cromwell renewed the East India Company's charter in 1657 (see Morineau, *Les grandes compagnies des Indes Orientales*). The privilege of trade beyond the Cape of Good Hope was maintained without restriction and the company could continue to act like a state in itself towards other states outside Europe. While from 1694 the company's privilege was called into question and competition came from a new firm, from 1708 after a merger of the two, there was again just a single company still known as the East India Company and enjoying the same privileges.

114 Kirti N. Chaudhuri, *The trading world of Asia and the English East India Company, 1660–1760*. (Cambridge University Press 1978), p. 10.

capital for commercial establishments to set up while imports, the level of which rose almost symmetrically, supplied thriving British and European markets. It should be noticed too that the structure of imports also changed substantially in the course of the century, which was not without repercussions on public debate. In the first half of the century, most imports were spices and especially pepper, whereas in the following decades textiles took over. Between 1664 and 1678, the proportion of pepper in the total value of imports varied between 15 and 30 per cent while that of cotton- and silk-based products fluctuated between 60 and 70 per cent.[115] This growth in the proportion of fabric imports was very substantial between 1660 and 1685 since nearly 300,000 pieces were imported in 1665 and 1,760,315 in 1686.[116] It was driven by a widespread fashion for lighter textiles that were easy to care for and by the ambition of the company directors to 'popularize' these products.[117] Conversely, tea made up just 1 per cent of imports in 1690 while coffee fluctuated between 1 and 2 per cent and indigo between 2 and 5 per cent. This growth slowed with Parliament's 1685 ban on importing silk and coloured or printed calico except for re- export.[118] Accordingly trade in these fabrics plummeted (155000 pieces of imported fabric in 1688 as against 46,258 pieces in 1692). Other bills for more or less radical bans flourished but were not passed before 1700, despite strong protests from wool merchants in particular. In 1700/1701 a new bill was introduced which was very similar in content to those of 1696 and 1697. However, despite the 1701 Calico Act, much printed and dyed cotton was smuggled into England[119] and the ban fostered the working of cotton by industrial processes to substitute for imports and caused the take-off of the cotton industries in the 18th century.[120] The new legislation cut imports, of course, but the slow down had to be combined with other factors including the outbreak of continental wars and shortage of money.[121]

2.2.1 A Highly Profitable Trade

Child took up Mun's argument: 'no man that understands any thing of the trade of the world, will affirm, that England loses by that trade [...] That is the

115 Chaudhuri, *The trading world of Asia and the English East India Company*, p. 97.
116 Morineau, *Les grandes compagnies des Indes Orientales*, 48.
117 Chaudhuri, *The trading world of Asia and the English East India Company*, 287.
118 Morineau, *Les grandes compagnies des Indes Orientales*, 48.
119 Angus Maddison, *L'économie mondiale, Une perspective millénaire* (Paris, O.C.D.E. 2001), p. 91.
120 Brasseul, *Histoire des faits économiques*, 166.
121 Chaudhuri, *The trading world of Asia and the English East India Company*, 295.

most beneficial trade this nation drives at present'[122] and yet the company imported far more goods from the region than it exported to it. The silver and gold losses were ultimately more than made good by sales on European markets: 'these goods exported, do produce in foreign parts, to returned to England, six times the treasure in specie that the company exports from'.[123] Davenant made the same observation, being 'clearly convinced in general, that the East-India trade is greatly beneficial to England'.[124] This induced many commercial trade flows in Europe.[125] Indeed 'By carrying to other places the commodities brought from India, we every where enlarged our commerce, and brought home a great overbalance, either in foreign goods, or in bullion. In Holland, we exchanged our wrought silks, callicoes, for their spices: by Indian goods, we could purchase, at a better rate in Germany, the linens of Silesia, Saxony and Bohemia. In times of peace we did, and may again traffic with France, for our India goods against the things of luxury, which will always be brought from thence; and thereby we may bring the balance more of our side between us and that kingdom'.[126] This trade also supported national output and employment: this trade involved the permanent use of a large number of ships, estimated at between 25 and 30, and the employment of many seamen (60–100 per crew). Holland was generally cited as the example to support their reasoning. The Dutch, it was claimed, primarily grew rich while being *carriers to the world*: 'they will endeavour still to be the chief carriers of the world, as they have been for many years'.[127]

2.2.2 The Argumentation of the Monetary Drain in Question!

To counter the chief criticism of the opponents of this trade (that it was a drain on monetary reserves), the authors did not argue that, all things considered, once the goods were ultimately sold off the stock of gold and silver would increase.[128] They maintained, instead, that accumulation should not be viewed

122 Child, *A New Discourse of Trade*, 171–172.

123 Child, *A New Discourse of Trade*, 172–173.

124 Davenant, *Essay on the East India trade*, 89.

125 These arguments are consistent with findings by historians; manufactured goods coming from Asia and re- exported on the European markets accounted for 22.5% of British exports for 1699–1701; see Chaudhuri, *The trading world of Asia and the English East India Company*, 13.

126 Davenant, *Essay on the East India trade*, 97.

127 Davenant, *Essay on the East India trade*, 116.

128 Between 1660 and 1700, some 702852 kg of silver and 20098 kg of gold were exported (Chaudhuri, *The trading world of Asia and the English East India Company*, 177). Europe obtained bullion from the mines of the Americas and it was that metal which was re-exported. It was about 15% in 1680; see Morineau, *Les grandes compagnies des Indes*

as an end in itself. What mattered above all was not the amount of cash but its sustained flow: 'It is not a great sum, employed two or three years in this trade, must preserve it to the kingdom, nor can the nation in general reap advantage by the fortunes which a few merchants may raise to themselves by skill and good conduct [...] but it is a large treasure running in this channel with a constant and continued course, that must enrich England, and not a few ventures made by starts at random, and in an unsettled manner'.[129] The accumulation of gold and silver was no longer the prime objective. What was important was to develop commercial activities, to meet the increasing demand for new goods, and indirectly to promote manufacturing, domestic employment and maritime employment. These authors acknowledged that the country was running a trade deficit, but they considered that ultimately 'Money is the serving of the trade'.[130]

2.2.3 A Free Trade in Favour of National Interest

Davenant bluntly acknowledged the problem of excessive consumption of luxury goods and the resulting drain on monetary reserves: 'If all Europe, by common consent, would agree to have no further dealings to those parts, this side of the world by such a resolution, would certainly save a great and continual expense of treasure'.[131] But he also wrote that 'As bread is the staff of life, so the woollen manufacture is truly the principal nourishment of our body politic'.[132] However, he developed more theoretical arguments by extending Child's claim whereby 'Liberty and property conduce to the increase of trade'.[133] Indeed, he defended the general idea that trade should not be restricted or burdened by taxes. In particular he argued that the trade of calicoes, far from being prejudicial to the English economy, was beneficial to it on two counts. First, competition should bring down the price of woolen goods[134] by playing the role of stimulant, a view widely held by supporters of the Company.[135] Secondly, Davenant outlined his thesis on the advantages of specialization by

Orientales, 48). This trade with the East Indies could not cause any significant loss. In addition, it was accepted that the Eastern market could not absorb very large quantities of European goods given their production costs, so the noble metals were unanimously accepted as means of payment in international trade.

129 Davenant, *Discourses on the public revenue and on the trade*, 129.

130 Davenant, *Discourses on the public revenue and on the trade*, 147.

131 Davenant, *Essay on the East India trade*, 91.

132 Davenant, *Essay on the East India trade*, 88.

133 Quoted by Thomas, *Mercantilism and East India trade*, 79.

134 Davenant, *Essay on the East India trade*, 90.

135 William Barber, *British Economic Thought and India, 1600–1858* (Oxford, Clarendon Press, 1975), 47.

each country in international trade. If one nation could not produce a good on better terms than another, then it was preferable for that nation to buy in that good and to concentrate all its efforts on the activities in which it enjoyed an advantage over other nations. The idea was for a nation to buy goods more cheaply than it could produce them under identical conditions, and to sell in greater quantity those goods that other nations were unable to sell so cheaply: 'If the people of England are willing and pleased to wear Indian silks [...] of which the prime cost in India is not above a fourth part of what their own commodities would stand them in here, and if they are thereby enabled to export so much of their own products, whatever is so saved is clear gain to the kingdom in general'.[136]

Bills seeking to restrict imports of Indian cotton fabrics and even prohibit the wearing of silks from India, Persia and Bengal and dyed and printed calicoes were 'absolutely destructive to the trade and very prejudicial to the kingdom'.[137] Prohibition of these goods would mean England buying them on the European markets at higher prices. The Dutch would fill the gap in the market: 'The Hollanders, at this time, are very powerful in India, they have many good forts and castles well provided, and large colonies of men; and they can, upon any occasion, call together there 40 strong frigates, so that it agreed with the present circumstances of their affairs in Europe, or with the nature of the alliance they are engaged in, it is undoubtedly in their power, to engross this rich traffic wholly to themselves, and to expel us for ever from those countries'.[138]

2.2.4 The Protectionist Opposition

The main criticism in this period was of the competition and the damage which English industrialists and wool traders in particular incurred. Demand for Eastern textiles was booming at the time and in direct competition with English textiles on local markets. Child admitted that real harm was suffered by wool traders. Manufacturers in Gloucestershire and Worcestershire had even raised a petition in 1674 against Indian calicoes, but Child reported their sales were expanding: 'They do now make and vend above twenty times the quantity of cloth which they did before the Company was erected'.[139] He failed, then, to understand this fierce opposition.

136 Davenant, *Essay on the East India trade*, 102.
137 Davenant, *Essay on the East India trade*, 90.
138 Davenant, *Essay on the East India trade*, 121.
139 Child, *A treatise concerning the East-India trade*, 38.

Although outgoings of bullion could be offset by incoming bullion from the re-export trade, some opponents of colonial trading posts maintained that the country's money reserves were being depleted. John Pollexfen, commissioner of trade and plantations and a staunch defender of the cause of the wool merchants, was one such opponent.[140] He claimed the trade was responsible for a loss to the treasury of £400,000 of gold and silver annually. Nor, he argued, did the East Indies trade enrich the nation.[141] But Pollexfen's main quarrel with this trade was that it harmed national industries; by promoting new tastes, it gave rise to fashions which harmed the wool merchants. He did not dispute that wool goods were not competitively priced. However, he maintained that cheap Indian cotton fabrics would completely destroy the English wool industry: 'People will go to the cheapest markets […] those from India must otherwise be cheapest'.[142]

Nor did he subscribe to the idea that importing cheap Indian products would bring down the prices of English goods: 'That we must therefore send our money to India to purchase the manufactured goods made in India to purchase the manufactured goods made those parts to be spent at home, and abroad, in the room of our own, in order to bring down the price of them, by making wool and labour cheap, are false conclusions drawn form true principles'.[143] He insisted on the nation's right not to open up its markets, rejecting the principle of entirely free trade, which would be the ruin of domestic industry.[144]

2.3 *Trading Posts in the East Indies Still in Debate in the First Part of the 18th Century: The Continuation of the Calicoes' Controversy*

Relations between England and the Asian trading posts continued to develop during the first half of the 18th century, particularly given that the disorganization of the central power after the death of Mughal Emperor Aurangzeb had an effect on European colonial practices. In the middle of the century, despite the persisting weakness of the European presence (75,000 Europeans compared with a local population in excess of 200 million), an economic, then a political, power was put in place (with stricter control of cotton fabric production

140 Thomas, *Mercantilism and East India trade.*

141 Istvan Hont, 'Free trade and the economic limits to national politics', in J. Dunn (ed.), *The economic limits to modern politics* (Cambridge University Press 1990), 96.

142 Pollexfen, *England and East India inconsitent in their manufactures*, 17–18.

143 Pollexfen, *England and East India inconsistent in their manufactures*, 20.

144 Hont, *Free trade and the economic limits to national politics*, 100.

areas[145]), growing ever stronger. Prohibitive laws were not enough to discourage European demand. Not only did the Calico Act of 1700 not discourage British demand, but it actually created greater discontent among wool manufacturers, because white calico (authorized for import) was less expensive and less heavily taxed than pre-painted cloths. Many cloths were dyed in England, generating a real industry, and sold at low prices. Furthermore, many painted cloths entered illegally from the Netherlands. Finally, a large portion of those painted cloths were sent directly to other zones (particularly America), creating additional competition for English wool products. The 1721 protectionist act put an end to the official importation of Indian calicos, with the exception of muslins, scarves, fustians and completely blue calicos.[146] Other products were the subject of more substantial trade during the 18th century, particularly tea and coffee. In 1717, tea represented 7% of the Company's imports, 20% in 1747, and 40% in 1760. Coffee, which accounted for 1–2% of the East India Company's imports in the 17th century, rose dramatically to 22% in 1724.[147]

2.3.1 The Debate between Wool Manufacturers and Importers of Colonial Products

The debate that was forming on trade with the colonial trading posts revealed, first and foremost, radically opposing interests between wool manufacturers and importers of colonial products. A related debate pertained to the risk of the decline of the British economy: it was claimed that the wool manufacturers' personal interests – damaged by other commercial interests – were contributing to the nation's industrial and commercial decline. More generally at the outset, some writers questioned the limitations of economic freedom. This was the case with Berkeley, who published *An essay towards preventing the ruin of Great Britain* (1721), a pamphlet in which he criticized the excesses in freedom that, according to him, were responsible for the South Sea Bubble.[148] More pragmatically, the merchants Blanch and Brewster attributed their country's decline to the exportation of raw wool to foreign factories, penalizing their country's own wool industry. This economic nationalism also led to criticism of the behavior of the East India Company. Blanch, on the other hand, believed that the success of a Scottish India Company would reduce England's advantages. Blanch observed that calico imports were not balanced, that they

145 The East India Company financed production, gave advances to craftsmen and thus enjoyed powerful means of pressure.

146 Thomas, *Mercantilism and East India trade*, 118–119.

147 Chaudhuri, *The Trading World of Asia and the English East India Company*, 97.

148 Hutchison, *Berkeley's Querist*, 3–4.

competed too heavily with local wool products and that they were accompanied by a net cash outflow: 'This trade deserves the favour of our nation'.[149] Brewster, who was very involved in overseas trade, but not with India, saw calico as dangerous competition, due to the low cost of Indian labor. In response, he suggested influencing the cost of labor through the procurement of foodstuffs, rather than by adjusting workers' wages: 'A penny a day were taken off every man's work, which might easily be done if provisions were lowered in proportion, and kept as they are now; but the misfortune of our conduct among other things in trade, is, that we make no provision for a time of scarcity'.[150] Cary criticized the Company, which encouraged the British population to wear Indian calicos, of selling too few British products on the colonial markets: 'I cannot see how that nation [India] can be supplied with manufactures hence fit for their wearing, answerable in price to their own, except they were a luxurious people'.[151] Even Defoe, who appeared to be more liberal with regard to that trade, changed his position and proposed, in 1707, that calicos be imported without restriction but be manufactured in England, so that the poorest members of its population might be employed.[152] All of these protectionist arguments were relayed in the *British Merchant*, which saw the protection of the British market as a factor in the support of domestic industry.

This debate on Indian calicos was a natural extension of the discussion begun in the late 17th century. The benefits of this type of trade went to private agents[153] or the East India Company which, theoretically, was the guardian of the public interest. In reality, Blanch considered that the Company's interests were most often limited to those of its leaders: 'This East-India trade has been chiefly managed by a few hands that have reaped the benefit thereof'.[154] His stance heralded the future debate that Edmond Burke would kick off on the EIC's abuse of power.[155]

2.3.2 The End of the Debate

As the calico debate had dropped after the 1720 act was passed, economists' perceptions of the advantages of that trade tended to stress the positive

149 Blanch, *The naked truth in an essay upon trade*, 6.
150 Francis Brewester, *New essays on trade* (London, H. Walwyn 1702), 54.
151 Cary, *A discourse concerning the East-India trade*, 8–9.
152 Moore, *Daniel Defoe, Citizen of the Modern World*, 315.
153 Cary, *A discourse concerning the East-India trade*, 3.
154 Blanch, *The naked truth in an essay upon trade*, 5
155 Alain Clément, 'Liberal economic discourse on the colonial practices and the rejection of British Empire (1750–1815)', *European Journal of the History of Economic Thought*, 21–24 (2014), 583–604.

contributions of those relationships to the trade balance. In Gee's words, for example: 'We send very great quantities of bullion thither, as well as some manufactures of this kingdom, which purchase there, at very low prices, the products and manufactures of India and China, which are brought home in our own navigation, out of which we supply ourselves with muslins, callicoes, and other cotton cloaths, sufficient for our own consumption as repay for all the bullion shipp'd out, and leave with us beside a very considerable balance upon that trade'.[156] These writers also underlined the low cost of raw materials like silk and its positive effect on domestic manufacturing. A new position, more favorable to global free trade, seemed to be taking shape, although it was only partially defended. Defoe was sympathetic to it, but with substantial reservations. Only Paterson could be qualified as an early liberal. His visionary, liberal side hoped to see his idea of a Scottish colony come to fruition, as a sort of global trade platform provided by the Isthmus of Panama's connection of the two oceans. His rejection of trade monopolies was not linked to the fact that he was not himself at the head of a monopoly. He was a staunch supporter of free, unrestricted trade and remained one of Smith's first forerunners.[157] He also promoted this campaign in a pamphlet published 1701, entitled *Proposals and reasons for constituting a council of trade*, in which he posited a number of reasons for the creation of a true trade office for Scotland and explained the main functions that the latter might have. The scope of that body was highly ambitious, as it could play the role of encouraging domestic industry,[158] as well as that of making public economic decisions –'to take off and publickly dispence with all such restraints and prohibitions, monopolys, premptions or exclusions [...] to have power to lay on, impose, collect and receive such dutys and impositions'[159] – but above all, that of fostering growth in trade and industrial progress: 'It will be absolutely necessary, that the weight of the present duties and impositions on foreign trade, should be partly removed and partly otherwise disposed and regulated'.[160] This would be one of the functions of that trade office.

156 Gee, *The trade and navigation of Great-Britain considered*, 43.

157 Hutcheson was fairly closely aligned with Paterson's theory, although he did accept certain exceptions to the principle of free trade; see Donald Rutherford, *In the Shadow of Adam Smith: Founders of Scottish Economics 1700–1900*, 19.

158 William Paterson, *Proposals and reasons for constituting a Council of trade* (1701), 17.

159 *Ibidem*, 21–22.

160 *Ibidem*, 26.

3 From the Liberal Opposition to Opposition to the Colonies

3.1 *Liberal Opposition or the Advantages of Unequal Trade*

An anonymous pamphlet '*Considerations on the East-India Trade*' published in 1701 and attributed to Henry Martyn, took a very different view of matters and also disputed the role of the East India Company in foreign trade. For Martyn, trade with the East Indies was based on an unequal exchange. The exchange of gold and silver for Indian products was the best means, the pamphleteer claimed, to obtain more value, allowing England to export more manufactured goods than it would otherwise have done, for the same amount of money: 'To export bullion for Indian manufactures, is to exchange less for greater value; it is to exchange bullion for manufactures more valuable, not only to the merchant but also to the kingdom'.[161] This trade was even more advantageous than the mere sale of manufactured goods made in England for the European markets: 'This trade is a continual exchange of the bullion procured by less for more and better manufactures; and therefore of less for more and better manufactures, it is therefore of all other trades, the most likely to increase our plenty of those too fast for our luxury and consumption [...] It is therefore most likely to increase our exportations'.[162]

Next, the pamphleteer challenged the protectionist arguments about the level of output and employment. In the calico controversy, Martyn spoke out against the 1697 and 1699 bills. He saw trade with the Eastern trading posts more as a stimulus than a threat to the national industry: 'we cannot be so much impoverished by the free and indifferent use of any manufactures'.[163] This opening up to international competition was a powerful driving factor behind English industry: 'The East India trade by the importation of cheaper, must needs reduce the price of English manufactures, nevertheless it is matter of fact, that the wages of men are not abated'.[164] Martyn argued that competition was a means of promoting technical advances in manufacturing thereby saving labour without calling wage levels into question. Competition led to lower production costs through technical progress. He believed that although some industries would disappear and some jobs too, others would develop: 'Some that were employed in those (manufactures), will betake themselves to other manufactures'.[165] On the other hand, employing people to manufacture

161 Martyn, *Considerations on the East-India Trade*, 556
162 *Ibidem*, 573.
163 *Ibidem*, 578.
164 *Ibidem*, 588.
165 *Ibidem*, 573.

goods which could be imported from India was a loss for the realm. His argument led to a true international division of labour. England might find it advantageous, he claimed, to specialize 'as long as any country possesses anything which England wants, Spain the gold and silver of America, Holland the fishing another trades, France the wines … English labour might be exchanged for other'.[166]

Lastly, Martyn advised pursuing this trade outside of any monopolistic structure. Trade organised by private agents operated in virtue of 'the effect of necessity and emulation, things unknown to a single company'.[167] Competition was more advantageous for the community as a whole if not for each individual merchant. Thus the nation would be 'by half a million yearly richer, as long as this trade is so much enlarged by the emulation of two companies, than if it were reduced to the joint-stock of one'.[168] However, Martyn did not overlook the matter of the infrastructures required to conduct trade, and, in particular, the construction of forts and commercial establishments. He suggested they should be financed from the public purse and dismissed the 'natural' monopoly argument defended by the East India Company. He claimed instead that these essential public investments would be largely offset by higher incomes (thanks to increased trade) derived from customs duties: 'this may be better paid by the greater gain of an open trade'.[169]

3.2 *First Oppositions to the Colonies: Petty and Coke*

Throughout the 17th century a minority of economists constantly opposed the proponents of the settlement of new lands and colonial trade.[170] Coke, Roberts and Petty were their standard bearers.

Coke and Petty alike regarded trade and more particularly foreign trade as the most profitable of activities: 'There is much more to be gained by manufacture than husbandry, and by merchandize than manufacture'.[171] But it was maritime trade which was perceived as the most lucrative of all. Foreign trade was the only means of enriching the realm.[172] However, for England, navigation was the only way of conducting trade (except for trade with Scotland). Therefore control of the seas was paramount, especially for Petty: 'Those who

166 *Ibidem*, 582.

167 *Ibidem*, 561.

168 *Ibidem*, 566.

169 Martyn, *Considerations on the East-India Trade*, quoted by Barber, *British Economic Thought and India*, 60.

170 Knorr, *British colonial theories, 1570–1850*, 59–62.

171 Petty, *Political Arithmetick*, 256.

172 Coke, *A Discourse of Trade in Two* Parts, 4.

predominate in shipping, and fishing, have more occasions than others to frequent all parts of the world, and to observe what is wanting or redundant everywhere, and what each people can do, and what they desire, and consequently to be the factors, and carriers for the whole world of trade'.[173] Trade had to be free to bring about enrichment and so these authors opposed the Navigation Acts.[174] Coke in particular advocated free trade (while Petty was more reserved about it) because he believed in the great project of international trade bringing all nations together: 'Our plantations and Ireland too would have been increased and enriched by a free trade, more than by this restraint; and by like reason the trade of England too would have been much more, and the nation much more enriched than now, if no restraint had been put upon the trade by the act of navigation'.[175]

Given the geographical situation of England, the development of trade with the colonies and Ireland could prove very lucrative because the country met all the required conditions: 'Every part of England, Scotland, and Ireland, is one with another, but twelve miles from the sea'[176] and since carriage by land was much more expensive than by sea, it followed that its natural advantages should lead England to develop its colonial activities. However, both Petty and Coke, were reserved about the benefits of colonies in terms of population and economics.

Despite their interest in maritime trade, Coke and Petty were hostile overall to the foundation of a colonial empire. Demographic reasons were evoked (see above) as well as economic reasons: the colonies (of settlement) would cost more than they would bring in. For Petty, settlers in New England could have farmed in Ireland in much better circumstances, but instead Ireland was abandoned and doomed to an extremely low level of economic development. With the colonies, in fact, the collective operating costs increased without any additional output because of the dispersion of the nation's vital forces: 'There is no doubt that the same people, far and wide dispersed, must spend more upon their government, and protection, than the same living compactly, and when they have no occasion to depend upon the wind, weather, and all the accidents of the sea'.[177] In his condemnation of the customs duties between the various lands brought under the authority of England, Petty seemed to have favoured a customs union with the colonies, forming a single market with common

173 Petty, *Political Arithmetick*, 258.
174 Appleby, *Economic thought and ideology in the seventeenth century* England, 120.
175 Coke, *A Discourse of Trade in Two* Parts, 33.
176 Petty, *Political Arithmetick*, 293.
177 Petty, *Political Arithmetick*, 300.

rules.[178] However interesting such a union might be, geographical dispersion remained a major obstacle. The possession of colonies was more expensive than if power were concentrated in a smaller area: 'The smaller kingdoms and dominions, instead of being additions are really diminutions'.[179] In this judgment, Petty was applying to the colonies aspects of his thesis on the advantages of economic concentration.[180] Finally he criticized the colonial monopoly. This system did not benefit the colonies. It meant goods bound for other areas had to go via England, burdening the colonies with dissuasive customs duties compounded by the costs of transport. Ultimately it was on the basis of this economic cost- benefit calculation that Petty rejected the colonial system and the additional burden it entailed.

3.3 *1740–1760: Increasingly Liberal Conceptions of Colonial Economics?*

In the following decades, from the 1740s to the 1760s, Massie,[181] Decker,[182] Townsend,[183] Wallace[184] and Tucker,[185] who were the major authors of that period, addressed economic questions and (for some) the issue of the colonies with a more liberal orientation, even if the subsequent 'free' translations and publication of Jérôme Savary's *Dictionnaire universel de commerce* by Malachy Postlethwayt and Richard Rolt between 1751 and 1766 somewhat toned down that change.

178 Alessandro Roncaglia, *Petty – The origins of Political Economy* (New York, M.E. Sharpe 1985), 39–40.

179 Petty, *Political Arithmetick*, 298.

180 Clustering activities and people would eliminate the costs of transporting goods from the place of production to the place of consumption. Petty's ideal, Dockès writes, was a short economic circuit where all activities were concentrated in a single city. This was one reason, Petty imagined, why London numbered 4, 690, 000 inhabitants whereas the remainder of England had a population of just 2.710.000.

181 Joseph Massie, *A state of the British sugar colony trade* (London, T. Payne 1759).

182 Decker, *An essay on the causes of the decline of the foreign trade.*

183 Charles Townshend, *National thoughts recommended to the serious attention of the public* (London, Dodsley 1751).

184 Robert Wallace, *A dissertation on the numbers of Mankind in Ancient and modern times* (London 1753; Reprint London, Routledge 1998).

185 This was the period when Josiah Tucker published *A brief essay on the advantages and disadvantages which respectively attend France and Great Britain with regard to trade* in 1750 and *Elements of commerce and theory of taxes* in 1752. However, his contributions to the issue of the colonies and the debate in which he participated pertained to a slightly later period, contemporary to Smith, Burke and Anderson (Clément 2014). For these reasons, his writings will not be covered in this article.

3.3.1 Matthew Decker: The Embodiment of the First Liberal Position

Decker was undoubtedly the most liberal writer of the period, even if he continued to champion the mercantilistic principle of the balance of trade. He was heavily involved in colonial trade, as the former director of the EIC, from 1713 to 1743.[186] In his 1744 pamphlet, *An essay on the causes of the decline of the foreign trade consequently of the value of the lands of Britain and on the means to restore both*, published one year after he left the EIC, he continued the debate on this decline, which was initiated by other writers in previous decades, but with completely different conclusions and proposals. This text was distributed widely, with seven additional editions published through 1756. Much more theoretical than his 1743 pamphlet (*Considerations on the several high duties which the nation in general, as well as trade in particular, labours under*), he explained the decline of foreign trade as the result of high taxes and the existence of monopolies. According to Decker, taxes prevented the country from being a global warehouse for merchandise,[187] slowed maritime transport,[188] prevented any increase in the number of sailors, '[t]he true strength of this nation',[189] encouraged illicit activities[190] and, contrary to mercantilist thought of the 1700s to the 1720s, ruined manufacturing and wool businesses, in particular.[191] These remarks pertained to both foreign trade and strictly colonial trade. Next, his criticism of the monopolies (of which he claimed there were six[192]) partially but directly referred to trading companies, including the East India Company, the South Sea Company and the Turkey Company. This criticism was all the more surprising in that it was made by a former head of the EIC. In reality, Decker left the Company in an atmosphere of financial scandal and strong shareholder discontent.[193] He built his theory of the negative effects of trading companies on three main arguments: Those companies limited the trade in manufactured goods abroad, because '[b]y being all of them confined to London, the prices of the woolens they export are enhanced by long

186 Cf. Lars Magnusson, in Donald Rutherford (ed.), *The Biographical Dictionary of British Economists*, 2 vol. (Bristol, Thoemmes Press 2004), 312–313.

187 Decker, *An essay on the causes of the decline of the foreign trade*, 151.

188 *Ibidem*, 152.

189 *Ibidem*, 152.

190 *Ibidem*, 155.

191 *Ibidem*, 156.

192 Aside from the trading companies' monopolies, Decker also attacked the monopolies of cities and corporations, the laws preventing the import of agricultural products from Ireland, the laws preventing the import of certain fishes from abroad, the Navigation Acts and the laws preventing the export of Irish woollens.

193 Chaudhuri, *The Trading World of Asia and the English East India Company*, 459.

land carriages up to town'.[194] He went on to remark that it was 'not the interest of the East-India Company to increase the quantities of the woollens they export [...] the smallness of the quantities naturally enhances the price; and if the company can gain as much on 5000 cloths as on 10000, it is not their interest to prefer the lesser quantity on account of the lesser quantity on account of the lesser disbursement and risk?'.[195] Finally, the status of its agents meant that 'they cannot naturally be supposed to be so industrious as those who trade only on their own stocks'.[196] In other words, those national companies did not develop their trade with the same objectives as private merchants. Another critique targeted the Navigation Act, which more directly concerned colonial trade and, according to Decker, raised the prices of imported products because they 'shall not be imported by the cheapest navigation but by a dear one'.[197]

Although the goal of colonial conquest was to enrich the nation, Decker concluded that it actually led to economic ruin. In the second part of his pamphlet, he gave a detailed account of the measures to be taken, based on the strengths of the English economy. He noted that England had significant assets it could use to fight economic decline and the decline in its trade. These assets included 'institutional' elements, including border security, government efficiency and environmental aspects like plentiful mining and agricultural resources, and the possession of abundant land in the plantation colonies, with the advantage of having access to timber there, a strategic raw material in the construction of boats. On that basis, he made 11 proposals, some of which directly concerned the colonies. The key measures naturally included the elimination or reduction of taxes, with Decker stressing the fact that it was important 'to make all our ports free'.[198] The only allowable taxes should be those pertaining to luxury goods. Without taxes, trade should increase, because the import of untaxed products would indirectly lead to 'labour being rendered cheap by the reduction of taxes and freedom of trade'.[199] Another effect would be the jobs created by such a measure. He challenged and explicitly criticized Gee's assessments, which he also cited in his *Tract on Trade*. He further wanted to prove that if 'our trade is quite free, no nation could hurt our staple, the woollen manufacture, and that if cheapness pours in goods to a country, we should do it on the French and Dutch, instead of they on us\; consequently

194 Decker, *An essay on the causes of the decline of the foreign trade*, 168.
195 *Ibidem*, 168.
196 *Ibidem*, 169.
197 *Ibidem*, 174.
198 *Ibidem*, 191.
199 *Ibidem*, 207.

that Gee's objection is void'.[200] Another more liberal and completely unheard-of measure was the freedom that he wanted to grant to the colonies' own trade, namely allowing them to export freely and directly to Europe.[201] This freedom that Decker wanted to give them was partially linked to a geographic advantage: 'by our plantations supplying part of those growths we now buy from foreigners, by their having a more convenient navigation to the Baltic and Mediterranean than they have to each other, by being cheap ship-builders'.[202] This freedom would result in an increase in the colonies' trade, because 'they supply the Baltic with the Southern Growths cheaper than the people on the Mediterranean'.[203] In the end, this boost in trade would make it possible for the home country to sell even more manufactured goods to its colonies. Decker pragmatically considered that the colonies' economic freedom would procure economic advantages for them, the home country and the other nations. This marked the dawn of the debate on the cost of the colonies and on the diversion of trade that Smith and the liberals would later highlight in the decades to come.

3.3.2 Individual Economic Interests Called into Question

Decker marked an important theoretical advance with regard to the mercantilistic ideology of the times. But over and above the perpetuation of this economic thought that continued to resonate (cf. below), Decker's approach was criticized internally, particularly by Joseph Massie, considered to be one of his opponents and a precursor to Smith, namely on the subject of taxes on profits.[204] Massie wrote a large number of texts and pamphlets on trade, currency and the colonies, and namely anticipated certain monetary aspects of Hume's thought.[205] He also compiled more than 2,400 texts, ranging from 1557 to 1763 and covering trade issues, and, in particular, defended the idea that trade should be a science, with its own laws: just as there are laws of physics, 'by parity of reasoning, the principles of commercial knowledge, whatever they are, must retain their nature and efficacy in all changes of application'.[206] Account taken of those assertions, he proposed a number of trade rules and, in

200 *Ibidem*, 224.
201 *Ibidem*, 263.
202 *Ibidem*, 266.
203 *Ibidem*, 266.
204 W. Cunningham, 'The progress of economic doctrine in England in the Eighteenth century', *Economic Journal*, 1 (1891), 73–94.
205 Cf. Terence Hutchison, *Before Adam Smith: The Emergence of Political Economy*, 1662–1776 (Oxford University Press 1988), 239–241.
206 Quoted in Hutchison, *Before Adam Smith: The Emergence of Political Economy*, 239–241.

particular, endeavored to define how they should be organized and structured. In a 1759 text devoted to the sugar islands, he outlined a few economic management rules and, although he spoke of economic 'laws', in reality they were, strictly speaking more rules than laws. In that text, he began by suggesting and reorganization of the plantation colonies by attributing the land to the colonists, thus entering into the field of an administered economy. To optimize the exploitation of colonial land, he proposed 'that such of those lands should be re-granted in shares of portions not exceeding 200 acres, not less than 20 acres to any one person'[207] and that they should be reassigned to new colonists –'British protestant subjects' – should any land be left uncultivated. Moreover, he criticized the varied points of view of merchants when they spoke of the question of trade, because he considered that they were driven more by personal feelings than by the public good. He did not believe in compatibility between individual interests and the general interest,[208] but in an opposition between them and, in that sense, foresaw the criticism that certain liberal economists would subsequently make on the lure of profits from the colonies, their pronounced taste in wealth and the little eagerness they showed in the economic exploitation of the colonial territories. His point of view entailed a change in the colonies' governance, with more a more involved, more directive political power: 'By these or some such means, I most humbly apprehend, the British sugar-colonies, and the trade thereof, may be brought into such a course of subordination and regularity, as comport with the dignity of the British Crown, and the public weal of this kingdom'.[209] This reorganization also applied to the purely commercial relations between the colonies and the motherland, particularly with regard to the importation of colonial products: 'That no sugar-planter, or other owner of a plantation, in any of the British sugar-colonies, should be capable of shipping from thence as merchandize on his or her own account, any sugar, rum, melasses, &c; but that those and all the other commodities produced there, should be bartered for commodities, manufactures, negroes, &c, brought to those colonies in British or British plantation ships, or should be sold to the commanders thereof, at such prices as shall be agreed upon, between them and the sugar-planters, or other planters'.[210]

207 Massie, *A state of the British sugar colony trade*, p. 94.

208 Cf. Cunningham, *The progress of economic doctrine in England in the Eighteenth century*, 81.

209 Massie, *A state of the British sugar colony trade*, 96.

210 *Ibidem*, 95.

4 Conclusion

Mercantilist economic thought first developed with the beginning of European colonial expansion. This coincidence was not, however, fortuitous. Economic theory was partly constructed on the promotion of trade with the East Indies: the many pamphlets published were often penned by leaders of large commercial companies (Misselden, Mun, Child, Davenant). Mercantilist ideas, which were based on power and wealth, were superbly illustrated by colonial expansion. Reciprocally, the important debates and intellectual exchanges which colonialism engendered made an essential contribution to the emergence of new concepts and mechanisms (balance of trade, international division of labour, etc.) and nurtured the emerging economics. But along the second part of the 17th and the fisrt part of the 18th century, the debate about the relationships between colonies and the mother country has opened the way to a new economic thought. The liberal thought which is coming, is founded on the limits of a protected economy, and on the advantages of a free economic trade. In background, the maintenance of colonial empire is called into question, *via* the reject of the old colonial system (Navigation Acts, Calico Acts, Sugar Act….) and of the chartered companies' commercial monopoly.

The Transplant and Adaption of Company Law in Colonial Victoria 1850–1900

Phillip Lipton

1 Introduction

This paper deals with the transplant and adaption of company law in the Australian colony of Victoria during the second half of the nineteenth century as part of a roundtable examining the influence of colonies on the development of commercial law and practice. In order to facilitate comparisons with other colonial experiences, this paper will attempt to place the development of company law in Victoria in its economic, social and institutional contexts. The interaction of economic development and the evolution of company law in colonial Victoria presents an interesting case study of a company law transplant because it allows for the examination of this interaction in the context of the development of a wealthy capitalist society over a relatively short period of time. It also enables us to examine the introduction of a body of law from the originating colonial power into a prosperous settler-society based upon the social and political institutions of the founding country.

Apart from some notable exceptions, surprisingly little has been written about the history of Australian company law,[1] possibly because it has been regarded as a mere copy of the English legislation with few if any distinguishing

---

1 Part of this paper draws upon an earlier article written by the author, 'A History of Company Law in Colonial Australia: Economic Development and Legal Evolution', *Melbourne University Law Review* 31 (2007), 805–836. Rob McQueen in particular has written a number of important works dealing with the history of company law in Australia. See for example, 'An Examination of Australian Corporate Law and Regulation 1901–1961', *University of New South Wales Law Journal* 15 (1992) 1; 'Company Law as Imperialism', *Australian Journal of Corporate Law* 5 (1995), 187; 'Corporate Law and Historical Methodology: a Critical Perspective', *Canberra Law Review 3 (1996)*, 7; 'Limited Liability Company Legislation: the Australia Experience', *Australian Journal of Corporate Law* 1 (1991), 22; and *A Social History of Company Law: Great Britain and the Australian Colonies 1854–1920 (Farnham:* Ashgate, 2009). John Waugh also wrote an historical analysis of Australian company law in terms of the deficiencies which were exposed by the crash of the 1890s and the resultant Victorian reforms in 'Company Law and the Crash of the 1890s in Victoria', *University of New South Wales Law Journal* 15 (1992), 356. For a history of the law of business corporations in Canada see R C B Risk, 'The Nineteenth-Century Foundations of the Business Corporation in Ontario', *University of Toronto Law Journal* 23 (1973), 270.

 | DOI:10.1163/9789004443075_009

features worthy of note apart from some local innovations in the 1870s and 1890s. This paper looks at the transplant and adaption of English company law in colonial Victoria and finds several noteworthy features which depart from the notion that the Australian colonial developments were largely a bland imitation of the law in England. In fact, there were innovative features in the development of company law which were specific to the Victorian colonial experience and which may subsequently have influenced the development of company law in the United Kingdom.

Part 2 discusses some of the theoretical arguments that have been put forward to explain why legal transplants may be successful or not and why some colonies such as Victoria became wealthy while others remained poor. It raises the important question whether the transplant of company law in Victoria facilitated economic development or whether it was predominantly aimed at furthering the colonialist objectives of British imperial interests. The most significant interpretations of the history of Australian company law are a series of articles by Rob McQueen in the early and mid-1990s which questioned whether the adoption of English company law by the Australian colonies was appropriate for the local conditions.[2] He described this adoption of English company law as 'company law as imperialism' serving English economic interests rather than assisting Australian economic development and he argued that the adoption of English company law was inappropriate for Australian conditions.[3] This paper reassesses the transplant of English company law in Victoria in terms of whether it was successful and appropriate and encouraged economic development. The development of sound institutions is generally regarded as conducive to strong economic growth and it is a central contention of this paper that the successful transplantation of company law was a significant institutional factor in the remarkable economic success of Victoria and the other Australian colonies in the latter half of the nineteenth century.

Part 2 also considers the question of why the exploitation of resources may be a blessing or a curse. In this regard several writers have emphasised the importance of the quality of institutions, including legal frameworks. The Victorian colonial experience appears to provide evidence to support the proposition that settler societies with transplanted, relatively high quality institutions were able to turn their resource abundance into a blessing and so became very wealthy societies during the nineteenth century. The initial transplant of

2 See the articles by Rob McQueen referred to in n 1 especially 'Company Law as Imperialism'; 'An Examination of Australian Corporate Law and Regulation 1901–1961'; and 'Limited Liability Company Legislation – The Australian Experience'.

3 McQueen, 'Company Law as Imperialism', 46–55.

company law and a preparedness to adapt it to suit local circumstances was an important part of this process.

Part 3 of this paper deals with the economic and institutional environments in which early Australian companies operated and legal developments which aimed, with varying degrees of success, to facilitate the formation of appropriate forms of business enterprises. This Part also considers the nature and financing of the very important gold mining industry as it changed from small-scale surface operations undertaken mainly by individuals or small partnerships to underground mining carried on by more highly capitalised pooled investment enterprises.

While this paper mainly focuses on the transplant of company law in Victoria in 1864 and subsequent amendments, as discussed in Part 4, the introduction of English companies legislation did not mark a complete break with the past as the underlying features of company law were generally well understood and limited liability companies and partnerships had already existed in the Australian colonies for some time. Unincorporated joint stock companies with transferable and tradable shares were already quite common in the colony of New South Wales from the 1820s and 1830s, well before the introduction of companies legislation and the establishment of formal stock exchanges. This suggests that companies would have continued to evolve as a matter of commercial practice, irrespective of legislative developments. Limited liability partnerships which as the name suggests, had some of the characteristics of companies, were introduced in New South Wales and Victoria in the early 1850s for the use of mining enterprises. This legal form was short-lived and was not widely used, but it indicates a preparedness of colonial governments to seek innovative responses to the needs of their business communities, especially in the gold mining industry, despite the absence of equivalent English legislation. At the same time as these experiments in forms of limited liability were taking place, its introduction in the companies legislation was still being vigorously debated in England and would not be introduced until 1855. This shows that even at a very early stage in the development of company law, there was a preparedness to adapt the law in innovative ways to better meet the needs of local conditions.

Part 5 discusses the introduction of English companies legislation in Victoria in 1864 and the main features of the legislation. This coincided with the early stages of a gold mining boom which was a major driver of economic growth. The facilitation of company formations in the gold mining industry was a significant or arguably, even a necessary factor in the development of this key industry and the enormous wealth it generated. Part 6 discusses the introduction of the no liability mining company in 1871. The no liability company was an innovative response to the requirements of the gold mining industry which occurred at a time of significant expansion in gold output and investment in gold mining company shares. This legislation was described as 'one of the most radical experiments in company law in the English-speaking world'.[4] It is worth noting that this type of mining company still exists in Australia. The investor protection reforms introduced in the 1890s are discussed in Part 7. These legislative changes were also innovative and highly progressive and while largely based on law reform proposals that originated in England, were introduced in Australia more than a decade before similar reforms were introduced in England and may well have strongly influenced the development of company law in England. These legislative amendments were a response to the widespread losses suffered by many investors in the aftermath of the boom and bust and severe depression of the 1890s and represented an early example of the introduction of investor protection legislation.

2 The Transplant of Colonial Institutions

It is of interest to consider the Australian experience in the context of the effects of colonialism. There are many former colonies of European powers that have adopted and retained institutional arrangements that were transplanted from their colonial founders. These former colonies vary considerably in their levels of economic well-being. Some such as Australia, Canada and the United States are relatively wealthy while others in Africa, Asia and South America are generally very poor. The economic success of the Australian colonies in the second half of the nineteenth century can be at least partially attributed to the abundance of natural resources.[5] However this in itself cannot be a complete explanation because there are many countries endowed with abundant natural resources which have failed to produce sustained economic growth. In fact many political scientists and economists have noted that abundant natural resources are more often a curse than a blessing for developing countries. Jones Luong and Weinthal suggest that this 'resource curse' stems from institutional weakness which in turn is related to ownership structure. The authors found that strong fiscal and regulatory institutions are more likely to emerge under private domestic ownership because a significant political and economic group has a mutual interest in establishing suitable institutional outcomes

4 Geoffrey Blainey, *The Rush that Never Ended: a History of Australian Mining*, 5th ed. (Carlton, Vic.: Melbourne University Press, 2003), 99.

5 Ian W McLean, *Why Australia Prospered: The Shifting Sources of Economic Growth* (Princeton, NJ: Princeton University Press), 15.

which reduce transaction and monitoring costs. They conclude 'the concentration of wealth impoverishes the state whereas the dispersion of wealth enriches the state'.[6]

Various ways have been put forward to explain such diverse economic performance among former colonies. These explanations have suggested factors such as legal origins,[7] geography and the prevalence of disease[8] and the proportion of European settlers in the colony's population,[9] affect the likelihood of growth-promoting institutions being introduced. The transplant of company law in colonial Victoria might usefully contribute to this discourse and enable comparisons to be made between different colonial experiences.

We have seen that the central drivers of the remarkable prosperity in the Australian colonies in the second half of the nineteenth century were the development of natural resources, most notably first wool and then gold. This raises the question whether an abundance of natural resources is in itself likely to result in sustained economic growth and prosperity. Empirical studies in development economics have shown that in many cases economies that have abundant natural resources have tended to stagnate or grow more slowly than economies which do not have abundant resources and this so-called 'natural resources curse' operates independently of any declining global demand for resources and falling prices.[10] This is not to say that all natural resource rich

---

6 Pauline Jones Luong and Erika Weinthal, 'Rethinking the Resource Curse: Ownership Structure, Institutional Capacity and Domestic Constraints', *Annual Review of Political Science* 9 (2006), 241, 259. Various theories explaining the negative relationship of resource abundance and growth are set out in Jeffrey D Sachs and Andrew M Warner, 'Natural Resource Abundance and Economic Growth', *National Bureau of Economic Research* (1995) This paper may be accessed at http://www.nber.org/papers/w5398.

See survey of literature dealing with the 'resource curse' in Gavin Wright and Jesse Czelusta, 'Mineral Resources and Economic Development', *Working Paper 209 Stanford Center for International Development* (2003), 1–3. This paper may be accessed at http://www-siepr.stanford.edu/workp/swp04004.pdf.

7 Rafael La Porta, Florencio Lopez-de-Silanes, Andrei Shleifer and Robert W Vishny, 'Legal Determinants of External Finance', *Journal of Finance* 52 (1997), 52; 'Law and Finance', *Journal of Political Economy* 106 (1998), 1113; and 'Investor Protection and Corporate Governance', *Journal of Financial Economics* 58 (2000), 1.

8 Daron Acemoglu, Simon Johnson and James A Robinson, 'Reversal of Fortune: Geography and Institutions in the Making of the Modern World Income Distribution', *The Quarterly Journal of Economics* 117 (2002), 1231.

9 Daron Acemoglu, Simon Johnson and James A Robinson, 'The Colonial Origins of Comparative Development: An Empirical Investigation', *American Economic Review* 91 (2001), 1369–1401.

10 Jeffrey D Sachs and Andrew M Warner, 'The Curse of Natural Resources', *European Economic Review* 45 (2001), 827–838.

economies have failed in economic terms. There are a number of countries rich in resources that have experienced sustained economic growth and have among the highest per capita incomes. These countries include Australia, Canada and Norway. A number of reasons have been put forward to explain the existence of the resources curse. One line of argument suggests that the development of natural resources creates excess demand for wages and other input costs and so crowd-out other activities, such as manufacturing, that are drivers of growth. Profits in manufacturing and other export sectors are squeezed by higher input costs and this leads to a decline in growth.[11] Other variants of the 'crowding-out' or 'Dutch disease' argument suggests that diversion away from education or entrepreneurial activity and innovation occurs, government corruption increases and the political process becomes captured by resource interest groups.[12]

There has been considerable recent interest by academics in a range of disciplines in determining key factors which encourage or discourage economic development. A number of studies have asserted that those former colonies which have developed strong institutions have experienced successful economic growth.[13] The concept of institutions in this context refers to the broad way the society is organised. 'Good' institutions are those that provide incentives and opportunities for investment.[14] They are characterised by secure property rights for a wide cross section of the society as opposed to what Acemoglu et al. describe as 'extractive institutions' which concentrate power in the hands of a small elite and create a high risk of expropriation for the vast majority of the population and discourage innovation and change which are seen by the elite as threatening. This type of analysis can explain the different economic histories of countries such as Australia and Argentina which were in similar stages of economic development during the second half of the nineteenth century.

11 Jeffrey D Sachs and Andrew M Warner, 'The Big Push, Natural Resources Booms and Growth', *Journal of Development Economics* 59 (1999), 43–76.

12 For examples of 'crowding-out' perspectives see Thorvaldur Gylfason, Tryggvi Thor Herbertsson and Gylfi Zoega, 'A Mixed Blessing: Natural Resources and Economic Growth', *Macroeconomic Dynamics* 3 (1999), 204–225; and Richard Auty, 'The Political Economy of Resource Driven Growth', *European Economic Review* 45 (2001), 839–846.

13 See for example Douglass C North, 'Institutions and Economic Growth: An Historical Introduction', *World Development* 17 (1989), 1319–1332; Halvor Mehlum, Karl Moene and Ragnar Torvik, 'Institutions and the Resource Curse', *Economic Journal* 116 (2006), 1–20; and Acemoglu, Johnson and Robinson, 'The Colonial Origins of Comparative Development'.

14 Referred to as 'institutions of private property' by Acemoglu, Johnson and Robinson, 'Reversal of Fortune', 1235.

Several writers have emphasised the importance of institutions in explaining why some countries are prosperous and others poor. Mehlum, Moene and Torvik noted that countries rich in natural resources could be either 'growth winners' or 'growth losers'. In explaining this divergence, the authors argue that the quality of institutions is the critical factor and in particular, how resource rents are distributed. Those countries whose institutions favour producers in the distribution of resource rents tend to take full advantage of their resource abundance, while those who favour 'unproductive grabbers' tend to be caught in a growth trap. Countries with grabber-friendly institutions typically are characterised by weak rule of law, high risk of expropriation and government corruption.[15]

Acemoglu, Johnson and Robinson also focus on the quality of institutions in seeking to explain why there are large differences in income per capita across countries. Their starting point is the notion that countries with better institutions, more secure property rights and less distortionary policies will invest more in physical and human capital and will use these factors more efficiently to achieve a greater level of income. They then seek to estimate the impact of institutions on economic performance in countries colonised by European powers. Acemoglu et al differentiated between different types of colonial policies which created different sets of institutions. At one extreme were 'extractive states' whose main purpose was to transfer as much of the resources of the colony to the colonizer. There was little protection against government expropriation or of private property rights. At the other extreme were colonies to which many European settlers migrated. They sought to replicate European institutions with strong property rights and checks on government power. As to which colonial policy was adopted in a particular colony depended on the feasibility of settlements which was in turn influenced by the disease environment. Colonies in Africa and Asia were mostly unfavourable for European settlement because of the high frequency of disease and its impact on mortality rates. Such colonies were more likely to be extractive states rather than settler colonies and even after the colonies gained independence, a path dependence had been established and the nature of the colonial state and its institutions persisted. The writers therefore argued that there was a link between early settler mortality, settlements and current institutions and economic performance.[16]

---

15 Mehlum, Moene and Torvik, 'Institutions and the Resource Curse', 3.

16 Acemoglu, Johnson and Robinson, 'The Colonial Origins of Comparative Development', 1373–1376. See also by the same authors 'Reversal of Fortune'. For an analysis of the replacement of local forms of business organisation by the introduction of English

La Porta et al., put forward the argument that the legal origins of the colonizer were critical in the development of financial institutions such as stock exchanges. They further put forward the claim that former British colonies that adopted the common law generally had better property rights, investor protection laws and more developed financial markets than those countries whose laws originated in civil law countries especially in France.[17]

The Victorian colonial experience indicates that resource abundance was a blessing and not a curse. This was because of the development of high quality institutions which showed a capacity to adapt to the changed economic conditions during the gold rush period. As settler societies, the Australian colonies replicated British institutions and benefited from being part of the British Empire. The institutions that developed in Australia favoured producers in the distribution of resource rents. The society was relatively egalitarian and so the distribution of profits from gold mining benefitted a large part of the society.

The economic success of the Australian colonies during the nineteenth century would indicate that the institutions which were transplanted from Britain were conducive to economic development largely because they encouraged investment from a wide cross section of the society through the protection of property rights. The successful transplantation of company law in Australia is consistent with the analysis of Jones Luong and Weinthal that dispersed income is beneficial for economic development. Share ownership was encouraged and became relatively broad-based. This encouraged entrepreneurship and innovation making the mining industry in particular, a very successful global competitor. From this perspective, the transplantation of English company law facilitated dispersed private domestic ownership of shares in gold mining and later other mineral companies together with strong regulatory and market institutions which enabled the abundance of resource wealth to be a blessing rather than a curse.

There has been considerable historical analysis in recent years which focuses on the evolution of corporate law and patterns of legal development in 'transplant' countries compared with those of 'origin' countries.[18] Pistor et al.

---

companal.y law as a tool of imperialism in India see Radhe Shyam Rungta, *The Rise of the Business Corporations in India 1851–1900* (London: Cambridge University Press, 1970).

17 La Porta, Lopez-de-Silanes, Shleifer and Vishny, 'Legal Determinants of External Finance', 'Law and Finance', and 'Investor Protection and Corporate Governance'.

18 See for example Katharina Pistor, Yoram Keinan, Jan Kleinheisterkamp and Mark D West, 'The Evolution of Corporate Law: A Cross-Country Comparison', *University of Pennsylvania Journal of International Law* 23 (2002), 791; Katharina Pistor, Yoram Keinan, Jan Kleinheisterkamp and Mark D West, 'Innovation in Corporate Law', *Journal of Comparative Economics* 31 (2003), 676; and Daniel Berkowitz, Katharina Pistor and Jean-François

claim that irrespective whether a country's corporate law origin lay in the common law or civil law, transplant countries exhibit different patterns of legal development than do the countries where the law originated.[19] The authors surveyed a number of countries across legal families which included both origin countries and countries where corporate law was transplanted. In a number of transplant countries they found extreme volatility in legal change after enactment of the initial companies' legislation. They interpreted this volatility as a response to the economic impact of the new law or as a rejection of parts of the imposed new law. They also found that in other countries, the legislation did not change for long periods despite considerable economic development. The Australian experience seems to indicate an initial preparedness to adapt the received law in response to local circumstances. This occurred in relation to the requirements of the mining industry to adopt the no liability form and the inclusion of more detailed disclosure requirements and investor protection measures as a result of the corporate collapses of the 1890s and the inadequacies in the law that they exposed.

In 'Evolution of Corporate Law' Pistor et al. attempted to determine how 'good' corporate law evolves. They argued that a continuous evolution of law was a key ingredient because the success of the corporation over a long period came about because of its capacity to adapt to a changing environment and corporate law evolves in close interaction with socioeconomic and political factors. Successful legal systems encourage and facilitate this adaption process and then respond to changed circumstances by amending the law to better suit the new conditions. The writers concluded that common law countries have been more innovative than civil law countries and in this respect, origin countries have been more successful than transplant countries. Pistor et al also considered that the common law countries developed more liberal corporate law systems complemented by control devices such as a greater role for the courts and securities market regulation. This enabled common law countries to rely less on legislated restraints and thereby encouraged more innovation in the uses of companies.[20] The evolution of transplanted corporate law was found to differ from the country of origin especially where complementary institutions were often not as fully developed as in the country of origin to support a flexible,

Richard, 'Economic Development, Legality and the Transplant Effect', *European Economic Review* 47 (2003), 165.

19 Pistor, Keinan, Kleinheisterkamp and West, 'The Evolution of Corporate Law', 797 and 870.

20 Pistor, Keinan, Kleinheisterkamp and West, 'The Evolution of Corporate Law', 868.

enabling system. Legal change can be either erratic or stagnant. The advent of legal change appears to indicate that a transplanted law has taken root.[21]

In an article which considered the transplant of law generally rather than the specific transplant of corporate law, Berkowitz, Pistor and Richard proposed that those countries which received transplanted law and adapted it to suit local conditions and had a population that was familiar with its basic legal principles, were more likely to build an effective legal system. On the other hand, where these conditions were absent, the recipient countries experienced difficulties in developing effective legal systems.[22] This characteristic of transplant countries is described in this article as the 'transplant effect'. The authors considered that the way in which the law was transplanted and the receptiveness of the transplant country are more significant than the particular legal family origin, that is, whether it is from the civil law or common law family of legal systems.

The Australian experience has exhibited a number of the legal transplant characteristics observed by the authors above. These include some innovative adaptions to local conditions, some erratic, idiosyncratic and self-interested responses in times of crisis and long periods of relatively little change. Australia adapted its corporate law to suit local circumstances and experience in the late nineteenth century and since the 1970s with a long period of relatively little change in between.

3 The Economic and Institutional Context

Prior to 1901 there was no sovereign entity of Australia. There were six independent colonies established at different times as part of the British Empire, each with their own legislatures, judicial systems and financial institutions. The Australian colonies were fortunate to have the highest standard of living in the world during most of the second half of the nineteenth century.[23] The main

21 Pistor, Keinan, Kleinheisterkamp and West, 'The Evolution of Corporate Law', 870.

22 Berkowitz, Pistor and Richard, 'Economic Development, Legality and the Transplant Effect', 168ff.

23 Various measures may be utilised to show this. In terms of GDP per capita, the Australian colonies ranked ahead of the United Kingdom as the highest GDP per capita by 1860 and retained its top ranking until overtaken by the United States at the very end of the nineteenth century. At the beginning of the twentieth century the countries with the highest income per capita levels were Australia, United States, United Kingdom, New Zealand, Switzerland, Belgium and the Netherlands. Of these seven wealthiest economies, three were originally British settler colonies. See McLean, *Why Australia Prospered*, 11–12

reasons for the early economic success of the Australian colonies were the development of the wool industry between 1820 and 1850 and gold mining between 1851 and 1890. The wool industry proved to be highly efficient in sustaining an export-oriented high wages and high income economy. The discovery of gold in New South Wales and Victoria in 1851 diversified the wealth-producing capacity of the economy and laid the foundation for sustained prosperity based upon agricultural and mining exports that remains to this day. The period of the gold boom saw a major population increase that ushered in three decades of economic growth and a further population increase of two million between 1861 and 1891.[24] This wave of migrants was largely comprised of single, mainly young males who had a high participation rate in the workforce and increased the birth rate in later years after arrival. Importantly, a large proportion of immigrants during this period stayed in Australia. This remarkable period saw population grow eight-fold while at the same time GDP per capita significantly increased. This boom ended with a severe depression during the 1890s.

The economy of the colony of Victoria in 1851 was based upon a widely scattered wool industry and was already showing a high degree of urbanisation with a population of 77,000 of which 23,000 lived in the capital city, Melbourne. There was very little company activity as the financial services required by the dominant wool industry were almost entirely met by a small number of colonial banks. Insurance services were mostly provided by agents of English insurance companies. There were very few pooled investment enterprises and so little or no dealing in shares whereas Sydney did have some share activity as it was a larger and more developed commercial centre than Melbourne. It was into this provincial, unsophisticated although well-ordered and already prosperous society that the gold rush erupted in 1851. This was a dramatic shock which doubled the population within a year and initially caused severe disruption and turmoil to the economy and society as a whole. The colonial society proved to be adaptable and resilient in meeting this major challenge and the economic benefits of the gold discoveries boosted the development of the economy and provided considerable business and employment opportunities to the rapidly expanding population.

---

referring to Angas Maddison, *Historical Statistics of the World Economy: 1–2008 AD* Groningen Growth and Development Centre, www.ggdc.net/maddison. McLean suggested that other measures of living standards and economic well-being which take into account factors such as inequality, real wages, leisure time, education attainment and life expectancy do not significantly alter the conclusions based upon GDP per capita.

24 McLean, *Why Australia Prospered*, 15.

The sudden rapid expansion of the economy and population provided a number of large-scale commercial opportunities which required pooled investment from a large number of investors. It was from this time that the early railways were constructed joining Melbourne to the gold fields. New banks, urban infrastructure, roads and port facilities were also required. A number of local companies were formed during the first year after the discovery of gold and share prices were first listed in newspapers indicating the beginnings of a share market.[25] Companies formed during this early phase faced a number of difficulties. The economy was severely disrupted during the early stages of the gold rush which caused labour shortages, scarcity of finance and increased costs. Company law was still undeveloped and uncertain and had not yet been adapted to meet the particular needs of a rapidly changing economy. The shareholders of the local companies whose shares were listed in 1852 did not have limited liability. In the following year, a number of listed companies went through the process of obtaining an Act of Incorporation which included limited liability. The process of incorporation was costly, drawn out and could be opposed by vested interests. It is not surprising that there was little support for the introduction of limited liability. Even in Britain at this time there was strong opposition to its introduction.[26] In the colonies where share trading was largely insignificant, the issue of limited liability was far less pressing at this time.

During the 1850s the number of companies slowly grew. The success of early banks, railway companies and public utilities encouraged an increased number of applications for incorporation during the second half of the 1850s. However the legal process was cumbersome and made incorporation on a case by case basis difficult to achieve. While there was a slow increase in the number of companies whose shares could be traded, turnover was low and the market was still very limited. Shares tended to have high par values with large unpaid amounts, so ownership was limited to a relatively small circle of wealthy investors. There was no formal stock exchange able to provide a uniform market but rather there were a number of agents who dealt in land and various commodities such as gold. Stockbroking on a small scale may also have been a part of these commercial activities. Share trading took place on an ad hoc basis where an individual broker would seek to match a client's order with that of a

25 The Melbourne *Argus* 18 October 1852, 4 listed the prices of 14 companies of which a number were London or Sydney based. Five were banks, three were railway companies and others included providers of gas and water, insurance and coastal shipping.

26 See the detailed discussion in McQueen, *A Social History of Company Law*, 78–96.

counterparty.[27] It was not until the late 1850s or early 1860s that a distinct stockbroking profession developed, the volume of shares in the market increased and the circle of investors grew. These developments led to growing calls for the establishment of a stock exchange.

In the 1860s the gold industry, in addition to playing a major role in the development of the Victorian economy, was also instrumental in the very important related institutional developments of the modernisation of company law and the formation of a Melbourne stock exchange. The gold industry played a crucial role in these developments because it was during this decade that large scale operations became necessary for underground mining and this required the widespread use of the company form with the features of limited liability and tradeable shares. In the early stages of the gold rush, miners looking for surface alluvial gold operated largely as individuals or in partnerships of usually three to six. The requirements for this type of mining were relatively simple as it was the most efficient form of organisation. There was no need for legal regulation beyond the traditional law of partnership. This straightforward picture started to change from the mid-1850s when easily accessible surface gold became scarcer and miners increasingly attempted to find alluvial gold in underground rivers and streams deep below the surface. As the depth of mine shafts often increased to 40 meters and more, so the organisational demands became more complex as larger partnerships were required to share the work and raise more capital. This led to the practice of forming a type of informal company with transferable and divisible shares that were often bought and sold as miners transferred between enterprises in the hope of becoming part of a major strike. This development also occurred without legal recognition apart from English law which had long recognised this type of unincorporated company as a form of partnership.

A Royal Commission established in 1855 after the Eureka rebellion to report on conditions on the goldfields recommended legislation to allow for mining partnerships along the lines of 'cost book' mining partnerships which had long been used by miners in Cornwall. This resulted in the 1855 Mining Companies Statute.[28] A feature of this Act was that it granted limited liability to shareholders of companies formed under the legislation. This attempt at providing law which met the needs of the mining industry did not prove to be popular. One reason for this suggested by Hall may have been the strong sense of independence felt by most miners. They very much favoured working small claims as

27 Alan R Hall, *The Stock Exchange of Melbourne and the Victorian Economy 1852–1900* (Canberra: Australian National University Press, 1968), 12.

28 18 Vic. No. 42.

individuals or in partnerships and strongly opposed the development of 'capitalist' mining organisations and being employed as paid labourers of companies working deep mines.[29] The restructuring of the administration of the goldfields in 1855 established local mining courts whose members were elected by holders of a mining right. This provided miners with strong democratic rights over the administration of their industry but also resulted in the continuation of the practice of providing the smallest possible claims for the largest number of miners. This system remained workable for as long as mining was carried out on or near the surface and it was convenient to use small scale partnership enterprises.

The 1855 Mining Companies Statute was premature and although unsuccessful, pointed the way forward to a time of large mining enterprises. By the early 1860s the surface alluvial fields had been largely worked out and mine shafts of more than 100 meters were commonly sunk seeking alluvial gold in underground rivers. Gold was also increasingly mined in quartz reefs which also required underground mining at considerable depths. These forms of mining required considerable capital outlays particularly for pumps and rock crushing machinery. Large numbers of men and considerable capital were needed and a long time usually passed before a deep shaft was sunk and gold could be extracted. This period saw the passing of the independent miner and the rise of large scale mining companies.

Two major legal changes were required to facilitate this transition to large scale company mining. First, the size of claims had to be increased to a much larger size than the previous 'smallest possible claims for the largest number of miners'. This was done through legislation providing for Crown leases of suitable size for deep underground mining. Larger sized claims had already occurred when adjoining partnerships amalgamated and combined their claims and the need for larger claims became increasingly accepted as the nature of mining changed. The second requirement was the further development of company law to encourage the formation of mining companies that were suited to the newly emerging industry. This occurred over several years. In 1858 and 1860 legislation was passed that simplified the procedure for the formation of mining companies and introduced limited liability for mining company shareholders.[30] Other laws were introduced to assist mining companies in financing their operations by providing banks with improved security over a gold mining company's assets. These included recognition of preferable liens on the first gold produced by a mine and the issue of mortgages over goldmining machinery.

29 Hall, *The Stock Exchange of Melbourne*, 15.

30 Known as *Ireland's Act* and *Pykes' Act* after their proposers.

The changing nature of gold mining and the related legal changes encouraging the formation of companies and their financing brought about a brief speculative mining boom in 1859 which saw a large number of company floats. The boom did not last long but by the end of 1859 there were 45 mining companies on the Melbourne share list.[31] The boom also led to the growth of the number of active stockbrokers. There were twenty to thirty firms in Melbourne and a further large number in the main goldfield towns, especially Ballarat and Bendigo.[32] The increased volume of share trading and the increased number of stockbrokers made it increasingly important that an organised share market be established that maintained an official list of buying and selling quotations rather than the cumbersome and uncertain process of brokers separately negotiating with each other. Melbourne's first stock exchange was established in 1861 when some thirty brokers agreed upon a set of rules based upon those of the London and Liverpool exchanges and became members.[33] After a troubled few years, during which share trading and the number of brokers declined, the Melbourne Stock Exchange was reconstituted in 1865.

The Melbourne Stock Exchange remained relatively small and was primarily a gold mining exchange whose main competitors were the provincial exchanges especially those in Ballarat and Bendigo. This reflected the composition of the Victorian economy where listed companies were predominantly gold miners with a relatively small number of banks, insurance companies and public utilities also listed. On the basis of market value, in 1865 gold mining companies comprised approximately 40 per cent of the total ordinary shares of listed companies. This fell to approximately 8 per cent in 1884.[34] In the mid-1860s there were over 500 limited liability gold mining companies and over the next decade a further 4,000 gold mining companies were formed. Of course the majority of these companies did not survive for long in a highly speculative activity however at any one time there were a large number of companies and some hundred or so may have figured prominently in the industry.[35] These figures greatly understate the importance of gold mining to the business of the stock exchange because turnover of gold shares was far greater than the turnover of shares in other sectors. Gold mining companies also paid much more in dividends to shareholders than did non-mining companies. During the

31 *The Argus* 29 December 1859, 4.

32 Hall, *The Stock Exchange of Melbourne*, 22–23.

33 These rules are set out in *The Stock and Share Journal* 8 April 1861.

34 Hall, *The Stock Exchange of Melbourne*, 58.

35 Hall, *The Stock Exchange of Melbourne*, 59. See also the table at p. 81 which shows new gold mining company registrations for the period 1868–72. This table indicates the great fluctuations in registrations from 329 in 1868 to 1,206 in 1871.

period 1868 to 1871 gold mining companies paid approximately three quarters of total dividends paid by all companies.[36]

The institutional arrangements in place during the early surface alluvial phase of the gold rush period minimised the potential for social conflict. Issues such as right of access to gold discoveries and participation in the distribution of proceeds from the exploitation of gold resources were resolved in ways that maximised opportunities for mass entry and widely spread the benefits arising from the gold discoveries. Mining during this period was generally carried out by small groups working small claims on the surface. When gold production largely shifted to more capital intensive quartz mining, companies were formed to raise the necessary capital to follow quartz reefs deep underground. Wage labour was employed at relatively high wages that matched wages paid elsewhere in the economy. From the beginning of the gold rush period there were strong societal factors that led to relatively egalitarian and widely dispersed distributional outcomes. This is in contrast to the early development of the pastoral industry where relatively few squatters were able to gain occupation of a large proportion of land and the benefits flowing from the wool industry.

4 Early Experiments in Limited Liability

Sole traders and partnerships were by far the most common forms of business organisation and both New South Wales and Victoria introduced legislation which recognized limited liability partnerships in the early 1850s.[37] These early forms of limited liability enterprises were little used[38] and were repealed by the Companies Act introduced in Victoria in 1864 which provided for the universal incorporation of companies with limited liability. Although the limited liability partnership Acts were short-lived and not widely used, they nevertheless reflected a preparedness of colonial governments to depart from English law and to adopt business forms suited to the local economic and business environment in response to the demands of some sectors of the local business

36 Hall, *The Stock Exchange of Melbourne*, 74.

37 *An Act to Legalize Partnerships with Limited Liability* 1853 NSW (17 Vic No 9) and *An Act to Legalize Partnerships with Limited Liability* 1854 Vic (17 Vic No 5). Limited Liability also generally prevailed in Canada even in the absence of express provision. See Risk, 'The Nineteenth-Century Foundations of the Business Corporation in Ontario', 295–298.

38 Ralph W Birrell, *Staking a Claim: Gold and the Development of Victorian Mining Law* (Carlton, Vic, 1998), 36 noted that according to the *Victorian Government Gazette* only 14 partnerships, of which six were mining enterprises, were registered under the Victorian Act.

community. In particular, the recognition of limited liability partnerships may have been a response to community concern during the economic downturn of the 1840s when large numbers of shareholders became liable for company losses.

During the period prior to the introduction of general incorporation legislation in 1864, there were several attempts to introduce limited liability as a means of encouraging the development of business. These attempts were made in response to perceptions of the needs of local business interests and were ahead of similar developments in England where limited liability was not introduced until 1855. The New South Wales Parliament passed several acts in the period 1848 to 1853 which incorporated some of the leading banks such as the Bank of New South Wales and later some mining, insurance and shipping companies. In most cases, the liability of shareholders was limited to twice the nominal value of shares held. This reflected the reluctance of British government authorities to authorise the incorporation of banks with limited liability, while being prepared to accept liability of double nominal value. It was for this reason that banks were excluded from the English limited liability legislation of the 1850s. In the Australian colonies, this double nominal value liability served as a model for incorporations in industries other than banking including the Great Nugget Vein Gold Mining Company, incorporated in 1852, despite the fact that this type of extended limited liability was rarely used in Britain.[39]

These incorporations led to increased company activity in Sydney where investors favoured shares which paid regular dividends, especially the large banks.[40] Melbourne investors focused on gold mining shares and were more speculative in their share dealings. Several advertisements in Melbourne newspapers sought investment funds and announced the intention to seek incorporation by act of the Legislative Council.[41] Company formations increased markedly after 1851 as New South Wales and the newly established colony of Victoria experienced rapid population increases following the discovery of

---

39 Stephen Salsbury and Kay Sweeney, *The Bull, the Bear and the Kangaroo: The History of the Sydney Stock Exchange* (Sydney, 1988), 33–34 quoted the *Sydney Morning Herald* 21 June 1853 which opposed the double nominal share value liability and favoured liability limited to the nominal amount of the shares. Double nominal value liability was also adopted by banks in Canada. See Risk, 'The Nineteenth-Century Foundations of the Business Corporation in Ontario', 295.

40 Salsbury and Sweeney, *The Bull, the Bear and the Kangaroo* note that in 1858 there were over 20 dividend-paying companies in New South Wales and this increased during the 1860s.

41 Birrell, *Staking a Claim*, 108.

gold in both colonies. At the same time there was large scale investment in the pastoral sector and railway networks developed to service the mining and agricultural sectors. The growth in equity markets and company formations was particularly marked in Victoria to the extent that by 1860 there were ten specialised broking firms in Melbourne and two in Sydney. This reflected the beginning of deep lead mining in Victoria which required substantial amounts of pooled investment finance from large numbers of investors organised into syndicates. Initially the membership of the syndicates comprised local miners, silent partners and merchant suppliers. This soon led to active share trading in a large number of relatively small mining companies.

To further encourage investment in the mining industry, Victoria passed a Mining Companies Act in 1855[42] which introduced a form of incorporation and limited liability for mining corporations and partnerships. The distinction between companies and partnerships remained blurred until the introduction of the companies legislation modelled on the 1862 English Act. The 1855 Victorian legislation enabled a company to be formed and registered with a local court although it was in many respects a partnership governed by partnership law. The structure of these companies was based on the 'cost-book'[43] system which was commonly used in Cornwall however this type of company proved to be cumbersome and unsuited to an environment where people moved frequently from one goldfield to another and from one claim to another. Shareholder meetings were required to be held every six months at which time the shareholders authorized the declaration of dividends or the making of calls on the shares. The shareholders were mostly miners who formed groups to sink shafts that were becoming necessary after alluvial gold petered out. Each miner in the group, which could comprise up to 80 members, received a share and shares were also issued to providers of mine materials. These shares could be divided so as to enable the holder to acquire money for living purposes. These interests in shares soon came to be traded at designated locations in the mining

42 *An Act for the Better Regulation of Mining Companies* 18 Vic No 42. This act was often referred to as *'Haines' Act'* after the Chief Secretary who presented it to the Legislative Council. See Birrell, *Staking a Claim*, 36–37.

43 Nathaniel Lindley (later Baron Lindley), *A Treatise on the Law of Companies*, 5th ed. (London 1889), 93–98 described these as a type of company governed under the law of partnership whereby the shareholders agree to share in a mining enterprise in certain proportions and appoint an agent as manager. The 'cost book' was a book in which was contained the agreement entered into by the venturers, the receipts and expenditures of the mine, the names of the shareholders and their accounts with the company and transfers of shares. A feature of such companies was their ability to sell shares on which calls were not paid.

towns from which early stock exchanges developed in Ballarat and Bendigo from the late 1850s.[44]

The concepts of paid up shares, minimum par value and the limiting of liability to the amount unpaid on shares were introduced in the legislation in 1858[45] and simplified in 1860.[46] This legislation represents an early example of the introduction of limited liability to mining companies that occurred almost contemporaneously with its introduction in England and it appears to have encouraged further investment in mining companies. A major impetus to investment in gold mining companies came after a change of government in 1858 which saw a change in policy, led by Melbourne business interests, in favour of mining companies and the encouragement of the inflow of capital into the industry. Mining companies had previously been viewed with suspicion and hostility by individual alluvial miners who saw them as a threat to their livelihoods and the government was responsive to their grievances in the years after the Eureka rebellion. By the late 1850s alluvial mining was in rapid decline. A necessary requirement for the development of mining companies was the granting of large leases which gave greater security of tenure. By the late 1850s stock exchange trading and the utilisation of limited liability mining companies as an investment vehicle had already become well established in Victoria despite the lack of a general incorporation procedure. The system of company registration had developed in an *ad hoc* way and was complex in that companies could be registered under several statutes. The 1855 Haines' Act was based on the cost book system and proved unwieldy and cumbersome, the 1858 Ireland's Act attempted to overcome some of these difficulties but was not widely used largely because it was interpreted so as to impose liability on wealthy shareholders[47] and the 1860 Pyke's Act which was simpler and ultimately the most successful of these legislative attempts to provide for registration of companies and limited liability.

There were many companies whose shares were actively traded and several of them, especially the banks, were quite large in terms of their issued capital. It is clear that there were entrepreneurs who wished to establish pooled investment business organisations and there were also investors seeking investments which offered returns with varying degrees of risk. Many of the investors in mining companies were the miners themselves who sought a stake in the mine

44 Birrell, *Staking a Claim*, 63–64. On page 112 Birrell says that in 1859 there were 27 Bendigo mines, 10 Castlemaine mines and 10 Maldon mines quoted on various stock exchanges.

45 *Mining Associations Act 1858* 21 Vic No 56 was often referred to as '*Ireland's Act*'.

46 '*Pyke's Act*' 24 Vic No 109.

47 Birrell, *Staking a Claim*, 68 quoting Vincent Pyke as describing it in Parliament as 'so cluttered with conditions as to be virtually useless'.

that they were working. A major development which was about to occur was the rapidly increased use of the company form by a large number of mining companies which came to dominate colonial stock exchanges. This development coincided with the introduction of what we can now identify as 'modern' companies legislation.

5 The Transplanting of the English 1862 *Companies Act*

Soon after the consolidation of the Companies legislation in England in 1862,[48] much the same legislation was passed in most Australian colonies.[49] The main features of this legislation were that it allowed for incorporation by lodgement of constituent documents, required associations of more than 20 members to incorporate by prohibiting them from operating as partnerships or unincorporated joint stock companies and introduced limited liability of members. These features were introduced by the 1856 English Act.[50] Within six months after the passing of the 1862 English *Companies Act*, a similar version was introduced into the Victorian Parliament although it took several further months before it was finally passed. Other Australian colonies adopted virtually the same legislation between 1863 and 1874. Prior to this, South Australia had passed legislation in 1847 based on the English *Companies Clauses Consolidation* Act 1845.[51] However this was little used and ultimately repealed in 1864 by legislation based on the English 1862 Act. Western Australia passed the *Joint Stock Ordinance* 1858[52] based on the English *Joint Stock Companies* Act 1856.[53]

As the Victorian *Companies Statute* 1864 and similar colonial legislation were based on the English *Companies Act* 1862, they contained few public disclosure requirements beyond the lodgement of the memorandum and articles of association on registration and subsequent lodgement of the register of members and summary of capital.[54] Information which was not generally available to the public therefore included financial information about the company's activities, the extent to which the company's issued capital had

48 *Companies Act* 1862 (25 & 26 Vic c. 89).

49 *Companies Act* 1863 Qld (27 Vic No. 4); *Companies Statute* 1864 Vic (27 Vic No 190); *Companies Act* 1864 SA (27 & 28 Vic No.13); *Companies Act* 1869 Tas (33 Vic No 22); *Companies Act* 1874 NSW (37 Vic No. 19).

50 *Joint Stock Companies Act* (19 & 20 Vict. c. 47).

51 *Joint Stock Companies Ordinance* 1847 SA 10 & 11 Vic No 5.

52 22 Vic No 6.

53 19 & 20 Vic c 47.

54 *Companies Statute* 1864 ss. 15 and 24.

been paid up in non-cash consideration and the nature and value of this consideration. There was no requirement to disclose details of contracts entered into by the company with its promoters so investors had little opportunity to ascertain related party transactions, conflicts of interest and other circumstances behind company promotions.

Apart from the important exception of the gold mining industry, initially there appeared to be little local demand for the companies legislation and it was not for another 20 years that the company form became widely used in other industries.[55] During the early 1860s the most important sectors for investment in company shares were in banking and mining companies and most large banks were either incorporated by Act of Parliament or were established in Britain. This slow development in the number of company incorporations outside the mining sector is consistent with developments in Britain where it also took several decades after the introduction of companies legislation in 1844 for company registrations to increase appreciably.

The Australian economy and business sectors were much smaller and far less diversified than was the case in Britain. Evidence of the lack of real interest in the introduction of the 1864 companies legislation is shown in the fact that the Act inadvertently repealed the *Mining Partnerships* Act 1860. This was much to the annoyance of mining interests which found the repealed Act far more suitable for their purposes than the later introduced *Companies* Statute which, Hall suggests, was 'obviously tailored to the requirements of relatively large-scale firms operating in England'.[56] This oversight was redressed within six weeks by the passing of a separate Act for mining companies, sometimes referred to as Frazer's Act, and the regulation of mining enterprises in Victoria remained separate from the general companies legislation for the remainder of the century. Even though the *Companies Statute* had little or no impact on most business organisations, it enabled companies, especially in the mining sector, to be incorporated far more easily and with a minimum of compliance requirements, the main one of which was to require annual reports to be lodged. However there was no prescribed form which had to be used and in any case, the enforcement of compliance requirements was generally lax. This ability to readily incorporate and seek listing on a stock exchange was very important for capital raising in the gold mining industry.

The market value of ordinary shares listed on the Melbourne Stock Exchange in 1865, soon after the Victorian *Companies Statute* was introduced, was nearly £9 million, of which bank shares comprised 45 per cent. There were 133

55 Hall, *The Stock Exchange of Melbourne*, 43.
56 Hall, *The Stock Exchange of Melbourne*, 43.

mining companies listed on the Melbourne Stock Exchange with a market value of £3,626,000 compared to 25 non-mining companies with a market value of £5,298,000.[57] In 1884, before the height of the boom of the 1880s, the market value of ordinary shares had increased threefold in twenty years.

This marked increase in the market value of listed shares shows that the transplant of company law legislation and limited liability in particular, in all likelihood, had the effect of encouraging the promotion of stock exchange listed companies and trading in their shares. Certainly the capital markets of the Australian colonies were less developed than their contemporary equivalents in Britain but by the 1860s, there was already significant and growing share market activity, especially in gold mining shares which led to the establishment of several stock exchanges. Blainey noted by way of example that within one year of the introduction of the Victorian *Companies Statute*, the isolated rural district and village of Woods Point had 262 registered companies comprising 13 per cent of Victoria's mining companies.[58] This exponentially increased share market activity fuelled the conversion of many co-operative mining companies into limited companies. The main reason for this adoption of the company form was that it allowed greater flexibility in the capital structure of the enterprise, especially by enabling the issue of large numbers of shares in the event of a company becoming successful. Co-operatives generally had a small number of shares and so gold mining companies registered under the *Companies Statute* were more accessible to large numbers of investors. Hall noted that in some cases the price of a company's shares rose to as much as £3,000 and even at this level there was a considerable volume of transactions.[59] This indicates the considerable wealth of a large number of investors and the strength of demand for speculative investment in gold mining shares at this time.

A characteristic feature of most early gold mining companies was the issue of high par value, partly paid shares. This adopted the prevalent practice in England during the boom in the shares of bank and finance companies of the 1860s, which culminated in the 'Panic of 1866' and famously the collapse of Overend, Gurney & Co Ltd.[60] The ability of gold mining companies to make

57 Hall, *The Stock Exchange of* Melbourne, 58. There seemed to be a similar trend in Canada. Risk, 'The Nineteenth-Century Foundations of the Business Corporation in Ontario', 278–279 noted that 1850 and 1860 Canadian legislation saw 220 incorporations of which 145 were for mining purposes.

58 Blainey, *The Rush that Never Ended*, 71.

59 Hall, *The Stock Exchange of Melbourne*, 61

60 J B Jefferys, 'The Denomination and Character of Shares, 1855–1885', *The Economic History Review* 16 (1946), 45. On the 'Panic of 1866' see Bishop Carleton Hunt, *The Development of the Business Corporation in England 1800–1867* (Harvard, 1936), 148–155.

calls of relatively large amounts was particularly useful to them given the nature of quartz mining with its continual high exploration and developmental costs. In the gold mining industry, very few mines were continuously profitable over a long period of time as deep leads changed course, ran into a neighbouring lease or yields fell, sometimes rising again at greater depth. When a rich ore body was found, this generated speculative activity in the share market. Calls on shares would typically be made by companies which owned the mines where ore bodies were discovered and owners of other mines in the vicinity were also encouraged to further explore their leases and make calls on their shareholders who were often prepared to pay the calls so as to enable further exploration. In most cases the extravagant expectations of investors were not met and the burst of speculation would be replaced by investors adopting a more cautious approach while share prices fell. Companies still required funding to keep sinking shafts so they continued to make calls, the payment of which operated as a dampener on share prices as it reduced the amounts available to purchase other shares and participate in the floats of new companies. The money paid for calls then fell as investors often chose to cut their losses or successful companies funded their development needs from profits. Eventually optimism would return after another rich strike in the vicinity and a new speculative cycle would begin. Hall considered that this cyclical nature of the gold mining industry played a positive role in encouraging investment into a key economic sector and enabled gold output to reach very high levels.[61]

A marked and rapid shift from underground alluvial to deep quartz gold mining took place in the late 1860s and early 1870s. In 1868 quartz mining companies paid a fifth of total dividends paid by all public companies in Victoria. In 1871, this proportion had grown to well over half.[62] This move to deep quartz mining greatly increased the complexity and scale of operations of mining companies and required the application of new technology such as dynamite, invented in the mid-1860s and more sophisticated machinery for pumping water and ventilation. These developments also required companies to be able to efficiently raise more capital and establish suitable management and administrative structures. The ability to tap the market for capital was particularly important because the nature of quartz mining was such that considerable expense had to be incurred and development work undertaken before any profit could be earned and dividends paid. These industry characteristics lent themselves to widely-held listed companies being the most efficient means of financing.

61 Hall, *The Stock Exchange of Melbourne*, 62.

62 Hall, *The Stock Exchange of Melbourne*, 74.

The Victorian mining companies and ultimately the mining industry itself, benefited greatly from the introduction of a general incorporation procedure and limited liability legislation. Co-operatives, which were the previously prevalent form of business organisation in the mining industry when it was smaller scale and mostly engaged in alluvial mining, were inappropriate and a highly inefficient means of conducting quartz mining. They issued relatively few shares and therefore could not raise capital from large numbers of investors and members retained unlimited liability. Co-operatives' shares were not freely transferable on a stock exchange and they were not conducive to the development of professional management structures as the shareholders were often active gold seekers. The practice of issuing partly paid shares was also a further advantage of the limited company form as it was advantageous in the gold mining industry that a company could retain the ability to seek further capital from its shareholders as the need arose especially during the exploration and development phases.

The importance of mining shares, especially in Victoria, gave share markets a highly speculative, high risk character.[63] Hall suggested that an important characteristic of the prosperity of the Victorian economy was the 'speculative spirit and haste to be rich' of Victorian investors in the 1880s.[64] This characteristic was probably already evident some time earlier when speculative share trading became popularised. The growth in market value of listed shares indicates that the introduction of companies legislation made a significant contribution to economic development and the high standard of living in the Australian colonies. The gold mining industry was particularly subject to speculative booms and downturns and a large number of investors necessarily displayed a considerable appetite for risk. This may have encouraged diversification of portfolios of gold mining companies on the expectation that for every successful company there would be several that would become worthless, making the introduction of limited liability a very important feature of the legislation.

Of course, as in England, the vast majority of small businesses outside the mining sector did not adopt the limited liability form but remained sole traders or partnerships. It was not until the 1880s, some 20 years after the introduction of companies legislation, that the number of company registrations significantly increased, although from a low base. McQueen calculated that in 1903 there were over 9,000 registrations of firms (being mostly partnerships) and 157 company registrations. On the basis of these figures he concluded that

63 Colin White, *Mastering Risk: Environment, Markets and Politics in Australian Economic History* (South Melbourne, 1992), 124 and Blainey, *The Rush that Never Ended*, 97–100.

64 Hall, *The Stock Exchange of Melbourne*, 198–199.

partnerships were chosen in more than 98 per cent of businesses as the preferred organisational structure. Part of the explanation he put forward for this slow uptake in the use of the limited liability company form was the 'prejudice and distrust prevailing among respectable people towards the corporate form'.[65] However the argument presented here is that this generally slow uptake does not indicate that the colonies were ill-suited to the introduction of companies legislation. It was only in some industries that the company form of business organization was advantageous. In order to determine whether the introduction of companies legislation was appropriate to the local conditions, it is necessary to consider the degree to which this form was utilised by particular key industries, most notably, the mining industry. It should be noted that there was also a slow uptake of limited liability companies by small businesses in England for several decades after the introduction of limited liability.[66]

6 Mining Companies and No Liability Legislation: 'One of the most radical experiments in company law in the English-speaking world'

While the Australian colonies initially adopted the English companies legislation in almost unchanged form, there was an early development in Victoria which marked a departure from the almost exact adoption of the English legislation. Given the importance of the gold mining industry in Victoria and the necessity of raising capital from large numbers of investors after the development of deep quartz mining, it is not surprising that legislative innovation in Victoria would address a difficulty which arose in relation to the raising of capital by gold mining companies and that it would be passed almost precisely at the time that quartz mining was becoming the dominant mining activity. The following background to the no liability legislation is largely based on the account by Hall.[67]

The cyclical nature of gold mining meant that companies found it relatively easy to raise capital at times of high speculative interest but at other times, it was common for investors to resist payment of calls despite the apparent legal obligation to do so. Companies often found it difficult to pursue shareholders who failed to pay calls and the costs involved often did not justify taking legal

65 McQueen, 'Company Law as Imperialism', 200.

66 Paddy Ireland, 'The Rise of the Limited Liability Company', *International Journal of the Sociology of Law* 12 (1984), 239, 244–245.

67 Hall, *The Stock Exchange of Melbourne*, 75–77. See also Birrell, *Staking a Claim*, 98–100 and Lipton, 'A History of Company Law in Colonial Australia', 818–822.

proceedings. Some shareholders sought to avoid liability to pay calls by use of the common practice of 'dummying'. This meant that a number of shareholders used false names in registering themselves with the company. This served as a type of insurance for shareholders who could choose to pay calls and remain shareholders if prospects looked favourable or in the event the prospects of the company looked bleak, or the company went into liquidation, the shareholder could 'disappear'. This situation created difficulties for the company which still had to meet the claims of creditors despite sometimes large numbers of shareholders reneging on their liabilities and also resulted in situations where shareholders failed to pay calls, but if the company later became profitable, they would pay the outstanding calls and become entitled to dividends and the benefit of a higher share price.

These factors created uncertainties that tended to discourage investment in mining companies because if the company failed, the burden of meeting the company's debts fell disproportionately on those shareholders holding partly paid shares who were traceable or who were wealthy. The technique which was often employed by companies to overcome these difficulties was to include provisions in the memorandum of association (part of the company constitution) to enable the forfeiture of shares on non-payment of a call. The forfeited shares could then either be purchased by existing shareholders or sold at auction. This provided a mining company with greater certainty of supply of capital as it received the proceeds of the sale of forfeited shares and thereby ensured that shareholders who provided calls during times of exploration or uncertainty would gain the benefit of share ownership if the company later became profitable. The practice of forfeiture and sale was an effective response to dummy shareholders and those who refused to pay calls. However doubts were cast on the validity of forfeiture provisions in the company constitution by a decision in the Court of Mines which held that such provisions were contrary to the *Mining Companies Act* of 1864 under which the company was incorporated.[68] The strong political influence of the mining industry is indicated by the almost immediate introduction into Parliament of a Bill aimed at overruling this decision.

This legal uncertainty remained for another year before the introduction of the no liability legislation which sought to formalise the practice of forfeiture of partly paid shares upon failure to pay calls.[69] This legislation still operates

68 Hall, *The Stock Exchange of Melbourne*, 76 referred to an 1869 decision of the Sandhurst Court of Mines in *Nash v Annabella Company* where the forfeiture provisions were held to be invalid. This decision was affirmed on appeal in the Chief Court of Mines. See Birrell, *Staking a Claim*, 66–67 for a description of the legislation which established Courts of Mines and their roles.

69 *Mining Companies Law Amendment* Act 1871.

today[70] so that shareholders of mining companies registered as no liability companies under the *Corporations Act* 2001 s 112 and its predecessors, are not contractually liable to pay calls, but if a call is unpaid the shares are forfeited and must be offered for sale at an advertised public auction. The effect of this legislation was to extend limited liability to unpaid share capital. From a creditor's point of view, this was a significant disadvantage especially if the company had issued shares of high par value and large unpaid amounts. The practice of companies issuing high par value shares was already becoming less common both in Britain and Australia as lower par value shares attracted more investors and enhanced the marketability of shares.

The *Mining Companies Act* 1871 introduced a stricter regulatory regime for mining companies in Victoria than that which applied to trading companies under the *Companies Statute* 1864. Mining companies were subject to more stringent disclosure requirements such as having to prepare a report of the company's prospects and assets and liabilities before a general meeting. Books of account were required to be kept and made available for inspection by shareholders and creditors and half yearly statements had to be lodged. Various criminal offences were created for breaches of duty and making false statements. These legislative provisions imposed a more rigorous statutory regulatory environment than existed in Britain and elsewhere in Australia and reflected a willingness of the Victorian legislature to adapt the transplanted legislation in innovative ways that met the needs of the business community. These stricter investor protection requirements reflected the fact that mining companies dominated the share market lists and they had the widest spread of shareholders. Despite these statutory investor protection provisions, in reality the government offices charged with responsibility for administering the legislation were largely incapable of ensuring widespread compliance with these legislative requirements.

The introduction of the no liability legislation in 1871 coincided with a period of intense speculation surrounding the sudden dominance of the Bendigo quartz mines which resulted in a marked increase in gold mining company registrations and investment. Share ownership was widely held across a wide cross section of society and the financing of Victorian gold mines depended on this domestic speculative investment as there was relatively little British investment in Australian gold mines before the late 1880s.[71] The total nominal capital of new registrations increased nearly three-fold in one year from £6

70 *Corporations* Act ss 112, 254M(2) and 254Q.

71 Blainey, *The Rush that Never Ended*, 100–102.

million in 1870 to nearly £17 million in 1871.[72] In the first 10 months of 1870, 765 new companies were registered at Bendigo and calls of £200,000 were made.[73] Either the legislation encouraged the increased capital raising activity or reflected the growing importance of the industry to the Victorian economy or as seems most likely, an interaction of both factors. Certainly extreme fluctuations in investment in the mining industry occurred from time to time and the timing of a speculative boom increased the urgency of legislation designed to assist capital raising. The wild fluctuations of the speculative mining boom can be seen in the capital raised in 1872 by new mining company registrations falling back to near 1870 levels. This raises the strong possibility that the boom in 1871 was directly related to the introduction of the no liability legislation or at the very least it significantly encouraged mining company investment.

Hall argued that the no liability legislation encouraged a regular supply of investment in an inherently risky but very important industry and he thought its continued existence for more than 140 years confirms its success in achieving this objective.[74] The relative importance of payment of calls in the gold mining industry can be seen from the fact that dividends paid by Bendigo gold mining companies in 1871 and 1872 amounted to nearly £1 million while calls made were a little over £600,000.[75] The weight of this overhang of unpaid liabilities operated as a dampener to new fundraising especially if it is borne in mind that relatively few companies were sufficiently successful to pay dividends but almost all issued partly paid shares and made calls when finance was required. Blainey described the no liability legislation as 'one of the most radical experiments in company law in the English-speaking world' and 'Victoria's revolutionary answer to the dearth of capital for mining'.[76] He considered that this legislation encouraged wealthy investors who had previously been suspicious of mining, to invest in gold mining companies. Birrell described the legislation as 'an excellent example of lateral thinking to come up with a novel and workable solution to a difficult problem'.[77]

McLean argued that the institutions which were in place ensured that resource abundance became a blessing rather than a curse and at least partly

72 Hall, *The Stock Exchange of Melbourne*, 81. Blainey, *The Rush that Never Ended*, 97 noted that Anthony Trollope said that Bendigo's vice was not drunkenness but share speculation. The speculative boom in Bendigo is described by Blainey, *The Rush that Never Ended*, 74–76; and Birrell, *Staking a Claim*, 115–116.

73 Birrell, *Staking a Claim*, 117.

74 Hall, *The Stock Exchange of Melbourne*, 77.

75 Hall, *The Stock Exchange of Melbourne*, 89–90.

76 Blainey, *The Rush that Never Ended*, 99.

77 Birrell, *Staking a Claim*, 99.

explained the economic success of the Australian colonies during the second half of the nineteenth century.[78] The introduction of companies legislation and the concept of the no liability company can be seen as beneficial institutional factors which encouraged investment in the gold mining industry. The decline of the mining sector after the turn of the century may be explained by the replacement of a large number of relatively small companies financed by investors who had a high appetite for risk with a smaller number of larger, more risk averse companies.[79]

McQueen regarded the practice of 'dummying' by mining company shareholders as providing an example of regulatory failure because there were no administrative means of preventing such malpractice. He argued that the introduction of no liability legislation was a direct result of this failure of enforcement and inability to ensure compliance.[80] While the practice of dummying may have been more common in Australia than in Britain, this may have been due to local factors such as a large immigrant population that was therefore more transitory and a large geographic area from which investors were drawn, rather than regulatory failure. In this era when there were relatively low expectations of government regulation and enforcement action, it would not have been expected that it was a role of government administrative and regulatory agencies to ensure that the members' register of a company was accurate and false names were not used. It was, and still is, a private matter for companies to enforce calls made on their shares. It is therefore an incomplete explanation of the no liability legislation to attribute its introduction to a regulatory failure to ensure all shareholders used their real names or could be readily found in the event of non-payment of a call. As discussed above, the introduction of this legislation coincided with a boom in gold mining share market activity and probably played a beneficial and significant role in encouraging this growth of investment in a critically important colonial export industry which depended for finance upon local listed company capital raising.

78 Ian McLean, 'Why was Australia so Rich?', *Explorations in Economic History* 44 (2007), 635, 637–639. McLean noted that Australia's per capita GDP was considerably higher than that of the US between 1870 and 1890.

79 Paul A. David and Gavin Wright, 'Increasing Returns and the Genesis of American Resource Abundance', *Industrial and Corporate Change* 6 (1997), 221 argued that nineteenth century US and Australian mineral law encouraged mineral exploitation through maintaining exploration incentives, respect for law and minimizing disputation. The authors pointed out at 235 that Australia was an underachiever in minerals other than gold in the twentieth century suggesting this was due to the absence of 'the atmosphere of buoyant expectations about major new discoveries'.

80 McQueen, 'Company Law as Imperialism', 196–197, 202.

7 The Reforms of the 1890s

The Victorian investor protection reforms of the 1890s were a response to the frauds and malpractices which became apparent during the boom of the 1880s and depression of the 1890s. The latter half of the 1880s saw a major speculative boom, especially in Melbourne, in shares of land companies and finance companies which speculated in mostly urban land, as well as mining shares in companies operating at Broken Hill and in Queensland and Tasmania. The land and mining booms were fuelled by heavy investment in public infrastructure works such as railways, irrigation works, roads, tramways, water and sewerage. The land boom was associated with building activity which saw Melbourne's suburbs greatly expand as the public transport system stretched out and the central business district was substantially rebuilt with what were at the time high rise buildings. The most prominent land speculators, described as 'land boomers', were several prominent politicians.[81] This unprecedented investment activity demanded more capital than was locally available and was financed by large amounts of British capital inflow attracted by higher interest rates than were available in Britain, which flowed into both the public and private sectors.

The boom of the 1880s brought about a substantial increase in the number of Victorian registered companies. From 1871 there had been two separate administrative schemes under which companies were incorporated and regulated. Mining companies fell under the jurisdiction of the *Mining Companies Act* 1871 (Vic) and other companies, described as 'trading' companies were formed and regulated under the *Companies Statute*. Trading company registrations were below 100 per year until the late 1880s when they jumped to 145 in 1887 and 343 in 1888 of which about a half were land and finance companies.[82] Relatively few companies were engaged in manufacturing which remained undeveloped and mostly in the hands of small sole proprietorships or partnerships. The activity of land companies was typically to purchase large tracts of agricultural land on the fringes of cities and then seek to subdivide and auction housing lots. The scale of these activities was largest in Melbourne where the population increase was greatest. Blainey considered that there was also more of a gambling culture in Melbourne than in the other large Australian city, Sydney.

81 The best known history of the personalities and their activities of this period is Michael Cannon, *The Land Boomers: the Complete Illustrated History* (Carlton, Vic, 1995).

82 McQueen, 'Limited Liability Company Legislation', 50.

> That Melbourne's land boom of the 1880s was wilder and more disastrous than Sydney's may partly be explained by Victorian gamblers turning from waning gold mines to a newer and faster set of dice, blocks of city and suburban land.[83]

In 1888, there were approximately 1500 companies registered under the *Companies Statute* in Victoria.[84] This figure understates the size of the corporate business sector because a large number of companies carrying on business in Victoria were incorporated in Britain or other Australian colonies. The value of shares listed on the Melbourne Stock Exchange increased from £7 million in 1865 to £65 million in 1889.[85] This nearly ten-fold increase in 24 years reflects the rapidly expanding economy and increasing maturity of the share market of colonial Victoria in the period following the introduction of the companies legislation. This increase in share market activity was particularly pronounced in 1888 when share turnover was three times that in 1887 which was itself a boom year.[86]

During this period of strong growth in the number and value of listed companies, the administration of companies by government regulatory authorities was haphazard by modern standards. McQueen drew attention to the *ad hoc* and undeveloped nature of colonial administrative bodies charged with the responsibility of administering the companies legislation. He put forward the argument that the introduction of limited liability legislation in the Australian colonies was a failure largely because of the absence of effective regulatory structures with enforcement arms to prevent malpractices.[87] The Board of Trade in England had a long history of overseeing commercial legislation with a specialised and experienced bureaucracy. In Australia, there were relatively few registered companies so administrative arrangements were made almost as an afterthought, being added to the responsibilities of existing functionaries. In South Australia and Queensland, administrative responsibility over companies was given to Masters of the Supreme Court, in New South Wales, it was the responsibility of the Registrar-General and in Victoria for a time, it was

83 Blainey, *The Rush that Never Ended*, 100.

84 Ernst Arthur Boehm, *Prosperity and Depression in Australia 1887–1897* (London, 1971), 248; John Waugh, 'Company Law and the Crash of the 1890s in Victoria', UNSW *Law Journal* 15 (1992), 358.

85 Hall, *The Stock Exchange of Melbourne*, 37, 169.

86 Waugh, 'Company Law and the Crash of the 1890s in Victoria', 357 quoting *The Argus* 1 January 1889.

87 McQueen, 'Company Law as Imperialism', 194–195.

the responsibility of the Titles Office.[88] Lacking expertise and resources due to inadequate funding, these functionaries concentrated on raising revenue from incorporations and lodgement fees rather than the more expensive and difficult task of enforcing compliance. This was also much the case in England where non-compliance with lodgement requirements was very widespread in the nineteenth century. The role of nineteenth century government regulators was far less developed than is the case today. Commercial activity was then largely seen as a private contractual matter with little role for government regulation including investor and creditor protection.

The severity of the depression in the 1890s and the losses suffered by many investors led to strong calls for legislative responses to address the perceived deficiencies in company law regulation.[89] Share market activity on the Melbourne Stock Exchange after the banking crisis in 1893 was significantly below that which occurred in the late 1880s and took some years after that to recover. The market value of ordinary shares listed on the Melbourne Stock Exchange declined from £65 million in 1889 to £47 million in 1900 and the number of listed companies declined during this period from 231 to 130.[90] Bank reconstructions, the prospects of paying calls and the bad experiences of shareholders discouraged investment in bank shares for a number of years and the dominant investment activity during the period between 1893 and 1900 was in mining, especially in companies operating in the newly discovered gold fields of Western Australia and copper mines of Tasmania. This compensated for the fall in silver prices which led to a temporary decline in the value of Broken Hill shares in the early 1890s.[91] Apart from high risk mining speculation, Hall noted that local private enterprise was hesitant and there was little capital formation financed through the stock exchange.[92] This background gave impetus for the introduction of highly innovative investor protection reforms that attempted to increase investment in listed companies.

A number of reform proposals were passed by the Victorian Legislative Council but were blocked in the other House of Parliament, the Legislative Assembly. This was probably because the Legislative Assembly was dominated by some of the most prominent land speculators, Matthew Davies who was Speaker, James Munro, who was Premier and Thomas Bent who was also

88 McQueen, 'Company Law as Imperialism', 195.

89 Waugh, 'Company Law and the Crash of the 1890s in Victoria', 381 footnote 175. See this article generally for a detailed discussion of the deficiencies of company law in addressing the malpractices of this period.

90 Hall, *The Stock Exchange of Melbourne*, 230.

91 Hall, *The Stock Exchange of Melbourne*, 221–240.

92 Hall, *The Stock Exchange of Melbourne*, 233.

Speaker and later became Premier.[93] The presence of leading politicians on the boards of some land companies gave an air of what turned out to be entirely undeserved respectability to these companies and also appeared to make the Parliament captive or at least receptive to the wishes of these men. Boehm quoted *The Economist* which commented that the need for law reform relating to land companies 'has been frequently pointed out, but it has to be confessed that Parliament has hitherto shown no disposition to encourage any efforts in that direction. Too many members have, in fact, become involved in company promoting'.[94]

During this period the *Voluntary Liquidation Act* 1891 was passed in Victoria at the time of a severe run on building societies and the collapses of a number of land companies. A number of these companies were threatened with compulsory liquidation under which a creditor could apply to the court for an order winding up the company on the grounds of its insolvency and if the order was granted, the court appointed a liquidator with powers to investigate misconduct by the directors.

The *Voluntary Liquidation Act* made it difficult to put a company (including a building society) into compulsory liquidation against the wishes of its directors by requiring a majority of creditors by number and value of debts to consent to the winding up proceeding in cases where the company was not already being wound up voluntarily.[95] Where the company was in the process of a voluntary winding up and had no creditors outside Victoria, a court order to wind up the company could not be made without the consent of one third of creditors by number and value of debts. Where the company did have creditors outside Victoria, the proportion of creditors required to approve a court order for winding up was one quarter by number and value of debts.[96] The lower creditor threshold where there were creditors outside Victoria was intended to placate British investors.[97]

---

93 A number of other prominent Parliamentarians who were directors of companies controlled by Davies were James Bell (Minister of Defence) and James Balfour. Other directors included Sir George Baden Powell who was a member of the British Parliament and Sir Graham Berry, a former Premier of Victoria and Agent-General in London for the Colony of Victoria.

94 Boehm, *Prosperity and Depression in Australia*, 266 footnote 1.

95 *Voluntary Liquidation Act* 1891 s 4.

96 *Voluntary Liquidation Act* 1891 s 3.

97 John Waugh, 'The Centenary of the *Voluntary Liquidation Act* 1891', *Melbourne University Law Review* 18 (1991), 170, 172. An example of the operation of the Act is provided at p. 173 in *Re Phillip Island Company Limited* (1892) 13 ALT 269 where a creditor bank which was owed £9343 was prevented from petitioning for the compulsory winding up of the debtor company in the face of opposition from other creditors who were owed £628.

The Preamble of the Act stated its purpose as being 'to prevent injury and loss to creditors by the compulsory winding up of companies and building societies against the will and interest of creditors'. The Attorney-General William Shiels described the object of the legislation as being to prevent the loss arising from compulsory liquidation by the actions of 'one litigious, cantankerous or mischievous person, or it might be a person simply bent on plunder and rapine'.[98] This seems to contemplate unworthy winding up applications being brought by creditors who sought to acquire a company's assets cheaply in a sharply falling market in circumstances where the company could realistically regain its solvency in the not too distant future and thereby ensure a better return to creditors as a whole. While other attempts to introduce remedial legislation over several years were unsuccessful, this statute was brought into the Legislative Assembly without notice and immediately passed both Houses within a day with only minor technical amendments. The Act commenced from its date of passage.

The *Voluntary Liquidation Act* was widely condemned by the business community who were not provided the opportunity to have input into the legislation. In practical terms it was difficult to meet the creditor approval requirements so that the creditor safeguards built into compulsory liquidation were effectively suspended. The main effect of the Act in preventing compulsory liquidations was that it enabled companies to go into voluntary liquidation without court supervision or control. This enabled greater secrecy and concealment of mismanagement, breaches of duty and fraud and the liquidator could be appointed from the directors or their associates who had most to conceal. It greatly reduced the role of creditors as supervision of voluntary liquidations was with shareholders and it took away the protection of court supervision and the possibility of binding compromises. At the conclusion of the liquidation, the books and records of the company could be destroyed if so directed by the shareholders' meeting.[99] This legislation can be seen as an example of changes to transplanted law in response to local conditions and circumstances where the change was brought about by political pressure from vested interest groups who sought to protect themselves at the expense of the broader commercial community. The legislation may ultimately have been self-defeating in that far from encouraging greater investment, it may have further undermined fragile investor confidence which was to be further shaken with the bank collapses over the next few years.

---

98 Trevor Sykes, *Two Centuries of Panic: a History of Corporate Collapses in Australia* (St Leonards, NSW, 1988), 151.

99 *Companies Act* 1890 (Vic) s 140.

At about the same time, New South Wales also passed legislation which was aimed at assisting companies to arrive at compromises with their creditors and reconstructions.[100] Where a numerical majority of creditors holding three quarters of a company's liabilities agreed to an arrangement with the company, this arrangement was binding on all creditors. This had the effect of preventing a single or small number of creditors forcing the company into compulsory liquidation. The provisions of this legislation were based on similar English legislation[101] and were more widely accepted than the counterpart Victorian legislation.[102]

After a prolonged period of deadlock between the Victorian Houses of Parliament, a change of government in 1894 resulted in Isaac Isaacs[103] becoming Attorney-General with a strong commitment to company law reform to address the misconduct which arose during the land boom and crash. He introduced a comprehensive Companies Bill in 1894 and after the usual protracted debates and deadlock between the Houses, it was ultimately passed in a reduced form at the end of 1896.[104] Isaacs introduced the legislation to deal with the types of cases of 'deliberate and widespread fraud' which were evident during the period leading up to the crash and which caused 'widespread ruin upon the people'.[105] This indicates the broad based nature of share ownership throughout the community and the political influence of small shareholders. The main impediment to the passage of the legislation was in the unelected Legislative Council where, according to *The Age*, 30 out of 48 members were themselves directors.[106]

The 1896 legislation introduced a number of modern disclosure requirements and prohibitions such as compulsory audit by certified auditors under a statutory duty to verify the accuracy of the accounts; requirements for sending to shareholders and filing an audited balance sheet in the prescribed form; prohibitions on misleading statements in prospectuses, the use of misleading company names (the use of the word 'bank' had mislead many land company

---

100 *Joint Stock Companies Arrangement Act* 1891 (NSW).

101 *Joint Stock Companies Arrangement Act* 1870 (UK).

102 Boehm, *Prosperity and Depression in Australia*, 268.

103 Later Sir Isaac Isaacs, Governor-General of Australia and Justice of the High Court of Australia.

104 *Companies Act* 1896 No 1482. Waugh, above 'Company Law and the Crash of the 1890s in Victoria', 382–385 described the passage of the legislation through the Houses and the various political alignments which formed during the debates on the legislation.

105 *Victoria Parliamentary Debates* 1896 Volume 81, 123.

106 Waugh, 'Company Law and the Crash of the 1890s in Victoria', 383 citing *The Age* 16 March 1896.

depositors and investors) and loans by a company secured by its own shares; and detailed winding up provisions which gave creditors greater protection.

Some of the provisions of the 1896 legislation adopted English legislation. This included s 38 from the 1867 *Companies Act* (UK) which required prospectuses to contain details of contracts entered into by the company with its directors and promoters and the *Directors' Liability Act* 1890 (UK) which overruled *Derry v Peek*[107] by allowing an action in deceit by shareholders against directors whose misstatements in a prospectus fell short of fraud. Most of the disclosure provisions of the 1896 *Companies Act* came from the recommendations of the 1895 report of the English Davey Committee. It is a strong reflection on the willingness of the Victorian Parliament to improve its company law regulation and respond to calls to overcome weaknesses apparent in the land boom period that its legislation contained the first modern disclosure provisions some ten years before similar requirements such as compulsory filing of balance sheets were incorporated into the English legislation. The concept of the proprietary (private) company was introduced and such companies were exempted from laying an audited balance sheet before members in general meeting. A proprietary company was defined as having no more than 25 members, not being able to borrow from non-members and meeting certain prohibitions on raising funds from the public. It also had to have the word 'proprietary' in its name. This distinction between public and proprietary companies still remains in the Australian companies legislation.

The *Companies Act* 1896 was a very progressive and far-reaching response to the abuses of directors and promoters during the previous decade and marked a significant change in regulatory policy towards greater investor protection after the relatively *laissez-faire* approach of the English legislation which had prevailed since 1856. It sought to guard the public 'on the one hand against ignorance and on the other hand against misrepresentation'.[108] A strong criticism of the legislation was that it did not apply to mining companies when they were the most common type of company formed at the time.[109] The exclusion of mining companies was repealed in 1910. These reforms were enacted because of the spectacular nature of the boom and bust which occurred in Victoria. The consequent widespread losses throughout the community had the effect of galvanising political support for the reforms put forward by Isaacs.

107 (1889) 14 App Cas 337.

108 Isaac Isaacs, *Victoria Parliamentary Debates* 1896 Volume 81, 124.

109 Isaac Isaacs, *Victoria Parliamentary Debates* 1896 Volume 81, 150.

8 Conclusion

The Victorian corporate law transplant experience in the 1860s came at a time of strong investment demand in the mining sector. Although the institutions necessary to encourage and facilitate company formation and investment were already established to some extent before the introduction of the English limited liability companies legislation in Victoria in 1864, the introduction of this legislation provided a stimulus to company formations, capital raising, widespread share ownership and the development of several stock exchanges throughout the colony. The economic success of Victoria in the second half of the nineteenth century can at least partially be attributed to the abundance of gold. However resources may be a curse as well as a blessing. Victoria also possessed 'good' institutions that replicated British institutions characterised by strong property rights, responsive law making and checks on government power. The transplant of English company law also provided incentives and opportunities for capital raising and investment so that the wealth generated by the extraction of gold was widely distributed rather than concentrated in the hands of a wealthy few.

The transplant of English company law in Victoria was successful because there was a preparedness of local legislators to adapt the transplanted law to suit local conditions. This can be seen in the introduction of the no liability company to assist the gold mining industry to raise capital and the investor protection provisions that were introduced in response to the inadequacies of the law that became apparent in the boom and bust of the late 1880s and early 1890s.

Acknowledgments

I am grateful to Richard Mitchell for his insightful comments and stimulating discussions which were of invaluable assistance in the writing of this paper.

Company Law Transplants and Change in Colonial Southeast Asia

Petra Mahy

1 Introduction[1]

Company law, for all that it establishes a technical instrument for the creation of business entities with legal personality, limited liability and asset shielding, is nonetheless an important lens through which to examine the exercise of, and resistance to, state power and the development of various economic ideologies.[2] Many studies of the early evolution of company law in 'origin' jurisdictions such as England and France have alerted us to the politically contested nature of this area of law, particularly during the period when the principle of the freedom of incorporation without overt interference from the state was being established.[3] Only relatively recently has there been a growth in studies which have analysed the 'transplant' and subsequent development of company law in colonial settings with such sensitivity to politics. Some of this scholarship has been framed as a corrective to the general assumption that colonial company law transplants were merely uninteresting copies of the law of the metropolis[4] or locating sources of underdevelopment in colonial company

1 Much of the archival work for this paper was conducted under the Australian Research Council Discovery Project titled 'Legal Origins: The Impact of Different Legal Systems on the Regulation of the Business Enterprise in the Asia-Pacific Region' (DP1095060) led by Richard Mitchell, Ian Ramsay, Sean Cooney and Peter Gahan. I also thank Jonathan P. Sale for his assistance in facilitating my research in the Philippines, as well as the organisers and participants of the workshop on 'The Influence of Colonies on Commercial Law and Practice' held in Fiskars, Finland, 7–8 January 2016.

2 See generally Iain Ramsay, 'The Politics of Commercial Law', *Wisconsin Law Review* (2001), 565–575.

3 See, e.g. Charles E. Freedeman, 'Joint-Stock Business Organization in France, 1807–1867', *The Business History Review* 39:2 (1965), 184–204; Michael Lobban, 'Corporate Identity and Limited Liability in France and England 1825–67', *Anglo-American Law Review* 25 (1996), 397–440; Ron Harris, 'Political Economy, Interest Groups, Legal Institutions and the Repeal of the Bubble Act in 1825', *The Economic History Review* 50:4 (1997), 675–696. More generally, see Ramsay, 'The Politics of Commercial Law', 565–575.

4 See, e.g., Phillip Lipton, 'A History of Company Law in Colonial Australia: Economic Development and Legal Evolution', *Melbourne University Law Review* 31 (2007), 805–836; Rob McQueen, 'The Flowers of Progress: Corporations Law in the Colonies', *Griffith Law Review* 17 (2008), 383–412.

 | DOI:10.1163/9789004443075_010

law.[5] Meanwhile, other papers have been written in direct critical response to the 'legal origins' thesis of the late 1990s.[6] The 'legal origins' theorists had implicitly assumed that transplants of company law had occurred in a straightforward and uncontested manner during the colonial era such that it was possible to causally link levels of shareholder protection in the present to the legal family of a country's former coloniser.[7]

These studies of company law development in different colonial contexts are posed around a number of interrelated questions: To what extent did colonial company law function as a tool of imperialism to facilitate both state and private exploitation of resources? To what extent was the initial transplant a direct copy of the law of the metropolis, and then to what extent did any subsequent changes continue to follow the pattern of the domestic law of the colonial power? To what extent was the law contested by local populations and/or adapted for their use? And further, was the law actually used in the colony and, if so, by which population groups? Beyond these historical points of interest, some of the studies are also concerned with more general theoretical questions about the evolution of law, the effects of legal transplants and any ongoing influence of styles of regulation based on legal family.

Providing a valuable foundation for such theoretical discussions, Pistor et al. (2002) argued that 'good' company law is not law which necessarily provides the highest levels of shareholder protection, but rather it is law which develops incrementally over time and is highly responsive to local social and economic contexts.[8] Their study was based on four 'origin' jurisdictions (France, Germany, England and the United States) and six 'transplant' jurisdictions (Chile, Colombia, Israel, Japan, Malaysia and Spain). Tracing company law evolution in each of these countries from the earliest point of introduction, they found that transplanted company law was unlikely to follow the same pattern of development as occurred in the country where it originated. Rather, transplanted company law tended, particularly in the early years following

5 Robert Charles Means, *Underdevelopment and the Development of Law: Corporations and Corporation Law in Nineteenth-Century Colombia* (Chapel Hill: The University of North Carolina Press, 1980).

6 See, e.g., Mariana Pargendler, 'Politics in the Origins: The Making of Corporate Law in Nineteenth Century Brazil', *American Journal of Comparative Law* 60 (2012), 805–850; Umakanth Varottil, 'The Evolution of Company Law in Post-Colonial India: From Transplant to Autochthony', *American University International Law Review* 31:2 (2016), 253–325.

7 Rafael La Porta et al., 'Legal Determinants of External Finance', *The Journal of Finance* 52:3 (1997), 1131–1150; Rafael La Porta et al., 'Law and Finance', *Journal of Political Economy* 106:6 (1998), 1113–1155.

8 Katharina Pistor et al., 'The Evolution of Corporate Law: A Cross-Country Comparison', *University of Pennsylvania Journal of International Economic Law* 23 (2002), 791–871.

the transplant, to undergo patterns of either legal stagnation or of erratic change – both of which, they argued, indicated a lack of connection between the demands of law users and the responses of legislative drafters. Pistor et al. noted that the law in such transplant countries is likely to have only recently shown signs of adaptability to local political and economic change. Of course, more general comparative law scholarship on legal transplants also notes that laws often behave very differently in a new environment compared to in their place of origin.[9]

Importantly, for Pistor et al., it was the fact of the law being transplanted from elsewhere that was key, rather than the mode or context of the transplant. So, for instance, they make no distinction between Spain, Chile and Colombia despite the obvious fact that the latter two countries were once colonies of the former. A separate set of research has suggested that 'colonial history' is significant,[10] and more specifically that different types of colony determined the political and legal institutions which were put in place and their long-term legacies. Acemoglu et al. (2001) notably drew a distinction between 'settler' and 'extractive' colonies and argued that the legal institutions established in extractive colonies were inferior to those of settler colonies.[11] Lange (2004), drawing on data about 33 former British colonies, reasoned that it was whether direct or indirect rule was used that mattered to the establishment of legal-administrative institutions.[12] Daniels et al. (2011), in a study of eight formerly British-controlled territories, found that the quality of legal institutions depended on the degree to which the indigenous population was represented in legislative bodies and to which indigenous legal principles were integrated into a localised jurisprudence.[13] The combined effect of this group of studies suggests that

9 See, e.g., Gunther Teubner, 'Legal Irritants: Good Faith in British Law or How Unifying Law Ends up in New Divergences', *Modern Law Review* 61:1 (1998), 11–32; William Twining, 'Diffusion of Law: A Global Perspective', *Journal of Legal Pluralism & Unofficial Law* 49 (2004), 1–45.

10 Daniel M. Klerman et al., 'Legal Origin or Colonial History?' *Journal of Legal Analysis* 3:2 (2011), 379–409.

11 Daron Acemoglu, Simon Johnson and James A. Robinson, 'The Colonial Origins of Comparative Development: An Empirical Investigation', *The American Economic Review* 91:5 (2001), 1369–1401. See also Daron Acemoglu, Simon Johnson and James A. Robinson, 'The Colonial Origins of Comparative Development: An Empirical Investigation: Reply', *The American Economic Review* 102:6 (2012), 3077–3110.

12 Matthew Lange, 'British Colonial Legacies and Political Development', *World Development* 32:6 (2004), 905–922.

13 Ronald J. Daniels, Michael J. Trebilcock and Lindsey D. Carson, 'The Legacy of Empire: The Common Law Inheritance and Commitments to Legality in Former British Colonies', *American Journal of Comparative Law* 59 (2011), 111–178.

more nuanced studies of company law transplants in colonial contexts may provide evidence towards revision and refinement of Pistor's et al.'s framework. This is particularly the case given their emphasis on the role of law users in relation to adaptability of the law, and arguably the importance of taking account of the identity and position of those law users within the context of the hierarchical systems of power that characterised colonial regimes.

Drawing on these theoretical considerations, this Chapter presents a comparative study of the evolution of company law in colonial Southeast Asia. It continues and extends my earlier individual research on the evolution of company law in the Netherlands Indies[14] and collaborative research on British Malaya (focussing on the Straits Settlements and Federated Malay States).[15] Here, I add newly gathered historical material on the Philippines during the Spanish and American eras to round out the comparison.

These neighbouring territories, which form present-day Indonesia, Malaysia, Singapore and the Philippines, provide particularly interesting subjects for comparison given that they share some basic similarities in terms of geographical region and colonial trajectories. In each place, colonialism developed originally through trade and control of relatively small trading enclaves. In later phases, the colonial powers extended their governmental control over increasingly wider territory in order to pursue local production through commercial plantations, mining and some early manufacturing. In other words, these were all 'extractive' colonies, and not 'settler' colonies.[16] At the same time, each territory was colonised by a different European (and in the case of the Philippines, also American) power which bequeathed distinct legal legacies to their respective colonies. Therefore, the choice of these countries allows me to begin to test the above-mentioned historical and theoretical questions about the evolution of company law – at least in relation to extractive colonies.

14 Petra Mahy, 'The Evolution of Company Law in Indonesia: An Exploration of Legal Innovation and Stagnation', *American Journal of Comparative Law* 61 (2013), 377–432.

15 Petra Mahy and Ian Ramsay, 'Legal Transplants and Adaptation in a Colonial Setting: Company Law in British Malaya', *Singapore Journal of Legal Studies* (2014), 123–150.

16 Note that Singapore was largely 'settled' as a result of the British presence (and indeed Daniels et al., 'The Legacy of Empire' classified Singapore as a settler colony), but the majority of settlers were not of British extraction. Singapore (as part of the Straits Settlements) was also closely tied politically and economically with the Federated Malay States which were far more straightforwardly classified as being 'extractive'.

2 A Note on Comparative Approach

Horowitz (1994) argued that developing systemic explanations of legal change should be high on the agenda of legal scholarship. And, to develop such explanations of legal change, he advocated taking a comparative approach because when systems are juxtaposed then changes that may appear natural in one system can begin to seem curious.[17] In other words, paying attention to individual incidents of change and longer-term trajectories across legal systems can permit identification of patterns and eventually theory building about legal evolution.

Pistor et al. devised a system for qualitatively mapping change in company law by using an open-ended list of legal indicators covering core areas of the law.[18] In determining the scope of this list of indicators, for practical reasons they chose to limit themselves to the main content of major company law statutes rather than seeking to include all possible laws that might be functionally relevant to shareholder protection. Using these indicators, they then traced changes in the law and noted the allocation of control rights over company affairs among different interests including shareholders, management, creditors, labour and the state. This approach aimed to depart from the traditional pre-occupation with the principal-agency problem in company law in order to include these other relevant parties. They also observed whether the rules allocating these control rights were mandatory or optional, and whether complementary control devices had developed in response to problems associated with greater flexibility. Pistor et al. limited their sources to formal statutory law and justified this on the basis that company law is mostly statutory in nature.

For the research that underpins this Chapter, I have adopted an approach inspired by that of Pistor et al. by using a similar open-ended list of key indicators on the core areas of company law in order to map legal change consistently across jurisdictions, to keep systematic track of the timing of legal changes, and to pay attention to the allocation of control rights in relation to these indicators. Using open-ended indicators is necessary in order to include any significant idiosyncratic developments that may not otherwise be captured. My approach in this Chapter, however, is much more historically contextualised than that of Pistor et al. and pays far greater attention to political and economic triggers for change (or lack of change). To do this, I draw on a wide range of primary and secondary materials as available. From this material,

17 Donald L. Horowitz, 'The Qur'an and the Common Law: Islamic Law Reform and the Theory of Legal Change', *American Journal of Comparative Law* 42 (1994), 233–293, 240.

18 Pistor et al., 'The Evolution of Corporate Law', 801–804.

I have pieced together detailed contextualised historical accounts of company law change in each jurisdiction, paying particular attention to where any changes were intended to respond to the local context. Like Pistor et al. I confine my definition of company law to the content of the major legislation that is defined as company/corporations law in a particular jurisdiction. In other words, this is a law-centred approach, where I start with the law and then look to political and economic developments to explain incidents of legal change. Of course, in electing to undertake a comparison, and to meet the practical space limits of this Chapter, I have necessarily considerably reduced the complexity and detail of the original research and only present brief overviews of each jurisdiction here.

The following sections of the Chapter trace the transplants and change in company law in the Netherlands Indies, British Malaya and then the Spanish and American Philippines.

3 Company Law in the Netherlands Indies: Race and Legal Pluralism

The Dutch expansion of power in the Indonesian archipelago began with the arrival of the United Dutch East India Company (*Verenigde Oostindische Compagnie* (VOC)) which traded there from 1602 to 1796. The VOC established various trading posts, including its main fortified base in Batavia, founded in 1619. The VOC, for the most part, was only interested in trade and not in governance and simply adapted to and used the existing political systems. The company was declared bankrupt in 1799, and subsequently the Dutch government assumed control of VOC holdings and began to extend colonial control throughout the archipelago – a process that was still ongoing in the early 20th century. Except for the British Interregnum (1811–1816), the Dutch retained control of the archipelago up until the Japanese occupation during World War II. Indonesia declared its independence in 1945, and the Dutch finally withdrew in 1949.

Dutch colonial economic policy progressed from the Cultivation System (*Cultuurstelsel*) introduced in 1830 which involved state-induced export crop production throughout the island of Java, through to the 'Liberal Policy' of 1870 which permitted private investment for the first time, resulting particularly in the development of tobacco and other plantations in eastern Sumatra. The Dutch colonial regime was largely built on the principle of indirect rule, with indigenous nobility filling out the lower positions in the governance structure. In 1901, Queen Wilhelmina announced a new 'Ethical Policy' aimed at the 'uplifting of the indigenous peoples' of colony. This eventually led to some experimentation with self-governance including the introduction in 1918 of the

Volksraad (People's Council) – a hastily created quasi-representative assembly with members partly appointed and partly elected.[19] The *Volksraad* began with purely advisory powers but was granted co-legislative powers in 1927, although the Governor-General retained powers of veto. The *Volksraad* did alter some government bills but only on very few occasions did it initiate new laws.[20] Due to its subordinate status, the *Volksraad* was distrusted by most Indonesian nationalist organisations.[21]

The pattern of company law development in the Netherlands Indies was particularly striking due to the extraordinarily long period of time during which it underwent no change.[22] The first company law was introduced on 1 May 1848 when the Dutch Commercial Code of 1838 (a redrafted version of the Napoleonic French Commercial Code of 1807) was extended to the colony.[23] This extension, which occurred during the Cultivation System period when private Dutch enterprise was restricted, was merely part of a general extension of Dutch law to the colony, rather than being specifically intended to create opportunities for the use of the company form. The Commercial Code, which had a scant 21 articles relating to joint stock companies (*Naamloze Vennootschap* (NV)), was to remain in force through to 1995 – for almost 150 years. This was despite the fact that the Netherlands itself substantially updated its own company law provisions in 1928. These 21 articles covered basic provisions on incorporation, company lifespan, division of capital into shares, management to be conducted by directors, shareholder voting rights and required automatic dissolution if the company should suffer a 75% loss of capital. Hence, the Commercial Code enabled and only very lightly regulated companies. This accords with Pistor et al.'s observation that original company laws, in both civil and common law jurisdictions, merely enabled incorporation and did not pay much attention to governance.[24]

In the beginning, the Commercial Code was only applicable to Europeans present in the Netherlands Indies based on the policy of racial legal pluralism and of leaving indigenous Indonesians to be governed by their own customary laws (*adat* law). Changes made in 1855 were to bring Chinese residents and

19 Harry J. Benda, 'The Pattern of Administrative Reforms in the Closing Years of Dutch Rule in Indonesia', *The Journal of Asian Studies* 25:4 (1966), 589–605.

20 George McTurnan Kahin, *Nationalism and Revolution in Indonesia* (Ithaca: Cornell University Press, 1952), 40.

21 Herbert Feith, *The Decline of Constitutional Democracy in Indonesia* (Ithaca: Cornell University Press, 1962), 5–6.

22 Mahy, 'The Evolution of Company Law in Indonesia'.

23 *Staatsblad* no. 23/1847.

24 Pistor et al., 'The Evolution of Corporate Law', 814.

other so-called 'Foreign Orientals' under the jurisdiction of the European Codes in order to protect Europeans who were doing business with them. Also in 1855, the Dutch required registration of the internal contracts of the Chinese *kongsi* partnership form with the local district court. Further formalisation of the *kongsi* occurred in 1927 when it was deemed by law to be a partnership with joint and several liability, and as a consequence many Chinese businesses turned to the NV company form instead which had the advantage of limited liability. Indigenous Indonesians were not given access to the European partnership and company forms until 1917 when a law was passed permitting them to individually voluntarily submit partially or fully to the Commercial and Civil Codes.[25] Few indigenous Indonesians took advantage of this, and instead often created business forms that did not accord with European law.[26]

Although the Commercial Code articles relating to the NV form were not altered during the colonial period, there was one notable innovation towards the very end of Dutch rule. In 1939, the *Volksraad* passed a special separate law to enable the formation of indigenous joint stock companies (*Inlandsche Maatschappij op Aandeelen* (IMA)).[27] This law was a product of complex interacting social and economic forces including the ongoing Ethical Policy, the rising Indonesian nationalist movement and its demands for more economic opportunities and the continuation of the race-based plural legal system in the colony under which indigenous Indonesians were still mostly subject to *adat* law. The IMA ordinance was a conscious and paternalistic attempt to encourage indigenous Indonesians to enter the modern (European) economy, and the IMA was made much cheaper and easier to establish than the NV. The law was also much more detailed than the Commercial Code indicating the colonial regime's desire for control over IMAs. The law conferred limited liability on IMA shareholders and also incorporated elements of the cooperative form such as requiring directors to be shareholders themselves. It also restricted the amount of land that the IMA could hold as a sop to European sugar interests which feared competition from new large sugar estates. Although there was

25 *Staatsblad* no. 12/1917.

26 Nono Anwar Makarim, 'Companies and Business in Indonesia' (Ph.D. dissertation, Harvard University Law School 1978), 145; J. Thomas Lindblad, *Bridges to New Business: The Economic Decolonization of Indonesia* (Leiden: KITLV Press, 2008), 33; 'Verslag van de Commissie voor Inlandsche Rechtspersonen Ingesteld bij Besluit van den Gouverneur-Generaal van Nederlandsche-Indië van 14 Mei 1929 no. 4x' [Report of the Commission on Native Legal Persons Installed by Order of the Governor-General of the Netherlands Indies on 14 May 1929] (Bataviacentrum: Landsdrukkerij, 1931).

27 *Staatsblad* no. 569/1939. This law came into force on 1 February 1940 (*Staatsblad* no. 717/1939).

interest in the IMA, and the law remained on the books until 1995, it was never much used in practice as entrepreneurs in post-independence Indonesia generally chose the NV form, apparently due to the perception of it being more modern and less paternalistic.

The story of company law in the Netherlands Indies was ultimately one of race and the dominance of the idea that European law was unsuitable for the native population until they had progressed further towards 'modern' economic life. The IMA represented a paternalistic half-step in this direction by providing native Indonesian entrepreneurs with an instrument thought to be tailored to their phase of development, which was in the end rejected in practice in favour of the outdated law of a century earlier. Overall, the pattern of legal stagnation predicted by Pistor et al. for transplants is fulfilled in the case of the Netherlands Indies given the extraordinarily long period during which the formal law was not updated.

4 'Imitatory Machinery' and English Company Law in British Malaya

As occurred in the Netherlands Indies, British power in Southeast Asia was pioneered by a great chartered trading company – in this case the (British) East India Company (EIC). It founded trading settlements on Penang in 1786 and on Singapore in 1819. Malacca was transferred to the company in 1824. These three territories were established as the Straits Settlements under the control of the EIC in 1826, and later became a separate Crown Colony in 1867 with its own Governor and Legislative Council. The Legislative Council comprised a handful of government high office holders or 'Official' representatives as well as 'Unofficial' non-government members, usually including one Chinese representative. In 1924, the Legislative Council was expanded to thirteen 'Official' and thirteen 'Unofficial' members who were all appointed by the Governor. According to Goh (2010), the sitting of the Council signified both an advance for the colony in imperial status as well as the transplantation of British civilisation to the Straits Settlements, but non-British interests were mostly only given symbolic recognition.[28] Thus, the Straits Settlements were ruled 'directly' with only limited involvement of local populations and with no popular elections until 1948.[29]

---

28 Daniel P.S. Goh, 'Unofficial Contentions: The Post-Coloniality of Straits Chinese Political Discourse in the Straits Settlements Legislative Council', *Journal of Southeast Asian Studies* 41:3 (2010), 483–507, 486.

29 Daniels et al. 'The Legacy of Empire', 136.

From their base in the Straits Settlements, the British began to encroach on the Malay Peninsula in 1874 by negotiating various treaties whereby the traditional rulers each accepted British Residents. This was a system of indirect rule – the Malay rulers retained constitutional and ceremonial roles, but ultimately executive power was in British hands with Residents' 'advice' bound to be followed in almost all matters. Councils in each state were responsible for passing (often identical) British-influenced legislation. In 1895, four of the Malay States – Negeri Sembilan, Pahang, Perak and Selangor – were amalgamated as the Federated Malay States. Although never formally designated as a Colony, the Federated Malay States were nonetheless essentially under direct British control. A Federal Council was established in 1909 consisting of the Malay hereditary ruler of each of the four states, the British Residents of each state and some other Official and Unofficial members, usually including one or two Chinese representatives.[30] The remaining 'Unfederated' states on the Malay Peninsula – Johor, Kedah, Kelantan, Perlis and Terengganu – nominally retained their independence but also all eventually accepted British Residents. Originally, the Malay Peninsula was a backwater compared to the trading harbours of the Straits Settlements, but the tin and rubber booms in the late 19th and early 20th centuries shifted the economic focus to a certain extent. Following World War II, the different British colonies were amalgamated, and independence was achieved in 1957. Singapore seceded from Malaysia in 1965.

The story of the evolution of company law in the Straits Settlements and the Federated Malay States was essentially one of keeping up with English legal developments but often with a substantial time lag, and with some copying among colonies rather than always taking the law directly from England. The first company legislation to have effect in the Straits Settlements was the *Indian Companies Act 1866*. This Act was closely based on the English *Companies Act 1862*. Then, the first locally produced law was passed in the Straits Settlements in 1889,[31] largely in order to resolve legal uncertainty caused by the passing of the *Civil Law Ordinance IV of 1878* and resulting confusion as to whether the *Indian Companies Act 1866* was still in force. This was followed a little less than a decade later by the first company laws in the Federated Malay States which were simultaneously enacted in each state in 1897.[32]

30 Chai Hon-Chan, *The Development of British Malaya 1896–1909* (Kuala Lumpur: Oxford University Press, 1964); Yeo Kim Wah, 'The Grooming of An Elite: Malay Administrators in the Federated Malay States 1903–1941', *Journal of Southeast Asian Studies* 11:2 (1980), 287–319.

31 *Straits Settlements Companies Ordinance no. V of 1889.*

32 *Perak Enactment No. 13 of 1897, Selangor Enactment No. 9 of 1897, Negeri Sembilan Enactment No. 11 of 1897, Pahang Enactment No. 19 of 1897.*

Essentially there were only two instances where the company laws in the Straits Settlements and the Federated Malay States departed from the pattern of England in order to respond to the local context. In 1903, identical amendments were passed in each Federated Malay State to allow an exception to the prohibition on large partnerships of more than 20 members.[33] This exception was explicitly for 'associations of miners working under the Chinese *hun* system'. Under the *hun* system, Chinese tin mine workers were not paid fixed wages but were considered to be shareholders and entitled to a share of the mine's profits. The amendment was not so much a legal innovation as simply a measure to maintain a division between the business practices of different population groups in the Malay Peninsula.[34]

The second instance, more significant than the first, was the legislative reaction to the collapse of the Kwong Yik Chinese bank in Singapore. The bank, founded in 1903 to serve Chinese customers who preferred not to use British banks, collapsed in 1913 after rumours of financial difficulties led to a run on the bank. It suspended payments to customers and subsequently became bankrupt. Many small depositors and local Chinese businesses lost substantial amounts of money as a result.[35] The bank's collapse was blamed on it having given unsecured advances to its directors and on poor auditing practices. In response to the resulting public outcry against Chinese business practices, the Companies Ordinance of the Straits Settlements was amended in 1914[36] to require half-yearly auditing of banks, publication of the audit statement, to prevent directors of banks from taking unsecured advances and to require all company books to be kept in English (and by implication not in Chinese). Proceedings of the Legislative Council indicate that the provision on advances to directors was actually watered down from being a total prohibition. This was in response to opposition from some of the Unofficial members of the Council, including the representative of the Singapore Chamber of Commerce, who argued that it was not part of the company law of any other British colony.[37]

The remainder of the colonial period in British Malaya, saw more mundane copying of the developments in English law, although the exception for *hun*

33 *Perak Enactment No. 4 of 1903, Selangor Enactment No. 2 of 1903; Negeri Sembilan Enactment No. 8 of 1903, Pahang No. 3 of 1903.*

34 Mahy and Ramsay, 'Legal Transplants and Adaptation', 132.

35 'Big Chinese Firm in Difficulties', *The Straits Times* (26 December 1913), 10; 'Kwong Yik Results', *The Straits Times* (3 December 1913), 8.

36 Straits Settlements *Companies (Amendment) Ordinance* (No. 9 of 1914).

37 Straits Settlements, *Proceedings of the Legislative Council* (27 February 1914, 13 March 1914). Note, however, that in Victoria, Australia, banking companies were prohibited from granting advances to directors or officers (*Companies Act 1896* (Vic.), ss. 45, 46).

mining and the 1914 amendments were carried forward through time as well. The major updates in the Straits Settlements were the Companies Ordinances of 1915, 1923 and 1940, while Enactments were passed in the Federated Malay States in 1917 followed by some minor amendments in 1927 and 1932. It seems that there was some involvement of the Singapore Chamber of Commerce and the Singapore Bar in the Straits Settlements Companies Ordinance 1940[38] – but overall limited popular interaction with the law-making process.

The 'imitatory machinery' in colonial Malaya was slow but regular, and the company laws of the colonies were periodically amended to reflect the law of England as it developed.[39] As noted, the laws were often copied from one colony to another rather than coming directly from England as might have been expected. And, there were just a couple of instances where the law was deliberately tailored to local circumstances. This pattern of company evolution does not match either of the patterns predicted by Pistor et al. for transplant countries – extreme volatility or a long period of legal stagnation – but rather can be characterised as a close adherence to the pattern of legal developments in the metropolis.

5 Company Law and the Dual Colonial Experience in the Philippines

The Philippines had a unique colonial history in the Southeast Asian context; it was a Spanish colony for over three centuries before sovereignty was acquired by the United States of America in 1898 – ultimately resulting in a hybrid civil law-common law legal system where the common law is dominant.[40] The Spanish arrived permanently in the Philippines in the late 16th century, established their main settlement in Manila, and began the galleon trade between Mexico and Manila to trade silver for Chinese goods. At the time, the Spanish lacked interest in local production beyond ensuring their own living

38 Straits Settlements, *The Companies Bill 1939: Report of the Companies Legislation Committee*, vii.

39 Mahy and Ramsay, 'Legal Transplants and Adaptation," 141; H.G. Calvert, 'Commercial Law' in *Malaya and Singapore, The Borneo Territories: The Development of Their Laws and Constitutions*, vol. 9 of *The British Commonwealth: The Development of Its Laws and Constitution*, eds. George Williams Keeton and L.A. Sheridan (London: Stevens & Sons Limited, 1961), 401.

40 Pacifico A. Agabin, *Mestizo: The Story of the Philippine Legal System* (Quezon City: University of the Philippines College of Law, 2011); Pacifico A. Agabin, 'Philippines: The Twentieth Century as the Common Law's Century', in Sue Farran et al. (eds.), *A Study of Mixed Legal Systems: Endangered, Entrenched or Blended* (Farnham, UK: Ashgate, 2014).

needs and kept the Philippines as a frontier entrepôt trading post through the greater part of the Spanish era.[41] This situation began to change from the mid-eighteenth century as the industrial revolution created a greater world demand for raw products and the Philippines began to produce agricultural products for export. From 1789, foreign traders were progressively allowed to visit Manila, and in 1834, Manila was made into a free port. From this point, British and American merchant houses came to dominate trade and were the driving force behind commercial development in the Philippines.[42]

The Spanish colonial administration of the Philippines placed a high degree of executive power in the person of the Governor and Captain-General as the representative of the King. The Governor could enforce the laws of Spain but also suspend them and issue his own decrees.[43] Hence, although Spain fairly regularly extended new laws to its overseas colonial territories, these were not always implemented.[44] The *Audiencia* was established in Manila in 1590 with administrative, legislative and judicial functions rolled into one, although its judicial functions were dominant and it eventually acted as a Supreme Court for the colony.[45] The *Consulado* of Manila was established by Royal Decree on 6 December 1769, although only became properly constituted in 1771, and functioned as a court of first instance for hearing commercial cases.[46] It is also worth noting that, unlike the Netherlands Indies and British Malaya, the

41 Chester Lloyd Jones, 'The Spanish Administration of Philippine Commerce', *Proceedings of the American Political Science Association* 3 (1906), 180–193, 183; John A. Larkin, 'Philippine History Reconsidered: A Socioeconomic Perspective', *American Historical Review* 87:3 (1982), 595–628.

42 Amando Doronila, *The State, Economic Transformation, and Political Change in the Philippines 1945–1972* (Singapore, New York: Oxford University Press, 1992), 10–11; Benito J. Legarda, *After the Galleons: Foreign Trade, Economic Change and Entrepreneurship in the Nineteenth-Century Philippines* (Quezon City: Ateneo de Manila Press, 1999).

43 MB Hooker, *A Concise Legal History of South-east Asia* (Oxford: Clarendon Press, 1978), 217.

44 David P. Barrows, 'The Governor-General of the Philippines under Spain and the United States', *The American Historical Review* 21:2 (1916), 288–311, 299; Hooker, 'A Concise Legal History', 222.

45 Charles Henry Cunningham, *The Audiencia in the Spanish Colonies: As Illustrated by the Audiencia of Manila (1583–1800)* (Berkeley: University of California Press, 1919); Manuel T. Chan, *The Audiencia and the Legal System in the Philippines (1583–1900)* ([The Philippines]: Progressive Printing Palace, 1998).

46 Carmen Yuste, 'La Fundación de la Junta de Professores Comerciantes o Consulado de Filipinas: Circunscripción, Atribuciones y Competencias [The Foundation of the Board of Professional Merchants or the Consulado of the Philippines: Cirumscription, Attributes and Competences]', *Revista Mexicana de Historia del Derecho* 28 (2013) 111–130; Maria Lourdes Diaz-Trechuelo, 'Eighteenth Century Philippine Economy: Commerce', *Philippine Studies* 14:2 (1966), 253–279, 263.

Spanish almost totally excluded local customary law from the colonial legal system in the Philippines.[47]

Most texts on company law in the Philippines only make mention of the extension of the Spanish Code of Commerce of 1885 to the Philippines in 1888. In fact, at least formally, earlier Spanish company laws were also made applicable to the Philippines. These Spanish developments were identified by Pistor et al. as displaying a pattern of extreme volatility,[48] and indeed this volatility was extended to Spain's colonial territories too. The *Spanish Code of Commerce* (*Código de Comercio*) of 1829/1830 established the *sociedad anonima* company form, and in a departure from the French model of the time, it embodied the principle of general incorporation, requiring only approval of the courts of commerce. This Code was extended to the Philippines in 1832, at the same time replacing the existing judicial functions of the *Consulado* of Manila with a Commercial Court.[49] However, in response to economic crisis and perceived abuse of the company form, Spain's *Joint Stock Companies Act* (*Ley de Sociedades por Acciones*) of 1848 was passed with much higher regulatory requirements than the *Code of Commerce* of 1829, that is, government authorisation was needed to form a company.[50] The 1848 law may have been directly extended to the Philippines – a letter survives dated 24 April 1850 in which the Governor of the Philippines requested a copy of the 1848 law and its regulations in order to implement a royal order that the law should be introduced.[51] Certainly, in 1862, the company law of Cuba and Puerto Rico from 1853 (based on the 1848 law), as amended in 1857, was formally extended to the Philippines.[52]

47 Owen J. Lynch, 'The Philippine Indigenous Law Collection: An Introduction and Preliminary Bibliography', *Philippine Law Journal* 58 (1983), 457–534, 458.

48 Pistor et al. 'The Evolution of Corporate Law', 842–843.

49 Royal Decree 26 July 1832 (*Real Cédula de 26 de Julio de 1832 de Comunicacion á Los Islas Filipinas*). The Commercial Court was later subsumed into the general court system in 1869.

50 Law of 28 January 1848 (*Ley de 28 de Enero de 1848, de Compañías Mercantiles por Acciones*); Regulations of 17 February 1848. See also Rafael Ansón Peironcely, 'La Ley y el Reglamento de 1848 sobre Compañías Mercantiles por Acciones' [The Law and Regulations of 1848 on Joint Stock Commercial Companies] (Doctoral thesis, Faculty of Law, Universidad Complutense de Madrid, 2015).

51 Ministerio de Ultramar, Aplicación en Filipinas de la Ley y Reglamento de Sociedades Anónimas [Application of the Philippines for the Law and Regulations on Companies], 1850. <http://pares.mcu.es/ParesBusquedas/servlets/Control_servlet?accion=3&&txt_tipo_busqueda=dl&txt_busqueda=&txt_correo=S&txt_id_desc_ud=2347899>. Note that some of the dates associated with the 1848 law and its regulations in the letter appear to be mistaken.

52 Royal Order of 5 May 1862 (*R.O. hacienda estensivas á las Islas la Real cédula de 29 de Noviembre de 1853, sobre Sociedades anónimas, y la Real órden de 8 de Setiembre de 1857*

Following the Glorious Revolution in Spain in 1868, the 1848 law was suspended and the *Code of Commerce* of 1829 temporarily reinstated.[53] The following year, the *Joint Stock Companies Act* of 1869 was passed.[54] However, it appears that only the 1868 decree, and not the 1869 law, was ever extended to Spain's overseas territories.[55] Hence, the *Code of Commerce* of 1829 formally governed companies in the Philippines from 1868 to 1888, when the Spanish extended their new *Code of Commerce* of 1885.[56] This new code was the result of a codification movement that had occurred in Spain, and a number of other codes, such as the Civil Code, were introduced to the Philippines in the same time period.

The sparse literature on the topic all suggests that *sociedades anonimas* were rarely used in the Spanish Philippines due to the prevailing social and economic conditions, and that where commercial enterprises were established they were much more likely to be formed as partnerships.[57] An insight into local practices is provided by Legarda's (1999) account of the beginnings of the famous San Miguel brewery company.[58] Founded in 1890 by the wealthy Enrique Ma. Baretto y de Ycaza, San Miguel was based on an arrangement with some business associates, including Pedro P. Roxas y Castro, under a notary joint account (*cuentas en participación*). Roxas became the manager, but in 1896, an embargo was put on Roxas' assets for involvement in the revolution against Spain. Roxas himself jumped ship in Singapore on his way to Spain in September 1896. The remaining associates then entered into lengthy civil court proceedings to argue that the San Miguel organisation was not just a contract for joint accounts but in fact a *sociedad anonima* with separate legal personality that was merely managed by Roxas, and hence that the embargo could be lifted on the asset portions of the other associates. In the end the decision was

[Royal Order extending to the Islands the Royal Decree of 29 November 1853 on Companies, and the Royal Order of 8 September 1857]), *Legislacion Ultramar*, volume V, p. 448.

53 *Gaceta de Madrid*, 29 October 1868, number 303, 6–7.

54 Law of 19 October 1869 (*Ley de 19 de octubre de 1869, sobre la libre constitución de sociedades mercantiles*).

55 Decree of 17 September 1869, *Coleccione Legislativa de España*, 1869, part II, 568.

56 Royal Decree of 6 August 1888, extending the Code of Commerce in force in the Peninsula to the Philippines.

57 Emilio M. Javier, 'A Comparative Study of the Laws of the Philippine Islands and of the United States of America Applicable to Private Corporations' (SJD Dissertation, University of Michigan Law School, 1932), 2–3; Juan T. Santos, 'Suggested Reforms on the Philippine Corporation Law', *Philippine Law Journal* VIII:4 (1928), 145–161.

58 Benito J. Legarda, *After the Galleons: Foreign Trade, Economic Change and Entrepreneurship in the Nineteenth-Century Philippines* (Quezon City: Ateneo de Manila Press, 1999), 331–332.

overtaken when a military judge dismissed the charges against Roxas for lack of evidence.

In 1898, following the Spanish-American war, Spain ceded the Philippines to the United States of America. In the early American era (1901–1916), the Philippine Commission (a small council of American officials under the leadership of William Taft) was in full command. Then, following the Jones Law of 1916, which was to begin the process of decolonisation, a fully elected Philippine legislature was established but with the appointed American Governor-General retaining executive power. From 1935, under the Commonwealth era, the executive office of President was also elected, local Filipino politicians had greater political power than ever before but there was still limited franchise. Some matters such as foreign affairs were retained by the United States, Philippine court decisions were still subject to review by the Supreme Court of the United States and the office of Governor-General was replaced with a High Commissioner. The Philippines gained full independence in 1946 following World War II.

Under the Philippine Commission, a new American-style Corporation Law was passed in 1906.[59] The US, which was motivated by an uneasy combination of desiring to both exploit economic opportunities and to civilise the Filipino people, quickly moved to reconstitute the legal system.[60] Most public and commercial laws were rewritten based on the American common law model, and indeed it was in the area of commercial law that the American attempt to recreate the Philippines in its own image was most evident.[61]

The 1906 Corporation Law was understood to be 'practically a codification of American Corporation Law'.[62] Prepared by Philippine Commissioner, James Francis Smith, the Law appears to have been based predominantly on the state laws of California and New York,[63] although Commission reports also made mention of public sessions held to discuss the proposed law and of a 'large

59 Act no. 1459.

60 Anna Leah Fidelis T Castañeda, 'Spanish Structure, American Theory: The Legal Foundations of the Tropical New Deal in the Philippine Islands, 1898–1935', in Alfred W. McCoy and Francisco A. Scarano (eds.), *Colonial Crucible: Empire in the Making of the Modern American State* (Madison: University of Wisconsin Press, 2009); Leia Castañeda Anastacio, *The Foundations of the Modern Philippine State: Imperial Rule and the American Constitutional Tradition in the Philippine Islands, 1898–1935* (Cambridge: Cambridge University Press 2016).

61 Agabin, 'Mestizo', 213.

62 *Harden v Benguet Consolidated Mining*, G.R. no. L37331 (18 March 1933).

63 Makalaya Jamir, 'Critical Analysis of Section 19 of the Corporation Law', *Philippine Law Journal* XVI:1 (1936), 1–35, 4.

number of communications containing suggested amendments'.[64] Indeed the Law contained some provisions of 'peculiarly local application'.[65] It permitted companies that had been formed under the Spanish Code of Commerce of 1888 to continue to be organised according to the principles in the Law if desired, but prevented any new *sociedades anonimas* from being formed. The law also contained a prohibition on any company doing business in the Philippines engaging in slavery. Eradicating slavery was a high priority at the time, as the United States was having trouble reconciling its own founding principles of individual freedom with its colonial role and the existence of slavery-like practices in some parts of the Philippines.[66] There were strong restrictions on foreign ownership of companies, although Americans were given exemptions to this. The company law also prohibited mining and agriculture companies from owning shares in other mining and agricultural businesses. Finally, there were detailed provisions for registration of foreign companies doing business in the Philippines.

The 1906 Corporation Law was amended some 28 times prior to Philippine independence. The majority of these were minor procedural amendments, but one set of amendments, passed in 1928,[67] was particularly significant and politically charged. In the lead up to the passing of the amendments, 'every resource of timidity and reaction was arrayed against the bill, and the debates over it filled not only the halls of the Legislature but public meetings outside as well as the columns of the daily press'.[68] The amendments permitted the issuance of shares without par value, the declaring of dividends in stock (instead of just in cash), and having more than one corporate purpose. These were based on American developments of the time. The amendments also relaxed the previously absolute prohibition on mining and agriculture companies owning shares in other mining or agriculture companies, in order to allow holdings of up to 15 per cent of the voting stock.

These amendments in 1928 seem to have occurred due to a confluence of interests meeting with the aim of promoting economic nationalism in the Philippines. The American Governor-General, Henry L. Stimson, and leading

64 Bureau of Insular Affairs, *Sixth Annual Report of the Philippine Commission*, 1905, Part 1, 117; Bureau of Insular Affairs, *Seventh Annual Report of the Philippine Commission*, 1906, Part 1, 131.

65 Sulpicio Guevara, *The Philippine Corporation Law* (5th edition, Quezon City: Central Lawbook Publishing Co., 1967), 1.

66 Michael Salman, *The Embarrassment of Slavery: Controversies over Bondage and Nationalism in the American Colonial Philippines* (Berkeley: University of California Press, 2003).

67 Act no. 3518.

68 Jose Palarca, 'The New Amendments to the Philippine Corporation Law (Act No. 3518)', *Philippine Law Journal* x (1930–1931), 226–262, 226.

Filipino politicians Manuel Quezon, Manuel Roxas and Sergio Osmeña made a show of united cooperation in respect to the issue (even though behind the scenes they continued their intrigues against one another).[69] Speaker of the Senate, Roxas, promoted the bill as being 'primarily designed to benefit Philippine corporations when competing with American corporations'.[70] Stimson presented justifications for the amendments in paternalistically benevolent terms, emphasising the need for the Filipino to 'achieve a position in the world of business for which no apology need be offered' and the Filipino's response to 'America's faith in the ... foundation of a self-governing democracy ... ha[d] been amply sufficient to entitle him to be trusted in this future venture'.[71] Concerns widely expressed that the changes would affect the laws protecting public lands were brushed aside by the promoters of the amendments.

Overall, it is clear that the Philippines during the Spanish era was merely a target for the extension of the law of home out to the periphery – with the extension of the commercial codes and individual company laws probably functioning more as symbolic reminders of power than any real expectation of the law being of use in the colony. Under the Americans, with their particular brand of benevolent colonialism and the graduated trajectory towards democracy and independence, the company law of the Philippines showed some key moments of innovation and response to the demands of law users.

6 Conclusions

Pistor et al. predicted that transplanted company law would undergo patterns of either erratic change or of long periods of legal stagnation where the law would simply sit on the books without being adapted to local context. In this study of three colonial territories in Southeast Asia it becomes clear that the patterns of legal evolution were quite idiosyncratic in each colony and do not easily fit Pistor et al.'s theory. In the Netherlands Indies, there was indeed a long period where the sparse provisions of the Commercial Code of 1848 did not change, which does suggest legal stagnation. The creation of the Indigenous Joint Stock Company in 1939, however, was a paternalistic innovation made in

69 Lewis E. Gleeck, *The American Governors-General and High Commissioners in the Philippines: Proconsuls, Nation-Builders and Politicians* (Quezon City: New Day Publishers, 1986), 230.

70 'The Amendments to the Corporation Law', *The Philippine Finance Review* I:11 (Dec 1928), 12–13, 33.

71 Henry L. Stimson, 'Amending the Corporation Law', *The Philippine Finance Review* I:9 (Oct 1928), 6, 30; Henry L. Stimson, 'Business Development is the Road to Freedom', *The Philippine Finance Review* II:1 (Feb 1929), 10–11.

an attempt to create a company form that would fit local requirements. In British Malaya, the pattern was for fairly regular updates in order to keep up with the developments of home. Indeed, English company law was more regularly updated and refined than that of the Netherlands. In only a couple of instances was the law specifically tailored to local conditions in British Malaya. In the Spanish Philippines, the law was also mostly synchronised with the volatile legal changes occurring in Spain and no adaptations to local context were made. In the American Philippines, the Corporation Law of 1906, though mostly an American transplant did contain some local peculiarities. The American allowance of graduated independence for the Philippines also meant that local politicians could shape the law themselves to some degree, as occurred in 1928.

To what extent did the 'extractive' nature of these colonies affect the evolution of company law? Certainly the general colonial institutions put in place were geared towards European control of territory and exploitation of local resources, with few gestures made to involving local populations in decision-making. The use of company law to do this, however, does not seem to have been high on any of the colonial powers' agendas. This was most likely because most business entities were being formed at 'home' with trade and investment carried out in the colonies, rather than much capital-raising originating in the colonies. It was only when the tides of ethical challenges to colonial practices began to occur, and early attempts at 'law and development' thinking emerged that any encouragement of colonial subjects to use companies for economic development purposes occurred.

Why then did the colonial powers even bother extending their company laws to the colonies in the first place? In part it was incidental to the extension of European law generally to the colonies, particularly as just one part of the larger commercial codes of the continental European powers. Symbolism also seems to have been a large factor whereby extending law to a colony was integral to actual military control and governance as well as maintaining an image of modernity. Perhaps more instrumentally, having the same laws in both metropolis and periphery might have been thought to facilitate efficient commercial practice.

As noted in the Introduction, Pistor et al. did not take account of the mode or context of transplants in developing their model of company law evolution. It seems clear from this comparative study in these colonies of Southeast Asia that the colonial context was highly determinative of the outcomes of the transplant of the first company laws and their subsequent development. The political and economic subordination of the colonised, the small classes of people likely to take advantage of the company form and their relatively small opportunities to influence policy-making seem to be key reasons for the low-levels of adaptability in the law.

From Denial to Opportunity: Chinese Access to Colonial Law in the Netherlands Indies (1800–1942)

Alexander Claver

1 Introduction

During the late colonial period (1800–1942) the Dutch purposefully and successfully used their system of law to keep the different population groups within the Netherlands Indies in check, and to consolidate their dominant position. In order to serve Dutch political and economic interests, elaborate legal arrangements to that effect were put in place and were strictly guarded. Denial or restriction of access to (parts of) the legal system by means of racial segregation formed a key component of this system. Within the existing legal constellation the Chinese constituted a separate element as was clearly mirrored in their treatment before the law. The law provisions in place affected Chinese lives and commercial activity to great extent. Sometimes, however, the law operated in rather unexpected and indeed beneficial ways, and Chinese entrepreneurs did not hesitate to exploit legal opportunities whenever the occasion arose.

Entrepreneurial room for manoeuvre in general depends upon access to security (i.e. the reduction of uncertainty), capital and information. These three notions are both complex, and related differently to each other. Here, the emphasis will be on the security options accessible to Chinese traders within the colonial context. More specifically, the article will zoom in on the (unintended) security options available to the Chinese business community, as was provided by the (commercial law) legislation of the Netherlands Indies during the late colonial period. As will be shown, the Chinese ethnic minority on more than one occasion managed to turn initial access denial rather unexpectedly into rewarding access opportunities. This suggests the potential value of accessibility as a research framework, and highlights the need to explore the theoretical and methodological implications of this concept in more detail. Here, a first glimpse is offered by focusing on the so-called Chinese 'access paradox' as is exemplified by three specific cases.

The first case looks at a change of law in 1855 with regard to the settlement of commercial disputes advocated by Dutch businessmen which unexpectedly backfired. Dutch entrepreneurs did evidently not anticipate that their Chinese counterparts could benefit from this change as well. The second case shows

 | DOI:10.1163/9789004443075_011

how a number of Chinese entrepreneurs managed to benefit from a change in legal status which was intended for Japanese citizens in 1899. This side-effect of the so-called *Japannerwet* (Japanese citizen law) was recognized by the Chinese and subsequently acted upon. The third case turns to the commercial pressure applied by Chinese merchants boycotting European companies on three separate occasions. In one instance the boycott victim remains unknown, in the other instance the subject was the *Handelsvereeniging Amsterdam*, a prominent Dutch wholesale trader. The HVA counteracted the Chinese course of action using all means at their disposal, but only to find out that existing law provisions applied to their adversaries as well. The description of the cases is preceded by a contextual paragraph offering a brief sketch of the religious and racial segregation in place in the Dutch colony. The concluding remarks will tentatively explore the concept of accessibility, which offers valuable insights into commercial mechanisms with regard to the aspects of security, capital and information.[1]

2 A Question of Race

Racial classification was a cornerstone of the late colonial administration.[2] Society within the Netherlands Indies was highly stratified and divided the

1 The different cases presented in this paper can be found in more detail in A. Claver, 'Struggling for Justice. Chinese Commerce and Dutch Law in the Netherlands Indies 1800–1942', in Peter Boomgaard, Dick Kooiman and Henk Schulte Nordholt (eds.), *Linking destinies: Trade, town and kin in Asian History* (Leiden: KITLV Press, 2008), 99–118; and A. Claver, *Dutch Commerce and Chinese Merchants in Java: Colonial Relationships in Trade and Finance 1800–1942* (Leiden and Boston: Brill, 2014). For the purpose of the paper they have been abbreviated, revised and updated.

2 See Albert Dekker and Hanneke van Katwijk, *Recht en rechtspraak in Nederlands-Indië* (Leiden: KITLV Uitgeverij, 1993), 12–13; Cees Fasseur, 'Cornerstone and stumbling block. Racial classification and the late colonial state in Indonesia', in Robert Cribb (ed.), *The Late Colonial State in Indonesia: Political and Economic Foundations of the Netherlands Indies 1880–1942* (Leiden: KITLV Press, 1994), 31–56, 31); Daniel S. Lev, 'Colonial law and the genesis of the Indonesian state', *Indonesia* 40 (1985), 57–74, 58–59; Daniel S. Lev, 'The origins of the Indonesian advocacy', in Daniel S. Lev (ed.), *Legal evolution and political authority in Indonesia* (Den Haag: Kluwer Law International, 2000), 245–283, 249; F.H. Visman, *Verslag van de commissie tot bestudeering van staatsrechtelijke hervormingen ingesteld bij gouvernementsbesluit van 14 september 1940*, 2 vols. (Batavia: Landrukkerij, 1941–1942). A detailed historical survey of the constitutional classification of the colony's population can be found in W.E. van Mastenbroek, *De historische ontwikkeling van de staatsrechtelijke indeeling der bevolking van Nederlandsch-Indie* (Wageningen: Veenman, 1934). The Chinese position has been dealt with extensively in Patricia Tjiook-Liem, *De rechtspositie der Chinezen in Nederlands-Indië 1848–*

population into three categories: Europeans, Natives (*Inlanders*) and Foreign Orientals (*Vreemde Oosterlingen*). The Chinese population group dominated the last category, but Arabs, Indians and other smaller population groups were included as well. Different treatment of these various groups was deeply embedded in legal and executive policy.

This had not always been the case. Under the Dutch East Indies Company (*Vereenigde Oostindische* Compagnie, VOC), religion – not race – had been central in distinguishing between Christians, including native converts, and Muslims or 'pagans'. In 1818 the first Government Regulation (*Regeeringsreglement*) for the Netherlands Indies came into effect. In this colonial 'constitution' no reference was made to racial classification. The introduction of the Cultivation System (*Cultuurstelsel*) in the 1830s changed this. Its compulsory labour services intensified awareness of the differences between Europeans and non-Europeans, between the rulers and the ruled. Besides promoting racial classification before the law, it also concentrated legal and executive powers in the hands of the civil servant, thereby weakening guarantees against governmental arbitrariness.[3] Autocratic governance was deemed indispensable to implement the Cultivation System successfully. The Dutch resident had to be allowed near-total command over his residency and control over the judiciary system was seen as part of successful policy implementation. As a result, courts turned more and more into tools of the colonial administration instead of being instruments for dispensing justice.

In 1848 a new law codification became valid, much of which was only applicable to Europeans. The indigenous population was governed by its own laws and customs. It now became even more necessary to distinguish between the different population groups, since in case of legal strife a decision needed to be made regarding which court was applicable. The new Government Regulation of 1854 cemented the clear-cut distinction between Europeans and

1942: Wetgevingsbeleid tussen beginsel en belang (Leiden University Press, 2009). See also G.K.N. Liem, *'Vreemde Oosterlingen'. Een verkenning in de Nederlands-Indische wetgeving met betrekking tot de Chinezen en haar invloed op het leven van deze bevolkingsgroep* (unpublished MA-thesis Universiteit van Amsterdam, 1997), 27. The situation of the Arab population with regard to colonial politics of race and restriction of movement reflected the Chinese position and is covered in Sumit Kumar Mandal, *Finding their place: A History of Arabs in Java under Dutch rule, 1800–1924* (Unpublished dissertation Columbia University, 1994), 53–94.

3 See Fasseur, 'Cornerstone and stumbling block', 32–34, 42–43; Lev, 'Colonial law and the genesis of the Indonesian state', 61; van Mastenbroek, *De historische ontwikkeling*, 9–10, 46; Eric Tagliacozzo, *Secret trades of the Straits: Smuggling and State Formation along a Southeast Asian frontier, 1870–1910* (New Haven, Connecticut, 1999), 258; Lea Williams, *Overseas Chinese nationalism: The Genesis of the pan-Chinese movement in Indonesia, 1900–1916* (Glencoe, Illinois: Free Press, 1960), 33–35.

Natives, with Foreign Orientals being equated with natives, not Europeans. With the introduction of this regulation the colonial population was officially divided according to race, resulting in a distinctly different treatment before the law.[4]

The law did offer one escape, since non-Europeans could be equated (*gelijkgesteld*) with Europeans by order of the Governor-General himself. This provision became increasingly popular as 'from time to time *Staatsblad* and *Javasche Courant* contain long-drawn-out lists filled with names of Chinese, who are equated with Europeans'.[5] Women married to European men were part of the European population group, as were their offspring, provided they were 'recognized' by the father.[6]

Disputes among Europeans were tried before a Council of Justice (*Raad van Justitie*) where three professional judges were given evidence by a prosecutor and defence lawyer. The indigenous population had its own administration of justice to which it resorted. Whenever a European or the colonial administration itself was involved, the case appeared either before the Local Court (*Landraad*), or the Police Court (*Politierol*) when dealing with minor offences. These courts compared unfavourably with the Council of Justice, where legal procedure regarding preventive custody, the rights of the accused, or the use of search warrants was well defined and better guarded[7]

In 1855 a change in law saw the legal position of the Chinese significantly altered. From now on Foreign Orientals had civil (including commercial) law in common with the Europeans (excluding family law for divorce and inheritance cases). Whenever a commercial dispute arose, Chinese and Arabs were seen as Europeans and therefore had their cases tried before a Council of Justice.[8]

In 1892 a new Dutch nationality law was drawn up withholding Dutch citizenship from all 'natives' and Foreign Orientals residing in the Netherlands

4 Howard Dick, et al., The emergence of a national economy. An economic history of Indonesia, 1800–2000 (Crows Nest (NSW) / Leiden: Allen and Unwin, 2002), 61; Van Mastenbroek, *De historische ontwikkeling*, 63, 66.

5 P.H. Fromberg, *Mr. P.H. Fromberg's verspreide geschriften verzameld door Chung Hwa Hui, Chineesche Vereeniging in Nederland* (Leiden, 1926), 415.

6 Van Mastenbroek, *De historische ontwikkeling, 68–81.*

7 Liem, *'Vreemde Oosterlingen',* ch. 5.

8 See Dekker and Van Katwijk, *Recht en rechtspraak in Nederlands-Indië*, 11–12, 17–18; Fasseur, 'Cornerstone and stumbling block', 35–36, 40–41; Fromberg, *Verspreide geschriften*, 115, 410; Lev, 'Colonial law and the genesis of the Indonesian state', 61; Tagliacozzo, *Secret trades of the Straits*, 258–259; Twang Peck Yang, *The Chinese business élite in Indonesia and the Transition to Independence, 1940–1950* (Kula Lumpur: Oxford University Press, 1998), 22–24; Williams, *Overseas Chinese nationalism*, 33–35.

Indies. This law clearly branded them as not Dutch and thus prevented them from exercising any political rights. In 1910 a new law provided 'natives' and Foreign Orientals alike with the rather peculiar legal status of 'Dutch subjects, non-Dutch' (*Nederlands onderdaan, niet-Nederlander*). In essence, racial classification and unequal treatment before the law remained in place until the proclamation of independence of the Indonesian Republic in 1945, which declared all Indonesian citizens equal before the law.[9]

3 The Chinese under Commercial Legislation

Since 1855 European law provisions had applied partly to Foreign Orientals.[10] This legislation seemingly benefited European traders in disputes with the Chinese, as the former preferred to do business with Foreign Orientals under Dutch civil and commercial law.[11] In previous years, European traders had consistently argued that there was a lack of sufficient guarantees for the observance

9 See Writser Jans Cator, *The economic position of the Chinese in the Netherlands-Indies* (Oxford, 1936), 31–96; Dekker and van Katwijk, *Recht en rechtspraak in Nederlands-Indië*, 16, 41; Fasseur, 'Cornerstone and stumbling block', 38–42, 54–55; Lev, 'Colonial law and the genesis of the Indonesian state', 63–67; van Mastenbroek, *De historische ontwikkeling*, 97–105; Bas Pompe, 'The effects of the Japanese administration on the judiciary in Indonesia', in Peter Post and Ellen Touwen-Bouwsma (eds.), *Japan, Indonesia and the war: Myths and realities* (Leiden: KITLV Press, 1997), 51–63; W.F. Wertheim, *De status van de Chinezen in vooroorlogs Nederlands-Indië: Zeer geheime documenten uit de jaren 1928–1932* (Leiden, 1997). Dutch law did not disappear with the proclamation of Indonesia's independence and its influence can still be felt in Indonesian society today. See Mason C. Hoadley, *The Role of Law in Contemporary Indonesia* (Lund: Centre for East and South-East Asian Studies, Lund University, 2004) for an analysis of the 'foreign-ness' of present-day law, i.e. the heritage of colonial law in Indonesia.

10 Claver, 'Struggling for justice', 107–111. See also the outstanding work of Tjiook-Liem, *De rechtspositie der Chinezen in Nederlands-Indië* on the judicial position of the Chinese population group in the Netherlands-Indies (1848–1942). Unfortunately Dr. Tjiook-Liem's dissertation is not available in English.

11 As early as 1842 – when asked their opinion regarding the commercial legislation for the colony – some merchants had complained about the 'most objectionable' behaviour of Chinese as well as Arabs in cases of disputes and/or defaults. In 1848 similar complaints resurfaced in an official memorandum summarizing proposed changes in the commercial jurisdiction of the Netherlands Indies. In 1852 and again in 1855 nearly all Batavian trading houses signed an address urging the Governor-General to recognize the problem of jurisdiction and have the law changed accordingly. See J. van Kan, 'Uit de geschiedenis onzer codificatie. 12. De wenken van den handel', *Indisch Tijdschrift van het Recht* 124 (1926), 346–356, here 346–347 and 354–356; and J. van Kan, 'Uit de geschiedenis onzer codificatie. 14. Een strijd om het adatrecht', *Indisch Tijdschrift van het Recht* 124 (1926), 449–468, here 460–461 and 467; Liem, *'Vreemde Oosterlingen'*, 23–24.

of business commitments in situations where they remained partly dependent on the laws and customs of the Chinese and were obliged to present their cases before the *Landraad*.[12] The Chinese, however, stood to benefit greatly from the new legislation.[13] The codified civil law, the ability to sue and have a case presented before a judge, and the reduction of *Landraad* arbitrariness were of great help to them.[14] These 'disadvantages' from the colonial perspective had been disregarded, and the eagerness which Chinese business showed in exploiting the offered legal opportunities had clearly not been foreseen. The benefits of improved legal security were far less tangible than expected and soon started to fade from Dutch memory.[15]

The legal provisions to which colonial business had to adhere since 1855 were transplanted from the Netherlands and therefore suited the Dutch situation. However, they encountered numerous and powerful objections from European traders within the colony. Nothing caused more offence than the so-called bankruptcy provisions. In cases of default and subsequent bankruptcy, the debtor's fortune would be seized in order to settle his creditors' bills. Ascertaining the available assets required the debtor to submit his books upon defaulting. However, Chinese traders could appeal to the judge, claiming to be unskilled in bookkeeping. And, if incompetence (*onbedrevenheid*) had indeed

---

12 Given the high interdependence of Chinese business ventures, Dutch law was not confined solely to the dealings between Chinese and Europeans, but was deliberately extended to cover business among the Chinese themselves. Since there were hardly any direct links between European and indigenous traders, the latter were simply required to subject themselves to Dutch private and commercial law for the term of the contract. The use of commercial instruments (e.g. contracts) common to European practice automatically implied submission to the European commercial code for the purpose of the given transaction, whether or not those involved were aware of it. See Lev, 'The origins of the Indonesian advocacy', 252.

13 As they were [...] far more gifted with the *Kampf um's Recht* than the Dutch [...]'. The German expression used translates into 'Struggle for Justice' (Fromberg, *Verspreide geschriften*, 417, 488). The Chinese readiness to go to court can be observed from the very beginning of the Dutch presence in the Indonesian archipelago. During the first half of the seventeenth century, for instance, Chinese were involved in at least half of all civil lawsuits in Batavia. In general, the Chinese easily found their way to city hall. See Hendrik Niemeijer, *Batavia: Een koloniale samenleving in de 17de eeuw* (Amsterdam: Balans, 2005), 77–78.

14 See Norbertus Petrus van den Berg, *Munt-, crediet- en bankwezen, handel en scheepvaart in Nederlandsch Indië: Historisch-statistische bijdragen* ('s-Gravenhage: Martinus Nijhoff, 1907), 378; Dekker and van Katwijk, *Recht en rechtspraak in Nederlands-Indië*, 13–16; Fromberg, *Verspreide geschriften*, 309, 416–417; Fasseur, 'Cornerstone and stumbling block', 37; Tagliacozzo, *Secret trades of the Straits*, 259.

15 Lev, 'The origins of the Indonesian advocacy', 252; Liem, *'Vreemde Oosterlingen'*, 23–24; Tjiook-Liem, *De rechtspositie der Chinezen*, 97–154.

prevented the debtor from keeping proper records, he would be completely discharged. The Chinese frequently resorted to this line of defence, and their pleas were accepted on many occasions. Proper and standardized bookkeeping methods were not general and so the Chinese were even exempted from the obligation to make up a yearly balance sheet. Moreover, the law permitted their books to be written in the Chinese language.[16]

Many European wholesale traders thus believed that the bankruptcy law was perverted by the cunning tricks of the Chinese.[17] In 1862 the first of many requests was addressed to either the Governor-General in Batavia (Jakarta) or the Minister of Colonies in The Hague, urgently requesting an end to the menace of Chinese bankruptcies. A change of law provisions was considered to be vital to the health of the trading sector, and this change required government intervention. The European banking and trading sector kept fulminating against the fact that the Chinese could keep their trade records in languages that were incomprehensible to their creditors. Between 1862 and 1902 at least eight official requests were made, for the greater part initiated by the Batavian financial and trading establishment. These petitions usually followed a period of economic downturn and heavy financial losses due to the collapse of Chinese trading businesses. They were accompanied by a flood of articles in newspapers and magazines, depicting the Chinese as utterly unreliable.[18]

16 Fromberg, *Verspreide geschriften*, 309–313, 316; P. Meeter, *Advies van een deskundige in zake boekhouding en faillissementen van Chineezen* (Soerabaia, 1881), 38, 64–66; J. van Gennep, 'De Vreemde Oosterlingen en de lijfsdwang', *De Economist* I (1884), 362–380.

17 Similar doubts were voiced in Singapore in the 1840s with the introduction of the 'Insolvent Law'. It was feared that this would enable the insolvent Chinese trader to send his assets secretly to China while his European creditors were busy making claims on his property. This was considered a distinct possibility since 'the bookkeeping of the Chinese is a mystery to all but themselves'. At worst, his eventual fate was imprisonment and then retirement to China to enjoy what he had saved from the hands of his creditors. The Insolvent Court, established in 1848, was largely ignored by European traders, partly because of the time-consuming procedure, and partly because the court officials had little knowledge of business transactions. See Wong Lin Ken, 'The trade of Singapore, 1819–1869', *Journal of the Malayan Branch of the Royal Asiatic Society* 33 (1960), 5–315, 164–165.

18 See F. Alting Mees, *De Indische groothandel en de Chineesche lijnwaadhandel*. Reprint of the original published by *De Economist*, February-March, 1–2; Fromberg, *Verspreide geschriften*, 311, 623; Meeter, *Advies van een deskundige*, 1, 4, 24, 54–55; Tjiook-Liem, *De rechtspositie der Chinezen in Nederlands-Indië*, 137–142; 'Adres in zake de boekhouding van Vreemde Oosterlingen' published in *De Indische Gids* 3:2 (1881), 948–963, especially 949, 951, 955, 957; *Indisch Weekblad van het Regt*, 11-02-1878, 134–135; *De Locomotief*, 04-04-1878.

The main recommendation continued to centre around the language issue.[19] Banks and trading houses were often on the losing end of Chinese bankruptcies, which might have been avoided if their debtors' books could have been understood and examined more thoroughly. Account books of Foreign Orientals should therefore be kept in one of the European languages or *Rumi* (Romanized Malay), as well as the original language of use (Chinese, Arabic, etc.). It is telling that the colonial government was never inclined to alter the law to meet this demand. It simply could not be convinced that the Chinese 'race' was by nature inclined to deception and fraud, and would not collectively punish a whole population group for alleged crimes.[20] There were more practical reasons as well. Although most Chinese businessmen had a (rudimentary) knowledge of Malay, the government thought it preposterous to assume that they could keep their books in that language. This demand was considered to be irrational and potentially obstructive to the Chinese intermediate trade in general, even when allowing for a transitional period of two to five years to master the Malay language adequately.[21]

This is not to say that the charges made by the European wholesalers and bankers were completely disregarded. After 1865 Foreign Orientals were no longer exempt from the requirements to make up a balance sheet every year, and were also obliged to save all their business correspondence. In 1872 Chinese fraudulent bankruptcy, formerly brought before the native *Landraad*, became a matter of the *Raad van Justitie*. And in 1890 *onbedrevenheid* could no

19 P.N. Kuiper, *The early Dutch sinologists: A study of their training in Holland and China and their functions in the Netherlands Indies (1854–1900)*, 2 vols. (Unpublished Dissertation, Leiden University, 2015), 494–500; Tjiook-Liem, *De rechtspositie der Chinezen*, 142–145.

20 Compare the experience of P. Meeter, a government interpreter of the Chinese language in the colony, upon his return to the Netherlands, where he learned from Dutch lawyers that bankruptcy fraud was as common as and even more sophisticated in the mother country than it was in the Netherlands Indies. Meeter was an expert in this matter as he had translated and investigated numerous Chinese account books. He judged that only illegal agreements with regard to repayment (so-called *sluipaccoorden* or stealth settlements) in the case of pending bankruptcy cases were more common in the colony, since European merchants counted on a higher degree of secrecy from the Chinese. See P.N. Kuiper, *The early Dutch sinologists*, 793–794.

21 Fromberg, *Verspreide geschriften*, 312–313, 624; Tagliacozzo, *Secret trades of the Straits*, 257–258; Tagliacozzo, *Secret trades of the Straits*,129; J.L. Vleming, *Het Chinese zakenleven in Nederlands-Indië* (Weltevreden, 1926), 15–16, 39–55. What also tended to be forgotten was the substantial number of Chinese traders seeing to the specific needs of the large Chinese population group. Earthenware, lamps, salted fish and vegetables, sacrificial items such as incense or thuribles, etc. were imported directly from China. This separated line of trade required no mediation from the European trading sector and hardly any knowledge of the Malay language (*De Java-Bode*, 01-06-1892).

longer be used to excuse a debtor's faulty administration. But these measures were incapable of redressing the advantageous legal position of Foreign Orientals vis-a-vis their suppliers/creditors. Even supporters of the Chinese acknowledged this. Although every trader could keep his books in the language he wanted, in practice the Chinese had a distinct advantage, as use of the Chinese language improved their chances of getting away with fabricated, bankruptcy-ready (*faillisementsklaar*) accounts.[22] The Chinese themselves fully understood this, as they asserted: *Wet bilang saja boleh simpan boekoe bitjara tjina.* ('The law merely states that it is allowed to keep books in Chinese').[23]

Naturally, the Chinese themselves were equally aware of the fact that in many instances, the legal courts were not up to the task of assessing the validity of a Chinese bankruptcy. There was hardly any doubt, both amongst the Chinese and the Dutch, that financial accounts were on occasion falsified – or at the very least prepared to suit the trader's purposes – in order to hide semi-legal or illegal behaviour (e.g. tax evasion, unjust withdrawal of money, deliberate undervaluation of assets, artificial raising of expenses, etc.). The fact that such acts were seldom detected, or almost impossible to prove, frequently led to an acquittal. This had as much to do with most judges' inadequate knowledge of Chinese business practices and its bookkeeping methods as with the use of the Chinese language.

In private conversations Chinese could be very outspoken on the legal situation in the Netherlands Indies. The acquittal of a Chinese trader suspected of fraudulent bankruptcy in Surabaya around 1880 elicited the following illuminating remark from one of his fellow countrymen. When asked his personal opinion concerning the verdict, he replied: *Betoel, Toean! Itoe toewan toewan Raad toelong pegang tanggah boeat orang tjina naik paliet.* ('Correct, Sir! The gentlemen of the Council [of Justice] are helping the Chinese by holding the ladder, enabling them to go bankrupt').[24] Almost two decades later P. Brooshooft recorded the following remarks, alleged to come from Chinese defaulters: 'The Dutch justice system treats us as if we are Europeans and this is our

22 See Fromberg, *Verspreide geschriften*, 312–314; Liem Twan Djie, *De distribueerende tusschenhandel der Chineezen op Java* ('s Gravenhage: M. Nijhoff, 1947), 37–38; Meeter, *Advies van een deskundige*, 30–31; Tagliacozzo, *Secret trades of the Straits*, 258.

23 Quoted in 'Adres in zake de boekhouding van Vreemde Oosterlingen', published in *De Indische Gids* 3:2 (1881), 959. See also Vleming, *Het Chinese zakenleven in Nederlands-Indië*, 17–18.

24 Quoted in Meeter, *Advies van een deskundige*, 44–45. The use of the expression *naik paliet* in this instance is a pun on the Malay expression for going bankrupt or more literally to go down: *djatoh paliet.*

salvation; if they were familiar with our tricks and better trained to recognize the hidden foul play, we would be lost'.[25]

The fact that Chinese traders could file for bankruptcy themselves was identified by many as being the main cause of the problem. Protagonists and adversaries of the Chinese alike expected much from a restriction of this legal right. Since it was the main obstacle to debtor imprisonment, withdrawal of this provision would undoubtedly increase caution. But, efforts in this direction also turned out to be futile; the government did not respond favourably, and debt imprisonment actually ceased to exist in all but name by 1906.[26]

In sum, whereas the restrictive (legal) policy of the Dutch suggests a successful subjugation of the Chinese, changing commercial legislation in this particular instance actually worked in their favour. Where the Dutch commercial world expected to gain in security, Chinese business actually reaped the greater benefits by the allowance of access to law provisions of a higher standard, better (equipped) courts, lawyers, and notaries. Paradoxically, their Dutch counterparts experienced a sense of access denial by law provisions such as the aforementioned filing for bankruptcy, bookkeeping obligations and – in particular – the lack of foreign language demands imposed upon Chinese entrepreneurs and the insurmountable lack of Chinese language skill on part of the European commercial community. It was for these reasons that the issue received such attention, as a fierce debate continued to rage for almost half a century.[27]

4 The Benefit of Multiple Nationalities

The limited liability company Kwik Hoo Tong Handelmaatschappij (KHT / Trading Company Kwik Hoo Tong, Ltd) was formally established on 1 June 1894 in Solo, Central Java. The main purpose of the company was 'the trade in sugar,

25 *De Locomotief*, 10-03-1898.

26 See van den Berg, *Munt-, crediet- en bankwezen*, 379–380; Fromberg, *Verspreide geschriften*, 316–320, 625–626; Van Gennep, 'De Vreemde Oosterlingen en de lijfsdwang', 362–380; J.W. Young, 'Eenige aanteekeningen betreffende de Chineezen in Nederlandsch Oost-Indië', *Tijdschrift voor Nederlandsch Indië* 19 (1890), 362–374, here 369–371; J.W. Young, 'Handelsgebruiken in China', *Tijdschrift voor Nederlandsch Indië* 21 (1892), 241–246, here 241–246.

27 See, for instance, the different issues of *De Locomotief* – with P. Brooshooft as editor-in-chief – in March 1892 (9, 10, 14 and 15) and March 1898 (10 and 11) or the series of articles published in *De Java-Bode* in June (1, 2, 7, 8, 16, 28) and July (12 and 13) 1892.

tea, rice, and other articles to be designated by a majority of shareholders'.[28] The company's shareholders were the Chinese merchants Kwik Hong Biauw, Kwik Djoen Eng, Kwik Ing Djie, Kwik Ing Sien and Kwik Ing Hie. The company's business slowly developed in the years which followed, which gave rise to a change in its articles of incorporation. On 7 July 1903, a special KHT shareholders meeting was held in Semarang.[29] The meeting had been convened by Kwik Hong Biauw who noted 'the considerable expansion in trade relations over the last few years'. According to him, KHT's management structure needed to be revised to be better prepared for whatever the future might bring. The introduction of a mid-management level was to be part of this.

An easily overlooked but curious change, however, was the addition of a single sentence to article 23. In the original version of July 1894, the article read as follows:

> Article 23
> The shareholders, the agents, the director, their replacements, as well as the representatives of shareholders at the general meeting have to be Chinese.30

The introduction of a mid-management level management structure required only slight alterations in the phrasing of article 23, which makes the sudden appearance of a second section in 1903 all the more puzzling:

> Article 23
> (1) The shareholders, director, deputy director, principal agents, agents, as well as the authorized representatives of shareholders at the general meetings have to be Chinese.
> (2) This provision, however, does not include the founders and their descendants, even if they should change to another nationality or be equated with it.31

The rationale behind this addition can be found in the possibility of reducing commercial risk by carrying multiple nationalities.[32] This practice was well

28 Claver, *Dutch commerce*, 299–304
29 *Javasche Courant*, 11-09-1903.
30 *Javasche Courant*, 19-10-1894.
31 *Javasche Courant*, 11-09-1903.
32 Man-Houng Lin, 'Overseas Chinese merchants and multiple nationality. A means for reducing commercial risk', *Modern Asian Studies* 35 (2001) 985–1009.

accepted amongst the overseas Chinese in Southeast Asia and was made possible by the flexible nature of the prevailing nationality laws at the time. China's failure to provide security for its citizens abroad and the feeble minority position of Chinese living abroad all contributed to this.

The so-called *Japannerwet* (Japanese citizen law) of 1899 provided a way out for some Chinese citizens.[33] This law equated Japanese with Europeans, and in so doing blurred the distinction between Europeans and Asians. The decision by the Dutch authorities to promulgate this law in the Netherlands Indies had been a political one. Japan was an emerging, powerful nation, assertive and very confident after its military victory over China in 1894. In concluding a commercial treaty with the Netherlands in 1896, the Japanese government insisted upon equal treatment of its citizens. The Dutch accepted, consoling themselves with the fact that there were only a few hundred Japanese in the colony.[34] Giving equal status to a tiny minority could therefore not make much difference. The Dutch however failed to foresee the impact of this change in law upon the large Chinese minority. The Chinese did not see why they could not follow the Japanese and enjoy new status and prestige as 'Europeans' as well. This sense of injustice was amplified by the fact that the Chinese had shared civil law with the Europeans for almost half a century. The fact that most Japanese had a very low social status, working as prostitutes, or within households as maids or servants, added insult to injury.

Japanese nationality also applied to the inhabitants of Japanese colonies such as Taiwan, which had been wrested from China in 1895. As a result, the legal nationality of the Taiwanese was in fact Japanese. This included those who took Japanese nationality from Taiwan, but stayed in China or Southeast Asia. Though generally resenting the Japanese, many Chinese in the Netherlands Indies were quick to recognize the advantages of registering as a *Taiwan sekimin* – meaning a 'person registered in Taiwan' – and thus obtaining a higher legal status in the sense that a European status offered better legal protection.

---

33 Patricia Tjiook-Liem, 'Feiten en ficties bij het ontstaan van de Japannerwet. Wijziging van art. 109 RR bij Stb. No. 121, Ind. Stb. 1899 no. 202' Rechtsgeleerd Magazijn THEMIS, 4 (2005), pp. 192–208; Tjiook-Liem, *De rechtspositie der Chinezen in Nederlands-Indië*, 260–275.

34 In 1896 there were 463 Japanese in the Netherlands Indies, comprising 376 (81%) women and 87 (19%) men. The majority of these women (219 or 58%) were prostitutes. In 1905 the number of Japanese had risen to 997, of which number still more than 80% were women. See Peter Post, *Japanse bedrijvigheid in Indonesië 1868–1942: Structurele elementen van Japan's economische expansie in Zuidoost Azië* (Unpublished dissertation Vrije Universiteit Amsterdam, 1991); Fasseur, 'Cornerstone and stumbling block', 37.

From his own bitter experience, Kwik Hong Biauw was very much aware of this. In July 1903 the local newspaper in Solo – De Nieuwe Vorstenlanden – reported the following:

> Yesterday morning, very early, the police had the houses of several well-to-do Chinese fenced off whereupon a search was conducted the moment the doors to the street were opened. It was well prepared. The occupants were surprised, and the police found what they were looking for, i.e. opium. All together it must have been a considerable result.
>
> The question is, however, whether a punishable act had been committed. After all, the wrapping of the opium belonged to the farmer. Right now, it seems obvious to assume that the farmer has disposed of his remaining opium at the last moment against reduced prices. How much is the maximum amount of opium one may have at home? In one Chinese house a basket full of empty opium cans was found.
>
> One may well wonder whether all that opium was for personal use or whether it had been (smuggled) traded as well. In any case, ever since January, so for well over half a year, the Government has sold far less opium than it could have sold had it not been for this final act of the farm. That meant a loss of profit, and one can assume that still more such opium is held by rich Chinese, who stocked up on a cheap supply at the end of last year. And then another question arises: Is the farmer not liable to punishment as well, for selling wholesale?
>
> Finally, we have been informed that the opium has been sent to Batavia for examination in order to ascertain that the opium does not originate from the Regie.[35]

In all, the houses of eight Chinese, including the home of Kwik Hong Biauw, were searched.[36] Three times the permitted amount of opium had been confiscated from his house, and part of the opium was suspected not to have been produced in the government opium factory in Batavia. Consequently, Kwik Hong Biauw was charged with possession of (illegal) drugs and could be sentenced to three months of hard labour. Solo was one of the last areas in Java where the system of selling opium through private traders had been replaced by the state-run *Opium Regie*. Understandably, the colonial administration

35 *De Nieuwe Vorstenlanden*, 22-07-1903.

36 Bank Indonesia (BI) / De Javasche Bank (DJB) 1408 Confidential and secret correspondence Solo branch office, 24-07-1903; BI/DJB 1344 Confidential and secret correspondence Semarang branch office, 28-06-1904.

tried to battle smuggling as it cut revenues. Drug smuggling cases were tried locally before the police roll and *Landraad*, and were often chaired by incompetent and far from impartial civil servants. Despite the fact that Kwik Hong Biauw's offence was rather negligible, he could therefore expect to receive harsh punishment, which was all the more likely should the authorities want to set an example.[37]

The elderly Kwik Hong Biauw feared the trial and was 'very depressed, wishing to die rather than endure the shame of *krakal* (hard labour)'.[38] Initially, the drug charge against Kwik Hong Biauw appeared to have been dropped and after 'a nerve-racking period he was released from prison'.[39] However, on 6 August Kwik Hong Biauw was sentenced by the dreaded Police Court to one month of labour (*voor de kost zonder loon*, i.e with food provided, but without pay). A request for clemency was denied on 12 September 1903 after which Kwik Hong Biauw served his sentence. The whole affair had another serious consequences; besides Kwik Hong Biauw, the telegraphic code of KHT had been seized as well, and remained in the hands of the *Opium Regie* for more than a year.[40] Deprived of this fast and reliable means of communication, KHT was seriously handicapped in its overseas business and suffered considerable financial damage.

The unpleasant confrontation with highhanded Dutch law enforcement and the biased judicial system of the colony convinced both Kwik Hong Biauw and Kwik Djoen Eng of the advisability of changing their legal status forthwith. The procedure was simple. It required a trip to Taiwan, which both partners immediately undertook after the release of Kwik Hong Biauw in October 1903, and where several pieces of land were bought. When the purchase deed was handed to the Japanese consulate general in Singapore on the return voyage, the owner would quietly receive the necessary paperwork proving him to be a *Taiwan sekimin* and therefore a Japanese national. Within half a year Kwik Hong Biauw and Kwik Djoen Eng had made use of this Japanese 'loophole' and registered themselves as citizens of Taiwan, which automatically gave them

37 J.R. Rush, *Opium to Java. Revenue farming and Chinese enterprise in colonial Indonesia 1860-1910* (Ithaca, 1990) 228–229.

38 BI/DJB 1408 Confidential and secret correspondence Solo branch office, 24-07-1903; BI/DJB 1344 Confidential and secret correspondence Semarang branch office, 28-06-1904.

39 BI/DJB 1413 Confidential and secret correspondence Yogyakarta branch office, 17-06-1908; Tjiook-Liem, *De rechtspositie der Chinezen in Nederlands-Indië 1848–1942*, p. 262.

40 BI/DJB 1344 Confidential and secret correspondence Semarang branch office, 28-06-1904.

European status upon their return to the Netherlands Indies,[41] ensuring better treatment at the hands of the colonial authorities. According to *Resident* De Vogel of Surakarta (i.e. Solo), Kwik Hong Biauw's swift actions (becoming a Japanese citizen as well as cutting off his Manchu ponytail as a means of showing his equation to European status) greatly impressed the Chinese community in town.[42]

In sum, a wicked consequence of the *Japannerwet*, one that was not foreseen by the Dutch colonial authorities, was that it offered (wealthy) Chinese citizens access to Japanese citizenship and thereby access to better and more even-handed judicial treatment. They realized that the obtained equality before the law offered them more and better tools to right their wrongs. Kwik Hong Biauw could have his case pleaded from now on by (expensive) lawyers before more competent judges with access to more secure and better law provisions. And, inter alia, probably have the denial of access of his telegraphic business code challenged with more chance of success than before. Protected by their Japanese passports, the Dutch for their part were denied recourse to their customary high-handedness in cases involving these particular Chinese-Japanese-Indies citizens.[43]

5 Boycotts

The application of (il)legal pressure of any kind in trading matters was a common enough phenomenon which occasionally took the form of a trading boycott by the Chinese.[44] They were not routinely applied, since boycott

41 BI/DJB 1346 Confidential and secret correspondence Semarang branch office, 19-02-1913.

42 Tjiook-Liem, *De rechtspositie der Chinezen in Nederlands-Indië 1848–1942*, 262.

43 The sources remain silent as to how many Chinese made use of this legal loophole and became naturalized Japanese citizens. Mention is made of 60,000 Chinese applications in 1901, but corroboration of this mass intent was not found by the Dutch authorities who stated in 1917 that 69 Japanese citizens of Chinese decent were registered on the island of Java. Tjiook-Liem, *De rechtspositie der Chinezen in Nederlands-Indië 1848–1942*, 274.

44 One of the earliest recorded Chinese boycotts took place in Batavia in 1655 and was aimed against the existing trading practices of the VOC. The Chinese traders involved resisted the fact that only a limited part of textile shipments from India was publicly auctioned, after which high-ranking VOC-personnel would secretly buy the remainder against lower prices. This course of action naturally gave the latter a financial advantage upon resale of the acquired goods. The Chinese textile traders thereupon agreed no longer to buy from the VOC upon payment of a fine. Despite the agreed penalty, the ensuing boycott lasted only eight days after which the first Chinese resumed their business with the VOC. When the agreement came to the knowledge of the Dutch, the three initiators of the boycott – Lacco, Oeco and Simko – were subsequently charged with undermining the trade

movements required managerial and logistical skills as well as monetary resources and sufficient power of will. Chinese traders participating in a boycott acted as an interest group: i.e. a group of individuals, conscious of sharing a common concern, cooperating on the borders of power, and seeking to increase their own benefits through bargaining with a political system they (have to) accept and (attempt to) influence but cannot control. To be more precise, the Chinese organizing themselves in a boycott movement acted as a non-associational interest group. By definition such groups are linked by family ties, ethnicity, status, class, or region. Its members are, however, not permanently organized, know little formal procedures, do not possess continuity in internal structure, and articulate their interests through influential individuals, family heads or representatives.[45]

Whenever initiated, most group actions of this kind were small-scale, often with only local implications. The great majority were not unanimously supported, were ill-organized, and could be easily bypassed due to the extreme competition among traders of all calibres. Thus, many collective exercises just faded away, seemingly without being noticed. Still, each and every time a boycott was announced, the Dutch were reminded of the potential of Chinese collective action.

5.1 *Ho Tsai Ing*

One example of a Chinese trading boycott case has been described by H. Borel, who worked as an Chinese interpreter in Surabaya in the late 1890s.[46] As the official responsible for Chinese affairs, he was regularly summoned to hearings of the Council of Justice in order to provide expert advice concerning Chinese bankruptcies. Through the investigation of the account books of numerous Chinese traders who failed to honour their business commitments, he acquired intimate knowledge of the trading system in general and Chinese business operations in particular.

In early 1898, Borel stumbled upon the case of Ho Tsai Ing, a trader in ironware, who had defaulted repeatedly in the preceding years and now offered to settle for the third time.[47] The previous settlements had led to a reconstruction

monopoly and authority of the VOC and ordered to pay one hundred and fifty *rijksdaalders* (Niemeijer, *Batavia*, 228–229).

45 Jessica Vance Roitman and Han Jordaan, 'Fighting a foregone conclusion. Local interest groups, West-Indian merchants and St. Eustatius, 1780–1810' *Tijdschrift voor Sociale en Economische Geschiedenis*, 12 (2015), 86–87.

46 H. Borel, *De Chineezen in Nederlandsch-Indië* (Amsterdam: L.J. Veen, 1900) 105–116; P.N. Kuiper, *The early Dutch sinologists*, 283–305, 341–386, 832–839.

47 Claver, *Dutch commerce*, 200–201.

of his debt and had seen repayments of 30% and 40% as part of the agreement. This seemed a quite reasonable percentage under the prevailing circumstances, but it became known that on both occasions friendly trading partners received a full 100% of the outstanding debt. In other words, Ho Tsai Ing showed no scruples in concluding a so-called *sluipaccoord* (stealth settlement), much to the detriment of other creditors. Borel regretted that this kind of behaviour was not punishable by law, and that it had become common practice among Chinese and European traders alike. He pointed out that both parties were to blame however, and that they were well-matched when it came to cunning business practices.

Ho Tsai Ing's proposal to settle his arrears once again was accepted by all of his European creditors with one exception. One trading firm had the books examined by an expert – most likely Borel himself – and upon hearing the results decided to press charges. Despite the fact that Ho Tsai Ing's business boasted an annual turnover of more than one hundred thousand guilders, he had only surrendered a list showing how much he owed his European creditors and how much he could claim from his Chinese and indigenous debtors. For want of other books it turned out to be impossible to make a reliable assessment of his total assets and liabilities, and judge whether he had masterminded his own default. It was therefore feared that he had withdrawn capital from the company for his own personal benefit. In the meantime Ho Tsai Ing claimed not to possess any other books. He simply declared that he had no need for them and only required the book which he had already turned in.

Borel found this to be utterly unbelievable. The fact that no ledger, cash book, stock register or balance sheet was present indicated clear fraudulent intent to him. It remained a mystery how much merchandise was supposed to be in stock, or what amount of money had to be in cash. There was no telling whether Ho Tsai Ing had pocketed money that was not his or had already cashed (part of) his company's assets. Fraud was also suspected, since Ho Tsai Ing had recently made a habit of buying on credit and selling for cash below prevalent market prices. Such transactions were proved as European firms had to hand over receipts showing all cash payments made to Ho Tsai Ing during the last six months. It turned out that Ho Tsai Ing had sold over ƒ 12,000 of ironware priced far too cheaply. He refuted this incriminating evidence by saying that he had merely intended to clear old stock at low prices. According to him, all the merchandise sold had been purchased long ago, at least more than six months before. With the absence of a stock register this could however not be disproved, and Ho Tsai Ing remained in the clear.

Notwithstanding all this legal haggling, the European trading firm on whose behalf the inquiry had been conducted found ample reason to bring the matter to court. To his surprise, Borel noticed that this was not at all appreciated by one of Ho Tsai Ing's biggest European creditors. However, he was truly aghast to see actual countermeasures taken by this particular firm. It managed to persuade the leading Chinese retail traders of Surabaya to sign a notarial deed, requiring them – under penalty of a heavy fine – to boycott the firm planning legal action if the charges were not immediately withdrawn. No matter how blunt this strategy was, it worked. In order to avoid the boycott, all charges were hastily dropped. Nevertheless, the case was continued by the public prosecutor who accused Ho Tsai Ing of misleading his creditors and of embezzlement, if not of destroying his account books. These accusations did not hold for lack of proof. After months of deliberation, the judges could only find Ho Tsai Ing guilty of failing to keep adequate account books, for which he was sentenced to six months of forced labour. At this point, in a final attempt to see some of their claims recovered, the misled creditors went as far as to petition for a pardon which, however, was not granted. Ho Tsai Ing remained incarcerated, and in the end was declared bankrupt. This left his creditors no other option than to swallow their loss and wait for the next episode in Surabaya's turbulent history of defaults, bankruptcies and boycotts.

5.2 'Bikin mati toko Amsterdam'

> Typical of the changed relations within the Indies trading world is the conduct in 1902 of the Soerabaia based Chinese traders towards the Agency of the Handelsvereeniging Amsterdam [...] their attempt to lock out (to boycott) that office in all its dealings with import houses, and by that means to wage a real trade war, [...] could only be brought to an end by making substantial financial sacrifices.[48]

With the boycott against the HVA starting in 1902, the Chinese traders of Surabaya sought to put an end to one of the most important Dutch trading houses.[49] Their aim was 'to finish off the Amsterdam shop' (*Bikin mati toko Amsterdam*). The only reason they had failed so far – according to pamphlets distributed in Java's interior in June 1904 – was the fact that the Chinese had run 'into the wall of millions behind which the *Handelsvereeniging Amsterdam* has entrenched itself'. According to public opinion, the HVA would have been forced into

48 Van den Berg, *Munt-, crediet- en bankwezen.*

49 Claver, *Dutch commerce*, 189–239.

submission a long time before had it not been for the financial leverage at its disposal.[50]

Preparations to boycott the HVA had commenced in the second week of August 1902 and became publicly known with a small announcement in the *Soerabaiasch Handelsblad* on 13 August 1902. Under the title 'A boycott movement', editor M. van Geuns reported that Chinese retail traders had recently started to organize themselves in an apparent attempt to deny the HVA any future orders. The Chinese had a contract drawn up by notary A.H. van der Does de Bije, which stated that the boycott was exclusively aimed at the import business of the HVA, while the export of agrarian products as well as the important trade in petroleum were deliberately excluded.[51]

The contract contained twelve provisions and each clearly indicated the determination of the boycotters. The penalty for breaching the boycott and resuming trading with the HVA was no less than ƒ 1,000 on the first occasion, ƒ 2,500 on the second, ƒ 5,000 on the third and ƒ 10,000 for each following violation. Anyone who wanted to be dismissed from his boycott obligation within five years after joining was obliged to pay a fine of ƒ 10,000. The boycott had an indefinite running period and could only be terminated with the explicit consent of all participants. Any attempt to influence those that wanted to continue the boycott was again punishable by a penalty of ƒ 10,000.

Furthermore, the boycotters agreed to try to prevent all trade in HVA merchandise by any of their commercial connections. Most European objections were raised against this article, since it attempted a complete block on the HVA's import trade. This was a frightening prospect for every European trader and/or banker. More than any other provision it seems to have convinced them of the need to counteract the Chinese measures.[52]

Adding to this was the number of Chinese retail traders that joined the boycott. In all, 85 Chinese traders and shopkeepers signed the boycott contract, making the boycott a highly organized and massive affair. It was unequalled, in both scale and ramifications, and was consequently perceived by the European wholesale traders as a danger.[53]

Initially, the HVA hardly reacted to all of this. It was convinced that the whole matter would peter out within weeks and assumed a haughty attitude. The Surabaya agency even failed to mention the particulars of the boycott in

50 *Soerabaiasch Handelsblad*, 21-05 1904; B.G. Setiono, *Tionghoa dalam pusaran politik* (Jakarta: Elkasa, 2003) 363–365.

51 The complete provisions of the contract were published in the *Soerabaiasch Handelsblad* on 5 September 1902.

52 *Soerabaiasch Handelsblad*, 05-09-1902; *Weekblad voor Indië* I 5 (29-05-1904), 5.

53 *Soerabaiasch Handelsblad*, 20-08-1902; *Weekblad voor Indië* I 5 (29-05-1904), 5.

its correspondence to the Amsterdam head office. However, news travelled fast and manufacturers and producers alike did not take the matter lightly and in Amsterdam started to inquire what was going on. With no answers, head office suddenly found itself in an embarrassing situation and communication with the branches in Java was stepped up. From the end of August the situation gained momentum. The HVA began to look for help, and approached the financial institutions in Java.

On 8 September a counter boycott was put into effect with the support of the four main banks as well as the Surabaya Savings Bank and the two English banks operating in the city. The banks were confident that their refusal to discount the acceptances of selected Chinese traders would end the boycott. However, the attempt hurt the European importers who had accepted IOUs from their Chinese clients in the belief that the signatures were good for the specified amount. The banks' refusal to discount these IOUs in the future rendered them worthless, and consequently plunged the wholesalers into a liquidity crisis.

The importers started to object to the banks' approach. In a letter dated 12 September 1902 they voiced their disapproval of the 'punishment' of a few selected Chinese and of the 'one-sided' point of view upon which the banks based their judgement. Information had been received from the HVA only and the Chinese case was totally disregarded.[54] The banks were asked to reconsider their counter boycott. The importers were however rebuffed, and even their plea to limit the punitive measures to a much smaller number of Chinese traders was rejected. The counter boycott nevertheless did not bring the Chinese to their knees and therefore failed within weeks of its inception.

Consequently, the HVA had to follow a new course. It now focused on the possibilities of a court proceeding. If the contract was breached and the court ruled that the perpetrator did not have to pay the stipulated fine of ƒ10,000, traders might be persuaded to give up the boycott. The HVA tried to find at least one trader willing to risk this procedure, guaranteeing to pay all possible damages, but not a single boycotter agreed. The HVA then called in the authorities. In January 1903, the Surabayan assistant-Resident Arends was found to be prepared to mediate.

Although the authorities in Surabaya had followed the boycott closely, they had not intervened, considering it to be primarily an economic dispute with no harmful political implications. But with the dispute dragging on and with no solution in sight it was thought prudent to respond positively to the HVA's request. The Assistant-Resident's intervention might have worked, were it not for

54 BI/DJB 5143, 13-09-1902; BI/DJB 78 No. 50, pp. 203–204.

the fact that he was also the acting chief of police and so presided over the indigenous court of justice. As the Chinese were well aware of how much depended on his benevolent attitude in legal cases, they could not view him as an impartial negotiator. Except for the HVA, the European importers were of the same opinion and immediately objected to his involvement by preparing a complaint, to be sent to the Governor-General, stating that the Surabaya authorities had no right to interfere. This proved to be unnecessary, because in February Arends gave up his attempt to negotiate without achieving a breakthrough.[55]

Confronted with yet another failure, the HVA changed tactics and decided to address both the Governor-General and the Minister of Colonies personally with a request for help.[56] Due to the inertia of the bureaucracy the HVA did not expect quick results and continued to work on other initiatives. On 30 April 1903 the situation was assessed at the Amsterdam head office. The boycott had been occasioned by two Chinese traders – Tjo Sik Giok and Tjo Tje An – aided and abetted by European competitors (Schnitzler & Co amongst others). The immediate reason for the boycott had been the refusal of credit facilities to the aforementioned Chinese on account of the new restrictive credit policy of the HVA. Convinced of this policy's soundness, the Directors and Commissioners decided not to deviate from the set course.[57] The HVA was capable of showing this kind of determination, because so far the boycott had not harmed its profitability. The Surabaya agency had managed to maintain its volume of trade for most products, and through much effort a sufficient turnover was accomplished. Nevertheless, a way had to be found to neutralize the boycott.

On 16 June 1903 the struggle entered a new round with the HVA suing Tjo Sik Giok and Tjo Tje An, demanding to be compensated for sustained damages.[58] At the same time 22 boycotters were called before the Assistant-Resident Arends to give a statement.[59] The Dutch lawyer of the two Chinese summoned to court asserted that the whole exercise was extremely nerve-wracking, as the two were made to wait seemingly endlessly, and were living in constant fear of being interned or expelled altogether from the Netherlands Indies. This investigation was followed by a second one conducted by the public prosecutor, who also heard the Surabaya traders on the conditions under which business was conducted in general and in particular by the HVA. Their statements did

55 BI/DJB 78 No. 52, p. 207; BI/DJB 77 No. 87, p. 119; *Weekblad voor Indië* I 5 (29-05-1904), 6.

56 *De Locomotief*, 19 and 21-12-1908; *Weekblad voor Indië* I 5 (29-05-1904), 6.

57 Nationaal Archief, The Netherlands, The Hague (NA) / Handelsvereeniging Amsterdam (HVA) 1 *Minute Book* 3, pp. 87–88.

58 BI/DJB 79 No. 23, p. 83.

59 *De Locomotief*, 21 and 22-12-1908.

not help the HVA as they appear to have made the boycott more understandable if not justifiable.

Whatever the reason, no charges were ever pressed against the boycotters. In the end, the Chinese scored an outright victory as the law suit against Tjo Sik Giok and Tjo Tje An was thrown out of court on 20 May 1904.[60] The HVA never recovered from this mental blow. It did appeal the court's decision but had essentially run out of options. From now on, it could only try to resist the boycott. For another year the adversaries tested each other's resolve. In May 1905 the Chinese renewed their proposal to end the boycott by buying them off. This time they offered to settle the matter provided that the HVA contributed ƒ 25,000 for the building of a Chinese school and another ƒ 5,000 to cover their legal expenses. Battle-weary, the Amsterdam office agreed to pay, against the advice of the Java branch offices.[61] After nearly three years the Chinese had won.

It stands to reason that the Dutch were not at all pleased with the effectiveness of the boycott, which received immediate and widespread recognition. The celebrated results obtained by boycotts or the mere threat of them found fertile ground in the imagination of the indigenous population. In popular speech the boycott instrument soon came to be called the *obat gandroong Tiong Kok*, or the 'medicine of which the Chinese are extremely fond'.[62] The economic balance of power had shifted, and European companies braced themselves for more (threats of) boycotts. The HVA, for instance, saw a renewed Chinese boycott in Semarang in 1908–1909. The difference was that in 1902 the Dutch commercial establishment and part of government circles still thought they could turn the tide and eradicate the problem; in 1908 the inevitable had been recognized and the HVA knew that it had to solve the problem itself.

In sum, successful boycotts like the one aimed at the HVA were a true shock to the Dutch colonial system, since it reversed the cards on the table. Deviating from the perceived natural order of things, Dutch commercial interests were denied access to their customer base at great expense in time, effort and money spent. In essence, the Chinese involved used a traditional network strategy, but cemented this legally by a binding notary deed. A course of action feasible by virtue of the commercial legislation in place. The HVA tried to respond by accessing its financial and government network, but to no avail. In a legal sense, the Chinese adversaries had to be treated as equals, which not

60 BI/DJB 81 No. 14, p. 51; SH, 21-05-1904; *Weekblad voor Indië* I 5 (29-05-1904), 6–7.

61 NA/HVA 1 *Minute Book* 3, p. 139; Nieuw Rotterdamsche Courant (NRC), 28-06-1905.

62 *Soerabaiasch Handelsblad*, 30-12-1908.

only levelled the playground, but in this case put the HVA at a serious disadvantage.

6 In Search for Access

As stated, entrepreneurial room for manoeuvre in the Netherlands Indies depended upon access to capital, information, and security. The notion of access seems to have been a precondition for the functioning of adequate survival mechanisms. Capital was of primary importance, acting at one and the same time as a means of information, security and – indeed – capital. Information and security in this equation were means to an end, since both are instrumental in securing capital. However, information was also instrumental in furthering security which, in turn, was a precondition for Chinese survival. The importance of the semantics and defining characteristics notwithstanding, it is clear that the concept of accessibility is essential to the considerations above.

Any degree of access is essentially a function of space, time and information.[63] Greater access is generated by reducing the space between the entity seeking access and the objective (physical or informational) being sought; by reducing the time needed for transport or communication, and by increasing the amount of information available about it. Access conveys benefits through these variables, which results in multiplier effects. Greater access increases available time by reducing the time needed for transport or communication. It increases the amount of usable space in which individuals or corporations can function (e.g., from local to global markets); and greater access to information benefits decision making by reducing the level of uncertainty.

This paper has focused in particular on the successful reduction of uncertainty by Chinese merchants. However, in all cases, accessibility issues have been vital in understanding the contribution to security enhancement. As evidenced, access to capital (hiring expensive lawyers or purchasing land in Taiwan) and access to information (implications of law changes or KHT's telegraphic code withdrawal) played a crucial part. In the cases presented here, Chinese entrepreneurs seized upon (unintended) access opportunities offered to them by groups (Dutch merchants, Japanese government) advocating different and/or contrary interests. The fact that they managed to cope with the

---

63 *How greater access is changing the world. A Landmark study on the relevance of access to people, businesses and nations* (Menlo Park, California; Stanford Research Institute (SRI), 2006); *The dynamic force of access. An update of the access index* (Menlo Park, California; Stanford Research Institute (SRI), 2008).

restrictions imposed upon them, and indeed on occasion turned them to their advantage, says much of their ability to access opportunities as well as their (subconscious) recognition of the importance of having a good access position. It is equally informative of the seminal role played by entrepreneurship; a role which has received much attention, but remains elusive so far, and fails to be captured in general conceptual models. It is therefore argued that the use of the concept of accessibility as a research tool within the context of entrepreneurship should be explored further as the cases presented in this paper clearly indicate its potential value.

Corporate Law in Colonial India: Rise and Demise of the Managing Agency System

Umakanth Varottil

1 Introduction

Conventional scholarship in corporate law ascribes the origins of governance debates to the seminal work of Berle and Means.[1] Through a study of US corporations during the period between 1880 and 1930, they concluded that there is a 'separation of ownership and control' in which the individual interest of shareholders is made subservient to that of managers who are in control of a company. Due to the diffusion in shareholding, the shareholders are unable to monitor the managers, as widely dispersed shareholders lack sufficient financial incentives to intervene directly in the affairs of the company. Left unchecked, the managers may abuse their position by acting in their own interests rather than in the interests of the shareholders, which they have a duty to promote.[2] Much of the effort in corporate law over the years has been to address the agency problem[3] between managers and shareholders as identified by Berle and Means, at least in countries where diffused shareholding is the norm. While the field of corporate governance has witnessed substantial progress, there is much to evolve.[4]

1 Adolph A. Berle, Jr. and Gardiner C. Means, *The Modern Corporation and Private Property* (New York: Transaction Publishers, 1932).

2 Brian Cheffins, 'The Trajectory of (Corporate Law) Scholarship', online: <http://ssrn.com/abstract=429624> (2003), 26.

3 For a detailed discussion on the concept of the agency problems in a company, see Michael Jensen and William Meckling, 'Theory of the Firm: Managerial Behavior, Agency Costs, and Ownership Structure', *The Journal of Financial Economics* 3 (1976), 305–360 at 310; Reinier Kraakman et al., *The Anatomy of Corporate Law: A Comparative and Functional Approach* (Oxford: Oxford University Press, 2009), 35.

4 For example, the Economist magazine portends the decline of the Western corporation. 'Death and transfiguration: The golden age of the Western corporation may be coming to an end', *The Economist* (19 September 2015). On the other hand, Bainbridge and Henderson propose a radical idea whereby corporate boards are substituted by board service providers who are themselves firms (either partnerships or corporations). Stephen M. Bainbridge and M. Todd Henderson, 'Boards-R-Us: Reconceptualizing Corporate Boards', *Stanford Law Review* 66 (2014), 1051–1119.

 | DOI:10.1163/9789004443075_012

This paper focuses on the managing agency system, a peculiar type of corporate governance arrangement that emanated in India during the colonial period, which not only preceded the Berle and Means corporation, but which has also largely escaped the attention of corporate law scholars. Although the managing agency system displayed more acute forms of agency problems between shareholders and management on account of the separation between ownership and control, it remained overshadowed by its well-known US variant. While the quest for appropriate mechanisms to resolve agency problems in the Berle and Means corporation is yet ongoing, the problems that plagued the managing agency system in India for over a century were resolved ultimately by a legislative fiat that sounded its death knell. The objective of this paper is to analyse the evolution of the managing agency system, its benefits, the agency problems it generated, and finally the attempts by corporate law in India to deal with those problems that led to its abolition.

The managing agency system emerged in India in the early part of the nineteenth century and gradually spread to certain other British colonies in Asia. Under this, a managing agent (typically a sole proprietorship, partnership or private limited company) would enter into a contract with one or more joint stock companies so as to manage those companies.[5] Although the managed companies would constitute their own board of directors, it was the managing agent that carried out all management functions, including establishing and running the business as well as raising finances.[6] The managing agent often held a limited number of shares in the managed company, but exercised significant control by virtue of the management contract and additional measures that included obtaining representation on the board of the company and soliciting proxies from other shareholders. British managing agents dominated the system for most of the colonial period. The business rationale for the system is understandable as it provided the much-needed impetus for entrepreneurship and financing at the time. However, by the latter half of the nineteenth

5 Andrew F. Brimmer, 'The Setting of Entrepreneurship in India', *Quarterly Journal of Economics* 69 (1955), 553–576 at 554. This was a form of external management, which is not altogether alien to contemporary corporate governance given that mutual funds and real estate investment trusts (REITS) are managed by external entities such as fund managers or investment advisors. Jill E. Fisch, 'Rethinking the Regulation of Securities Intermediaries', *University of Pennsylvania Law Review* 158 (2010), 1961–2041 at 1968. It is a different matter that external management is at present largely confined to the investment industry, unlike the management agency system that was broader and covered manufacturing and trading activities.

6 Robert C. Rosen, 'The Myth of Self-Regulation or the Dangers of Securities Regulation without Administration: The Indian Experience', *Journal of Comparative Corporate Law and Securities Regulations* 2 (1979), 261–302 at 263.

century, the system had fallen victim to failures in the form of large-scale abuse by some managing agents who were only interested in perpetuating their control over the managed companies for their private benefits, much to the detriment of their shareholders who remained rather passive due to their low individual shareholdings.

The composition of the managing agents and the managed companies altered over a period of time with greater Indian involvement. While the later part of the colonial period witnessed greater participation by Indian shareholders and directors on managed companies and also the emergence of Indian-owned managing agents, following India's independence there was a gradual retreat of British business interests who divested their stakes in the managing agents in favour of Indian businesses that ended up holding the skeletal remains upon the demise of the system.

The legal responses to the managing agency system are somewhat remarkable. For a century since its inception, the concept did not receive any recognition whatsoever under Indian law. The constant protestations by shareholders from the mid-nineteenth century onwards, regarding wholesale abuse of the system, fell on deaf ears. The colonial government refused to legislate on the matter until 1936, when companies' legislation in India imposed some restrictions on the operation of managing agencies and limited the scope of their control. Although there were calls for the abolition of the system by the time India gained independence in 1947, the independent Government refused to accede to these requests, although it did impose additional controls. It was only in the 1960s that the noose around the managing agency system was tightened further, culminating in its abolition with effect from 1970.

As is elaborated in this paper, the legal responses to the managing agency system were affected by several considerations, including economic, social and cultural factors. The colonial government did not possess adequate momentum to rein in changes to the system, as it would have impinged upon British business interests in India. It was only towards the end of the colonial period, when Indian influence in the legislative process became more pronounced, that checks and balances were in fact introduced. The effect of interest groups and rent-seeking behaviour continue to manifest themselves even in the post-colonial period.

Part 2 of this paper discusses the evolution of the managing agency system. It seeks to ascertain the reasons for its origin, and the institutional, economic and social factors that led to its prominence. Part 3 analyses the contractual structure and the relationship between the managing agent and the managed companies, and identifies the various corporate governance problems that arose from the structure as well as from its operation in practice. Part 4 charts the legislative response to the managing agency system. A century of inaction led to the imposition of the restrictions on the system followed by its abolition. Part 5 concludes with a discussion of the key lessons arising from the managing agency episode.

2 Evolution of the Managing Agency System

Given the uniqueness of the managing agency system to colonial India, the concept cannot be examined in isolation. The institutional, economic and social circumstances prevailing at the time of its emergence as well as its evolution thereafter take on tremendous significance. The necessity for its introduction as well as its subsequent distortion must be examined in these specific contexts, as this part seeks to do.

2.1 *Origins*

The emergence of the modern business corporation in India can be attributed to the establishment of the English East India Company ('EIC') in 1600, which was granted a royal charter that effectively conferred upon it a monopoly on trade in India.[7] EIC officials were barred from undertaking private business, but towards the end of the eighteenth century, several agency houses sprung up that were established and managed by ex-officials of the EIC.[8] These agency houses performed the role of facilitating remittances between British citizens residing in India and London, but they thereafter also began undertaking trade and commerce generally.[9] While little is known about the precise nature of the agency houses' activities, they shot into prominence when the EIC's monopoly on trade in India came to an end in 1813.[10] There is a consensus that the agency houses acted as precursors to the more organized form that took on the character of managing agents.

The precise timing of when the agency houses metamorphosed into managing agents is much less settled. Rungta identifies features of the managing agency system among life insurance companies in the first two decades of the

7 Ron Harris, 'The English East India Company and the History of Company Law', in Ella Gepken-Jager, Gerard van Solinge and Levinus Timmerman (eds.), *VOC 1602–2002 – 400 Years of Company Law* (Deventer: Kluwer Legal Publishers, 2005) 219–247 at 219.

8 B.R. Tomlinson, *The Economy of Modern India: From 1860 to the Twenty-first Century*, 2nd ed. (Cambridge: Cambridge University Press 2013), 78.

9 Dwijendra Tripathi, 'Indian Entrepreneurship in Historical Perspective: A Re-Interpretation', *Economic and Political Weekly* 22:6 (1971), M59–M66 at M-61.

10 Tomlinson, *The Economy of Modern India*, 78.

nineteenth century.[11] However, Kling points to the establishment of Carr, Tagore and Company in 1834 for the origin of the system.[12] Interestingly, this was a partnership between William Carr, a British trader, and Dwarkanath Tagore, a wealthy merchant in Calcutta. In 1836, Carr, Tagore and Company undertook the management of the Calcutta Steam Tug Association, and subsequently added other joint stock companies to its managed portfolio. The promise of an Indo-British joint venture was short-lived, as the partnership came to an end in 1847 due to its inability to deal with a financial crisis and also because of internal mismanagement.[13]

The uniqueness of the managing agency system to colonial India can be related to the trade and investment relationship between Britain and India, and 'can be seen as an institutional innovation for directing capital flows and ... to alleviate agency problems in the context of long-distance investment for the British'.[14] Its close association with British enterprise in India is without doubt, as it began in India and then went on to the port cities of British colonies in Southeast Asia and East Asia, and 'that there appears to be an assumption that it represented some special adaptation of British business practices to the peculiar economic environment of Asia'.[15]

Brimmer suggests that the system was necessitated on account of (i) the lack of entrepreneurial capacity on the one hand, and (ii) a shortage of financing on the other.[16] Since Indian businessmen were engaged in traditional trading and financing, the British managing agency firms who had gained knowledge not only of local markets in specific industries, but also of foreign markets and sources of supply, were able to fill the gap quickly with their superior technology and managerial skills.[17] Similarly, on the financing side, the managing agents played an important role. When either the managing agent or a group of businessmen came up with a business idea, it was possible to raise financing

11 Radhe Shyam Rungta, *The Rise of Business Corporations in India 1851–1900* (Cambridge: Cambridge University Press, 1970), 222–224.

12 Blair B. Kling, 'The Origin of the Managing Agency System in India', *The Journal of Asian Studies* 26 (1966), 37–47 at 38.

13 Tomlinson, *The Economy of Modern India*, 78; Rungta, *The Rise of Business Corporations*, 226.

14 Bishnupriya Gupta, 'Community Networks and Capital Flows in Colonial India: A Tale of Two Cities', online: <http://www.iga.ucdavis.edu/events/Research/All-UC/Gupta%20paper.pdf> (2010), 19–20.

15 J. Forbes Munro, 'From Regional Trade to Global Shipping: Mackinnon Mackenzie & Co within the Mackinnon Enterprise Network', in Geoffrey Jones (ed.), *The Multinational Traders* (London, New York: Routledge, 1998), 48–65 at 51.

16 Brimmer, 'The Setting of Entrepreneurship in India', 560.

17 Tripathi, 'Indian Entrepreneurship', M-62.

through investments by shareholders in a joint stock company promoted by the managing agent.[18] It was the managing agent's capabilities and reputation that attracted businessmen to invest on the understanding that they would not be involved in the management of the business, as they were themselves handling their own businesses and had limited time to devote to the affairs of the joint stock company.[19] This helped fill the funding gap, as it provided comfort to investors to infuse funds into the managed company without considerable oversight.[20] It has been noted that in the early stages, it fitted well with the needs of the Indian business environment and that there was indeed no alternative to this mechanism.[21]

At the same time, the evolution of the managing agency system cannot be viewed as a mere business phenomenon or a financial venture, as it is ensconced in a combination of geographical considerations and factors of ethnicity that require examination.

2.2 *Geography, Ethnicity*

The evolution of the managing agency system is closely related to the geographical diversity in business activities in colonial India. Historians have been occupied with the divide between the eastern part of India (focused on Calcutta) and the western part (focused on Bombay and Ahmedabad). Business activities evolved rather differently in these two regions. British businesses dominated eastern India with control over jute mills, collieries and tea plantations.[22] One rationale for this phenomenon is that these businesses were export-oriented, wherein British businessmen possessed the expertise and contacts for international trade.[23] Conventional accounts indicate that the entry and expansion of British businesses in the eastern region was made possible because the local population was not entrepreneurially driven, but also

18 Ananya Mukherjee Reed, 'Corporate Governance Reforms in India', *Journal of Business Ethics* 37:3 (2002), 249–268 at 251.

19 Rungta, *The Rise of Business Corporations*, 228; Tirthankar Roy, *The Economic History of India, 1857–1947*, 2nd ed. (New Delhi: Oxford University Press, 2006), 260.

20 Thus, the seeds of shareholder passivity were sown at the very outset.

21 Palamadai Samu Lokanathan, *Industrial Organization in India* (London: Allen & Unwin, 1935), 23.

22 Omkar Goswami, 'Sahibs, Babus, and Banias: Changes in Industrial Control In Eastern India, 1918–50', *The Journal of Asian Studies* 48 (1989), 289–309 at 290.

23 Morris David Morris, 'South Asian Entrepreneurship and the Rashomon Effect, 1800–1947', *Explorations in Economic History* 16:3 (1979), 341–361.

that the British businesses imposed significant high barriers to entry due to their dominance in the region.[24]

By the end of the nineteenth century, British businesses maintained a strong foothold over the eastern region, particularly in the three industries of jute, collieries, and tea plantations. Consistent with this account, British managing agencies also acquired dominance in the region. Goswami finds that in eastern India at the eve of World War I, 'Of 849 tea plantations, 729 (89 percent) were managed by Britons ... all fifty jute mills were under the control of European managing agencies, and ... the major collieries – commanding greater capital and larger mining rights – were joint-stock firms, and 89 percent of these were controlled by European, mostly British, managing agencies'.[25] By this time, British businesses began sharing their existence with the commercially influential community of the Marwaris, who had migrated to Calcutta and established themselves as traders and investors in the stock market.[26] Although the Marwari community initially operated in a different field, they would subsequently threaten the dominance of the British managing agencies by staging takeovers of some of the managed companies and eventually of the managing agency firms themselves.

In the western part of colonial India, however, indigenous business initiatives were more prominent. Business communities in Bombay such as the Parsis and the Gujaratis had been experienced traders. Moreover, the principal industry that developed in the western region was cotton textiles, which was focused on import-substitution, and also attracted the required amount of domestic entrepreneurship and capital.[27] Similarly, the managing agents themselves began taking on an indigenous tone with business groups such as the Tatas arriving on the scene.[28] Hence, the British managing agents were unable to make as much inroads in Bombay as they did in Calcutta and the eastern region.

Some historians have ventured to explore the differences in management style between the British and Indian firms. Brimmer finds that while British

---

24 However, this account has attracted some challenge on the ground that it is overdrawn. Tirthankar Roy, 'Trading Firms in Colonial India', *Business History Review* 88 (2014), 9–42 at 13. Furthermore, it does not explain the subsequent entry and expansion of some domestic ethnic groups into the core of Calcutta's business sphere. Goswami, 'Sahibs, Babus, and Banias', 291.

25 Goswami, 'Sahibs, Babus, and Banias', 292.

26 Tirthankar Roy, *Company of Kinsmen: Enterprise and Community in South Asian History, 1700–1940* (Oxford: Oxford University Press, 2010), 124.

27 Gupta, 'Community Networks and Capital Flows', 2.

28 Rungta, *The Rise of Business Corporations*, 238.

managing agency firms were set up by one or two members of a family who would continue to maintain control over the firm, they were keen to attract external talent by inducting partners.[29] On the other hand, the Indian managing agents were strongly driven by their sentiment towards their communities, where strict succession rules and the need for stability prevented the induction of outsiders. It was common for Indian business families headed by a '*karta*'[30] to control managing agencies, which in turn managed several joint stock companies.[31] In that sense, indigenous business forms had an important role to play in operating Indian-owned managing agency firms. Brimmer argues for the aforesaid reasons that the British managing agents portrayed the desirable aspects of the system. While this might be true from an entrepreneurship perspective, both types of managing agents were afflicted with similar agency problems when it came to corporate governance, as will be discussed further in this paper.

Finally, for most of the colonial period, barring exceptions such as Carr, Tagore and Company, there is little evidence of collaboration and business relationships between the British and Indian businesses. As Misra notes, 'British law and institutions were becoming more influential from the late nineteenth century, while Indian and British business communities were becoming more isolated from one another. This suggests that institutional explanations must be placed in a broader social and cultural context'.[32]

This brings us to the question of how these developments can be considered from an institutional perspective. Such an understanding would provide the framework upon which the corporate governance issues and legal responses can be analysed.

Before examining the institutional implications, it is worth noting that from a geographical standpoint the managing agency system transcended beyond India's shores and found a significant presence in East Asia and Southeast Asia as well, mostly in port cities with British business influence. Leading agency houses such as Jardine Matheson dominated the business scene in Hong Kong during the colonial period.[33] British managing agencies flourished in Singapore

29 Brimmer, 'The Setting of Entrepreneurship in India', 556–559.

30 A '*karta*' is the head of a Hindu undivided family who manages the property and business of the family.

31 Subhash Chandra Das, *Corporate Governance in India: An Evaluation* (New Delhi: Prentice-Hall of India, 2012), 9.

32 Maria Misra, *Business, Race, and Politics in British India, c. 1850–1960* (Oxford: Clarendon Press, 1999), 56–57.

33 David R. Meyer, *Hong Kong as Global Metropolis* (Cambridge: Cambridge University Press, 2004), 34.

and Malaya as they managed the rubber estates in Malaya during the rubber boom in the early part of the twentieth century.[34] The system extended to other Asian cities such as Penang, Sarawak, Shanghai and Yokohama.[35] While the underlying reasons for the emergence of the managing agency system in those locations comport with those in India, the system took on very different overtones and did not receive the type of scrutiny it did in India. Hence, much less is known about the benefits and abuses of the system in non-Indian territories.

2.3 *Institutional Framework*

Extensive literature seeks to explain the emergence of institutions and organizations, including why individuals would commit themselves to mutually beneficial arrangements.[36] It posits that specific organizational forms emanate to fill a number of institutional voids confronting the prevailing society. For example, where legal systems are weak and informational asymmetries are rampant, the role of community and kinship based arrangements acquires importance.[37] In their detailed overview of the literature on family groups in emerging markets, Khanna and Yafeh note:

> 'Limited contract enforcement, weak rule of law, corruption, and an inefficient judicial system should all lead to high transaction costs between unrelated parties. Under such circumstances, intragroup trade, within the context of long-run relationships supported by family and other social ties may be relatively cheap and efficient'.[38]

These institutional imperatives are evident in the emergence of managing agents, and more importantly in the dualism between the British and Indian managing agents (and businesses more generally). One explanation for the divergent flow of businesses relates to the 'comparative advantage enjoyed by

---

34 W.G. Huff, *The Economic Growth of Singapore: Trade and Development in the Twentieth Century* (Cambridge: Cambridge University Press, 1994), 181–188. In addition, the European managing agencies undertook business in banking, shipping and tin mining. Goh Chor Boon, *Technology and Entrepot Colonialism in Singapore, 1819–1940* (Singapore: Institute of Southeast Asian Studies, 2013), 37.

35 Michael Carney, *Asian Business Groups: Context, Governance and Performance* (Oxford: Chandos, 2008), 43; Stanley Chapman, *Merchant Enterprise in Britain: From the Industrial Revolution to World* War I (Cambridge: Cambridge University Press, 1992), 108.

36 Avner Grief, *Institutions and the Path to the Modern Economy: Lessons from Medieval Trade* (Cambridge: Cambridge University Press, 2006).

37 Gupta, 'Community Networks and Capital Flows', 30.

38 Tarun Khanna and Yishay Yafeh, 'Business Groups in Emerging Markets: Paragons or Parasites?', *Journal of Economic Literature* 45:2 (2007), 331–372 at 341.

social groups in information and the role of social networks in determining entry and creating separate spheres of industrial investment'.[39] Hence, while the British businesses were more knowledgeable in the export-oriented businesses of tea and jute, the Indian businesses enjoyed greater awareness of the indigenous cotton textiles industry.

The informational asymmetry problem arises in other ways as well, i.e. between the investors and managers. By definition, the managing agency system acknowledges the existence of this asymmetry as it emerged to enable investors who are less knowledgeable and uninterested in management to entrust their funds to managers who enjoy informational advantage. If the economic and legal systems are incapable of addressing this asymmetry (as was the case in the early colonial period in India),[40] the informational gap can be filled either (i) through the reputation that the managing agency firm has established for honest dealing, or (ii) by limiting financing among communal or familial groups with deep ties.[41] A closer analysis would indicate that the British and the Indian managing agents resorted to each of these distinct mechanisms.

The British-owned managing agents attracted a heterogeneous investor body,[42] which consisted of investors who resided in Britain and also those who resided in India. Over a period of time, indigenous investors were brought in as well. In these circumstances, it was the reputation of the managers for good management that attracted the investors.[43] The information asymmetry was bridged by the reputation of the managing agent.[44] On the other hand, different factors operated in the case of Indian managing agents. The common origins of the investors and the managers and the communal ties between the two groups ensured that any abuse of the investing relationship could result in social sanctions.[45] In fact, there is ample evidence to indicate the classification

---

39 Bishnupriya Gupta, 'Discrimination or Social Networks? Industrial Development in Colonial India', online: <http://wrap.warwick.ac.uk/56607/1/WRAP_twerp_1019_Gupta.pdf> (2013), 1.

40 Contemporary corporate and securities laws are meant to address this asymmetry in a more sophisticated manner through governance and disclosure norms prescribed by regulation, which is supported by an appropriate enforcement mechanism through the imposition of legal sanctions.

41 George A. Akerlof, 'The Market for 'Lemons': Quality Uncertainty and the Market Mechanism', *The Quarterly Journal of Economics* 84:3 (1970), 488–500 at 497–498.

42 Akerlof, 'The Market for 'Lemons', 498.

43 Roy, *Company of Kinsmen*, 121–122.

44 Gupta, 'Discrimination or Social Networks?', 14–15.

45 Roy, *Company of Kinsmen*, 121; Susan Wolcott, 'An Examination of the Supply of Financial Credit to Entrepreneurs in Colonial India', online: <http://www.binghamton.edu/economics/research/old-working-papers/docs/WP0704.pdf>, 33.

of firms across various communities such as the Parsis, Gujaratis, Bengalis and Marwaris.[46]

While the initial establishment of the managing agency system fits within the institutional paradigm discussed above, the subsequent expansion of the system resulted in its abuse and gradual breakdown. Roy argues that with the further evolution of company law and the introduction of the limited liability principle in India, investments transcended beyond kinship to outside investors as well.[47] The familiarity between the managing agents and the investors diminished, thereby diluting the reputational incentives as well as social sanctions. The establishment of the Bombay Stock Exchange in 1875 added to the anonymity of the shareholder body. The absence of the two mechanisms that helped address the information asymmetry problem resulted in wholesale mismanagement and fraud, whereby the agents acted to enrich themselves rather than in the interests of the managed companies and their shareholders.[48] In such circumstances, it would have been necessary to resort to the legal system to address the asymmetry, but that would not occur until much later.

As we have seen, the managing agency system's peculiarity is closely tied to several economic, social, cultural and institutional factors that were at play in colonial India at the turn of the nineteenth century. An understanding of these factors is essential in order to analyse the corporate governance problems produced by the system and also the efficacy of the legal response in addressing these problems.

3 Managing Agency System: Structure and Governance Problems

Different approaches may be adopted when considering the structure of the managing agents and their relationship with the managed company. Institutional economists consider the managing agent to be the 'firm', which is the decision-making authority, and the managed companies merely as the operating units of the firm.[49] They argue that it is necessary to avoid becoming preoccupied with the legal aspects of the managing agency system. In that sense, the system generates benefits such as integration and synergies through economies

46 Akerlof, 'The Market for 'Lemons', 497; Rungta, *The Rise of Business Corporations*, 241.

47 Roy, *Company of Kinsmen*, 122.

48 Roy, *The Economic History of India*, 261.

49 Brimmer, 'The Setting of Entrepreneurship in India', 563; Nasir Tyabji, 'The Politics of Industry in Nehru's India', online: <https://mpra.ub.uni-muenchen.de/62260/1/MPRA_paper_62260.pdf> (2015), 6.

of management and administration,[50] for which reason the system has been compared with the *zaibatsu* system in Japan that existed following the Meiji Restoration in 1868 and is the predecessor of the *keiretsu* system that is currently in vogue.[51] Under the *zaibatsu* system, wealthy Japanese families exercised control over corporate groups by organizing them into pyramidal structures.[52]

However, in order to examine the corporate law and governance implications of the managing agency system, it is necessary to treat the managing agent and each of the managed companies as separate entities and to identify the exact legal relationships involved. Viewed as such, it would be possible to examine four specific areas: (i) the nature of the managing agency contract between the managing agent and the managed company; (ii) the nature and extent of shareholding of the managing agent in the managed company, and the exercise of voting rights in respect of those shares; (iii) the role of the board of directors of the managed companies; and (iv) the interrelationship among the managing agent and various managed firms under its control, especially on financial matters.[53] I will now elaborate on each of these areas.

3.1 *Management Contract*

The most distinctive feature of the managing agency system is the management contract entered into between the agent and the managed firm. Compared to other companies, particularly those with diffused shareholding, it is the extensive powers granted to the agent under the management contract that not only conferred excessive control upon the agents but also gave rise to distorted incentives on their part and enabled them to subject the system to abuse.

---

50 Misra, *Business, Race, and Politics*, 67–68. Rosen notes that 'managing agents developed a system of administrative integration, the forerunner of modern corporate conglomerates'. Rosen, 'The Myth of Self-Regulation', 263.

51 Neil Charlesworth, *British Rule and the Indian Economy 1800–1914* (London: MacMillan, 1982), 47.

52 Randall Morck and Masao Nakamura, 'Been There, Done That: The History of Corporate Governance in Japan', online: <http://ssrn.com/abstract=422120> (2003), 1–2. A principal difference between the two systems is that control is exercised in the *zaibatsu* through a holding company, whereas in the managing agency system control is exercised through the management contract in the absence of a holding company structure.

53 Brimmer, 'The Setting of Entrepreneurship in India', 567.

3.1.1 Powers of the Managing Agent

The scope of the managing agents' powers was rather extensive, to the extent that the exercise of all crucial decision-making powers pertaining to the managed companies were conferred upon the managing agent. For example, a managed company in its contract to the managing agency pertaining to the first cotton mill in Bombay stated: 'The entire management of [the establishment of the cotton mill] is entrusted by us, of our own will and pleasure, to you, and you will continue to do so in the course of your lifetime'.[54] Brimmer's study of twenty-four management contracts indicates that the managing agent can carry out the 'general conduct and management of the business of the company',[55] although subject to the overall supervision of the board of directors of the managed companies. As we shall see later, the exercise of supervision by the board turned out to be extremely weak. In any event, one might imagine that the agent would be subject to duties and liabilities under contract law as a fiduciary, but the historical accounts do not allude to this legal technicality and how they were treated by the legal system.

The other powers of the managing agent included the power to enter into contracts on behalf of the managed companies, undertake the purchase and sale of goods and materials, initiate legal proceedings, receive monies on behalf of the managed company, issue financial instruments, and also engage and dismiss employees.[56] All of these suggest that the managing agents effectively exercised complete management control over the companies.[57]

Managing agents enjoyed some flexibility in terms of engaging in competing businesses. While the agents themselves could not enter into a business in the same field as a managed company, nothing prevented them from managing multiple companies within the same industry.[58] Given the extensive role and powers of the managing agents, this would clearly have given rise to sensitivities in terms of using competitive information to the disadvantage of one or more managed companies and their shareholders.

The problems with excessive control were exacerbated by the structure of the managing agents themselves. They were largely constituted as sole

---

54 Rungta, *The Rise of Business Corporations*, 228.

55 Brimmer, 'The Setting of Entrepreneurship in India', 569.

56 Brimmer, 'The Setting of Entrepreneurship in India', 569.

57 In contemporary corporate law, one can imagine such powers being conferred upon the managing director of a company, albeit within strict limits and subject to conditions. The risk of conferring such significant powers on the managing agent is that they are augmented by the other relationships the agents enjoyed with the managed companies, which enhances the shareholders' exposure to the vagaries of the agent.

58 Brimmer, 'The Setting of Entrepreneurship in India', 568–569.

proprietorships or partnerships, and at most as private limited companies. Only in exceptional scenarios were they public limited companies. Arguably, such entity structuring on the part of the managing agencies was by design. Establishing closely held firms would ensure that control would remain with a small group of individuals. This would extend both to control over the managing agents and indirectly to managed firms as well. Misra notes that in 1930–31, 'of the thirty-six largest managing agency firms active in Calcutta only seven held limited liability status'.[59] The compulsion to maintain tight control was so strong that the managers were willing to sacrifice the benefits of limited liability when they confined themselves to non-corporate entities.

3.1.2 Term of the Managing Agency Contracts

The structure of the management contracts ensured that the managing agents' positions in the managed companies were well entrenched without any risk of removal. Terms of managing agency arrangements were extremely lengthy, and 'usually ran for twenty or thirty years'.[60] There were also instances where managing agents were appointed for life, or where their appointment was secured by incorporation in the articles of association.[61] Moreover, it was almost impossible for shareholders to remove managing agents as that required the support of a two-thirds majority of the shareholders, which was difficult to obtain since managing agents themselves either held shares or solicited proxies to defend their position in the company.[62] Hence, shareholders were left without recourse even if managing agents engaged in serious misconduct and destroyed corporate value.

3.1.3 Remuneration of the Managing Agents

The managing agents were rewarded handsomely, irrespective of whether they performed to create value for shareholders. The management contracts

59 Misra, *Business, Race, and Politics*, 75.

60 Misra, *Business, Race, and Politics*, 69–70. Buchanan finds that the term sometimes extended to fifty years. Daniel H. Buchanan, *The Development of Capitalistic Enterprise in India* (New York: MacMillan, 1934), 165.

61 Rungta, *The Rise of Business Corporations*, 228, 231. The Bose Committee highlights the severity of a clause in a managing agency agreement in which the managing agent's compensation for early termination was the amount that equated to the total remuneration the agency would have earned during the unexpired term of the contract. In such a case, the agent would obtain the entire amount upfront upon termination rather than over the term of the agreement if it continued. Bose Committee – Government of India, *Report of the Commission of Enquiry (Inquiry of the Administration of Dalmia-Jain Companies)* (1962).

62 Misra, *Business, Race, and Politics*, 70; Lokanathan, *Industrial Organization in India*, 28.

provided for three kinds of remuneration payable by the managed companies to the agents.[63] The first was a percentage of the profits. This aligned the incentives of the managing agents and the shareholders as it motivated the agents to work in the interests of the managed companies and their shareholders. There seems to have been a considerable variation in the percentage levels, but some of the better-known managing agents pegged their earnings at ten per cent of the profits.[64] However, in several cases, the managing agent's profits were linked to the turnover of the company. This distorted the incentives, as it allowed the agents to focus on production and sales rather than profitability. While higher productivity would benefit the managing agents, this system did not provide adequate motivation for them to increase profitability even though that is what matters for shareholders.

The second method of payment from companies to the managing agents was a commission on purchases and sales. Rungta notes that the 'standard pattern ... was to charge a commission of 1/4 *anna* or 3/8 of a penny per pound of yarn and/or cloth produced in the mill'.[65] The payment of commissions is common in the case of normal agency arrangements. But, the important feature of the managing agency system was that these commissions were in addition to other forms of remuneration. Their entrenchment in the company through the managing agency contract would ensure a constant flow of earnings through the commissions whether or not they delivered results for their shareholders.

As a third form of payment, the managing agents were paid a 'head office allowance', essentially as a mechanism for reimbursement of costs. While the agents earned profits and commissions, they did not have to incur significant costs of their own as those were met by the managed companies, which effectively made the agent's financial outlay rather negligible.

This combination of payment obligations that managed companies carried towards their agents created distorted incentives, which hardly motivated them to act in the interests of the companies. The agents were interested in perpetuating their own rewards even though they came at the cost of the shareholders.[66] The problem was compounded because several managing

63 Misra, *Business, Race, and Politics*, 69. Oonk elaborates on the types of payments sought by managing agents and how they changed over the years, arguing that the 'managing agency system was an extremely dynamic and flexible system'. Gijsbert Oonk, 'Motor or millstone? The managing agency system in Bombay and Ahmedabad, 1850–1930', *Indian Economic Social History Review* 38 (2001), pages 419.

64 Rungta, *The Rise of Business Corporations*, 237.

65 Rungta, *The Rise of Business Corporations*, 230.

66 Such arrangements involving 'pay without performance' have come under severe attack in the contemporary corporate governance discourse. Lucian Bebchuk and Jesse Fried,

agents entered into similar arrangements with multiple companies. Even though the agents acted on a part-time basis without necessarily devoting the required care and attention to managed companies on an individualized basis, they were able to reap excessive rewards with almost no risk.

3.2 *Shareholding and Voting Rights*

The managing agents bolstered their contractual protection by acquiring shares in the managed companies that conferred them with an element of corporate control. Unlike in a typical pyramidal structure, the managing agents did not own a significant amount of equity in managed companies. They only held a minority stake, usually ranging between 15 and 20 per cent.[67] This was sufficient to bestow control in favour of the managing agents as the remaining shareholding of the managed companies tended to be dispersed among a large number of shareholders. There is evidence that whenever the managing agents floated the shares of a managed company on the stock exchange, they would ensure that the shares were allocated to outside shareholders, such that the managing agent could exercise control despite owning a small number of shares.[68] It is this aspect of the managing agency system that bears similarities with the Berle and Means corporation as it aggravates the agency problems between the shareholders and managers. The managers are in a position to exercise significant control despite having invested only a limited amount in the shares, thereby having very little 'skin in the game'. The collective action problems among the outside shareholders impede their effective exercise of monitoring the managers. Buchanan's observations are characteristic of this phenomenon: 'The shareholders' meetings are often summoned only to say "aye" to what has already been laid down by the agency firm. As an example, one firm advertised the half-yearly meetings of five large jute mills in five successive periods of five minutes each'.[69]

If agency problems between managers and shareholders existed by virtue of the limited financial investment by the managing agents, that was exacerbated

---

Pay Without Performance: The Unfulfilled Promise of Executive Compensation (Cambridge, MA: Harvard University Press, 2004).

67 Misra, *Business, Race, and Politics*, 70; Goswami, 'Sahibs, Babus, and Banias', 294. However, this was not always the case as in some cases, managing agents held a larger stake in managed companies so as to exercise control through shareholding. Chikayoshi Nomura, 'The Origin of the Controlling Power of Managing Agents Over Modern Business Enterprises in Colonial India', *Indian Economic Social History Review* 51 (2014), 95–132; Lokanathan, *Industrial Organization in India*.

68 Goswami, 'Sahibs, Babus, and Banias', 293–294.

69 Buchanan, *The Development of Capitalistic Enterprise*, 169.

through additional features of the agents' shareholding in the managed companies. Brimmer refers to the use of deferred shares, which were allotted to managing agents.[70] While these shares carried low denominations, thereby limiting the agents' financial investments into the companies, they conferred disproportionate voting rights that rendered them on par with ordinary shares. Hence, managing agents were able to exercise greater control with far limited financial investment, which created a disparity between economic rights and control rights.

Another rampant practice was that managing agents solicited proxies from other shareholders so as to enhance their voting rights.[71] This would ensure that managing agents were able to obtain shareholder affirmations on key decisions taken by them. Further, it enabled the agents to enhance their control over the company in a manner that was disproportionate to their financial investments. Finally, managing agents could always increase their shareholding in the company by acquiring further shares, an option they exercised only when their position in the company was threatened by one or more shareholders intending to take over control. Presumably, this was a fall-back option since it involved financial outlay, but that may not have been a significant constraint given that managing agents were earning attractive remuneration from the company that they could utilize to buy more shares. Even if such remuneration was not forthcoming due to unfavourable business conditions, managing agents could resort to borrowing from the companies at reduced interest rates so as to preserve their hold over the companies. All of these conferred undue benefits to managing agents at the cost of shareholders.

In an account that challenges conventional wisdom, Goswami finds that in the eastern region of India, these protective measures adopted by the British managing agents to maintain control over the managed companies were not effective in preventing the ingression of indigenous Marwari shareholders who managed to wrest control over some companies towards the later part of the colonial period.[72] The managing agents were unable to obtain proxy support when there were wild swings in market prices, as existing shareholders became keen to cash out their holdings. Taking advantage of such opportunities, the Marwaris began creeping up their shareholding in companies through the stock markets and even demanding seats on the board of managed companies.

70 Brimmer, 'The Setting of Entrepreneurship in India', 573.

71 Goswami, 'Sahibs, Babus, and Banias', 294.

72 Goswami, 'Sahibs, Babus, and Banias', 294–296. Misra also notes that in case of scarcity of capital, if managed companies were unable to raise funding through the managing agents, they may have to look to Indian investors for such capital, in which case the agent's shareholding was likely to be diluted. Misra, *Business, Race, and Politics*, 75.

Goswami also highlighted another practice that enabled Marwaris to obtain additional shares in companies. During periods of cash shortages, the managing agents began obtaining loans at attractive interest rates from the Marwaris against a pledge of shares which they held in the managed companies. In several instances, the Marwaris invoked the pledge on account of failure by the managing agencies to repay the loans, which resulted in the Marwaris acquiring control over the companies. Thus, there is some evidence of a market for corporate control in managed companies in the 1920s.[73]

Barring the occasional takeover of managed companies by local businesses, the shareholding structure devised through the managing agency enabled the agents to cement their positions in the managed companies without external threats. Despite holding relatively low (non-controlling) shareholding percentage in the managed companies, the agents were able to exert significant influence on the companies due to the dispersed nature of the remaining shareholdings, which they supported through mechanisms such as shares with disproportionate voting rights, proxies and even exercising, when it became necessary, the option of shoring up the agents' shareholding in managed companies to preserve their position. Arguably, such undue entrenchment by managing agents was inimical to the interests of the shareholders of the managed companies.

3.3 *Structure and Role of the Board of Directors*

In corporate law, the primary power for superintendence and management of a company rests with its board of directors.[74] However, the position was not straightforward under the managing agency system. While the boards may in theory have possessed significant powers, they rarely exercised them, instead leaving all matters of management to the agents. Although the law treats board members as fiduciaries, the managing agency system rendered them superfluous.

At the inception of the managing agency system during the early part of the nineteenth century, joint stock companies were not required to have boards of directors.[75] In such a milieu, the need for and role of the managing agents is understandable. It is possible to visualize a scenario whereby the vacuum

73 Goswami, 'Sahibs, Babus, and Banias', 296. The market for corporate control suggests that inefficiently run companies with dispersed shareholding could be subject to a takeover by an outside acquirer. Frank H. Easterbrook and Daniel R. Fischel, 'The Proper Role of a Target's Management in Responding to a Tender Offer', *Harvard Law Review* 94 (1981), 1161–1204.

74 Kraakman et al., *The Anatomy of Corporate Law*, 12–14.

75 Rungta, *The Rise of Business Corporations*, 228.

created by the absence of a specific corporate organ to carry out management functions was filled in by the management agency system. This disposition prevailed for nearly a century since the inception of managing agents.

However, when a legislative mandate for elected corporate boards was introduced in 1913, it resulted in an overlap between the roles of the managing agents and the boards of directors of the managed companies. Any friction over the exercise of management functions was expediently avoided when managing agents invited family and friends to take up directorial positions.[76] Hence, the boards came entirely within the control of the managing agents. It was common for a partner of the managing agency firm to be the *ex officio* chairman of the companies it managed.[77] Due to the dispersed nature of the managed companies, the agent was in a position to control the composition of the board even though it held a stake that was far less than majority.

Brimmer offers useful insights into the composition of the managed company boards.[78] In addition to directors nominated by the managing agent, the board primarily consisted of 'prestige directors' who were appointed for their position in society rather than for their contribution towards management strategy or monitoring. According to him, 'managing agency directors held an average of 4.7 directorships in the controlled companies and prestige directors held an average of 2.5 each. On the other hand, nonagency and non-prestige directors held only 1.1 directorships…'[79] Given such a board composition, it is unrealistic to expect the boards to monitor the actions of the managing agent or to raise objections if those actions go contrary to the interests of the shareholders. This went against the grain of corporate law which recognizes the primacy of the board of directors on matters of superintendence and management of the company. To quote Brimmer:

> While the managing agent presumably functions under the supervision of the board of directors, the latter is frequently nothing more than a fiduciary body which exists to persuade the public to invest and fulfill legal requirements. A look at the large number of 'prestige' directors – 'Sirs', 'Rajas', 'Rao Bahadurs', etc. – on the boards of Indian companies will make this suggestion quite obvious. Thus, the managing agency firm is

76 Lokanathan, *Industrial Organization in India*, 20; Kamal Ghosh Ray, 'The forgotten managing agency system: a nineteenth century model of Indian corporate governance', *Social Responsibility Journal* 5 (2009), 112–122 at 114, 118.

77 Misra, *Business, Race, and Politics*, 69.

78 Brimmer, 'The Setting of Entrepreneurship in India', 575.

79 Brimmer, 'The Setting of Entrepreneurship in India', 575.

responsible for practically all decisions made in the company under its control.[80]

From a corporate law perspective, the managing agency system introduced parallel centres of power. While the board of directors is possessed with *de jure* powers to control the management of companies, the powers were exercised *de facto* by the managing agents, thereby rendering the board of directors redundant. Although one might expect the board of directors to be in a better position to protect shareholder interest, the managing agency system vested all powers in the agents who were largely interested in perpetuating their holds over the companies.

3.4 *Financial Relations between the Managing Agent and Companies*

From an industrial organization perspective, the managing agency system has been advantageous as it allowed the companies not only to take advantage of economies of scale and superior management, but it also allowed for diversification of businesses by way of a de-risking strategy. Moreover, the competence and reputation of the managing agents enabled portfolio companies to raise the required finance. The agents even went to the extent of guaranteeing loans and deposits availed of by the managed companies.[81] However, the benefits of the group structure were overshadowed by its abuses, as will be discussed below.

Essentially, the managing agents treated all companies within their portfolio as part of a single unit without regard to the separate legal personality and the separate interests of the shareholders of the individually managed companies. The managing agents handled the financial matters commonly across the group as it if it were a single entity. For instance, monies raised by one company by accessing the capital markets would be routinely transferred to another company that may have developed a dire need for finances.[82] Similarly, managed companies would make loans and advances to one another and buy or sell products or raw materials, in each case on terms that were not necessarily consistent with the market price. These transactions may not have been carried out on an arm's length basis, due to which one company's shareholders may have benefited, while the other company's shareholders may have been adversely affected.[83]

80 Brimmer, 'The Setting of Entrepreneurship in India', 556.

81 Roy, *Company of kinsmen*, 122.

82 Brimmer, 'The Setting of Entrepreneurship in India', 570.

83 Contemporary corporate governance is rather circumspect about such transactions as they are related party transactions that amount to tunnelling. Marianne Bertrand et al.,

Such attitude by the managing agents adversely affected the shareholders' interests. While the agents were responsible for, and earning income from, several managed companies, and were largely indifferent to inter-company transactions within the group, this left shareholders vulnerable as their interest was confined only to one company. For instance, nothing prevented the managing agent from shifting funds from one managed company to another, by which it 'can nourish or strangle any company under his control to any extent [it] desires'.[84] At the same time, the boards were powerless to intervene. While there are examples of shareholder rebellions against such conduct by the managing agencies, they were rendered futile and did not result in significant improvements to governance. Managing agents also enjoyed informational advantages, which they were not required to share with shareholders. Legal requirements relating to the disclosure of financial information and auditing standards were weak.[85]

In concluding this part, I stated that while the managing agency system was devised to address certain needs that arose in the business relationships between Britain and its colony, its structure was open to abuse by the agents in its actual operation. While shareholders were aggrieved, they were unable to bring about changes through the exercise of their voting control, due to a combination of the dispersed shareholding in which individual shareholders held limited number of shares and also the additional entrenchment mechanisms deployed by the managing agents. That leads to the next question, whether shareholders or others impacted by the adversities of the system could benefit through governmental intervention. I will now turn to the legislative responses and examine their nature and effect (or lack thereof) in addressing the problems generated by the managing agency system.

4 Legislative Responses to the Managing Agency System

In this part, I will discuss the governmental efforts to rein in the managing agency system and the resistance by businesses, especially when the agencies were still in British hands. The underlying political and economic factors had a significant role to play in the legislative outcome. This part is divided into two sub-parts, the first of which relates to the period up to 1936 when managing

'Ferreting Out Tunneling: An Application to Indian Business Groups', *The Quarterly Journal of Economics* 117 (2002), 121–148.

84 Brimmer, 'The Setting of Entrepreneurship in India', 570.

85 Brimmer, 'The Setting of Entrepreneurship in India', 570; Misra, *Business, Race, and Politics*, 81.

agents enjoyed a free hand, and the second deals with the subsequent period, when they were regulated and finally abolished.

4.1 *Origin to 1936: Freedom from Regulation*

Beginning with the history of corporate law in India, companies were established and carried on business in India without the existence of a specific body of law regulating them. Specific company legislation made its debut in India only in the year 1850 when an Act for Registration of Joint Stock Companies was passed.[86] This was based essentially on the then prevailing Companies Act 1844 in England, and marks the beginning of an era when legislative developments in the corporate field in India merely kept up with developments in England.[87] It was only in 1857 that limited liability was conferred upon companies other than banking and insurance companies.[88] New pieces of companies' legislation were introduced periodically in India, usually to track the legislative developments in England.[89] The last piece of legislation in the colonial period was the Indian Companies Act, 1913, which was subject to significant amendments in 1936.

4.1.1 The Philosophy of Corporate Lawmaking in the Colonial Era

Here, I seek to analyse the impact that corporate legislation had on Indian businesses in the colonial period, and also the possible motivations behind the introduction of such legislation. Any attempts to regulate the managing agency system must be viewed in this context. Two trends are quite evident in the colonial period. First, the transplant of English corporate law into India was to serve British business interests rather than to modernize Indian corporate law. Second, English company law as transplanted to India operated as an instrument of market regulation, a sort of 'colonial *laissez faire*'.[90]

The motive behind transplanting English company law into India was to facilitate better trade between Britain and India, which could be accomplished

---

86 Rungta, *The Rise of Business Corporations*, 36.

87 Umakanth Varottil, 'The Evolution of Corporate Law in Post-Colonial India: From Transplant to Autochthony', *American University International Law Review* 31 (2016) 253–325, at 263.

88 Banking companies were conferred limited liability in 1860 and insurance companies in 1866. Varottil, 'The Evolution of Corporate Law', 264; Rungta, *The Rise of Business Corporations*.

89 For details of these legislative developments and corresponding English companies' legislation, see Varottil, 'The Evolution of Corporate Law', 266.

90 Ritu Birla, *Stages of Capital: Law, Culture, and Market Governance in Late Colonial India* (Durham: Duke University Press, 2009), 243.

if there was symmetry in the corporate legislation between the two countries.[91] In other words, the familiarity of the British businesses with Indian corporate law was thought to minimize their risk in trading with that colony. Rungta is unequivocal in his analysis:

> If there is any underlying theme running through the company legislation of a full half century in India, ... it is a steadfast adherence to the policy that what was good for Britain must also be good for India. It was not that the legislators responsible for these Acts were not able men, some of them were well qualified and experienced in company affairs in India. ... What they seemed to lack the most was the will, rather than the wisdom, to change.[92]

Narrowing this discussion to the managing agency system, despite the close cross-referencing of Indian developments (both in the business and legislative spheres) with Britain, the evolution of the system in India bears little connection with Britain and emerged on account of specific local requirements. The system was born out of the need to ensure British trade and investments in India. Intriguingly, a business innovation in the Indian context was sought to be governed by laws that originated in Britain. Here, the knowledge and familiarity of British businessmen with corporate law in India can be considered an imperative to enhance business activity. The idea was to promote British business interests in India, which were dominated by managing agency firms controlled by them.

However, the transplant of English law into India so as to favour British businesses was accompanied by a consequential impact, in that it often ran counter to local business interests.[93] Hence, even when indigenous shareholders acquired large stakes in companies managed by British managing agents, the legal system failed to provide recourse to them. Given that the managing agency system was not prevalent in Britain, the legislation did not contain any specific protections for shareholders. The impulsive transplant of English legislation to India without consideration of the local circumstances meant that the managing agency system avoided any treatment under the Indian legal system,

---

91 Rungta, *The Rise of Business Corporations*, 68; Rob McQueen, *A Social History of Company Law: Great Britain and the Australian Colonies 1854–1920* (Surrey: Ashgate, 2009), 10.

92 Rungta, *The Rise of Business Corporations*, 214. Although these observations pertain to the second half of the nineteenth century, they largely hold good for the remainder of the colonial period spanning the first half of the twentieth century.

93 McQueen, *A Social History*, 10.

and was able to operate for over a century without any legal constraints. As Lokanathan astutely observes:

> One of the unfortunate results of reproducing English legislation in the entirely different industrial conditions of India is the lack of control over the managing agency system of industrial management. The Government did not realize that the managing agency system was quite different from the English method of industrial management, and that the company law should recognize this vital distinction. …
>
> …
>
> Nothing has done more to enable abuses to creep into the system than the failure of the Indian Companies Act to distinguish between the British system and the Indian system of company management.[94]

Moving to the second factor, since the transplanted law was intended to operate for the benefit of British traders, it adopted a largely free-market ideology. This was also consistent with developments within England at the time. During the colonial period, law was used as an instrument to facilitate trade. As Birla notes:

> I would like to reconsider the performance of colonial sovereignty, this time as a staging of market actors and as an implementation of a certain kind of colonial laissez-faire, manifest in legal frameworks standardizing the 'free circulation' of credit and commodities, most especially in the institutionalization of the law of contract as operative mode for market exchange.[95]

This philosophy resonates with the legislative approach taken towards the managing agency system. The free-market ideology meant that managing agents and the managed companies were free to establish their relationship through contract, with no interference whatsoever from the government. This was consistent with a similar approach followed in company law as a whole. The result was that shareholders were left to fend for themselves against abuses by management. Without additional legislative support, they were unable to make much headway, and were left at the mercy of the managing agents who enjoyed tremendous freedom.

---

94 Lokanathan, *Industrial Organization in India*, 331, 351.

95 Birla, *Stages of Capital*, 243.

In this background, the paper will proceed to deal with some of the attempted reforms during the initial period, until 1936.

4.1.2 The (Non-)Regulation of Managing Agents

Interestingly, the first attempts at reform came directly from shareholders who sought to alter corporate practice without governmental intervention. Since the 1870s, shareholders of some companies had succeeded in replacing their managing agents with managers operating under the direct supervision of the board of directors, and others succeeded in varying the terms of the management contract to introduce favourable terms such as limiting the tenure of office to ten years and the remuneration to ten per cent of the profits of the company.[96] But, these developments failed to gain more widespread support without legislative intervention and remained sporadic. It is also puzzling that despite the concerns with the managing agency system, no alternative mechanism that addressed those was forthcoming.

The ill effects of the managing agency system appeared in the legislative debates as early as 1882 when a Companies Bill was being considered for enactment. Birla identifies the concerns:

> As the official responses to the Companies Bill elaborated, British directors and managing agents speculated on invested share capital, transferred shares between a variety of companies they controlled, and in the process produced a chain of bankruptcies that financed new concerns. As bankruptcies became common, directors absconded with the share capital of populations of largely 'native' shareholders.[97]

The underlying tension between British managers and indigenous shareholders is largely evident in this episode. However, the result of the debates was that the Companies Act of 1882 sought to address the problem by streamlining the procedures for dissolution and winding up of companies.[98] The managing agency system itself was left untouched.

When company law next came up for reform in 1913, further attempts were made to ensnare managing agents within the sphere of regulation. The Secretary of Commerce and Industry Department sought to prevail on the Government to deal with the problems of the managing agency system, explicitly recognising that 'English Company Law when imported into the country requires

96 Rungta, *The Rise of Business Corporations*, 236–237.

97 Birla, *Stages of Capital*, 41.

98 Birla, *Stages of Capital*, 41.

special modifications if it is to deal with conditions which do not exist in England'.[99] The concern was that managing agencies were being allowed to get away with conflicts of interests, which would not be allowed in the case of directors (even under English law), presumably indicating that the managing agency system provided for a regulatory arbitrage in India that was unavailable in England. The valiant attempt to constrain the freedom of managing agents was set at naught when the proposals were met with severe objections, particularly from the Bengal Chamber of Commerce.[100] The Government caved in, and did not incorporate any suggestions to provide for specific treatment of the managing agency system.

During the initial period, we find that sufficient support was being mustered for regulating managing agents (and even for abolishing the system altogether). But, the attempts failed. Several reasons could be attributed to this outcome. The primary reason was the effect of legal transplants and path dependence whereby there was a lack of impetus to deviate from legislation in England. The managing agency system suffered the most from this inertia because it did not receive any treatment whatsoever in English legislation as the system originated and existed only in the colonies and did not affect domestic companies' legislation in England. At the same time, even though it did not affect the management and operation of British companies, the legislation had a role in ensuring that British interests in India were protected. Since British agents dominated the managing agency system, the lack of regulation worked to their advantage. Although there is no direct evidence, it is reasonable to conclude that the colonial government played up to British business interests during the period. The indigenous shareholders and businessmen were not influential within the political circles so as to have exerted pressure to push legislation through. But, this was to change in the next phases, to which I will now turn.

4.2 *1936–1970: From Regulation to Abolition*

During the first half of the twentieth century, there were significant economic and political changes both within India and around the world that had an impact on the managing agency system and its regulation. From an economic standpoint, businesses were subject to greater uncertainties due to the two World Wars. Moreover, the interwar period saw the Great Depression that plagued the global economy for several years since its onset in 1929. This added a greater element of risk to Indian companies, especially those involved in the

99 Rungta, *The Rise of Business Corporations*, 215.
100 Rungta, *The Rise of Business Corporations*, 216.

export market, although some did benefit from the excessive demand for certain products arising from the World Wars.

Domestically, the managing agency system witnessed substantial alterations. Indian shareholders had by then acquired significant shareholdings in companies managed by British managing agents, and had begun to assert themselves. The voices against the abuse of the managing agency system grew louder. More importantly, the Indian businessmen became more influential in the political system, and their opinions began receiving deference from the colonial Government. As Misra notes: 'an increased involvement in politics and a close relationship with Congress enabled some Indian businessmen to promote legislative bills designed to limit the sphere of operations of British firms on the grounds that they excluded Indian capital, management and employees'.[101] She also argues that the British managers were not only disinterested in developing ties with the Indian businesses, but that they also adopted a largely apolitical attitude showing apathy towards government relations. This may have resulted in their waning influence compared to previous years. It is in this background that legislative reforms commencing in 1936 must be viewed.

4.2.1 Company Law Amendments in 1936

Following the enactment of the English Companies Act of 1929, significant amendments were made to Indian law by way of the Companies (Amendment) Act, 1936. A unique aspect of this legislative effort is that the Indian legislature decided to embark upon a process of amending the then existing Indian Companies Act, 1913 rather than a re-enactment along the lines of the 1929 English legislation, indicating for the first time a hesitation in having a wholesale transplant. The Statement of Objects and Reasons of the 1936 amendments suggests that it was decided not to adopt the wholesale English legislation due to some unfavourable criticism it attracted, and also because of the recognition that problems peculiar to India had to be dealt with, particularly those relating to the managing agency system.[102]

The 1936 amendments for the first time expressly recognized as well as defined a managing agent. Several restrictions were imposed on their activities under sections 87A to 87I of the Indian Companies Act, 1913. The term of office of the managing agents was limited to a maximum of twenty years. Provisions were made for vacation of office by managing agents or even removal by

101 Misra, *Business, Race, and Politics*, 124.

102 Bhabha Committee – Government of India, *Report of the Company Law Committee* (1952), 17.

shareholders in certain circumstances such as where the agents had been convicted of certain offences. This ensured that managing agents' ability to continue was dependent upon shareholder decision-making, due to which they may be motivated to act in the interests of the shareholders. Remuneration of managing agents was limited to a percentage of the net profits of the company to be computed in the prescribed manner. Any other form of remuneration was possible only with the approval of shareholders through special resolution. This limited the ability of managing agents to charge commissions or to peg their remuneration to turnover rather than profits. Transactions involving intercompany loans and share transfers were restricted when they were carried out either between the managing agent and a company or between the managed companies themselves. This curbed the ability of managing agents to move funds among companies so as to adversely affect the interests of shareholders of some companies for the benefit of others through transfer of value. Managing agents were prohibited from engaging in businesses that competed with managed companies. They were also permitted to appoint no more than one-third of the board of directors. This diminished their role on the boards, whose altered composition would confer upon it greater powers.

The set of amendments in 1936 is significant in that it symbolised the onset of restrictions over the free market under which managing agents were operating until then. Their powers were significantly curbed. At the same time, 'it appears merely to have undermined their position rather than changed their behaviour', as they simply buttressed their diminished powers by acquiring controlling shareholdings in managed companies.[103]

The subsequent period witnessed India's independence in 1947, following which legislative powers were exercised by the government in free India under its Constitution that came into force in 1950. While it is reasonable to assume that decolonization would have brought with it a major shift in corporate law in India, the reality turned out to be different. Signs of change emerged only a few years later.

4.2.2 First Companies' Legislation in Post-colonial India

By the time of decolonization, the managing agency system had become a significant economic institution in India exercising dominance over business. While British managing agents continued to be active, several Indian agents also began providing competition. The new government's policy towards the managing agency system as well as business in general lacked clarity. There were different factions within the ruling Congress party: one that advocated

103 Misra, *Business, Race, and Politics*, 84.

the model of 'Fabian socialism' with state ownership and regulation of key sectors of the economy, and the other that sought to pursue liberal economic policies by providing incentives to private investment.[104] The government's mixed attitude towards business became evident even in the first legislation after independence, i.e. the Companies Act, 1956.

The inspiration for a new companies' legislation in post-colonial India arose from the appointment of the Company Law Amendment Committee in England (known as the Cohen Committee), which suggested far-reaching changes to the then applicable English company law, whose recommendations resulted in the enactment of the English Companies Act of 1948. After some initial law reform efforts, the Indian Government appointed a committee under the chairmanship of C.H. Bhabha, which undertook an extensive exercise (including interviewing experts across the country) and submitted its 477–page report to the Government in March 1952. The Bhabha Committee Report is striking in many ways. Despite the momentous shift in India's destiny through decolonization, the reliance on English laws as the model for Indian corporate law was unaffected. The tenor of the Bhabha Committee Report is such that on every aspect of the law, it largely referred to the developments in English company law and considered whether that would be relevant to the Indian context or not. There was no intention whatsoever to frame an indigenous legislation that would be appropriate to India's changed circumstances.

While the Bhabha Committee considered the various issues plaguing the managing agency system, it did not find the need to abolish the system, but only to make incremental changes.[105] It observed:

> Having regard to all the circumstances, we consider that under the present economic structure of the country it would be an advantage to continue to rely on the managing agency system ... We feel that, shorn of the abuses and malpractices which have disfigured its working in the recent past, the system may yet prove to be a potent instrument for tapping the springs of private enterprise ... [and] the recommendations that we make are designed only to tighten up the relevant provisions of the Indian Companies Act...[106]

The Committee went on to recommend changes to processes relating to the appointment of managing agents, their conditions of service, remuneration,

104 Varottil, 'The Evolution of Corporate Law', 272.

105 Bhabha Committee, Ch. x.

106 Bhabha Committee, 84–85.

powers and matters pertaining to intercompany relations. Since the changes to the managing agency system were expressed in measured terms, the Bhabha Committee recommendations suffered a backlash from certain political quarters, and its recommendations were referred to a parliamentary standing committee which tightened them further.[107] The Companies Act 1956 as enacted contained further restrictions on remuneration of managing agencies, limits on the number of managed companies under one agent and a prohibition on certain types of intercompany transactions such as loans. At no point during this process was there an adequate legislative will to address the matter radically by eliminating the managing agency system altogether due to its mounting ill effects.

In all, although the Indian Parliament was presented with the opportunity following independence to alter the nature of company law radically, especially given the altering economic sentiment, it chose to adopt the path dependence approach and continued to rely on transplanted law from England. In other words, decolonization did not represent any break whatsoever from the past.[108] Limiting the discussion to managing agencies, Goswami argues that 'the impact of decolonization on European business was not discontinuous and centered on 1947'.[109] The decline of the system and the process of tighter regulation began in the 1930s, and the events surrounding India's independence can be said to be a continuation of that process rather than any sharp shift initiated by the independent government. This also explains why we do not see a swift retreat of British managing agency firms from India as a consequence of decolonization, although there was a sharp shift in the nature of their operations as they became more collaborative with Indian businesses and also raised more capital from and shared their stake with Indian shareholders.[110] But, change became evident, albeit gradually and incrementally, in the two decades following India's independence.

4.2.3 Abolition of the Managing Agency System

India's corporate law began witnessing a departure from its colonial past only from the early part of the 1960s. The socialist ideology of the Government appears not to have taken effect immediately upon decolonization, but only in the years that followed.[111] The managing agency system was also caught by the rising tide of socialism. This was coupled with some high profile episodes of

107 Misra, *Business, Race, and Politics*, 191.

108 Varottil, 'The Evolution of Corporate Law', 277.

109 Goswami, 'Sahibs, Babus, and Banias', 302.

110 Misra, *Business, Race, and Politics*, 194.

111 Dwijendra Tripathi and Jyoti Jumani, *The Oxford History of Indian Business* (New Delhi: Oxford University Press, 2007), 26–27.

mismanagement by certain managing agents that demonstrated the abuse of the system, which evoked significant political and popular sentiment. For example, a controversy surrounding the Dalmia-Jain group of companies attracted investigation by a specially constituted committee that unearthed numerous wrongdoings in an 815–page report.[112]

Other committees that were appointed during the period also came up with scathing attacks on the managing agency system. The Shastri Committee discussed the differing points of view on whether the system should be continued or abolished, and called upon the Government to take a definitive stance.[113] Subsequently, the Patel Committee considered in detail the advantages and disadvantages of the system.[114] Based on its analysis, the Committee concluded that the advantages of the system were largely exaggerated, and hence should be discontinued, but in a phased manner. Even among the academic community, there were growing calls for abolition, primarily on the grounds that the system engendered concentration of ownership and control of companies, and prevented competition.[115] Heeding to these calls, the managing agency system was abolished by the Companies (Amendment) Act, 1967, which finally came into effect in 1970. Even though several recommendations of Government-appointed committees called for a phased abolition, it was finally decided to put an end to the system in one fell swoop.[116]

By the time of its abolition, most British managing agencies had changed hands and transitioned into the control of Indian business groups.[117] However, the legacy of some of the former managing agencies continues to be carried on by businessmen, although those firms are currently operating other businesses.[118]

112 Bose Committee.

113 Shastri Committee – Government of India, *Report of the Companies Act Amendment Committee* (1957), 129.

114 Patel Committee – Government of India, *Report of the Managing Agency Enquiry Committee* (1965), 15.

115 R.K. Hazari, 'The Managing Agency System: A Case for Its Abolition', *The Economic Weekly NRO* (1964) February, 315–322; R.K. Hazari, 'The Managing Agency System: Far From Dead', *The Economic Weekly NRO* (1965) July, 1101–1108.

116 In that sense, the legislative effort is similar to other more recent scandal-driven responses in corporate governance in the form of the Sarbanes Oxley Act of 2002 in the US following the Enron scandal, and stringent measures in the Companies Act, 2013, in India following the Satyam corporate governance scandal.

117 Misra, *Business, Race, and Politics*, 209.

118 Examples include Williamson Magor & Company, Greaves & Company, Gillanders & Arbuthnot & Company. Rungta, *The Rise of Business Corporations*; Misra, *Business, Race, and Politics*, 209.

Furthermore, the managing agency heralded the ascent of another mechanism of corporate governance in the form of 'business houses' that operated large businesses in India. This form of family ownership continues to be dominant in Indian corporate governance, including in listed companies.[119] The owners of erstwhile managing agencies became controlling shareholders of family business groups.[120] This opened a new phase of corporate governance in India during the 1970s and thereafter following India's economic liberalization in 1991, wherein the problems between controlling shareholders and minority shareholders took centre-stage.[121]

Elsewhere, in South Asia and Southeast Asia where managing agencies also existed, there is little evidence of legislative or regulatory responses to deal with the managing agency system. It appears that the system was not subject to the kind of abuses that were experienced in India. Consequently, the system quietly faded away into oblivion as it was overshadowed or succeeded by the more modern forms of business organizations such as the multinational corporations.[122]

5 Lessons and Concluding Remarks

This paper is essentially a longitudinal analysis of the managing agency system using a corporate law and governance framework. It is possible to take away some key lessons from this analysis. First, the system is indeed peculiar in that it was born out of the trading and investment needs of British businesses in certain colonies. While it emanated in India and spread to other British colonies in Southeast Asia and East Asia, nowhere did it acquire the kind of prominence and controversy as it did in India. Arguably, it was the unique circumstances present in India's colonial industrial and social setting that may have enabled it to proliferate. Curiously enough, the system did not receive any recognition or acceptance within Britain itself for its domestic business concerns. In that sense, it can be considered to be a targeted innovation arising from colonial influence on overseas trading that has had an impact on corporate law

119 Praveen B. Malla, *Corporate Governance: Concept, Evolution and India Story* (New Delhi: Routledge, 2010), 178–180.

120 Reed, 'Corporate Governance Reforms', 252.

121 Varottil, 'The Evolution of Corporate Law', 308–311.

122 Geoffrey Jones and Asli M. Coplan, 'Business Groups in Historical Perspectives', in Asli M. Coplan, Takashi Hikino and James R. Lincoln (eds.), *The Oxford Handbook of Business Groups* (Oxford: Oxford University Press, 2010), 73–75.

and practice, and influenced the business relationships between the colonies and the Empire.

Second, the managing agency system was conceived to fill a gap in the entrepreneurial needs of British businesses in India. However, once the system gained popularity and became entrenched in India's corporate ecosphere, Indian businessmen also began to adopt the system, although their needs were arguably somewhat different (albeit with some overlaps). In that sense, the innovation was put to use for reasons beyond those that related to its appearance in the first place.

Third, it is nobody's case that the managing agency system is inherently problematic. It did perform a useful role at the relevant time. However, over the years, the practices that surrounded its implementation became rather devious in that the system was subject to capture by managing agents who were interested only in enriching themselves at the cost of the shareholders. This gave rise to the acute agency problem between shareholders and the managers. Unlike the Berle and Means corporation, the managing agency system furthered the interests of the managing agents through other mechanisms such as a one-sided management agency contract. This resulted in severe abuse of the system, perhaps an unintended consequence.

Fourth, the factors relating to ethnicity seem to have an important role to play, given that the literature is replete with discussions of the conflicts between British managing agents and mostly Indian shareholders. There is some indication that this may have been the reason for the lack of political will within the colonial government to address the problem through corporate law, at least until the very end of the colonial period.

Fifth, there is sufficient correlation between the aforesaid economic, social and political factors and the nature of the legislative responses to the excesses of the management agency. Given that corporate law in India until 1936 was essentially a transplant of English company law, the system was left untouched, as it was a concept which was alien in English law. Moreover, this was consistent with the *laissez faire* attitude adopted by English company law. It was only from 1936 that the system was reined in gradually, and that too when Indian businesses (and shareholders) obtained a political voice.

Finally, decolonization does not appear to have been the primary reason for the demise of the managing agency system. Even in independent India, the system had its sympathizers both within government and among the business and intellectual elite. Moreover, both British and Indian managing agents continued to thrive, although the balance between the two had by then substantially shifted eastward. It was only the rise of socialism and the magnitude of scandals involving managing agencies that mustered the will required to abandon it.

Although the managing agency system was unique to certain colonies of the British Empire and has been defunct now for nearly half a century, the rich lessons in corporate law and governance it offers cannot be ignored.

Acknowledgements

I would like to thank all participants at the conference as well as my colleagues Michael Dowdle, Arif Jamal, James Penner, Stephen Phua, M. Sornarajah, Tan Cheng Han, Tan Yock Lin, Tan Zhong Xing, Hans Tjio and Helena Whalen-Bridge for comments and discussions on a previous version of this paper, and also Shreya Prakash for excellent research assistance. Any errors or omissions remain mine.

'Neither the state nor the individual goes to the colony in order to make a bad business': State and Private Enterprise in the Making of Commercial Law in the German Colonies, CA. 1884 to 1914

Jakob Zollmann

1 Questions of a Proto-colonial Society: Can Germany Afford Colonies?[1]

The pros and cons of the possession of overseas colonies was a hotly debated issue in Germany prior to and after the unification of 1871. Chancellor Otto von Bismarck (1815–1898), Imperial Germany's dominating political figure, was no friend of colonies. Colonial enthusiasts in Germany tirelessly worked for years to convince him of the 'necessity' of colonial possessions. Colonies, it was said, would accommodate the masses of German emigrants, keep them under German authority, and would solve the 'social question'. Furthermore, it was argued, with reference to Britain's or Holland's economic success, that colonies would be financially necessary for an expanding German economy in need of both raw materials and additional export markets. However, for a long time Bismarck declined any overseas project. He openly doubted that colonies were profitable and, more specifically, he questioned whether Germany could afford such a 'luxury'. When in 1870/71 some Hansa merchants, who had built up trade relations along Africa's Atlantic coast and in the Pacific region, argued for the German take-over of Cochinchina or some other places from defeated France, the Chancellor scornfully responded with a famous aphorism: 'A colonial policy for us would be just like the silken sables of Polish noble families who have no shirts'.[2] Also, France's politicians hoped that they could divert the German appetite for annexations to Asian territories, but Bismarck repudiated such insinuations with irony and reference to financial constraints: 'O! O! Cochinchina! This is a very juicy nugget [*fetter Brocken*] for

1 Quotation in the chapter title taken from Theodor Leutwein, *Elf Jahre Gouverneur in Deutsch-Südwestafrika*, 2nd ed. (Berlin: E.S. Mittler, 1907), Vorwort: '*um ein schlechtes Geschäft zu machen, geht der Staat so wenig wie der einzelne in die Kolonie*'. Unless otherwise stated, all translations into English are my own.

2 Quoted and translated in Louis L. Snyder, 'The Role of Herbert Bismarck in the Angra Pequeña Negotiations between Germany and Great Britain, 1880–1885', *Journal of Negro History* 35 (1950):435–452 (436).

 DOI:10.1163/9789004443075_013

us' However, we are not rich enough to be offered the luxury of colonies'.[3] Indeed, he rather bowed to the pressure from the general staff and agreed to the annexation of Alsace-Lorraine.

But still, rumours abounded that Germany had aspirations for some ports around the globe. For example, in 1872 the German government denied an attempt to purchase Delagoa Bay (Mozambique) from the Portuguese.[4] Over the next ten years, pressure was put on the Emperor and his Chancellor by figures such as mission inspector Friedrich Fabri and others. They dreamt of a 'German India' and calculated the national economic loss due to higher import prices from British or French colonies or due to German emigration to the US, Brazil or elsewhere. They asked 'Does Germany Need Colonies?', the title of Fabri's bestseller of 1879, and answered in the affirmative.[5] Still, the Chancellor remained steadfast in his rejection of colonies. In 1881, he declared categorically: '*As long as I am Chancellor, we will have no colonial policy*'. He considered colonies as an expensive means of 'providing sinecures for officials'.[6]

And when, in 1884, Bismarck finally agreed to grant German 'protection' to the 'possessions' of the rather obscure Bremen merchant Adolf Lüderitz in southwestern Africa, he called his change of policy a 'fraud' (*Schwindel*) that he needed in order to win the elections in 1884 with little success, however.[7] Subsequently, territories in modern-day Togo, Cameroon, East Africa (Tansania),

3 Otto von Bismarck, *Die gesammelten Werke, Friedrichsruher Ausgabe*, vol. VII (Berlin, 1924), 382, cit. in Horst Gründer, *Geschichte der deutschen Kolonien*, 5th ed. (Paderborn: F. Schöningh, 2004), 51.

4 Raymond W. Bixler, 'Anglo-Portuguese Rivalry for Delagoa Bay', *Journal of Modern History* 6 (1934), 425–440, 438.

5 Friedrich Fabri, *Bedarf Deutschland der Kolonien? Eine politisch-ökonomische Betrachtung* (1879; 3rd edition 1883), an English translation can be found at <http://germanhistorydocs.ghi-dc.org/pdf/eng/618_Fabri_Germany%20Colonies_198.pdf> [visited 6/11/2015]; cf. Klaus J. Bade, *Friedrich Fabri und der Imperialismus in der Bismarckzeit: Revolution, Depression, Expansion* (Freiburg: Atlantis Verlag, 1975). See for example the newspaper report in Das Bayerische Vaterland, no. 97, p. 1, 25.4.1880 'Über das neue Auswanderungsfieber'. Reporting on the latest numbers of German emigrants to the United States (600.000 in eight years), the Munich newspaper bewailed: '*Dies ist nun ein empfindlicher Verlust für Deutschland an Geld und Arbeitskraft, an Gewerbe und Landwirthschaft*'. Quoting the Deutsche Reichszeitung the newspaper underlined '*Die Auswanderung aus einem Lande ist immer ein Zeichen politischen Mißbehagens und socialer Umstände. Sie ist insbesondere für das neudeutsche Reich eine unheilvolle offene Wunde*'.

6 '*Solange ich Reichskanzler bin, treiben wir keine Kolonialpolitik*': quoted in Gründer, *Geschichte der deutschen Kolonien*, 51; Holger H. Herwig, *'Luxury' Fleet. The Imperial German Navy 1888–1918*, London 1980, 95; cf. Otto Pflanze, *Bismarck: Der Reichskanzler* (Munich: Beck, 1998), 370–374.

7 '*Schwindel*' quoted in Jean Stengers, 'Review Article. The Partition of Africa. L'impérialisme colonial de la fin du XIXe siècle. Mythe ou réalité', *Journal of African History* 3 (1962), 469–491, 487; Gründer, *Geschichte der deutschen Kolonien*, 58.

and New Guinea were also granted German 'protection' after 'protection treaties' between local chiefs and German merchants or explorers were concluded. Much to the chagrin of the British, the German gun-boat 'Möwe' with a handful of marines sailed along Africa's west coast, hoisted the German flag, and represented the Imperial authority. The domestic and foreign motives for 'Bismarck's sudden leap across principles and oceans troubled contemporaries and has puzzled historians ever since'.[8] Despite decades of research, as one reviewer put it succinctly, 'decrypting the primary reasons for the acquisition of German colonies seems not yet over'. Bismarck considered the German overseas possessions as a 'means to an end' in order to please the colonial enthusiasts in Germany who hoped for a new space for German migrants and new export markets. The Chancellor was vying for their votes. At the same time, he aimed at an *entente* with France by provoking the British government under Gladstone – after all, the territories which had been under German protection since 1884 were located mostly in regions previously considered to be British spheres of influence. Given the ill health of Emperor Wilhelm I, an Anglo-German crisis, which only he could solve, would have proven to the German 'liberal' circles around Crown Prince Frederic that Bismarck was indispensable as Chancellor.[9]

Bismarck, conscious of his own political, and most of all economic, objections against the maintenance of colonies by state administrations, explained to the members of the *Reichstag* in 1884 that he did not desire formal 'colonies' but rather territories which stood under German 'protection' (*Schutzgebiete*, i.e. protectorates). They ought to be administered 'in the style of the English Royal Charters' by merchants. Thus, Bismarck wanted to evade the question of German 'sovereignty' in Africa. The *Reich*'s financial and legal involvement was to be kept to a minimum. A 'complicated colonial administration with German

---

8 Fritz Stern, *Gold and Iron: Bismarck, Bleichroeder and the Building of the German Empire* (New York: A.A. Knopf, 1979; orig. 1977), 409; see Jonathan Steinberg, *Bismarck. A Life*, (Oxford: OUP, 2011), 418; Ulrike Jureit, *Das Ordnen von Räumen. Territorium und Lebensraum im 19. und 20. Jahrhundert*, (Hamburg: HIS, 2012), 91.

9 Ulrich Lappenküper: Rezension von: Winfried Baumgart (Hg.): *Bismarck und der deutsche Kolonialerwerb 1883–1885. Eine Quellensammlung*, (Berlin: Duncker & Humblot, 2011), in: sehepunkte 11 (2011), Nr. 12 [15.12.2011], URL: http://www.sehepunkte.de/2011/12/20625.html [22/6/2017]. on the state of the art; see Konrad Canis, *Bismarcks Außenpolitik 1870 bis 1890: Aufstieg und Gefährdung* (Paderborn: Schöningh, 2004); Bernhard Gissible, Imagination and beyond. Cultures and geographies of imperialism in Germany, 1848–1918, in: MacKenzie, John M. (ed.), *European empire and the people. Popular responses to imperialism in France, Britain, the Netherlands, Belgium, Germany and Italy*, Manchester 2011, 158–194, 166 on contemporary discourse; overview in Sebastian Conrad, *Deutsche Kolonialgeschichte* (Munich: Beck, 2012), 22–29.

civil servants …[and] garrisons with German troops were to be avoided', he said.[10] However, the merchants who had previously pressured politicians into the overseas territories now proved to be very reluctant to continue to follow the path they and their supporters had opened. Bismarck's administrative plans, his idea of a 'commercial sovereignty under protection' of the German state, were soon revealed to be illusory as in the case of most of the other European colonies.[11] Privately financed 'protection charter' (*Schutzbrief*) companies, as were once employed in British India or Canada, were nothing more than '[a] relic from a past [mercantile] age'.[12] The German merchants in question were neither willing nor capable to finance the 'administration' of territories in Africa or along the Southern Pacific. Bismarck's arrangement soon proved inadequate, and so did hopes for Africans willingly accepting German 'protection'. The Chancellor soon lost any interest in colonial affairs.

Still, in German Southwest Africa, the privately financed *Deutsche Kolonialgesellschaft für DSWA* set up a small military detachment in 1888. It consisted of three German officers and twenty African commoners. Unable to exert any power over the Africans to whom the Germans had promised 'protection', Germany's first commissioner of the colony, Heinrich Göring (1838–1913), requested a force of between 400 and 500 men. Considering these costs and his intention not to spend public money on the colonies, Chancellor Bismarck rejected Göring's request. In January 1889, however, the *Reichstag* in Berlin agreed that under the private command of Captain Curt von François (1852–1931) around fifty German 'mercenaries' would be detached to GSWA and financed by the *Reich*. An increase in 'rebellions' led to the deployment of more troops.

There were similar developments in Germany's other 'protectorates' that were not meant to be colonies. In the beginning, they had a 'mediated

10 RK Bismarck to Emperor Wilhelm I, 19.5.1884, in: Otto von Bismarck, *Gesammelte Werke* (NFA), vol. 6, Schriften 1884–1885, Paderborn 2011, 166, Doc. no. 124.

11 SBRT 5. Legislatur Periode, 4. sess., vol. 2, 42. Session of 26.6.1884, p. 1062 '*nach Gestalt der englischen Royal Charters*'; '[*unter*] *Protection stehende kaufmännische Souveränität*'; cf. Jörg Schildknecht, *Bismarck, Südwestafrika und die Kongokonferenz: Die völkerrechtlichen Grundlagen der effektiven Okkupation und ihre Nebenpflichten am Beispiel des Erwerbs der ersten deutschen Kolonie* (Hamburg: LIT, 2000), 58–62; Dirk van Laak, *Imperiale Infrastruktur: Deutsche Planungen für eine Erschließung Afrikas 1880 bis 1960*, (Paderborn: Schöningh, 2004), 106–108; Norbert B. Wagner, *Die deutschen Schutzgebiete: Erwerb, Organisation und Verlust aus juristischer Sicht* (Baden-Baden: Nomos, 2002).

12 Crawford Young, *The African Colonial State in Comparative Perspective* (New Haven: Yale University Press, 1994), 103; cf. Winfried Speitkamp, *Deutsche Kolonialgeschichte* (Stuttgart: Reclam, 2005), 30–35. 1884/85 German 'Protectorates' were 'established' in: German East Africa, Cameroon, German South-West Africa, Togo, New Guinea; later included: Samoa, Caroline Islands, and Tsingdao.

government' (*mittelbare Regierung*), as lawyers later called Bismarck's arrangement. The territorial government by colonial companies (*Kolonialgesellschaften*) and not by state authorities was practised in German East Africa and German New Guinea and its adjacent Islands. Following the Buschiri Rebellion in 1890, the *Deutsch Ostafrikanische Gesellschaft* relinquished its rights to exert any form of sovereignty (*Hoheitsrechte*).[13] In the German Pacific territories, New Guinea, the Marshall, the Caroline, and Mariana Islands, Palau, and since 1900 parts of Samoa, company rule lasted considerably longer, even though it remained difficult to find enterprises prepared to exercise sovereignty (and pay for it).[14] The rule of the *Neu-Guinea-Kompagnie* in New Guinea lasted until 1900, when the company renounced its rights. Here also, no private enterprise was willing to take over and the Imperial government had to assume responsibility for the administration.

With regard to the Marshall Islands, 'Bismarck tried to persuade the firm of *Robertson & Hernsheim* to accept full responsibility for the administration of these territories. Robertson, however, made clear to the Chancellor that the firm was unwilling to accept a charter since the financial responsibilities would be too heavy. For three years the Imperial Commissioner in the Marshall Islands was without a budget or staff'. Only in 1888, with the support of the financiers Gerson Bleichröder (Bismarck's private banker) and Adolf von Hansemann, was the Jaluit Company set up. The company also rejected Bismarck's idea of a *kaufmännische Souveränität* by a charter, but it agreed to defray to the German Empire the expenses of the Islands' administration (around 80,000 marks annually). In return, the company was granted a monopoly on the exploitation of the pearl grounds and the guano exports, and was entitled to 'appropriate unoccupied land'. This arrangement lasted – to the satisfaction of both the company and the German government – until 1906, when the Jaluit Company became embroiled in a dispute about landing rights with the government of Australia. Subsequently, the German government took over direct responsibility for the Islands.[15] In the end, all protectorates, now increasingly called 'colonies', were directly administered by the *Reich*.[16]

13 Hans Gmelin, 'Kolonieen', in Fritz Stier-Somlo and Alexander Elster (eds.), *Handbuch der Rechtswissenschaften*, vol. III (Berlin: de Gruyter, 1928), 627–630.

14 Cf. Hermann Hiery, *Das Deutsche Reich in der Südsee (1900–1921). Eine Annäherung an die Erfahrungen verschiedener Kulturen* (Göttingen: Vandenhoeck & Ruprecht, 1995).

15 William Otto Henderson, 'Chartered Companies in the German Colonies':, *Studies in German Colonial History*, 2nd ed. (London: Cass, 1976; orig. 1962), 11–31, 26 f.

16 Gmelin, 'Kolonieen', 630.

A constantly growing colonial administration was set up, overseen since 1890 by a new section of the Foreign Office, the Colonial Department. In 1906, an independent Colonial Office (*Reichskolonialamt*) was set up. In addition, the German military (navy and army) was heavily involved in colonial affairs.[17] In Africa, the *Schutztruppe*, as the colonial army had been called since 1891, was continually increased. In German East Africa, the company troops of the *Deutsch Ostafrikanische Gesellschaft* were reorganized and financed according to the German *Schutztruppen* law (1891; 1896) and subsequent Imperial decrees that provided for German officers and African rank-and-file. In GSWA, the *Schutztruppe* – also no longer a private enterprise – had grown to 540 German soldiers in 1894, fully financed by the Imperial budget.[18] In Wilhelminian Germany, the question of whether the nation could afford colonies was barely opportune any longer; Germany did afford colonies as the Empire was pursuing a course of *Weltpolitik* to obtain a 'place in the sun'.[19] Millions of public money were spent. The new question was rather when the nation would profit financially from the colonies.

2 How to Make a Profit from Colonies? A State-Budgetary Perspective

2.1 *Expenditures for Colonies as Economic Policy*

Colonialism was expensive. This was a Bismarckian perspective, and given the Reich's financial dire straits, the overall economic crisis after the crash of 1873, and the Chancellor's intention to minimize frictions in the field of foreign policy, his reluctance with regard to possible German colonies seems

17 See Hermann Hiery, Die Kolonialverwaltung, in: Horst Gründer and Hermann Hiery (eds.): *Die Deutschen und ihre Kolonien. Ein Überblick*, (Berlin²: be.bra, 2018), 179–200.

18 See André Tiebel, *Die Entstehung der Schutztruppengesetze für die deutschen Schutzgebiete Deutsch-Ostafrika, Deutsch-Südwestafrika und Kamerun (1884–1898)*, (Frankfurt/M.: Lang, 2008), 65–78; Tanja Bührer, *Die Kaiserliche Schutztruppe für Deutsch-Ostafrika: Koloniale Sicherheitspolitik und transkulturelle Kriegführung, 1885 bis 1918* (München: Oldenbourg Verlag, 2011), 35–90; it is important to bear in mind that 'military conquest [of GSWA] was neither the intention of Berlin nor of [GSWA]'s first Governor, Major Leutwein'; Helmut Bley, *South-West Africa under German Rule, 1894–1914* (Münster: LIT, 1996), xviii. Orig. *Kolonialherrschaft und Sozialstruktur in Deutsch–Südwestafrika 1894–1914* (Hamburg, 1968); cf. Canis, *Bismarcks Außenpolitik*, 211, 222–225; Wagner, *Die deutschen Schutzgebiete*; David Simo: 'Colonization and Modernization. The Legal Foundation of the Colonial Enterprise. A Case Study of German Colonization in Cameroon', in: Ames, E./ Klotz, M./Wildenthal, L. (eds.): *Germany's Colonial Past*, Lincoln 2005 97–112, 101f.

19 Konrad Canis, *Von Bismarck zur Weltpolitik. Deutsche Außenpolitik 1890 bis 1902* (Berlin²: Akademie, 1999).

comprehensible. On the other hand, there were a number of Hansa merchants involved in commercial overseas activities, in particular with West-Africa and the South Pacific. They lobbied for a more substantive support of the German government, since they grew increasingly nervous about possible tax and customs discriminations by British, French, or Portuguese officials in Africa and the Pacific region. The period of global free trade, it seemed, was drawing to a close. It was expected that governments would become more involved in questions of international trade, and Bismarck's government slowly adapted to this new notion of the meaning of economic policy. However, when he tabled the famous *Samoa-Vorlage* in April 1880, a legislative proposal that would have aided, using public money, the bankrupt trade house in Samoa of the Hamburg merchant Johan C. Godeffroy, the proposal was narrowly defeated in the *Reichstag*. In 1881, the German government, in a memorandum, suggested improving the German ship services to East Asia and Australia to further German trade, but in 1884 a law to this respect that would have involved a financial engagement of the Reich was again rejected by the *Reichstag*; a similar proposal in 1885, however, was accepted by a more colonial-friendly *Reichstag*.[20]

These bills were first steps towards an explicitly supportive governmental foreign trade policy that blends into an overall picture of what historians have later called the 'beginnings of the modern interventionist state, which … sought to master the problem of uneven industrial growth'. As historian Hans-Ulrich Wehler explained years ago, the interventionist state and organized capitalism 'attached decisive importance to the promotion of an export offensive and to the winning of foreign markets, either through the methods of informal empire or through direct colonial rule'. For Germany, Wehler recognized the development of 'a broad ideological consensus [that the welfare of the country was dependent on the successes of informal and formal expansion] … from the end of the first depression (1878–9) onwards, and subsequent German overseas expansionism rested upon this consensus'.[21]

It is one thing to recognize the intention of an 'anti-cyclical economic policy' in the foreign expansion that finally led, certainly against Bismarck's own plans, to formal German colonial possessions in some of the areas targeted by German merchants;[22] it is another thing to ask how much the state profited

20 See Canis, *Bismarcks Außenpolitik*.

21 Hans-Ulrich Wehler, 'Bismarck's Imperialism 1862–1890', *Past and Present* 48 (1970), 119–155, 121 f.; cf. also Hans-Ulrich Wehler, *Bismarck und der Imperialismus*, 2nd ed. (Köln: Kiepenheuer & Witsch, 1970), 112–120; Markus Denzel, 'Die wirtschaftliche Bilanz des deutschen Kolonialreichs', in: Horst Gründer and Hermann Hiery (eds.): *Die Deutschen und ihre Kolonien. Ein Überblick*, (Berlin²: be.bra, 2018), 144–160 (145).

22 Wehler, 'Bismarck's Imperialism', 122.

financially from its anti-cyclical policies that were, after all, implemented to overcome the economic crisis. The legislation that granted subsidies to ship lines or overseas merchants and that allowed for the payment of soldiers and officials working in the *Schutzgebiete* caused – first of all – additional expenses for the Reich budget. The sceptics among the members of *Reichstag* were still numerous and they soon asked how the 'colonies' could be used to re-pay the original expenses to the *Reich*.

Bismarck, after giving in to the pressure to change the informal indirect free trade expansionism into a direct and formal colonialism, remained sceptical about the effects colonial possessions would have on the German economy. As historian Horst Gründer underlines, it would be 'unrealistic' to assume that the chancellor expected substantial short or medium-term economic effects from the *Schutzgebiete*. Rather, he was well aware of the immediate financial burden which the direct colonial activities put on the Imperial budget.[23] Indeed, Germany's early 'colonial budgets' spoke an unambiguous language: there were additional expenses included in the budget of the Foreign Office (*Auswärtiges Amt*); but there was no income to off-set these costs.

2.2 *Taxing Trade, Consumption, and Income: The Example of German Southwest Africa*

The Imperial government assumed that the tasks of the Imperial Commissioner in GSWA, Heinrich Göring, would be limited to maintaining peace among Africans (and the very few Europeans) in GSWA. Yet even these most elementary tasks came at a cost, as the 1885 supplementary budget (*Ergänzungsetat*) of the Foreign Office revealed. It allocated, for example, 30,000 marks for the erection of an office building in Angra Pequeña, GSWA (soon re-named Lüderitzbucht).[24] This was a lot of money for one building – and more money would be spent. These expenses were also part of the active involvement of the administration in all questions of economic policy around the globe. The state administrator was meant to support the merchant in increasing his income and earning more – a cycle that would have been concluded with increased tax payments by those who profited from the state support.

Commissioner Göring understood his (economic) role in GSWA as twofold: First, he wanted to transmit his knowledge and insights to the local merchants; and second, he wished to 'draw the attention of German capitalists … to undertakings that would promote the economic growth of the country

23 Gründer, *Geschichte der deutschen Kolonien*, 52, 59.

24 'Denkschrift', in *Drucksachen RT, 6. Legislaturperiode II*. Sess. 1885/86, vol. 1, Nr. 21, A, p. 7.

[GSWA]'.[25] Over the years, government measures taken to promote the economy in the colonies were manifold and can be described in the 'categories of development policy'.[26] The 1901 Imperial budget for GSWA (RGBl. 1901, p. 92), for example, listed expenses for new buildings, roads, wells, dams, improvement of agriculture and stock farming, expansion of the harbour in Swakopmund, etc. However, despite these expenditures, neither GSWA nor any other German colony ever developed into 'what it is supposed to be, an export market for Germany'. Instead, in around 1900, most of the Europeans lived 'almost exclusively on the money ... that the military and officials bring into the [colony]'.[27] Given these realities, in 1899 the journal *Grenzboten* bemoaned that in the case of the economic gains from the *Schutzgebiete*, their 'benefit [*Nutzen* for Germany] was currently minimal ... and, to make things worse, bureaucracy began to spread, which, with its decrees and paperwork' was working against the merchants who needed 'free movement'. Regarding the colonial administration, it was acidly said that 'It is a pure end in itself [*Selbstzweck*]'.[28] Indeed, colonial administrators began to regulate trade and did levy fees, taxes, and custom duties from traders (see below) to generate some revenues for the treasury. However, 'currently [1899] the expenditures of the administration [of GSWA] are five times higher than the revenues, and these revenues are composed mostly of customs duties, which are paid by the military and the officials'.[29]

---

25 'Berichtdes kaiserlichen Kommissars für das südwestafrikanische Schutzgebiet, Dr. Göring, d.d. Angra-Pequena, den 22. Februar 1886', in: *Drucksachen des Bundesraths* 1886, Bd. 2, Nr. 75, 8. '*die Aufmerksamkeit der deutschen Kapitalisten auf ein ... den wirthschaftlichen Aufschwung des Landes förderndes Unternehmen [etwa die 'Errichtung einer zuverlässigen Absatzstelle für Vieh'] zu lenken*'; critical of these beginnings Friedrich Bruck, 'Die Zukunft Deutsch-Südwestafrikas', *Die Grenzboten* 1/1899 (59.Jg), 289–299, 290.

26 Speitkamp, *Deutsche Kolonialgeschichte*, 86 'mit Kategorien von Entwicklungspolitik.'

27 Curt von Francois, 'Unsere südwestafrikanische Kolonie', *Die Grenzboten* 56:4 (1897), 67–72 '*was sie sein soll, ein Abfluß und Absatzgebiet für Deutschland*'. *Europeans lived 'fast ausschließlich von dem Gelde ..., das die Schutztruppe und die Beamten ins Land bringen*'.

28 *Grenzboten*, 1/1899, 346; '*ihr Nutzen, war vorerst gering ... und zum Überfluß begann sich die Bürokratie dort breit zu machen, die mit ihren Verordnungen und Schreibereien dem auf freie Bewegung angewiesenen Großkaufmann ein Greuel ist*'; '*Sie ist reiner Selbstzweck*'; cf. Bruck, Die Zukunft Deutsch-Südwestafrikas', 295; for details on the critique of colonial administration Maria-Theresia Schwarz, *Je weniger Afrika desto besser* (Frankfurt am Main: P. Lang, 1999).

29 Bruck, 'Die Zukunft Deutsch-Südwestafrikas', 295 '*Zur Zeit [1899] betragen die Kosten der Verwaltung fünfmal soviel als die Einnahmen, und diese Einnahmen setzen sich zum großen Teil aus den Zöllen zusammen, die von den Schutztruppen und Beamten aufgebracht werden*'.

After fifteen-odd years of formal colonialism, the sceptics, who had aired their doubts about the opinion widespread in 1885 'that tropical vegetation [always] comes with fertile soil', were apparently proven right. 'Rather, all of Africa is a poor [continent]; do not look there for a second India; only through hard labour can something be earned in the Dark Continent'. In 1885, in the journal *Export*, the trade specialist M. Schwert warned his readers of '*Schwärmereien* for Africa', which could cause only 'quixotic expectations'.[30] Indeed, most observers had the wrong expectations about African (or other) colonies, since barely anything was known to the wider public about these territories. The alleged 'tropical vegetation' of Africa (where allegedly coconuts and oranges would grow by themselves) often turned out to be deserts or semi-arid grassland (as in GSWA) or impenetrable forests (as in Cameroon or New Guinea). The Tsetse fly prevalently hindered livestock farming. It would be an undeniable challenge for German settlers and merchants to produce and sell anything deriving from these meagre soils.[31]

The history of taxes in the German colonies attests to these sobering economic realities. It was not the farmers or miners who were the first to be asked to contribute to the state budget of GSWA, but the innkeepers and their traders who catered for the liquor needs of Africans and Germans (most of them officials or soldiers). The introduction of an alcohol tax, trade tax, and income tax for non-Africans in GSWA on June 30, 1888 was, however, more an attempt at regulating the staggering consumption in beer and liquor than a spirited effort to offset the costs of formal colonialism. While it has been stated about the Gold Coast (Ghana) that the 'financing of colonial rule ... was largely based on liquor revenues',[32] in GSWA such revenues may have taken up a considerable

30 Quote in H. Jehring, 'Die deutsche Auswanderung und ihre Zukunft', *Unsere Zeit. Deutsche Revue der Gegenwart*, 10 (1885), 433–450; 11; 620–635, 634. '*daß mit tropischer Vegetation auch Reichtum des Bodens verbunden sei. Ganz Afrika ist vielmehr ein armes Land; ein zweites Indien ist dort nicht zu suchen, und nur durch harte Arbeit ist dem dunklen Erdteil etwas abzuringen*'; '*Schwärmereien für Afrika*'; '*überspannte Erwartungen hervorrufen*'.

31 Denzel, 'Die wirtschaftliche Bilanz', 148.

32 Emmanuel Akyeampong, 'AHR Conversation. Explaining Historical Change; or, The Lost History of Causes', *American Historical Review* 120:4 (2015), 1369–1422, 1400, who recalls the concerns of his Ghanaian professors with regard to his dissertation topic, 'the social history of alcohol' in Ghana. When Akyeampong presented his archival evidence, '[m]y professors were stunned to discover that the financing of colonial rule in the Gold Coast before 1930 was largely based on liquor revenues. I was given the stamp of approval'. Cf. also Emmanuel Akyeampong, *Drink, Power, and Cultural Change: A Social History of Alcohol in Ghana, c. 1800 to Recent Times* (Portsmouth, N.H.: James Currey, 1996); on alcohol consumption in GSWA Jakob Zollmann, *Koloniale Herrschaft und ihre Grenzen: Die Kolonialpolizei in Deutsch-Südwestafrika 1894–1915* (Göttingen: Vandenhoeck & Ruprecht, 2010): 250–258.

proportion of all state revenues, but still the total amounts were rather small. A decree of the German commissioner stipulated that traders of alcohol had to purchase a license for 300 marks. To open their business, an innkeeper also required an official permit, which had to be presented inside the bar and which detailed when and how alcohol could be sold.[33] Financially, German colonial rule remained largely based on Imperial subsidies.

Trade tax (*Gewerbesteuer*) was hesitatingly introduced in GSWA, but after two decades the legal provisions dealing with all kinds of salespersons and their rights and duties developed into a rather dense net. If there are any particularities in German colonial commercial law, they are to be found here. To begin with the early provisions: persons pursuing a trade had to pay trade tax annually. A 'progression' was to be achieved by classifying different trades into several groups that had to pay fixed amounts of taxes: the first group was composed of craftsmen, traders, and hawkers who had to pay either 40 or 80 marks (according to income); the second group consisted of innkeepers, merchants, commercial agents, technicians (120 marks and 240 marks); the highest amounts (400 marks and 600 marks) had to be paid by wholesale traders and trading companies.[34] Iterant trade tax (*Wandergewerbesteuer*) had been levied since 1895 and was subdivided into three classes: trade without carriage (25 marks p.a.); trade with cart (75 marks p.a.); and trade with carriage (125 marks p.a.). Proprietors of ox wagons – *the* hauling means all over southern Africa, which lost much of its business to the railway after 1900 – had to pay a wagon fee (*Wagenabgabe*) annually; it was first levied in 1901 and in 1909 the fixed amount was 40 marks per wagon.[35]

In order to contextualize these dense provisions related to trade duties and taxes,[36] it is important to recall that 'the itinerant trader' was the quintessential

---

33 Edler v. Hoffmann, 'Das deutsche Kolonial-Gewerberecht',*Zeitschrift für Kolonialpolitik, Kolonialrecht und Kolonialwirtschaft* 8 (1906), S. 164–195; 285–323 [Sonderdruck, Berlin 1906], 36. Verordnung vom 18. 12. 1900; cf. also Kurt v. Stengel, *Die Rechtsverhältnisse der deutschen Schutzgebiete*, (Tübingen 1901), 95.

34 For details see Eugen Kade, *Die Anfänge der deutschen Kolonial-Zentralverwaltung*, Phil. Diss. Berlin (Würzburg, 1939), 117f.

35 Otto Mathies, *Die Beschränkungen der Gewerbe- und Handelsfreiheit in den deutschen Schutzgebieten* (Hamburg: Friederichsen, 1916), 56: §1 *Wandergewerbeordnung vom* 14.6. 1912; cf. ibid, 69; Friedrich Weber, *Die koloniale Finanzverwaltung* (Münster: Coppenrath, 1909), 223.

36 As to the levying of fees (*Gebühren*) in the colonies, i.e. amounts charged for the execution of official acts by public administrators: the Emperor was entitled to empower the colonial administrators to levy fees. If fees were regulated by the Imperial justice laws (*Reichsjustizgesetze*; e.g. RStPO; CPO), the Emperor was empowered according to §3 No. 1 *Schutzgebietsgesetz* (§6 No.7 iFv 1900) to stipulate amendments; cf. Kurt von Stengel, 'Die

non-state representative of the pre- and early colonial society. Even more so, the itinerant traders and the (unwritten) customs related to their trade with Africans while roaming Namaland, Hereroland, and Ovamboland in search of ivory, ostrich feathers, horns, and cattle since the first half of the nineteenth century, were far older than the German colonial state. One of these traders, many of whom were of British, Swedish, or Afrikaaner origin, found a telling comparison for these proto-colonial days: 'As dawn precedes sunrise, a kind of twilight-zone of European civilization was spreading [with the traders] over the interior [of southwestern Africa], far in advance of real colonial power'.[37] Considering the often explicit intention of these traders to refuse to accept German 'interference' (i.e. laws) with their trade and the at times ruthless trading practices that bore more resemblance to (stock) theft or duress of their African trade 'partners', the German officials were overwhelmingly concerned with controlling these men and their comportment. Colonial tax and commercial law, in this political context, was closely intertwined with the policing efforts of maintaining peace in the colony. At the same time, the economic advancement of the colony and the traders involved had to be ensured by the policy makers in the Governorate in Windhoek and the Colonial Department/Office in Berlin. After 1900, increasingly these goals seemed to be mutually exclusive. Open conflicts between Africans and traders (and the growing numbers of German settlers eager to obtain their private tract of land from the colonial government or directly from an African chief) erupted, most of all in Hereroland. In 1903/04, the OvaHerero and other peoples of southwestern Africa rebelled against their colonial exploitation. The resulting wars against OvaHerero and Nama (1904–1908) were led with genocidal violence and ended in a moral and financial disaster. A shocking percentage of the African population (and from a colonial perspective, the work force) was either dead or had fled the colony. The wars had cost the Empire around 400 million marks. Given these expenses and the experience of the previous twenty years of colonial rule, it was unlikely that German colonialism would ever 'pay'.[38]

deutschen Schutzgebiete, ihre rechtliche Stellung, Verfassung und Verwaltung', *Annalen des deutschen Reiches* (1895), 244.

37 Gerald McKiernan 1879, quot. in Alvin Kienetz,: 'The Key Role of the Orlam Migration in the Early Europeanization of South West Africa (Namibia)', *International Journal of African Historical Studies* 10 (1977), 553–572, 553; cf. Lorena Rizzo, *Gender and Colonialism. A History of Kaoko in north-western Namibia, 1870s – 1950s*, (Basel: BAB, 2012), 40; Marion Wallace, with John Kinahan, *A History of Namibia. From the Beginning to 1990*, (Oxford: OUP, 2012), 86f.

38 Matthias Häussler, *Der Genozid an den Herero. Krieg, Emotion und extreme Gewalt in 'Deutsch Südwestafrika'* (Weilerswist: Velbrück, 2018).

After the wars, the colonial administration and the Imperial government in Berlin aimed at a more 'efficient' German colonialism. One day soon, it was hoped, GSWA would also be able to offset the costs it had caused to the *Reich* – or, at least (similar to Togo or Samoa), the annual revenues would suffice for the colonies' expenses without the need for further subsidies from Germany. The new colonial secretary Bernhard Dernburg was a former banker (who specialized in rescuing enterprises at the brink of collapse – mockingly he was referred to as *Herr Sanitätsrat*), not a lawyer.[39] More affluent settlers and thus better taxpayers were to be brought into the colony; (cattle) farming and mining were now recognized as the economic backbone of GSWA.[40]

But 'efficiency' also meant better control of the African population as stipulated by three so-called 'native decrees' (*Eingeborenen-Verordnungen*) of August 18, 1907, on the 'control of natives', on their 'passports', and on 'service and labour contracts with natives'. These new legal provisions required all Africans to register with the local authority and obliged them to carry passes and demanded permits in case of any travel. The labour relations between European employers and African workers were to be supervised by the colonial police and other administrators. They were required to control the situation to ensure that both contractual parties duly fulfilled their legal obligations out of their service or labour contracts (i.e. to work and to pay wages/provide sufficient food which often did not happen).[41] Subsequently, the colonial administration entitled municipalities to impose a 'native tax' on the wages of African workers. This tax was to be expended 'exclusively for the profit of the natives' (*zum Besten der Eingeborenen*). The municipality of Windhoek, for example, levied the tax since 1912 and financed the drilling of boreholes inside the town's major 'native compound' with the 'native tax'. In 1913, the town's 'native tax' income reached around 14,500 marks.[42]

In addition, the commercial laws of the colony were used for the aim of gaining better control of the population. The itinerant trade decree (*Wandergewerbeordnung*) of 1912 regulated in great detail on when the colonial district offices were entitled to provide the applicant with an itinerant trade license and the reasons for refusing the application: among them, insanity or

39 Werner Schiefel, *Bernhard Dernburg 1865–1937: Kolonialpolitiker und Bankier im wilhelminischen Deutschland* (Zürich: Atlantis, 1975).

40 Birthe Kundrus, *Moderne Imperialisten. Das Kaiserreich im Spiegel seiner Kolonien*, (Cologne: Böhlau, 2003), 44–77.

41 Jakob Zollmann, *Koloniale Herrschaft und ihre Grenzen: Die Kolonialpolizei in Deutsch-Südwestafrika 1894–1915* (Göttingen: Vandenhoeck & Ruprecht, 2010), 99–106.

42 National Archives of Namibia (NAN) ZBU 162, A VI a 8, fol. 88, annual report Native Commissioner Windhoek, 1.4.1913 – 31.3.1914.

potential threat to public order. An entire list was compiled stipulating the goods that could not be distributed by itinerant traders (guns, liquor, hogs, and poultry, etc.). The governor was free to declare additional prohibitions. Also, exhibitions 'without higher artistic or scientific interest' required an itinerant trade license.[43] Evidently, these nit-picking provisions did not only mirror the tendency of the modern state administration to regulate the details of everyday life, nor were they first of all focused on increasing tax payments, but they were also a means of restraining the liberties of Africans and their way of life. To them, the itinerant trade decree of GSWA applied in the same way as it did to Europeans, and their chances of transgressing an individual provision was considerably higher given that most of them could not read. It would be necessary, however, to do more archival research to see whether Africans in GSWA applied at all for an itinerant trade license.

Income tax was levied in GSWA only from officials, managers, administrator, and craftsmen. For an annual income of between 1,000 and 1,500 marks they had to pay 6 marks to the colonial administration. Higher earnings were to be taxed with 2 per cent.[44] When in 1908 diamonds were discovered in the desert of GSWA (near Lüderitzbucht), the economic fortune of the colony seemed to change for the better. It cannot be the task of this article to detail the monopolistic *Diamantenregie*, the corporate and tax regime developed by Dernburg's Colonial Office in order to maximize the state revenues from diamonds. He did so much to the chagrin of individual miners and traders who deplored that inside the special diamond area it was prohibited for anyone but employees of the *Deutschen Kolonialgesellschaft für Südwest-Afrika* to search for diamonds.[45] So complicated

43 Mathies, *Die Beschränkungen der Gewerbe- und Handelsfreiheit in den deutschen Schutzgebieten*, 56 (on §1 *Wandergewerbeordnung vom* 14.6. 1912), 69; Weber, *Die koloniale Finanzverwaltung*, 223.

44 Cf. Weber, *Die koloniale Finanzverwaltung*, 226. Similar to municipalities in Germany, also dog owners (German or African) had to pay dog tax (30 marks p.a.) to the colonial administration.

45 Horst Drechsler, *Südwestafrika unter deutscher Kolonialherrschaft, Band 2: Die großen Land- und Minengesellschaften (1885–1914)* (Stuttgart: Steiner, 1996), 277–283; for a contemporary (less than favourable) view see Paul Rohrbach, *Dernburg und die Südwestafrikaner. Diamantenfrage. Selbstverwaltung. Landeshilfe* (Berlin: Deutscher Kolonialverlag, 1911); on legal details see Kurt Perels, *Das Bergrechtsabkommen vom 17. Februar / 2. April 1908 und die bergrechtliche Stellung der Deutschen Kolonialgesellschaft für Südwest-Afrika unter besonderer Berücksichtigung der Rechtsverhältnisse im Lüderitzbuchter Diamantspergebiet* (Berlin: Mittler, 1910); Karl Ritter, *Das Koloniale Bergrecht* (Nürnberg: Sebald, 1912), 93; W. Westhoff, 'Geschichte des deutschen Bergrechts. Aus dem Nachlasse herausgegeben und bearbeitet von Oberbergrat W. Schlüter. Teil E. Das Bergrecht in den deutschen Schutzgebieten', *Zeitschrift für Bergrecht* 51 (1910), 217–276; 'Denkschrift betreffend die Verhältnisse im südwestafrikanischen Diamantengebiet vom 6. Januar 1910', *Drucksachen*

were these regulations that finally even the Supreme Court (*Reichsgericht*) in Leipzig had to clarify the legal situation.[46] Instead, it must suffice here to state that these additional tax revenues did not suffice to cover all the expenses of the colony. During the last years of the German rule, the arrangement with the Imperial government was mainly based on the following formula: the colonial government covers (with its own revenues) the expenses for the civil administration, and the Imperial government pays for the military and the police.[47]

Table 1 *Budget of German Southwest Africa*[48]

Year	Revenues	Subsidies
1900	993	7.181
1902	1.824	7.635
1904	2.720	9.810
1906	1.824	90.389
1907	3.616	65.071
1908	5.304	38.067
1909	8.348	17.125
1910	13.559	14.425
1911	18.613	11.416
1912	17.606	13.828
1913	15.884	14.627

These few hints about the nature of state revenues in GSWA indicate that, on the one hand, the legal forms of tax payments were rather similar to metropolitan provisions. The colonial administration in Windhoek and Berlin had any interest to increase the tax payment given that until 1910 Imperial subsidies were considerably higher than the revenues. Colonial critics in parliament never grew tired of pointing out the disproportionate expenses for the *Reich*, and contrasted this with the alleged 'purpose' of colonies to contribute to the

des Reichstages, 12. Legislatur Periode 181 (1910), 18; Ernst Radlauer, 'Über den Umfang der Geltung des preußischen Rechts in den deutschen Schutzgebieten', *Jahrbuch der hamburgisch wissenschaftlichen Anstalten* 28:6 (1911), 13.

46 RGZ 80, 99; RGZ 81, 237; cf. Jakob Zollmann, Bausteine einer kolonialen Geschichte des Privatrechts. Das Reichsgericht und die deutschen Kolonien, 1888–1920', *Rechtskultur – Zeitschrift für Europäische Rechtsgeschichte* 5 (2016): 14–36 (34).

47 Cf. Schiefel, *Bernhard Dernburg 1865–1937*, 90.

48 In thousand marks; summary of: *Statistisches Jahrbuch für das Deutsche Reich*, vols. 1900–1914.

wealth of the nation. The special provisions on the taxing of (itinerant) trade, on the other hand, lost its relevance when other businesses grew in importance. It was also from a tax perspective that by 1910, the 'Southwestern' ox wagon trader seemed a relic of the past.

2.3 *Customs* (Zoll)

'Germany's colonial trade policy contrasted with her national policy: the open-door principle was maintained throughout the [colonial] period [1884–1915]'.[49] This somewhat simplifying characterisation requires some qualifications as 'open-door' did not mean that no regulations applied or no customs duties were levied in the German colonies. Most of all the 'open-door principle' meant that most custom tariffs in the colonies did not discriminate against foreign traders or products of foreign production (as, for example, the Portuguese colonial custom tariffs did). Contemporaries were already airing the assumption that the Imperial government maintained this form of free trade policy for the German colonies in order to avoid foreclosing the much more relevant colonial export markets (e.g. India, Indochina, or South Africa) of other colonial states. In the German case, the numbers were particularly telling: even in 1913, 2.5 per cent of all German exports went to British India and Dutch Indonesia, but only 0.5 per cent went to the German colonies. And the German colonies received only a part of their imports from Germany: in 1900 42 per cent, in 1913 only 34 percent, the neighbouring colonies or other states were thus more important.[50]

It was regarded as a 'general policy of all colonial powers, to hitherto consider the colonies as foreign territory with regard to customs duties [*Zollausland*]'.[51] Also the German colonies were not integrated into the customs union of the German Empire (article 33 German constitution, 1871), they therefore remained 'with regard to customs and tax legislation [§1 II Zolltarifgesetz of 25.12. 1902 (RGBl. 303)] without any doubts foreign territories [*Ausland*]'.[52] Each colony

49 Paul Bairoch, 'European trade policy, 1815–1914', *The Cambridge economic history of Europe*, vol. VIII. The industrial economies, (Cambridge: CUP, 1989), 1–160, 121, who mentions the numbers indicated below.

50 Speitkamp, *Deutsche Kolonialgeschichte*, 89.

51 Fritz Sabersky, *Der koloniale Inlands- und Auslandsbegriff*, Berlin 1907, 30: *Zwar war es die allgemeine Politik der Kolonialmächte, bisher die Kolonien als Zollausland zu betrachten.* '[*E*]*ine Änderung dieser Politik* [*würde*] *England zu gleichen Maßnahmen veranlassen*', p. 31.

52 Hansjörg Michael Huber, *Koloniale Selbstverwaltung in Deutsch-Südwestafrika: Entstehung, Kodifizierung und Umsetzung* (Frankfurt am Main: Lang, 2000), 36: '*im Sinne der Zoll- und Steuergesetzgebung zweifellos Ausland*'; see already Georg Meyer, *Die staatsrechtliche Stellung der deutschen Schutzgebiete*, Leipzig 1888, 93.

constituted its own customs territory with its own import and export custom duties. Commercial treaties of the German Empire were not valid for the colonies, except if they were explicitly integrated into the treaties' customs provisions. Since 1893, the most-favourite-nations clause was applied to all German colonies; this provision was codified in §1 III *Zolltarifgesetz* (1902). According to this law, the *Bundesrat* (the first chamber of parliament) was entitled to stipulate those (most favourable) custom duties for the German colonies that had been agreed upon with other nations in treaties of commerce and navigation.[53] At the same time, with regard to custom duties and other provisions concerning trade, the German colonial administration was bound by several international treaties. In particular, the Berlin (Congo) Act (1885) and the Brussels General Act (1890), attempting to limit the trade in weaponry and liquors, are to be mentioned in this respect.[54]

For example, in GSWA the Imperial commissioner Göring published his first custom duties decree (*Zollverordnung*) in 1888. He stipulated the amounts to be paid upon the export from GSWA of cattle, horses, sheep and goats, ostrich feathers, ivory, and rawhides; in addition, customs were levied for the transport of these goods across GSWA to any third country. A more detailed customs decree was published in 1896 by the *Landeshauptmann* (governor) Leutwein.[55] Such decrees were legally based on the right of delegation, which was stipulated in the German Colonial Law of 1886/88 [*Schutzgebietsgesetz*]. Thereby, Emperor and Chancellor were entitled to delegate their empowerments to the governor or lower colonial officials.

In GSWA's harbour towns Swakopmund and Lüderitzbucht, a proper customs administration was set up with its own officials (often supported by soldiers), headed by a *Zollamtsvorsteher*.[56] The decree of 1896, and a new one of 1903, levied import duties on 'almost everything, even goods necessary for life and also merchandise whose value and the [small] customs duties are barely worthwhile the trouble which arises from levying it' as was argued critically by a

53 F.J. Sassen, 'Die staatsrechtliche Natur der deutschen Schutzgebiete', *Zeitschrift für Kolonialpolitik, Kolonialrecht und Kolonialwirtschaft* 8 (1906), 594–620, 617.

54 For details and further international conventions see von Stengel, 'Die deutschen Schutzgebiete', 246–248; cf. Matthew Craven, 'Between Law and History. The Berlin Conference of 1884–1885 and the Logic of Free Trade', *London Review of International Law* 3:1 (2015), 31–59.

55 Ernst Backhaus, *Das Verordnungsrecht in den deutschen Kolonien*, diss.iur. Heidelberg, Berlin 1909, 35; A. Zimmermann (ed.), *Die deutsche Kolonial-Gesetzgebung. Sammlung der auf die deutschen Schutzgebiete bezüglichen Gesetze, Verordnungen, Erlasse und internationalen Vereinbarungen*, Teil II 1893–1897, Berlin 1898, Nr. 450. (*Zollverordnung* of 10.10.1896).

56 See B.v. König, 'Die Kolonialbehörden, deren Zuständigkeit und Verfahren', *Beiträge zur Kolonialpolitik* 2 (1901), 1–11, 7.

contemporary academic.[57] The administration granted individual (politically motivated) tariff reductions when the (rather high) tariffs threatened the viability of the business and exports were no longer economically feasible. The guano export from GSWA was a case in point. In other cases, higher tariffs aimed at reducing the level of imports (of alcohol); tariffs were also raised in order to protect local production from competitors in the neighbouring colonies (sisal in GEA) or overexploitation (natural rubber and ivory). Export bans and prohibitive export duties on livestock could be decreed, which aimed at strengthening local stocks (Angora goats in GSWA and Ostriches in GEA). The level of the custom tariffs varied greatly and fluctuated in different years. In 1911, the level of import tariffs ranged from 5.4 per cent (to GSWA) to 20.8 per cent (to Togo). Imports on account for the colonial administration (*Schutzgebietsfiskus*) were exempted from all custom duties. Altogether, the import and export custom duties were 'the most important source of revenue' of the German colonies.[58]

Against the provisions of the custom duties decree of 1903 declaring as 'foreign' all territories that do not belong to GSWA,[59] patriotically motivated resentment was expressed: 'Motherland and colonies are destined to form a greater fatherland and to this customs barriers do not fit well'.[60] In this respect also the economic interests of the trader in Germany were mentioned, since the trader was considered eager to purchase the German colonial goods at a lower price 'than if he had procured them from English colonies'.[61] The fact that customs were levied on products from the German colonies being imported to Germany or any other German colony has been described by historians as 'hindrance to the economic development of the German colonies',[62] also blocking the 'economic integration of the colonial empire'.[63] However, the above-cited free trade arguments for the equal treatment of German and foreign goods by German custom officials in the colonies and the metropole were macroeconomically more relevant than any colonial 'tax patriotism'. Furthermore,

57 Weber, *Die koloniale Finanzverwaltung*, 227: '[*unterwarf*] *nahezu alles der Zollpflicht, auch notwendige Lebensbedürfnisse und auch solche Waren, bei denen die Zolleinnahmen kaum die Erschwerungen und Mühen lohnten, welche die Erhebung mit sich brachte*' – on p. 228 f. a detailed list of tariffs (1908).

58 Denzel, 'Die wirtschaftliche Bilanz', 148.

59 §1 *Zollverordnung für Deutsch-Südwestafrika* (1903): 'Als Zollausland werden alle nicht zu Deutsch-Südwestafrika gehörenden Gebiete angesehen'.

60 H. Schwörbel, Die staats- und völkerrechtliche Stellung der deutschen Schutzgebiete, diss.iur. Erlangen, Berlin 1906, 30 '*Mutterland und Kolonien sind dazu bestimmt, ein größeres Vaterland zu bilden und dazu passen Zollschranken schlecht*'.

61 Sassen, 'Die staatsrechtliche Natur', 617 '*als wenn er sie aus englischen Kolonien sich kommen läßt*'.

62 Denzel, 'Die wirtschaftliche Bilanz', 148.

63 Speitkamp, *Deutsche Kolonialgeschichte*, 89.

the *Schutzgebiets* budgets remained dependent on the tax revenues. Therefore, the German colonies were never integrated into the German customs union.

3 How to Make a Profit from Colonies? A Commercial Perspective

3.1 *Company Profits, in Germany or Elsewhere?*

Prussia's Prime Minister Bismarck, in a different age, had foreseen the discrepancy between state expenditures and private gains that would later on characterize German colonial policy so dramatically. In 1868, he wrote to his Minister of War, Field Marshall Roon:

> 'On the one hand the advantages for trade and industry of the motherland, which are expected from the possession of colonies, are – for the most part – based on illusions; because the costs caused by the establishment, support and maintenance of colonies often exceed the benefit enjoyed by the motherland, as the experiences of England and France prove. Furthermore, it is difficult to justify making the entire nation pay, via taxation, for the benefit of certain branches of trade and industry'.[64]

The latter sentence described properly the situation in the German colonies as it evolved up to the First World War.

Despite the fact that a number of well-known Hansa merchants had been involved since the 1860s in trade relations with the territories that later on became German territories, until the mid-1880s, as historian Horst Gründer emphasizes, the 'overwhelming majority of Hansa merchants and their banks were followers of free trade and opponents of colonies'.[65] Nevertheless, the German Colonial Association (*Deutscher Kolonialverein*) grew in importance and influence. In 1884, it had 43 local chapters and around 9,000 members, many of them owners of small and medium-sized companies, but more than this its membership 'read like a "Who's Who" of prominent figures in the

---

64 *'Einerseits beruhen die Vortheile, welche man sich von Kolonien für den Handel und die Industrie des Mutterlandes verspricht, zum größten Teil auf Illusion. Denn die Kosten, welche die Gründung, Unterstützung und namentlich die Behauptung von Kolonien veranlaßt, übersteigen, wie die Erfahrungen der Kolonialpolitik Englands und Frankreichs beweisen, sehr oft den Nutzen, den das Mutterland daraus zieht, ganz abgesehen davon, daß es schwer zu rechtfertigen ist, die ganze Nation zum Vorteil einzelner Handels- und Gewerbezweige zu erheblichen Steuerlasten heranzuziehen'.* Hans Spellmeyer, *Deutsche Kolonialpolitik im Reichstag* (Stuttgart: Kohlhammer, 1931), 3 cit. in: Michael Fröhlich, *Imperialismus: Deutsche Kolonial- und Weltpolitik 1880–1914* (München: DtV, 1994), 32.

65 Gründer, *Geschichte der deutschen Kolonien*, 43.

German business world': among them Krupp, Haniel, Hoesch, Oppenheim, Hansemann, Schwabach, Bleichröder, Mendelssohn and many others, including institutions such as the *Centralverband deutscher Industrieller* or several chambers of commerce.[66] They all were united in their assumption that colonies offered commercial opportunities not to be missed (any longer), either for Germany as a nation or, concretely, for the enterprise they represented.

But what kind of trade, what kind of products offered such promising opportunities? And how much did the German capitalists and their followers know about the territories under German protection since 1884/85?[67] In the pre-colonial period, Hansa companies such as *C. Woermann*, or *Jantzen & Thormälen* maintained more than twenty trading posts (*Faktoreien*) in Africa, from Liberia to the Kongo River. *Woermann* alone was said to hold 25 per cent of the entire trade along the coast of the Cameroons. The Hamburg companies *Godeffroy* and others were active in the Pacific region . *Godeffroy* held a 'quasi-monopoly' on exports from Samoa and Tonga.[68] The profits were made by importing cheap merchandise such as spirits, guns, gunpowder, salt, or textiles to Africa or the Pacific, and exporting expensive colonial products like palm oil or ivory (and later caoutchouc) to Europe.[69] Most of the German exports to Africa were, much to the chagrin of missionaries, in fact alcohol products (*Branntwein*). In southwestern Africa, German missionaries had, in competition with British, Swedish, and Afrikaaner traders, set up a *Missionshandels-Aktiengesellschaft* (MHAG) in 1868 that was intended to bring the gospel and European products to the Africans. However, the idea of financing mission efforts directly through missionaries and their trade was unrealistic. Due to mismanagement, the MHAG had to be liquidated in 1873.[70] German missionaries and traders remained in the region, but trade interests here were considerably weaker than

---

66 David Blackbourn, *The Long Nineteenth Century: A History of Germany, 1780–1918* (New York: OUP, 1998), 333; cf. Stern, *Gold and Iron*, 412; Pflanze, *Bismarck: Der Reichskanzler*, 374.

67 On the history of 'academic colonial knowledge' in Germany, see Anne-Kathrin Horstmann, *Wissensproduktion und koloniale Herrschaftslegitimation an den Kölner Hochschulen. Ein Beitrag zur «Dezentralisierung» der deutschen Kolonialwissenschaften*, (Frankfurt am Main: Lang, 2015).

68 Aleš Skrivan, 'Das hamburgische Handelshaus Johan Cesar Godeffroy & Sohn und die Frage der deutschen Handelsinteressen in der Südsee', *Veröffentlichungen des Vereins für Hamburgische Geschichte* 81 (1995), 129–155.

69 Gründer, *Geschichte der deutschen Kolonien*, 82.

70 Thomas Braun, *Die Rheinische Missionsgesellschaft und der Missionshandel im 19. Jahrhundert* (Erlangen: Verlag der Ev.-Luth. Mission, 1992); Curt von François, *Deutsch-Südwestafrika: Geschichte der Kolonisation bis zum Ausbruch des Krieges mit Witbooi* (Berlin, 1899), 8 f.

along the central African coastline frequented by the Hansa merchants. When Adolf Lüderitz negotiated in 1883 with Nama *Kaptein* Joseph Fredericks about the 'purchase' of land around Angra Pequeña (in exchange for 260 old rifles and 600 Pound Sterling), he hoped to find gold and copper, but to no avail. Returning from Angra Pequeña one year later, the German consul Gustav Nachtigal, who represented Germany along west Africa's coast, admitted to the American consul in Luanda, Robert S. Newton, that 'it [Angra Pegueña] seems but a poor place to establish a Colony and more resembles a desert than anything else'.[71] A few days later, Nachtigal sent a disillusioned report to Chancellor Bismarck, which painted a rather dark picture of the economic prospects of the territory. Significantly, the report was kept secret.[72]

As it turned out, the German merchants and their financiers knew very little about the economic realities of Africa. Apart from the export of liquors and the import of some 'exotic' raw materials like ivory or palm oil, the trade volume was rather minuscule. Over the following three decades two main features characterized economic relations between Germany and its colonies: the government was the main investor, and German capitalists remained notoriously 'timid' in investing in the colonies, as Bismarck had already lamented. However, it should be noted that it was a common feat of African colonies, whether they were ruled by Britain, France, Portugal or Germany, that 'public investment during that period [prior to the First World War] was small, and private capital influx even smaller'.[73]

With regard to GSWA, the government in Berlin – remaining unable to mobilize the German economy to invest in the German colonies (gold and diamonds had not yet been found) – turned to British capital. The grant of the *Damaraland-Konzession* to the South West Africa Company (SWAC), founded in 1892 and under the influence of Cecil Rhodes, Prime Minister of the Cape Colony, was supposed to open a new chapter in the development of mining, farming and railroads in the colony. The German Colonial Law (*Schutzgebietsgesetz* of 1888) had, in line with the Bismarckian idea of a colonial government by chartered companies, stipulated special provisions for the concessionaires, which resulted in tax relief and other privileges for the involved companies (see below 4.). As a result of the *Damaraland-Konzession*, the rather counter-intuitive situation came into being that by around 1895, British-South

71 National Archives and Records Administration (Washington D.C.) RG 84, Loanda, v.3, US Consul to Secretary of States, 9.9.1884; 13.12.1884; cf. Lynn Berat, *Walvis Bay. Decolonization and International Law*, (New Haven: Yale University Press, 1990), 44.

72 Gründer, *Geschichte der deutschen Kolonien*, 53.

73 Young, *The African Colonial State*, 136; on Bismarck see Stern, *Gold and Iron*, 412, 434.

African capital dominated GSWA.[74] This was heavily criticized by German colonial enthusiasts who bemoaned that most of the mine concessions available in the colony were sold to British companies. It was argued that the German state should have kept the rights for itself in order to profit from future discoveries (many still dreamt of a second Transvaal with plenty of gold deposits). Instead, it was claimed, the Germans had 'only worked for England ... this is unbelievable'.[75] In 1897, GSWA's former governor Curt von François also complained about these developments. According to him, most of the public funds spent on the colony had gone to merchants and companies in the Cape Colony, while British (and German) companies had done next to nothing to develop the colony.[76] François and other contemporaries were understandably disappointed. Indeed, the influx even of British capital remained very limited. The SWAC and six other companies who obtained concessions for large tracts of land from the German government were underfinanced and their shareholders remained risk averse and passive. One subsidiary enterprise of SWAC commenced in 1906 with the mining of copper. In 1908, on land for which another company, the *Deutsche Kolonialgesellschaft für Deutsch-Südwestafrika*, had a concession, diamonds were found accidentally. Four out of seven colonial companies in GSWA never paid dividends.[77]

Given this failure, how could German private capital be induced to invest in German colonies? One of the foremost problems in all colonies was the transport capacity to the nearest harbour. Only with a functioning railway system could raw materials be transported to the world markets. Only then would the colonial exports contribute to make colonialism profitable. Also in parliament, colonial critics pointed to these elementary prerequisites of a functioning economy.[78] In GEA, the first railway tracks were laid in 1893, in GSWA in 1897, in Togo in 1904, and in Cameroon in 1906. Given the limited knowledge about the

74 George Paish, 'Great Britain's capital investements in individual colonies and foreign countries', *Journal of the Royal Statistical Society* 74 (1911): 167–200; Frank R. Cana, 'German aims in Africa', *Journal of the Royal African Society* 14 (1915): 355–365, 357 SWA 'mainly exploited by British capital'; Drechsler, *Südwestafrika* vol. II, 81–191.

75 Bruck, 'Die Zukunft Deutsch-Südwestafrikas', 299. '*nur für England gearbeitet ... das ist schier unglaublich. Deutscher Michel, wann wirst du dich auf deine Kraft besinnen und dich endlich einmal deiner ehrlichen Haut wehren?*'.

76 von Francois, 'Unsere südwestafrikanische Kolonie', 67–72, 71; id., 'Staat oder Gesellschaft in unseren Kolonien?' Referat, erstattet für die 11. Hauptversammlung des Bundes der Deutschen Bodenreformer (Berlin: Harrwitz 1901).

77 Drechsler, *Südwestafrika* vol. II, 277.

78 SBRT 8. L.P. I.Sess. 1890/92, vols. II, 57. Session of 4.2. 1891, p. 1299. Ludwig Bamberger explained with regard to possible copper or gold deposits in GSWA: '*in einem so neuen Lande, in dem es keinen Weg und keinen Steg, keine Kohle und keine Industrie in der Nähe dieser*

economic prospects of individual colonies, e.g. knowledge about meaningful iron ore or copper deposits, the German colonial administration found it hard to convince any financiers to invest money in the improvement of transport capacities. The railways built in German colonies were therefore overwhelmingly financed with public funds and loans (*Anleihen*); at times the construction was executed by the military (including forced labour by prisoners of war) for military purposes during the colonial wars.[79]

Evidently, a number of private companies profited greatly from the millions in public money spent on the colonies. Most profits of companies were related to the military, the shipping and railway lines, and the mining industry. One of the *Kaiserreich*'s leading parliamentarians, Matthias Erzberger of the Catholic Centre Party, an outspoken critic of Germany's colonial engagement, spoke of *Millionengeschenke*, also the title of one of his pamphlets.[80] Particularly during the wars in German East Africa and German Southwest Africa the squandering of public money and at times undeniable corruption were apparently rampant in the German colonial economy. As a side remark it should be noted that since the 1950s the economic mismanagement of the colonies and the alleged 'monopolies' had been a focus of East-German Marxist-Leninist historiography on German colonialism.[81]

Bernhard Dernburg, when he took over the helm of the Colonial Department (soon Colonial Office) in 1906, hoped that greater financial autonomy would help the colonial administration in the colonies to make more prudent decisions and to induce more private capital to seek its fortune in the colonial

---

angeblichen Lager giebt, [*wäre*] *selbst das Ausbeuten von recht reichen Lagern noch wahrscheinlich ein schadenbringendes*'.

79 Nina Kleinöder, 'A "Place in the Sun"? German Rails and Sleepers in Colonial Railway Building in Africa, 1905 to 1914', *Zeitschrift für Unternehmensgeschichte* 65,1 (2020), 9–31; Speitkamp, *Deutsche Kolonialgeschichte*, 85.

80 Matthias Erzberger, *Millionengeschenke: Die Privilegienwirtschaft in Südwestafrika: Mit einer Materialsammlung über die bergrechtlichen Verhältnisse dieses Schutzgebietes* (Berlin: Verlag der Germania, 1910).

81 See Drechsler, *Südwestafrika* 2, 274; Elfriede Rehbein, *Studien zur Geschichte der imperialistischen deutschen Eisenbahnpolitik in den Jahren von 1890–1914: Habilitationsschrift* (Halle [Saale], 1958); Horst Drechsler, *Südwestafrika unter deutscher Kolonialherrschaft: Der Kampf der Herero und Nama gegen den deutschen Imperialismus*, 3 rd ed. (Berlin: Akademie-Verlag, 1986; 1st ed. 1966); Dieter Schulte, 'Die Monopolpolitik des Reichskolonialamts in der 'Ära Dernburg' 1906–1910. Zu frühen Formen des Funktionsmechanismus zwischen Monopolkapital und Staat', *Jahrbuch für Geschichte* 24 (1981), 7–39. E.g. Wolfgang Carlé, 'Podbielski bat zur Kasse. Vor 75 Jahren. Volksaufstand im Südwesten Afrikas', *Wochenpost* 4 (1979), 12 on the corruption scandal involving the company Tippelskirch & Co, the Prussian minister of agriculture, General a.D. Viktor von Podbielski, and the Colonial Department with regard to overpriced uniforms and other military deliveries (1906).

economy. But he also knew that the state would still play a leading role, most of all as facilitator and guarantor of the money invested. For larger investments to realize in the mining, railway, and banking industry in the colonies, the only solution at hand seemed to be loans guaranteed by the Imperial government. The *Reich* would be liable for the payment of interests and the debt retirement/liquidation of the loan. Through guaranteed above-market-interest rates, the investment became attractive and, even better, the risk for individual investors was minimized; thus, more investors became interested in the colonial economy. Since 1908, the colonial treasuries were allowed to draw loans on the capital market. The *Reich*'s laws which were stipulated in this respect also form part of the commercial-legal arrangements found to 'make colonialism work'. The Imperial subsidies, on the other hand, were supposed to decline over the years, once the colonial economy had improved based on the private investments.[82] And indeed, compared with 1904, the capital of colonial trading houses grew, according to historian Mary Townsend, from 185 million marks to 505 million marks in 1912. In 1914, around 400 companies were active in the colonies, among them ten banks, nine shipping lines (the de-facto monopoly of the *Woermann* shipping line had been a constant bone of contention in early years of German colonialism), 47 mining companies, 188 plantation companies, and 109 different industrial companies.[83] Mining and the related questions of mining law became increasingly relevant for investors in GSWA after the Otavi copper mine and most of all the diamond mines near Lüderitzbucht turned out to be quite profitable. In 1913, GSWA exported minerals valued at 37 million marks. The exports of other 'colonial' products such as ivory, sisal, coffee, or caoutchouc from German East Africa, Togo, or Cameroon rather stagnated; the amounts involved barely reached into the millions.[84]

However, all this was far away from the relevance colonial enthusiasts of the 1870s and 1880s had once assumed colonies would have for the German national economy. The German capital export to all German colonies (500 million marks in 1912) remained minimal in comparison to other foreign markets (it was said that even before the beginning of the South African war in 1899, German capitalists had invested '500 million marks' in Transvaal alone[85]).

82 Schiefel, *Bernhard Dernburg*, 89.

83 Mary E. Townsend, *Macht und Ende des deutschen Kolonialreichs* (Leipzig: Schulz, 1932), 220–222.

84 Paul Sprigade and Max Moisel (eds.), *Deutscher Kolonialatlas mit illustriertem Jahrbuch 1914* (Berlin: Reimer, 1914), 26, 13.

85 J.J. Van-Helten, 'German Capital, the Netherlands Railway company and the Political Economy of the Transvaal 1886–1900', *Journal of African History* 19 (1978), 369–390, here 376, 387f.

Merely 2 per cent of the German foreign investment reached the German colonies. The extraction of raw materials (mostly based on the expropriation of Africans and their exploitation in mines, farms, or plantations) and their import to Germany was barely felt on a national scale. In 1913, all German colonies imported goods valued at 143,678,936 marks and exported goods valued at 120,880,128 marks.[86] Imports from the German colonies constituted barely 0.5 per cent of Germany's overall imports. As we have seen already, in 1913 Germany's exports to its colonies stood equally at minuscule 0.5 percent of all German exports. Until 1905, beer was Germany's leading export product to GSWA; and also in later years it remained staggeringly high on the list.[87] In sum: Bismarck's prediction of 1868 had come true. The 'entire nation pa[id], via taxation, for the benefit of certain branches of trade and industry', most notably those involved with the military procurement for the colonies. But the 'advantages for trade and industry of the motherland, ... [remained] based on illusions'[88] given the overall picture: German colonies were next to irrelevant for German capitalists and the national economy.

3.2 *Individual Profits: The Example of the Colonial Trade and Credit System in GSWA around 1900*

The itinerant traders of GSWA must have understood, as was mentioned above, the German fiscal and commercial provisions as an intrusion into their previously enjoyed proto-colonial economic liberty. The tax and license system was one grave concern for these men, a few of whom were indeed fined by colonial officials for their contraventions.[89] The intention of the German colonial administration to also interfere with the widely used credit system, however, was nothing less than a complete reversal of the way commercial interactions were undertaken in GSWA.

The purchase of goods based on credit and at times horrendous interest rates had developed a long time before the arrival of German officials. It would

86 Sprigade and Moisel, *Kolonialatlas*, 12; Speitkamp, *Deutsche Kolonialgeschichte*, 89.

87 *Statistisches Jahrbuch des Deutschen Reiches*, vol. 28 (Berlin, 1907), 369, and vol. 35 (1914), 460. In Germany, it was know that 'alcohol abuse in the colonies is extremely widespread' (*dass der 'Alkohol-Mißbrauch in den Kolonien außerordentlich verbreitet* [*ist*]. *Seine Hauptursache ist sicherlich mit, soweit eben der Europäer in Frage kommt, die Langeweile'*) *Die Kolonial-Hygiene*, Nr. 11 (1913), 8; similar consideration on the 'excessive' alcohol consumption in British colonies in Ronald Hyam, *Britain's Imperial Century, 1815–1914. A Study of Empire and Expansion*, (New York: Palgrave, 2002), 290.

88 See note 64 above.

89 NAN ZBU 146, A VI a 3, Bd.1, Bl. 10, Hptm. v. Francois to RK v. Caprivi, 31.12.91, reported about six cases: *'Geldstrafe von min. 30 – max. 600 M, und 2 Freiheitsstrafe*[*n*] *von min 10 Tagen Haft – maxim. 2 Monaten Gefängniß'*.

be too far-fetched to call these customs a Southwest African *lex mercatoria*, but over the years the need to change these customs became more and more evident to German officials for one particular reason: the latter noticed that many European traders unscrupulously took advantage of the African population in particular. One of the first German officials to work in GSWA, constable Hugo von Goldtammer, shortly after his arrival in 1886 reported about traders who made 150 to 200 per cent profit from bartering (very little) tobacco against (a lot of) cattle.[90] Complaints were rampant. A 'rebellion' was likely to break out given the abuses and the resulting impoverishment of the African population. Due to the barter of imported products, Africans were forced to give away their only means of production: cattle and land. To be sure, in 1901 the local court (*Bezirksgericht*) in Swakopmund also described the indebtedness and the credit lines of the German population as 'difficult' (*schwierig*).[91] However, this never reached the degree of the complete over indebtedness of many Africans in Hereroland or elsewhere in GSWA. Governor Leutwein attempted in vain to counter steer. He started to publish 'urgent' warnings against the 'granting of unjustified credits to natives'. However, these warnings were barely a means against practices of traders to hold liable entire families or 'tribes' for the debts of individual members.[92] Given such commercial practices, in 1903, the German chief official of the Karibib district spoke of the '*Creditunwesen*'.[93] The inspector of the Rhenish Mission, Gottlob Haußleiter mentioned the term '*Raubhandel*'. A decree of the Governor was intended to limit strictly the granting of credit. Scheduled to be enforceable on 1 January 1899, it never came into effect; otherwise, the 'credit economy of the Herero would have found a bloodless end', as Haußleiter assumed. Africans, missionaries, and colonial officials continued to complain about the 'credits'. A new decree of the Chancellor on

90 Bundesarchiv Berlin (BAB) R 1001/9328, Bl. 1452, v. Goldtammer an Nels betr. Dienstreise von Otyimbingue nach Otyiambi und zurück, 8.8.1886. Writing about the Swartbooi: '*Besonders wirtschaftlich scheinen sie mit ihrem Viehbestande nicht umzugehen. Für Taback und Kaffee verkaufen sie selbst ihr letztes Stück Vieh. Die Hauptschuld, daß dieser Stamm immer mehr verarmt, scheint die Händler zu treffen, denn diese arbeiten bei demselben nach Abzug sämmtlicher Auslagen mit 150 bis 200% Gewinn. Ich selbst bin Augenzeuge gewesen, daß die Leute von den Händlern für eine Kuh nur Pfund 2, für einen Ochsen nur 2.10 und für 1 Schaf nur 6/- in Waaren erhalten haben*'.

91 DSWA-Zeitung, III. Jg. 22, 30.10.1901, Beilage, p. 1; cf. Külz, 1909, 366.

92 NAN GWI 760, Gen VIII 9, Bl.20, LHpt to Court Windhoek, 27.8.1898; *Windhoeker Anzeiger*, I. Jg. 11, 2.3. 1899, 1.

93 NAN ZBU 715, F V o 2, Bd.1, Bl. 72, DA Karibib to Governor, 4.8.1903.

the credit system (July 23, 1903) was based 'essentially on Leutwein's proposals. However, it was four years late!'[94]

Missionaries had no doubt that it was the traders with their 'stores' and the *Borg* system (from German *borgen*: to borrow, to loan) who 'were to be blamed' for the ever-growing impoverishment of the OvaHerero and Nama.[95] It is difficult to find sources that attest to African perspectives on this history. The texts available in archives and secondary sources are overwhelmingly written by Germans who took for granted institutions that were related to profit making. However, a few remarks have survived from African leaders, which demonstrate to their incomprehension towards German undertakings that ran counter to their notions of equity, profit, or the manner of running a business. Hendrik Witbooi (~1835–1905), the Nama-leader who was a faithful ally of the German colonial administration until he rebelled in late 1904,[96] explained to a colonial official: 'I know that [in the German colony] there is no place for me amongst you', and he predicted the death of his people under the colonial yoke. The Germans, in the areas of GSWA already under their control, forced upon the Africans their legal regime, a system that in many respects stood in sharp contrast with the customs of the latter. This became particularly evident in the ensuing conflicts over property of land and land use. While the inhabitants in Hereroland and Namaland did not previously recognize exclusive land tenure or land use by 'proprietors', the German settlers attempted to 'purchase' (or rather barter against European goods like rifles, gun powder, or liquor) for their exclusive use as much land and as many watering places as possible. Once the 'contract' was concluded, the settlers argued with (German) property rights that entitled them to exclude others. In a letter to *Kaptein* Josef Frederiks, Hendrik Witbooi observed the following about his own people, the Nama:

> They do not make prohibiting laws against each other, concerning water, grazing or roads; nor do they charge money for any of these things, No, we [the Nama, "rooi menschen"] hold these things to be free to any traveller

---

94 *Berichte der Rheinischen Missionsgesellschaft*, Nr. 5, 61. Jg. (1904), S.142. '*hätte die Schuldenwirtschaft der Herero wahrscheinlich damals ein unblutiges Ende gefunden*'; '*prinzipiell auf dem Boden der Leutweinschen Vorschläge. Aber sie kam eben vier Jahre zu spät!*'.

95 Archives of the Evangelical Lutheran Church in the Republic of Namibia (Windhoek), C I 1.40, Bl.1, Präses Viehe to Governorate, o.D. [~1903]. '*In den letzten Jahren hat die Verarmung der Herero ...ganz bedeutend zugenommen ... Die Schuld hieran tragen wesentlich die Stores*'.

96 Gunther Pakendorf, 'Witboois Verweigerung', in Carlotta von Maltzan, Akila Ahouli and Marianne Zappen-Thomson (eds.), *Jahrbuch für Internationale Germanistik 134, Grenzen und Migration: Afrika und Europa* (Bern: P. Lang, 2019), 21–37.

> who wishes to cross our land, be he Red, White, or Black ... But with White people it is not so at all. The White men's laws are quite unbearable and intolerable to us Red people: they oppress us and hem us in all kinds of ways and on all sides, these merciless laws which have no feeling or tolerance for any man rich or poor.[97]

Even the sons of important chiefs had escaped to northern Ovamboland, 'because of their level of debt with white traders', as governor Leutwein wrote to his superiors in Berlin.[98] The decree of 1903 on the limits of credits and their enforceability, however, had the immediate effect that 'now the traders acted particularly reckless', since according to its provisions from 1 April 1904 debts were to lapse after 12 months.[99] Subsequently, the traders panicked that they would lose their claims against (African) debtors. The ensuing conflicts about the payment of merchandise or the value of land or cattle often turned into violence. In January 1904, OvaHerero took to arms. One reason for the outbreak of war between Germans and OvaHerero was the trade and credit system, as becomes evident from Herero Chief Daniel Kariko's description of the 'creation' of debts by German traders and the manner of paying off these debts.

> 'Our people ... were being robbed and deceived right and left by the German traders, and their cattle were taken by force. They were flogged and ill-treated and got no redress. In fact, the German police assisted the traders instead of protecting us. Traders would come along and offer goods. When we said that we had no cattle to spare as the rinderpest had killed so many, they said they would give us credit. Often when we refused to

97 Transl. in Werner Hillebrecht, 'The Nama and the war in the south', in Jürgen Zimmerer and Joachim Zeller (eds.), *Genocide in German South-West Africa. The Colonial War of 1904–1908 and its Aftermath, translated and introduced by E.J. Neather* (Monmouth Press, 2008), 143–158, here 146; cf. also Andreas Eckert, 'Land-rights, land-use and conflicts in Colonial Cameroon. The case of Douala', in Jaap de Moor and Dietmar Rothermund (eds.), *Our Laws, Their Lands: Land Laws and Land Use in Modern Colonial Societies* (Münster: LIT, 1994), 25 f.

98 BAB R 1001/1491, Bl.137, Gouv to Colonial Dpt, 9.11.03 '*wegen ihrer starken Verschuldung bei weißen Händlern*'; see Bley, *Kolonialherrschaft*, 179; Nils Ole Oermann, *Mission, Church and State Relations in South West Africa under German Rule (1884–1915)* (Stuttgart: Steiner, 1999), 91 f.

99 *Berichte der Rheinischen Mission*, Nr. 4, 61. Jg. (1904), 110 (FN): *Ab dem 1.4.1904 sollten 'die Schulden der Eingeborenen nach einem ... Formular nur innerhalb von zwölf Monaten noch einklagbar sein, darnach also verjähren. Die Folge war, daß eine Unzahl von Schuldklagen mit allen ihren Folgen anhängig gemacht wurde. Eine Notiz in der Südwest-Afrikanischen Zeitung besagt, daß von den Kaufleuten nicht weniger als 106.000 Exemplare besagter Formulare bestellt wurden. Darnach kann man ermessen, in welchem ausgedehnten Maße dieses verhängnisvolle Borgsystem geübt worden ist'.*

> buy goods, even on credit, the trader would simply offload goods and leave them, saying we could pay when we liked, but in a few weeks he could come back and demand his money or cattle in lieu thereof. He would then go and pick out the very best cows. Very often one man's cattle were taken to pay other people's debts. If we objected and tried to resist, the police would be sent for and, what with floggings and threats of shootings, it was useless for our poor people to resist ... they fixed their own prices for the goods but would never let us put down our own valuation on our cattle'.[100]

Also chief Samuel Maharero argued in a similar vein when he explained to governor Leutwein what had caused the war:

> 'I had not started the war that year [1904], but it was started by the whites, as you know how many Herero the whites had killed, especially traders with their guns and in prisons. And when ever I brought up the matter in Windhoek, the blood of my people merely costs some small stock, that is to say 50 or 15 [animals]. The traders increased our misery by, on their own initiative, lending things to my people ... These were the things that caused the war'.[101]

The war ended in a 'genocidal escalation' in late 1904.[102] Since 2015, the 'extermination order' of General Lothar von Trotha against the OvaHerero nation and the brutal policies resulting from it have been the subject of

---

100 Daniel Kariko, quoted in Department of Information and Publicity. SWAPO of Namibia, *To Be Born a Nation: The Liberation Struggle for Namibia* (London, 1981), 18; others gave similar testimonies: '*Die Schuld am Kriege tragen die Händler, die uns mit ihrem Handel drangsaliert haben; kauften wir nicht bei ihnen auf Schuld, so war's ein Unglück; kauften wir auf Schuld, so war's auch ein Unglück; sie quälten uns eben immer*'. Zit. in *Berichte der Rheinischen Missionsgesellschaft*, Nr. 6, 61. Jg. (1904), 225.

101 '*Der Anfang des Krieges ist nicht jetzt in diesem Jahre [1904] durch mich begonnen worden, sondern er ist begonnen worden von den Weißen, wie Du weißt wie viele Herero durch die weißen Leute, besonders die Händler mit Gewehren und in den Gefängnissen getötet sind. Und immer, wenn ich diese Sache nach Windhoek brachte, immer kostete das Blut meiner Leute wenig Kleinvieh, nämlich 50 oder 15. Die Händler vermehrten die Not noch in der Weise, dass sie von sich selbst meinen Leuten Sachen auf Borg gaben. ... Diese Dinge sind es, die den Krieg in diesem Lande erweckt haben*'. S. Maharero to Leutwein, 6.3.04, Archiv der Vereinten Ev. Mission Wuppertal, RMG 2.615, quot. in W. Wienecke, 'Der Befreiungskampf der Herero in ihrem Selbstverständnis und im Urteil der Missionare. Einige persönliche Erfahrungen', in: Ulrich v. d. Heyden and Holger Stoecker (eds.), *Mission und Macht. Europäische Missionsgesellschaften in politischen Spannungsfeldern in Afrika und Asien zwischen 1800 und 1945*, (Stuttgart: Steiner, 2005), 507–524,(510).

102 Häussler, *Der Genozid an den Herero*, 11.

Namibian-German governmental consultations. They will have the likely outcome of reparation payments and an official German apology for the mass killings that have already, in line with the terminology used by most historians, been officially acknowledged as 'genocide'.[103]

With the end of the war against the OvaHerero and Nama in 1907/08, the commercial relations between colonizers and colonized were also reformed through the so-called native decrees. The granting of credit to African customers was restricted. As paid labourers for European employers, Africans were supposed to become part of a cash economy. The catastrophic results of the credit system until 1904, however, warned the colonial administrators to remain alert of excesses of the market forces. Since 1906, access to the northern regions of GSWA (Ovamboland) were formally prohibited for all 'non-natives'. This provision chiefly targeted the remaining itinerant traders who would have liked to proceed with their business in areas not yet thoroughly penetrated by formal colonialism. However, the colonial police was strictly advised not to let pass any 'white' beyond a certain 'domestic borderline' defining the so-called 'police zone', where most Africans were dispossessed and farmland was allotted to settlers after 1907.[104]

4 A Better Law for More Profits? The Colonial Companies

Even before the onset of formal imperialism in the last quarter of the nineteenth century, German practitioners of international and colonial trade were well aware that at times the commercial practices in British, Portuguese, or French spheres of influence in Africa or Asia were ruled by special legal

103 https://www.bundestag.de/dokumente/textarchiv/2016/kw11-de-voelkermord-afrika/413646; http://m.windhuk.diplo.de/Vertretung/windhuk/en/03/Bilateral_Relations/Bundestag_20printed_20paper_20no._3A_2018-8859_20of_2022.06.2016.html [22.6.2017]; Andreas Eckl and Matthias Häussler with Jekura Kavari, '*Oomambo wandje komuhoko wOvaherero*. 'Words to the OvaHerero nation'. The Extermination Order of Lothar von Trotha', in: Wolfram Hartmann (ed.), *Nuanced Considerations. Recent Voices in Namibian-German Colonial History*, (Windhoek, Orumbonde, 2019), 109–116.

104 Cf. Giorgio Miescher, *Namibia's Red Line. The History of a Veterinary and Settlement Border*, (New York: Palgrave, 2012), 44–51; Bley, *South-West Africa under German Rule*, xix; Gregor Dobler, *Traders and Trade in colonial Ovamboland, 1925–1990. Elite Formation and the Politics of Consumption under Indirect Rule and Apartheid*, (Basel: BAB, 2014), 19; Wolfgang Werner, 'A Brief History of Land Dispossession in Namibia', *Journal of Southern African Studies* 19 (1993): 135–146, 140; in 1907, police protection for life and property of settlers had been confined to the 'police zone', the central and southern parts of GSWA within reach of railway lines and main roads; cf. Zollmann, *Koloniale Herrschaft*, 45 f.

provisions that differed from the laws applicable in the mother countries. German expert journals like the *Zeitschrift für das gesamte Handelsrecht* therefore also paid attention to the new developments in this field that were mostly related to the shipping of goods. For example, readers were informed about a new British 'Merchant Shipping Act (Colonial)' of 1869 that detailed the competences to regulate 'coasting trade' in the colonies.[105]

Still, once Germany had acquired overseas possessions, German legal academia concerned with commercial law was – contrary to their colleagues from the constitutional law branch[106] – slow to appreciate the colonies as a new field of research. The ordinary commercial law treatises that introduced law students to the subject and its pitfalls barely even mentioned the term 'colonies'. For example, the classic *Lehrbuch des Handelsrecht* by Edgar Heilfron referred to 'colonies' only in the introduction, with regard to the history of 'trade policies' of mercantilism during the seventeenth and eighteenth century. Heilfron had much more to say about the German consuls as representatives of German trade interests abroad: in 1910, Imperial Germany had 768 consulates, among them 137 '*Berufskonsulate*', whose head of mission was often sent directly by the Foreign Office.[107] Given the fact that trade with foreign countries, including foreign colonies, was much more relevant for Germany's national economy than the trade with its own colonies, this silence on German colonial trade seems comprehensible. For students of German commercial law it was more important to learn about German consuls abroad and the laws concerning their work than about German administrators in German colonies. For these students, one question which may have arisen was whether there was a particular German colonial commercial law. At least in one aspect, this was indeed the case.

If any, the only recurring subject in commercial law treatises related to 'colonies' was the law of the colonial companies (*Kolonialgesellschaften*). When summarizing the development of the German stock corporation law (*Aktienrecht*) since the 1850s, the treatises of the law professors Karl Lehmann and Julius von Gierke mentioned the change from the 'concession system' (*Konzessionssystem*) to the 'normative system' (*Normativsystem*) of corporations based on the law reforms in 1870 and 1884. However, the strictness of the provisions

105 F. Mittermaier, 'Englische Handelsgesetzgebung von 1869', *Zeitschrift für das gesamte Handelsrecht* 15 (1870), 356–385, 383.

106 Marc Grohmann, *Exotische Verfassung: Die Kompetenzen des Reichstags für die deutschen Kolonien in Gesetzgebung und Staatsrechtswissenschaft des Kaiserreichs (1884–1914)* (Tübingen: Mohr Siebeck, 2001).

107 Edgar Heilfron, *Lehrbuch des Handelsrechts*, vol. 1, 2nd ed. (Berlin 1910), 13 (on *Kolonialsystem*) and 34 f. (on *Reichskonsuln*).

of the 1884 *Aktiennovelle* made it difficult in 'certain circumstances' to set up a stock corporation. Therefore, two laws were enacted by the *Reichstag* that enabled 'special forms of stock corporation'. The GmbH-law of 1892 and the Colonial Law of 1888 (*Schutzgebietsgesetz*) whose Section 8 (section 11 in the revised law of 1900) allowed for the purpose of colonial enterprises to administrate stock corporations with special provision;[108] thereby the old *Oktroisystem* was reintroduced. The term *Oktroi* referred to the international trade companies that had – since the seventeenth century – a concession from and that were regulated by the government. The 'constitution' of these companies was regulated by the *Oktroi* granted by the government.[109]

108 *Schutzgebietsgesetz* (September 10, 1900), RGBl. 1900, Nr. 40, 812–817 (excerpt) '*§.11. Deutschen Kolonialgesellschaften, welche die Kolonisation der deutschen Schutzgebiete, insbesondere den Erwerb und die Verwerthung von Grundbesitz, den Betrieb von Land- oder Plantagenwirthschaft, den Betrieb von Bergbau, gewerblichen Unternehmungen und Handelsgeschäften in denselben zum ausschließlichen* [816] *Gegenstand ihres Unternehmens und ihren Sitz entweder im Reichsgebiet oder in einem Schutzgebiet oder in einem Konsulargerichtsbezirke haben oder denen durch Kaiserliche Schutzbriefe die Ausübung von Hoheitsrechten in den deutschen Schutzgebieten übertragen ist, kann auf Grund eines vom Reichskanzler genehmigten Gesellschaftsvertrags (Statuts) durch Beschluß des Bundesraths die Fähigkeit beigelegt werden, unter ihrem Namen Rechte, insbesondere Eigenthum und andere dingliche Rechte an Grundstücken zu erwerben, Verbindlichkeiten einzugehen, vor Gericht zu klagen und verklagt zu werden. In solchem Falle haftet den Gläubigern für alle Verbindlichkeiten der Kolonialgesellschaft nur das Vermögen derselben.*

Das Gleiche gilt für deutsche Gesellschaften, welche den Betrieb eines Unternehmens der im Abs. 1 bezeichneten Art in dem Hinterland eines deutschen Schutzgebiets oder in sonstigen dem Schutzgebiete benachbarten Bezirken zum Gegenstand und ihren Sitz entweder im Reichsgebiet oder in einem Schutzgebiet oder in einem Konsulargerichtsbezirke haben.

Der Beschluß des Bundesraths und im Auszuge der Gesellschaftsvertrag sind durch den Reichsanzeiger zu veröffentlichen.

§12. Der Gesellschaftsvertrag hat insbesondere Bestimmungen zu enthalten:

1. über den Erwerb und den Verlust der Mitgliedschaft;

2. über die Vertretung der Gesellschaft Dritten gegenüber;

3. über die Befugnisse der die Gesellschaft leitenden und der die Leitung beaufsichtigenden Organe derselben;

4. über die Rechte und Pflichten der einzelnen Mitglieder;

5. über die Jahresrechnung und Vertheilung des Gewinns;

6. über die Auflösung der Gesellschaft und die nach derselben eintretende Vermögensvertheilung.

§13. Die Gesellschaften, welche die im §. 11 erwähnte Fähigkeit durch Beschluß des Bundesraths erhalten haben, unterstehen der Aufsicht des Reichskanzlers. Die einzelnen Befugnisse desselben sind in den Gesellschaftsvertrag aufzunehmen'.

109 Karl Lehmann, *Lehrbuch des Handelsrechts*, 2nd ed. (Leipzig: Veit, 1912), 380 f.; Julius von Gierke, *Handelsrecht und Schiffahrtsrecht* (Berlin: de Gruyter, 1921), 171; see also Karl Lehmann, 'Über Kolonialhandelsgesellschaftsrecht', *Zeitschrift für das gesamte Handelsrecht* 53 (1911), 1 ff.; Christian Schubel, *Verbandssouveränität und Binnenorganisation der Handelsgesellschaften* (Tübingen: Mohr, 2003), 515.

The colonial company as it was legalized in 1888 was factually a stock corporation (according to the law it was merely a corporate enterprise, but the form of stock corporation was chosen by the shareholders) that was regulated by special provisions. Similar to the English chartered company, the colonial company received its articles of incorporation (*Statut* or *Gesellschaftsvertrag*) by special government act (Act of the *Bundesrat*), and it was controlled by the Federal Chancellor. By this government act, the colonial company became a legal entity (§23 BGB).[110] According to Section 12 of the Colonial Law (SGG), the *Statut* of the colonial company had to regulate a number of points, such as membership, legal representation *vis-a-vis* third parties; allocation of profits etc. The *Bundesrat* was not bound by the provisions of the law on stock corporations. The *Statut* of the colonial companies often deviated from the provisions of the German *Handelsgesetzbuch*, in order to 'moderate' the strict provisions of the latter with regard to stock corporations. For example, the minimum-nominal sum for shares (*Nennbetrag des Anteils*) was reduced to 100 marks (§180 I HGB required 1.000 marks) and there were voices who demanded for policy reasons for a further reduction in this amount.[111] Also, the requirements of the HGB on incorporation and balancing of accounts did not apply to colonial companies; the increase of share capital was simplified.[112]

110 Paul Oertmann, *Kommentar zum Bürgerlichen Gesetzbuch und seinen Nebengesetzen. Allgemeiner Teil*, 3rd ed. (Berlin: Heymanns, 1927), 100: '*Juristische Personen §22f. BGB, Verleihung der Rechtsfähigkeit des Vereins durch jeweiligen Bundesstaat; §23 BGB 'Einem Verein, der seinen Sitz nicht in einem Bundesstaate hat, kann in Ermanglung besonderer reichsgesetzlicher Vorschriften Rechtsfähigkeit durch Beschluss [des Bundes/Reichsrats] verliehen werden*'. On this Oertmann: '[*§23*] *macht* [*anders als §22*] *zwischen wirtschaftlichen und nichtwirtschaftlichen Vereinen keinen Unterschied. Es gehören dahin:* (*a*) *Vereine, die ihren Sitz in einem* (*etwa künftigen*) *deutschen Kolonial- oder Schutzgebiet haben*'. ... '*Die Rechtsfähigkeit der unter §23 gehörigen Vereine regelt sich* (*a*) *nach den etwaigen besonderen Reichsgesetzen. So für Kolonialgesellschaften nach §11 des SGG von 10.9.1900 und des §8 des Gesetzes v. 15.3.1888* (*Beschluss des Bundesrats auf Grund eines vom Reichskanzler genehmigten Gesellschaftsvertrages*)'.

111 von Gierke, *Handelsrecht und Schiffahrtsrecht*, 177. '*Aktie' als 'Anteil* (*Bruchteil*) *des Grundkapitals*'. *§178 HGB. 'Das deutsche Gesetz verlangt ... daß sie* [*die Aktie*] *auf eine bestimmte Geldsumme lautet* (*Summenaktie*) *§180 HGB. ... 'Die Summenaktie muß auf den Betrag von mindestens 1000 Mk. Lauten. §180 I. Nur ausnahmsweise sind auch Aktien bis herunter zu dem Mindesbetrage von 200 Mk nach dem HGB zugelassen sog. Kleinaktien §180 II-IV HGB. ... Weitere Ausnahmen kommen in Betracht nach Konsularrecht und für die Kolonialgesellschaften* (*Nennbetrag bis herunter auf 100 Mk*) ... *Wenn der deutsche Gesetzgeber den normalen Mindesbetrag so hoch beziffert hat, so geschah dies in der Absicht, kleine Leute von der AG fernzuhalten. Mit Rechte wird aber de lege ferenda eine freie Zulassung von Kleinaktien gefordert*'.

112 Lehmann, *Lehrbuch des Handelsrechts*, 466 f. See also Lehmann, 'Über Kolonialhandelsgesellschaftsrecht', 7; Keyßner Förtsch, Lehmann, Scharlach and Bornhaupt, 'Zur

Another major facilitation for the colonial companies in comparison with other German stock corporations was mentioned by the law professor Paul Krückmann in his seminal *Institutionen des Bürgerlichen Gesetzbuches*. He referred to the colonial companies when explaining the term 'legal entity' (*juristische Person*) and its origins:

> For the commercial associations AG, GmbH, Genossenschaft … there are particular requirements as to their form [in order for them acquire legal capacity] … Other commercial associations need to be granted the status of legal entity by the state [concession], because [the state] aims to avoid that economic associations hide behind the easier form requirements of the BGB and thereby bypass the [strict] requirements made for the AG, GmbH, Genossenschaft that protect all participants and the general public. … when we still had colonies, the concessioning was used to support the colonial companies, because thereby they were freed from a number of taxes and fees.[113]

As an aside, it needs to be added that, legally speaking, the *Kolonialgesellschaften* survived the end of the German colonial empire and the Treaty of Versailles. The SSG remained the legal basis for the existence of the colonial companies as stipulated in a decree on 'the settlement of colonial affairs' (March 21, 1924). After the Second World War, another law 'concerning the legal relationships of colonial companies' was promulgated. Only in 1975 was the liquidation of all German *Kolonialgesellschaften* declared, with the abrogation of these laws. The companies could be transformed into limited liability companies (GmbH).[114]

Frage der Genußscheine', *Beiträge zur Kolonialpolitik und Kolonialwirtschaft* 1 (1899), 321–313; Bornhaupt, 'Zur Frage der Genußscheine', ibid., 267; Hermann C.O. Nollau, *Das Recht der auf Grund des Reichsgesetzes betreffend die Rechtsverhältnisse der deutschen Schutzgebiete errichteten Kolonialgesellschaften* (Berlin: Süsserott, 1904).

113 Paul Krügmann, *Institutionen des Bürgerlichen Gesetzbuches*, 5th ed. (Berlin: Verlag von Georg Stilke, 1929), 92. '*…Andere wirtschaftliche Vereine müssen sich staatlich die juristische Person verleihen lassen, weil es verhindert werden soll, daß die Vereine zu wirtschaftlichen Zwecken sich hinter die unverfänglichen Formvorschriften des BGB stecken und die zur Sicherheit der Beteiligten wie der Allgemeinheit vorgeschriebenen Formen der AG, GmbH, Gen. umgehen. … Von der Konzessionierung wurden früher, als wir noch Kolonien hatten, Gebrauch gemacht, um die Kolonialgesellschaften zu unterstützen, denn sie wurden damit frei von mancherlei Steuern und Gebühren*'.

114 *Gesetz über die Auflösung, Abwicklung und Löschung von Kolonialgesellschaften* (August 20, 1975; BGBl. I: 2253) '*§4 Das Schutzgebietsgesetz idF vom 10.September 1900 … und die*

5 Epilogue: Prolegomena to a History of Private Law in the German Colonies

Given that the profits derived from German colonial possessions remained rather limited if not illusory for most of the individuals and companies involved, and considering the huge losses incurred by the German state, which continued to subsidize the colonial undertaking as a whole until 1914, historians tend to agree that German colonialism 'did not pay' financially, it was a 'losing deal'.[115] Nevertheless, the effects – social, economic, administrative and otherwise – were profound for most societies involved in this history. After all, in 1914, all German colonies were inhabited by around 13 million people, among them 24,389 German nationals.[116]

The history of labour and capitalism in Africa is currently being rewritten,[117] and the work of historians will profit greatly from giving the law its apposite share in this history. If the 'emergence of capitalist social relations of production and the development of productive forces' is a striking feature of twentieth-century sub-Saharan Africa, as economists John Sender and Sheila Smith argued years ago in unmistakably Marxist terms, then historians must also ask about 'changes in ownership and control of the means of production'. The terms 'ownership' and 'control', by their very nature, involve legal questions; all the more so since the role of the state – the governments, the administration, the courts, the parliaments – has to be taken into consideration.[118]

The law's role in German colonialism, or more specifically, the law's role in making possible the rule over the German colonial territories and their inhabitants – settler and native population – has been given some prominence by historical research over the last two decades or so. However, it is evident

Verordnung über die Regelung der kolonialen Angelegenheiten vom 21. März 1924 ... treten mit Ablauf des 31.Dezember 1976 außer Kraft. ...'.

115 Drechsler, *Südwestafrika*, 328; Speitkamp, *Deutsche Kolonialgeschichte*, 89, 'Verlustgeschäft'.

116 Sprigade and Moisel, *Kolonialatlas*, 12.

117 See e.g. Frederick Cooper, *Africa in the World: Capitalism, Empire, Nation-State* (Cambridge: Harvard University Press, 2014); Andreas Eckert, 'What is Global Labour History Good For', in Jürgen Kocka (ed.), *Work in a Modern Society: The German Historical Experience in Comparative Perspective* (Oxford: Berghahn Books, 2010), 169–181; see also the project 'General Labour History of Africa' at the Amsterdam International Institute of Social History, <https://socialhistory.org/en/projects/general-labour-history-africa> [accessed July 1, 2016].

118 John Sender and Sheila Smith, *The Development of Capitalism in Africa* (New York: Routledge, 2011; orig. 1986), 1; for an early consideration on the relevance of law cf. Richard Roberts and Kirsten Mann (eds.), *Law in Colonial Africa* (Portsmouth: Heinemann, 1991).

that questions of international, public, or criminal law have received the greater emphasis.[119] Considerations of private and commercial law in the German colonies and their intricacies are rare and have not yet reached monographic dimensions.[120] Yet, the examinations undertaken so far have shown how legal history can be fruitfully employed to shed light on labour or family relations within the context of German colonialism.[121] The history of the commercial relations of the German colonies with the rest of world as well as within the colonies (and the role of the law in this context) remains to be written. After all, what was 'colonial' about these commercial relations? What was different from other German contexts? Was it, for example, the relative 'freedom' of the colonial administration to create law by administrative decree (*Verordnung, Verfügung*) without much parliamentary involvement?[122] And what resulted from this 'freedom', for what purpose was it used, to whose advantage, and how did this affect the societies involved? *Nolens volens*, these decrees also comprised fields of law which touched upon private law, even though the *Bürgerliches Recht* was supposed to be exempted from the colonial ordinances of the Emperor or colonial governors (cf. §3 *Schutzgebietsgesetz* [1900] and §19 *des Gesetzes über die Konsulargerichtsbarkeit*).

In this context, it is worth referring to a contemplation by Max Weber, in his seminal *Economy and Society* (1920), who concluded, when writing about 'the most general relations between law and economy' that 'Under certain conditions a "legal order" can remain unchanged while economic relations are undergoing a radical transformation'. Weber chose the 'extreme' example of the introduction of 'a socialist system of production'. However, we can pursue

119 Cf. Margitta Boin, *Die Erforschung der Rechtsverhältnisse in den 'Schutzgebieten' des Deutschen Reiches* (Münster: LIT, 1996); Martin Schröder, *Prügelstrafe und Züchtigungsrecht in den deutschen Schutzgebieten* (Münster: LIT, 1997); Schildknecht, *Bismarck, Südwestafrika und die Kongokonferenz*; Grohmann, *Exotische Verfassung*; Ralf Schlottau, *Deutsche Kolonialrechtspflege: Strafrecht und Strafmacht in den deutschen Schutzgebieten 1884–1914* (Frankfurt/M.: Peter Lang, 2007).

120 For a contemporary analysis see Edler von Hoffmann: 'Das Deutsche Kolonial-Gewerberecht', *Zeitschrift für Kolonialpolitik, Kolonialrecht und Kolonialwirtschaft* 8 (1906), 164–195, 285–323; see Zollmann, 'Bausteine einer kolonialen Geschichte des Privatrechts', 14–36.

121 Udo Wolter, 'Deutsches Kolonialrecht – ein wenig erforschtes Rechtsgebiet, dargestellt anhand des Arbeitsrechts der Eingeborenen', *Zeitschrift für Neuere Rechtsgeschichte* 17 (1995), 201–244; Ulrike Schaper, *Koloniale Verhandlungen* (Frankfurt/M.: Campus, 2012), chapter on family law.

122 Ignacio Czeguhn, 'Das Verordnungsrecht in den deutschen Kolonien', *Der Staat* 47 (2008), 606–633.

Weber's diagnosis about a 'most unlikely' example[123] into the real world by asking: how can we analyse the introduction of a colonial order of production and its relations to the BGB that was also introduced in the German colonies in 1900? What parts of the '"legal order" … remained unchanged', and what did change? And what role did the different stakeholders in the colonies play in these developments? This task seems worthwhile, considering that the 'economic relations' in the colonies were – in part – 'radically' different (or 'transformed') compared to those in metropolitan Germany. Using Weber's insight that law can remain the same in different (political and economic) contexts, one might ask about the possibility of writing a colonial history of the *Bürgerliches Gesetzbuch* (BGB) and the German commercial code (*HGB*). Whereas the history of these codes in different ideological and political contexts of German history over the past century has been written,[124] the colonial episode is conspicuously missing from this history.[125] We should start working on this.

123 Max Weber, *Economy and Society: An Outline of Interpretive Sociology*, (eds.) Guenther Roth and Claus Wittich (Berkeley: University of California Press, 1978), 333 f. (The Economy and Social Norms Cpt. 1.4).

124 See e.g. Hans-Peter Haferkamp, *Das Bürgerliche Gesetzbuch während des Nationalsozialismus und in der DDR: mögliche Aspekte und Grenzen eines Vergleichs* (Köln: Otto Schmidt, 2005); Thorsten Keiser, *Eigentumsrecht in Nationalsozialismus und Fascismo* (Tübingen: Mohr Siebeck, 2005); Werner Schubert, *Das Familien- und Erbrecht unter dem Nationalsozialismus: ausgewählte Quellen zu den wichtigsten Gesetzen und Projekten aus den Ministerialakten* (Paderborn: Schöningh, 1993).

125 But see Zollmann, 'Bausteine einer kolonialen Geschichte des Privatrechts'.

Customs Law in the Congo: On the Fiscal Bargaining Process between the Colonial State and Private Enterprise in Africa (1886–1914)

Bas De Roo

1 Introduction

Colonial law and legal practice was never simply transplanted from Metropole to colony.[1] Instead, colonial legal systems were negotiated by different stakeholders on the colonial level.[2] This chapter demonstrates how commercial law in the Congo Free State and Belgian Congo was developed through the interaction between the private sector and the state; two actors with both competitive and complementary interests. As Anthony Hopkins argues, the state relied on firms for fiscal revenue and hence promoted trade – for example through investments in infrastructure – but also feared the consequence of unregulated private enterprise. The private sector needed the colonial state to secure public order and to underpin confidence and credit-worthiness, but disliked the regulations and fiscal burden that went along with growing state presence and economic intervention. Moreover, firms often felt that colonial support was insufficient.[3] This contribution argues that, in the economic domain, the lawmaking process in the pre-war Congo essentially consisted of finding a balance between private and public interests on the colonial rather than on the metropolitan level.

This chapter focuses on customs law, as this set of regulations had a huge impact on colonial enterprises in the pre-war Congo. First of all, customs law largely determined how much and which kind of tariffs trading firms and concession companies had to pay to the state – virtually every colonial enterprise in the Congo was active in the export of commodities. Secondly, customs law regulated the export of primary products and the import of manufactured

1 Lauren Benton, *Law and Colonial Cultures. Legal Regimes in World History, 1400–1900* (Cambridge: Cambridge University Press, 2002).

2 John L. Comaroff, 'Reflections on the Colonial State in South Africa and Elsewhere: Factions, Fragments, Facts and Fictions', *Social Identities* 4:3 (1998), 321–361.

3 A.G. Hopkins, 'Big Business in African Studies', *The Journal of African History* 28:1 (1987), 131–134.

 | DOI:10.1163/9789004443075_014

goods. From the perspective of the colonial state, customs duties were a vital source of income, necessary to survive without metropolitan support.[4]

This contribution demonstrates that the Free State and Belgian Congo had a hard time balancing the annual budget through the collection of export and import duties, as the interests of trading firms and concession companies had to be taken into account when new customs regulations and tariffs were devised. The hardest part about taxation is to get the taxpayer to pay. A state can force taxpayers to comply, or depend on their consent. Consent produces better results more cheaply, but requires bargaining with the taxpayer who expects the state to provide public services in return, and wants to have a say in lawmaking. Moreover, consent depends on the perceived fairness of taxation and the legitimacy of the state. As the state was forced to bargain with the taxpayer, the latter had a large heavy influence on decision-making about the tax burden, the mode of taxation, and even the allocation of tax receipts.

In this chapter, the taxpayers are the leading European trading firms and concession companies that were active in the Congo and who paid the greater part of colonial customs duties. These enterprises imported products to pay for Congolese rubber and ivory or cash crops such as palm nuts, which they exported back to Europe. The biggest players in the Congolese market were trading houses such as Daumas Béraud et Compagnie, the Nieuwe Afrikaansche Handels-Vennootschap, and the Société Anonyme Belge pour le Commerce du Haut-Congo – henceforth called Société Anonyme Belge as it was in colonial times – and concession companies such as Abir, the Société Anversoise, Compagnie du Kasaï, and the Compagnie du Lomami.[5]

Trading firms simply bought exports from local producers or intermediaries with imports or accepted currencies in the Congo. Concession companies operated differently. African producers, merchants or local elites were paid with similar imports for the ivory and rubber they turned over to a company. However, local producers gained little from compulsory production. Concession companies held a trade monopoly and used coercive methods, and this enabled them to pay producers very little, and that in cheap manufactured goods.

4 Leigh Gardner, *Taxing Colonial Africa: The Political Economy of British Imperialism* (Oxford: Oxford University Press, 2012); Bas De Roo, 'The Trouble with Tariffs: Customs policies and the shaky balance between colonial and private interests in the Congo (1886–1914)', *Tijdschrift voor Sociale en Economische Geschiedenis* 12:3 (2015), 1–21; Ewout Frankema and Marlous van Waijenburg, 'Metropolitan Blueprints of Colonial Taxation: Lessons from Fiscal Capacity Building in British and French Africa, c. 1888–1940', *The Journal of African History* 55:3 (2014), 371–400.

5 Frans Buelens, *Congo 1885–1960: Een financieel-economische geschiedenis* (Berchem: EPO, 2007).

However, coercion required additional imports. *Capitas* – the African intermediaries who stood between the producer and the concession company and were often ex-merchants – and local chiefs had to be armed and paid.[6]

The first section of this Chapter demonstrates that the Free State was forced to raise the tariff burden continuously and implement new customs procedures to make ends meet from 1885 to 1892. Some trading firms considered the tax policies and commercial activities of the state as unfair and illegitimate and complained that the burden of tariffs and control procedures was too high. As a result, every new customs law was met with fierce resistance. Section 2 shows that the customs dispute cooled down and was not revived after 1892. The tariff burden did not prove to be as intolerable as private enterprise had feared, and all parties got their fair share of the wealth that was generated by the rubber boom that took place from 1896 to 1913. The Belgians reformed the customs system and raised the tariff burden. However, no new disputes arose as the new colonial regime restored the fiscal contract with the commercial sector by abolishing the concession system that had been implemented at the end of 1892. Moreover, the Belgians felt less pressure to balance the annual colonial budget and could make more concessions to the corporate taxpayer.

This chapter also argues that is it crucial to take into account the close relationship between the colonial state and certain corporate taxpayers in order to understand commercial lawmaking in the pre-war Congo. As in other African colonies, the Congolese administration depended on companies for tax revenue and the latter needed the state to create a growth inducing context through public investment, labour mobilization and price policies. However, the prewar Congolese state and private enterprise were also strongly intertwined on an institutional, practical, and personal level.[7] This chapter demonstrates that a company's connections with Brussels and Boma heavily affected how both actors negotiated customs law.

6 Robert Harms, 'The end of red rubber: a reassessment', *The Journal of African History* 16:1 (1975), 73–88; Robert Harms, 'The World Abir Made: The Maringa-Lopori Basin, 1885–1903', *African Economic History* 12 (1983), 125–139; Daniël Vangroenweghe, *Rood rubber: Leopold II en zijn Kongo* (Brussels: Elsevier, 1985); Osumaka Likaka, 'Rural Protest: The Mbole against Belgian Rule, 1897–1959', *The International Journal of African Historical Studies* 27:3 (1994), 589–617; Catherine Coquery-Vidrovitch, *Le Congo au temps des grandes compagnies concessionnaires 1898–1930* (Paris: Ed. de l'Ecole des hautes études en sciences sociales, 2001).

7 Jean-Luc Vellut, 'Hégémonies en construction: Articulations entre Etat et Entreprises dans le bloc colonial Belge (1908–1960)', *Canadian Journal of African Studies / Revue Canadienne des Etudes Africaines* 16:2 (1982), 313–330; Jean-Luc Vellut, 'Réseaux transnationaux dans l'économie politique du Congo Léopoldien, c. 1885–1910', in Laurence Marfaing and Brigitte Reinwald (eds.), *Afrikanische Beziehungen, Netzwerke un Räume* (Berlin: Lit Verlag, 2001), 131–146.

2 Negotiating Customs in the Face of Looming Colonial Bankruptcy (1885–1892)

This first section studies the fiscal bargaining process during the first years of colonial rule, when the new-born Free State desperately tried to develop a tax system that would generate sufficient revenue to balance the colonial budget.[8] The first three subsections deal with the grievances of trading firms. Subsection 4 examines whether the Free State took these complaints into account.

The main taxpayers in this period were the Dutch Nieuwe Afrikaansche Handels-Vennootschap, the Société Anonyme Belge, and the French Daumas, Béraud et Compagnie. The Dutch and the French firm had been active in the Congo estuary before the Congo basin was officially divided between the Free State, France, and Portugal in 1885. During the 1880s, both firms ventured into the Congolese interior in search of ivory and rubber. The Société Anonyme Belge was established at the end of 1888 by its parent company, the Compagnie du Congo pour le Commerce et l'Industrie, to buy ivory and rubber in the Upper Congo. A number of other large trading firms such as the Sanford Exploring Mission, Hatton and Cookson or the Companhia Portugueza do Zaire were also active in the Free State.[9] Unfortunately, these firms hardly left a trace in the colonial archives and are hence not dealt with here. Information on the numerable smaller trading firms, run by Portuguese or Greek merchants, is even harder to access. The colonial custom system was virtually blind to African trading networks that were also active in trans-border trade.[10]

2.1 *An Excessive and Ever-Increasing Fiscal Burden*

Every single time the Free State increased the tariff burden, the Nieuwe Afrikaansche Handels-Vennootschap and Daumas, Béraud et Compagnie

8 Lewis H. Gann and Peter Duignan, *The Rulers of Belgian Africa, 1884–1914* (New Jersey: Princeton University Press, 1979); Jean Stengers and Jan Vansina, 'King Leopold's Congo 1886–1908', in J.D. Fage and Roland Oliver (eds.), *The Cambridge History of Africa* (Cambridge: Cambridge University Press, 1985), 315–358.

9 James P. White, 'The Sanford Exploring Expedition', *The Journal of African History* 8:2 (1967), 291–302; Lysle E. Meyer, 'Henry S. Sanford and the Congo: A Reassessment', *African Historical Studies* 4:1 (1971), 19–39; Herman Obdeijn, 'The New Africa Trading Company and the Struggle for Import Duties in the Congo Free State, 1886–1894', *African Economic History* 12 (1983), 195–212; Jelmer Vos, *The Kingdom of Kongo and Its Borderlands, 1880–1915* (University of London, 2005).

10 Jean-Luc Vellut, 'Katanga, Bié, Benguela and Beyond: The Cycle of Rubber and Slaves, 1890–1910', *Portuguese Studies Review* 19:1–2 (2011), 133–152; Bas De Roo, 'The blurred lines of legality: Customs and contraband in the Congolese M'Bomu region (1889–1908)', *The Journal of Belgian History* XLIV:4 (2014), 112–142.

complained loudly that venturing into the African interior was costly enough as it was. Customs duties not only made things worse, the tariff burden simply rendered trade in the Upper Congo unprofitable. Initially, both firms had given the yet-to-be-born Free State the all clear when Brussels disclosed the plans to introduce export duties. The French firm called the burden of the new tax 'minimal'.[11] Export duties did not seem excessive to the Dutch trading house either.[12] However, the resistance of both firms grew once the customs system actually started to take shape.

In 1886, the Nieuwe Afrikaansche Handels-Vennootschap and Daumas, Béraud et Compagnie joined forces with a number of other trading houses to write an open letter to the Free State. The companies complained that the burden of the recently introduced export tariffs on rubber, ivory and cash crops was too high. European demand for African commodities had decreased. Moreover, trading firms had to pay more to African producers and middlemen because an exceptionally heavy rainy season had significantly reduced the supply of Congolese products. If the high cost of transport and insurance was added to the equation, tariffs made trade in the Congo unprofitable.[13] Trading firms and the Free State held different views on the appropriate tariff burden. The Nieuwe Afrikaansche Handels-Vennootschap for example suggested that copal tariffs should be lowered by 90% and palm oil tariffs by 60%.[14]

In 1890, Brussels and Boma were forced to increase export tariffs to balance the colonial budget. Rubber and ivory exports were henceforth taxed at a rate of 0.5 and 2 francs respectively per kilogram instead of the previous rates of 0.2 and 0.5 francs per kilogram.[15] Daumas, Béraud et Compagnie called the new rubber tariff 'exorbitant' and the new ivory tax 'ruinous'. Moreover, the French firm argued that the new tariffs did not take into account the fact that ivory prices depended on the size and shape of a tusk and hence disproportionally

11 Archives du Ministère des Affaires Etrangères Belge (AMAEB). Archives Africaines (AA). Etat Indépendant du Congo (EIC). Finances (FIN).863.1.33 – Daumas, Béraud et Cie à l'Administrateur Général des Finances (17 September 1886).

12 AMAEB.AA. Classement Provisoire (CP).2571 – l'Administrateur Général des Finances à l'Administrateur Général au Congo (23 July 1886).

13 AMAEB.AA.CP.2571 – De Bloem (NAHV), Mac Creadie (Hatton & Cookson), Lasthou (Daumas Béraud et Cie), Frazer (British Congo Company), d'Oliveira, de Ribeiro, Abseio (Companhia Portugueza do Zaïre), de Souza, Lopo, Borges, Valle et Azevede, Ferreira d'Acosta, Real, de Freitas et da Sylva à l'Administrateur Général au Congo (10 June 1886).

14 AMAEB.AA.EIC.FIN.863.1.46 – Le NAHV à l'Administrateur Général des Finances (27 August 1886); AEB.AHD.2 – l'Administrateur Général des Finances à l'Administrateur Général au Congo (24 August 1886).

15 Droits de sortie (15 December 1885), BOEIC, 1885, pp. 40–42; Droits de sortie (15 June 1890), BOEIC, 1890, pp. 81–83.

burdened smaller tusks. According to Daumas, Béraud et Compagnie, the new tariffs made trade in the Upper Congo impossible.[16]

In 1891, the Free State introduced an ivory tariff of 25% *ad valorem* on ivory bought inside the private domain of the state, which comprised a large part of the Congolese interior.[17] Once more Daumas, Béraud et Compagnie claimed that this 'monstrous' tariff rate made commerce unprofitable and would prevent companies from venturing into the Upper Congo.[18] Contrary to its French counterpart, the Nieuwe Afrikaansche Handels-Vennootschap welcomed the introduction of export duties on products from the Upper Congo. The Dutch firm hoped that Leopold II's agents would stop buying ivory in the Haut Congo if the Free State could raise sufficient revenue through tariffs.[19] However, tariff rates were excessively high according to the Nieuwe Afrikaansche Handels-Vennootschap. The customs system also did not take price fluctuations on the world market into account. In addition, the state did not seem to realize that the ivory price depended on the size and quality of each specific tusk. Rubber also came in different qualities, affecting prices.[20] Moreover, it was hard to allocate the cost of customs duties to the African producer: if Africans were paid less, they simply offered fewer exports or sold their commodities to a competitor.[21]

When the Free State unveiled its plans to introduce import duties, the Nieuwe Afrikaansche Handels-Vennootschap and Daumas, Béraud et Compagnie did everything that was in their power to block the introduction of the new tax. Import duties seemed to have been the final straw for both trading

16 Nationaal Archief (NA). Buitenlandse Zaken (BZ).A.214 – Daumas-Béraud et Compagnie au Ministre du Commerce et des Colonies de la France (16 August 1890); Archives nationales d'outre-mer (ANOM). Fonds Ministériels (FM). Service Géographique (SG). Afrique (AFR).VI.80a – Daumas-Béraud et Compagnie au Ministre des Affaires Etrangères de la France (21 August 1890).

17 Modifications à certains lois d'impôts (19 February 1891), BOEIC, 1891, pp. 23–26.

18 ANOM.FM.SG.AFR.VI.94a – Daumas-Béraud et Compagnie au Ministre du Commerce et des Colonies de la France (28 January 1891); Archives de l'Etat Belge (AEB). Archives du Palais Royal (APR). Cabinet du Roi Leopold II (CRL). Développement extérieur de la Belgique (DEB). Correspondances avec diverses personnes (CD).106 – Thys au Roi (6 June 1891).

19 NA.BZ.A.213 – De NAHV aan de Minister van Buitenlandse Zaken van Nederland (5 October 1889).

20 NA.BZ.A.214 – De NAHV aan de Minister van Buitenlandse Zaken van Nederland (18 August 1890).

21 NA. Nieuwe Afrikaansche Handels-Vennootschap (NAHV).246.656 – De NAHV aan de Minister van Buitenlandse Zaken van Nederland (18 August 1890); *La conférence antiesclavagiste et les droits d'entrée dans l'Etat du Congo par un négociant hollandais* (Rotterdam: D. Van Stijn & Fils, 1890), 10–14.

firms. Once more, the Dutch and the French firm argued that the burden of import duties rendered trade unprofitable.[22] The commercial sector was still in its infancy and could not yet bear such a heavy tax burden.[23] Especially considering that additional taxes on trading firms had been introduced.[24]

The Nieuwe Afrikaansche Handels-Vennootschap and Daumas, Béraud et Compagnie were also dissatisfied with the 'torturous', 'impractical' and 'nitpicking' customs procedures that slowed down trade.[25] Each new customs measure increased the level of red tape. Daumas, Béraud et Compagnie even suspected the Free State of making customs procedures extra complex to hinder trading firms.[26] The French company – joined by the Nieuwe Afrikaansche Handels-Vennootschap – was, for example, disgruntled with the new customs regulations that were implemented in 1890, which obliged all steamers to stop at the first customs post they encountered to declare their merchandise on their journey downstream from the Congolese interior to the Atlantic coast.[27]

While the Nieuwe Afrikaansche Handels-Vennootschap and Daumas, Béraud et Compagnie denounced every new customs law, the Société Anonyme Belge struck a far more positive note. When the Free State informed the management of its plans to introduce import duties, the Belgian company responded that this would increase the total tax burden to about 125% of the firm's profits. However, the trading house stressed that it accepted the principle of taxation and was 'happy' to comply.[28] The Société Anonyme Belge welcomed import duties because the firm hoped that these taxes would serve as an alternative for the recently implemented direct taxes on companies which

22 AEB. Archive Hubert Droogmans (AHD).32 – Report of the Proceedings of the Conference of African Merchants on the Congo Free State and Import Duties (4 November 1890).

23 F. de Bas, *Een onpartijdig advies in het Congo-vraagstuk* (Schiedam: H.A.M. Roelants, 1890), 4.

24 ANOM.FM.SG.AFR.VI.80a – Daumas-Béraud et Compagnie au Ministre des Affaires Etrangères de la France (30 December 1890).

25 NA.BZ.A.214 – de NAHV aan de Minister van Buitenlandse Zaken van Nederland (18 August 1890); ANOM.FM.SG.AFR.VI.80a – Daumas-Béraud et Compagnie au Ministre des Affaires Etrangères de la France (30 December 1890).

26 ANOM.FM.SG.AFR.VI.80a – Daumas-Béraud et Compagnie au Ministre des Affaires Etrangères de la France (30 December 1890).

27 AMAEB.AA.EIC. Affaires Etrangères (AE).204.35.5/17-18 – Daumas-Béraud et Compagnie au Ministre des Affaires Etrangères de la France (10-09-1889); NA.BZ.A.214 – Daumas-Béraud et Compagnie au Ministre du Commerce et des Colonies (16 August 1890); NA.NAHV.246.656 – De NAHV aan de Minister van Buitenlandse Zaken van Nederland (4 April 1891).

28 AEB.APR.CRL.DEB.CD.106 – Thys au Roi (1890).

were far more burdensome.[29] The Belgian trading house never once openly complained about the tariff burden.

The Dutch, French and Belgian trading firms did agree on one important matter. All three companies repeatedly demanded more stability. Both the Nieuwe Afrikaansche Handels-Vennootschap and the Société Anonyme Belge denounced the ever-changing customs laws in the Congo. The fiscal and legal instability rendered the climate for investment unpredictable; tariffs could increase at any given moment.[30] The two companies also complained that the Free State did not give them sufficient time to adapt to the many fiscal reforms and communicated poorly about coming changes.[31] The Société Anonyme Belge expressed the desire that the introduction of import duties would be the last major fiscal change.[32]

2.2 *The Free-Rider Issue*

Initially, the Société Anonyme Belge never complained about free-riding, contrary to the Nieuwe Afrikaansche Handels-Vennootschap and Daumas, Béraud et Compagnie. The latter regularly protested that the tariff burden was not equally distributed. The Dutch and the French firm mainly denounced the unfair competition by the Free State. Desperate for more income the new-born state also bought ivory and rubber in the Upper Congo and competed with trading firms. However, the colonial administration traded at a lower cost because it did not have to pay tariffs, while private enterprise was heavily taxed.[33]

29 In 1890, Brussels and Boma brought the following two taxes into force: a patent tax on ivory and direct taxes on the buildings and boats that trading companies owned. MG, 1890, p. 101 – Société Belge du Haut-Congo. Emile Banning, *Mémoires, politiques et diplomatiques: Comment fut fondé le Congo Belge* (La Renaissance du livre, 1927).

30 NA.NAHV.246.656 – De NAHV aan de Minister van Buitenlandse Zaken van Nederland (18 August 1890); ANOM.FM.SG.AFR.VI.94a – Daumas-Béraud et Compagnie au Ministre des Affaires Etrangères de la France (7 November 1891).

31 AMAEB.AA.EIC.AE.207.53 – De NAHV aan de Minister van Buitenlandse Zaken van Nederland (12 November 1886); NA.NAHV.246.656 – De NAHV aan de Minister van Buitenlandse Zaken van Nederland (18 August 1890); Nieuwe Afrikaansche Handels-Vennootschap. *Réplique à l'Africain, auteur de la brochure: Réponse au mémorandum, publié par la Nieuwe Afrikaansche Handelsvennootschap sur les récents décrets de l'Etat-Indépendant du Congo* (Rotterdam: D. Van Sijn & Fils, 1890), 3; NA.NAHV.145.364 – Note (26 May 1891).

32 Mouvement Géographique (MG), 1892, pp. 117–119 – l'Assemblée générale de la Société du Haut-Congo.

33 NA.BZ.A.213 – De Nederlandse Consul in de Kongo Vrijstaat aan de Minister van Buitenlandse Zaken van Nederland (5 September 1889); AMAEB.AA.EIC.AE.204.35 – Daumas-Béraud et Compagnie à l'Administrateur Général des Affaires Etrangères (10 September 1889); ANOM.FM.SG.AFR.VI.94a – Daumas-Béraud et Compagnie au Ministre du Commerce et des Colonies (28 January 1891).

Daumas, Béraud et Compagnie calculated that the operating expenses of the state were 40% lower than the costs of trading firms, which had to pay export tariffs, direct taxes, and import duties.[34]

In the eyes of the Nieuwe Afrikaansche Handels-Vennootschap, the Société Anonyme Belge abused its close connection with the Free State. The Dutch company was convinced that the Belgian firm received preferential treatment. The Nieuwe Afrikaansche Handels-Vennootschap believed that the customs system was not only designed by the Free State to benefit colonial commercial activities but also those of the Société Anonyme Belge.[35] According to the Dutch trading house, the Belgian firm never complained about colonial customs law because Leopold II bribed them with privileges.[36] Some Dutch agents even believed that the Free State repaid some of the customs duties that it collected from the Société Anonyme Belge.[37] The Nieuwe Afrikaansche Handels-Vennootschap also feared that the Free State would abuse the fact that import duties were collected *ad valorem* to give preferential treatment to the Belgian firm.[38]

Another frustration of the Nieuwe Afrikaansche Handels-Vennootschap was that customs regulations were not abided by everyone. The company often complained that the excessive tax burden and strict customs regulations only played to the advantage of 'dishonest' merchants that disregarded commercial law.[39] The Free State was not capable of imposing customs regulations to the letter and curbing contraband. As a result, fraudulent traders had an unfair advantage. Smugglers did not pay taxes and could hence outcompete honest firms such as the Nieuwe Afrikaansche Handels-Vennootschap.[40] The Dutch

34 ANOM.FM.SG.AFR.VI.80a – Daumas-Béraud et Compagnie au Ministre du Commerce et des Colonies (26 December 1890).

35 *l'Etat Indépendant du Congo et le commerce: Réponse à la brochure 'La Conférence de Bruxelles et les Pays-Bas' par 'Un ami de la Vérité'* (Rotterdam: D. Van Sijn & Fils, 1890), 30–31.

36 NA.BZ.A.213 – De Nederlandse Consul in de Kongo Vrijstaat aan de Minister van Buitenlandse Zaken van Nederland (5 September 1889).

37 NA.BZ.A.215 – de la Fontaine Verwey aan het NAHV management in Rotterdam (18/21 November 1890).

38 NA.NAHV.246.656 – De NAHV aan de Minister van Buitenlandse Zaken van Nederland (28 February 1891).

39 *l'Etat Indépendant du Congo et le commerce. Réponse à la brochure 'La Conférence de Bruxelles et les Pays-Bas' par 'Un ami de la Vérité'*, 13; NA.BZ.A.217 – Le NAHV à l'Administrateur Général des Finances (6 November 1886); AMAEB.AA.EIC.AE.294.375 – Consul de l'Etat Indépendant du Congo à Rotterdam à l'Administrateur Général des Affaires Etrangères (28 January 1889); AEB.AHD.2 – l'Administrateur Général des Finances à l'Administrateur Général au Congo (24-08-1886).

40 AMAEB.AA.EIC.FIN.863.1.27 – Réclamations de la NAHV au sujet des contrats de vente, mesurage des propriétés et droits de sortie (5 June 1886).

firm was unhappy for instance that the collection of import duties was based on the declaration of the importer. This was to the advantage of unscrupulous merchants who could simply under-declare the value of their imports to pay less taxes.[41] The company even frequently informed the Free State about the illegal activities of Portuguese firms that were active in the Congo estuary.[42]

Finally, the Nieuwe Afrikaansche Handels-Vennootschap was frustrated that trading firms always had to pay the colonial bill.[43] When import duties were implemented, the company complained: 'What more do they want from the small group of traders in the Congo? Why exactly does the money always have to come from their pockets [...]?'[44]

2.3 *State Legitimacy and a Broken Fiscal Contract*

The Congo Free State was created during the Berlin Conference in 1884 and 1885.[45] The Act of the Berlin Conference regulated commercial law in the Congo Basin and set down the civilization mission of colonial states in Africa. From the perspective of trading companies, Sections 1, 3, 4 and 5 of the Berlin Act determined the fiscal contract between the commercial sector and the state. The business lobby often referred to these sections in their complaints about the Leopoldian customs regime.[46] In short, the Berlin Act stated that the colonial administrations in the Congo Basin had to provide security to merchants and promote the development of free trade. In exchange for providing these services, colonial states were allowed to collect a fair fiscal contribution from commerce. The Nieuwe Afrikaansche Handels-Vennootschap, Daumas, Béraud et Compagnie and the Société Anonyme Belge all felt that Brussels and Boma broke this contract in several ways.

The Dutch and the French firm both acknowledged the right of the Free State to tax, and claimed to be willing to contribute to the colonial effort. Nevertheless, both trading houses felt that Leopold II's administration did the exact opposite of what was promised to them in 1885. The Free State overburdened

41 *La conférence anti-esclavagiste et les droits d'entrée dans l'Etat du Congo par un négociant hollandais* (Rotterdam: D. Van Stijn & Fils, 1890), 12.

42 AMAEB.AA.EIC.FIN.863.1.41 – l'Ambassadeur Belge à Lisbonne à l'Administrateur Général des Affaires Etrangères (1886).

43 *La conférence anti-esclavagiste et les droits d'entrée dans l'Etat du Congo par un négociant hollandais*, 15–16.

44 *l'Etat Indépendant du Congo et le commerce. Réponse à la brochure 'La Conférence de Bruxelles et les Pays-Bas' par 'Un ami de la Vérité'*, 17.

45 Jean Stengers, 'The Partition of Africa: L'Impérialisme Colonial de la fin du XIX-Siècle: Mythe ou Realité', *The Journal of African History* 3:3 (1962), 469–491.

46 See for example: *La conférence anti-esclavagiste et les droits d'entrée dans l'Etat du Congo par un négociant hollandais.*

trading firms with customs procedures and high tariffs, to the point where commerce became unprofitable. Moreover, the state traded on its own accord.[47] The Nieuwe Afrikaansche Handels-Vennootschap bitterly wrote to the Dutch foreign affairs department: 'There is no need to explain how it feels to pay taxes to a state that is a competitor at the same time'.[48]

The Nieuwe Afrikaansche Handels-Vennootschap was also dissatisfied with the services that the Free State provided in exchange for their fiscal commitment. The colonial state even failed to protect companies. For example, the Dutch firm was furious when the *Force Publique* had shown up too late and with too few soldiers when its Malella post was attacked by a local chief.[49] A pamphlet of the Dutch firm clearly stated: 'who is protecting the small group of Europeans and negros that man trading posts? The few state posts that are established here and there at large intervals? No!'.[50] In fact, the Nieuwe Afrikaansche Handels-Vennootschap felt that the Free State did the opposite of protecting merchants. Sometimes the company even preferred that the *Force Publique* did not intervene. The violent behaviour of Leopold II's army generally gave rise to new retaliations against Europeans.[51] Moreover, agents of the Nieuwe Afrikaansche Handels-Vennootschap often fell victim to state violence themselves. For instance, the Free State had opened fire at the SS Frederiksen, without any warning, when the steamer did not anchor in Bangala to have its cargo checked.[52]

The Free State also broke the fiscal contract according to the Société Anonyme Belge. The company, for example, carefully noted that the introduction

47 AMAEB.AA.EIC.AE.204.35.5/17-18 – Daumas-Béraud et Compagnie au Ministre des Affaires Etrangères de la France (10-09-1889); ANOM.FM.SG.AFR.VI.77a – Daumas-Béraud et Compagnie au Ministre des Affaires Etrangères de la France (19 July 1889); NA.BZ.A.214 – Daumas-Béraud et Compagnie au Ministre du Commerce et des Colonies de la France (16 August 1890); NA.NAHV.246.656 – De NAHV aan de Nederlandse Minister voor Buitenlandse Zaken (18 August 1890); NA.BZ.A.215 – Adresse de Daumas et Cie à MM. les Sénateurs et MM. les Députés (25 April 1891).

48 NA.BZ.A.213 – De Nederlandse Consul in de Kongo Vrijstaat aan de Minister van Buitenlandse Zaken van Nederland (5 September 1889).

49 NA.BZ.A.217 – De NAHV aan de Nederlandse Minister voor Buitenlandse Zaken (10 March 1887).

50 *l'Etat Indépendant du Congo et le commerce. Réponse à la brochure 'La Conférence de Bruxelles et les Pays-Bas' par 'Un ami de la Vérité'*, 23.

51 *l'Etat Indépendant du Congo et le commerce. Réponse à la brochure 'La Conférence de Bruxelles et les Pays-Bas' par 'Un ami de la Vérité'*, 23; Nieuwe Afrikaansche Handels-Vennootschap, *Réplique à l'Africain, auteur de la brochure: Réponse au mémorandum, publié par la Nieuwe Afrikaansche Handelsvennootschap sur les récents décrets de l'Etat-Indépendant du Congo* (Rotterdam: D. Van Sijn & Fils, 1890), 7.

52 NA.NAHV.145.364 – Note (26 May 1891).

of import duties substantially changed the economic context that existed when the company was created.[53] Nevertheless, the tariff regime was never the real issue for the Belgian firm. In the eyes of the company, the Free State broke the fiscal contract by competing with trading houses. The Belgian company acknowledged the state's need to raise revenue and understood that a lack of income forced the Free State to trade and compete with private enterprise. The firm figured that the colonial administration would no longer need to trade if it managed to collect more taxes.[54] This is an important reason why the company never denounced Leopold II's tariff measures. Once the Belgian trading firm realized that a higher tax burden went hand in hand with more restrictions on free trade and growing competition from state agents, the firm and the Free State had a falling out.[55]

Another important reason why the Société Anonyme Belge responded so differently to the tariff policies of the Free State is that the firm had a different understanding of the legitimacy of taxation and Leopold II's state. The Nieuwe Afrikaansche Handels-Vennootschap and Daumas, Béraud et Compagnie acknowledged the Free State's right to tax but clearly regarded Leopold II's administration as a competitor more than as a state. In the eyes of the Dutch and French firm, tariffs were not collected to fund the colonial effort but to outcompete them and to monopolize trade by raising the cost to such a level that trading houses were forced to leave the Congo.[56] The Free State was often compared to a charter company or called the 'state-competitor' or 'government-merchant'.[57] The fact that the Dutch firm made a big fuss about having their steamers sail under the colours of the Free State is quite telling of the company's reluctance to recognize the legitimacy of colonial rule.[58] The Belgian firm

53 MG, 1892, pp. 75–76 – Une lettre de Georges Brugmann à Monsieur Van Eetvelde.

54 MG, 1890, p. 101 – Société Belge du Haut-Congo.

55 AEB.AHD.37 – Lettres & documents ayant trait aux réclamations formulées en 1892 par le Société Anonyme Belge pour le Commerce du Haut-Congo relativement à l'exploitation du domaine de l'Etat (1893).

56 ANOM.FM.SG.AFR.VI.94a – Daumas-Béraud et Compagnie au Ministre du Commerce et des Colonies de la France (28 January 1891).

57 AMAEB.AA.EIC.AE.204.35.5/4 – le Secrétaire d'Etat des Affaires Etrangères à La Légation de France en Belgique (28-06-1890); *l'Etat Indépendant du Congo et le commerce. Réponse à la brochure 'La Conférence de Bruxelles et les Pays-Bas' par 'Un ami de la Vérité'*; AEB.AHD.31 – Publicatie met klachten van verschillende handelsorganisaties met betrekking tot het schenden van de vrijhandel in de Onafhankelijke Congostaat zoals werd vastgelegd tijdens de conferentie van Berlijn in 1885 (1890).

58 NA.NAHV.145.364 – Diversen, tekeningen en kaarten, ingekomen correspondentie met diversen en handelsagenten, rapporten en verslagen diverse agenten in Afrika (1854–1925); NA.BZ.A.206 – Congo aangelegenheden (1885–1894).

was more convinced of the legitimacy of the Free State and customs law. The trading house accepted that the state needed to raise revenue to stick to its part of the fiscal contract which was to promote the development of commerce in the Congo Basin.[59]

2.4 *Taking into Account the Grievances of the Trade Sector*

Though the Nieuwe Afrikaansche Handels-Vennootschap and Daumas, Béraud et Compagnie often complained about not being heard, the Free State did pay attention to the grievances of trading firms. For instance, the introduction of export tariffs and customs procedures was postponed twice, from 25 March to 15 May, and eventually to 1 July 1886, because trading houses complained they had not been given sufficient time to adapt to the new fiscal regime.[60] The Free State also adjusted its first customs law to introduce different tariffs on white copal and the more valuable red variant; just as the Nieuwe Afrikaansche Handels-Vennootschap had requested.[61] Similarly, the Free State also listened to the Dutch firm and Daumas, Béraud et Compagnie, and reformed the way ivory exports were taxed. The new system differentiated between three categories based on the size and hence value of each single tusk.[62]

The Free State also adjusted customs procedures to meet the demands of trading firms. For example, the colonial administration made an arrangement with the Nieuwe Afrikaansche Handels-Vennootschap about transit goods in the Congo estuary. The Dutch company centralized all its activities in Banana at the Congolese coast. From these headquarters the company provisioned its posts in Angola, Cabinda, French Congo and the Free State. Banana was also the place where the Nieuwe Afrikaansche Handels-Vennootschap gathered its exports from the Congo estuary before the goods were shipped to Rotterdam, Liverpool or Antwerp.[63] The export regulations that Brussels and Boma

---

59 MG, 1890, p. 101 – Société Belge du Haut-Congo.

60 AMAEB.AA.CP.2571 – Le Gouverneur Général à l'Administrateur Général des Finances (11 May 1886); AMAEB.AA.CP.2571 – l'Administrateur Général des Finances au Roi (15 June 1886).

61 AEB.AHD.2 – l'Administrateur Général des Finances à l'Administrateur Général au Congo (27 November 1886); AEB.AHD.3 – l'Administrateur Général des Finances à l'Administrateur Général au Congo (28 October 1887).

62 NA.BZ.A.214 – Daumas-Béraud et Compagnie au Ministre du Commerce et des Colonies de la France (16 August 1890); NA.BZ.A.214 – De NAHV aan de Minister van Buitenlandse Zaken van Nederland (18 August 1890); ANOM.FM.SG.AFR.VI.80a – Daumas-Béraud et Compagnie au Ministre des Affaires Etrangères de la France (21 August 1890).

63 AMAEB.AA.EIC.FIN.863.1.36 – le NAHV à l'Administrateur Général des Finances (5 October 1886); AMAEB.AA.EIC.AE.207.53 – De NAHV aan de Minister van Buitenlandse Zaken van Nederland (12 November 1886).

introduced in 1886 interfered with the firm's trans-colonial activities. Transit goods had to be accompanied by a certificate to prove that the exports came from another colony and could be exempted from customs duties. However, for a while the French and Portuguese did not issue certificates of origin. Once they did, it still required considerable time to first pass by one of the few posts that were manned by French or Portuguese officials to acquire such a certificate. As a result, it was difficult for the Dutch firm to comply with export regulations.[64] The Free State however allowed the company to use documents such as shipping logs to prove the foreign origin of transit goods.[65]

The above-mentioned examples of changes to customs law were only small concessions. Brussels and Boma did not give in to the main demands of some companies. However, this does not mean that decision makers were unwilling to meet the wishes of trading firms. The Free State could simply not make any major concessions as this would mean it would have to stop buying ivory, lower ivory and rubber tariffs, impose less customs procedures and refrain from taxing imports. Complying to these demands would drastically reduce the only two real sources of income in the colony at a time when bankruptcy loomed.[66]

The fact that the Free State did not meet any of the main demands of trading firms does not mean that policymakers tried to hinder their activities as some companies claimed. Policymakers continued to stress the importance of good relations between the state and the commercial sector, claiming that both parties relied on each other. The Free State wanted to develop trade to broaden and deepen the tax base on which it could draw.[67] Decision makers argued that the Congo and its riches were large enough for both parties to thrive.[68] Once the fiscal regime of the Free State had definitely taken shape in 1892, the Free State tried to straighten things out with the Nieuwe Afrikaansche Handels-Vennootschap and Société Anonyme Belge.[69]

The Free State only made one important concession to the private sector. Trading companies lobbied fiercely against the 25% tariff on ivory from the

64 NA.BZ.A.217 – le NAHV à l'Administrateur Général des Finances (6 November 1886).

65 NA.BZ.A.217 – Ordonnance n°10 (1 October 1886).

66 Jean Stengers, 'La dette publique de l'Etat Indépendant du Congo', in *La dette publique aux 18e et 19e siècles: son développement sur le plan local, régional et national* (Bruxelles: Crédit communal de Belgique, 1980), 297–312.

67 AEB.AHD.2 – l'Administrateur Général des Finances à l'Administrateur Général au Congo (23 July 1886).

68 AEB. Archive Edmond Van Eetvelde (AEVE).151 – Van Eetvelde à Thys (4 June 1892).

69 NA.NAHV.237.631 – Notulen der commissie van toezicht van de Nieuwe Afrikaansche Handels-Vennootschap (11 November 1891); NA.BZ.A.215 – Handelsbelangen in de Congostaat (1890–1894); Banning, *Mémoires, politiques et* diplomatiques, 332.

private domain of the state instead of the regular 10% tax. The commercial sector was lucky that the Free State and France were negotiating a tariff union at the time. Daumas, Béraud et Compagnie managed to influence the French position in the negotiations. In the end, the Free State gave in to the French request to only tax tusks at a rate of 10% *ad valorem*.[70] The Société Anonyme Belge also had an important hand in this decision. Its manager, Albert Thys, did everything in his power to convince the Free State to abolish the 25% tax rate. For a long time, Leopold II stubbornly refused. His colony needed all the tax revenue that could be raised.[71] Eventually, the Free State caved to the demands of the French Government and the Belgian firm.

The rather uncompromising position of the Free State was not only fuelled by revenue constraints. Another important explanation is the lack of trust in trading firms. Many decision makers were convinced that trading companies exaggerated. In reaction to the complaints about the burden of the newly introduced export duties in 1886, Brussels argued that the new tariffs were far from excessive. Exports were only taxed at a rate of 2% to 5% ad valorem.[72] Moreover, Leopold II was convinced that import duties would not harm trading firms.[73] In 1892, State Secretary of Finances Van Eetvelde wryly remarked that the Société Anonyme Belge still managed to pay 'abundant' dividends, despite all the allegedly detrimental effects of the colonial tax system.[74] Policymakers also argued that the fiscal contribution of the trade sector effort paled in comparison to the funds that Leopold II invested each year.[75] Brussels and Boma were not only convinced that trading firms could bear the rising tariff burden, but the administration also firmly believed that it was the duty of private enterprise to contribute to the colonial effort to open up new markets in the Congolese interior, because trading firms were the ones that benefited from the expansion of colonial rule.[76]

---

70 ANOM.FM.SG.AFR.VI.80a – Affaires diplomatiques: Conférence de Bruxelles. Dépêches du Ministre des Affaires Etrangères (1889–1890); ANOM.FM.SG.AFR.VI.94a – Affaires diplomatiques: Congo indépendant. Tarifs douaniers: Convention du 9 février 1891 (1890); AMAEB.AA.EIC.AE.326.458 – l'Administrateur Général des Finances à l'Administrateur Général des Affaires Etrangères (24 June 1891).

71 AEB.APR.CRL.DEB.CD.106 – Thys au Roi (6 June 1891); Banning, *Mémoires, politiques et diplomatiques*, 227.

72 AAB.CP.2571 – l'Administrateur Général des Finances à l'Administrateur Général au Congo (23 July 1886).

73 AEB.APR.CRL.DEB.CD.9 – Le Roi à Banning (1 December 1890).

74 AEB.AEVE.152 – Van Eetvelde à Beernaerts (1892).

75 BOEIC, 1890, pp. 101–105 – Rapport au roi (14 July 1890).

76 AMAEB.AA.EIC.FIN.863.1.28 – l'Administrateur Général des Finances au NAHV (1886); AEB.AHD.32 – Report of the Proceedings of the Conference of African Merchants on the Congo Free State and Import Duties (4 November 1890).

Van Eetvelde neatly summarized the position of the Free State in an angry letter to the president of the Société Anonyme Belge: 'You know that the annual deficit of the state is large. We cannot let it exceed three million francs. Belgium gives two million, the King one million. We want to, and have to, extract from Africa whatever revenue that covers the remainder of our recurrent expenses which largely exceeds four million. [...] we have been patiently running considerable annual deficits, [...] is it reasonable that the trade sector does not understand that it has to temporarily make a little contribution too [...]? The ivory trade alone already allows you to reimburse your capital. You have just paid out a dividend of 12% to your shareholders. [...] Until now you have only exploited ivory [...] you can create other revenue streams [...] Do not forget that the possibility of penetrating Central Africa, which has allowed the expansion of commerce, has been created thanks to the millions that have been generously spent by the state'.[77]

Not only did policymakers believe that the commercial sector could and should make a bigger contribution to the colonial effort, they also suspected trading firms of smuggling. The Nieuwe Afrikaansche Handels-Vennootschap was accused of systematically sending African traders who sold ivory and rubber from the Free State through to their posts in the French Congo, where export duties were introduced much later. Upon arrival in the French Congo the local agent of the Dutch firm bought the rubber and acquired a certificate of origin from the French administration that stated that the rubber came from the French territories. The rubber was then exported via the main post of the Nieuwe Afrikaansche Handels-Vennootschap in Banana in the Free State. As a result, the Free State missed out on customs duties as transit trade could not be taxed in the Congo Basin.[78] Similarly, the Société Anonyme Belge was accused of bypassing the Free State's customs regime by smuggling the ivory it bought in the Upper Congo to Brazzaville instead of paying tariffs in Leopoldville or Matadi.[79]

To conclude this first section, during the first years of colonialism in the Congo, the influence of trading firms on customs law was limited as the revenue imperative – the pressure to balance the annual budget – forced the newborn Free State to trade tusks, to introduce burdensome verification procedures and to raise the tariff burden through the constant increase of ivory and

77 AEB.AEVE.157 – Van Eetvelde à Brugmann (n.d.).

78 AMAEB.AA.EIC.AE.207.55 – Rapport du Commissaire de District de Léopoldville au Gouverneur Général (27 October 1887).

79 AMAEB.AA.EIC.AE.204.32.2/132 – Le Vice-Gouverneur Général à l'Administrateur Général des Affaires Etrangères (10 February 1891).

rubber tariffs and the introduction of import duties. The Nieuwe Afrikaansche Handels-Vennootschap, Daumas, Béraud et Compagnie, and the Société Anonyme Belge largely failed to stop the Free State from increasing export tariffs and introducing import duties. However, this representation might be somewhat misleading. If it was not for the business lobby, the Free State might have introduced even higher tariffs and more red tape.

3 Negotiating Customs after 1892

3.1 *1892–1908: Fiscal Stability*

In the early 1890s, the dispute between the Free State and trading firms such as the Nieuwe Afrikaansche Handels-Vennootschap and Daumas, Béraud et Compagnie about the implementation of import duties and the ever-increasing burden of tariffs and red tape gradually made way for an even fiercer row about the *régime domanial*. This exploitation system made large parts of the Congo off-limits to the companies that were active in the Upper Congo at that time. Instead the colonial state and concession companies were the only actors allowed to exploit the majority of the Congo. This new quarrel only cooled down in 1894.[80] The disagreements on the colonial customs systems were however not resurrected.

From 1894 till 1908, trading firms hardly complained about customs law, and neither did concession companies. The absence of new disputes has a number explanations. First of all, customs regulations did not change all that much in comparison to the fundamental changes that were introduced during the late 1880s and early 1890s. Moreover, customs tariffs remained largely unchanged. Export tariffs on rubber were only increased in 1899, 1906 and 1907. Import tariffs were changed once in 1902 and liquor tariffs in 1900 and 1907.[81] Companies got exactly what they wanted: fiscal stability.

80 Gann and Duignan, *The Rulers of Belgian Africa, 1884–1914*; Vangroenweghe, *Rood rubber: Leopold II en zijn Kongo*; Buelens, *Congo 1885–1960: Een financieel-economische geschiedenis*.

81 Bulletin Officiel de l'Etat Independant du Congo (BOEIC), 1898, p. 346 – Caoutchouc – taxe – date de perception (29 August 1898); BOEIC, 1898, pp. 141, 142 – Droits d'entrée et de sortie (5 May 1898); BOEIC, 1900, pp. 115, 116 – Droits d'entrée sur les spiritueux (12 June 1900); BOEIC, 1902, pp. 135, 136 – Droits d'entrée (28 June 1902); BOEIC, 1906, pp. 285, 286 – Caoutchouc des herbes – taxe (3 June 1906); BOEIC, 1907, pp. 384, 385 – Droits de sortie (2 July 1907); BOEIC, 1907, pp. 523, 524 – Droits d'entrée sur les spiritueux (12 November 1907).

Secondly, the Free State was quicker to comply with the wishes of trading firms and concession companies. Decision makers wanted to avoid any new disputes with the commercial sector. In 1902, the Free State was hesitant to increase import tariffs from 6% to 10% *ad valorem*. Policymakers were afraid that this increase would provoke protest among enterprises, especially in the lower Congo where firms had recently petitioned the state to reduce the tax burden.[82] In 1905, Brussels and Boma were afraid to antagonize trading firms and concession companies by increasing rubber tariffs.[83] In both cases, the increases were implemented because the Free State did not want to break the tariff union with the French. In 1907, the Free State increased rubber tariffs once more as rubber prices had risen considerably. However, this measure was postponed to give companies sufficient time to adapt.[84]

Thirdly, the tariff burden was not as intolerable as the commercial sector had feared. The rubber boom created more than enough wealth for both private enterprise and the state to enrich themselves, whereas both actors had competed over the scarce Congolese wealth in the 1880s and early 1890s, fearing that they would be left out when the colonial riches were divided. The few tariff changes that were implemented were in line with rising commodity prices. In addition, the customs department adopted a tolerant attitude towards importers and exporters in Matadi.[85]

It had also become easier for companies to allocate the tariff burden. In the late 1880s and early 1890s trading firms had a hard time allocating the costs of customs duties to African middlemen or producers as they had to compete with their counterparts. In the 1890s, the competition among the many trading firms in the Kasai region, for example, caused rubber and ivory prices to rise.[86] Concession companies were in a much stronger position vis-à-vis African producers and middlemen as they held monopolies, though these monopolies were never fully enforceable. Secondly, concession companies used force to

82 AMAEB.AA.CP.617.3 – Note (1902).

83 Archives Diplomatiques (AD). Correspondance politique et commerciale (CPC). Afrique Equatorial (AE).3 – La Légation de France en Belgique au Ministre des Affaires Etrangères de la France (20 April 1907); AMAEB.AA.CP.617.3 – Le Vice-Gouverneur Général au Secrétaire d'Etat (18 September 1907).

84 AMAEB.AA.CP.617.3 – Modification à l'article 2 du protocole du 8 avril 1892 (1907).

85 AMAEB.AA.CP.2571 – Droits de sortie: déclaration des produits avant leur embarquement (25 January 1890); AMAEB.AA.CP.2571 – l'Administrateur Général des Finances au Gouverneur Général (2 April 1891).

86 Recueil Financier (RF), 1914, pp. 1158–1160 – Compagnie du Kasaï; Jan Vansina, *Being Colonized: The Kuba Experience in Rural Congo, 1880–1960* (Madison: The University of Wisconsin Press, 2010).

pay a price that they determined for rubber and ivory although coercion definitely did have its limits as it instigated all sorts of resistance.[87]

3.2 *1908–1914: Consent between Private Enterprise and the State*

The Belgians completely reformed the colonial fiscal system and substantially increased rubber tariffs in 1909 and 1910 and refrained from lowering these taxes when world market prices steadily decreased from 1911 onwards. However, there is no sign of any new customs-related disputes. In part, this might be a skewed interpretation, caused by the general lack of sources for studying the brief Belgian era before World War I. However, the tariff payer also had little to complain about.

By abolishing the monopolistic domanial system, the Belgians restored the fiscal contract. The crux of the Belgian legal reforms was rather straightforward: the state would abolish the *régime domanial* and would open up the Congo Basin to all traders, and the ensuing loss of in-kind tax income and concession dividends would be compensated by growing customs revenue, paid by the private sector that would expand rapidly as companies ventured into those parts of the Congo Basin that had been off-limits until then.[88] This is exactly what trading firms had asked for in the late 1880s and early 1890s: a state that spent tariff receipts to facilitate free trade.[89] The restoration of the fiscal contract largely explains why trading companies did not seem to mind the rising tariff burden. The Société Anonyme Belge, for example, called the new export tariffs 'reasonable'.[90]

The Belgian fiscal system was designed to benefit trading firms. Tariffs were to become the main source of colonial revenue. To increase customs revenue the Belgians wanted to expand the tax base by stimulating trade. 'More trade equals more tax revenue' became the colonial credo. Therefore, the Belgians tried to limit the customs burden as much as they could. Brussels and Boma were afraid that excessive taxation and time-consuming procedures would

---

87 Gann and Duignan, *The Rulers of Belgian Africa, 1884–1914*; Harms, 'The World Abir Made: The Maringa-Lopori Basin, 1885–1903', Vangroenweghe, *Rood rubber: Leopold II en zijn Kongo*; Coquery-Vidrovitch, *Le Congo au temps des grandes compagnies concessionnaires 1898–1930*.

88 AEB.AHD.149 – Discours prononcé par M. Renkin Ministre des Colonies (15 December 1909).

89 MG, 1905, pp. 653–659 – Compagnie du Congo pour le Commerce et l'Industrie. Assemblée générale ordinaire du 18 décembre 1905; MG, 1910, pp. 403–412 – L'Œuvre africaine du Roi Léopold II. Conférence du Colonel Thys.

90 Musée Royal de l'Afrique Centrale (MRAC). Papiers Félix Fuchs (PFF).225 – Note (12 August 1912); AMAEB.AA.CP.543.20.1-I.C1 – Instructions from the MC to the GG: organization of the customs service (30 January 1913).

hinder international trade in the long run, which would affect customs receipts.[91] The upcoming mining industry was not even taxed at all. In addition, the Belgians tried to make customs procedures more effective and efficient. More effective customs procedures reduced free-rider issues as smugglers would get caught more easily, making it harder for them to compete unfairly with 'honest' firms. More importantly, these procedures would save time for the companies.

The renewal of the fiscal contract between the state and private enterprise is not the only reason customs related disputes did not arise after 1908. Two other factors have to be taken into account. First of all, the Belgians were less pressured by the revenue imperative. As a result, Brussels and Boma could more easily meet the demands of private enterprise.[92] For example, the investments in better customs infrastructure in Boma, Matadi and Stanley Pool were partly inspired by the frequent complaints by the business lobby.[93] The Compagnie du Kasaï and the Chamber of Commerce of Boma and Matadi had complained that a lot of merchandise was simply left to rot because it took such a long time to clear customs in the main Congolese ports.[94]

The Belgians also cooperated with companies such as the Compagnie Maritime Belge and the Compagnie du Chemin de Fer du Congo to make customs procedures faster and more effective.[95] In addition, the Belgians involved private enterprise in lawmaking. Companies were consulted about the transformation of *ad valorem* import duties to fixed tariffs in 1914.[96] The idea of letting

---

91 MRAC.PFF.225 – Le Gouverneur Général au Chambre du Commerce de Boma (n.d.).

92 De Roo, 'The Trouble with Tariffs'.

93 AMAEB.AA.CP.543.20.1-I.C2 – Le Chargé de Mission Douanière au Gouverneur Général (23 August 1913); AMAEB.AA.CP.543.20.1-I.C1 – Le Ministre des Colonies au Gouverneur Général (30 January 1913); BOCB, 1914, pp. 747–773 – Entrepôts – réglementation (20 June 1914).

94 AMAEB.AA.CP.1233 – Le Compagnie du Kasaï au Ministre des Colonies (30 September 1909); MRAC.PFF.225 – Note (12 August 1912); AMAEB.AA.CP.543.20.1-I.B1 – Le Directeur de la Marine et des Travaux Publics au Gouverneur Général (23 September 1912); AMAEB.AA.CP.543.20.1-I.B1 – Rapport sur le service des douanes de la colonie par le Directeur des Finances a.i. Périer (18 September 1912).

95 AMAEB.AA.CP.543.20.1-I.B1 – Le Directeur de la Marine et des Travaux Publics au Gouverneur Général (23 September 1912).

96 Bulletin Officiel du Congo Belge (BOCB), 1914, pp. 315–324 – Tarif des douanes. – Conversion de droits 'ad valorem' en droits spécifiques équivalents (2 March 1914); AMAEB.AA.CP.544.20.3-I. – Le Ministre des Colonies à Belgo-Katanga, Société Alimentation Bas-Congo, Société Commerciale & Minière de Congo, Société Anonyme Belge pour le commerce du Haut-Congo, Compagnie du Kasaï, Société Commerciale et Financière Africaine, Comptoir Commercial Congolais, Compagnie du Congo Belge, La Mercantile Anversoise, Compagnie Citas, Produits Végétaux du Haut Kasaï, Compagnie du

Congolese imports clear customs in Antwerp to speed up verification procedures was also discussed with colonial firms.[97] Another example of the influence of the business sector is the reduction of the tariff on imported fuels. The Société Anonyme des Pétroles du Congo and Union Minière du Haut Katanga had complained that fuels and coal were too expensive in the Congo and had asked for an exemption.[98]

The relatively low pressure from the revenue imperative only partially explains the close cooperation between the state and private enterprise in the field of customs. In 1913, the rubber crisis hit both the state and private enterprise. Though tax receipts did plummet as a result of the crisis, rubber tariffs were reduced to come to the aid of trading firms and concession companies that could not cope with the substantial price drop and had appealed to the state for help.[99] Policymakers estimated that the first tax cuts would cost 2.5 million francs, almost a third of tariff revenue in 1912.[100] The colonial administration was even prepared to make considerable fiscal sacrifices to assist private enterprise during a period when the revenue imperative forced the state to cut costs drastically and raise more revenue.

To conclude Section 2, trading firms and concession companies and the colonial state were more or less on the same page after 1892. The revenue imperative did not put as much pressure on decision makers as it had done before the start of the rubber boom, which widened the opportunities for taking the interests of private enterprise more into account when devising commercial law. Moreover, policymakers wanted to avoid new tax disputes. The tariff burden also proved to be manageable and was predictable. The Belgians turned the fiscal system upside down and raised the tariff burden. In return for the contribution of the private sector, the state promoted the commercial development of the colony. As a result, new disputes on customs law did not appear.

Chemin de Fer du Bas Congo au Katanga, American Congo, Union Minière du Haut Katanga, Compagnie Urselie, Société Equatoriale Congolaise Lulonga Ikelemba, Comptoir Belgika, Compagnie Forestière et Minière, Intertropical Anglo-Belgian Trading Company, Compagnie du Lomami et Maison Gomez (10 March 1913).

97 AMAEB.AA.CP.543.20.1-I.C2 – Pour le Ministre le Directeur Général Délegué aux Entreprises belges ayant un ou plusieurs sièges d'opérations au Congo et Katanga (19 September 1914).

98 AMAEB.AA.CP.2047 – Finances/Douanes. Droits d'entrée houille charbon et huiles minérales (19 November 1914).

99 MG, 1913, pp. 376–378 – La taxe sur le caoutchouc et l'avenir de notre colonie; AP.CR. Séance du 1 janvier 1914 (n° 5). Budget des recettes et de dépenses du Congo Belge pour l'exercice 1914, pp. 37, 65.

100 Conseil Colonial. Compte rendu analytique des séances (CC.CRAS), 1912–1913, pp. 418–488 – Séance du 5 juillet 1913; CC.CRAS, 1912–1913, pp. 489–512 – Séance du 26 juillet 1913.

4 The Importance of Being Well-Connected

When it comes to pre-war Congo and the making of customs law, one has to take into account that the distinction between taxpaying companies and the state was often blurry. The close relationship between the state and a number of large colonial companies had two important consequences. First of all, some enterprises close to the Royal Palace and the General Secretariat of the Free State or the Ministry of Colonies were more successful in their attempts to influence lawmaking. Secondly, it can be difficult to discern which actor was the dominant partner in the lawmaking process.

During the first years of the Free State's existence, the Nieuwe Afrikaansche Handels-Vennootschap and Daumas, Béraud et Compagnie responded very differently to customs laws than did the Société Anonyme Belge. The Dutch and French firms had similar strategies to influence decision-making in Brussels and Boma. The first step always consisted of contacting the Free State directly. However, both companies regularly complained that their complaints fell on deaf ears. The Nieuwe Afrikaansche Handels-Vennootschap was especially sensitive to the idea that its voice was not being heard. As the main Congolese trading house, the firm made the biggest fiscal contribution and hence felt it was entitled to have a say in tax policies.[101] If the Free State did not take their demands into account, the Dutch and the French firm called in the Foreign Affairs Ministries of the Netherlands or France to put pressure on Brussels and Boma.

The Nieuwe Afrikaansche Handels-Vennootschap maintained close ties with the Dutch government. For instance, representatives of the company were part of the Dutch delegation to the Berlin Conference and Brussels Convention – the Brussels Convention was gathered in 1889 to amend the Berlin Act so that the colonial states in the Congo Basin could tax imports in order to raise more revenue to finance the fight against the slave trade and liquor abuse in Africa.[102] The Netherlands largely adopted the company's discourse and fiercely defended the interests of the firm. The most far-reaching example of the close relation between the Nieuwe Afrikaansche Handels-Vennootschap and The Hague was the anchoring of the warship H.M. Sommelsdijck in the Congo estuary.

101 NA.BZ.A.217 – Le NAHV à l'Administrateur Général des Finances (6 November 1886); F. de Bas, *Een advies in het Congo-vraagstuk* (Schiedam: H.A.M. Roelants, 1890), 4–5.

102 Emile Banning. *L'acte général de la conférence de Bruxelles devant les chambres françaises: réflexions d'un homme politique* (Saint-Cloud: Imprimerie Belin Frères, 1891).

During a trip back to the Netherlands, the H.M. Sommelsdijck had stayed in the waters of the Free State on the request of Frederik de la Fontaine Verwey. This man was the Dutch consul in the Congo and head agent of the Nieuwe Afrikaansche Handels-Vennootschap in Banana. He had complained to The Hague that the ever-increasing tax burden ruined Dutch commerce in the Congo. The presence of a warcraft would 'encourage the Belgians to moderation' and 'protect Dutch trade interests from the Free State's arbitrary rule'.[103] If the Dutch Foreign Ministry and Nieuwe Afrikaansche Handels-Vennootschap had had their way, other warships would have regularly been sent to strong-arm the Free State. Nevertheless, the Dutch Minister of the Navy did not approve of such gunboat diplomacy. His preference for a more diplomatic approach quickly ended the military involvement of the Netherlands.[104]

Daumas, Béraud et Compagnie had a more complex relation with Paris. Before 1890, the French government simply relayed the firm's complaints to Brussels or Boma and did not really defend the interests of the company. During the Brussels Convention, French diplomats did protect the interests of the firm. However, it took a large-scale media campaign in France and a speech in Parliament before Daumas, Béraud et Compagnie managed to rally the support of the French government.[105] France had its own fiscal interests to defend in the Congo Basin. Nevertheless, eventually, the Quai d'Orsay was forced to yield to the lobbying of the French firm, which blocked an agreement on common tariffs in the western part of the Congo Free Trade Zone until Leopold II ordered Thys to have the Société Anonyme Belge buy the company, which quickly put an end to its protest.[106]

---

103 NA.BZ.A.215 – de la Fontaine Verwey aan de Minister van Buitenlandse Zaken van Nederland (11 December 1890); NA.BZ.A.215 – Captain Steyn aan de Minister van Marine van Nederland (13 December 1890); NA.BZ.A.215 – De NAHV aan de Minister van Buitenlandse Zaken van Nederland (20 January 1891).

104 NA.BZ.A.215 – De Minister van Buitenlandse Zaken van Nederland aan de Minister van Marine van Nederland (13 December 1890).

105 Médard Béraud, *Les intérêts du commerce français au Congo belge considérés dans leurs rapports avec la convention franco-congolaise du 9 février 1891* (Paris: Imprimerie Chaix, 1891); NA.BZ.A.215 – Adresse de Daumas et Cie à MM. les Sénateurs et MM. les Députés (25 April 1891); AMAEB.AA.EIC.AE.300.399 – Chambre des Députés. Session de 1891. Annexe au procès-verbal de la séance du 20 juin 1891. Rapport fait au nom de la commission chargée d'examiner le projet de loi portant approbation de l'Acte général de la Conférence de Bruxelles du 2 juillet 1890, de la déclaration en date du même jour et du Protocole signe à Paris le 9 février 1891.

106 MRAC. Papiers Albert Thys (PAT).1. Cahier 30. Lettre n° 40 – Le Roi à Thys (25 April 1891); AEB. Archive du groupe Compagnie du Congo pour le Commerce et l'Industrie (CCCI).483 – Comité permanent. Procés-verbaux des réunions (24 March 1892); AMAEB.AA. Ministère

Apart from calling in Dutch and French diplomacy, the Nieuwe Afrikaansche Handels-Vennootschap and Daumas, Béraud et Compagnie also tried to put pressure on the Free State by joining forces and developing a common stance, often together with other trading firms that were active in the Congo Basin.[107] Moreover, they published numerous pamphlets to substantiate their complaints and suggest alternatives.[108] Both companies also called in the press to influence the public opinion. As the dispute with the Free State grew fiercer, so did the tone of the articles written by company agents.[109] Both the Nieuwe Afrikaansche Handels-Vennootschap and Daumas, Béraud et Compagnie, for instance, regularly accused the Free State of buying and employing slaves to undermine Leopold II's argument that the Free State needed import duties to finance the fight against the slave trade in the East.[110]

Contrary to the Nieuwe Afrikaansche Handels-Vennootschap and Daumas, Béraud et Compagnie, the Société Anonyme Belge remained awfully quiet. The interaction between the Belgian firm and the colonial state mainly took place behind the scenes and never got out of hand as did the dispute between the Dutch and French trading houses and the Free State. One man was responsible for the good relationship between the Belgian trading firm and the colonial administration. Thys wore three hats and it was not always clear which one he was wearing: he was aide-de-camp to the Belgian King; the co-founder and member of the board of directors of the Compagnie du Congo pour le Commerce et l'Industrie and chairman of the Société Anonyme Belge; and he was the temporary treasurer of the Free State in 1886, acting as Secretary General of Interior Affairs in 1889 and a special envoy who negotiated a tariff union with the French Congo on behalf of Brussels and Boma in the early 1890s.[111]

des Colonies (MC). Statuts (ST) – Statuts du société Daumas-Béraud et Compagnie (1887–1892).

107 See for example: AMAEB.AA.CP.2571 – De Bloem (NAHV), Mac Creadie (Hatton & Cookson), Lasthou (Daumas Béraud et Cie), Frazer (British Congo Company), d'Oliveira, de Ribeiro, Abseio (Companhia Portugueza do Zaïre), de Souza, Lopo, Borges, Valle et Azevede, Ferreira d'Acosta, Real, de Freitas et da Sylva à l'Administrateur Général au Congo (10 June 1886).

108 See for example publications such as: *l'Etat du Congo et son avocat. Réponse à la brochure: 'l'Etat Indépendant du Congo et la Compagnie de Rotterdam par un Ami de la Vérité' par un négociant hollandais* (Rotterdam: M. Wyt & Zonen, 1890); Béraud, *Les intérêts du commerce français au Congo belge.*

109 See for example: AMAEB.AA.EIC.AE.207.53 – 'Oeconomische en Financieele Mededeelingen. Kongo', *Nieuwe Rotterdamsche Courant* (8 July 1887).

110 See for example: NA.BZ.A.206 – 'Lettre d'un employé d'une maison française au Congo', *Le Temps* (13 June 1892).

111 Biographie Colonial Belge (BCB): Thys (Albert, Jean-Baptiste, Joseph); Julien Vanhove, *Histoire du Ministère des Colonies* (Bruxelles: Académie Royale des Sciences d'Outre-Mer,

Thys managed to reconcile the often opposite interests of the colonial state and the Société Anonyme Belge on many occasions.[112] One of Thys' biggest achievements was to convince Leopold II to drop the 25% export tax on ivory in 1890 and 1891.[113] Thys was not always successful. During the negotiations on import tariffs in 1891, the French proposed a rate of 6% *ad valorem*, while the Free State had always talked about 5%. Via Thys, the Société Anonyme Belge agreed on a 6% tariff for general imports but tried to reduce customs duties on imported cloth. Nevertheless, the King did not give in this time.[114]

Once the domanial regime was established in 1892, the distinction between taxpaying companies and the state became blurred. The once-defiant trading firms were embedded in the *régime domanial*. Daumas, Béraud et Compagnie was absorbed by the Société Anonyme Belge. This Belgian firm and the Nieuwe Afrikaansche Handels-Vennootschap evolved into holding companies that had large stakes in a number of concession companies, such as the Compagnie du Kasaï, to which large parts of the Congolese territory were conceded.[115]

Concession companies and the colonial states were closely knit on an institutional and practical level: the colonial treasury relied on the dividends and customs duties that concession companies paid, while the latter depended on the backing of the *Force Publique* and the state's steamer service.[116] In addition, both parties had close personal connections. The state had representatives on the executive board of most firms as it became the main shareholder in return for granting commercial monopolies. The colonial administration recruited in the business community and major corporations often hired former

1968). See Chapter 4 for more information on how Thys negotiated a common tariff with Paris and Brazzaville.

112 AEB.APR.CRL.DEB.CD.106 – Correspondence Albert Thys; MRAC.PAT.1 – Correspondence Leopold II – Albert Thys.
AEB.CCCI.467 – Procès-verbaux des assemblées générales ordinaires et extraordinaires, allocutions Présidentielles à l'occasion des assemblées générales, correspondance concernant notamment les publications légales dans la presse en Belgique et au Congo (1887–1978); AEB.CCCI.483 – Comité permanent. Procés-verbaux des réunions (1887–1972); Banning, *Mémoires, politiques et diplomatiques*.

113 AEB.APR.CRL.DEB.CD.9 – Banning au Roi (1 December 1890); AEB.APR.CRL.DEB.CD.9 – Banning au Roi (2 December 1890).

114 Banning, *Mémoires, politiques et diplomatiques*, 217.

115 The SAB for example had an important share in the Anversoise, the Compagnie du Kasai and the Compagnie du Lomami. The Nieuwe Afrikaansche Handels-Vennootschap was a key shareholder of the Compagnie du Kasai. The Free State owned between 25 and 50% of the shares of all three concession companies.

116 Gann and Duignan, *The Rulers of Belgian Africa, 1884–1914*, 129–130; Vellut, 'Réseaux transnationaux dans l'économie politique du Congo Léopoldien, c. 1885–1910'.

administrators.[117] The careers of Van Eetvelde, Droogmans and Nicolas Arnold were characteristic of the cross-breeding between the colonial state and private enterprise.

Van Eetvelde was the State-Secretary of Finances from 1892 to 1894, when he was promoted to Secretary-General of the Free State. His successful colonial career ended in 1906. As a representative of the Free State, Van Eetvelde had always had a seat on the executive board of the Société Générale Africaine et Banque de Commerce et d'Industrie and held the position of President of the Compagnie des Chemins de Fer du Congo Supérieur aux Grands Lacs Africains. After his colonial career, he became the vice-president of both firms.[118] Droogmans succeeded Van Eetvelde as State-Secretary of Finances. In 1908, he once more followed in Van Eetvelde's footsteps when he was promoted to Secretary-General of the Ministry of Colonies. Droogmans ended his colonial career in 1911 but remained president of the Comité Spécial du Katanga – he had held this position since 1900 and continued to do so until 1928.[119] Arnold was promoted to Director-General of Finances of the Belgian Congo in 1908 and hence succeeded Droogmans as State-Secretary of Finances of the Free State. In 1911, he took over Droogmans' position again. He held the post of Secretary-General of the Ministry of Colonies until 1925. During his colonial career Arnold represented the Belgian interests in key companies such as the Comité Spécial du Katanga, the Société de Kilo-Moto, and Forminière.[120]

The colonial state and major corporations were closely related in multiple ways. This makes it difficult to identify who received the short end of the stick when customs reforms were negotiated. Consequently, this study can only refer to the work of Vellut to argue that companies with good connections in Brussels had considerable influence over colonial customs policies and that this is an important reason why the Free State and Belgian Congo took commercial interests into account and made sure that its fiscal strategies did not provoke any disputes. Vellut argues that the private sector and the colonial state were not always as thick as thieves, but were generally on the same page. However, private enterprise was clearly the dominant partner in the close relationship between the state and certain companies.

117 Gann and Duignan, *The Rulers of Belgian Africa, 1884–1914*, 129–130; Vellut, 'Hégémonies en construction: Articulations entre Etat et Entreprises dans le bloc colonial Belge (1908–1960)'; Vellut, 'Réseaux transnationaux dans l'économie politique du Congo Léopoldien, c. 1885–1910'.

118 BCB – Eetvelde (Van) (Edmond).

119 BCB – Droogmans (Hubert).

120 BCB – Arnold (Nicolas).

5 Conclusion

This chapter demonstrates that commercial law in colonial Congo was not simply transferred from the Metropole to the colony. Commercial law developed on the colonial level through the interaction between the state and the private sector which had complementary and opposite interests. This claim is based on a study of lawmaking in the field of customs. This legal domain affected both the state and private enterprise in a fundamental manner as it constituted the fiscal contract between both actors. Moreover, customs revenue was a key source of revenue for the state and an important cost for the commercial sector which of course demanded a say in lawmaking and expected the state to implement growth inducing policies. Coercion never suffices to collect taxes. Like most states, the Free State and Belgian Congo mainly relied on taxpayer consent. Consent was only achieved through bargaining with the commercial sector that paid tariffs. As a result, the corporate taxpayer had a heavy influence on customs law in the pre-war Congo.

In the Free State and Belgian Congo, customs law was the result of a difficult balancing act between the fiscal health of the colony on the one hand, which required the increase of tariffs so as to maximize revenue raising and a rigid enforcement of import and export regulations; and on the other hand the interests of trading firms and concession companies, enterprises that aimed to minimize their fiscal contribution and expected the Free State and Belgian Congo to pursue growth-inducing economic policies in return – which included the cutting of customs related red tape.

During the first years of colonial rule, the revenue imperative forced the Free State to increase the tariff burden continuously and impose stricter customs regulations. These measures antagonized firms such as the Nieuwe Afrikaansche Handels-Vennootschap and Daumas, Béraud et Compagnie. According to both trading houses the tariff burden was excessive. Moreover, the constant tariff increases and the introduction of new customs duties made the future uncertain. The Dutch and the French company were also frustrated by the fact that not everyone chipped in. Smugglers and fraudulent merchants did not pay tariffs and the Société Anonyme Belge received preferential treatment. Moreover, it was unfair that the state always looked to the commercial sector for additional receipts. However, the most frustrating issue for both trading firms was the fact that the Free State also bought ivory in the Upper Congo without having to pay any taxes at all. In the eyes of the Nieuwe Afrikaansche Handels-Vennootschap and Béraud, Daumas et Compagnie, the Free State was a competitor rather than a state that promoted the development of trade in exchange for a fair contribution from trading firms.

Unsurprisingly, the Nieuwe Afrikaansche Handels-Vennootschap and Béraud, Daumas et Compagnie did everything they could to block any customs reform. To little avail; budgetary constraints only allowed the Free State to make minor concessions to the trade sector. Moreover, Brussels and Boma did not fully trust trading firms. Decision makers believed that the commercial sector could and should make a bigger fiscal contribution. Not every trading firm protested against the customs measures that were introduced during the first years of colonial rule. The Société Anonyme Belge preferred to keep the tariff burden as low as possible but never openly attacked the customs policies of the Free State. The Belgian firm did not mind paying taxes to the state as it allowed the latter to promote the commercial development of the Congolese hinterland. Moreover, the state could stop trading ivory if it managed to generate sufficient revenue through the collection of export and import duties.

After the initial development of the fiscal system, new customs disputes did not occur. The Free State only made minor changes to the customs system. Companies received the legal and fiscal stability they desired. Moreover, the rubber boom generated more colonial income, thus allowing the state to be more compliant towards the business sector. The tariff burden also proved to be manageable: the rubber boom created more than sufficient surplus, export tariffs were only increased in accordance with the rising rubber prices on the world market and the cost of customs duties could be allocated to the African producer by concession companies. The Belgians drastically reformed customs law. Export taxes were raised and many changes were introduced. Moreover, Brussels and Boma restored the fiscal contract by abolishing the domanial regime and by pursuing growth-inducing policies. As a result, the trade sector did not mind the growing tariff burden. In addition, the relatively low pressure to balance the budget created more room to take the interests of companies into account when devising customs law.

In the pre-war Congo, the State was closely linked to some of the main trading firms and concession companies. As a result, it is hard to identify which actor influenced the other. However, we can assume that the business sector was the dominant partner in the close relationship between private enterprise and the colonial state. This partly explains why the Société Anonyme Belge responded differently to the customs reforms of the late 1880s and early 1890s than did its Dutch and French counterparts. The close relations between the state and private enterprise also explains why no new disputes arose after 1892, Brussels and Boma being largely on the same page as trading firms and concession companies, because the latter had much influence over colonial decision making.

The Birth of a Colonial City: Tianjin 1860–1895

Luigi Nuzzo

1 A Really 'Dapper' Guy[1]

'We were waiting to board ship, the North German Lloyd building at our backs and the sun in our eyes. The Kaiser stood on a platform high above us and gave a spirited speech out over our heads. We had these new broad-brimmed hats to keep the sun out. Sou'westers, they were called. We looked real dapper. The Kaiser, though, he wore this special helmet with the eagle shining against a blue background. He talked about solemn duties and the cruel foe. We were all carried away. He said, 'Keep in mind the moment you land: No mercy shall be shown, no prisoners taken…' Then he told the story of King Attila and the Huns. He praised them to the skies even though they wreaked all kinds of havoc … He ended with our orders for China: 'Open the way to culture now and forever!' We gave three cheers … When we finally landed in Tientsin they were all there: the British, the Americans, the Russians, even real live Japanese and small troops from minor countries. The British turned out to be Indians. There weren't many of us to start with, but luckily we had the new five-centimeter rapid-fire cannons, the Krupp ones, and the Americans were trying out their Maxim machine gun, which was one hell of a weapon. So Peking fell in no time. In fact, by the time our company marched in, everything seemed over and done with, which was a pity. Though some of the Boxers were still making trouble. They were called Boxers because they had this secret society they called *I Ho Ch'uan* or 'righteous fists' in our language. That's why the English – and then everybody else – talked about the Boxer Rebellion. The Boxers hated foreigners because they sold the Chinese all kinds of stuff. The British particularly liked selling opium. That's why things went the way the Kaiser ordered: There were no prisoners taken'.[2]

These were the words, addressed to his girlfriend, of the protagonist of a short story by Günter Grass. He was a Bavarian soldier departed from Bremen,

1 This paper is a larger version of an article published in the Leiden Journal of International Law, 31, 3, 2018. It is part of a larger project, entitled *Space, Time and Law in a Global City: Tianjin 1860–1945*, that has been developed during the academic year 2014–2015 at the Institute of International Law and Justice at the New York University School of Law within the Hauser Global Fellow Program. The project received a grant by the Fondazione Monte dei Paschi di Siena.

2 Günter Grass, *My Century*, (trans.) M. Henry Heim (New York: Hartcourt, 1999), 1–3.

 | DOI:10.1163/9789004443075_015

with in mind the rousing words of Wilhelm II, and arrived in Tianjin when there was already little to do. The German writer entrusted the soldier to remember the famous speech delivered in the port of Bremen on 27 July 1900 by the Kaiser to the troops ready to embark for China.[3] A few days before their departure, the Allied powers, Italy, the US, the UK, France, Austria, Russia, Japan, and Germany, had freed the foreign concessions in Tianjin and had triumphantly entered the Chinese city, but the Boxers had not yet been defeated and the district of the foreign legations in Beijing remained under siege.[4]

For Germany, however, it was not simply a matter of participating in an international police operation. As was evident from the speech of Wilhelm II reported by Grass, it was something more. What was at stake was the very idea of German honour. On the 20 June 1900, in fact, a captain of the Imperial Guards Brigade murdered the German Ambassador Clemens von Ketteler, automatically placing the Chinese outside the great Family of Nations and its law. 'The Chinese have overturned international law',[5] Wilhelm II stated, and with it the universal values which it expressed.

The Kaiser's quotation deserves our attention. On the one hand, one cannot but underline the paradox: the murder of an ambassador was a denial of a law to which China until then had not had full access. On the other hand, the murder committed by the imperial guard, followed the next day by the declaration of war against the Allied Powers, had become a crime for which an entire nation was responsible. It provided not only a cause for military intervention, but it also allowed the use of violence against the Chinese, which was absolute, pure, devoid of any filter or any of the limits that even international law could have provided.

'Just as a thousand years ago' – the Kaiser noticed in a famous passage from of his speech, later taken out from the official versions – 'the Huns under their king Attila made a name for themselves, one that even today makes them seem mighty in history and legend, may the name German be affirmed by you in such a way in China that no Chinese will ever again dare to look cross-eyed at a German'.[6]

3 Wilhelms II, In Bremer Haven, 27 Juli 1900, in Johannes Prenzler (ed.), *Die Reden Kaiser Wilhelms in den Jahren 1896–1900*, B. II (Leipzig: Reclan, 1904), 209–212.

4 Paul Cohen, *History in Three Keys: The Boxers as Event, Experience and Myth* (New York: Columbia University Press, 1997).

5 Wilhelms II, In Bremer Haven, cit., 210.

6 The passage cut in the official version was the following: '*Kommt ihr vor den Feind, so wird derselbe geschlagen! Pardon wird nicht gegeben! Gefangene werden nicht gemacht! Wer euch in die Hände fällt, sei euch verfallen! Wie vor tausend Jahren die Hunnen unter ihrem König Etzel sich einen Namen gemacht, der sie noch jetzt in Überlieferung und Märchen gewaltig erscheinen läßt, so möge der Name Deutscher in China auf 1000 Jahre durch euch in einer Weise bestätigt*

The exceptional nature of the response to the crime was, therefore, justified, and offered further confirmation that China was not able to satisfy the principle of reciprocity, conforming its own actions to the laws and practice of the (Western) international community. At the same time, the murder of Ketteler also testified the persistence of a deep cultural and historical gap. It made the formation of a legal conscience/consciousness impossible and prevented China from the production of international law, excluding any guarantee of legal certainty in the processes in which Western citizens or Western interests were involved. According this interpretation, these reasons led the country to a hostile policy towards international trade as well as toward the presence of Western traders and Christian missionaries.

If twenty-five years before it still seemed possible to wonder 'to what extent and under what conditions the international unwritten law was applicable to the Eastern European nations', at the beginning of the new century that question had lost all its meaning.[7] If, in other words, in the seventies of the nineteenth century, the differences between the East and the West had prevented European jurists nor from including the Eastern populations in the international legal community neither from launching broad debate within the *Institut de Droit International* on the transplant of international law beyond its natural boundaries, the Boxer Rebellion transformed those same social, cultural and economic differences into an insurmountable barrier. Such issues not only continued to divide the West from the rest of the world, but it made superfluous any theoretical reflection on the universality of international law.

In October of 1900, three months after the Kaiser had delivered his famous speech, Georg Jellinek, one of the leading scholars of German public law, published a short article about China in the *Deutsche Juristen Zeitung*, where he attempted to read the dramatic war events of the earlier months according to the categories of international law. According to Jellinek, it was worth reflecting in an international law perspective on the relationship between China and the Western '*Kulturstaten*' after the German army landed in China to avenge 'rightly' the grievance to which they were subjected.

From his perspective, however, it was not simply a matter of ascertaining the violations that international law had suffered as a result of China's conduct,

---

werden, daß es niemals wieder ein Chinese wagt, einen Deutschen scheel anzusehen!' It has been reprinted in Manfred Görtemaker, *Deutschland im 19. Jahrhundert. Entwicklungslinien* (Opladen: Verlag für Sozialwissenschaftren, 1996), 35. v. <http://germanhistorydocs.ghi-dc.org/sub_document.cfm?document_id=755>.

7 Martti Koskenniemi, *The Gentle Civilizer of Nations* (Cambridge: University Press, 2001), 132–136; Luigi Nuzzo, *Origini di una scienza. Diritto internazionale e colonialismo nel XIX secolo* (Frankfurt-am-Main: Klostermann, 2012), 202–221.

or to ascertain whether its transfer was still possible, but to use the ongoing conflict in a comprehensive manner in order to rethink the legal form of the future relations with China. In the light of this goal, it seemed to be an unnecessarily strenuous exercise to continue to question the legal qualification of the actions taken by the allies against China. From a strictly legal point of view, the fundamental question was not in fact to decide whether such actions could be regarded as a 'true' war, an intervention, or a simple retaliation, but rather the question was '*in welchem Masse sind die Beziehungen der zivilisierten Mächte zu China nach Volkerrecht zu beurteilen?*'.[8]

To properly answer this question, Jellinek thought that it was necessary to clear away the myths and the 'popular beliefs': international law was not 'necessary' law and therefore always applicable. On the contrary, its validity was limited to the States that recognized it and that accepted its binding character.

It was not a return to the old representation of international law as a law with an effectiveness limited to the space of Christian countries of the West. The entrance of Turkey into the European Concert and even more the adhesion of Japan to Western values, showed that the German jurist clearly did not see a limit for its expansion in the religious/cultural matrix that constituted the foundation of international law. The Chinese case seemed to be completely different. It was in fact 'unprovable' to argue that China had adopted Western international law. Bowing to Western pressure, China had only broken its traditional closed-door policy, accepting to have relations with the 'civilized' countries, but it did not deny its premises.

China continued to represent itself as the Middle Kingdom, to consider the foreign States as vassals, and to recognize the privileges and not the rights of their diplomatic representatives. The consequences were very serious and bore witness once again to a cultural lag: '*Ein Angriff auf einen Gesandten bedeutet daher für einen China bloß einen Vertragsbruch, nicht Verletzung einer grundsätzlich anerkannten Norm des Völkerrechts*'. China, in other words, lacked the awareness (*Bewusstsein*) that the progress that international law had made over time was inextricably linked to the recognition of the necessity and binding nature of the international agreements and treaties. '*Ein Völkerrecht* – Jellinek stated with his usual clarity – *gibt es aber erst der Zeit, da die Staaten erkannten, daß sie durch die von ihnen vollzogenen Vereinbarungen und Verträge*

8 Georg Jellinek, *China und das Völkerrecht*, (Deutsche Juristenzeitung 1900) in Id. *Ausgewählte Schriften und Reden*, B. 2 (Berlin: Häring, 1911), 491. On Jellinek's article, see also Stephan Kroll, *Normgenese durch Re-Interpretation China und das europäische Völkerrecht in 19. und 20. Jahrhundert* (Baden Baden: Nomos, 2012), 44–45.

unabhängig von den wechselnden Forderungen der Tagespolitik gebunden seien. Diese höhere Stufe hat China bis heute noch nicht erreicht, darum und kann dort ein oder der andere Satz des Völkerrechts vorübergehende Anerkennung finden; das ändert aber nichts an der Tatsache, daß es bis heute sich außerhalb der Gemeinschaft des Völkerrechts gestellt hat'.[9]

The recently ended war confirmed China's estrangement from the 'values' system and the progress of the West, but also, at the same time, it showed how that same alleged foreignness would allow, on the one hand, the justification of the violence in a response free from the limits imposed by international law; and on the other hand, to exclude any infringement of it. There could be no fractures or breaches of international law, nor could it be appealed, as was noticed by Jellinek, by countries like China that were not able to grasp its 'spirit'.

One day, perhaps, Jellinek sustained, if China agreed to rethink profoundly the relationship with its own tradition, and introducing the reforms requested by the West, it could be admitted into the club of civilized nations and enjoy its rights.

In the meantime, in the long and uncertain wait, Jellinek entrusted China to the humanity that the victorious powers are obliged to respect as civilized nations, regardless of the barbarity of their enemies. At the same time, however, international lawyers started important reflections on the limits of the concept of sovereignty on the grounds of an analysis of the relationship between the State and the territory. They tried to overcome the embarrassment that was concealed behind words like 'curiosity', 'novelty', 'anomaly', 'nonsense', and 'irregularity', when the jurists tried to describe the uniqueness of the non-Western world with an overall interpretation that brought the whole phenomenon of exceptionality within the legal horizon.[10]

'In the reality of international life' – Arrigo Cavaglieri wrote referring to Jellinek – 'there is nothing that can be said to be absurd and unreasonable. In order to exclude it, it is sufficient to recall the very existence of that particular

9 Jellinek, *China und das Völkerrecht*, 493.

10 Johann Kaspar Bluntschli, *Le Congres de Berlin et sa portée au point de vue du droit international*, 5e article *Les nouveaux états de formation incomplète*, *Revue du droit international et de législation comparée* 13 (1881), 586; Travers Twiss, *The Laws of the Nations Considered as Independent Political Communitie: On the Right and Duties of Nations in Time of Piece* (Oxford: Clarendon Press, 1884), 120; Franz von Holtzendorff, 'Das Landgebiet der Staaten', in Franz von Holtzendorff (ed.), *Handbuch des Völkerrechts, Bd. 2: Die völkerrechtliche Verfassung und Grundordnung der auswächtigen Staatsbeziehungen* (Hamburg: Richter, 1887), 245; Fyodor Fyodorovich Martens, *Völkerrecht: Das internationale Recht der civilisirten Nationen systematisch dargestellt* Bd. 1, (trans.) C. Bergbohm (orig. 1881; Berlin: Weidmann, 1883), 361, 364; Henry Bonfils, *Manuel de droit international public* (*Droit des gens*) (Paris: Rousseau, 1894), 180.

phenomenon, which, therefore, no matter how seemingly bizarre and new, it certainly has in itself a reason to exist and cannot be overlooked. It is up to the lawyers to study it without preconceptions in its manifestations and legal consequences, searching among the existing or, if necessary, building ex novo the scheme within which it falls'.[11]

This was certainly not an easy task, but it was now a duty which even the most sensitive jurists could no longer escape.[12]

In Italy, this task was taken up by two international lawyers: Enrico Levi Catellani, always attentive to the colonial phenomena with a series of studies on China; and Cavaglieri himself, who made the relationship between the State and the territory and the categories used to define it, which was the subject of three important articles published in Italian legal journals between 1903 and 1906.[13] In the same period some French minor jurists such as Perrinjaquet, Gerard, and Alfonsi catalogued the *cessions temporaires* and *cessions déguisées* of territory in international law; while in Germany, Boghitchiévitch dedicated his dissertation to the concept of semi-sovereignty, emphasizing the relationship with the notion of autonomy.[14] A few years before, in 1896, in Germany Conrad Bornhak, a lawyer who worked with much awareness of colonial law in the wake of Jellinek's *Die Lehre der Staaten Verbindungen,* published an essay on the 'unilateral dependence conditions'. In 1896, Georg Jellinek's *Staatsfragmente* was printed as a text destined to leave a mark in the debate on public law doctrine of the twentieth century.[15]

---

11 Arrigo Cavaglieri, *Contributo alla definizione di alcune figure del diritto pubblico contemporaneo* (Roma: Tipografia dell'Unione cooperativa editrice, 1906), 16. In the same way Gennaro Mondaini, 'Il carattere di eccezionalità della storia e del diritto coloniale e le nuove forme giuridiche d'espansione nelle colonie', *Rivista Coloniale* 2 (1907), 6–32.

12 Arrigo Cavaglieri, *Il diritto internazionale e alcune recenti concessioni di territori* (Verona: Manuzio, 1903); Cavaglieri, *Contributo*, 8–12.

13 Arrigo Cavaglieri, *Il diritto internazionale ed il rapporto giuridico tra Stato e territorio, Archivio giuridico* 73 (1904), 77–127; Enrico Levi Catellani, *I 'settlement' europei e i privilegi degli stranieri nell'Estremo Oriente* (Venezia: Ferrari, 1903); Enrico Levi Catellani, *L'Estremo Oriente e le sue lotte* (Milano: Treves, 1904); Enrico Levi Catellani, 'I privilegi degli stranieri in Oriente e nell'Estremo Oriente: condizione attuale e tentativi di riforma', *Rivista di diritto internazionale* 9 (1915), 3–22; Enrico Levi Catellani, *La penetrazione straniera nell'Estremo Oriente: Sue forme giuridiche ed economiche* (Firenze: Barbera, 1915).

14 Louis Gerard, *Des cessions deguisées de territoires en droit international public* (Nancy: Imprimerie Nancienne, 1903); Jean Perrinjaquet, *Des cessions temporaires de territoires* (Paris: Giard & Brière, 1904); M. Boghitchiévitch, *Halbsouveranität: Administrative und politische Autonomie seit dem Pariser Vertrag* (Berlin: Springer, 1903).

15 Conrad Bornhak *Einseitige Abhängigkeitsverhältnisse unter den modernen Staaten* (Leipzig: Duncker & Humblot, 1896); Georg Jellinek, *Ueber Staatsfragmente* (Heidelberg: Koester, 1896).

For the Austrian jurist, to understand the reality and placing it within (new) legal categories was possible only through an awareness of the limits of the concepts of sovereignty and State.

The categories of sovereign rights, territory and subjects still constituted the necessary elements of statehood, but the absence of one of them, even the most important such as the governmental power, did not necessarily condemn the political formation which was missing within simple administrative authorities. Outside the borders of the Western States, sovereignty could lose exclusivity and indivisibility, coexisting with the recognition of broad spheres of autonomy. For Jellinek this meant that sovereignty was no longer an essential feature of the State, but only 'a historical category necessary for an understanding of the contemporary State system, but not the State in it itself'.[16] Jellinek could not get rid of the *idolon* of sovereignty, and continued to use it in his observations and reconstructions of the international order. At the same time, however, he was well aware that only an approach free from 'doctrinal preconceptions' could notice the existence of ambiguous political subjects. Provided with territory, subjects and more or less degree of legislative, administrative and jurisdictional autonomy they could be defined 'fragments of State *Staatsfragmente*.

It was an extremely flexible category able to include the Danubian principalities or other territories of the Ottoman Empire, to explain the particular legal nature of Finland, or to be applied to the German colonial possessions in Africa and finally to the foreign concessions in China.

China, in fact, despite the compression suffered by its territorial sovereignty, could not be obviously qualified as a States' fragment, nor as a semi-sovereign State. On the contrary the new category invented by Jellinek could provide a theoretical key to qualify the territorial concessions made, since 1842, by China to the Western powers, Russia and Japan, and to understand what was happening in Tianjin and China after the Boxers Rebellion.

The history of the Western presence in Tianjin begins officially between 1860 and 1861 when, according to the Beijing Convention, seventy-six and sixty acres of land were, respectively, leased in perpetuity to the British and French government, with a small ground rent paid annually to China.[17] In addition, the American concession was granted in the same years, but it never developed

16 Jellinek, *Ueber Staatsfragmente*, 11.

17 See *infra*. some general information in Francis Clifford Jones, *Shanghai and Tientsin, with Special Reference to Foreign Interests* (Oxford: Oxford University Press, 1940), 120 ff.; Otto Rasmussen, *Tientsin: an Illustrated Outline History* (Tientsin: The Tientsin Press Ltd., 1925).

properly, and in 1891 it was given back to the Chinese Government (but the United States retained the right to have a concession and the possibility of exercising it in the future) and in 1902 it was placed under the control of Britain.[18]

More than thirty years later, concession rights were given to Germany in 1895 and to Japan in 1896, when they joined the Western powers already established in the city.[19] But it was only at the beginning of the twentieth century with the Boxers' defeat and the occupation of the city by the allied army (USA, Great Britain, France, Japan, Russia, Germany, Austria-Hungary, and Italy) that Tianjin changed definitively. In the Boxer Protocol, signed in 1901 at Bejing, the allied powers gained the right to occupy '*certains points, à determiner par un accord entre elles, pour maintenir les communications libres entre la capitale et la mer. Les points occupés par les Puissances sont: Houang-Ts'oun, Lang-Jang, Yang-Ts'oun, Tien-Tsin, Kiun-Léang-Tchang, T'hang-Kou, Lou-Tai, T'ang-Chan, Louan-Tcheou, Tchang-Li, Ts'in-Wang-Tao, Chan-Hai-Kouan*'.[20] In reality they had already taken possession of part of the Chinese territory. In April 1901, for example, well before the bilateral agreement between Italy and China (1902) and before the Peking Protocol was signed, the commander of the Italian garrison, lieutenant Valli, published an advice in Italian and in English in the Tien-Tsin Express which defined the confines of the Italian concession, inviting the Italian citizens and foreigners who claimed ownership of land or buildings within these boundaries to present their titles to the Legation in Beijing or to the military command of Tianjin.[21]

Between 1901 and 1903 also Austria, Belgium and Russia, as well as Italy, always through a private law agreement, obtained their own concession and they

---

18 On the American presence in Tianjin see the PhD thesis of Lewis Bernstein, *A History of Tianjin in the early modern times, 1800–1910* (Ann Arbor, 1988); and now Nicolais Vaicbourdt, *De la 'me too policy' aux ambitions contradictoires: la brève histoire de la concession américaine de Tianjin, 1860–1902*, in *Outre-Mers. Revue d'histoire*, 382/383 (2014), 27–46.

19 Mark Peattie, *Japanese Treaty Port Settlements in China 1895–1937*, in Peter Duus, Ramon H. Myers and Mark R. Peattie, *The Japanese Informal Empire in China, 1895–1937* (Princeton: University Press, 2014), 166–209; some information about the German presence in Tianjin in F. Koberstein, *Tientsin und Umgebung* (Tianjin: Verlag der Brigadezeitung, 1906). To understand the German strategies of colonization in China see Klaus Mühlhahn, *Herrschaft und Widerstand in der 'Musterkolonie' Kiautschou: Interaktionen zwischen China und Deutschland, 1897–1914* (München: Oldenburg, 2000).

20 Boxer Protocoll, Peking, 7.9.1901, art. IX, in http://www.chinaforeignrelations.net.

21 The text (1 April 1901) is in Archivio Storico del Ministero degli Affari Esteri, (thereafter ASMAE), serie P, pos. 86/37, pac. 426 (1901), see Luigi Nuzzo, 'Italiani in Cina: la concessione di Tien Tsin', in Aldo Mazzacane (ed.), *Diritto, istituzioni e economia nell'Italia fascista* (Baden Baden: Nomos, 2002), 255–281.

started to enjoy formally the rights over the Chinese territory that they had already physically occupied.[22] At the same time, France, England, Germany and Japan obtained an enlargement of their previous concessions, creating a metropolitan space with more than one million inhabitants composed of two distinct but connected entities – the Chinese city and the foreigner concessions – crossed by a multiplicity of physical, legal and social boundaries.

This space, or rather the process of the definition of the territorial space of British, France and American concessions in Tianjin, is the object of this article. In recent years, international lawyers returned to study the so called 'unequal' treaties, producing interesting works focused on the Western representations of Chinese law, its jurisdictions, or dealing with the position of China in the international legal order.[23] However, the foreign concessions of Tianjin have not received particular attention and remained a field of research entrusted to sinologists. This, in my opinion, has prevented to measure the relevance of law and legal discourses both for the conquest and the administration of these Chinese territories, and for the construction of the legal relations with the local populace. At the same time the delay of the jurists in focusing on this topic has contributed to hidden the relevance of the colonial dimension in the process of construction of the modern international law.

On the contrary, legal texts and juridical paradigms also played an important role in the Chinese colonial discourse. Jurists, colonial administrators, and military authorities bridled spaces and subjectivities into a textual network of laws and regulations, constructing new spaces and producing new social lives. By fixing the stereotypes of Chinese otherness they formed Chinese subjectivity, and contextually this made it possible to normalize it, and naturalized the racial and cultural differences that marked the stereotypes themselves. In this way, China and its populations were represented as being different on the basis of cultural and historical diversity, in order to justify the Western presence and the compression of Chinese sovereignty.[24] I think, therefore, that the best way

22 For the Austrian concession see the PhD thesis of Günter Hörtler, *Die Österreich-Ungarische Konzession von Tientsin* (Vienna, 1984).

23 Wang Tieya, 'International law in China: historical and contemporary perspectives', *Recueil des cours, Collected Courses* 221 (1990), 195–369; Matthew Craven, 'What happened to the Unequal Treaties? The Continuities of Informal Empire', *Nordic Journal of International Law* 74 (2005), 335–382; Anne Peters, 'Unequal Treaties', in Rüdiger Wolfrum, *Max Planck Encyclopaedia of Public International Law* (Oxford: Oxford University Press, 2012), 38–50.

24 See Lidia Liu, *The Clash of Empires. The Invention of China in Modern World Making* (Cambridge: Harvard University Press, 2004); Rune Svarverud, *International Law as World Order in Late Imperial China: Translation, Reception and Discourse* (Leiden: Brill, 2007); and from

to try to understand these related processes of construction of space and production of subjectivity is to choose a single place. This should be a place with its own characteristics and its own memories, but also a place that at the same time may be considered as a model for reading the Western theoretical discussions on the exceptionality of non-Western spaces and their populations (and obviously the solutions offered by international lawyers), and to understand the political and legal transformation in China in the first half of the twentieth century. In this way, Tianjin is not only the subject of my history, but it is also a decentralized platform of observation for the Western discourse of international law and its projections outside its borders. Tianjin, the only Chinese city where up to nine foreign concessions coexisted is, in other words, a unity of space, time and action, through which it becomes possible to 'spatialize' the legal discourse.

On the one hand this means that a spatial perspective must be taken, and within it, proceed to the reconstruction of the complex network of legal, political, social, and economic relations. On the other hand, the assumption of a spatial approach is not only the premise of the analysis, but its definition is an objective of the analysis itself. Therefore, the assumption of a spatial approach is a methodological instrument of analysis and, at the same time, its definition is an objective of the analysis itself. As Emile Durkheim and Marcel Mauss already stressed at the beginning of the last century, space is not homogeneous, universal or constant. By overcoming the classical representation of Newton and Cartesio as well as the Kantian identification of space and time as kinds of pure and *a priori* intuitions, they revealed its social dimension.[25] Seventy years later, this dimension of space was deeply stressed by Henry Lefebvre who analysed, from a Marxist perspective, the relationships of economy and politics with space, identifying this last one with a social institution shaped itself by social, political and economic contexts.[26] I cannot summarize here the huge theoretical debate on the concept of space that from Durkeim and Mauss, and including Foucault and Lefebvre, was channelled into postmodern geographers'

a legal perspective Teemu Ruskola, *Legal Orientalism: China, the United States, and Modern Law* (Cambridge: Harvard University Press, 2013).

25 Émile Durkheim and Marcel Mauss, 'De quelques forme primitive de classification: Contribution à l'étude des représentations collective', *L'Année sociologique* 6 (1903), 1–72. Pietro Costa has recently stressed the relevance of this article in a seminal work, 'Uno spatial turn per la storia del diritto? Una rassegna tematica', *Max Plank Institut for European Legal History Research paper Series* 7 (2013), 1–30.

26 Henry Lefebvre, *La production de l'espace* (Paris: Anthropos, 1974); Henry Lefebvre, *De l'État* (Paris: Uge, 1976–1978).

theories, such as those of Harvey or Soya.[27] But it is useful to stress that from these theoretical critics of the conception of space of Newton it has been possible to rethink the image of the homogeneity of the State space offered by Western public lawyers between the nineteenth and the twentieth century, and at the same time to challenge the existence of a unitarian concept of sovereignty.[28] In this sense, my aim, is not only to assume Tianjin as a determined space in which texts, institutions and subjects were placed, but also to understand how this space has been imaged, looking at which economic, political and social strategies of governance were involved in its construction, and which forms of resistance or negotiations were put in place by Chinese elites.

2 Legal Stereotypes

According the Western representation, China was not a fully 'civilized' State. It was still living in a condition of exceptionality that justified the compression of its sovereignty and the introduction of new legal regimes.

It was indeed a paradoxical situation that was no different to what happened with regard to the Ottoman Empire: a new feeling of universalism and humanitarianism led the international lawyers to desire a broader application of international law, so as to be able to go beyond the Christian West, but also to limit the internal sovereignty of Eastern States in defence of the Western economic interests. This set of circumstances legitimated, first, the application of consular law and later, when it became necessary, a military intervention. In both cases it was an exceptional answer that produced a restriction of the Chinese territorial sovereignty. As a matter of fact the religious, cultural and historical gap that marked the Chinese legal and political life imposed diplomats and international lawyers to break the relationship between sovereignty, subjects and territory. This allowed spaces and subjects within the Chinese territory to be placed outside its *imperium*.

The so called 'unequal' treaties signed by China at the end of the First Opium War (1839–1842) testified it, showing how, outside the borders of Western States, the efficacy of the principle of legal territorial sovereignty had faded away.

---

27 Michael Foucault, 'Des espaces autres', in Michael Foucault, *Dits et écrits*, vol. 6 (eds.) D. Defert and F. Ewald (Paris: Gallimard, 1994), 752–762; David Harvey, *The Urban Experience* (Baltimore: John Hopkins Press, 1989); Edward Soja, *Postmodern Geographies: the Reassertion of Space in Critical Social theory* (London: Verso, 1989).

28 Luigi Nuzzo, 'Autonomia e diritto internazionale: Una lettura storico giuridica', *Quaderni Fiorentini* 43 (2014), 651–686.

In 1842, in fact, with the Treaty of Peace and Friendship of Nanking that put an end to that war, England ensured the right to conduct business without the exorbitant and arbitrary intermediary of the merchant guild of Hong Co. It also obtained a reasonable indemnity for the costs of war and the drug loss; the settlement of Hong Kong and the opening of five ports (Guanghzhou, Fuzhou, Ningbo, Xiamen, Shanghai) to English commerce with the right of residence for British subjects and their families; the presence of a consul in each of them; reliable and fair customs taxes; and finally the recognition of a 'perfect equality' between the Chinese emperor and the English Queen.[29] The following year a new agreement (*The Supplementary Treaty*) signed in Hu-men-chai by Henry Pottinger and Qi-ying supplemented the Treaty of Nanking, allowing Britain to gain further advantages. It introduced the most favoured nation clause, by which the privileges and immunities that China would grant in the future to other foreign countries were to be considered as automatically extended to the United Kingdom together with the application of the principle of extraterritoriality.[30]

The treaties that the Celestial Empire signed in 1844, in Wanghia (Wangxia) and Whampoa (Huangpu), with the United States of America and France, were also characterised by the same trade privileges, producing a similar restriction of Chinese sovereignty. However, the two Western powers, represented respectively by Caleb Cushing and Théodose de Lagrené, did not only assume the Anglo-Chinese agreements as a model, they also succeeded in getting further benefits, being able to better regulate the competences of the consuls and the implementation of the principle of extraterritoriality.[31] The American and French consuls were required to supervise and regulate everything concerning American and French citizens living in the five ports. This meant transforming the territory assigned to them into a new social space. From an urbanistic point of view, it meant proceeding with their requalification, buying in the name of their respective governments the land required for the construction of warehouses, hospitals, churches, and cemeteries; and also to

29 Treaty of Nanking 29.8.1842, Wilhelm Grewe (ed.), *Fontes iuris gentium*, Bd. 3,1 (Berlin: de Gruyter, 1988), 258–262.

30 *The Supplementary Treaty*, 8.10.1843, William L. Tung (ed.), *China and the Foreign Powers: The Impact of and the Reaction to Unequal Treaties* (New York: Oceana Publications, 1970), 436.

31 *Treaty of Peace, Amity and Commerce between the United States of America and Chinese Empire* (3.7.1844), and *Traité d'amitie de commerce et de navigation conclu, le 24 septembre, 1844, entre la France et la Chine* both edited in *China Imperial Maritime Customs, III Miscellaneous Series: n. 30, Treaties Conventions, etc., China and Foreign States*, vol. 1 (Shanghai: Statistical Department of the Inspectorate of Customs, 1908), respectively, 76–83, 49–58.

mediate between Western merchants in search of land and buildings to buy and the Chinese interested in doing business with the newcomers (Wanghia, art. 17; Whampoa, art. 22). From a legal point of view, the Westernization of the new territories was possible, on the one hand, by overcoming Chinese sovereignty and by the rigorous application of the principle of legal personality in criminal proceedings (Wanghia, art. 21; Whampoa, art. 27); and on the other hand through the use of equitable remedies and alternative forms of administration of justice that, however, emphasized the superiority of the consular judiciary (Wanghia, art. 16; 24; Whampoa, art. 10, 25).

This implied the exclusion of any intervention by the Chinese government in dispute settlement concerning 'property rights or personal rights' between Western citizens. Their resolution was left to the consul when plaintiff and defendant had the same nationality or was left to the treaties in force between the nations the parties were citizens of (*Wanghia* art 25; *Whampoa*, art 28). However, in case of civil law complaints between Chinese and Western citizens, contract law, commercial fraud, debt recovery, the consular office had to filter the claims for damage and evaluate the possibility of any attempt of conciliation. In the same way, with full reciprocity in the Wanghia Treaty, the local officials had a analogous function to intermediate when the plaintiff was a Chinese citizen (*Wanghia*, art. 16). Nevertheless, in both treaties the consul continued to be the only authority to legitimize a conciliation independently from the plaintiff's nationality and, as established in the General Regulations, it was always the consul who invited a Chinese officer to participate in a mixed commission in order to decide the case according to equity when the dispute could not be resolved in a friendly way (*Wanghia*, art. 24; *Whampoa*, art. 25). Commenting this provision in 1915, Enrico Catellani noted that 'nella cooperazione di due magistrati di così diversa origine e di così diversa coltura, il criterio informatore di tali regole di equità non potesse riuscire sempre uniforme; e come, dato l'indirizzo assunto dalle potenze d'Europa nei loro rapporti colla Cina, e la parte preponderante ch'era assegnata all'ufficiale consolare in tale procedura relativa ai processi misti, il criterio di equità dell'ufficiale consolare dovesse finire per prevalere sempre, anche quando si trattato di un convenuto cinese e pertanto di un caso di evidente ragione di prevalenza della legge e della competenza territoriale'.[32] According to the treaty of *Wanghia* and *Whampoa*, the diplomatic relationships between the Chinese Empire and the Western powers were merged in a exceptional dimension, and the same Italian International lawyer seemed to be conscious of it. Formerly, however, the two treaties described China, the United States and France in terms of full equality

32 Catellani, *La penetrazione straniera nell'Estremo Oriente*, p. 41.

and absolute reciprocity.[33] As a matter of fact the articles reproduced article 11 of the Anglo-Chinese Treaty of 1842 when for the first time an official diplomatic instrument recognized the perfect equality between the Chinese Emperor and the British Queen, and extended the effects to France and America as well. The prevision of a perfect equality between the two sovereigns was an extremely delicate issue of the relationship between China and England and a strongly persecuted goal of the British diplomacy. It was connected with the battle the latter led to eliminate from the official documents the letter 夷 (*yi*) which is the letter used by Chinese to identify foreigners, assuming its possible translation with the term barbarians. Putting the reciprocal relationship on a base of absolute equality meant to compel China to overcome a sinocentric vision of the world based on a deep sense of superiority witnessed by the equation yi/barbarian and at the same time intended to prepare the entrance of the Celestial Empire into the 'great family of civilized nations'. The meaning to be assigned to a grammatical sign overcame the limits of linguistics and became a serious politic-juridical problem. It coagulated the British resentment for an offense coming from a civilization they considered inferior and was seen as a threat for the construction of an Eurocentric system of international relationships.

Recently, historiography turned on the Chinese letter 夷 (*yi*) and the equation yi/barbarians and showed its relevance in the construction of British colonial strategies. Through a careful historic semiological reconstruction, Lydia Liu proved the paradox of an identity between foreigner and barbarian unknown in Chinese documents in the first half of the nineteenth century, but on the contrary, first produced and imposed by the Anglo-Saxon diplomatic and legal discourse and then passively accepted by much of the contemporary historiography seeing in this identity an irrefutable prove of Chinese xenophobia. In the eighteenth and the nineteenth century, the letter 夷 (*yi*) simply meant the foreigner and it was used in this meaning in diplomatic relationships. The semantic passage from foreigner to barbarian happened later, in the 30s of the nineteenth century, coinciding with the transformation of the Chinese Secretary' Office in a government office competent for the translation of all diplomatic instruments and marking also rhetorically the radicalization between the British government and the Qing dynasty that would lead a few years later to the first Opium War.[34]

33 *Treaty of Peace* (*Wanghia*), art. 30; *Traité d'amitié* (*Whampoa*), art. 33.

34 Lydia Liu, *Legislating the Universal. The Circulation of International Law in the Nineteenth Century*, in Id. (ed.), *Tokens of Exchange: The Problem of Translation in Global Circulation*

The Anglo-Chinese Treaty of Tientsin (Tianjin) of 1858, signed at the end of the second Opium War, made this identity 'official' and eliminated the risk that translations could produce other 'illegal' stories. With article 51, the letter 夷 (*yi*) was banned from any diplomatic instrument and was no longer applied to the British government and subjects. But at the same time it changed into a *hetero-linguistic sign*.[35] It had become a 'super sign', different from the Chinese language, formed by Chinese character, by the transliteration of the pronunciation I and the English translation barbarian and at last gifted, thanks to the legal recognition of an official diplomatic instrument, with performative power.[36] The possibility to translate the letter 夷 (*yi*) with the term barbarian, banned from any public document and at the same time fixed irrevocably by the same article that introduced it in contempt of the Chinese language, was confirmed by another disposition of the treaty where only the English language was recognized as official. From then onwards, supposing that there was a difference in meaning between the English version of a treaty and the Chinese one, only the English version would have prevailed.[37]

(Durham: Duke University Press: 1999) 131–134, Id., *The Clash of Empires. The Invention of China in Modern World Making* (Cambridge: University Press, 2004) 31–69.

35 'It is agreed (*Treaty of Peace, Friendship, Commerce and Navigation between her Majesty the Queen of Great Britain and Ireland and the Emperor of China*, 26.6.1858, art. 51, ed. *Treaties*, p. 19)– that henceforward the charachter夷 'I' (Barbarian) shall not be applied to the Government or subjects of Her Britannic Majesty, in any Chinese official document issued by the Chinese authorities, either in the capital or in the provinces'. In the North American (art. 7, ed. *Treaties*, 11–20), French (art. 4, ed. *Treaties*, 59–71), and Russian (art. 2, ed. *Treaties*, 101–112) version of the treaties of Tianjin there is a obligation to communicate on a base perfect equality treaties. Also the first *Trattato di amicizia, commercio e navigazione* signed on 26.10.1866 between the Kingdom of Italy and China (*Treaty of Peking*, ed. *Treaties, Conventions, etc., between China and Foreign States*, vol. 2, 1145), affirmed the perfect equality between the Italian king and the Chinese emperor (art. 5), but the art. 51 provided that: 'Il carattere cinese 夷, *I*, non sarà adoperato in alcun documento uffiziale emanato dalle Autorità cinesi della capitale o delle provincie per designare il Governo o i sudditi di Sua Maestà il Re d'Italia'. S. Andrea Francioni, '*Il banchetto cinese*'. *L'Italia fra le treaty powers* (Nuova immagine: 2004) 16–33.

36 'That is to say – according to Liu, *The Clash of Empires*, 37 – whoever violates the integrity of the super sign risks violating the international law. The risk, of course, was always there; so was the fascination with the exclusive signification of yi in terms of the English word "barbarian". The legal injunction of Article 51 catapulted what seemed at first a trifling matter of translation into the broader realm of international conflicts with major implications for our understanding of narratives of civilizational clash, past and present'.

37 In the same way also art. 3 of the *Treaty of Peace, Friendship, Commerce, and Navigation between France and China* (27.6.1858) ed. *Treaties*, 59–71: 'Les communications officielles des agents diplomatiques et consulaires français avec les autorités Chinoises seront écrites en français, mais seront accompagnées, pour faciliter le service, d'une traduction

Apart from linguistic issues, the Tientsin treaty extended also to the British the privileges and the immunity in legal and economic matters as had already been granted to Americans and French in Wanghia and Whampoa, and transformed, through the clause of the most favored nation, the concessions made into a kind of 'common law of all foreigners'.[38]

As a matter of fact with these treaties the Western powers revisited previous agreements, obtaining a wider protection of their economic interests, new treaty ports, the right of free commerce and navigation along the Yangzi, and the possibility of travel within China.[39] They moreover forced China to accept the presence of Christian missionaries, imposing the duty on them to protect their missionary activity (art. 8) and the right to establish diplomatic delegations in Beijing (art. 2; 3). It was a goal which had been pursued by Western powers for a long time and that would lead, according to the British plenipotentiary James Bruce, Earl of Elgin, to overcome the mediation of the provincial authorities in dealing with the emperor, thus simplifying and facilitating relationships. This would have pushed China to participate fully in the international legal and political system.

But times were not right, and the Tianjin treaties hampered Chinese sovereignty more than it already had been by the previous agreements China was forced to sign. The possibility for Western diplomacy to open its diplomatic offices in Beijing and to deal directly with the emperor, and the right of merchants and missionaries to travel inside the interior of the vast empire, together with the increasingly broader competences of consular jurisdiction constituted a serious violation of Chinese sovereignty over its own territory, which

Chinoise aussi exacte que possible, jusqu'au moment où le Gouvernement Impérial de Pékin, ayant des interprètes pour parler et écrire correctement le français, la correspondance diplomatique aura lieu dans cette langue pour les agents française, et en chinois pour les fonctionnaires de l'empire. Il est convenu que jusque-là, et en cas de dissidence dans l'interprétation à donner au texte français et au texte chinois, au sujet des clauses arrêtées d'avance dans les Conventions faites de commun accord, ce sera toujours le texte original qui fera foi. Cette disposition est applicable au présent traité et dans les communications entre les autorités des deux Pays, ce sera toujours le texte original et non la traduction qui fera foi'.

38 Catellani, *La penetrazione straniera nell'estremo Oriente*, 25; s. also Marcel Baudez, *Essai sur la condition juridique des étrangers, en Chine*, (Paris: Pedone, 1913) and Roland H. Ouang de Soutchéou, *Essai sur le régime des capitulations en Chine*, (Paris: Sirey, 1933).

39 The treaties signed at Tientsin were ratified at Pechino on 24.10.1860; cf. Dong Wang, *China's Unequal Treaties: Narrating National History* (Lanham: Lexington Books, 2005), 16–19; s. also John K. Fairbanks, 'The Creation of the Treaty System', in John K. Fairbanks (ed.), *The Cambridge History of China, vol. 10: Late Ch'ing 1800–1911* (Cambridge: Cambridge University Press, 1978), 213–263.

was incompatible with the images of State or nation that the Western legal doctrine was constructing in those same years.

It was necessary, therefore, to rethink the relationship between sovereignty, territory and subjects, as I have previously stated, admitting that outside the boundaries of the Christian West, the principle of the territoriality of a sovereign State, a modern conquest of the European nations, could not still have an unconditional application. Since it was not acceptable to leave the Western citizens to the abuses of a judiciary system represented as unreliable, it became necessary to limit the sovereignty of the Eastern States. An old legal fiction, that of extraterritoriality, enabled the Western diplomacy to achieve this goal. Viewed with suspicion by the international lawyers, outside Western territorial boundaries, it became a fundamental legal principle of a new colonial order. It allowed the Western powers to de-territorialize Western citizens that had settled in Eastern countries, freeing them from the *imperium* of the local authority and entrusting them to their own consuls.

Outside the borders of Christendom the necessity was imposed to broaden the powers and privileges that were normally accorded to consuls. They were really public ministers, and they enjoyed all the prerogatives of diplomatic agents: judicial immunity, inviolability, rights provided by the diplomatic ceremonial, tax and customs exemptions, a body of troops, and mainly an 'exceptional' jurisdictional competence.[40] As a matter of fact, the exceptional prerogatives enjoyed by the consuls in the East reflected an exceptionality inherent to the same consular law. Searching for a difficult compromise between a universal international law, based on morality, and a positive international law, grounded on the common Christian conscience of the Western States (and thus only applicable to them) rather than on the civilized States' will, the consular law was a good tool for regulating relations between States and those political entities that were considered to be at a lower level of civilization, while at the same time not hampering the scientific representation of international law as a positive law with a universalistic appeal.[41]

The whole non-Western world, in different forms and degrees, was considered as exceptional, as well as the measures adopted by legal science and practice in order to rule that reality. In both cases, human beings and texts were

40 August von Bulmerincq, 'Consularrecht', in Franz von Holtzendorff (eds.), *Handbuch des Völkerrechts, Bd. 3: Die Staatsverträge und die internationalen Magistraturen* (Hamburg: Richter, 1887), 723–727.

41 Luigi Nuzzo, *Origini di una scienza: Diritto internazionale e colonialismo nel XIX secolo* (Frankfurt am Main: Klostermann, 2012), with reference to the Ottoman Empire see Eliana Augusti, *Questioni di Oriente: Europa e Impero ottomano nel diritto internazionale dell'Ottocento* (Napoli: Edizioni Scientifiche Italiane, 2013).

physically moved from the West to the East and then to Africa, and Western legal concepts were incorporated into non-European contexts. At the same time the legal transplants were the result of discursive strategies that imposed the direction, making their content opaque and defining their limits. It was a multiplicity of shared representations founded on widespread and resistant stereotypes. They were able to make the non-Western world as they imagined it had to be, and capable of producing a self-consciousness based on the idea of the superiority of Western legal and political structures and on a negative dialectic of the recognition. So these legal translations did not transfer something that already existed, but they produced betrayals, adaptations and profound changes. Furthermore, they were not only horizontal (and unidirectional), internal to the same temporal dimension, moving of people and texts from the West to the East and then to the African colonies, but were also vertical.[42] The European lawyers moved freely through time, using for the interpretation of the colonial reality legal categories from the old regime and rediscovering outside the Western borders the centrality of the executive power now incompatible with the separation of powers of the Rule of Law. It was a complex operation that can be found in the early twentieth century, and it shows surprising similarities with other 'borderline' cases (such as the state of siege, the state of exception, the international emergency, or the military occupation). In these hypotheses, the resistance of the legal order seemed to be assured only through the suspension of the guarantees of the Rule of Law.

The exceptionality of the non-Western World produced a temporal displacement. It seemed to exist in a different time period to that of the metropolis, in a period that could be compared with that of the European *Ancient Regime*. Juridical modernity resurrected pre-modernity and, citing the temporal difference between the centre and the periphery, defined the latter as different. It appeared as a remnant of the past or a remote realm which could be penetrated by the advantageous effects of the modern era and could become an object of its myths. However, the history of the colony had yet to begin, or had begun at precisely the same moment that European colonization started. Through this temporal disconnection, it was possible to maintain a unified concept of the legal order. It permitted the co-existence of the exceptionality of consular and colonial law, on one hand, and of the Rule of Law of the metropolis, on the other hand, and it thereby created a unique cross-temporal

42 Luigi Nuzzo, *Spatial and Temporal dimension of Legal History: International Law, Foreign Policy and the Construction of a Legal Order*, in Gunther Hellmann, Andreas Fahrmaier, Milos Vec (eds.), *The Transformation of Foreign Policy. Drawing and Managing Boundaries from Antiquity to the Present* (Oxford University Press, 2016), pp. 158–161.

unity between the pre-modern past of Christian Europe and the colonial present.

The entrance of China into the 'family of nations', therefore, was possible by suspending the application of international law and by devolving the relations between Western States and the Celestial Empire to diplomatic practice and to consular law. China still had limited legal subjectivity. It lived in an exceptional condition that prevented it from participating in the production of international law which justified the application of exceptional measures. It was a country with limited sovereignty in which the modern principle of legal territoriality was replaced by the pre-modern principle of legal personality. Apart from Christianity, whose missionary activity has been largely tolerated in China, the Middle Kingdom had not reached a sufficient level of civilization that would have allowed it stand on an equal footing with the United States and the European powers. In the meantime, diplomacy, since the 1840s, had allowed China to enjoy the (poisoned) fruits of the Christian international law, projecting into the East the system of capitulations to which the Muslim countries had been subjected from the previous century.

3 The Ambiguous Origins of a Colonial City

The treaties of 1858 which ended the second Opium War also traced the beginning of Tianjin's history as an imperial location. However, in the homonymous treaties China stipulated with Great Britain and France, it did not show the list of the new open ports.[43] Its inclusion was decided only two years later with the

43 *Treaty of Peace, Friendship, Commerce and Navigation between her Majesty the Queen of Great Britain and Ireland and the Emperor of China*, 26.6.1858, in *Treaties between the Empire of China and the Foreign Powers together with Regulations for the Conduct of Foreign Trade, Conventions, Agreement, Regulations* (1877), by William Frederick Mayers, 5. ed. (Shanghai: North Herald, 1903), art 11: 'In addition to the Cities and Towns of Canton, Amoy, Foochow, Ningpo and Shanghai, opened by the Treaty of Nanking, it is agreed that British subjects may frequent the Cities and Ports of Newchwang, Tängchow, Taiwan [Formosa], Chawchow [Swatow] and Kiungchow [Hainan]. They are permitted to carry on trade with whomsoever they please, and to proceed to and fro at pleasure with their Vessels and Merchandise. They shall enjoy the same privileges, advantages and immunities at the said towns and Ports as they enjoy at the Ports already opened to trade, including the right of residence, of buying or renting Houses, of leasing Land therein, and of building Churches, Hospitals and Cemeteries'. In the homologous treaty ratified with France on 27 June 1858 art. VI 'Experience proves that opening new ports to trade from abroad is one of the needs of the times, and so it has been agreed that the ports of Qiongzhou and Chaozhou in the Guangdong Province; Taiwan [Taibei] and Tanshui in the Isle of Formosa, Fujian Province; Dengzhou in Shandong Province; and Nanjing in Kiang-nan

Bejing Convention, the agreement following the entrance of Anglo-French troops into this city and the destruction of the Summer Palace. The Convention decreed, with the exchange of ratifications, the going into effect of the Tianjin treaty, setting the compensation China had to pay to France and Great Britain to sixteen million *taels*, and finally decreed that both the town and the harbour of Tianjin should be open to Western trade under the same conditions as those established for the other treaty ports of the empire.[44]

A few months later, between the end of 1860 and the first months of 1861, the Chinese authorities allowed the British and French and, by virtue of the clause of the most privileged nation, the Americans, three plots of land along the Hai River for the construction of their settlements. The British settled a few miles south of Tianjin in an area inside the Southern walls of the town and the river.

In the table of contents of the volume of the *Treaties Series* dedicated to the treaties stipulated between Great Britain and China the agreement concerning Tianjin is listed as signed only on September 3, 1861 and as the last in a series of leases allowing the European power to have its own concessions in Chinkiang (23 February 1861), Hankow (21 March 1861), and Kiunkiang (25 March 1861), and to widen the already existing one in Canton.[45] But this contract seems to have disappeared. As the British consul Byron Brennan wrote to Thomas G.

[Jiangsu] Province, will enjoy the same privileges as Canton [Guangzhou], Shanghai, Ningbo, Amoy [Xiamen] and Fuzhou. As for Nanjing, French agents in China will deliver no passports to their citizens for that city, except when the rebels there have been driven out by imperial troops' (English version online at <http://www.chinaforeignrelations.net/node/162>). The ports open for Russian trade and people were Shanghai, Ningpo, Fuchow-fu, Amoy, Canton, Taiwan-fu (on the Isle of Formosa), Khioung-Cheou-fu (on the Isle of Hainan) (Treaty of Tianjin 1/13.6.1858, art. 3 <http://www.chinaforeignrelations.net/node/233>). The United States, by a clause for the most favoured nation, obtained the right for their citizens to live in any port or place open to Western powers (Treaty of Tianjin 18.6.1858 art. XIV, <http://www.chinaforeignrelations.net/node/206>).

44 The opening of the port of Tianjin was foreseen in art. IV of the Beijing convention ratified with Great Britain on 24 October 1860 and art. VII of the homologous convention between France and China was ratified on the following day. Also the Czarist Empire signed an agreement with China. Anyhow, the Russian 'version' of the Beijing Convention did not consider Tianjin, but foresaw the opening of Kashgar to Russian trade 'on the same basis as at Ili and Tarbagatay. At Kashgar, the Chinese cede a lot big enough to hold a warehouse and all associated buildings, such as dwellings, stockrooms, church, and also a lot for a cemetery, and pastures as well, as at Ili and Tarbagatay. Orders will immediately be given to the governor of Kashgar to work out these concessions'. The Conventions ratified in Beijing by China, Great Britain, France and Russia are published on line in <http://www.chinaforeignrelations.net>.

45 Annex 7, Tien-Tsin, British Concession, in Lease Treaty Series N. 34 (1925), List of Treaties, &c., between Great Britain and China (1842–1922), including International Treaties, and

Grosvenor, British chargé d'affaires in Beijing, in fact, 'no formal lease for the British concession at Tientsin has been issued by the Chinese Government'.[46] Thus the only prove of the existence of the agreement is a receipt issued by the Chinese district officer concerning the payment of the annual fee carried out by the British consul and diligently reported in the volume: 'To annual rent for the year ending, paid to the Chinese – Government for the British concession at Tientsin, known by the name of Tan Chu Lin, viz., 412 mou, 6t. 5m. Se. at 1,500 copper cash per mou = 618,987 copper cash'.[47]

FIGURE 1 Plan showing the present state of the British settlement of Tientsin[48]

Treaties between Great Britain and Foreign Powers relating to China, London printed and published by his Majesty's stationery office, 1925, p. 26 [s. also n. 72].

46 Brennan to Grosvenor, Tienstin, 15, February 1883, in National Archives (thereafter TNA), FO 228/731. Brennan reported a dispatch of January, 6, 1877 written by the British consul in Tianjin, Mongan. The same statement is reported with no indication of the source in the Annex 7 Tien-Tsin, British Concession, p. 26.

47 Annex 7, Tien-Tsin, British Concession, p. 26.

48 TNA: FO, MPKK 1/50/9, Plan showing the present state of the British Settlement of Tienstin 1865.

Already in August 1860, however, Tientsin had been occupied by the allied forces. The Chinese authorities had been allowed to continue to administer the city, but they were now placed under the strict British control and had to work together, providing adequate assistance to the British troops who moved on to conquest Beijing. To this end Admiral James Hope had left in Tianjin his interpreter, Harry Parkes, who took charge to select the most suitable accommodation for Lord Elgin and find the buildings that could have been allocated to the public service.[49] One month after the Beijing Convention had transformed Tianjin into an open port, the same Parkes issued a memorandum in which he singled out the borders of the British settlement. This seems to be the first and unique document that recognized and presupposed the right of Great Britain to have its own space, fixing the lines of the future development of the British concession.[50] But yet at the first glance this text presents relevant problems. I do not know if somewhere in the files of the National Archive there is a official copy that I was not able to find, but the version I saw is so hurriedly written, so full of corrections and cuts that it is hard to consider it more than a simple draft.[51] Thirteen years later, a more readable copy is attached, together with other relevant documents, to a letter written by the English consul at Tianjin, Mongan, and addressed to Hornby, Chief Justice in Shanghai. If this confirms the importance of the Parkes' memorandum and reinforces its image as constitutive act of the English presence in Tianjin, the strange feeling of uncertainty and ambiguity that it transmit does not however disappear. On the one hand it seems to be destined to both Chinese and Britons. A Chinese officer and a member of prince Sengerinchen's Committee of supplies are mentioned assisting Parkes in the procedure of border's definition, the Chinese village is named with its own Chinese name, the unit of land measurement is a Chinese one, the *zhang*.[52] On the other hand the document was signed only by Parkes, the annual rent to be paid to the Chinese government had to be determined and also the dimension of the area had not still been exactly calculated.

Parkes, anyway, estimated it correctly at around 430/440 mou, fixed the rates of the land tax and traced the borders of the settlement.[53] They run clearly

---

49 Harry S. Parkes to James Bruce, Lord of Elgin, Tientsin, August, 26, 1860, in *Correspondence respecting Affairs in China*, 1859–1860 (Harrison and Sons, 1861) 127.

50 Harry S. Parkes, *Land Memorandum*, Tientsin, November, 25, 1860, in TNA: FO, 674/1.

51 A easier version to read is in TNA: FO 656/44 as attachment to a letter written by the British consul at Tianjin, Mongan, on 26 august, 1873 at Tientsin and addressed to Edmund Hornby, Chief Justice in Shanghai.

52 In the version enclosed to the letter of 1873 (TNA: FO 656/44) addressed to Hornby, the Chinese village is no more written with Chinese characters.

53 'The whole of this ground – stated Parkes, *Land Memorandum*, TNA: FO, 674/1 – is classed as *yuen te* or garden ground and it pays land tax at the various rates. The amount due on

from north to south following a line of about one kilometres belong the river and assuming as point of reference trees, docks, huts and wells. The Northern end on the river side was marked 'by a large tree, at the foot of which are two wells and a small boat dock'. In the same way a 'large single tree on the East bank of the river in line with a small single tree on the West side a short distance from the bank' marked the southern limit of this line. Finally a hut within a few feet of that point had the task to make still more clear the terminal point of the line. For this purpose Parkes carved on one of the beams of the roof of the hut the following inscription: '255 *chang* Nov. 23. 1860' and wrote the same thing on a sheet posted on the wall of the hut itself.

On the opposite side, Taku road, the main road, marked the Western boundaries. 'At the Northern end it is a 120 *chang* from the river's bank to the road. At the southern end it is 91 *chang* from the River to the road'.[54]

Situated two miles south of the Chinese city of Tianjin, the site that has been selected, however, was a not blank space. And probably this was the main problem. It included a Chinese village and a village meant huts, graves and buildings to demolish and people to move. As a matter of fact Great Britain as well as all the occupying allied forces could not accept the Chinese presence for different reasons that affected, as we will see, the symbolic, the economic and the legal level. The memorandum, therefore, had to fix clearly the terms of the expropriation, compensation and expulsion of the people of the Zizhulin village from their own land.

Every landowner was entitled to receive 30 taels per mou plus another 10 taels as compensation for having be removed. The value of huts and buildings had to be refunded, but as long as the Chinese continued to occupy the ground, the English were exempted to pay the land tax to the Chinese Government.[55]

The memorandum does not add anything more and it substantially improved the right of occupation recognized by Article IV of the Beijing Convention, giving legal shape to the agreements reached by Harry Parkes and captain Gordon with the Chinese authorities. We have to look at others lease agreements stipulated by the British Crown for the settlements of Canton, Chinkiang, Hankow and Kiunkiang, in order to identify the legal theoretical framework within which we can trace back the Tianjin agreement. In all these cases, the Crown in fact turned to a standardized model. It was a strange

---

the whole area which can be accurately ascertained by the magistracy will probably be found to be under eighty taels which sum it is agreed is to be paid by the English and French if they join the arrangement'.

54 Harry S. Parkes, *Land Memorandum*.

55 If the English were exempted to pay the land tax to Chinese government until the Chinese refused to leave their properties, they were not allowed to build new buildings.

contract of tenancy without a temporary expiry concerning a variable plot of land, the rent of which was to be paid annually. With the signing of the contract and the concurring payment of the first year's rent, the land might be considered the property of the British Crown and subject to the full jurisdiction of the consular magistracy. As is shown from the lease concerning Hankow, a densely populated fluvial town that towards the end of the nineteenth century became also the seat of the German, French, Russian and Japanese settlements, the British consul, the Chinese district prefect and the magistrate should have summoned the land and stock owners within the concessions, asking them to present their instruments, and then look to the payment of the indemnity of expropriation. Possible conflicts would then have been resolved by referring to equative criteria.[56]

But go back to Tianjin. Just few days after Parkes issued his memorandum, Lord Elgin requested Prince Gong to lease in perpetuity an area of 440 mou south of Tianjin with the agreement that the Chinese inhabitants should be evacuated and their possessions expropriated, and confirmed the indemnity at 30 taels per mou. Contextually Gong asked to the Viceroy of Zhili to collaborate with the English in the management of the lease agreement and in the construction of the consulate building.[57]

According to the instructions of Parkes and Prince Gong, by the end of December 1860, Mongan, appointed the same month as acting consul at Tianjin, had marked the borders of the settlement and planted four boundary stones. In the first months of the following year, he sent to the British ambassador in Beijing, two plans executed by captain Gordon. The first one concerned the settlement and showed the project of land division in lots, the proposed position of the street, the site of the factories and finally the Chinese properties within the site. The second plan focused on the Chinese city and its suburbs, pointing out the quarters occupied by the allied troops. Mongan asked that both plans would be lithographed and published in the *North Chinese*

56 Annex 2, Hankow Lease (March, 21, 1861), in Lease Treaty Series N. 34 (1925), 19: 'the authorities will then and there decide the price to be paid in each case - whether the property to be purchased consist of Government buildings or temples, or of houses, huts, or other constructions belonging to the people - according to the size, description, and situation of the land or building, the people not being allowed to raise their prices, nor the British subject being at liberty to compel the people to accept his valuation, but equity in every case being so maintained that neither one party nor the other shall incur loss. The removal of the houses and the delivery of the land shall take place simultaneously with the payment of the money, and the land may be entered on and possessed as British property from the date of the payment'.

57 National Archives, TNA: FO 682/1993/93, Lord Elgin to Prince Gong 04.12.1860; Prince Gong in TNA: FO 682/1993/97.

Herald of Shanghai.[58] The future of the settlement passed through the quick sale of the lots. It was therefore necessary to attract investors, by defining a clear development plan that let glimpse real prospects for enrichment. Tianjin had a bad reputation. Only two years before, Laurent Oliphant entering in the city with James Bruce, had written that 'to contain half a million of inhabitants, Tientsin was the most squalid, impoverished-looking place we had ever been in. [...] In no part of the world – he wrote – have I ever witnessed a more squalid, diseased population than that which seemed rather to infest than inhabit the suburbs of the city. Filth, nakedness and itch, were their prevailing characteristics'.[59] Years later, Alexander Michie, in an article published in the *Tienstin Express* and William Mc Leish, in a conference held at the China Society of London, added the 'well known' aptitude to crime and violence of Tianjin 'bullies', 'the most wicked and predatory turbulent race in the Empire'.[60] Not only the people but also the nature was hostile in Tianjin. The winters were freezing and the summers humid and hot. And the Hai, the great river that puts Tianjin in communication with Beijing and the see, runs impetuously 'in the shape of corncrew' carrying with it a large quantity of mud and rendering difficult the navigation.[61] As the Western military and civil reports stressed, due to the inadequacy of the leaves and the lower level of the belonging grounds, the river frequently flooded and wiped out the huts that were along the banks.[62]

58 Mongan to Bruce, April, 4, 1861, in TNA: FO, 674/1.

59 Laurent Oliphant, *Narrative of the Earl of Elgin's Mission to China and Japan in the Years 1857, 1858, 1859*, vol. 1 (Blackwood and Sons: 1859) 385 and 399.

60 A large passage of the Alexander Michie's book, published in 1886 in the Tientsin Express, is quoted by Rasmussen, Tientsin, 37. Willian Mc Leish, Life in China Outport (Tientsin: press limited: 1917) 24. The text of Mcleish, former secretary to the British Municipal Council of Tianjin, is now more easily accessible thanks to the Virtual Tianjin project (http://tianjin.virtualcities.fr/Texts/E-Library?ID=250).

61 *Guide to Tientsin* (Tientsin: press: 1904) 1. 'The Chinese authorities – we red in the report of the British Consul J. Mongan, *Report on the Trade of Consular District of Tientsin for the year 1866*, Tientsin: April 17, 1867, in *Accounts and papers of the House of Commons*, vol. 68, 144 have endeavored to mitigate the evils arising from the sinuosity of the stream, and the number of the grain junks, by fixing the strong wooden posts at eight of the sharpest bends in the river to aid vessels in hauling round these bends, and by framing regulations for the junks to prevent collisions between them and foreign vessels'.

62 The mud carried by the Hai River affected heavily on the water's level and consequently caused serious inconvenience to navigation. For example, the German consul remembered the case of a boat that had been moored at a point of the river where the water depth was 11 eet. The next day it was founded resting on the bottom, because during night the stream had deposited a layer of mud 3 feet tall. The boat had taken had taken 14 days to cover the 40 miles necessary to reach Dagu. The debris and mud dragged by the river and even more

At the same time, the river determined the strategic importance of Tianjin on an economic, a political and a military level. Situated at the center of a great water basin, Tianjin could become an extraordinary market for the Indian opium and the British products (especially cotton and woolens goods) in the north of China, as well as a good port from which Chinese cotton and tobacco could be exported to the United Kingdom. Not by chance the British and the other foreign settlements were placed along both sides of the Hai River and all the consuls deserved a great attention to the river, planning strong interventions to facilitate the navigation, to ensure the river conservancy and protect the ground along the river. As Shirley Ye recently pointed out, this led in 1897, just after the great flood of the year before, to the founding of the Hai River Conservancy Commission. It was an interesting mixed commission appointed by Li Hongzang, the governor general of Zhili, the consuls of Great Britain and France and the chairman of the general commerce chamber of Tianjin, with which Chinese and Western actors tried to find a way of cooperation in order to overcome the problems affecting the Chinese and Western vessels.[63]

The first British Consul in Tianjin, James Mongan, was also conscious that the future of the city and the English settlement depended on the river. On the one hand, it was necessary to control militarily the river traffic by imposing limits on the navigation of Chinese junks and harshly suppressing smuggling and piracy. On the other hand it was crucial, at the time when the river was opened, to fix certain customs rules. The Custom Houses system, re-established in 1854 at Shanghai with the participation of foreigners as inspectors, was going to be extended also in Tianjin, but the condition of trade still looked a little confused.[64] In April 1861 the inspector general of Maritime Customs Horatio

the stream of the river as well as the antagonistic action of the waves of the sea have formed a great submerged shoal called the bar (Mongan, *Report*, 1459). S. also the report of the U.S. Liutenant J.t. Dickman, Pekin, 5, November 1900, in *Report on Military Operations in South Africa and China* (Washington: Government printing office, 1901) 493–498.

63 Shirly Ye, Interport Printing Enterprise: Macanese Printing Networks in Chinese Treaty Ports, in Robert Bickers and Isabella Jackson (eds.), *Treaty Port in Modern China: Law, Land and Power* (London: Routledge, 2016) 121–138.

64 Hans Van de Ven, *Breaking with the past The Maritime Customs Service and the Global Origins of Modernity in China* (New York: Columbia University Press, 2014) 31. The first board of Inspectors consisted of Arthur Smith, interpreter at the France Consulate Lewis Carr, interpreter at the American Legation Thomas Francis Wade, British Vice-Consul who was the first inspector general (1854–1855). The board was appointed on July 1854. A good synthesis in Robert Bickers, 'Good Work for China in every possible direction'. The Foreign Inspectorate of Chinese Maritime Customs 1854–1950, in Bryna Goodman and David S.G. Goodmann, (eds.), *Twentieth-Century Colonialism and China: localities, the everyday and the world* (London: Routledge, 2012) 25–37.

Lay was leaving for Great Britain, formally 'on sick leave', and came back to China only two years later.[65] Fitzroy and Hart were appointed by prince Gong to exercise the functions of inspector general from May on but, as Mongan wrote to Bruce, 'the arrival of foreign shipping may be daily expected'. Thus it was not possible to wait any longer. It was necessary to introduce immediately that system of policing and taxation which characterized the Chinese custom institutions, pursuing at the port of Tianjin a close cooperation between British and Chinese officers. Therefore, in agreement with Chung Hou, the Superintendent of Trade of the three northern ports, Mongan elaborated a short regulation and on March 12 sent it to Bruce in Shanghai.[66] Obviously the consul knew that it could be only a temporary set of rules and that it probably would have to be modified by the Custom service when Tianjin was included within the system of the Custom Houses. His regulation was very short, only six articles. It provided for the opening of a Custom House for foreign shipping at the northern extremity of the settlement and for an Office of general Inspection at Dagu. In this way any British merchant vessel entering in the Hai River could easily be boarded and visited by a Custom House Officer who would remain on board until they reached the point of anchorage at Tientsin. The day after the anchorage, according to the prescription of art. 37 of the treaty of Tianjin, the ship's papers had to be lodged to the consul who, within the next twenty-four hours, reported the name and the tonnage of the ship as well as the nature of the cargo to the Superintendent of Custom in order to determine the amount of the duties and custom charges.[67] On April 19th Chung Hou officially opened a new Custom House along the Hai River at the Chinese village of Zizhulin, that was exactly within the English settlement. The new Custom

65 Mongan to Bruce, Tientsin, March 12, 1861, in TNA: FO 674/3. Lay went back in China on may 1863 and was replaced by Hart in November 1863 following the clash with the prince Gong on control, use and financing of the British fleet of warships known with the name of Lay-Osborne Flotilla. See Van de Ven, *Breaking with the past The Maritime Customs Service and the Global Origins of Modernity in China* (New York: Columbia University Press, 2014); Jack Gerson, *Horatio Nelson Lay and Sino-British Relations, 1854–1864* (Cambridge: Harvard University Press, 1972).

66 Mongan to Bruce, Tientsin, March 12, 1861, in TNA: FO 674/3. Bruce shall acknowledge receipt of the letter on June 4, 1861.

67 Mongan to Bruce, Tientsin, March 12, 1861, in TNA: FO 674/3. The problems produced by the frequent and rapid change of the depth of Hai River's water level justified, in the Mongan's regulation, the introduction of a derogation of art. 37 of Tianjin treaty: 'The time allowed in Art. 37 of the Treaty of Tientsin – we read in the art. 4 – for lodging the ship's papers in the hands of the consul at Tientsin, is extended to seventy two hours in the case of a merchant vessel whose draught of water is such as to necessitate her anchoring outside the bar of the Peiho; and if this rule be not complied within ninety six hours, the penalties which are laid down, in the above named article of the traty aforesaid will be enforced'.

House was added to the old one and, according to the Superintendent, would have to collect the duties on all goods imported and exported by foreign merchant vessels. On the contrary the old Custom House would be competent in the event that the goods had travelled on native crafts, and if it were Chinese products.[68] But paradoxically, while Chung Hou was still referring to the Chinese village as spacial marker of the Custom House's site, the village itself was going to disappear. As a matter of fact, between March and April 1861, Mongan had partitioned the ground in 30 lots, and reserved four for Consular purpose, and was planning the sale of the remaining 26 others.[69] Thanks to the Hai River and its huge basin and net of canals, Tianjin became the hub of the British Empire in northern China. In this way the British settlement would have attracted the interest of the investors. The English Consul was sure to receive a great number of applications as well as to sell quickly the lots along the Hai River. He believed that buying up one of these lots would have been so important for the development of the entrepreneurial activity that he requested the purchasers not only to contribute like everyone else at the urbanization process of the settlements (provision of roads, leveling of land etc.) but also to build the bund along the water front on their own expenses. At the same time, in addition to the cooperation to which the English businessmen were invited, Mongan was equally convinced that the involvement of the Chinese government was necessary for a rapid improvement of the English settlement and paradoxically to free the settlement itself from the Chinese that lived there.

As Parkes had already pointed out in his memorandum, the Chinese had in fact to leave their land and properties. It was therefore necessary to proceed to a careful list of all Chinese householders and to the determination of the value of each house. At the same time the English officers were required to check their results with the data held by the Chinese government and balance the amount of the reimbursement they proposed with the economical requests demanded by the Chinese government. Finally he presented his idea of development of the settlement suggesting to Bruce some solutions concerning the lots for sale. As regards the place and the mode, trying to prevent speculations or concentrations of real estate in the hands of few investors, Mongan would have preferred to sale the land to the local residents and exclude the possibility to apply, at least in first instance, for more than one lot. If there were several requests for the same lot, it should have been sold by public auction on the

68 Chung Hou to Mongan, Tienstin April 19, 1861, in TNA: FO 673/1.

69 Mongan to Hornby, Tientsin 26 August 1873, in TNA: FO 656/44. 'The four lots situated on the Northern side of the settlement, adjoining the French concession, were afterwards given up by Mr. Gibson to Chung Hou, the Chinese Minister superintendent who had applied for some land in that position as a site for the Foreign Custom House'.

principle of the highest bidder. If on the contrary some lots did not receive an offer, the limitation of one lot per head would be removed.

Finally as regards the time of the sale Mongan suggested that all the applications were to be sent by May 31st at the British Consulate at Tianjin and that the sale would take place the day after, giving before the end of April sufficient notice of the plans of the site, the conditions of the sale and of the detailed schedule of each lot together with the assessed value of Chinese buildings eventually encompassed within the single lots.[70]

A few days before, the acting Inspector general Robert Hart and the French secretary of legation and Commissioner of Custom at Tianjin, Michael Kleczkowski, arrived in town in order to carry into effect the prescriptions concerning the custom aspects of the treaty of Tianjin. At the same time Chung Hou sent the final Tientsin Custom House regulations to Mongan, asking him to transmit them to the British merchants residing at that port.[71]

On 29 August 1861, Gibson who, due the illness of Mongan, was acting consul, started the first land sale. One month later, Bruce authorized the addition of another tract of land on the southern side of the settlement that had to compensate the four lots placed at the of the Chinese Government. At the beginning of 1862, he sanctioned 'the purchase of a new strip of land on the south side for the excavation of a canal from the Peiho River on the East, and to the Taku road on the West', establishing definitively the southern border of the concession. The sales were a great success and at the end of September 1863 all the lots had been sold. A formal lease agreement was still missing but the receipt of the first ground rent paid to the Chinese Government could be considered by now as a sufficient proof of the English rights on Tianjin. Nevertheless, between 1863 and 1865, there were still disagreements between Gibson and the Tianjin authorities on the extension of the concession and consequently about the rent to pay. According to the information sent by Mongan, it was estimated at mou 425 5.5.6 and rent at copper cash 638.732. In 1865 Mongan resumed the charge of Consul and compared the English land register with the leases, ascertaining that 'the total area of all the lots was mou 412 6.5.8 and that the total of the ground rent payable on these amounts at 1500 copper cash per mou; if computed in the aggregate, itwas 618.987, and 618.985 if computed *seriatim*'. Thus he proposed to the Chinese local authorities to accept the aggregate of these rents as the annual rent for the whole settlement payable each year. They agreed and Mongan received the approval by sir Alcock, the British plenipotentiary minister and Chief Superintendant of the Trade. Since then the annual

70 Mongan to Bruce, Tientsin April, 4, 1861, in TNA: FO 674/1.

71 Chung Hou to Mongan, May 22, 1861 in TNA: FO 673/1.

ground rent amounted to 618.985 copper cash, testifying that 'the Tse-Chu Lin is in consideration of the above yearly payment rented in perpetuity by the British Government'.[72]

Within the settlement every leases lasted for 99 years, foresaw the payment of a rent of 1.500 copper cash per *mou*, and compelled the leaseholders to contribute to the cost of building, repair and lighting of the road in the concession, to its security, and generally to its improvement.[73] In 1862 the land renters elected the municipal council and between the end of October 1863 (27 October) and 1 June 1864 the first local land regulations of the concession were published. Yet in November 1866 they were abrogated by Rutherford Alcock, the British plenipotentiary minister and Chief Superintendant of the Trade, who took care of the issue of new regulations for the lands within the concession and for the administration of the consular district of Tianjin.[74] Both were issued by virtue of an Order in Council for China and Japan of the year before, which reserved to the Crown the right to issue the necessary regulations for the good administration of its consular districts and for the good government of the British living within the treaty ports. The Tientsin local land regulations and general regulations were binding for every British citizen dwelling or living within the settlement.

Four boundary stones marked the borders and delineated the space of the British concession from the French and American ones. The simple definition of a British area was not sufficient to guarantee its transformation into a new social space. In order to reach this aim, it was necessary that the territory, once militarily occupied, conceded and measured, was actually inhabited, in other words spoke English. This meant traces indelibly showing the authority of the British Crown were necessary. New political, economic, juridical, and architectonic practices were able to impress the territory of the concession with a deep

72 Mongan to Hornby, Tientsin, August, 26 1873, in TNA: FO 656/44. The receipt of 1865 became the official receipt and was edited in Annex 7, Tien-Tsin, British Concession, in Lease Treaty Series N. 34 (1925), List of Treaties, &c., between Great Britain and China (1842–1922), including International Treaties, and Treaties between Great Britain and Foreign Powers relating to China, London printed and published by his Majesty's stationery office, 1925, p. 26. [s. n. 45].

73 A list of the first owners is in Foreign Office, Consulate of Tientsin, TNA: FO 678/1292. Other information about the first European living in Tianjin in Rasmussen, *Tientsin*, 39–44.

74 *Tientsin Local Land Regulations and General Regulations*, 26.11.1866, (Hong Kong: Noronha, 1866). Thirty-three years later on the occasion of the enlargement of the concession the British government issued new Land Regulations, Tientsin, 31.3.1899, *Land Regulations*, Bundesarchiv, Berlin Lichterfelde, R 901/30918, 4–23.

social transformation.[75] This was not a simple operation. The British settlement as well as the French and the others ones which were set up during the nineteenth and the beginning of the twentieth century, were a legally ambiguous space that seemed to be still menaced by ageless medieval categories of *dominium directum* and *dominium utile.* The recourse to the concept of concession and the payment of a yearly fee to the local authorities allowed to recognize at least formally the Chinese sovereignty over the territory of the concession. At the same time the continuation of the assignment, the forced expropriation of Chinese property, the expulsion of local people and the recognition of a full jurisdiction in favour of the occupying powers seemed to break irreparably the relationship between the Chinese State and the territory within the concessions, making the cession perfect and creating real territorial rights. Thus, the Local Land Regulations and the General Regulations were the first attempt to give the new space a juridical order and represented a model for all the other concessionary powers. As a matter of fact they are detailed regulations aimed at carefully and accurately regulating the life inside the settlement, proceeding towards the definition of the inner and outer space of the concession. After fixing its borders, identifying the plots to be subleased, and determining the cost of each unit (*mou*) of land, the Crown was concerned with making the territory of the concession homogenous by defining the qualifications required in a land renter. Citizens and naturalized British should obviously be the first lessees of the territories within the concessions, but foreigners were not excluded.[76] They could also buy plots of land, provided that they both observed expressly the norms contained in the Land Regulations and in the Bye Laws issued for the concession, and that they obtained 'the officially certified consent of their national authority'. But what about the Chinese? Could they be considered foreigners in their mother country and thus legitimized to buy land within the concession? Or did the formal fact of the recognition that the territory within the British settlement belonged to China and that it was the owner of an ultimate sovereignty withdraw them from the status of foreigners and, at the same time, seemed paradoxically not sufficient to protect them from expulsions and forced expropriations? The Land and General Regulations did not offer a clear and direct answer to this question, but they offered meaningful directions. Indeed, they gave the consular authority the right to rescind the subleases stipulated with foreign citizens when the

75 On the architectural transformations in the English settlement s. Dana Arnold, *Construire la modernité urbaine: la concession britannique à Tianjin, 1860–2013*, in *Outre-Mers. Revue d'histoire*, 382/383 (2014), 89–102.

76 British citizens also might lease land outside the settlement. The General Regulations following the Land Regulations foresaw as well the possibility of a lease by Chinese citizens presenting an instance to the consul containing any necessary data.

concessioner violated any regulations. Independent from the concessioner's nationality, however, it was possible to rescind the leasing contract and take back the possession of the land if the lessee allowed that Chinese citizens built or occupied a house inside the concession. The architectural, cultural, economic, social and juridical homogenization of the territory could support the presence of other Western citizens, if they respected British rules, but not the persistence of Chinese citizens. On the one hand it was necessary to carry out the expropriation of their possessions and the expulsion of those who were still within the concession, just as Lord Elgin had been asking prince Gong to do since 1860; on the other hand it had to be avoided (or at least try to avoid) a situation where the Chinese came back to live within the concession.[77]

Reaching these goals meant to define an efficient administrative system able to connect the government and renters. The concession had to become a British trade outpost in northern China, but the entrepreneurs had to take the burden of Chinese land tax on them, essentially repaying the Crown the sums advanced to lease the land, and the expenses necessary for the development and the administration of the concession.[78]

The entrepreneurs themselves, called annually by the consul – who was the chairman ex officio of all the general meetings of land renters – established how much each leaser had to pay in proportion to the land owned and defined the scale of wharfage dues and mooring charges. During this meeting the assembly elected an executive committee composed of three to five members and a chairman. The committee had the power and authority to levy and apply the rates and taxes, to administrate the municipal funds and to issue normative measures (Bye-Laws) necessary to reach the goals fixed by the assembly of leasers. Once adopted by the assembly and approved by the consul, the Bye-Laws issued by the committee had the same efficiency as did the Land and General Regulations.

---

77 In 1873 the British Consul Mongan, writing to Hornby, Tientsin, August, 26 1873, in TNA: FO 656/44, stressed the importance of a relaxed application of the prohibition to sell a lot of the English settlement to a Chinese: 'the progress of events within the last six years (which period has been commercially characterized, first by the substitution of shipping agencies for the more purely mercantile agencies at this port, and secondly, by the establishment of a Chinese steamer company, which now competes with our steamer in the carrying trade), has rendered it still further expedient to relax the provision made in Rule IV against a Chinese subject being allowed to become a land renter'. According to Mongan it would be sufficient on the one hand that the Chinese obtained a special permission by the English Ambassador; on the other hand that he accepted to conform 'to the same conditions of tenure as those under which land is now held in the settlement by other non-British subjects'.

78 The tax amounts to 1500 copper cash per *mou* and had to be paid within 21 days after 30 September, every year (art. 6).

The consul also had the duty of calling the assembly when it seemed necessary, or when the chairman of the land renters' committee or at least five owners asked for it. The validity of the decisions taken by the general assembly on questions of municipal character and of general interest was also subordinated to the chairman's approval. It was possible to present an appeal against the decision of the consul to the ambassador in Beijing within seven days.

The consular police and the private police corps chosen by the land owners had the right to arrest anyone who was caught red-handed within the settlement in not particularly serious circumstances such as public nuisance, theft, drunkenness or other 'disorderly' behaviours. The consul then had to verify the accusations and make a decision in obedience to British law if the accused was of British nationality. Otherwise he had to transfer the charge to the accused person's consular authority and entrust him to its custody. For accused people wo did not have a consular representative in Tianjin, however, the only option was the Chinese jails, and the only Western 'guarantee' was assured by the presence of a consular official (assessor) in the court.

The administrative system chosen by the Crown produced the expected fruits and soon the settlement became a model for the other European powers. As was pointed out in August 1896 in a memorandum written by the German Consul in Tianjin, Ludwig Loeper, and addressed to the Ambassador in Beijing, Gustav Adolf Freiherr Schenck zu Schweinsberg, the Crown and the municipal authority had been very skilled to define which lands were to be subleased to the best bidder and which were to be destined to public purposes. Above all, by identifying clear rules to avoid real estate speculation, the development of the concession had been ensured. Thanks to the surplus resulting from the sale of land, from the revenue generated by the taxes on the vessel traffic and to the choice to impose on investors the urbanization costs of the neighbouring areas to the individual lots purchased, the Crown had been able to anticipate the sums needed for expropriation and the expulsion of the Chinese. At the same time, it had been able to carry out the necessary measures in order to replenish the lands along the river and to provide the settlement of docks and an adequate road network. Without the Chinese and well organized, the settlement had begun to attract British and Western investors, and only few lands were now owned by the Crown. This had led to fast rising prices within the settlement and to a new interest toward the Chinese properties that were outside the settlement itself or within the Chinese city of Tianjin.

Without hiding his amazement, the German consul pointed out that, in 1893, 24000 taels had been offered for a not particularly interesting plot of 11 *mou*, that was far from the river and without usable buildings. Three years later the offer was 27,000 taels against a request of 36,000. Outside the settlement the prices required by the Chinese owners had increased to 300 taels per *mou* if the land was located in the area between the settlement and the Chinese city while they oscillated, according to the replenishments required, between 100 and 140 taels per *mou* for the lands which were within the Chinese walls.[79]

At the end of the century, the land speculation had crossed the boundaries of the settlement and had reached the Chinese area. The British municipality, taking advantage of China's political weakness and fearing the competition of Japan, Germany and other Western powers that had already arrived or were ready to land in Tianjin claiming their share of the booty, began to buy land outside the settlement and prepare for the expansion of the settlement. The extension also resulted in the introduction of a new contractual system according to which the buyer no longer had to pay the entire price due for the 99 years of rent at the time of the contract, but just an annual fee. The lessee continued to have his title as a real owner, always without being formally authorized to sell to Chinese, but the lessor could easily adjust the rent to the rise in prices or to the increase of the demands.

4 The French Concession

Formally speaking, the English were not the first to obtain the recognition of the right to a concession on the right bank of the Hai River. On 29 May 1861 the commercial superintendent of the three northern ports, Chung Hou, issued a *Proclamation* establishing the borders of the future French concession and officially announcing its existence.[80] It was the response to a direct request by Auguste Trève, head of the French consulate in Tientsin, which the Chinese official had found established 'in law and justice'. In the archives of the Ministry of Foreign Affairs, the French request seems to have unfortunately disappeared. However, the *Proclamation* of Chung Hou allows us to understand more about the beginning of the French presence in the city of Tianjin.[81] Nevertheless it is the first official recognition of a French concession in Tianjin, the

79 Ludwig Loeper to Gustav Adolf Freiherr Schenck zu Schweinsberg Auswärtiges, August 1895, *Promemoria betreffend die Gründung einer deutschen Niederlassung in Tientsin*, in Politisches Archiv des Auswärtiges Amt, Berlin, RZ 9208 R 1040, B. 2, August 1895–Oktober 1895.

80 On the French presence in Tianjin Pierre Singaravélou, 'Dix empires en un mouchoir de poche, le territoire de Tienstin à l'épreuve de phénomène concessionaire (années 1860–1920)', in Hélène Blais, Florence Deprest and Pierre Singaravélou (eds.), *Territoires impériaux: Une histoire spatiale du fait colonial* (Paris: ed. de la Sorbonne, 2011), 271–295; and now Pierre Singaravelou, *Tianjin Cosmopolis. Une autre histoire de la mondialisation*, Paris, Seuil 2017.

81 Proclamation du Surintendant des trois ports du Nord à Tien-Tsin, 29, 5, 1861 in Archives du Ministère des affaires Étrangèrs (thereafter AMAE) (Paris), NS Chine, vol. 286, Concession française de Tientsin 1861–1897 (148 CPCOM P/19231).

latter was not simply the result of Chung Hou's act of grace, but it was founded on the formal authority of article 10 of the French and Chinese Treaty of Tianjin of 1858, expressly cited in the text. In fact, for French diplomacy, both from a legal and a symbolic point of vue, it appeared to be much more effective to ground the legitimacy of the French occupation on an international treaty rather than on an administrative act mentioning the unilateral intention of an 'obscure' Chinese superintendent.

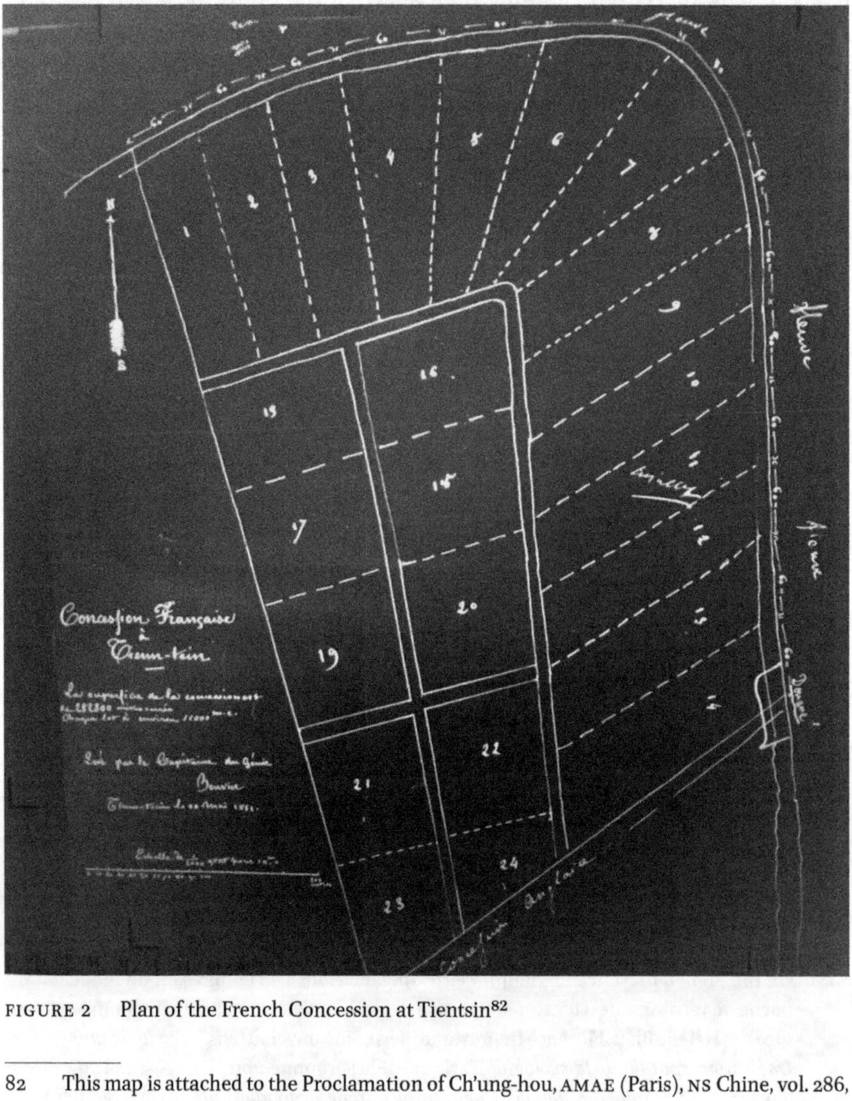

FIGURE 2 Plan of the French Concession at Tientsin[82]

82 This map is attached to the Proclamation of Ch'ung-hou, AMAE (Paris), NS Chine, vol. 286, Concession française de Tientsin 1861–1897 (148 CPCOM P/19231).

A few days later, the centrality of Article 10 was also confirmed by the *Règlement relatif à l'affermage à perpétuité des terrains dans les limites de la concession française a Tientsin* (2, 6, 1861), namely by the regulation that had been released on the basis of the declaration signed by the French secretary of legation, Michael Kleczkowski, and by the same Chinese superintendent.[83] In its introduction, it seemed appropriate to cite the present article also attributing to the French concession the right of perpetuity and full authority. Nevertheless, the article calls exclusively for the possibility of '*louer des maisons, des magazins ou bien affermer terrains et y bâtir lui-même des maisons et des magasins*', establishing its objective as the construction areas dedicated to the investment of French businesses in cities open to foreign commerce.[84] The perpetuity was therefore only a temporal factor which qualified the tenancy contract of the concession, but there was no element which imposed this

83 The regulation is attached to a letter from the French consul at Tianjin, Charles Dillon, adressed to the French Ambassador in Peking Fréderic Albert Bourée, Tientsin July 1881, AMAE (Nantes), Ambassade de France à Pékin 513po/1/262, Concession de Tientsin, dossier 36.

84 *Treaty of Peace, Friendship, Commerce and Navigation*, 26.6.1858 art. XII 'British subjects, whether at the Ports or at other places, desiring to build or open Houses, Warehouses, Churches, Hospitals, or Burial-grounds, shall make their agreement for the land or buildings they require, at the rates prevailing among the people, equitably and without exaction on either side'; 'Traité d'amitié, de commerce et de navigation conclu à Tien-Tsin, 27.6.1858', in Lucien de Reinach (ed.), *Recueil des Traités conclus par la France en Extrême Orient (1684–1902)* (Paris: Ernest Leroux, 1902), 52–53, art X: 'Tout Français qui, conformément aux stipulations de l'art. 6 du présent Traité, arrivera dans l'un des ports ouverts au commerce étranger, pourra, quelle que soit la durée de son séjour, y louer des maisons et des magasins pour déposer ses marchandises, ou bien affermer des terrains, et y bâtir lui-même des maisons et des magasins. Les Français pourront, de la même manière, établir des églises, des hôpitaux, des hospices, des écoles et des cimetières. Dans ce but, l'autorité locale, après s'être concertée avec le consul, désignera les quartiers les plus convenables pour la résidence des Français, et les endroits dans lesquels pourront avoir lieu les constructions précitées. Le prix des loyers et des fermages sera librement débattu entre les parties intéressées, et réglé, autant que faire se pourra, conformément à la moyenne des prix locaux. Les autorités chinoises empêcheront leurs nationaux de surfaire ou d'exiger des prix exorbitants, et le consul veillera, de son côté, à ce que les Français n'usent pas de violence ou de contrainte pour forcer le consentement des propriétaires. Il est bien entendu, d'ailleurs, que le nombre des maisons et l'étendue des terrains à affecter aux Français, dans les ports ouverts au commerce étranger, ne seront point limités, et qu'ils seront déterminés d'après les besoins et les convenances des ayants droit. Si des Chinois violaient ou détruisaient des églises ou des cimetières français, les coupables seraient punis suivant toute la rigueur des lois du pays'.

solution in the article or in fact in the entire treaty. The concession came about from the violence of a territorial occupation which no extensive interpretation of the treaty could have ever legitimised, and which the Chinese Empire would have been forced to endure under the principles of the most favoured nation whenever a new power requested it.

A few months later, the need to respond to the provisions in the Tianjin Treaty led Chung Hou to another declaration, the subject of which, this time, was a large plot of land along the Hai River, 60 miles east of Tianjin, in an area located amongst the Dagu Forts.[85]

The concession, situated in a strategic position from a military standpoint, should have strengthened the French presence in the area. The forts had been at the centre of the second Opium War and their conquest had determined the victory of the Anglo-French troops. To have control of the forts meant having control of the Hai River and access to the city of Tianjin, therefore also guaranteeing the strengthening of foreign concessions.

In the letter that accompanied the translation of Chung Hou's declaration, the French consul in Tianjin, Henri-Victor Fontanier, informed the legation secretary of the concession's location, attaching some of his sketches, underlining the importance and giving news of the tenancy request of a fort within the concession which had been forwarded to him by a protected French citizen. We do not know whether the request was accepted or whether the Italian 'subject' Sandri was the first tenant of one of the forts, and, in truth, it is not relevant to find out. It was indeed the first tenancy request to arrive at the consulate. It was a particularly awaited request, because a year and a half after the first declaration of Chung Hou there were very few Westerners in the French settlements. They were desperately needed to affirm the French identity in the concession. A new social space could not simply be the product of new territorial definitions or mapping. On the contrary, it required signs which indelibly characterised the territory, making it homogenous and clearly indicating the French authority. There was an ulterior motive which could explain the courteous insistence of Fontanier in order that Kleczkowski accepted the request of Sandri: it would have allowed the consul to *'faire valoir immédiatament nos traités'*.[86]

85 AMAE, Ambassade de France à Pékin 513po/1/262, Concession de Tientsin dossier 42/1862, Proclamation, 16.12.1862.

86 Fontanier a Kleczkowski, December 1862, AMAE, Nantes, Ambassade de France à Pékin 513po/1/262.

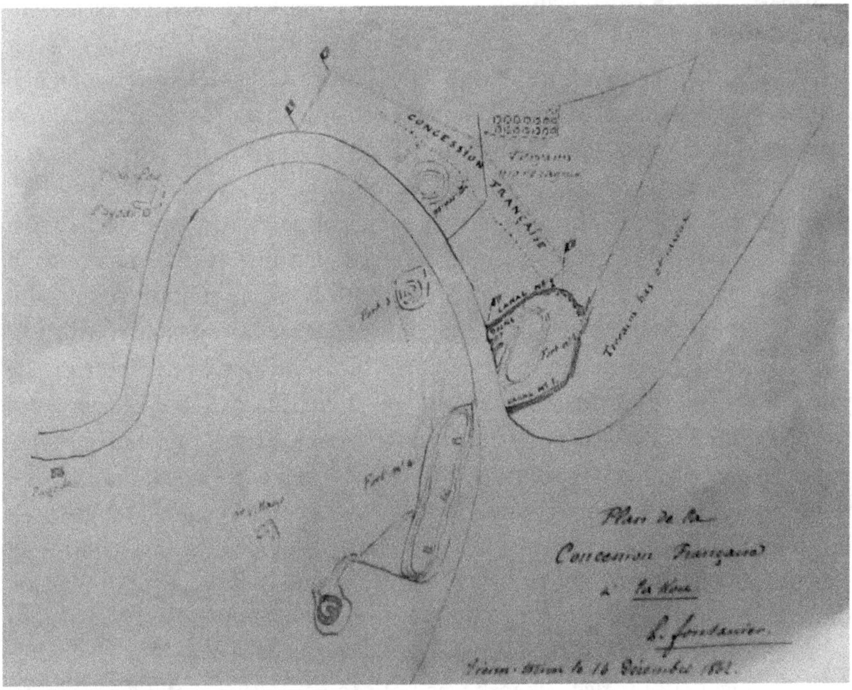

FIGURE 3 Plan of the French Concession at Ta-Kou[87]

It would have been the instrument used to strengthen an agreement whose legal foundation was not easy to identify. France too should have had a concession in Tianjin and France should have been granted the perpetual right to the property included in the concession, but its prerequisite could not be the unilateral declaration of a Chinese official. On the one hand, French privileges formally deferred to the regulatory force of an international treaty, which had sanctioned the different value of the two contracting parties and which, in this case, voided Chung Hou's provisions, transforming them into acts of duty, devoid of any discretion. On the other hand, those privileges tangibly needed to be enjoyed. Their very existence was unthinkable without their execution. The occupation of Chinese land therefore constituted the originating deed from which legitimacy, agreements and declarations could be drawn, and concurrently the necessary conditions so that those same agreements could carry out their constitutive validity.

87 The map is attached to the Proclamation of Chung Hou, 16.12.1862, AMAE, Ambassade de France à Pékin 513po/1/262.

Nevertheless, the factual dimension on which the concession was based was not without problems. Around twenty years after its formal opening, Charles Dillon, consul in Tianjin from 1870 to 1883, confessed in a letter to the French ambassador in Beijing, Fréderic Albert Bourée, that due to a fire at the French consulate, nine years after his arrival he had only just managed to find the agreement of 29 May and a map of the concession.[88]

However, judging by the tone of the letter, it appears evident that their discovery had not helped the French officials to determine exactly the extent of the concession, and which rules to follow both in the formation and assignment of the plots and the establishment of compensation owed to the dispossessed Chinese citizens. Yet the regulations of 2 June 1861 clearly indicate the process by which citizens and the protected French should have had access to the distribution of concession land. The recourse to an administrative procedure seemed to be the best solution, able to guarantee certainty of the expectations. It would have allowed France to measure its conceded land, transform it into plots to assign to French businessmen and merchants, and control its repartition and its use. The consul was entrusted with the task of overseeing the whole procedure, bringing about communication between two distant worlds. Those interested had to address their request to him, and, in agreement with the local authorities, his task was both to verify the application conformity by means of a plot inspection, and to follow the very delicate procedure of dispossession.

In the hope of generating interest in the concession plots, the consulate even prepared pre-filled applications in which investors could easily add their details and supporting statements in order to submit their applications. However, the application forms were given the more delicate task of integrating and clarifying the administrative regulations. If, in fact, its twelve articles were exclusively addressed to French citizens and those under French protection, in the application forms, it acknowledged the right of all westerners to invest in the concession on the condition that they were pre-emptively authorised by the French consul and recognised his jurisdiction. On the contrary, natives were expressly denied the right to purchase concession land.[89] Due to the very limited number of compatriots present in Tianjin or interested in settling in the

88 Dillon a Bourée, Tientsin July 1881, AMAE, Ambassade de France à Pékin 513po/A/262, Concession de Tientsin, dossier 42/1862.

89 '… *dans le cas de vente ultérieure de nos droits d'affermage de ces terrains nous nous engageons expressément a ne pas les vendre à des Chinois … et nous nous engageons à en observer toutes les obligations – notamment elle de ne transférer nos droits à aucun étranger, sans l'autorisation du consul de France et à la condition par l'acquéreur étranger de se soumettre formellement à la juridiction consulaire française*'. The application form to buy land

concession, the French authorities believed that an immediate expropriation of all land owned by Chinese was 'contrary to equity and justice', preferring instead to decide in each instance when the applications were received.

On the more profitable land by the river, the consul had to collect from the buyer half of the total price (60 *taels* per *arpent*) and deliver it to the owner who had been subjected to dispossession. The other half was allocated to the cost of the transcription of the act, the construction and maintenance of roads, bridges, and quays, and lastly to the institution and maintenance of a police force. For all the other plots of land the compensation owed to the Chinese consumed the financial duties of the French investors.

Nonetheless, this was not limited to the expropriated land, but it was extended to the property present on the land and even included a small sum in compensation for the inconvenience endured by the Chinese families for their *déplacement*. Both the Chinese and the real estates had been meticulously recorded by the magistrate of Tianjin, listed and delivered to the French first legation secretary. Signed and sealed by the two authorities, the list became an authentic legal act which certified the Chinese presence within the concession, avoiding, as was the French intention, an increase in the number of Chinese residents and excluding any form of reimbursement for buildings built after the proclamation of the regulation.[90]

On 15 December every year, the buyer had to deposit the continual rental charges (2000 *sapeche* per *arpent*), designating half to the Chinese government and half to the consulate to be utilised for the improvement and security of the concession. At the same time he received an authentic act '*de bail a perpétuité*' from the consul which, paradoxically, constituted a property deed with a perpetual guarantee of his right.

Some years later, in 1865, a translated copy of the regulation was sent to the English consul. In the accompanying note Gabriel Deveria, consular interpreter and at that time undertaking consular functions, reminded the English consul that the French government had to integrate the administrative regulations, in order to offer his compatriots the opportunity of investment in the concession. Even if the twelve articles of the regulations were addressed exclusively to French citizens, the serious scarcity of investors and the limited economic activities in general encouraged the consular authorities to consider the nationality of Western concessionaires and the eventual presence of locals far

within the French Concession of Tianjin, dated 1862, is in AMAE, Ambassade de France à Pékin 513po/A/262, Concession de Tientsin, dossier 42/1862.

90 The Chinese were able to continue to build, but they would not receive any compensation for new buildings (art. V, *Règlement*).

less relevant. The latter were prevented from buying land within the concession, but they were allowed to live within the concession.[91]

The only two limits expressly recorded by Deveria regarded, on the one hand, the French character which the settlement should maintain and could not be challenged; on the other, the concession's particular legal system to which every resident had to submit.

Foreign investors and Chinese residents did not appear to constitute a threat to the development and the identity of the concession, according to the indications laid out three years previously in the application forms. Nine years later, the regulation had still not been integrated and it was still not clear whether other Westerners were allowed to invest in the concession. On receipt of an application from a Portuguese investor interested in opening a recreation arcade on the river, the French consul, Dillon, had to take advice from his ambassador in Peking. The regulation, in its silence, excluded this as a possibility, however, it was time to move in another direction. '*Nous sommes si peu de Français en Chine que si l'on ne permet pas aux étrangers d'acheter un lot de terrain, jamais la concession française d'ici ne parviendra à être habitée*'.[92]

The concession land was still not raising sufficient interest, and in the hope of launching the concession's economic development it was necessary to open up opportunities to foreign investors. The absence of buyers was indeed the most serious danger for the production of a new social space and the building of the French identity in the concession.

At the same time, the few investors who had appeared to be interested clashed with the uncertainty of the administrative procedures and the fluidity of the borders of the concession. The administrative regulation of 1861 contained very precise indications in which, nevertheless, each consul in his practical interpretation had introduced his own system for the distribution of plots and his own method for the editing of applications. Moreover, the floods of the Hai River had caused the disappearance of the stone which marked the Western border of the concession, allowing the Chinese owners to redefine the concession's borders to their advantage, and to construct new buildings with the conviction that they would never be dispossessed.

This seemed to be confirmed in 1872 in the words of the French ambassador in Bejing, Geofroy, according to whom the substantial disinterest shown by the French towards the concession prevented the request for asking a rigorous

91 AMAE, Consulate de Tientsin, 691/po/1/180, Gabriel Deveria to James Mongan, Tientsin, 7.1.1865.

92 AMAE, Consulate de Tientsin, 691/po/1/173, Charles Dillon to Louis de Geofroy, Tientsin, 18.2.1874. The application of the Portuguese citizen De Castro is dated 18.2.1874.

respect of its borders and a serious application of the 'indisputable right' that France had on that territory. Nine years later the situation appeared to be even more serious and dictated, according to consul Dillon, that they act outside of legal logic, assuming equity, convenience and interests as guiding criteria in political action.[93]

In a long message despatched to the French ambassador Bourée in July 1881, Dillon cited having always acted according to the instructions of the Embassy, and claimed merit for improving the administrative procedure for the application for land, including introducing a new application model at the beginning of his term. Nonetheless, his letter revealed his preoccupation with being considered responsible for the lack of intervention by the consulate to avoid the preoccupation of the Western side of the concession by the Chinese. It was true that the Chinese had maliciously taken advantage of the disappearance of the liminal rocks and the investors were still few, but the fact that the consul had noticed neither the concession's border variation nor the buildings that the Chinese were constructing within the land only nine years after his arrival, could appear to be a very serious oversight.

The regulation of 1861 had already provided away out, allowing after its proclamation for the destruction of the buildings with no compensation. Dillon, nonetheless, preferred not to adopt this strategy, opting to take the completely opposite direction. Reprimanding Geofroy, on the one hand he evoked both the lack of proof which could identify who was responsible for moving the border stones and the solely theoretical nature of French law in view of demolition, and on the other he stressed its deep material injustice. The concession's border cut straight through a housing cluster rented out by the village chiefs to particularly disadvantaged Chinese families, who had been previously expelled by the English concession and then later by the French. These people were probably not faultless, demolishing their houses appeared to be an excessive form of punishment which could have brought about the risk of being '*mal compris du public et de surreter contre nous, dans la localité, le sentiment national des indigenes*'. It was therefore necessary to acknowledge that the occupied land had an extremely limited extension, and that no one had applied for it in all those years. At the same time it was just as necessary to appear firm in the face of the excessive Chinese requests. In fact, the Taotai of Tianjin requested the written surrender of not only the right of expropriation without compensation, contained in the regulations of 1861, but also the right of purchase of Chinese properties outside the concession, which were

93 Geofroy's letter of 13.07.1872, was addressed to Dillon and reported by Dillon himself.

considered to be an entitlement of France according to an extensive interpretation of article 10 of the Tianjin treaty.

Aware of the difficulty in which the concession was placed, and the risks brought about by the eventual hostility of the local population, Dillon preferred a change of interlocutor and he turned to the viceroy, whose decision seemed to offer both parties an honourable compromise. The French were granted the right to go ahead in a census and in the measurement of the (new) buildings present along the border within the concession, allowing Dillon to affirm that in this way the viceroy had implicitly acknowledged the concession and had accepted the (new) Western border. Concurrently, the viceroy would consider the presence of new buildings as *fait accompli* and likewise implicitly affirmed the right of the Chinese owners to compensation in the case of expropriation.

The Taotai was not happy with this decision and continued to obstruct the measurement's operations, stirring up the Chinese residents and openly declaring that the '*force resterait à la loi*'. Once again the intervention of the viceroy resolved a situation which was becoming difficult. He called for the Taotai and, in the presence of the consul, he reprimanded him to the point that the official himself declared to Dillon that he was ready to help them 'underhandedly' to purchase houses from the owners that were situated on the other side of the concession border.

However, the life of settlement was not easy: investors were still few and the work of urbanization continued slowly. The decision not to proceed to the immediate expropriation of Chinese property and the subsequent expulsion of residents by anticipating the necessary sums had proven unsuccessful. As we have seen, the French system, based on the consul and its mediation activity, foresaw that for the lands along the river, namely the more lucrative land but also the ones that needed more work, the sums for the replenishment activities, the construction of docks, bridges and road network came from half the agreed price (the other half would be delivered by the consul to the expropriated as compensation). Subordinating the urban planning to the sale of land lots was, however, a shaky move, and its consequences impacted adversely on the prospects of development of the concession, making embarrassing the comparison with the English settlement.

French investors had not arrived, and without them there was little that could be done. Not only the expulsion of the Chinese residents could not be pursued, but it had been also impossible to avoid that the French concession became the place of residence of Chinese officials and well funded natives. If we cross the information that gives us the map of the concession attached to the municipal regulations of 1894 with those offered by the German memory written by the consul of the Reich in Tianjin that we have previously examined, the reasons of its non-development are even clearer.

In the concession the consulate and the municipal government occupied two lots, the Chinese government owned three lots and on them there were the Custom House, the Telegraph and the Admiralty Office. A French citizen owned three small plots and a Russian citizen was the owner of two larger ones located along the river. All the others belonged to the Jesuits and Lazzaretti. In fact, the two religious orders, taking advantage of the French protection of the Christian missionaries, of the lack of competition, of the public auctions, and of a price per *mou* that ranged between 30 and 60 taels (in the same years in the English concession it arrived at 2000 taels per *mou*) had moved as skilled speculators. They bought up most of the land and waited for the best time to sell.

In 1894, that time had not yet arrived, because the construction works were lacking and the concession was still inhabited by the Chinese, but also because it was in a position that was objectively less favourable than the English one. Firstly the land was largely marshy, requiring a large scale remediation to adapt it to the European standards; secondly, the possibility of docking along that stretch of the river flowing belong the concession was by no means easy.

Two years later, however, the conditions for its relaunch were beginning to appear. The dramatic rise in land prices within the English settlement due to the decline in supply and the growth of business and entrepreneurial activities were pushing an increasing number of Europeans and European companies towards the French concession. The Jesuits and Lazzaretti finally began to sell.

5 A Nonexistent Concession

The origins of the American concession are even more uncertain. The United States did not take part in the second Opium War and also remained neutral in the two years between the Tianjin treaty and the convention of Beijing.[94] In any case, applying to the clause of the most favoured nation, they had obtained the same territorial privileges as had the other treaty powers. A 'tract of land'

94 Still useful is the classic work of Tyler Dennett, *Americans in Eastern Asia: A Critical Study of the policy of the United States with reference to China, Japan and Korea in the 19th Century* (New York: MacMillan, 1922); John King Fairbanks, *Trade and Diplomacy on the China Coast: The Opening of the Treaty Ports, 1842–1854*, 2 vols. (Cambridge: Harvard University Press, 1953). With a closer reference to the legal aspect the recent book of Ruskola, *Legal Orientalism*; now also Jedidiah Kroncke, *The Futility of Law and Development: China and the Danger of Exporting American Law* (Oxford: Oxford University Press, 2016).

above the Hai River was thus also let to them, but as we learn from the correspondence between Charles Denby, the American ambassador in Beijing, and Richard Olney, the Secretary of State, in 1895 the archives of the United States consulate in Tianjin had no official document relating to the possible acquisition of territory, not even a simple receipt of payment as in the British case, and did not offer any information about the way by which the distribution of plots of land to the American citizens living there had been carried out.[95]

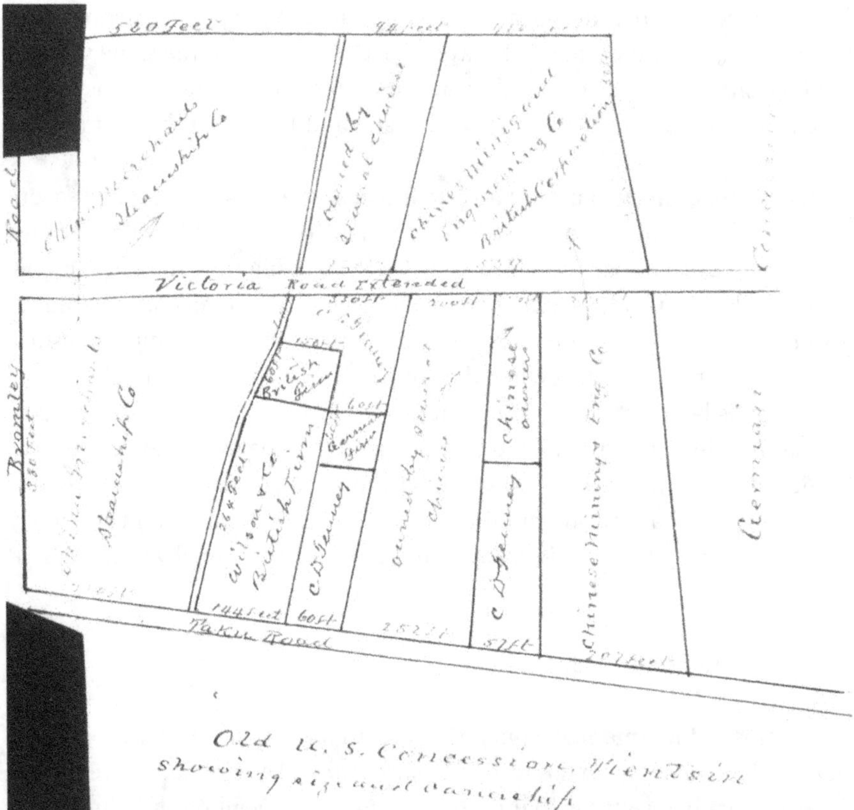

FIGURE 4 Map of the U.S. Concession at Tientsin[96]

95 Charles Denby, *The American Concession at Tientsin*, 4 (enclosure 1 to Denby's letter to Olney, 3 August 1895), in National Archives and Records Administration at College Park, MD (hereafter NARA), Microfilm Publications, Despatches from U.S. Minister to China (1843–1906), M 92, R 99.

96 The map of the American Concession is enclosed to a letter written by the US ambassador in Beijing Edwin H. Conger to the Secretary of State John Hay, 21 January 1902 (1843–1906), m 92, r 116. It has been published also by Nicolais Vaicbourdt, De la 'me too policy' aux ambitions contradictoires: la brève histoire de la concession américaine de Tianjin, 1860–1902, in *Outre-Mers. Revue d'histoire*, 382/383 (2014), 33.

The reason for this silence, according to the American diplomat, was due to the absence of an ambassador in Bejing until the arrival of Burlingame in July 1862, and to the appointment of a consular representative at Tianjin itself only in 1866.[97] Anyhow, according to what Denby stated, there was no lack of evidence for a legitimate American presence. In the mid-eighties, faced with the German aggressiveness, aiming at opening their own settlement in Tianjin, and asking for areas dangerously close to those assigned to the United States, Charles Denby tried to re-direct the State Department's policy towards Tianjin, hoping that the United States' government would take a more active role in the promotion of American entrepreneurial and commercial activities. The archive's papers proved, according to him, that the United States had obtained in October 1860, together with Britain and France, a plot of land from Chung Hou, the Chinese Superintendent of northern Trade, the borders of which could be determined and over which for twenty years the United States' consuls had exercised full jurisdiction.[98] However, none of these documents survived, and even in Denby's words an important proof was given by the presumption that if the American entrepreneurs had reached that far, even if there were more 'desirable' places, then there had to be an 'understanding, perhaps a definitive agreement' (p.8) determining their presence. A further, maybe definitive, confirmation finally results from the memories of the first official United States representative in Tianjin, Meadow, collected by William Pethick, another American vice-consul, and forwarded by him in a letter of 8 September 1883, to consul James C. Zuck.[99]

Pethick joined the American consulate at Tianjin in 1872 as an interpreter, later holding the position of a vice-consul a first time from 1873 to 1875 and a second time from 1885 to 1893. So, he knew the problems of the concession very well, and was aware of the chaos in the consular archive.

Meadow had forwarded all the documents in his possession to his successor, Sheppard, and Pethick himself had catalogued them, but discovered neither a

97 Denby, *The American Concession at Tientsin*, 5–6. The first consular representative of the United States was actually a simple American citizen, Meadow, living in Tientsin who in 1866 'was appointed acting U.S. consul'. On the role of Burlingame see John Schrecker, 'For the Equality of Men – for the Equality of Nations': Anson Burlingame and China's First Embassy to the United States, 1868', *Journal of American-East Asian Relations* 17:1 (2010), 9–34.

98 The American settlement extended itself on an area 23 acres, from the river to Taku Road and from the Southern part of the British concession to the cemetery (Denby, *The American Concession at Tientsin*, 4). Short notes in Rasmussen, *Tientsin*, 36; Jones, *Shanghai and Tientsin*, 129–130; Bernstein, *A History of Tianjin*, *op. cit.*

99 William N. Pethick, Letter to Zuck, U.S. Consul of Tientsin, 8.9.1883 in NARA, Microfilm Pubications, Despatches from U.S. Consuls in Tientsin (China, 1868–1906), M1114 R 5.

founding title, nor indications useful to understand how the distribution of the land occurred and who the legitimate owners had been. The interviews they had with the then elderly Meadow were not very useful. The official was present when Chung Hou chose the land for the British, French and American concessions and was able to indicate the borders of the concession clearly. But in those days, at the end of the seventies and the beginning of the eighties, there was no reason to continue the research, or more generally to worry about sure evidence. The American right to own a concession was not questioned and once obtained, even in an almost undocumented way, the North American investors and traders bought land inside the concession from the beginning of the sixties. They were certain to be subjected to the control of the government of the United States of America. 'There were plenty of equally desirable lots with water frontage still obtainable at that early time in the English and French Concession but the Pilgrim Fathers did not choose to locate elsewhere'.[100]

In addition, the British, and particularly Morgan, the first British consul with whom Pethick had also examined the ditch within the English settlement that had been assumed as a boundary between the two concessions, considered the American concession to be a fact, and recognized the American consul's authority, to the extent that they invited a fellow citizen of theirs, the only one living within the concession, to turn to the American consul if he had problems with the Chinese.

In the same way there was evidence that the Chinese also officially recognized the existence of the American concession. Mr. Chu, after inheriting from his brother a plot of land along the Hai River in the American area, decided to invest on that land. He had built 'godowns' (warehouses), shops and houses, and also giving the consulate the opportunity to build a quay on his own expense. He guaranteed that he would maintain a police force and cover all sanitary expenses. In exchange he asked for the payment of the wharfage dues and mooring fees. Even if it was to be rejected, Chu's request was decisive. Consul Denny from now on had a different view of the concession, and he established a local police force, began to tidy up and clean the roads, and introduced a light taxation system on houses and shops getting, as Pethick says, the residents' approval. The land within the concession began to show clear signs of American governmental power. The American sovereignty was evident, and both the Western nations and the Chinese took note of it. Pethick insisted on underlining that never, in the several conversations he had had with Chinese Customs' Taoai about the concession, the American right to have a concession or the

100 Pethick, *Letter to Zuck*, 8.

continuity shown by the United States of America exercising its sovereignty had been questioned.

So what led to the severe situation of neglect into which the concession had fallen after 1880, that is to say when consul Magnum even proposed the demotion of the concession to the Chinese government, reserving for the consular authorities only the right to establish suitable municipal regulations whenever it seemed desirable? Why should the funds at their disposal be used to build an impressive protection wall for the consulate instead of using them to improve roads and quays? Why had the efficient local police force been cast off? And why, finally, was the arrival of 'five Chinese soldiers in rags' sufficient to justify the evacuation of a settlement that after two years of real occupation had become 'very sleek and well-dressed'[101]?

In his letter, Pethick does not allow us to understand the reason for such a neglect, and neither does he offer answers. In any case, it was still worthwhile to take up the control of the concession even if there were no fellow-countrymen nor evident economic interests. For the United States diplomat, an act of defence of their rights would help all the foreign settlements: 'Passing across the boundary of any foreign settlement into Chinese quarters is like stepping from a garden into a sty; the further off we can keep the sty, the better it will be for us – if not for our bacon'.[102]

Twelve years had passed without anything relevant happening. For Denby, the American concession had not left the situation of uncertainty and neglect into which it had fallen apparently without any reason. Understandably, the Chinese authorities had taken Mangum's offer seriously and tried to take advantage of it. On the one hand they actually announced that they would adopt all those measures fit for guaranteeing American interests, but on the other they reserved for themselves the right, in case the American consuls would again take control of the concession, to verify the existence of impedimental conditions and to determine again the formalities of its administration.

Anyhow, for Denby, it had been only a proposal which, notwithstanding the impossibility of finding the original contract, the lack of exercise of municipal functions, and the lack of progress of the American settlement especially if compared to the British and French ones, did not let assume the absence of a legitimate title, nor could it be understood as a complete renunciation of its own rights by the United States government.[103]

101 Pethick, *Letter to Zuck*, 9.

102 Pethick, *Letter to Zuck*, vol. 5.

103 Denby, *The American Concession at Tientsin*, 29 'Their [of United States] title exists today unweakened by the failure of the United States Government to take the same advantage

Unlike France and Britain, the United States had not looked after the distribution of the plots of land within the concession, and neither did they take steps for their sale, thus compelling the American buyers to buy directly from the Chinese government. However, there is no doubt, as Denby said, that they got their concession at the same terms and times as the two European powers and, in spite of everything, they continued to be, formally, its legitimate owner. Moreover, insisted the ambassador, the two European powers had enlarged the originally foreseen prerogatives. At the same time no concession was based on a treaty but on the contrary was the result of unpredictable practices, habits and uses. It is not clear whether Denby referred to the three concessions in Tianjin or more generally to the settlements opened within the Chinese treaty ports. In any case, it is a very strong statement, pitilessly revealing the ambiguity of the legal discourse within colonial or semi-colonial contexts. Beyond the borders of the Occident, there was an overlap between rules and exceptions, and between rights and privileges, to the extent that it was ultimately no longer possible to differentiate between them. The result was the acquisition of legitimacy from practices and powers that had nothing to do with the rule of Law, international law, or even with consular law.

At the same time, Denby's words reveal the weakness of the American claims. Outside the law, the law could be respected only by transforming the social space; in other words, transforming a part of China into something similar to the United States where the authority of the American consuls would be visible. The delay in the urbanization of the concession, the lack of exercise of the legal powers and finally Mangum's letter to the Chinese governor weakened Denby's arguments. But in 1895 the problem did not affect the re-expansion of Chinese sovereignty over the territory 25 years before it had been assigned to the United States. 'I do not propose at this time' – wrote the ambassador on 31 July 1895 to *Tsungli Yamen* – 'to present a full argument on the question of the right of my Government to retake jurisdiction over the ceded territory. It will be time to do this when the right is disputed'.[104] The United States had never shown a particular interest towards this strip of land along the Hai River, but followed it by expressing their concern regarding the colonial policy of the other powers interested in opening their settlements in Tianjin and in strengthening their presence in the area. This was not a theoretical problem:

---

thereof as was taken of similar grants by other powers but on the contrary that the extensive exercise of jurisdiction by such powers [England and France] was entirely unforeseen in the original grants'.

104 Mr Denby to the Zongli Yamen, 31.07.1895, p. 3 (enclosure 3 Denby's letter to Olney, 3.8.1895).

the German Reich was trying to obtain a lease agreement, and the new Eastern power, Japan, after assuming control over Korea with the victory in the war against China, would not delay starting an expansionist policy inside the Chinese ports.[105] 'I have understood' – Denby wrote both to the Tsungli Yamen and to the viceroy – 'that proceedings are pending having for their object to cede the territory mentioned to one or more other powers. Against such cession or attempt at cession I enter my solemn protest'.[106] His aim was simple, and consistent with the diplomatic strategy he had followed during his ten years of direction at the American embassy in Beijing: to protect and boost the U.S. entrepreneurs' investments and commercial activities in northern China. This also meant avoiding in any way the formal cession of even a small part of the American concession.

A few days after these two letters, the memoirs on the American concession and a short introductory text were sent to Washington. In his answer, the Secretary of State, Richard Olney, shared Denby's analysis, but not his conclusions. In the mid-nineties, the prolonged interest of the State Department towards what was going on in far China began to be replaced by a more and more conscious awareness of the economic relevance of the Chinese market, and by the desire to play a more important role on the eastern chessboard. This notwithstanding, the policy of non-interference had not yet been abandoned. Olney actually asked Denby not to take any further initiative. On the one hand the economic interests and the American properties were guaranteed by unequal treaties; they were the legal framework within which all the Western policy in China took place, and where the rivalry between the different powers developed and the entrepreneurial activity of traders and commercial companies was defined. On the other hand, legally speaking, the United States had never had any jurisdiction over the so-called concession. Their claims on that territory did not derive either from a lease agreement, of which no documental evidence existed, or from the actual exercise of a normal administrative activity, which had already been abandoned for a long time, but simply from the diplomatic courtesy of the Chinese government. China, in Olney's eyes, recognized that the United States only had 'a right of comity' and the legitimate claims of the United States dated back to this. In other words, the strange *comitas* in an oriental version imagined by Olney not only obliged China to accept limitations to its own

105 Sara Paine, *The Sino-Japanese War of 1894–1895: Power, Perceptions, and Primacy* (Cambridge: Cambridge University Press, 2003).

106 Denby to His Excellency the Viceroy s.d. (enclosure 2 to Denby's letter to Olney, 3 August 1895). On the lines of Denby's diplomat policy see David Anderson, *Imperialism and Idealism: American Diplomats in China 1861–1898* (Bloomington: Indiana University Press, 1985), 144 ff.

jurisdiction, even if there was no reciprocity, but had even produced a further compression of Chinese sovereignty, granting the United States the right to obtain, as Britain and France had done, a plot of land and to call it the 'American Concession'. This right was in no case followed by a real interest: the United States government had not bought any territory nor made formal agreements. On the contrary, they had abandoned all those powers which had been given to them many years before. In the light of these considerations he did not consider his country to be in the position 'to maintain that we are entitled to resume jurisdiction over the tract, even if it is considered desirable to do so'.[107]

We do not know Denby's reaction to this. We can only imagine that the content of Olney's letter was no surprise to him. Looking at Tianjin from Washington, a small American concession might not have been attractive or strategically relevant neither on an economic nor on a political level. Observing the situation from the inside instead was different, and Tianjin might have become an outpost of American commercial imperialism in the way that it became more and more important for Germany and Japan.

The history of the Western concessions in Tianjin is not a story that can be told from an exclusively national point of view.

Tianjin was a complex, hybrid space, between East and West, defined by social practices, symbolic representations, and legal categories, which did not coincide simply with the area defined by the entity as a state, nation, or city. On the contrary, it was an imperial location placed under different foreign powers but at the same time in competition and cooperation between them, and crossed by different and unstable strategies of governance as well as equally different and unstable Chinese forms of resistance or negotiations. This continuous uncertainty and the multiplicity of interests involved is reflected as a thread running through Olney's and Denby's papers, emerging from the letters of the consuls in Tianjin, and it is confirmed by the Chinese Taotai's request, projecting on the small plot of land along the Hai River, known as the American concession, the uncertainty of the United States' diplomacy in China.

A few days after Olney had sent his letter and before Denby had confirmed its receipt, the political scene in Tianjin had definitely changed: on 30 October 1895 Germany had obtained its settlement and now asked the United States not to raise objections to the works necessary to extend the two roads linking the new German settlement with the British concession.[108] As a matter of fact

107 Richard Olney to Charles Denby, Washington 18.10.1895, in NARA, Microfilm Publications, Diplomatic Instructions of the Department of State (1801–1899), M 77 R 42, 265–268.

108 Denby received Olney's letter at the beginning of December 1895. His answer is dated 25 January 1896, in NARA, Microfilm Publications, Despatches from U.S. Minister to China (1843–1906), M 92 R 100, 1–4.

the two roads necessarily had to cross a territory that formally still belonged to the United States, and which was one that the Reich wanted to buy. Getting the assurance that his fellow citizens could dwell and buy land within the German concession under the same conditions foreseen in the British settlement, Denby invited the American consul in Tianjin, Sheridan P. Red, to release the necessary authorizations and informed the Secretary of State.[109] 'The ultimate question' still concerned the 'so called American concession'. It still was not clear what was to be done. The indications received from Washington and above all events going on in Tianjin induced Denby to consider that a re-assumption of the American jurisdiction was unlikely. In any case, the matter continued to have an importance, such as that it 'may well be kept under advisement'. Only thirty days later the situation became clearer. The American consul in Tianjin, in a letter addressed to Denby asking for further instructions, confirmed the inappropriateness of resuming jurisdiction on the 'so-called' American concession. According to him, due to the work of American officials, the Chinese government would still prefer that the United States to exercise once again their jurisdiction on the concession, but too many things had changed: the State Department thought that there was no longer any use in remaining in Tianjin, the Germans pressed for a definite answer, and finally inside the American concession there was very little land left at the disposal of American investors. The concession seemed indefensible, and also Denby was convinced that 'it was inadvisable to make any claim whatever. We have not a single American merchant at Tientsin. The American missionaries already own valuable tracts of land. There seems to be no reason why we should be embarrassed with a useless jurisdiction'. Anyhow, the ambassador insisted on his request to the State Department in order to get simple and clear instructions on how to deal with the German claims, and above all whether he should notify the *Taotai* of the abandonment of the claim of any legal right on the land in question.[110]

While Denby was waiting for further information from the State Department, much more serious problems worried the Western community living in the north of China. The defeat of China in the first Sino-Japanese war and the opening of a German and Japanese concession had modified the fragile Tianjin's political balance, and at the same time the resentment and anger of the

109 The official answer of the German consul in Tianjin to Denby's request is enclosed in the letter addressed to Olney dated 25 January 1896, also in NARA, Microfilm Publications, Despatches from the U.S. Minister to China (1895–1896), M 92 R 100.

110 Charles Denby to Richard Olney, Peking, 2 April 1896, in NARA, Microfilm Publications, Despatches from U.S. Minister to China (1895–1896), M 92 R 100, 2.

Chinese for the intrusive presence of the Western powers and the Christian missionaries were coalescing in the Boxer movement. On 20 June 1900, while the first Western contingents had already arrived, the German ambassador had been killed, causing the outrage in the international community and a violent reaction by Germany. Only seven days after the murder of Ketteler, the German sailor who we met at the beginning of this story embarked from the port of Bremen, with his soul inflamed by the Kaiser's words: the Chinese would never again dare to look cross-eyed at a German. A new history of Tianjin was about to begin.

Experiences and Experimentations: Two Words between Two Worlds

Bernard Durand

1 Introduction

A biologist who studied the world of bacteria noted the ability of some of them to mutate, and explained how they do. On the one hand they only mutate if the conditions of their live become more severe, forcing them to accelerate some of their genes to allow their evolution. But, as the choices they make can be disastrous, it is sometimes only a portion of the population (one percent) which begins to mutate, and if that mutation appears to be interesting, all the population can share the benefits. Being a pessimist, he concluded that this way of experimentation did not exist in human society.[1]

Is there in any colonial law an original 'bacterium-law' that we might call '*mutabilis colonarius jus*', whose properties lead to behave the same way, that is to say, able to mutate in the colonial territory, where the constraints, the circumstances, the 'localities', harder than in the mainland, dictate the experimentation with new rules? Does it transfer to other colonies or to the home country the newly acquired characteristics, or a few of them, once their relevance has been verified? And how could we interpret these transportations or transplantations: as experiences, experimentations or imitations, having in mind the three steps expressed by Auguste Comte in his lectures on positive philosophy?

In philosophy, authors expressed the idea that a distinction should be made between experience as a principle, and scientific experience for which they use the word experimentation. In this respect, the scientific object is produced by learned concepts in a system carefully designed and tested in order to 'experiment'. On the contrary, in colonial affairs, experience means that we draw lessons from the observation of reality, of what exists, and these lessons are put into law, and possibly can be reproduced elsewhere. The conditions of the experiments are not necessarily identical, and the mutations of human societies

1 Miroslav Radman, *Sciences et avenir*, avril 2004, p. 40 sq.

DOI:10.1163/9789004443075_016

prohibit arrested conclusions. However, the question of these 'legal experiments' that result in 'exported laws' still remain interesting.[2]

The first thing to consider is related to the law of the country which colonized. We can imagine that, at the beginning, the law was a 'model' to be respected, or at least a law which was easy to transplant. But rapidly the colonizers saw that the model was at variance with the new country and its way of life. Moreover, none of the colonizing nations had rules which were readily transferable. In addition, few men were able to know them exactly: amateurism characterised the first judges, who were often farmers and 'neighbours', loyal 'toward their local communities rather than the government'.[3] In some colonies, settlers came from different countries and applied different customs. Finally, they were confronted with spaces already inhabited by 'strange' populations, whose laws and way of life were very different. It all sets the stage whose elements may be summarized by reference to a 'model' confronted with a new space, where law and institutions could not be the same. And indeed, the model could not only be unenforceable or otherwise voluntarily dismissed by the settlers, but – especially while crossing a 'border' – the transfer could never be done without changes: 'it is not a branch of law', wrote Matter in his preface to the *Traité de droit colonial* 'which, transplanted to the colonies, would suffer more or less profound transformations' to the point sometimes that the imagined system is 'superior to that of the metropolis' and could be transported to it. By this 'special law, whose characteristics are always more and more outstanding', both in the content of the rules and in the principles behind them, everything is questioned again! Now, the colonial adventure has faced in the first place its 'borders', that of the 'world of the Sea'.[4]

The Odyssey tells us that the return of Odysseus to Ithaca was a journey of ten years with a sea that refused to take him home, a dark world filled with non-human landscapes, new plants, new entities which make travellers forget where they wants to go. That is the subject of the story about the confrontation with the people of the Lotus Eaters, that caused *Lothos*'s lapse of memory. It is also a world of dangers, a world without borders and in terms of institutions, of non-compliance (or conformity) with the home institutions … which requires a work of memory. Moreover, during this period – between the sixteenth and the seventeenth centuries – the history of international relations came to be

2 Bernard Durand, 'Migration et expérimentation en droit: l'exemple "colonial" français', in *Les collectivités locales et l'expérimentation: perspectives nationales et européennes* (Paris: Documentation française, 2004), 135–153.

3 Lisa Ford, *Settler Sovereignty, Jurisdiction and Indigenous People in America and Australia, 1788–1836* (Cambridge, Mass.: Harvard University Press, 2011), 123.

4 P. Matter, 'Preface', in Paul Dareste, *Traité de droit colonial*, t. I (Paris, 1931).

dominated by the overseas rivalries, specifically in two fields of confrontation: commercial and military. Colonization became a matter of maritime powers and control of the sea. It was maritime trade which was perceived as being the most lucrative. Foreign trade was the only means of enriching the realm. The new colonial system, in the second half of the seventeenth century, helped to triple the number of English ships and to pass additional and more detailed navigation acts about trade with the New World. Commercial practices applicable to overland trade could not be transposed to maritime trade. The extension of national power, the expanding economic universe, the accumulation of capital, the link between commercial supremacy and predominance in manufacturing and industry, and the regulations governing them were all different from those governing territorial trade. According Tomas de Mercado, in the colonies, different commodities which were contained in a ship were not separated, and that would be sold as the whole cargo of a ship. In the colonies, the fleet would arrive and it would be immediately attributed as '*de un solo concerto*', a price for the whole cargo of the ship, which would generate strange effects on the price of the individual goods.

The Ocean means also the freedom of war that knows neither *ortung* (*orientation, determination*) nor *recht*[5] which affects the freedom of trade. War indeed means 'open' space, strong law, the 'total' character of naval warfare, catches on neutral, confiscation of goods, blockades, ruled by ordinances of each state, while international law struggled to enforce common rules. The increase of trade launched a 'commercial revolution' and provoked military confrontations: in the third quarter of the seventeenth century the contest for trade caused no less than three wars between England and Holland! Therefore control of the seas became paramount, and England was reluctant to accept legal constraints in this area. For England, navigation was the only way of conducting trade (except for trade with Scotland). In determining the status of neutrality, the eviction of privateers, control of trafficking and pirates, it would make the 'ocean common space for all the prey of a single nation'. The strong and pragmatic British traditions and averse institutional models, will gradually be projected on the colonies, at least initially, as 'marine' approaches. Somehow, colonial law would learn from the 'open sea' by inheriting its characteristics. The 'Empires' kept the memory of the ocean routes operated by ships, and of occupied islands penetrated via the terrestrial waterways.

5 Filipo Ruschi, 'Leviathan et Behemot. Modeli Egemonici e spazi coloniali in Carl Schmitt', *Quaderni fiorientini* 33–34 (2004–2005), 396; and Carl Schmitt, *Terra e Mare*, Angelo Bolaffi (trans.) (Milano: Giuffré editore, 1986), 54–71.

Seamen assumed a new place, the so-called 'Tar Jack', in the system of international capitalism. The new routes of trade, organized around bulk goods, forced the merchants 'to mobilize huge amounts of labour to move their commodities on a regular basis'. As was stated by Markus Rediker, 'Labour-intensive shipping grew at the pace of expanding production and at the pace of the exploitation of slave labour in the New world'.[6] Seamen became free and mobile workers in an expansive international economy, heralding the transition to capitalist labour relations: new contracts, a new world of struggle and negotiation, a new subculture of a class segregated by sex and restricted to men, the constant threat of eventual strikes or mutinies, new forms of mutiny (such as the 'Round Robin', which expressed the collectivistic ethos of the seamen's opposition culture), new relations between seamen linked to the confrontation with nature, a sense of unity, and mutual responsibilities and egalitarianism. Through the ages, sailors had built an extraordinary tradition of labour militancy. In the eighteenth century they were one of the groups of British workers most likely to strike, as they did in Boston in the 1690s and 1740s; in Philadelphia in 1741, 1742, 1759–1769; in New York in 1705; 'and in all of these cities in the 1760s and 1770s'. Indeed, the very term 'strike' evolved from the collective decision of London seamen to 'strike the sails' of their ships in 1768, halting the flow of commerce and the accumulation of capital. Even if labour militancy was 'an attractive theory' (because four years later the London tailors had gone on strike),[7] stoppages of seamen were dangerous for the colonial trade of the East India Company, especially since the strict execution of laws was impossible without the help of armed forces, something which was 'politically sensitive'. So, magistrates – often mocked by seamen – were inclined to take the role of mediator and to prefer conciliation and arbitration, which were finally institutionalized. R.C. Dobson, in his *Masters and Journeymen*, calls seamen one of the 'three most conspicuously militant groups of the eighteenth-century English workers. The seaman was confined within a spatially limited labouring environment, forced to cultivate regular habits and keep regular hours, and placed in cooperative relationship with both other workers and the supervisors of his labour'. In all of these ways, the seaman's experience foreshadowed that of the factory worker during the Industrial Revolution. New patterns of

6 Marcus Rediker, *Between the Devil and the Blue Sea, Merchant Seamen, Pirates, and the Anglo-American Maritime world, 1700–1750* (Cambridge: Cambridge University Press, 1987), 19.

7 C.R. Dobson, *Masters and Journeymen: A Prehistory of Industrial Relations, 1717–1800* (London: Croom Helm, 1980), 19.

authority and discipline were crucial to the process of industrialization.[8] Seamen were also instrumental in the formation and extension of plebeian culture, and influenced both the form and the content of plebeian protest by their militant presence in seaport crowds. They served as a medium for the exchange of experience and information within a more broadly defined culture of the labouring poor: seamen were crucial to the cultural dimensions of class formation.[9]

However, inside the new territories too, constraints existed which necessitated new administrative or political rules. In real colonial life, a number of reasons can be discovered which prove that a true centrifugal colonial law existed. It included the choice of British, German, French, or Spanish district officers, who decided not to obey the central decisions, or not to apply legislation, saying '*obedezco pero no cumplo*'.[10] We can also understand that many 'officers' (governors, judges) or merchants could have different views of trading interests and local trading values. Moreover, in settlers' countries, when new population arrived after forty or fifty years, they transported with them new political and economic values. However, broadly speaking, transplanted laws were unlikely to follow the same patterns of development as in the country from which they originated. They rather tended to undergo different stages, particularly in the early years, of either legal stagnation or of erratic change, both of which indicate a lack of connection between the demands of the users of law and the legislative drafters. Scholars noted that in such settlers colonies transplanted law was likely to have only recently shown signs of adaptability to local political and economic change. Other, more general, scholarship on legal transplants also notes that laws behaved very differently when copied from one place to another. At the same time, legal transplants were often the result of discursive strategies that imposed a new direction, making their content opaque, and defining their limits. It was a multiplicity of shared representations based on widespread and resistant stereotypes, which were able to create a reality that was different to that which they intended to describe. Transplants produced a self-consciousness and superiority of their legal and political structure through a negative dialectic of its recognition. In other words, these legal translations did not transfer something which already existed, but produced betrayals, adaptations and profound changes. *Luigi Nuzzo*

8 Dobson, *Masters and Journeymen*, 206.

9 Dobson, *Masters and Journeymen*, 294.

10 Lewis Hanke, *The Spanish Struggle for Justice in the Conquest of America* (Oxford University Press, 1959), in particular Chapter XII about Francisco de Toledo, vice-king of Peru.

evokes a 'Temporal and spatial disconnection', a 'temporal displacement', that he interprets in a moving of people and texts from the West to the East, and then to the African colonies. These movements were not only horizontal and unidirectional to the same temporal dimension, but also vertical. The European lawyers moved freely through time, using, for the interpretation of the colonial reality, legal categories from the old regime. The exceptionality of the non-Western world, its 'difference', seemed to exist in a different time period to the metropolis, in a period which could be compared with that of European *Ancient Regime*, and thus commanded a law of 'ancient regime after the ancient regime'. Through this temporal disconnection, it was possible to maintain a unified concept of the legal order, connected with 'borderline cases' such as military occupation, or the exception of consular and colonial law. The reconstruction of the category of exception, its applicability to the non-Western world, and the analysis of the temporal disconnection between centre and periphery allows *Nuzzo* to explain particularly Tianjin, in China, and its 'real' *Rechtsordnung*. It was a country with limited sovereignty, in which the modern principle of the territoriality of the law was replaced by the pre-modern principle of the personality of the law. Tianjin, therefore, appears as a unity of space, where identity and difference, past and present, inclusion and exclusion, are indissolubly intertwined.

If all of this is true, is it possible to speak of 'experiences' – and of experiences in commercial law – as asserted by scholars who have studied 'colonial law and justice', and believe that colonial experiences influenced the commercial practices of the major colonial Empires 'as well in their relations with the overseas colonies as on an international level'? In some fields of colonial law, legislation had certainly been, according to Arthur Girault, 'an extremely interesting field of experience'. These new countries developed a new form of organization, or new rules which were transposed to other colonies who adapted them, and sometimes were even extended to the mainland, either in their entirety or in some elements only. One can indeed observe that – either under exceptional circumstances or on an *ad hoc* basis for economic reasons of greater efficiency – French national law took some lessons from the colonies and applied the rules which originated from the colonies. This is for example the case in matters of statutory orders, procedure, and the direction of the trial, the organization of the courts, the status of judges and juries, and the use of civil imprisonment. Colonial imitation can still be observed recently when France created in the 1960s large regions for economic reasons. So, what has been said by the contributors to this book on commercial law can be summarized in two words: why, and how far, did these experiences flourish in the field of colonial commercial law?

2 Why Such Experiences in Commercial Law?

The colonial venture was highly significant because it was seen as if it could bolster the power of the state, and be a source of monetary enrichment. It could also be a source of enrichment through the supply of commodities which were needed for the home nation's manufacturing activities, and an important source of raw materials, which could be obtained at less expense from the colonies. The same economic discourse persisted during the first half of the eighteenth century. First, for mercantilists, such imposed dependence required a lawful basis, which was given, for the British Empire, in the maintenance of the Navigation Acts. It also involved a reserved trade from the colonies to the metropolis by forcing the colonies not to buy or sell goods other than with England. With a relative degree of reciprocity colonial products were generally granted a monopoly on the national market (Alain Clément). In this intellectual context, the mercantilist doctrine was dominant, even if the results were more apparent than real, and the difficulty in stopping trade liberty was great. In Spain, for example, the two main principles that characterized Habsburgs' trade policy were monopoly and single harbour policy. Trade monopoly was the basic principle of all Hispanic trade with the Indies. This new form of colonial expansion was conducted under the authority and responsibility of large private companies, to which a monopoly was granted. The example was set by England, which created the East India Company by a decision of Queen Elizabeth in 1600. The United Provinces followed in 1602 with the VOC. In France, after several attempts, Colbert founded the Eastern Company of France mainly out of public monies.

The regulation of trade and navigation between Spain and the Indies during the sixteenth and seventeenth centuries shows a clear intention to affirm the exclusive presence of the Hispanic Government over America: a *Casa de Contratación de Sevilla* (House of Trade of Seville) was founded in 1503, as 'an answer given by the Catholic Kings to the problems related to the incipient trade with the Indies' (Cruz Barney). This state agency was in charge of controlling and managing trade over all goods coming from or going to the Indies, and to collect taxes for them.

However, an anonymous pamphlet 'Considerations on the East-India Trade' published in 1701 stands a very different view. The author saw trade with the Eastern trading posts more as a stimulus than a threat to the national industry. He argued that competition was a means of promoting technical advances in manufacturing, thereby saving labour without calling wage levels into question. Competition led to lower production costs through technical progress. Finally, a new concept emerged (of trade balance), and a new theory of international trade which was closer to the liberal analysis of the eighteenth century than it was to the traditional mercantilist outlook. Some authors explained that trade, and more particularly foreign trade, were the most profitable of all activities: 'There is much more to be gained by manufacture than husbandry and by merchandize than manufacture'. Trade had to be free to produce enrichment; and some authors thus began to go against the Navigation Acts.

To develop commercial activities, to meet the increasing demand for new goods, and indirectly to promote manufacturing, domestic employment, and maritime employment – i.e. all these 'beginnings' – it was necessary to have a modern interventionist state and the help of governments and new legislation, which '…sought to master the problem of uneven industrial growth'. As Parry wrote, 'colonial mercantilism, though its assumptions were being questioned, was by no means extinct, and the Colonial Office was constantly pressed to protect British mercantile interests overseas, to ensure supplies of essential commodities, to insist that the fiscal arrangements in the colonies should not hamper British exports'. The 'right' to trade anywhere, to sell goods to anyone who would buy them, always needed annexations, armed interventions and minor wars to protect and support the merchant in the pursuit of trade.[11] All nations had to grant subsidies to ship lines or overseas merchants, allow for the payment of soldiers and officials, causing thus initially additional expenses for the State's budget. In nineteenth century Germany, for larger investments to be realized in the mining, railway and banking industries in the colonies, the only solution at hand seemed to be loans guaranteed by the Imperial government. The *Reich* would be liable for the payment of interest and the debt retirement/ liquidation of the loans. The *Reich*'s laws formed part of the commercial-legal arrangements to 'make colonialism work'. Evidently, numerous private firms profited greatly from the millions of public money spent for the military, shipping, railway lines, and mining industry in the colonies.

In the commercial field, of course, we cannot reject offhand the hope of every colonial power that they could take advantage of the significant costs incurred on each of the confiscated territories, and to transfer its own law. National law primacy was, during these centuries, the will of all states involved in colonial ventures, and they tried to build a law to preserve their rights of jurisdiction. Since 1509, Spain had issued regulations to bring more security to the ships, trying to avoid every possible risk, stating the minimum number of crew members, equipment and weaponry for defence against pirates. Company law

11 See J.H. Parry, *Trade and Dominion: European Overseas Empires in the Eighteenth Century* (London: Cardinal edition, 1974), 438 and 445.

(*Petra Mahy*) was originally a colonial era transplant, intended primarily to facilitate colonial enterprises. In each case, the colonial power exported their own version of company law to their colonies. The Dutch extended their Napoleonic Commercial Code to the Netherlands Indies in 1848. In British Malaya, the Indian Companies Act of 1866 was extended to the Straits Settlements, and this was followed by a local version in 1889. In the Philippines, the Spanish Commercial Code introduced in 1888 was replaced by an American-style Corporation Code in 1906. Finally, the transplant of English corporate law into India was intended to serve British business interests, to facilitate better trade and minimize risks between Britain and India, which could be accomplished if there was symmetry in the corporate legislation between the two countries.

But, all these decisions were at variance with the massive presence of autonomous forces producing and projecting their own rules on the colonized land, and the progressive demands by settlers that they should have their own laws. Moreover, the legal origins theory is largely discredited on a number of methodological and analytical grounds. In fact, the 'transplant effect' from one jurisdiction to another cannot operate in exactly the same way, given the cultural and legal system differences in the new location.

We have to understand what Tomas de Mercado was saying in the sixteenth century. According to him, a collateral effect of the practice of credit was that the use of commerce for credit also spread across Europe, producing innumerable side effects concerning operations that were hiding usury. He already anticipated the increasing involvement and interest of Europe in this new commerce, and the changing characteristics of commerce in the future. The new merchants were forced by the new routes to mobilize huge amounts of labour to move their commodities on a regular basis. Trade was accompanied by military actions, the growth in shipping tonnage, new navigations Acts, and new links between hunters, farmers, planters, merchants, craftsmen, free-wage labourers and state officials. Trade also resulted in new joints between local, regional, national and international economies, and in new regulations about seamen. In this context, innovations tended to help commercial development in a very different way, and sometimes without receiving any recognition within Britain itself or acceptance for its domestic business. Very soon, legislation was centred on the goals of each country, due to commercial practices imposed by a plurality of ethnicities, local strategies, and the preference for bargaining and transactions.

2.1 *Commercial Practices and the Plurality of Ethnicities*

Commercial law is not much concerned by the status of merchants. Due to the involvement of even more ethnicities in trade, usages and customs had to be fitted to the new expectations of trade. This is already illustrated in some speeches or letters in Antiquity. Although it had few overseas colonies (*David Mirhady*), Athens' large population and naval forces made it the dominant player in the eastern Mediterranean grain trade throughout the fifth and fourth centuries BC. None is referred to with either an ethnic reference or a reference to an Athenian *deme* membership, and commercial activities involved *metics* or slaves. The sources moreover suggest that the litigants requested private arbitration in order to avoid the more stringent evidentiary rules of the popular court, perhaps as a result of Alexander's new cosmopolitan worldview. When, at the turn of the first and second century AD, two business partners in the Roman 'frontier' province of Britain corresponded by letter regarding their joint business activities, they described a commercial practice rather than the formalized rules of Roman law. They were concerned primarily with the continuing profitability of their undertaking within a larger context, where trust and good faith among merchants were paramount. The Romans probably identified elements of this in the term *bona fides*. Where the parties and their business were dependent upon the continuing trust of other traders, it was important to fulfil all contractual obligations promptly and not to renege on contracts. This would create a bad atmosphere and might harm future business. And the nearest *colonia* (where Roman law applied in theory) was very far away. It seems much more likely that what the business partners were relying on in this case was 'mercantile custom'. As suggested (by *Paul Du Plessis*), this custom was not based on a view of law either as a territorially based system radiating out from the centre, or a question about the nature of the law (as in Egypt), but according to a more useful question, namely, 'what did the parties in their writing thought that they were doing?'.

When commercial courts are created, references to 'usages' and commercial practice are paramount, as was the case with consulates, due to the need for specialized courts in commercial matters and whose judges and consuls were elected by merchants. In this sense, they acted as special courts to resolve commercial disputes between its members with the express prohibition for ordinary courts to intervene in such matters. No jurists or professional judges intervened, but rather merchants knowledgeable of the trade, its problems and its customs. Disputes were settled on the basis of *usus mercatorum* or usage of trade and the written rules of each Consulate. We must emphasize that from 1494, with the establishment of the Consulate of Burgos, the decisions dictated by the Prior and Consuls had the characteristics of arbitration coupled with an undeniable enforceability. Two ways to solve the disputes were available: the special jurisdiction of the Consulate, and traditional arbitration. Before Tunisia became a French protectorate, the French consul had been granted the power to judge commercial conflicts of nationals or protected people. When a protectorate was created, the French authorities projected – without success – to create a mixed chamber within the civil courts, a project finally limited to a 'Tribunal mixte immobilier' which expressed the participation of all skills, whether those of the French judges and auxiliaries, the Muslim jurists as the Tunisian secular judges. In the Congo, most of the affairs related to trade issues and economic legislation broadly were managed by native tribunals – and often, when Europeans were to be tried, administrative disputes were settled with transactional fines.

In some way, arbitration was a direct antecedent of the 'capitulations' and consular jurisdiction in solving commercial disputes, given the need for expeditious resolutions. The capitulations in ancient times already offer lessons on arrangements imagined between states, such as Egypt or Persia, although, as noted in an article from Jacques Vanderlinden,[12] the 'texts' cannot – without a knowledge of Archives (if any) – make us understand how these provisions could apply when compared to national powers. At least, they allow us to understand how 'Travelling Laws', on the occasion of explorations and business operations, were effected. Foreigners passing through or requesting installation, sought to be judged impartially but what could they expect? Some received only a single guarantee, that of an impartial judgment; some got real concessions, assigning them judicial powers; others, supported by their countries, had the benefit of a treaty (a 'contract' or a 'capitulation') and developed mixed jurisdictions. In fact, in Egypt, given the presence in the middle of the nineteenth century of more than 150,000 foreigners engaging in commercial activities, it is clear that some important cases escaped the jurisdiction of the court that had been established. In 1875, three first instance District Courts were established in Alexandria, Cairo and Mansoura, as well as a Court of Appeal in Alexandria. The history of their jurisdiction is that of a progressive extension, provided, however, that they excluded the personal status matters entrusted to the countless religious courts (Muslim, Coptic, Orthodox Christians, Catholics and Rabbinical). However, in civil and commercial matters, they had exclusive jurisdiction over lawsuits between foreigners of different nationalities, between foreigners and Egyptians and, without reference to nationality, in disputes concerning the ownership of land. Soon, the question

12 Jacques Vanderlinden, 'La justice européenne d'Outre-mer avant la colonisation. Fragments en guise d'ouverture à une recherche', in Bernard Durand and Martine Fabre (eds), *Le Juge et l'Outre-mer : Phinée le devin ou les leçons du passé* (Lille, 2006), 43–72, 47.

arose of whether the word 'foreign' concerned only nationals who signed the treaty, or whether their jurisdiction extended to all foreigners. The Court of Appeal upheld that interpretation, including 'National Ottomen' and adding all the trials about 'mixed interests', even when the two parties were 'foreign or indigenous' or when in a trial 'foreign interests were engaged' without involving a third person, such as a foreign creditor in a bankruptcy!

This principle proved to be useful in cases of company law, by granting the Egyptian nationality to companies benefiting from foreign capital, even partially, within the jurisdiction of mixed classes. Thus, the Suez Canal Company, the entire banking system and even government departments in which foreign interests were concerned, as for example the Public Debt Committee, benefited from this measure. Moreover, Egyptian nationals, although often showing a preference for the Egyptian capital corporations, opened share subscriptions to foreigners to take up mixed classes, which had the advantage of increasing the confidence in foreign capital. Sometimes the name of a foreign (not concerned) party was introduced into a trial, under the guise of a complaint, endorsement, or sale, for the sole purpose of making blended tribunals competent.

Even before the onset of formal imperialism in the last quarter of the nineteenth century, German practitioners of international and colonial trade were well aware that at times the commercial practices in the British, Portuguese, or French spheres of influence in Africa and Asia were ruled by special provisions that differed from the laws applicable in the homeland. Given the fact that trade with foreign countries, including foreign colonies, was much more relevant for Germany's national economy than the trade with its own colonies, it appeared more important for students of German commercial law to learn about German consuls abroad and the laws concerning their activities than about German administrators in the German colonies.

2.2 *Localities' Strategies*

The colonial space is concerned with the primacy of 'circumstances', those which are named '*localités*' by French officers. By studying the records of the first civil court in New South Wales, Bruce Kercher explained that 'many of its decisions owed much more to local circumstances than to the legal traditions received from England', which was increasingly the way towards colonial legal autonomy. It is probable that some colonies were more concerned by this approach, due to governors or chief justices with liberal ideas in the field of criminal law, for instance. However, as Francis Forbes who was accused in Newfoundland of following 'commercial customs even over the strict laws of England', the answer could be that 'the essence of the law was … British freedom'.[13] Nevertheless, they often considered that the most important aspect was to decide according to 'community needs and expectations … and the rotten nature of local practices'. So did Forbes in a case from 1833 concerning higher interest rates than in England by validating a local rule (rather an accepted usage than a strict custom) or in allowing people 'to make contracts that suited themselves'. It is true that this tendency often led to clashes between local and English legal ideas, when lawyers asserted that the closer the law 'came to England, the nearer they were in perfection'. This included commercial law, with a slavish but unsuitable legislation and its absurd results.[14] The 'localities' reforms could proceed from harsh conditions such as in Australia where debtors were imprisoned in miserable conditions in tents. In South Australia or in Victoria, it was agreed that the local law did not allow for the arrest of debtors, one year before the imperial parliament decided the same. Finally, concerning imprisonment for debt and its abolition, an Act was passed in 1843 by New South Wales, 26 years before the English reform. The same colony also passed a bankruptcy law for all debtors decades before England. Even if it was for special reasons – and did not mean a true abolition of imprisonment – these reforms demonstrate the originality of colonies and their capacity to stop innovations and finally adopt the new laws from England.[15] This was because time and space changed, forcing the country to think up new rules to deal with new problems in certain 'frontier' territories and to refer to English solutions – or not – in more modern towns. This was the case with Sydney and Adelaide, separated by 50 years, but linked however by the same problems concerning complex commercial disputes.

These disputes also reveal that the nature of commercial enterprises within empires was not simply one of economic benefit. It was also a political one, a search for peace and for consolidation of the settlers' sovereignty in charge of more diplomacy and successful negotiation rather than for jurisdiction and trials.[16] In fact, beyond the vague reference to 'circumstances', the first 'locality' need for commercial law was 'peace' with local populations; convicts in Australia, or Indians elsewhere. This is always the lesson to be learned in territories which are 'middle-grounds', a term popularized by Richard White.[17]

---

13 Bruce Kercher, *An Unruly Child: A History of Law in Australia* (Allen & Unwin, 1995), ix and 83.

14 Kercher, *An Unruly Child*, 92–102.

15 Kercher, *An Unruly Child*, 112–118.

16 See, for Georgia and New-South Wales, the Policy of Pluralism in Ford, *Settler Sovereignty*.

17 Richard White, *The Middle Ground: Indians, Empires and Republics in the Great Lakes Region, 1650–1815* (Cambridge: Cambridge University Press, 2011).

Maintaining peace must be understood broadly speaking. The concept of institutions in this context refers to the broad way in which a society is organized. The need to secure property rights for a wide cross-section of the society and not only for a small elite created a high risk of expropriation for the vast majority of the population. Sometimes the purchase of goods had developed a risk of 'rebellion'. In South West Africa the need to change these behaviors became more and more evident to German officials for one particular reason: the African population took advantage of many European traders who made 150 to 200 per cent profit from bartering (very little) tobacco against (a lot of) cattle, and complaints were numerous (*Jakob Zollmann*).

However, 'peace' could also be a 'good' institution providing to local merchants or investors strong guarantees or incentives and opportunities for investment. In Australia, although the limited liability partnership acts were not widely used, they nevertheless reflected a preparedness by colonial governments to depart from English law. Jurists wanted to adopt business forms which were suited to the local economic and business environment, in response to the demands from some sectors of the local business community. In particular, the recognition of limited liability partnerships may have been a response to the widespread losses suffered by many investors in the aftermath of the boom and bust and severe depression of the 1890s, thus representing an early example of the introduction of investor protection legislation.

In addition, the former colonies which developed strong institutions experienced successful economic growth, even during wars, and even when foreigners were in charge of trade. The chronicle of a commercial litigation concerning Panton Leslie's business firm (*Matthew Mirow*) – an example of a British company in a small northern outpost of the Spanish empire – demonstrates both the legal sophistication and the institutional limits of local actors. East Florida was a mix of populations (British, Spanish peninsular and various Indian nations), and each group brought different and competing ideas about commerce, law, and practices, combined with different languages, expectations, and cultures. This trading firm had over fifteen trading outposts and company stores that covered a region encompassing the states of Florida, Alabama, Mississippi, Louisiana, and Tennessee. Indeed, one of Panton Leslie's prime functions was to keep peace with the many Indian tribes to ensure peaceful coexistence and military allegiances. Doing so meant advancing the interests of the Spanish crown, and working for the Spanish defence of East Florida, even when Britain was at war with Spain. This is why Panton Leslie was often the recipient of particular favours and privileges granted by one government or another. When Spain and Great Britain entered into the Anglo-Spanish War of 1797 and Britain blockaded the Spanish colonies in the Americas, reasons of state centring on maintaining supportive and peaceful relations with the Indians led Spain to allow Panton Leslie to continue its activities during the war. In truth, Spain had no merchants ready to step into the shoes of Panton Leslie. The firm had access to highly appraised English goods, an established trade network, ships to manage it, an established knowledge of the customary practices, and personal contacts with the Indian leaders. And when, in the middle of June 1802, a petition sought to stop Panton Leslie from operating its trading post at Picolata and, alternatively, to expel the trading firm from East Florida because it was a foreign firm, the firm's answer was that 'it did not matter that Governor Enrique White was born in the province when ruled by Spain and that he called himself Spanish, if under British rule he was English'. He was neither Spanish nor English but a guardian of his own convenience'. Hence, the resolution of this dispute rapidly turned in favour of Panton Leslie, the Captain General having answered that closing Panton Leslie's trading posts 'in whatever way you look at it, was very prejudicial to the State and to royal interests'.

2.3 *Commercial Bargaining*

Colonial law seems to be, as a principle of organization, a discipline confined within its borders. However, when it is confronted with important firms and the decision not to jeopardize the success of a business, it has to deal with bargaining, even on the part of Foreign Offices, and organize the settlements decided by means of transactions. All legal fields were concerned with 'bargaining', and the best example was France's incapacity to fulfil in its colonies the law which separated Church and State.

Commercial bargaining with trading firms was permanent. Before the colonies were settled, trading firms were already active, and when national control was established, the colonizing nations discovered that commercial control was often in the hands of foreign firms. In German Cameroon and in French Congo English firms were in control. Planting and trading were their chief activities but some firms, such as the Company of Victoria, traded, had plantations, ran a narrow-gauge railway for the transportation of goods, acquired mining rights etc. In German South-West Africa (*Jakob Zollmann*), the government in Berlin – still unable to mobilize the German economy to invest in the German colonies (gold and diamonds had not been found yet) – turned to British capital. The grant of the *Damaraland-Konzession* to the *South West Africa Company* (SWAC), founded in 1892 and under the influence of Cecil Rhodes, Prime Minister of the Cape Colony, was then supposed to open a new chapter in the development of mining, farming and railroads in the colony. As a result of the *Damaraland-Konzession*, the rather counter-intuitive situation that has arisen is that around 1895 British and South African capital dominated the

GSWA. This was heavily criticized by German colonial enthusiasts who bemoaned that most of the mine concessions available in the colony were sold to British companies.

Complaints also came from companies. In German Cameroon, the constitutional laws of 1886, and later of 1888, organised all colonial affairs in accordance only with national German law. Colonial stock companies for example would in the future be formed under stipulation drawn up by the chancellor in consultation with the *Bundesrat*. This zeal to curtail the Kaiser's powers imposed great handicaps on such companies. Many firms did not seek incorporation under the regulations of 1888, and there were frequent complaints that conditions in Cameroon did not attract capital. In the Free State of Congo (*Bas de Roo*), when colonial expenditure rose much faster than fiscal receipts, bringing the colony to the brink of bankruptcy, export duties were introduced to generate revenue. Policymakers were forced to increase the tariff burden year after year and to negotiate with the different stakeholders customs policies on international, colonial and local level. Consent often produced better and less expensive results, but required bargaining with the taxpayer who expected something in return for his fiscal contribution and depended on the fairness of taxation. The firms acknowledged the Free State's right to tax, but clearly considered Leopold's administration more as a competitor than as a state. The Free State was often compared to a chartered company and was called the 'state-competitor' or 'government-merchant'. They were also dissatisfied with the 'torturous', 'impractical' and 'nit-picking' customs procedures which slowed down trade.

Trading firms could simply comply and pay tariffs, or try to evade customs procedures and taxes, or use more radical responses such as smuggling or fraudulent declarations. Trading companies could try to negotiate and change customs policies by focusing on a different Congolese export sector, less burdened by tariffs and customs procedures. They could also relocate to more business-friendly environments by moving their headquarters to another colony. In 1886, a company claimed that it moved because import duties made the tax burden unbearable. Another option could consist of contacting the foreign affairs ministry of the Netherlands or France, who would then contact the Free State. Via their respective metropolitan foreign affairs departments, the companies could indeed influence the outcome of the Berlin and Brussels Conferences where the colonial powers negotiated the scope for fiscal policymaking in the Congo basin. The most far-reaching example of the NAHV's successful attempts to involve the Dutch government was the anchoring of the warship H.M. Sommelsdijck in the Congo estuary. Companies sometimes called in the press to influence the public opinion, and they published numerous pamphlets that substantiated their complaints and called for alternative policies. When, after 1908–1914, the Belgian administration significantly changed the fiscal system of Leopold II's Free State and substantially raised rubber tariffs, it was done with the consent of private enterprises and colonial policymakers, a reform which worked to the advantage of trading firms, making customs procedures more effective.

So, colonial law was not sometimes an internal and sometimes an external law; it was continuously both, according to the type of cases involved and to a projection that required constant integration of both aspects.

3 Implementing These Experiences in Commercial Law?

From the seventeenth to the nineteenth century, colonization was a 'competitor scene' controlled internationally in order to keep an eye on commercial choices and to rule the 'geography' of land and sea. Sometimes, competitors abandoned the settlements which were deemed insignificant or useless in terms of interest. States had to create law that encompassed all at once internal and external requirements and shaped colonization in a global dimension. They had to admit that there could be colonial spaces where it was not possible to reproduce perfectly the path of European state borders. In this general breakdown, each colonized territory was a territory 'aside', a precarious and a poorly secured area, at least for a time. This meant that the law of a colonial territory could be permanently threatened or directly affected by the redistribution of spaces. Being reshaped, that space required a new colonial law able to satisfy the population and the economy of the colonizing country. Moreover, even in pacific spaces, 'time' was paramount and laws were changing rapidly under the impact of colonization, so much so that legal traditions had to be replaced constantly. Later came the colonial adventure in Africa. Italy measured how quickly each country imposed its own economy and that there could be several economies in the same area. In short, the colonial 'concrete' economy, as Labanca wrote, is a space of '*incontri, scontri, contrattazioni, mediazioni*'. Somehow 'models', rushed through both time and space, and one can see over time a territory make different choices and peripheral areas deconstruct national choices.[18]

However, the transfer of colonies from one state to another led the new occupants to take into account the existing rights and, most often, to make the

18 Nicola Labanca, *Oltremare: storia dell'espansione coloniale italiana* (Bologna: Il Mulino, 2002).

choice to promise populations to uphold their rights. When the promise was not formally made, the colony was transferred anyway according the principles commonly accepted in case of conquest or cession, i.e. the conservation of ancient law as 'common law of the country' as long as it is not repealed by a new law or custom! It is easy to imagine the uncertainties when some territories, as was the case from 1760 to 1815 for several conquered islands, sometimes passed from one sovereignty to another several times. From the seventeenth century, in the Cape of Good Hope, Java, Borneo, Sumatra and other Dutch facilities of the East Indies, Curacao in the West Indies or Guiana, the two major companies, the Dutch East India (1602) and the Dutch West India (1621), had brought the legal system – with some modifications in each colony – that prevailed in the United Provinces and Holland. When the Cape, occupied by the Dutch in 1652, then conquered by England in 1795 and kept until 1803, and then taken again by Batavia in 1806, was definitively ceded to England by treaty in 1814, no mention was made about maintaining the law which had been in force. But 'Roman-Dutch' was retained as 'common law' so that in the twentieth century it continued to be the law of reference. The same applied for Ceylon, where the Dutch settled in 1656 and the English in 1796. As for 'Guyana'– later British Guiana – which was repeatedly transferred from 1796 to 1814, Roman-Dutch Law continued to be applied by a similar provision, included in the patent letters of 4 March 1831, and was attended by the three institutions of Essequibo, Demerara and Berbice in a single colony. Colonies of 'conquest' followed the organization and transitional justice that English conquerors brought in with, it seems, some difficulty to define because of different regimes.[19] It was the same in South Africa where, over the territory of Cape extension, civil Roman-Dutch Law was accompanied by 'accretion', sometimes without the need for legislation. When in the middle of nineteenth century annexations began, all the territories confirmed the 'Roman-Dutch Law'. Louisiana shows even an increased complexity both because of the plurality of competing laws, but also because of the choices finally decided on. Other colonies immediately adopted a new law, because they had been little marked by the law of the first occupant, because they were simple passage territories or because the poverty of implantation. Such was the case for Jamaica. Identically, Trinidad received all the rules borrowed from England or other British colonies.

On the contrary, when occupations were stabilized, the law – and particularly commercial law – had to adapt itself constantly to new exigencies. In the

19 J.C. Leslie, 'Roman-Dutch Law in British Guiana and a West Indian court of appeal', *Journal of the Society of Comparative Legislation* 17 (1917), 210–222.

British colonies, the introduction of English legislation was probably necessary in the light of the important economic role played by several companies, most notably the large banks that expanded prior to the introduction of that legislation. The main importance of the adoption of the English *Companies Act* was that it became easier to float companies and raise capital, and this enabled the mining industry to flourish and contribute strongly to the prosperity of colonial Victoria, thus laying the foundations for the modern Australian economy. Commercial law worked both to tie disparate parts of colonial Empires together, and to lay the basis for exchanges of all sorts between politically and culturally separate imperial or colonial powers. Lawyers, merchants, and companies tried to adapt constantly to new needs and, in accompanying this stream year after year, some of the former law was lost.

Some changes nevertheless were not made to introduce the rules of a new nation, but rather to harmonize those which, sometimes after half a century, were no longer suited to the requirements of a world that had changed. This was the case in Ceylon, where, 'even if it belonged to the admirers of Roman-Dutch-Law', it had to be admitted that it not always responded to the need for legal innovations in trade.[20] In some countries, it is possible to note four or five different phases of law in only one century. Often, the debates in Quebec, St. Lucia, and Mauritius only attested the need for adaptation. Quebec, with respect to maritime law, opted for solutions brought by English and American law, and Mauritius introduced English commercial law and repealed the French Code of Criminal Procedure. At the same time, trade flows could have changed, forcing the law to adapt to this new economy, without totally expelling the trade law which had a common foundation. Already by the 1820s, a Ceylon chief justice declared that Roman-Dutch Law 'hardly serves as a guide in a special case ... But luckily it happens that the large commercial code, called the custom of merchants, has its foundations in this law and it is composed of rules established by the consent and practice of the merchants of Holland. We look at every decision of Westminster Courts on this subject as a comment on the Dutch commercial law'.

Sometimes, reforms simply scratched old institutions when massive 'legal injections' were decided. That was the case in criminal proceedings or in commercial law. In commercial law, maritime law, or banking law, it was easy to introduce English law by including several Acts in their entirety. When the Quebec Act restored French private law, this was done with the exception of

20 Sidney Abrahams, 'The Colonial Legal Service and the Administration of Justice in Colonial Dependencies', *Journal of Comparative Legislation and International Law* 30 (1948), 1–11.

commercial law: mercantile law (including marine, life and fire insurance) would be administered in compliance with the laws of England at the corresponding period, unless Quebec made other provisions. In 1852, an ordinance decided that Ceylon should apply the law of 'promissory notes and checks'; another 1866 order did the same about the law for 'partnerships, joint-stock companies, corporations, banks and banking, principals and agents, carriers by land, life and fire Insurance'. In British Guiana, an 1864 ordinance issued that: 'Ships and the property therein, and the owners thereof, and the behaviour of the master and mariners and their respective rights, duties, and liabilities as regards the carriage of passengers and goods by ships, stoppage in transit, freight, demurrage, insurance, salvage, average, bills of lading, and all rights, liabilities, claims, and in matters arising in respect of any ship or any such issues as foresaid – shall be adjudged, determined, construed, and enforced by the law of England applicable to such boxes and the like'. Yet another order introduced (in part or in full) English law of 'bills of exchange, joint-stock companies, insolvency and obvious'. In Cape Town, significant changes were made by an Act of 1879 which introduced English law in all matters concerning the 'shipping' and 'fire, life, and marine insurance, stoppage *in transitu* and bills of landing'.

Legal voluntarism in British Guiana was the driving force of a law now fully 'native', designated by some authors as a 'home grown law'. In June 1912 the Governor decided to appoint a commission 'to investigate and report if some changes are not recommended and if the substitution of English law or otherwise should not be done'? The commission sat during May–June 1913, and consulted many people and particularly legal practitioners and 'legal officers'. Asked for their opinion, they pronounced almost unanimously in favour of English common law, some arguing, however, for a change that would not be too brutal. English law should be introduced in most subjects (commercial matters, family, criminal, etc.) except for the right of 'real property' that had to be excluded because of 'complicated incidents in this field'. The Roman-Dutch Law could be kept with some changes in other areas, for example for the 'dirty, leasing and mortgaging of land'.

Sometimes, the attempt to respect the influences of many legal systems created discontent with the impeding of easy and just trade. From 1764 to 1774, the governance of Quebec was a welter of chaos. Many of the French and English legal provisions ran concurrently and created a disorderly and tense situation (*David Gilles*). In some instances, the Canadians would follow English law, while in others they would prefer French laws and customs, depending on the advantages that might be gained from one or the other. The population was uncertain as to the laws that were to be followed. In 1845, the author of a pamphlet emphasized the need to ensure that commercial law approximated as much as possible that of its most important trading relation: 'Our position should make us to desire to assimilate as much as possible our commercial code to commercial ties, those of England, the United States and Upper Canada because of our relationship with them'. The provisions of the Code which was brought into force in 1866 would not exactly be English or French, because 'French and Dutch civil lawyers built most of the provisions in the seventeenth and eighteenth centuries and these provisions were applied by courts and merchants of all European countries'. The complexity of the sources of the Quebec civil code did not accommodate the current simplification of placing the original civil law provisions in French law and those of commercial law provisions in English law. In each aspect, Canadian codified law was a 'mashup law', a new law.

In any case, it was clear that the complement of British sources would produce a 'home-grown legal system', caused by an interaction between several legal systems which forced judges to determine the one that, within particular cases, should be considered.[21] Slowly, decisions constructed an amalgam which created an 'indigenous system'. This caused a reflection on the exact meaning that should now be attributed to the expression 'common law'. Roman-Dutch Law is often said to be the 'common law of Sri Lanka', as it is said that 'common law' is that of England; but generally it means that this system is not the result of legislation but of a 'law created by the customs of the people and the decisions of judges'.[22] In this stream, experiences played their part in promoting radical experiments, as did the capacity of merchants to demonstrate their adaptability.

3.1 *Radical Experiments*

If we look at the transplantation and adaptation of English company law in colonial Victoria (Philip Lipton), we can find several noteworthy features which depart from the idea that the Australian colonial developments were largely a bland imitation of the laws in England. Referring to these colonial Acts which 'preceded major English law reforms by decades' or 'were entirely original and in direct conflict with basic English legal principles', Bruce Kercher confirms that 'Politics was more important in many of these repugnancy

21 See the developments on these 'mergings' in Bernard Durand, *Introduction historique au droit colonial: un ordre 'au gré des vents'* (Paris: Economica, 2015), 285–332.

22 L.J.M. Corray, 'The reception of Roman-Dutch Law in Sri Lanka', *The Comparative and International Law Journal of Southern Africa* 7 (1974), 295–318.

decisions than adherence to legal theory'.[23] According to him, the Victorian Companies Act 1871, which allowed shareholders of mining companies to avoid liability up to the amount of their shares (soon copied by others colonies), was based on the belief that the British statutes did not suit the speculative nature of the Australian mining industry.[24] Commercial law was not the only field which was concerned with 'politics', and it is well known that women had more rights in colonies than they did in their own nation as far as dowry, propriety and divorce were concerned. New South Wales or Victoria received the most liberal divorce laws in the Empire, almost fifty years before England, due to the nonexistence of an established Church in these territories.

In fact, there were innovative features in the development of company law which were specific to the Victorian colonial experience, mostly confined to miners, and which may subsequently have influenced the development of company law in the United Kingdom. This legal form was short-lived and was not widely used, but it indicates a preparedness in colonial governments to seek innovative responses to the needs of their business communities, especially in the gold mining industry, and despite the absence of equivalent English legislation. At the same time, as these experiments in the form of limited liability were taking place, its introduction was still being vigorously debated in England and would not be introduced until 1855. That legislation is described as 'one of the most radical experiments in company law in the English-speaking world'. This shows that even at a very early stage in the development of company law, there was a preparedness to adapt the law to best meet the needs of local conditions. Limited liability companies and partnerships had already existed in the Australian colonies for some time. Unincorporated joint stock companies with transferable shares and share trading were already quite common in the colony of New South Wales from the 1820s and 1830s, well before the introduction of companies' legislation and the establishment of formal stock exchanges. This suggests that companies would have continued to evolve as a matter of commercial practice, irrespective of legislative developments. Both these legislative developments can be seen as an example of legal evolution and economic development operating in a complementary way.

However, the transplant of English law into India so as to favour British businesses was accompanied by a consequential impact, in that it often ran counter to local business interests. Given that the managing agency system was not prevalent in Britain, the legislation did not contain any specific protections for the shareholders. Hence, even when indigenous shareholders acquired large

23 Kercher, *An Unruly Child*, 103.

24 Kercher, *An Unruly Child*, 134–135.

stakes in companies managed by British managing agents, the legal system failed to provide recourse to them. The impulsive transplant of English legislation to India without consideration of the local circumstances meant that the managing agency system avoided any treatment under the Indian legal system, and was able to operate for over a century without any legal constraints.

'Radical experiments' also concerned new discoveries, new obstacles too, and the need to react rapidly to these. In Western Australia, the discovery of gold in 1893 was an event of tremendous importance from an economic and political point of view, and it had a considerable effect on the legal system. There was an increase in the population with people coming from other Australian colonies, which meant that Western Australia needed to be treated as a part of an emerging nation and not as an isolated colony, and it was petitioning for federation. The discovery affected the legal system through the need to build up a body of mining law. These regulations were obviously drawn up after having taken into consideration the mining legislation in other colonies, and they adopted the same principles as were in force in other parts of Australia. In addition, it was necessary to appoint wardens with the power to determine the boundaries of claims and to set up special courts to deal with mining disputes. Each new act regularly gave the wardens discretionary powers with a very wide jurisdiction.[25]

In the 1860s the gold industry, in addition to playing a major role in the development of the Victorian economy, was also instrumental in the very important and related institutional developments of the modernization of company law and the formation of a Melbourne stock exchange. It was during this decade that large scale operations became necessary for underground mining when easily accessible surface gold became scarcer and miners increasingly attempted to find alluvial gold in underground rivers and streams deep below the surface. As the depth of mine shafts increased to 40 meters and more, the organizational demands became more complex as larger partnerships were required to share the work and raise more capital. This required the widespread use of the company form with the features of limited liability. This legal form was short-lived and was not widely used, but it indicates a preparedness by colonial governments to seek innovative responses to the needs of their business communities, despite the absence of equivalent English legislation.

25 Enid Russell (edited and completed by F.M. Robinson and P.W. Nichols), *A History of the Law in Western Australia and its Development from 1829 to 1979* (Nedlands: University of Western Australia Press, 1980), 286.

3.2 *Merchants' Adaptability*

In all colonial territories, many of the mechanisms used came about from strong practical needs related to colonial constraints: the scarcity of settlers, long distances, difficult communications, climate, scarcity of personnel, need for order, difficulty to involve citizens in the action of justice, etc., so that the institutions being implemented did not necessarily state a particular origin, and neither were legal borrowings necessarily marked. Similarities, therefore, do not justify an inspiration. In fact, regarding the mutations themselves, there is little to cause hesitation: the colonial legal and judicial history is the permanent theatre of merchants' adaptability to local commercial struggles.

For instance, in colonial India, the evolution of the managing agency system was closely related to the geographical diversity in business activities. The system was necessitated on account of the lack of entrepreneurial capacity on the one hand, and a shortage of financing on the other. Since Indian businessmen were engaged in traditional trading and financing, the British managing agency firms who had gained knowledge not only of local markets in specific industries, but also of foreign markets and sources of supply, were able to fill the gap quickly with their superior technology and managerial skills. Similarly, on the financing side, the managing agents played an important role. It was the managing agent's capabilities and reputation that attracted businessmen to invest on the understanding that they would not be involved in the management of the business as they were themselves handling their own businesses, with limited time to devote to the affairs of the joint stock company (Umakanth Varrotil). The eastern part of India (focused on Calcutta) was different to the western part (focused on Bombay and Ahmedabad), so that business activities evolved rather differently in these two regions. British businesses dominated eastern India with control over jute mills, collieries and tea plantations. One rationale for this phenomenon is that these businesses were export-oriented, and British businessmen possessed the expertise and contacts for international trade. Conventional accounts indicate that the entry and expansion of British businesses in the eastern region was made possible because the local population was not entrepreneurially driven, but also because the British firms imposed significant high barriers to entry due to their dominance in the region. So, innovations had only practical views, as did the managing agency system in India with its special adaptation of British business practices to the peculiar economic environment of Asia.

Adaptability can exist in a number of pending cases, and merchants were able to get round the legal hindrances, as can be seen in the Mixed Court of Shanghai. Sometimes merchants obtained their recognition as citizens under the treaty's power from a foreign Consul, so that they could be outside the

Chinese magistrate's jurisdiction and sue before the Consul instead.[26] In the same way, before the International Mixed Court, when a Chinese defendant was in foreign employ, it was said that this constituted a sufficient foreign interest to enable the Assessor of the nationality concerned to displace the Assessor of the day.

Civil, criminal, and commercial law provisions could and did have a real impact on individuals' personal lives and livelihood. In Shanghai, not only 'foreign mixed courts, but International Mixed Court realized how Chinese law contained nothing with regard to mercantile contracts, trust, property, or the law relating to debtor and creditor'. This absence of anything like a system of commercial law, in a great open port of commerce and a city where the major part of litigation involved commercial matters between foreigner and Chinese, obliged them to take into account frequent litigations and the need to conciliate Western Law and Guild's arbitrations. Because of a lack of proper legislation, the whole structure of Chinese business life was directed by commercial associations. If the mixed Court succeeded in introducing principles of western jurisprudence, there was for a long time no possibility of obtaining satisfactory results in fields such as bankruptcy proceedings, with the City Magistrate considering it to be its privilege to decide the bankruptcy cases.[27] In 1905, the inauguration of a Chinese General Chamber of Commerce, and in 1907 a Bankruptcy Code sanctioned by Imperial Edict (but repealed in 1908), gave it 'almost unlimited power to dispose of matters and provided for the 'local authorities' (the Courts) a comparatively modest role'. After 1908, the Mixed Court was confronted with new difficulties, and to solve the problem, choose to follow the Bankruptcy Code 'in practice', adding however under each article comments such as 'applied' or 'applied but instead of local authorities read International Mixed Court' or 'not applied'. For instance, with the articles concerning mortgages (33–38), the Court's practice was 'not applied, the issues being left at the discretion of the Court upon the report of the Official Court accountants and application of the interest of parties' Several articles were followed by the comment 'The Court reserves his right to decide the question upon its merits in every particular cases' or 'left at the entire discretion of the Court'.[28]

26 Thomas B. Stephens, *Order and Discipline in China: The Shanghai Mixed Court 1911–1927* (Seattle: Washington University Press, 1992), 53.

27 Anatol M. Kotenev, *Shanghai: Its Mixed Court and Council* (Shanghai, 1925), 166–167.

28 Kotenev, *Shanghai: Its Mixed Court and Council*, Chapter XV: 1911–1924, pages 251–273: 'The Mixed Court and Shanghai General Chamber of Commerce'.

By means of elaborate legal arrangements, colonial powers could consolidate their dominant (economic) position which contributed significantly to the long-lasting subjugation of many communities and especially those of merchants who were placed in an inferior position. That was the case everywhere, and this Dutch strategy could be verified in the Indonesian archipelago (Alexander Claver), where the Chinese constituted a separate community, which was clearly lowered in their treatment and their commercial activity before the law. For instance, trade needs access to capital and access to information, which the Chinese community lacked. However, the Chinese coped with the restrictions imposed upon them and succeeded to turn them to their advantage, proving their capacity of adaptability. They did it, first, in 1892 when a new Dutch nationality law was drawn up, withholding Dutch citizenship from all 'natives' and foreign Orientals residing in the Netherlands Indies. This legislation benefited European traders in disputes with the Chinese, as the former preferred to do business with foreign Orientals under Dutch civil and commercial law. And the Chinese felt unjustly treated because they had shared civil law with the Europeans for almost half a century.

Nothing caused as much offence as the bankruptcy provisions. Upon defaulting, the debtor had to submit his books. The Chinese, however, stood to benefit greatly from the new legislation and they could appeal to the judge, claiming to be unskilled in bookkeeping. The Chinese frequently resorted to this line of defence, and their pleas were accepted on many occasions. Moreover, the law permitted their books to be written in the Chinese language.[29] Although every trader could keep his books in the language he wanted, in practice the Chinese had a distinct advantage, as the use of the Chinese language improved their chances of getting away with fabricated, bankruptcy ready accounts. Whereas the restrictive policy of the Dutch suggested a successful subjugation of the Chinese, commercial legislation worked in their favour.

The same was the case also when the Japanese citizen law of 1899 provided a way out for some. This law equated the Japanese with the Europeans, and in so doing blurred the distinction between Europeans and Asians. In concluding a commercial treaty with the Netherlands in 1896 the Japanese government insisted upon equal treatment of its citizens. The Dutch however failed to foresee the impact of this change in the law upon the large Chinese minority, for Japanese nationality also applied to the inhabitants of Japanese colonies such

29 Too often neglected, the language could be a means of keeping out of things or of winning the allegiance. In Québec, the allegiance of Canadians lay in the imposition of as few of the English laws as possible. Furthermore, applying all English legal frameworks would be impracticable until the population had been educated in the English language and laws.

as Taiwan, which had been wrested from the Chinese in 1895. As a result, the legal nationality of Taiwanese was in fact Japanese. This included those who took Japanese nationality from Taiwan but who stayed in China or Southeast Asia. Many Chinese in the Netherlands Indies were quick to recognize the advantages of registering as a *Taiwan sekimin* – meaning a 'person registered in Taiwan' – and thus obtaining a higher legal status in the sense that a European status offered better legal protection. The manoeuvre only required a trip to Taiwan where a piece of land had to be bought and then the person could be registered as a citizen of Taiwan. This procedure automatically gave them European status upon their return to the Netherlands Indies, ensuring better treatment by the colonial authorities and direct access to means of information, security and – indeed – capital.

Turning to China, it was seen that in concessions granted by China – such as in TianJin but also in Macao[30] or Hong-Kong – not only were the residents guaranteed the free exercise of commercial activities under the protection of the law of their own nationality, but it also allowed them a more active role in the administration of the concession. When the new concessions and the enlarged old ones changed Tianjin spatiality completely, they became a Western trading outpost in China, providing residents the freedom to pursue their business under the protection of their own laws. However (as Luigi Nuzzo writes) the organization and exploitation of the colonial territory was not always easy. The Western states often manifested deep uncertainties about the strategies of legal and economic policy that they had to follow and they were torn between the desire to administer their own concession directly and to hand over its management to commercial companies, financial groups, or banks.

At the same time, China still exercised its sovereignty over the concessions. A new social space required a new order, a different code that presupposed and at the same time produced a new life. In a Concession such as Shanghai, this 'new life' was a result of the struggle between consuls and the 'group-disciplinary organization of Chinese merchant communities, in all the trade disputes, administration of bankruptcies, and all such commercial causes' because, according to the Chinese, Chinese interests lay with the Chinese Chamber of commerce and the Guild, and not with the State. In addition, merchants resisted this in order to keep their power while the consuls were seeking to take it from them, so that meetings were arranged for an exchange of views, gathering foreign assessors from the mixed court, representatives of the

30 Jean Escarra, *Le regime des concessions étrangères en Chine*, Académie de droit international t.27, (Paris, , 1929), 5–140.

Chamber of commerce, the Chinese banks, the guilds, and the Chinese merchant community.[31]

Is it possible to conclude that these attitudes of transplantation, of 'experiences', can be summed up by some principles such as 'imitation' or 'experimentation'? Or only by a concrete adaptability to commercial and political needs? It could certainly be seen that commercial legislation was transplanted in other colonies. British managing agencies flourished in Singapore and Malaya as they managed the rubber estates in Malaya during the rubber boom in the early part of the twentieth century. The system extended to other Asian cities such as Penang, Sarawak, Shanghai and Yokohama. However, the managing agency system suffered the most from its inertia because it did not receive any treatment whatsoever in English legislation, as the system originated and existed only in the colonies and did not affect domestic companies' law in England. It is true also that the 'projection on motherlands' is very rarely noted for commercial law even if it can be agreed that, in fact, legislative changes in Australia were also innovative and highly progressive. While largely based on law reform proposals that originated in England, they were introduced in Australia more than a decade before similar reforms were introduced in England and it is not impossible that they may have strongly influenced the development of company law in England. The experiences were many, and there is no reason to be surprised. This 'experiment', which involved a transcendental vision (the adjective is from Roland Drago[32]) – or is it a philosophical one – refers simply to the very history of law and institutions. Institutions, somehow, acquire a life of their own, made of evolution – this is already known – but also made of an ability to reproduce, to adapt, to change. Institutions are modigiable organisms able to adapt in a colonial territory. New problems generate new rules which can serve as models and thus 'return' to the mainland as such, to inspire even the very institutions that gave birth to them. It is then not necessary to solve the problem of experimental intention. Institutional tests do not need always to state their intentions; they are simply experiences. Somehow, they illustrate these ruses of history of which Hegel spoke. Applied to the colonial legislature, they refer, without any a *priori*, to new reflections on its own law, and equate the 'returns' to a 'reflexive law' or a '*spiegelrecht*', often unexpected or unacknowledged.

---

31 Stephens, *Order and Discipline in China*, 51.

32 Roland Drago, 'L'administration coloniale, laboratoire de la réforme administrative', in André Breton and Fernand Derrida, *Mélanges en hommage à André Breton et Fernand Derrida* (Paris: Dalloz, 1991), 83–92. And *Les Collectivités locales et l'expérimentation: perspectives nationales et européennes.*

Of course, the gradual implementation of rules inspired by the metropolis must not mask the amount of mechanisms which had been established very early on and which may have, to varying degrees, left their mark on colonial politics. There is no doubt they served as lessons for the choices made on other territories, since the law of imitation is fairly common and understandable here, both for theorists or for the actors of colonization. It can be seen that in French or British colonies, governors and judges were 'men of the world', circumnavigating from one colony to another and carrying practices and ideas which could be conservative or liberal.[33] Moreover, this inspiration could be very diverse, and it was seen that 'reminiscences' of the ancient regime were present in some colonial institutions. But other 'projections' are possible and some years ago, participants in a symposium on dictatorships between the two World Wars evoked the supposed role played by the colonies, both as inspiration and as a support for totalitarian ideas (see Hayek), as a preparation of minds (see Arendt), or as an experimentation in fascist ideologies (see Ethiopia with Italy) or national Socialism (see the German colonial Empire).[34]

Acknowledgements

I have tried, in these conclusions, to take my own views into account – inspired by some readings and books cited in the footnotes – and supplemented by the views of the contributors of this book.

33 See for instance Bridget Brereton, *Law, Justice and Empire: The Colonial Career of John Gorrie, 1829–1892* (Kingston: University of the West Indies Press, 1997).

34 Bernard Durand, 'Les colonies et l'économie des dictatures: Expérimentations et projections', in Gerd Bender, Rainer Maria Kiesow and Dieter Simon (eds.), *Die andere Seite des Wirtschaftsrechts: Steurerung in den Diktaturen des 20. Jahrhunderts* (Frankfurt am Main: Klostermann, 2006), 143–186.

Index of Names

Index of Places

Index of Subjects